FOURTH EDITION

EFFECTIVE
SMALL BUSINESS
MANAGEMENT

RICHARD M. HODGETTS · DONALD F. KURATKO

Florida International University   Ball State University

The Dryden Press

Harcourt Brace College Publishers

Fort Worth · Philadelphia · San Diego · New York · Orlando · Austin · San Antonio ·
Toronto · Montreal · London · Sydney · Tokyo

Acquisitions Editor   Scott Isenberg
Manuscript Editor   Karen Carriere
Production Editor   Jennifer Johnson
Designer   James Hughes
Art Editor   Susan Holtz
Production Manager   Alison Howell

ISBN: 0-15-520904-3

Library of Congress Catalog Card Number: 91-72313

Printed in the United States of America
2 3 4 5 6 7 8 9 0 1   039   9 8 7 6 5 4 3 2 1

The Dryden Press
Harcourt Brace College Publishers

Cover
Illustration by Robert LoGrippo/Frank & Jeff Lavaty Agents

Photo Credits
Page 2 Taurus Photos.   *14* Tom Tracy/Photophile.   *78* HBJ Picture Library.   *172* Tom Tracy/Photophile.
200, 205 HBJ Picture Library.   *270* Tom Tracy/Photophile.   *350, 370* HBJ Picture Library.
384 © Wesley Allison.   *412* Courtesy of Frieda's, Inc.   *430* Dick Luria/FPG.   *498* Tom Tracy/Photophile.   *527, 596* HBJ Picture Library.

Preface

THE IMPACT OF SMALL BUSINESS TODAY

The United States is a nation of small businesses. Individuals and giant corporations alike rely on small businesses for goods and services. Small businesses greatly outnumber large businesses, and thousands of new small businesses are formed each day in this country. Interest in small business continues to grow. Governmental bodies, public and private educational institutions, and a variety of economic development groups have joined the business community in recognizing the importance of small business to our country and its economy. As the nation moves towards the year 2000, effectively managed small businesses are critical to our economic success.

OBJECTIVES OF THE BOOK

Effective Small Business Management, Fourth Edition, provides an introduction to the world of small business and to the fundamentals of effective small business management—the fundamentals of such diverse activities as organizing and controlling, pricing, advertising, financial analysis, record keeping, budgeting, purchasing and controlling inventory, franchising, and acquiring capital. The book also provides much useful information about specific current concerns of small business, including computerization, crime, insurance needs, family business, ethics, and the global marketplace.

This textbook is designed for courses in small business management that involve three distinct but related constituencies. First, the textbook is designed to be useful to professors who relate the latest research to each topic as they teach the course. Second, the textbook has been written for students to *read.* The subject matter is presented in an interesting, easy-to-understand style. Finally, the specific needs of active small business owner–managers have been considered. The textbook's coverage of all aspects of small business management will help them to improve their management effectiveness on the job.

DISTINGUISHING FEATURES

A number of distinguishing features make this textbook informative, up-to-date, and useful.

COMPREHENSIVE ORGANIZATION

The textbook has seven distinct parts. Part One answers the question, What is small business? It explains the nature of small business, the factors that bring success *and failure* to new enterprises, as well as the characteristics of successful entrepreneurs and the unique concerns of family businesses.

Part Two describes how to prepare a business plan and then discusses the various ways individuals can get into small business—by buying an ongoing concern, by purchasing a franchise, and by starting a business from scratch.

Part Three discusses the special problems faced by new businesses. Special attention is given to financing, location, layout, and legal forms of organization.

Part Four focuses on how to manage a small business operation. Attention is directed to the nature of the managerial process including planning, organizing, directing, and controlling. The human resource management functions are examined as well as discussion of the unique challenges confronting the growing small business.

Part Five explains how goods and services are marketed. The topics include market research, pricing, advertising, selling, and customer credit.

Part Six deals with finances and inventory control. It covers financial statements, record keeping, financial analysis, budgeting, purchasing, and inventory control.

Part Seven is devoted to small business concerns specific to the 1990s. It focuses on such issues as computerization, ethics, social responsibility, crime, insurance needs, legal concerns, and government assistance available to small business.

The subject matter of the textbook moves from consideration of small business in general to the very specific needs of individual owner–managers. As with the previous editions, the underlying theme is *effectiveness;* that is, the textbook tells the small business owner–manager what he or she needs to know in order to ensure that costs are as low as they can be and that profits are as high as they can be.

PEDAGOGICAL AIDS

ILLUSTRATIONS   Numerous tables, charts, and exhibits present data, summarize information, and reinforce important concepts.

BOLDFACED TERMS   Key terms and concepts are highlighted with boldface type when they are introduced and explained.

LEARNING OBJECTIVES   Attainable learning goals are stated clearly at the beginning of each chapter. In each chapter, the student learns to identify, define, describe, discuss, and compare essential components of small business management.

CHAPTER SUMMARIES   Every chapter concludes with a concise, point-by-point summary of key topics.

REVIEW AND DISCUSSION QUESTIONS   Relevant questions address the major chapter concepts at the end of each chapter.

SUGGESTIONS FOR FURTHER READING   Numerous footnotes refer students to primary sources of information—most of them journal articles. These readings can be used to supplement the textbook material and as sources of information for writing projects. The references have been thoroughly updated for this edition.

GLOSSARY   The glossary defines important terms and concepts explained in the textbook. It is designed to help students speak the language of the small business entrepreneur.

SUBJECT INDEX   A comprehensive index helps students locate information quickly.

NAME INDEX   A comprehensive name index helps students locate specific names efficiently.

INTEREST-BASED FEATURES

SMALL BUSINESS SUCCESS   To stimulate innovation and enthusiasm for small business, the story of a successful small business is featured in each chapter. Many of these boxed inserts have been adapted from key entrepreneurial success stories featured in *Inc., Venture,* and *Entrepreneur* magazines. This is a new feature for this edition.

SMALL BUSINESS OWNER'S NOTEBOOK   Every chapter features a short informational item that is designed to identify key issues that affect the small business owner/manager. These helpful hints are adapted from some of the latest publications, and each "notebook" item relates to the chapter in which it appears. This is a new feature for this edition.

CASE STUDIES   At the end of each chapter are two short case studies that provide students the opportunity to apply what they have learned in the chapter to actual small business problems.

"YOU BE THE CONSULTANT" CASES   Also at the end of each chapter is a longer case study entitled "You Be the Consultant." The problems posed by these cases are more comprehensive; they call for the application of all of the material in the chapter as well as the student's experience and prior education.

A COMPLETE BUSINESS PLAN   The appendix to Chapter 4 presents a complete student-prepared business plan for a 1950s-style diner.

INTEGRATIVE CASES   Each major part of the textbook concludes with a comprehensive case study that integrates a multitude of relevant chapter topics. These cases were professionally prepared, presented, and referreed by professors who are members of the Midwest Society for Case Research.

ENTREPRENEURIAL SIMULATION FEATURE   Each part of the textbook also features an entrepreneurial simulation case that ties directly into the Entrepreneurial Simulation Program (E.S.P.), which was written specifically for this textbook by Thomas Penderghast of Pepperdine University.

SUPPLEMENTS AND TEACHING AIDS

STUDENT RESOURCE MANUAL

Developed by Donald F. Kuratko of Ball State University, this manual will help the student to profit from the textbook material. It contains chapter outlines, review questions, and exercises for each chapter of *Effective Small Business Management*, worksheets for developing expertise in small business management, fourteen biographies of small business entrepreneurs, fourteen complete journal articles, and generous lists of suggestions for further reading.

INSTRUCTOR'S RESOURCE MANUAL

Developed by Donald F. Kuratko and Douglas W. Naffziger of Ball State University, this manual contains chapter outlines, learning objectives, lecture outlines, teaching suggestions, answers to the review and discussion questions, and suggested solutions for the case studies. It also provides a Test Bank of more than one thousand true/false and multiple-choice test questions. It is a comprehensive Instructor's Resource Manual.

ENTREPRENEURIAL SIMULATION PROGRAM (E.S.P.)

Thomas Penderghast of Pepperdine University has written a computer-based instructional package that enables students to gain practical hands-on experience as small business owner–managers. Designed for use on IBM® PC systems, the package includes a single disk (that can be copied) and an *Instructor's Manual*. The *Student Manual* contains study units, exercises, and tear-out worksheets. Students compete as small business owner–managers by making decisions about store location, inventory, pricing, personnel, marketing, and advertising. Data entry can be controlled by the instructor; students are not required to use the computer directly. At the end of each session, the program prints operating results to aid the student in making further decisions. At the end of the semester, each student sees a profit or a loss from the sale of the business.

ACKNOWLEDGMENTS

We are indebted to many people for their help in preparing this new edition. In particular, we express our thanks to our wives, Sally Hodgetts and Deborah Kuratko, for their love, support, and patience. In addition, we thank the many colleagues who have helped us, especially Charles Nickerson (Dean of the College of Business at Florida International University), Dana Farrow (Chairman of the Management Department at Florida International University), Neil A. Palomba (Dean of the College of Business at Ball State University), William R. LaFollette (former Chairman of the Management Science Department at Ball State University), and Jatinder N. D. Gupta (Chairman of the Management Science Department at Ball State University).

We also gratefully acknowledge the authors from the Midwest Society for Case Research for their work on the integrative cases that conclude each of the seven parts of the textbook. They are Cyril C. Ling (Illinois Wesleyan University), R. F. Reimer (Indiana University Southeast), Norman J. Gierlasinski (Central Washington University), and Herbert E. Brown, Nabil Hassan, and Paula M. Saunders (Wright State University).

Thanks, also, to our reviewers for their helpful suggestions. They are Joseph Abbruscato (Scottsdale Community College), Robert Carrel (Vincennes University), Van Clouse (University of Louisville), Robert Cobb (Merced College), O. R. Edmondson

(Mira Costa College), Carol Hande (Spokane Falls Community College), Neil Humphryes (Virginia Commonwealth University), Rudolph Kagerer (University of Georgia), Bruce Kemelgor (University of Louisville), John S. Leahy (San Marcos Community College), Edward Menge (Franklin University), Richard Randall (Nassau Community College), Donna Schaeffer (Florida International University), Steve Stryker (University of the District of Columbia), W. W. White (University of Wyoming), and Larry Williams (Palomar College).

Many, many students have enriched our lives, our teaching, and our writing through the years. We would be remiss if we did not acknowledge their contributions here. We are especially grateful to Scott G. Voegele for allowing us to present his business plan as the appendix to Chapter 4.

Finally, we express appreciation to our colleagues and friends at Harcourt Brace Jovanovich, in particular to Scott Isenberg, acquisitions editor; Karen Carriere, manuscript editor; Jennifer Johnson, production editor; James Hughes, designer; Susan Holtz, art editor; and Alison Howell, production manager.

RICHARD M. HODGETTS
DONALD F. KURATKO

ABOUT THE AUTHORS

Richard M. Hodgetts, Ph.D., is a professor of business at Florida International University, with a Ph.D. from the University of Oklahoma and an MBA from Indiana University. He has been named an outstanding teacher of the year twice, at both the University of Nebraska and Florida International University, most recently in 1988. He has lectured in Mexico, Venezuela, Jamaica, Peru, Denmark, Kuwait, and many U.S. colleges and universities. He has worked with Burger King, Exxon International, CIGNA Dental, Eastern Airlines, the government of Kuwait, and the revenue department of Mexico, among many others. Professor Hodgetts is a fellow of the Academy of Management and serves on the review boards of five journals. He is the author of *Modern Human Relations at Work; Management: Theory, Process, and Practice;* coauthor with Fred Luthans of *Business;* and author of several other texts. He also writes a weekly column on small business and entrepreneurship for the *Ft. Lauderdale News and Sun Sentinel.*

Donald F. Kuratko, D.B.A., is the Stoops Distinguished Professor in Business and Director of the Entrepreneurship Program, College of Business, at Ball State University. He is the first professor to be named a Distinguished Professor for the College of Business at Ball State University. He has published more than 80 articles on aspects of entrepreneurship, new-venture development, and corporate intrapreneurship. He has also been a consultant on corporate intrapreneurship to major corporations such as GTE, Blue Cross/Blue Shield, AT&T, and Union Carbide Corp. Professor Kuratko's work has been published in such journals as *Strategic Management Journal, Journal of Small Business Management, Entrepreneurship Theory & Practice, Training and Development Journal, Entrepreneurship Development Review, Management Advisor,* and *Journal of Education for Business.* Professor Kuratko has written five books, including *Entrepreneurship:*

A Contemporary Approach (Dryden/HBJ, 1992) and *Management* (Harcourt Brace Jovanovich, 1991).

The academic program in entrepreneurship that Dr. Kuratko developed at Ball State University has received national acclaim with such honors as the George Washington Medal of Honor (1987); the Leavey Foundation Award for Excellence in Private Enterprise (1988); and the National Model Entrepreneurship Program Award (1990).

Dr. Kuratko was named Professor of the Year for five consecutive years at the College of Business, Ball State University; Outstanding Young Faculty for Ball State University in 1987; and was recipient of Ball State University's Outstanding Teacher Award in 1990. Dr. Kuratko was also honored as the 1990 Entrepreneur of the Year for the State of Indiana (sponsored by Ernst & Young, *Inc.* magazine, and Merrill Lynch) and inducted into the Institute of American Entrepreneurs Hall of Fame in 1990.

Brief Table of Contents

Contents

Part Two

Getting into Small Business

Part Three

Start-up Problems

Part Four

Managing Operations 270

Part Five

Marketing Goods and Services

Part Six

Finances and Inventory Control

430

Part Seven

Current Issues in Small Business   498

Glossary

Index

FOURTH EDITION

EFFECTIVE
SMALL BUSINESS
MANAGEMENT

Part One

An Introduction to Small Business

■ *Part One is designed to introduce you to the field of small business. In so doing we will answer the question, "What is small business?"*

*In Chapter 1 the focus of attention is on the nature of small business. We will define the term **small business** and make a comparison between small and large firms. You will learn that although large companies account for most of the employment in the United States, small businesses are the backbone of our economy. Without small businesses to support them, most large firms would not be as profitable as they are. Large firms depend on small businesses for many inputs that they themselves cannot produce as profitably. In Chapter 1 you will also learn some of the major advantages and disadvantages of going into business for yourself. In particular, we address the question, "What are the characteristics of successful small business entrepreneurs?"*

Chapter 2 examines failure and success in small business. You will see the business failure record in the United States and learn why companies fail. Particular attention is given to some common management traps that small business people need to avoid and success factors that help explain why some small enterprises survive and grow.

Chapter 3, the final chapter in Part One, examines the unique aspects of family businesses. You will learn the managerial as well as emotional differences that family businesses possess. Particular attention is focused on the succession issue—the continued existence—that plagues contemporary family firms.

When you have finished reading the material in Part One, you will be able to define small business; identify some of the advantages and disadvantages of going into business for yourself; relate particular characteristics that successful small business owners tend to process; and understand the common management traps that hurt many small businesses. In addition, you will have a greater understanding of the unique challenges confronting family businesses in the United States today.

The Nature
of Small Business

Objectives

The first objective of Chapter 1 is to define the term small business *using practical examples, identifying characteristics, and looking at the sectors of the economy in which small businesses tend to predominate. The second objective is to study some of the advantages and disadvantages of going into business for oneself. The third objective is to describe the traits generally attributed to successful small business owners. When you have finished studying Chapter 1 you will be able to:*

1. *Define what is meant by the term* small business.

2. *Cite some illustrations of small businesses in the manufacturing, merchandising, and service sectors of the economy.*

3. *Discuss the advantages and disadvantages of going into business for oneself.*

4. *List some of the traits believed to contribute to the successful operation of a small business.*

5. *Identify the characteristics of high achievers and the steps for developing personal high achievement.*

6. *Define the term* creativity.

7. *Describe the four major creative processes.*

SMALL BUSINESS: A DEFINITION

We will begin our study of small business with a definition of the term as provided by the Small Business Act of 1953. According to this Act, a **small business** is one that is *independently owned and operated and not dominant in its field of operation.* The Act also authorized the Small Business Administration (SBA) to develop a more detailed definition that takes into account such criteria as sales volume and the number of employees in the firm. Incorporating these criteria into workable guidelines for use in determining loans, the SBA has established the upper limits for small firms in this manner:

- ☐ MANUFACTURING 250 or fewer employees. (If employment is between 250 and 1,500, a size standard for the particular industry is used.)
- ☐ WHOLESALING $9.5 million to $22 million in annual sales, depending on the line of wholesaling.
- ☐ RETAILING $2 million to $7.5 million in annual sales, depending on the line of retailing.
- ☐ SERVICE Not exceeding $1.5 to $10 million in annual sales, depending on the line of business.[1]

It is important to recognize that an appropriate definition of a small business depends largely upon the policy issue being analyzed. A small business may appropriately be defined as one having fewer than 100 employees in a discussion of retail stores, because most retail establishments have few employees and most retail firms (enterprises) have few establishments. The average entity in the industry, whether establishment or enterprise, is small, and that smallness is captured within the under-100-employees size limit. In some industries, such as automobile manufacturing, the typical establishment may be larger than 100 employees, and a definition of small businesses as those having fewer than 500 employees accurately captures the fact that a firm with 300 or 400 employees may be small relative to the industry average.

The Small Business Administration reports that definitions of small business may vary from those having fewer than 100 employees to those having fewer than 500 employees. A more detailed employment breakdown also used is as follows: under 20 employees, very small; 20–99, small; 100–499, medium sized; and over 500, large. These size breaks are consistent with standard business employment, asset, and receipt size classes established on May 18, 1982, by the Office of Management and Budget to be used by all federal agencies when publishing business data.[2]

FACTS ABOUT SMALL BUSINESS

In terms of sheer numbers, small business dominates the American economy. Consider some of the following facts about small business:

1. Currently there are approximately 20.1 million U.S. businesses, based upon IRS business tax returns. Fewer than 7,000 qualify as large firms (over 500 employees). This represents 106 million jobs in the economy. See Table 1-1.

2. Over the last few years, small independent firms created 2,650,000 new jobs, more than compensating for the 1,664,000 jobs lost by large industry.

3. Women-owned businesses are growing at an all-time high. In 1985, 2.8 million sole proprietorships were owned by women (4 times the number in 1977). Including partnerships and corporations, the number exceeded 3.7

---

[1]*Facts about Small Business and the U.S. Small Business Administration* (Washington, D.C.: Small Business Administration, 1985), p. 7.

[2]*The State of Small Business: A Report to the President,* (Washington, D.C.: U.S. Government Printing Office, 1990), p. 10.

Table 1-1 Nonfarm Business Tax Returns, 1980–1989 (thousands)

YEAR	CORPORATIONS (Forms 1120 and 11205)	PARTNERSHIPS (Form 1065)	PROPRIETORSHIPS (Schedule C)	TOTAL
1989E	4,270	1,950	13,839	20,059
1988	4,027	1,826	13,126	18,979
1987	3,829	1,824	12,633	18,286
1986	3,577	1,807	12,155	17,499
1985	3,437	1,755	11,767	16,959
1984	3,167	1,676	11,327	16,170
1983	3,078	1,613	10,507	15,198
1982	2,913	1,553	9,877	14,343
1981	2,813	1,458	9,345	13,616
1980	2,676	1,402	8,944	13,022

Source: *The State of Small Business: A Report to the President,* (Washington, D.C.: U.S. Government Printing Office, 1990), p. 11

million, or 25 percent of all small businesses. In 1987 the number increased to 28 percent. By the year 2000 it is expected to be close to 50 percent.

4. Small businesses account for nearly $8 of every $10 earned by construction firms and $7 of every $10 earned by wholesalers and retailers.

5. Small business directly or indirectly provides the livelihood of more than one hundred million Americans.

6. Small business (excluding the farm sector) represents 58 percent (58%) of all U.S. business employment.

7. Almost one-half of the gross national product (GNP) is attributable to small business.

8. Ninety-eight percent (98%) of all businesses in the U.S. are considered small by the SBA's definition and size standards.

9. Ninety percent (90%) of the small businesses in the U.S. employ less than ten people.

10. In 1989, 677,394 new business incorporations occurred, which reflects the overall trend in the growth of small businesses throughout the 1980s.[3] See Table 1-2.

It is also important to realize that small businesses play a major role in the economy by providing both employment and goods and services. They also complement large businesses by doing things that large firms either cannot or will not do, as is shown in the following examples:

1. Small firms play an important role in the introduction of new goods and services to the marketplace.

[3]Adapted from *A Tribute to Small Business: America's Growth Industry* (Washington, D.C.: Office of Private Sector Initiatives, U.S. Small Business Administration, 1987), pp. 1–7; and also from *The State of Small Business: A Report of the President* (Washington, D.C.: U.S. Government Printing Office, 1990).

Table 1-2 New Business Incorporations, 1981–1989

INCORPORATIONS	
1989	677,394
1988	685,095
1987	685,572
1986	702,101
1985	668,904
1984	634,991
1983	600,400
1982	566,942
1981	581,661

Source: *The State of Small Business: A Report to the President,*
(Washington, D.C.: U.S. Government Printing Office, 1990), p. 15.

2. In addition to serving localized markets, small firms are important suppliers in other, very specialized markets. Many small firms exist to serve particular demands, as in the case of consumer goods, for which there is considerable diversity of taste. Also, small firms are important suppliers of very specialized **intermediate goods;** that is, goods used in the production of other goods.

3. Small firms purchase, use, and often revitalize used capital equipment. This practice reduces the risk and long-run costs of entry and expansion for all firms. Also, the use of capital equipment that might otherwise lie idle helps to maintain higher output levels, which in turn adds jobs to the economy.

4. Many small firms act as market-demand "shock absorbers." By employing flexible production technologies (emphasizing the use of labor and less specialized capital goods), small firms have greater flexibility than large firms in adjusting their relative production levels and are thus better able to accommodate random, short-term fluctuations in demand. By acting as demand shock absorbers, small firms help to satisfy temporary demand increases without causing sharp price increases.

5. The significant involvement of small firms in market entry and exit helps ensure mobility of capital resources. In order for capital markets to operate efficiently, capital must be free to flow, for example, from industries with low rates of return to industries with higher rates of return. The entry and exit of small firms facilitate these flows.

6. Small firms are more likely to employ less-skilled workers and individuals with no prior work experience. This employment practice benefits the economy in two ways. First, small firms employ workers that might otherwise have difficulty securing employment, thereby reducing the duration of transitional (frictional) unemployment among these individuals. Second, the employment of these workers raises their productivity by giving them on-the-job training and work experience.

7. Because of their size, small firms are less likely to encounter problems that can arise from the complex, multi-echelon management structures that are common in large firms. Complex organizational structures tend to increase

Figure 1-1
Small Business
Health Index and
Index of Net
Business Formation,
First Quarter 1980
through Fourth
Quarter 1989

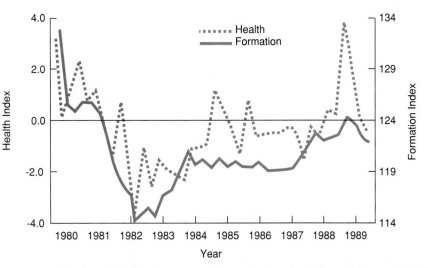

Sources: For Small Business Health Index: U.S. Business Administration Office of Advocacy. For Index of New Business Formation: U.S. Department of Commerce Bureau of Economic Analysis, 1990.

the cost of transferring information within firms and generally result in more rigid decision-making processes.

8. A small firm typically has less diffused ownership, and the owner is more likely to be directly involved in management. Thus, a small firm is less likely to experience the problems that arise when a firm's managers pursue goals that conflict with the owner's goals. Also, by virtue of the small firm's size, owners and managers can more easily (and at less expense) observe and ensure the productivity of the employees.[4]

Small businesses also provide important economic advantages for minorities and women. For example, the federal government reports that approximately 2 percent of all minorities own their own businesses.[5] These businesses account for well over $30 billion annually in receipts. Women-owned businesses take in over $45 billion annually, which represents approximately 7 percent of all U.S. business receipts, excluding those of large corporations.[6] The estimates showing that 28 percent of all U.S. businesses are currently run by women with a projected increase to 50 percent by the year 2000 indicates that more and more women will be reaching for the opportunities offered in the field of small business.[7]

Table 1-3 illustrates the numerous statistics involved with small business in the economy by summarizing various highlights. In addition, Figure 1-1 provides an

---

[4]*The State of Small Business: A Report of the President* (Washington, D.C.: U.S. Government Printing Office, 1987), pp. 108–9.

[5]*The State of Small Business: A Report of the President* (Washington, D.C.: U.S. Government Printing Office, 1987), p. 223.

[6]Carole E. Scott, "Why More Women Are Becoming Entrepreneurs," *Journal of Small Business Management,* October 1986, pp. 37–44; See also, Lois A. Stevenson, "Against All Odds: The Entrepreneurship of Women," *Journal of Small Business Management,* October 1986, pp. 30–36.

[7]*"New Economic Realities: The Rise of Women Entrepreneurs,"* House of Representatives Report No. 100–736 (Washington, D.C.: U.S. Government Printing Office, 1988).

Table 1-3 Who's Starting Small Businesses?

AGE		SOURCE OF IDEAS FOR BUSINESS	
20–29	25%	Prior job	42%
30–39	39	Personal interest	18
40–49	24	Chance	10
50 or over	11	Suggestion	8
PARENTS OWNED AN INDEPENDENT BUSINESS		Education	6
		Family business	6
Yes	45%	Friends/relatives	6
No	54	Other	4
No answer	1		
SEX		**INITIAL INVESTMENT**	
Male	77%	Under $5,000	17%
Female	22	$5,000–9,999	14
No answer	1	$10,000–19,999	16
PREVIOUS EMPLOYER		$20,000–49,999	25
		$50,000–99,000	15
Small business	46%	$100,000–249,999	8
Large business	16	$250,000 or more	3
Own business	14		
Medium business	12		
Other	12		

Source: National Federation of Independent Business, 1987.

illustration of the small business health index combined with the Index of New Business Formations from 1980–1989.

Of course, big businesses dominate some sectors of the economy, such as mining and auto manufacturing. On the other hand, there are a number of sectors such as manufacturing, merchandising, and service industries where small businesses predominate. The following section examines each of these latter sectors in detail.

MAJOR SMALL BUSINESS SECTORS IN THE ECONOMY

Small business opportunities exist in *all* sectors of the economy. However, since space limits the number of areas that can be given consideration, we will focus on those sectors often regarded as the major areas of business activity: the manufacturing of products, the distribution or merchandising of products, and the rendering of services. (See Small Business Owner's Notebook: Future Trends for the 1990s.)

MANUFACTURING

There are many types of small **manufacturing firms.** They include job printing shops, ice cream plants, bakeries, toy factories, furniture manufacturers, machine shops, clothing manufacturers, and cabinet shops, to name just a few. All, however, perform the same basic function. They convert raw materials into a useful end product, such as furniture hardware, for either the final customer or some other

■ SMALL BUSINESS OWNER'S NOTEBOOK ■

Future Trends for the 1990s

 Five major trends that are emerging in the 1990s will directly affect small business owners. The small businessperson who is prepared for these trends may find that they provide special opportunities rather than disruptive roadblocks.

Trend #1: The Aging Labor Market

The majority of American workers fall into the category known as the "baby boomers." Born between 1946 and 1964, 75 million workers are approaching or into their 40s. By the year 2000, the bulk of the work force will be in the 45 to 54-year-old age group. Conversely, the 16- to 24-year-old sector of the work force will decrease by 12 percent.

Trend #2: Women and Minorities

Of the 25 million new jobs generated between 1972 and 1985, 64 percent were filled by women. By the year 2000 it is estimated that women will account for nearly half of the U.S. labor force. In addition, the number of self-employed women grew by 86 percent during the 1975–1985 period (3 times greater than men). In terms of new entrants to the labor force, white males will account for only 8.5 percent, while Hispanics, Blacks, and Asians will account for almost 60 percent.

Trend #3: Growth in the Service Sector

The service segment of the economy is expected to add 16.6 million jobs by the year 2000, while the goods producing sector will add only 500,000. In fact, it is predicted that service jobs will account for more than 70 percent of the Gross National Product by the year 2000.

Trend #4: Computers

Computers are a key to business productivity. The computer age is upon us with almost 100 percent of large firms now using computers and 70 percent of small firms employing computers. It is expected that computer and data processing services will increase as an industry by 77 percent as we approach the year 2000.

Trend #5: International Opportunities

With the global economy becoming a reality, U.S. businesses are increasing their international involvement. Most regions of the world will grow more rapidly than the U.S. domestic market. East Asia, the Middle East, Latin America, and Japan will all grow at an annual rate of more than 4 percent, while U.S. growth will be under 2.4 percent.

Source: *Small Business Survival Guide, Indianapolis Business Journal,* Summer 1990, pp. 26–29.

manufacturer who performs further processing, such as the cabinetmaker who incorporates another manufacturer's furniture hardware in the end product.

In the area of further processing, large companies are most dominant. During the last decade, for example, it has been reported that approximately 70 percent of all manufacturing employment has been accounted for by only 3 percent of the firms. Despite such developments, the number of small manufacturing companies (one–four employees) continues to grow. One of the major reasons is that big manufacturing firms depend on small ones. For example, the giant auto manufacturers, radio makers, aircraft manufacturers, and home appliance builders all depend heavily on small subcontractors to build many of the parts that go into their finished products. One large manufacturer may require the services of 1,000 smaller ones. In fact, it has been estimated that there are probably no more than 500 firms in the mass-production industry that employ more than 1,000 workers each, while more than 300,000 firms have fewer than 500 workers. This works out to approximately 600 small manufacturers for every large-scale producer.

Small business manufacturers today are following one of two routes: producing goods for other manufacturers or manufacturing for local consumer markets. In the latter category are some of the types of firms mentioned earlier—bakeries, cabinet shops, and job print shops. These kinds of enterprises are found all over the United States, and as the local community grows so does its need for these manufactured products. For many small manufacturers, then, opportunity is tied directly to community growth.

MERCHANDISING

Merchandisers are middlepersons in the channel of distribution who either sell products to the final consumer (**retailers**) or buy goods for resale to retailers (**wholesalers**). Of the two, there are more retailers than wholesalers. Typical retail establishments include food stores, automotive dealers, gasoline service stations, eating and drinking establishments, furniture stores, and drugstores. Most retail stores are small; in fact, approximately 70 percent of them have less than four paid employees, and 95 percent of the retail establishments in this country are small-scale independents. Retail stores have sales of $1–4 trillion annually.

Most wholesalers have between four and ten employees, although they are like retailers in that they gross less than $600,000 annually. In recent years the growth of wholesale establishments has not kept pace with the growth of the population. The reason can be traced principally to such developments as the rise of chain stores and department stores that perform the wholesale function for themselves. Nevertheless, wholesale establishments remain an important part of the economy, accounting for total sales of well over $2 trillion annually.

SERVICE ENTERPRISES

In recent years the number of **service enterprises** has increased dramatically. One reason for this growth has been the increase in purchasing power of the average consumer. For example, in families where both spouses work there has been an increase in the amount of money spent for home cleaning services and laundry. Many working families do not have time for these household chores so they are having others do the work for them. Some service enterprises, such as hotel chains, are very large; most others, however, such as dry cleaners, shoe repair stores, barbershops, and restaurants, are small, require a minimal investment to get started, and rely heavily on close personal supervision. This leads to another reason for the huge increase in the number of service enterprises: lack of mechanization. The service industry as a whole is not highly mechanized. For example, a waiter can serve only a limited number of tables; if more customers show up, more waiters must be hired. Likewise, a ski instructor can teach only a limited number of skiers, and a barber can give only a limited number of haircuts. As a result, as more money is spent on these services the number of business opportunities increases. Another reason for the growth of the service industry is the large increase in funds spent on leisure activities. Now more than ever, people are bowling, skiing, boating, or doing something else that is relaxing with their leisure time. This has led to the growth of such service enterprises as travel agencies and small resort hotels.

Why do people choose to open a small manufacturing firm or go into merchandising or service enterprises? It must be that the advantages of doing so outweigh the disadvantages. The following section examines the advantages and disadvantages of going into business for oneself.

ADVANTAGES OF GOING INTO BUSINESS FOR ONESELF

There are a number of advantages of going into business for oneself:

1. independence
2. financial opportunities
3. community service
4. job security
5. family employment
6. challenge

INDEPENDENCE

Most small business owners enjoy being their own boss; they like the freedom to do things their way. While there is often a great deal of responsibility associated with this independence, they are willing to assume it.

FINANCIAL OPPORTUNITIES

Another major reason for going into business for oneself is financial opportunity. Many small business owners make more money running their own company than they would working for someone else.

COMMUNITY SERVICE

Sometimes an individual will realize that a particular good or service is not available. If there is reason to believe that the public will pay for such output, the person will start a company to provide it.

JOB SECURITY

When one owns a business, job security is ensured. The individual can work as long as he or she wants; there is no mandatory retirement.

FAMILY EMPLOYMENT

Another advantage is the opportunity to provide family members a place of employment. This has several benefits. First, many owner-managers want to perpetuate their business, and how better to do so than to get children or relatives to take it over? Second, there is usually higher morale and trust in family-run businesses than in others. Third, in times of severe economic downturn, small business owners can provide employment for family members.

CHALLENGE

Many small business owners are lured by the challenge that accompanies going into business for oneself. Research reveals that most successful small business owners like to feel that there is a chance they will succeed (they want to know success is possible), and a chance they will fail (success is not a sure thing). But one thing is certain: *the final outcome depends heavily on them.* They want to win or lose on their own abilities. This challenge gives them psychological satisfaction.

DISADVANTAGES OF GOING INTO SMALL BUSINESS FOR ONESELF

There are numerous disadvantages associated with going into business. Some of the major disadvantages include the following:

1. sales fluctuations
2. competition
3. increased responsibilities
4. financial losses
5. employee relations
6. laws and regulations
7. risk of failure

SALES FLUCTUATIONS

Because a person working for a large firm is paid regularly, the employee can budget food expenditures, plan vacations, and buy clothing. The owner-manager, however, often faces sales fluctuations. In some months sales are very high, while in others they drop off dramatically. The individual must balance cash inflows with cash outflows so that there is always enough money to meet expenses. Sometimes this will require the owner to take a short-term loan (30–90 days) to help the business get through a slack period. And virtually every small business has sales fluctuations. For example, auto dealers have their best sales months when the new models come out (November and December) and the summer (June and July) when people again start thinking about buying a new car. Retail stores find that their greatest sales volume occurs during the end-of-year holiday season. Manufacturers of swimwear obtain their largest sales prior to summer, when they sell their merchandise to wholesalers and retailers. Construction firms have their best months during the summer when the weather is good.

COMPETITION

A second disadvantage of owning a business is the risk of competition. In particular, an individual may start a business and prosper for three or four years before meeting insurmountable competition. Or there may be changes in market demand and the owner will find that this new demand is being satisfied by large competitors. For example, small restaurants and diners may find that they have lost customers to fast-food chains.

INCREASED RESPONSIBILITIES

Small businesses face many responsibilities, especially as their operations get larger. For example, owners not only have to make more decisions on major matters but have to become knowledgeable in many different areas. A successful owner is often a bookkeeper, accountant, salesperson, personnel manager, and janitor all rolled into one. The individual works long hours and, in many cases, six or seven days a week. This is in direct contrast to workers who hold full-time 9-to-5 jobs where salary is guaranteed and raises and promotions can be counted on.

FINANCIAL LOSSES

When all major decisions are made by the owner, it is inevitable that some of them will be wrong. On occasion, inventory will be too high (or low); a product line that was developed at great expense will not sell; a price reduction will not increase demand for the product, with a resulting decline in total revenue; an advertising campaign will not pay for itself; an increase in the sales force will prove to be a mistake and excess personnel will have to be laid off.

In all these cases the owner will face a financial loss, and if enough of them occur, bankruptcy may result. However, this is not what usually happens. Rather, the owner simply ends up making less money, resulting in a small return on investment for a great deal of effort, work, and risk. Additionally, it is important to note that unless the business is incorporated, the owner is *personally* responsible for all losses. This means the individual could lose everything he or she owns, although in some states the person's home is protected from creditors until the individual chooses to sell it.

EMPLOYEE RELATIONS

The small business owner also needs to be concerned with employee relations. If the workers are not content, sales will suffer. For example, in many retail stores employees are not allowed to talk or socialize on the job. Workers are expected to remain at their sales counters and stay alert for customers who need assistance. Management believes that if the employees begin talking to each other they will lose potential sales. On the other hand, research reveals that if employees feel isolated or alone, their attitudes toward the job will decline. This, in turn, will affect their sales ability. They will be rude or curt to the customer, who will then refuse to buy. Thus, a balance must be struck regarding how much socialization can be allowed. Solving this problem requires human relations skills.

So do many other problems faced by the owner. For example, friction between workers who do not like each other requires the owner to resolve the conflict by either getting the employees to put aside their personal differences or by firing one or more of them. Another common problem is job assignment. Who will do what? The owner must be careful not to overload one person with work while another does virtually nothing. There is also the matter of financial compensation. How much should each person be paid? When should raises be given? How large should each raise be? Finally, should salaries be secret or should the owner let everyone know how much each person is being paid?

Questions such as these exemplify the employee relations problems that must be resolved by the owner. As the enterprise grows and more people are hired, more issues present themselves. Some of the most common relate to medical insurance, retirement programs, other fringe benefits, and unionization. In short, as the company grows so will the employee relations issues that will have to be addressed.

LAWS AND REGULATIONS

Small businesses are subject to a multitude of laws and regulations. For example, federal law requires the owner to pay social security taxes for all employees as well as to withhold federal taxes from each person's pay and remit these funds to the government. At the state level, in addition to employee taxes, there is often a state sales tax to be collected and sent to the proper state agency. Also, for some fields the state requires that a license be secured before doing business; typical examples include restaurants, barber shops, beauty salons, and liquor stores. At the local level laws often regulate the days of the week and hours of the day during which business can be conducted. In addition, there are safety and health requirements related to fire prevention and the avoidance of job hazards. Finally, building and zoning regulations limit the type of structures that can be built and where they can be located. For example, in most cities, office and business buildings are not allowed in the same locale as residential homes.

RISK OF FAILURE

The ultimate risk faced by the small business owner-manager is that of failing, usually with a loss of most, if not all, of the money invested in the enterprise. In Chapter 2 we will focus on the specific causes of failure and ways to avoid them. For the moment let us look at business failure in general. All owners face this risk, and despite experience and business knowledge, many fail because of factors beyond their control. For example, a major recession hits most small businesses very hard. Meanwhile, despite precautions, every year some companies are forced into bankruptcy because their funds are embezzled by insiders who systematically drain the company's financial resources. Then there is the unexpected tornado that tears through the town, totally demolishing many businesses. In each of these cases the company may be forced to close its doors. In most instances, however, failure is caused by poor management.

THE SUCCESSFUL SMALL BUSINESS OWNER

The word used most often to describe a small business owner is **entrepreneur.** This is an individual who organizes, owns, manages, and assumes the risks of a business. As noted previously, the entrepreneur is a keystone of the American enterprise system. For this reason researchers have long sought to determine what characteristics result in entrepreneurial success. No universal list of traits and characteristics describes *every* entrepreneur.[8] However, *most* entrepreneurs show strength in certain traits, including technical competence, initiative, personality, understanding, attitude, emotional maturity, and efficiency. In a small manufacturing firm, technical competence and good judgment are extremely important. In a computer sales organization, personality and drive are of major value. In a motel/hotel operation, communications ability and dependability are required. In banking,

---

[8]Thomas M. Begley and David P. Boyd, "Psychological Characteristics Associated with Performance in Entrepreneurial Firms and Smaller Businesses," *Journal of Business Venturing*, Winter 1987, pp. 79–93.

initiative, confidence, and innovation are critical.[9] Thus the specific traits and characteristics necessary for success in particular businesses vary.[10] Nevertheless, several of them warrant our close attention. (See Small Business Success: The Institute of American Entrepreneurs.)

CHARACTERISTICS FOR SUCCESS

Five characteristics have primary importance for entrepreneurial success. Although not all-inclusive, *most* successful small business owners possess these traits:

1. technical competence
2. mental ability
3. human relations skills
4. high achievement drive
5. creativity

TECHNICAL COMPETENCE

The characteristic most important for success in a small business is **technical competence**—the owners need to know what they are doing. The retailer who does not know how to sell merchandise, the landscape architect who designs an eyesore, and the garage mechanic who tunes a car improperly will soon find themselves out of business. The first thing the entrepreneur must know is the "how-to-do-it" side of the job.

MENTAL ABILITY

Mental ability, roughly defined, is the capacity to know or understand. The entrepreneur uses this mental ability to develop competitive strategies. To develop such strategies the owner should also be a generalist. A **generalist** is a person who possesses the ability to view operations in broad terms. While technical knowledge enables one to understand how specific things work, a generalist approach helps the owner-manager understand how all of the jobs interrelate, which is necessary for developing overall business objectives and plans. It is the ability to "pull everything together."[11]

---

[9]Ray V. Montagno, Donald F. Kuratko, and Joseph H. Scarcella, "Perception of Entrepreneurial Success Characteristics," *American Journal of Small Businesses,* Winter 1986, pp. 25–32.

[10]For additional examples of entrepreneurial characteristics, see James W. Carland, Frank Hoy, William R. Boulton, and Jo Ann C. Carland, "Differentiating Entrepreneurs from Small Business Owners: A Conceptualization," *Academy of Management Review, April 1987,* p. 356; and John Hornaday, "Research about Living Entrepreneurs," *Encyclopedia of Entrepreneurship,* Calvin Kent, Donald Sexton, and Karl Vesper, editors (Englewood Cliffs, NJ: Prentice-Hall, Inc., 1982), pp. 26–27.

[11]Donald L. Sexton and Nancy Bowman, "The Entrepreneur: A Capable Executive and More," *Journal of Business Venturing,* Winter 1985, pp. 129–40. See also Harris M. Plotkin, "Portrait of a Successful Small Business Owner," *Small Business Reports,* January 1990, pp. 15–19.

The Institute of American Entrepreneurs

Each year Ernst & Young, Merrill Lynch, and *Inc.* magazine sponsor regional competitions to identify state or regional "Entrepreneurs of the Year." In each of these regions special ceremonies are organized to honor the award recipients chosen through a statewide nomination process. The honorees receive a specially designed trophy that represents the "Entrepreneur of the Year" program.

To further commemorate the achievements of those successful entrepreneurs, the Entrepreneur of the Year Hall of Fame was established by the Institute of American Entrepreneurs. Each year a special national ceremony is held to induct the new members into the Hall of Fame, which is located at the Kenan Institute of Private Enterprise on the campus of the University of North Carolina. The names of all of the honored entrepreneurs are engraved on plaques and prominently displayed. Biographies and background information about the inductees are also available.

Membership in the Institute of American Entrepreneurs is limited exclusively to "Entrepreneur of the Year" award recipients. Once inducted, members have a lifetime membership in the Institute.

Source: Institute of American Entrepreneurs, Kenan Center: University of North Carolina at Chapel Hill, Chapel Hill, N.C. 27514.

HUMAN RELATIONS SKILLS

Successful entrepreneurs have good **human relations skills**—that is, they know how to get along with others, including their employees, business associates, suppliers, and customers. In particular, they know how to communicate, motivate, and lead—three of the major human relations skills.

COMMUNICATION Communication involves the transmission of meanings from sender to receiver. If the manager cannot communicate properly, directions will be misunderstood, orders will be placed incorrectly, and general chaos will result. These problems can be prevented, however, if the owner ensures that his or her directives are clearly understood.

MOTIVATION Motivation is the process of inducing people to do something. In many cases, entrepreneurs report that independence is a strong motivator. Certainly it is an important consideration in motivation, but it can be misleading. While independence often motivates small business owners, it does not always motivate employees. Workers and managers are also motivated by job security, wages, and interesting work assignments, among other critical factors.

LEADERSHIP Leadership is the process of influencing subordinates to direct their efforts toward attaining specific objectives. Small business leaders tend to have the same leadership traits as their counterparts in large organizations.

Effective leadership style depends on the situation. Sometimes an autocratic leader is most effective; other times a democratic leader is best; still other times a laissez-faire leader is preferred. In *most* cases, however, the democratic leader is superior because situation variables usually favor that style.

HIGH-ACHIEVEMENT DRIVE

Successful entrepreneurs are high achievers. They both want and need to get things done. They are action-oriented and gauge their performance in terms of results; that is, "Was I successful in my efforts?" Research shows that only 10–13 percent of the U.S. population is strongly motivated to achieve. This need is a result of many factors including childhood and occupational experiences. However, without it, the small business owner is in trouble.

CHARACTERISTICS OF HIGH ACHIEVERS   Researchers like David C. McClelland of Harvard University have provided a number of important insights into the question "How do you identify the high achiever?"[12] In particular, three important characteristics have been found.

First, high achievers like situations in which they take **personal responsibility** for finding solutions to problems. These individuals want to play an active role in determining the outcome, rather than relying on chance or luck. They want to make their own opportunities. Among small business owners, for example, high achievers delegate minor decisions but make the important ones themselves. For them, the buck does indeed stop here.

Second, high achievers tend to be **moderate risk takers** rather than low or high risk takers. Many students of small business find this difficult to believe, but an analysis of the logic should resolve any doubt. If the high achiever made only low-risk decisions, the person would never really take any chances. When the high achiever is placed in a low-risk situation, the person tends to manipulate something to increase the risk. Things would be too calm and predictable otherwise. Conversely, if the decisions involved high risks, the individual would be playing long shots all the time. The entrepreneur would feel that success entailed luck, not skill. Remember, a high-risk situation only exists when the chances for success are small and the person cannot improve the chances through hard work or skill. Such conditions are unacceptable to the high achiever. Therefore, the person will accept moderate-risk situations where there is a chance of losing but with **personal effort** the chance is reduced. Keep in mind that in some cases high achievers make decisions that appear to be high-risk. However, while this might be true for the average person, for the high achiever it is not, because the person has determined how he or she can improve the chances of success through some special effort or strategy.

Third, high achievers like **concrete feedback** on how well they are doing. They want to know the score. Entrepreneurs are continually looking at the profit and loss statements, studying the costs of production, examining sales figures for the different product lines, and determining where they have been successful and where they have not. This feedback serves as a basis for future action; high achievers will not

---

[12]For more on this subject see David C. McClelland, *The Achieving Society* (Princeton, NJ: Van Nostrand Reinhold Co., 1961).

keep a product line that is a loser or offer a particular service once it has been established that the demand will not cover the costs involved. High achievers like concrete feedback because it helps them monitor their performance and gives them a basis for patting themselves on the back when they have done a good job.

DEVELOPING HIGH ACHIEVEMENT Not every small business owner is a high achiever—at least when starting out. However, achievement drive can be at least partially developed. Research shows four basic steps that can help.

First, the individual needs to strive for feedback. By looking for job-related results (sales, profits, margins) the entrepreneur can obtain reinforcement for success. This will strengthen the person's desire to achieve more.

Second, the individual needs to seek out successful people in the same line of work to emulate. In short, copy success!

Third, the entrepreneur should continually modify his or her self-image by imagining himself or herself as someone who needs success and challenge.

Fourth, the entrepreneur needs to control his or her daydreaming by thinking and talking inwardly in positive terms. By imagining oneself as facing difficult business problems and succeeding, internal confidence is created. Furthermore, business situations in which one is likely to find oneself mentally rehearsing makes it easier to cope with them.[13]

High achievers, especially in small business, tend to be more successful than average or low achievers. This is because they are realistic, hardworking, and convinced that they will make their business a success.[14]

CREATIVITY

Another characteristic of successful small business owners is **creativity,** which can be defined as the ability to process information in such a way that the result is new, original, and meaningful. Creativity is shown in many ways. In particular, there are four major creative processes: innovation, synthesis, extension, and duplication.

INNOVATION Innovation refers to original thinking. Some people can come up with new ideas that result in business success because of their innovative thinking. Conrad Hilton, the late founder of the Hilton Inn Corporation, said he became a success by taking advantage of opportunities that other people failed to notice. This statement reflects an important characteristic of creative people. They are bright but not necessarily brilliant. Hilton believed that others could have done what he did; they just lacked the originality to see it. He was not a genius, just a perceptive, innovative entrepreneur. Other examples of innovative businesspeople include the inventor of the ballpoint pen and Edwin Land, the developer of the Polaroid camera.

---

[13]For more on the development of high achievement see David Miron and David C. McClelland, "The Impact of Achievement Motivation Training on Small Businesses," *California Management Review,* Summer 1979, pp. 13–28.

[14]For an interesting discussion see Thomas M. Begley and David P. Boyd, "A Comparison of Entrepreneurs and Managers of Small Business Firms," *Journal of Management,* Spring 1987, pp. 99–108.

SYNTHESIS   Synthesis involves combining information from many sources and integrating it into a new, useful pattern. Discount stores are a post-World War II phenomenon. The distance between the manufacturer and the consumer has been reduced by eliminating some of the middlepersons. This approach was hailed as a major breakthrough. Yet any businessperson who understood marketing should have been able to develop this idea into a successful strategy. However, it took a handful of creative marketers to do so.

EXTENSION   Extension involves expanding current boundaries by applying ideas that work in one area to another area. For example, during the 1950s, Ray Kroc bought McDonald's and proceeded to make it a national organization with units located in almost every city and town in the United States. Other people have copied this approach with different products. Today fast-food outlets sell chicken, pizza, ice cream, and an assortment of other goods. By extending the basic idea into other areas, creative people have developed opportunities for themselves.

DUPLICATION   Duplication is best defined by the cliche "If you can't be original, copy good ideas." This approach is followed by many small businesses. By being alert to what other firms are doing, a company can modify its own goods or service and remain competitive. Collecting ideas, sorting them out, and then determining which are most useful to the firm is one of the easiest ways to introduce creative goods and services. Many business people will work as salespeople for a firm, watch the way the company does business, and then go off on their own and do basically the same thing. To a large degree, this is duplication, but it also illustrates a creative process.

In most cases creative thinking combines these four processes. There will be, for example, some synthesis, extension, and duplication in a creative idea. There may also be innovation, the most difficult of the processes because it demands the most originality.

Creativity is often regarded as something one either has or does not have. However, research shows that it can be improved within the individual.[15] Four ways of doing so are explained here.

First, loosen up emotionally and intellectually. Creative people give free rein to their thinking. They are not bound by old ways of looking at problems; they go beyond the familiar.

Second, discipline yourself to think creatively. The creative person recognizes that creativity is both necessary and desirable.

Third, in group settings, use approaches like brainstorming. This technique involves assembling a group for the purpose of formulating creative solutions. The group is told about the problem and encouraged to suggest solutions. No matter how wild the solution, criticism is forbidden. "Piggybacking," using someone else's idea as a basis for another new idea, is encouraged.

---

[15]For additional studies on creativity see Eugene Raudsepp, *How to Create New Ideas for Corporate Profit and Personal Success* (Englewood Cliffs, NJ: Prentice-Hall, Inc., 1982); David Campbell, *Take the Road to Creativity and Get off Your Dead End* (Greensboro, NC: Center for Creative Leadership, 1985); and Frank J. Sabatine, "Rediscovering Creativity—Unlearning Old Habits," *Mid-American Journal of Business,* Fall 1989, pp. 11–13.

Fourth, creativity is most likely to occur when the "climate" is right. No business will have creative owners and managers if creativity is not encouraged. Certain characteristics support a **creative climate:**

☐ willingness to accept change

☐ enjoyment of experimenting with new ideas

☐ little fear of negative consequences for making a mistake

☐ selection and promotion of employees on the basis of merit

☐ use of techniques that encourage ideas, such as suggestion systems and brainstorming

☐ sufficient financial, managerial, human, and time resources for accomplishing goals

■ SUMMARY

The term *small business* has been defined in a number of ways. The Small Business Administration (SBA) had defined small business as one that is *independently owned and operated* and *not dominant in its field of operation.* This is the definition that will be used throughout this book; most businesses in our economy fall into this definition. Approximately 90 percent of all enterprises have fewer than 20 employees, and 70 percent of all the firms in the country have annual gross sales of less than $200,000.

Despite the fact that large businesses dominate certain industries, there is a great deal of opportunity for small businesses in the economy. For example, the giant firms in manufacturing depend heavily on smaller firms to serve as subcontractors. Other small manufacturers supply local markets and find that as the communities in which they are located grow, their businesses grow as well. As a result, small business opportunities in manufacturing are good.

The same is true in the merchandising field, in which retailers and wholesalers serve as middlepersons between the manufacturer and the final consumer. Today approximately 95 percent of all retail establishments are small in terms of the guidelines set forth by the SBA. Wholesalers are larger, in both the number of employees and in gross sales, but they, too, for the most part, fit under the basic SBA definition of small business.

So do most service enterprises. Today this sector of the economy is growing rapidly as more and more people use their purchasing power for such services as haircuts, auto repair, dry cleaning, shoe repair, and recreational activities.

Going into business has a number of advantages. They include independence, financial opportunities, community service, job security, family employment, and challenge. On the other hand, there are also disadvantages. They include sales fluctuations, competition, increased responsibilities, financial losses, employee relations, laws and regulations, and the risk of failure.

In determining whether small business ownership should be a career goal, one has to carefully weigh the growth that is expected in the particular industry and then weigh the advantages and disadvantages discussed in this chapter. Additionally, one has to know why some firms succeed and others fail. That is the subject of Chapter 2.

While there are many ways to describe a small business owner, the word most often used is *entrepreneur*, which is defined as "the organizer of a venture, especially one who organizes, owns, manages, and assumes the risks of a business." What personal traits contribute to small business success? Many have been mentioned by various researchers, but the most agreed upon characteristics include technical competence, mental ability, human relations skills, high-achievement drive, and creativity.

High-achievement drive is possessed by those who both want and need to get things done. The three overriding characteristics of high achievers are that they take personal responsibility for finding solutions to problems, they tend to be moderate risk takers, and they like concrete feedback on their performances.

Creativity is the ability to process information in such a way that the result is new, original, and meaningful. The four major creative processes are innovation, synthesis, extension, and duplication.

■ REVIEW AND DISCUSSION QUESTIONS

1. What is your personal definition of a "small" business? What criteria did you use in formulating your definition?

2. In which area of the economy, merchandising or services, do you believe a small business has the best opportunity for growth? Why?

3. What are the advantages of going into business for oneself? List and explain at least four.

4. What are some of the disadvantages of going into business for oneself? List and explain at least four.

5. Most businesses in the economy are small businesses. Is this an accurate statement? Support your answer.

6. What is an entrepreneur?

7. Which characteristic is most important for entrepreneurial success? Explain.

8. What are the characteristics of high achievers? How can high-achievement drive be developed? Explain.

9. What is creativity? What are the four major creative processes? Describe each.

Case Studies

Judd's Dilemma

■ Just about every home in the United States seems to have a vacuum cleaner. As a result, when Judd Kannt set up his vacuum cleaning and repair store he felt sure that there would be more than enough business to ensure himself a good living. However, after three years in operation he is thinking about closing the store. There are a number of reasons for this.

First, Judd has found that the large retail stores can sell some models of vacuum cleaners at a lower price than his. Second, while he sells many models below the average retail price, not many people purchase from him. Judd has a large service business but does not sell many new vacuum cleaners. Apparently, people would rather purchase their machines from a large retailer or discount store and, when the warranty runs out, bring it to Judd for repairs. Vacuum cleaner repair, despite what the average person thinks, is not a great chore, and the repair charge is sufficient to ensure Judd a good living. However, what has Judd most upset is that he had hoped to make his living selling vacuum cleaners, not repairing them. He considers himself to be a salesperson, not a repairman.

Another thing that upsets Judd is that sales are not steady throughout the year. Most of his sales occur around the winter holidays. Otherwise, he notices that people come in on a random basis. He believes that most of his customers are buying the machines as gifts. This sales fluctuation requires him to budget his expenditures very carefully. Because he is continually making estimates of monthly income and expenditures, Judd sometimes feels as if he is more of an accountant than a businessperson.

Finally, what seems to discourage him most is that he works an average of ten hours a day Monday through Friday and a half-day on Saturday. The amount of money he grossed last year was only 7 percent more than his cousin made working as a packer at a local manufacturing plant. When one adds in the fringe benefits that his cousin receives from the company, such as hospitalization, retirement, and so on, Judd is making less money. Judd's big question right now is, "Why am I knocking myself out for nickels and dimes? I'm not doing any better than the average packer at a production company and I'm putting in a lot more hours, have a great deal more responsibility, and face the risk of financial loss and perhaps even bankruptcy. Maybe I should get out while I'm ahead."

1. What are the disadvantages of Judd's being in business for himself? Explain each.

2. What is the major reason Judd is thinking about closing up his business?

3. What advice would you give Judd? Why?

Doing It Better

■ It is seldom easy to create new products. However, Wayne Harrison has been quite successful at it, and his sales to retailers across the country have increased by 20% annually each of the four years he has been in business. Wayne uses a two-pronged approach. First, he stays alert for all new, inexpensive products that came on the market. Second, he buys those he believes are easiest to duplicate and then produces them at less cost than the competition.

Wayne generally starts out by looking for a good that is produced and shipped from another section of the country. If it is coming any great distance, there are shipping costs involved; and if Wayne can produce the product locally, he sometimes can undercut the competition. Since he lives in a Northwestern state, wood-related products are good ones with which to compete. Last month, for example, he found small computer tables being offered for $40 each at a computer store. These tables are designed to hold the computer, the disk drive, and the keyboard. They were produced and shipped by a large national manufacturer. Wayne bought one, carefully examined its dimensions and construction, and determined that he could produce the same product locally for $9 including labor. He made one and took it to six competitive computer stores, offering them the tables for $18 each. He received orders for 180 tables. Wayne then went to five large retailers and received orders for another 400.

"It's really not difficult to compete with other firms," he explained. "All you have to do is figure out what is selling and select those goods that you can produce more cheaply. Of course, I'll never be able to compete on a national level, but who cares? I'm doing great right here. I'll gross $5,220 from the 580 tables I sold last week, and it won't take me more than two weeks to deliver them. I'm having the wood precut; I've purchased the glue, screws, and other materials I'll need, and I have three people lined up to assemble them. It should take no more than fifteen minutes to put each one together. You know, the markup on goods by middlemen is so great that if you can sell direct, it's possible to make a large profit and still beat the competition."

1. Which creative process does this case study illustrate? Identify and describe it.

2. Is Wayne creative? Defend your answer.

3. What does this case illustrate about the relationship between creativity and small business success? Explain.

You Be the Consultant

A BUSINESS OPPORTUNITY

Acme Cleaners is a small laundry and dry-cleaning establishment in a large Northwestern city. The owners, Don and Paula Eiburg, have run the business for 25 years. During that time they have increased their total sales volume from $4,000 in the first year to over $210,000 last year. After all expenses except taxes last year, Don and Paula cleared $37,000.

The cleaners is open six days a week, from 8 A.M. to 8 P.M. on weekdays and a half-day on Saturday. Either Don or Paula is there at all times. In addition, three full-time employees each work 40 hours per week.

Don has noticed that during the last ten years there has been a sharp increase in business as more and more people have begun sending their clothing out to be cleaned. He attributes most of this increase to the fact that many people are

working and do not have time to do their own cleaning. In many cases, both spouses have full-time jobs. With their increased income they prefer to have others perform certain services for them, such as cleaning, rather than to come home from work and have to do the laundry themselves. Additionally, many of the people work in organizations that require them to dress "professionally," so more clothing than ever has to be dry-cleaned.

Don enjoys running his own operation. However, last week he went for his annual physical and the doctor noticed that Don was extremely nervous. After completing the physical the doctor recommended that Don take some time off. "You've worked hard all your life, Don," he told him. "Now it's time to slow down. Take a year off to relax and enjoy yourself. You and Paula have saved enough money to go on an extended vacation. Turn your business over to someone else for awhile and start being concerned with your own personal welfare."

Don and Paula have given this advice a lot of thought and concluded that the doctor is right. They are going to step out of the business, at least for awhile. Rather than turn the business over to some stranger, however, they have been thinking about their nephew Charles.

Last week they and Charles had dinner, and Don explained the situation to him. He told Charles that running the business is not very difficult. The average person could learn all there is to know within a month. Additionally, Charles, who is twenty-four years old and has been working as a salesperson in a retail store for five years, has been looking around for a better opportunity. Don and Paula told him that if he runs the store successfully for the year they are gone, they will strike a deal with him when they return. Charles will become a full partner with 40 percent interest in the operation, and over the next ten years they will gradually turn over the entire operation to him in return for a small percentage of the gross revenues. "We've saved a lot of money over the last 25 years," Don told their nephew, "so we won't really need much. What we want is to be sure the business is in good hands."

Charles has promised to think the matter over and reach a decision within two weeks. Charles's greatest concern right now is that of weighing the advantages and disadvantages of going into a small business. He does not want to pass up a golden opportunity, but he does not want to end up working long hours in a dull job for very little money.

■ **YOUR CONSULTATION** Imagine you are Charles's best friend and that he has just asked for your advice. In particular he would like to know what you consider to be the advantages and disadvantages of getting into the business venture. Cite all the advantages and disadvantages you can think of, and then tell Charles whether or not you believe he should accept his relatives' offer.

CHAPTER 2

Examining Failure and Success in Small Business

Objectives

Virtually every day of the year some small businesses fail. Most of them have been in operation less than five years. In this chapter we will examine failure and success among small businesses. The first objective is to review the record of business failure. The second is to study why businesses fail. The third is to examine the factors that account for business success. When you have finished studying Chapter 2 you will be able to:

1. *Define what is meant by business failure.*
2. *State the trend of business failures over the last 50 years.*
3. *Describe seven specific causes that, year after year, account for business failures.*
4. *Identify some management traps that bring about business failures.*
5. *Discuss the four factors that help account for business success.*
6. *Explain what is meant by the statement, "Most small business managers use common sense, and that is not enough to ensure success."*

BUSINESS FAILURE: A LOOK AT THE RECORD

Every year many business firms cease operations. The most frequent cause is failure to pay debts, in which case it is common for the owners to declare bankruptcy and to seek to make some accommodation with the creditors, such as paying them 25 cents on the dollar. In other instances, businesses go out of existence because the owners realize that, while they are currently solvent, if they continue operations they will incur debts that they cannot meet. In these instances, **business failure** can be defined as *a halt of operations.*

Figure 2-1
The Failure Record

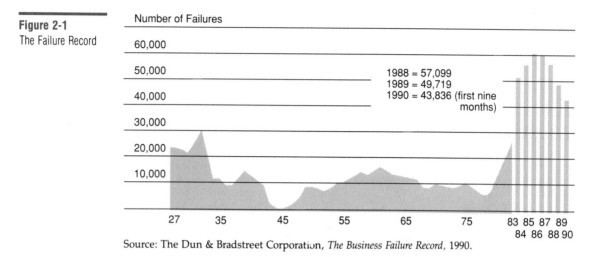

Number of Failures

1988 = 57,099
1989 = 49,719
1990 = 43,836 (first nine months)

Source: The Dun & Bradstreet Corporation, *The Business Failure Record*, 1990.

How great has business failure been in the recent past? As seen in Figure 2-1, the rate of failure per 10,000 firms has fluctuated since 1970. The 1980s saw more business failures than at any time over the past 20 years.

In examining failures more closely, two conclusions can be reached. First, the failure rate varies by region of the country. For example, after three years of a steady decline, U.S. business failures increased 14.5 percent in 1989, yet two regions actually reported *decreases* in failures during that period. During the first part of 1990, every region of the U.S. reported increases in business failures. Yet the New England states had a dramatic 192.8 percent increase in failures, whereas the South Atlantic region was reporting a 20 percent increase. See Table 2-1 for a complete breakdown. Keep in mind, of course, that many of these businesses merge with others or are bought out by larger firms. Not all are financial failures.

The second conclusion that can be reached about business failures is that the failure rate varies by industry. For example, as seen in Table 2-2, mining companies

Table 2-1 Business Failures by Region—Ranked by liability percent change. First nine months 1989 vs. first nine months 1990

| | 1989 | | 1990 | | % CHANGE | |
REGION	Number	Liabilities	Number	Liabilities	Number	Liabilities
Middle Atlantic	2,925	$1,930,304,181	4,816	$12,994,424,702	64.6%	573.2%
East North Central	6,743	$1,430,380,334	6,168	$4,767,780,624	− 8.5%	233.3%
New England	750	$1,240,164,338	2,196	$3,993,124,870	192.8%	222.0%
South Atlantic	5,823	$3,420,746,575	6,993	$10,093,286,419	20.1%	195.1%
East South Central	2,097	$557,086,446	2,618	$1,422,727,054	24.8%	155.4%
West North Central	2,377	$527,297,182	2,829	$1,035,815,253	19.0%	96.4%
Mountain	3,366	$2,961,767,803	3,544	$3,797,810,645	5.3%	28.2%
West South Central	6,480	$16,115,126,940	7,209	$11,303,506,804	11.3%	− 29.9%
Pacific	7,735	$5,931,190,011	7,463	$3,090,099,068	− 3.5%	− 47.9%
Total	38,296	$34,114,063,810	43,836	$52,498,575,439	14.5%	53.9%

Source: The Dun & Bradstreet Corporation, Economic Analysis Department. Reprinted by permission.

Table 2-2 Business Failures by Industry—U.S. Census Region
First nine months 1989 vs. first nine months 1990*

INDUSTRY	PACIFIC 1989	1990	% Change	TOTAL U.S. 1989	1990	% Change
Agriculture/forestry/fishing	192	146	− 24.0%	1,081	1,160	7.3%
Mining	8	10	25.0%	270	257	− 4.8%
Construction	914	790	− 13.6%	5,285	5,857	10.8%
Manufacturing	614	665	8.3%	2,904	3,469	19.5%
Transportation & public utilities	295	296	0.3%	1,520	1,826	20.1%
Wholesale trade	509	451	− 11.4%	2,740	3,106	13.4%
Retail trade	1,297	1,443	11.3%	8,329	9,372	12.5%
Finance/insurance/real estate	454	385	− 15.2%	2,111	2,767	31.1%
Services	3,429	2,839	− 17.2%	13,615	14,777	8.5%
Nonclassifiable establishments	23	438		441	1,245	
Total	7,735	7,463	− 3.5%	38,296	43,836	14.5%

*Data for 1989 are final; figures for 1990 are preliminary.

Source: The Dun & Bradstreet Corporation, Economic Analysis Department. Reprinted by permission.

have a failure rate more than twice that of wholesale trade companies and three times that of manufacturing firms. Similarly, agriculture, forestry, or fishing companies are more than twice as likely to fail as are retail firms. Research shows that 184 out of every 10,000 transportation equipment firms fails. For printing and publishing firms, textile product manufacturers, and paper and allied product companies, the rate per 10,000 firms is in the low 80s.

Why do some firms fail while others continue to remain successful? The following sections examine some of the underlying causes for failure and some of the major reasons for success.

WHY BUSINESSES FAIL

There are many reasons why businesses fail.[1] Dun and Bradstreet, which keeps a record of business failures and analyzes them in order to determine the specific causes, reports that the basic factors *remain the same.* In addition to these specific causes, one can also attribute failure to **poor management,** which consists of a series of **management traps.** The following examines both the specific causes of failure and the most important management traps.

SOME SPECIFIC CAUSES OF FAILURE

Year after year, the major reason businesses fail is **incompetence.** (See Table 2-3, Experience Causes.) The owners simply do not know how to run the enterprise. They make major mistakes that an experienced, well-trained entrepreneur would quickly see and easily sidestep.[2]

[1]See Hugh M. O'Neill and Jacob Duker, "Success and Failure in Small Businesses," *Journal of Small Business Management,* January 1986, pp. 30–37.

[2]William P. Sommers and Aydin Koc, "Why Most New Ventures Fail (and How Others Don't)," *Management Review,* September 1987, pp. 35–39.

The second most common reason businesses fail is **unbalanced experience.** By this we mean that the owners do not have well-rounded experience in the major activities of the business, such as finance, purchasing, selling, and production. Because the owner lacks experience in one or more of these critical areas, the enterprise gradually fails.

A third common cause of business failure is **lack of managerial experience.** The owners simply do not know how to manage people. A fourth common reason is **lack of experience in the line,** that is, the owner has entered a field of business about which he or she has very little knowledge.

Other common causes of business failure include neglect, fraud, and disaster. **Neglect** occurs whenever an owner does not pay sufficient attention to the enterprise. The owner who has someone else manage the business while he or she goes fishing often finds the business failing because of neglect. **Fraud** involves intentional misrepresentation or deception. If one of the people responsible for keeping the business's books begins purchasing materials or goods for himself or herself and having the company pay for them, the business might find itself bankrupt before too long. Of course, one can sue the individual for recovery of the merchandise and have them sent to jail, but that may all happen after the firm's creditors have demanded payment for their merchandise and the owner has had to close the business. **Disaster** refers to some unforeseen happening or "act of God." If a hurricane hits the area and destroys materials sitting in the company's yard, the loss may require the firm to declare bankruptcy. The same is true in the case of fire, burglary, or extended strike.

In all of these instances reference has been made to "underlying causes of failure." However, in most cases, these problems could have been prevented if the owners were capable managers and did not fall into management traps.

FAILURE: MANAGEMENT TRAPS

Many businesses fail during slow economic times. During periods of prosperity, however, few should go out of business.[3] Those that do must have some basic problems worthy of attention by anyone studying small business. In a study reported by the Small Business Administration, ten firms that had failed during prosperous years were compared to ten similar companies that had been successful during the same period. An analysis of the two groups revealed eighteen avoidable management traps related to three major areas:

1. poor financial planning
2. poor coordination between manufacturing and selling
3. poor general administration

The eighteen management traps are described here.[4]

---

[3]See Harriet Buckman Stephenson, "The Most Critical Problem for the Fledgling Small Business: Getting Sales," *American Journal of Small Business,* Summer 1984, pp. 26–32; and Robert L. Rose, "An Expansionary Tale," *Wall Street Journal,* May 15, 1987; p. 5d.

[4]A.M. Woodruff, *Traps to Avoid in Small Business Management,* Management Aids for Small Manufacturers, Annual No. 6 (Washington D.C.: U.S. Small Business Administration).

Table 2-3 Causes of Business Failure, 1986

	AGRICULTURE, FORESTRY, FISHING	MINING	CON-STRUC-TION	MANU-FAC-TURING	TRANSPOR-TATION, PUBLIC UTILITIES	WHOLE-SALE TRADE	RETAIL TRADE	FINANCE, INSURANCE, REAL ESTATE	SERVICES	TOTAL
Neglect Causes	**2.3%**	**0.9%**	**1.8%**	**2.1%**	**2.1%**	**2.2%**	**2.2%**	**1.6%**	**1.6%**	**1.8%**
Bad habits	32.7%	62.5%	23.1%	29.6%	15.1%	25.9%	18.2%	31.2%	22.8%	23.4%
Business conflicts	6.6%	0.0%	16.9%	23.5%	20.8%	18.3%	16.8%	22.2%	11.7%	15.9%
Family problems	6.6%	0.0%	2.3%	4.1%	11.3%	2.9%	7.2%	4.4%	7.4%	6.0%
Lack of interest	14.8%	25.0%	15.4%	19.4%	22.5%	26.0%	19.9%	11.1%	11.7%	17.0%
Marital problems	21.3%	0.0%	14.6%	5.1%	5.7%	6.7%	16.5%	13.3%	19.4%	14.7%
Occupational conflicts	0.0%	0.0%	4.6%	3.1%	5.7%	5.8%	5.2%	6.7%	5.5%	4.8%
Poor health	18.0%	12.5%	23.1%	15.3%	18.9%	14.4%	16.2%	11.1%	21.5%	18.2%
Disaster Causes	**0.5%**	**0.1%**	**0.4%**	**0.9%**	**0.4%**	**0.8%**	**0.8%**	**0.3%**	**0.2%**	**0.5%**
Act of God	57.2%	100.0%	19.4%	7.3%	20.0%	8.1%	10.6%	33.3%	15.8%	14.9%
Burglary	14.3%	0.0%	3.2%	0.0%	0.0%	2.7%	9.7%	0.0%	5.3%	5.8%
Employee fraud	14.3%	0.0%	3.2%	0.0%	20.0%	13.5%	2.7%	11.1%	10.5%	6.1%
Fire	7.1%	0.0%	16.1%	39.0%	30.0%	32.4%	53.1%	0.0%	34.2%	37.3%
Death of owner	7.1%	0.0%	58.1%	53.7%	30.0%	43.3%	23.9%	55.6%	34.2%	35.9%
Strike	0.0%	0.0%	0.0%	0.0%	0.0%	0.0%	0.0%	0.0%	0.0%	0.0%
Fraud Causes	**0.2%**	**0.5%**	**0.4%**	**0.4%**	**0.2%**	**0.8%**	**0.4%**	**0.9%**	**0.2%**	**0.4%**
Embezzlement	0.0%	20.0%	44.0%	14.3%	16.7%	26.3%	7.8%	28.0%	11.4%	19.1%
False agreement	0.0%	60.0%	4.0%	9.5%	0.0%	7.9%	11.8%	20.0%	13.6%	11.8%
False statement	25.0%	0.0%	12.0%	4.8%	0.0%	7.9%	11.8%	4.0%	6.8%	8.2%
Irregular disposal of assets	75.0%	20.0%	28.0%	47.6%	33.3%	29.0%	39.2%	44.0%	47.7%	39.1%
Misleading name	0.0%	0.0%	8.0%	4.8%	33.3%	2.6%	7.8%	0.0%	11.4%	6.8%
Premeditated overbuy	0.0%	0.0%	4.0%	19.0%	16.7%	26.3%	21.6%	4.0%	9.1%	15.0%
Economic Factors Causes	**80.0%**	**79.0%**	**69.8%**	**66.0%**	**68.6%**	**67.7%**	**68.3%**	**63.2%**	**75.7%**	**70.6%**
Bad profits	77.1%	69.5%	74.2%	72.8%	73.0%	70.1%	70.9%	72.7%	79.9%	75.0%
High interest rates	5.4%	0.6%	0.6%	0.1%	1.5%	0.5%	0.3%	0.6%	1.2%	1.0%
Loss of market	4.1%	18.8%	11.6%	12.9%	9.7%	13.4%	8.3%	11.9%	9.4%	9.9%
No consumer spending	11.3%	7.6%	8.8%	5.9%	10.5%	8.1%	14.9%	10.6%	6.0%	9.4%
No future	2.1%	3.5%	4.8%	8.3%	5.3%	7.9%	5.6%	4.2%	3.5%	4.7%

Table 2-3, *continued*

	AGRICULTURE, FORESTRY, FISHING	MINING	CON-STRUC-TION	MANU-FAC-TURING	TRANSPOR-TATION, PUBLIC UTILITIES	WHOLE-SALE TRADE	RETAIL TRADE	FINANCE, INSURANCE, REAL ESTATE	SERVICES	TOTAL
Experience Causes	**14.8%**	**12.6%**	**21.2%**	**20.9%**	**21.8%**	**19.4%**	**22.4%**	**19.4%**	**18.3%**	**20.7%**
Incompetence	58.5%	38.2%	50.8%	48.8%	47.1%	46.7%	45.9%	46.3%	43.5%	43.8%
Lack of line experience	6.2%	15.7%	8.3%	13.1%	13.3%	14.2%	17.6%	12.6%	15.0%	13.3%
Lack of managerial experience	13.4%	19.1%	14.3%	7.3%	17.8%	11.8%	14.1%	9.9%	13.2%	12.3%
Unbalanced experience	21.9%	27.0%	26.6%	30.8%	21.8%	27.3%	22.4%	31.2%	28.3%	30.6%
Sales Causes	**6.9%**	**7.1%**	**13.1%**	**11.8%**	**12.5%**	**12.5%**	**14.5%**	**11.0%**	**10.5%**	**11.7%**
Competitively weak	12.7%	13.8%	19.4%	21.1%	35.1%	19.0%	26.1%	14.4%	17.2%	21.0%
Economic decline	50.8%	38.5%	26.9%	13.1%	16.6%	16.5%	12.5%	23.0%	19.0%	18.5%
Inadequate sales	34.8%	47.7%	53.1%	64.2%	47.4%	60.3%	56.4%	62.3%	62.7%	58.1%
Inventory difficulties	0.6%	0.0%	0.4%	1.1%	0.3%	2.7%	3.0%	0.0%	0.4%	1.3%
Poor location	1.1%	0.0%	0.2%	0.5%	0.6%	1.5%	2.0%	0.3%	0.9%	1.1%
Expenses Causes	**7.4%**	**5.9%**	**7.2%**	**8.3%**	**8.5%**	**6.7%**	**7.3%**	**7.9%**	**7.1%**	**8.4%**
Burdensome institutional debt	68.2%	40.7%	38.2%	38.7%	33.9%	43.1%	45.2%	70.0%	49.4%	40.0%
Heavy operating expenses	31.8%	59.3%	61.8%	61.3%	66.1%	56.9%	54.8%	30.0%	50.6%	60.0%
Customer Causes	**0.5%**	**0.3%**	**1.5%**	**1.3%**	**1.2%**	**1.3%**	**1.1%**	**0.5%**	**1.1%**	**1.1%**
Receivables difficulties	46.2%	33.3%	81.9%	58.1%	67.7%	73.0%	28.3%	66.7%	29.5%	47.5%
Too few customers	53.8%	66.7%	18.1%	41.9%	32.3%	27.0%	71.7%	33.3%	70.5%	52.5%
Assets Causes	**0.6%**	**0.1%**	**0.5%**	**0.5%**	**0.7%**	**0.2%**	**0.6%**	**1.2%**	**0.4%**	**0.5%**
Excessive fixed assets	41.2%	0.0%	33.3%	30.4%	52.9%	36.4%	16.1%	38.2%	33.3%	30.2%
Overexpansion	58.8%	100.0%	66.7%	69.6%	47.1%	63.6%	83.9%	61.8%	66.7%	69.8%
Capital Causes	**0.5%**	**0.7%**	**0.9%**	**0.9%**	**0.7%**	**0.7%**	**1.1%**	**0.8%**	**0.5%**	**0.7%**
Burdensome contracts	0.0%	16.7%	18.3%	28.6%	15.8%	8.6%	9.8%	30.4%	12.5%	14.4%
Excessive withdrawals	78.6%	50.0%	65.0%	21.4%	47.4%	51.4%	46.1%	47.9%	58.3%	50.7%
Inadequate start capacity	21.4%	33.3%	16.7%	50.0%	36.8%	40.0%	44.1%	21.7%	29.2%	34.9%

Note: Due to the fact that some failures are attributed to a combination of causes, the total of the major categories exceeds 100.0%.

Source: The Dun & Bradstreet Corporation, 1987.

1 INADEQUATE RECORDS   Nine bankrupt firms had inadequate records. One of them, for example, had often bid unsuccessfully on government contracts. The bids were consistently too high. Unable to land any contracts this way, the company then hired a consultant who not only cost them a lot of money but got them into a disastrous subcontract. Unable to establish an adequate record-keeping system, however, the firm simply had no basis for estimating its costs and correcting the problem. Another firm had a good product line but failed to keep revenue and expense records. The partners never knew where they were in terms of finances. During the bankruptcy proceedings, the accountants admitted that they were unable to reconstruct even the simplest form of income statements from the records they had found. In fact, the office records consisted of piles of unsorted papers jammed into an old-fashioned safe.

2 CUMULATIVE LOSSES   Half the bankrupt firms had cumulative losses. In most cases these losses consisted of insignificant financial leaks. The management was unaware of these little problems, which collectively led to large losses. Most of these leaks could have been detected by the owners if they had had a suitable reporting system. However, among the five firms suffering this problem there were no suitable reports. The reports were either too cumbersome for analysis or took too long to get to the manager for timely action.

3 LACK OF TAX KNOWLEDGE   Some of the firms overlooked tax benefits in their financial planning. For example, a couple firms failed to take depreciation write-offs on their equipment. Another firm was the low bidder on a large contract but had failed to include social security and unemployment taxes in its computations. When the company failed to pay these taxes, it eventually ran into trouble with the government.

4 EXPANSION BEYOND RESOURCES   Some of the firms had grown rapidly and their bookkeeping systems were not designed to handle dramatic growth. In three cases management simply tried to save money on its bookkeeping system by taking shortcuts—all with disastrous effects.

5 INADEQUATE COST ANALYSIS   Three firms did not have adequate cost analysis for control purposes. In some instances operating reports were skimpy, while in others they were overly detailed. The former failed to provide the firms with sufficient information, while the latter made such analyses difficult. As a result, the companies did not have a clear-cut basis for controlling operations. One company had six identical operations. Two of these cost $10 per unit, two others cost $25 per unit, and the last two were somewhere in between. Due to its poor cost data reporting, such facts were difficult to uncover and were not used as a basis for cost control.

6 LACK OF PRODUCT DEVELOPMENT   Nine firms suffered from a lack of product development. The companies tended to retain outmoded or obsolete product lines. When they did change to a more up-to-date product it was usually after everyone else had done so. As a result, they were continually chasing the market instead of leading it. Over time customers began to realize that these firms did not offer the latest products in the field, and they began switching their patronage. Unable

to maintain their market niche, the firms lost sales. Bankruptcy was but a short time away.

7 LACK OF PRODUCT DIVERSIFICATION Most of the unsuccessful companies lacked product diversification and engaged in no product research at all. This was in direct contrast to the successful firms, nine of which strongly emphasized product diversification. As some product lines began to lose market appeal, the successful firms were able to substitute other products for them. This resulted in maintenance of overall sales revenue. Conversely, the unsuccessful firms found that as sales declined they had no new products to offer. At best, they found themselves engaged in a game of "catch-up."

8 LACK OF INFORMATION ABOUT CUSTOMERS Half the unsuccessful firms lacked information about their customers. For example, one company had been shipping goods to customers without making credit investigations. As a result, its receivables were in terrible shape. Most of the accounts were 90 days or more in arrears. Additionally, one of its customers was bankrupt and had not made a payment in over a year, and the company continued to ship goods to it.

9 FAILURE TO DIVERSIFY MARKET Three firms failed to diversify their markets and wound up selling their goods to a mere handful of customers. A loss of any one would have had a tremendous effect on overall revenue. One company contracted all of its output to just one buyer! When that buyer canceled the contract, the company went bankrupt.

10 LACK OF MARKETING RESEARCH Two firms undertook major ventures without conducting any marketing research, while three adopted a rather simple solution to their marketing problems by contracting their entire plant output to a single buyer. In all cases, changes in market conditions left them in a very poor position.

11 CONTINUED POLICIES OF BANKRUPT PREDECESSOR One firm had taken over the assets as well as the policies of a bankrupt company. Additionally, it undertook a substantial tool-up that cost almost $1 million, although there was no basis for believing that potential sales warranted such an expansion. As a result, the new company was never able to achieve its break-even point.

12 LEGAL PROBLEMS One company tried to save money on legal fees. However, when long, drawn-out patent infringement proceedings became necessary, the company was ill-prepared to deal with them. Had they exercised foresight and gotten competent legal advice from the beginning, many of these problems could have been avoided.

13 NEPOTISM In three instances favoritism toward family members helped bring about failure of the enterprise. One of the most typical examples was the carrying on the payroll of family members who received high salaries but contributed little to the overall running of the business. Additionally, in certain cases, meddling by these family members in important business matters resulted in severe financial setbacks.

14 LACK OF ADMINISTRATIVE COORDINATION Three companies were unable to coordinate their manufacturing and selling activities. Largely, this was due to recordkeeping systems that did not tell management which lines were most profitable and which were marginal. Additionally, in those firms that expanded operations it was found that poor communication of company policies, and failure to pay adequate attention to administrative problems resulted in poor overall coordination and inefficient operation.

15 ONE-PERSON MANAGEMENT In three cases, one-person management led to company failure. This occurred in one instance when the individual who had built the firm from nothing began to experience poor health and sold out to a group of investors. The investors did not realize that the man's technical genius was the reason for the company's success. Without that, the business failed within a year.

16 LACK OF TECHNICAL COMPETENCE Two companies suffered from a lack of technical competence. One had been purchased by a group of investors that had little technical knowledge and lacked the expertise for choosing a technically skilled vice-president. The firm's previous reputation carried the company for a while, and it had no difficulty landing a contract to supply gun parts. However, the first two shipments were rejected because they did not meet the quality called for by the contract. Eventually, the contract was canceled and the firm went bankrupt.

17 ABSENTEE MANAGEMENT One firm had a long period of profitable operation. Then it went through a number of years of absentee management. The owner stayed away constantly, and operations gradually deteriorated. Financial records were neglected, and the bookkeeper failed to make several years' tax payments. Given such developments, the company failed.

18 INTERNAL CONFLICT In one firm, internal conflict between the partners resulted in its ultimate failure. The individuals fought among themselves, made allegations about various kinds of scandalous misconduct, manipulated their expense accounts, and conducted secret negotiations for sales contracts. These actions eventually resulted in the failure of the firm to continue operations. (See Small Business Owner's Notebook: Owner Compensation.)

SUCCESS FACTORS

Now it is time to identify and describe those factors that help account for business success. There are four major factors:

1. the existence of a business opportunity
2. management ability
3. adequate capital and credit
4. modern business methods

THE EXISTENCE OF A BUSINESS OPPORTUNITY

The primary factor in the success of any small business is the existence of a real business opportunity.[5] There must be some customers in the marketplace who want to buy the good or service that is being offered.

---

[5]Robert Stuart and Pier A. Abetti, "Start-up Ventures: Towards the Prediction of Initial Success," *Journal of Business Venturing*, Summer 1987; pp. 215–30.

■ SMALL BUSINESS OWNER'S NOTEBOOK ■

Owner Compensation: What's Really Happening?

In 1990, *Inc.* magazine, in association with Coopers & Lybrand, conducted a survey of small business owners concerning their compensation. Based on the 823 business owners who responded, *Inc.* was able to create a profile of the "typical" company. The average respondent showed a sales level of $5 million and employed 66 people. The average sales growth for 1988–89 was 10 percent with 31 percent of sales going towards payroll. A majority of the companies, 97 percent, were privately-owned. The average CEO (Chief Executive Officer) compensation was $100,984 with $79,854 going into base salary. The CEOs' executive benefits are summarized below:

EXECUTIVE BENEFITS

Company Car	77%
Supplemental Life Insurance	54%
Tax Return Preparation	46%
Supplemental Medical Insurance	34%
Personal Financial Planning	28%
Supplemental Retirement Benefits	13%
First Class Air Travel	9%
Golden Parachute	3%

Source: Adapted from "*INC*'s 1990 Executive Compensation Survey," *Inc.*, November 1990, pp. 64–76.

A PRODUCTION ORIENTATION There are two ways of identifying a real business opportunity. The first, and least scientific, way is to start with the belief that the marketplace can always use another good product sold at a low price. This may be basically true, but there is always the danger that the customers will not buy the good or service. Two reasons can be cited: one attacks the "good product or service" idea; the other, the "low price" idea.

Many of the products or services considered "good" by the public are those with which they have had no problems in the past. In short, the quality was more than adequate. Given this fact, a small business has to prove to its potential customers that the good or service it is offering is even better than what is currently available. This is an uphill fight.

Additionally, consider the fact that when people do not know which specific good or service to buy they tend to be swayed by advertising. For example, when asked to give the brand name of the television with the highest quality, many customers say Zenith. No small business manufacturer is going to be able to compete with Zenith on the basis of quality. The TV giant is simply too entrenched. Thus, having a good product does *not* automatically ensure success. One has to consider the competition and the customer and see what the market currently looks like.

Nor does low price ensure success. In fact, a low price is self-defeating if people assume that low price means low quality. A restaurant with low prices will not attract businesspeople who are entertaining clients and want to impress them with a higher-priced menu. Low-priced perfumes and cosmetics often sell poorly, because women are accustomed to paying a higher price for quality merchandise and will not buy "obviously inferior" cosmetics. When is "low price" a good strategy? When the market is highly competitive, people know what the product does, and there is little difference between one firm's product and another's. In short, there is keen competition and a knowledgeable buyer.

Of course, there are many instances of a small business starting out by offering a good product at a low price because it felt sure there was a market there. How did the owner know? The only answer the individual could give would be, "I know if I were buying this type of product, I'd buy the one we're making." Some people call this approach intuition or gut feeling. Its basic characteristic is a **production orientation.** A good product sells itself.

A MARKETING ORIENTATION   The other approach to determining a real business opportunity is to use a marketing orientation. This method requires the small business owner to answer the question, "What good or service will the customer buy?" In this case, the individual does not answer the question by giving an intuitive response such as "Well, I think most people want a low-priced, quality lawn mower." That answer is simply an *opinion.* The owner may be right, but it makes better business sense to go out and ask potential customers and/or analyze information that has already been collected from them. This calls for **marketing research.**

There are two basic ways to conduct marketing research. One is to determine the potential market by interviewing the customers in an effort to discover what kinds of new goods and services they would like. This will give the firm information not possessed by anyone else. (Unless, of course, they, too, conducted such interviews.) Such data collection always questions a random sample, for it would be far too expensive to interview everyone in the potential market. If this sample is indeed representative it will be possible to generalize to the overall population. This means that if 20 percent of the interviewed groups say they would buy a particular good or service, then it would be possible to say that 20 percent of the entire market would want the good or service. When information is collected by means of interviews or questionnaires, it is referred to as **primary research.** This kind of research is most helpful when companies are thinking about bringing out a new good or service. However, it can be an expensive process.

Many small businesses are ill-equipped to either afford or conduct primary research. They therefore opt for **secondary research.** In this process the information has already been collected and merely needs to be analyzed. Some of the most common sources of such information include business and government publications. For example, "In what kind of business would one face the least chance of bankruptcy?" This question could be answered through a review of government data on business failures in different industries. All the business owner would have to do is visit a Small Business Administration office, go to a library, or write a firm like Dun & Bradstreet that collects such statistics.

Another question that could be answered via secondary research is "In what city would one have the best chance of operating a successful restaurant?" One key factor would be population. Another would be the number of restaurants currently located there. Consider these statistics:

CITY	NUMBER OF RESTAURANTS	POPULATION	INCOME PER CAPITA	PEOPLE PER RESTAURANT
A	850	600,000	$9,850	700
B	870	700,000	9,825	805
C	920	800,000	9,900	870
D	980	900,000	9,875	918
E	1,000	1,000,000	9,885	1,000

City E has the fewest restaurants per capita. Since the per capita incomes are similar, this city may be the best place to open a restaurant. In any event, this information was derived from secondary sources.

When a firm approaches its analysis of a real business opportunity via marketing analysis it is using a **marketing orientation.** This approach, although sometimes costly and time consuming, is more scientific than the production-oriented one. Remember, in order to determine if a real business opportunity exists, it is necessary to examine the market.

MANAGEMENT ABILITY

The second success factor is management ability.[6] The owner must know how to handle money, machinery, people, and materials. Specifically, he or she must be capable of getting things done through others.

In addition, the manager should know quite a bit about the business line, or at least a closely related line. Otherwise, the individual is going to be at a loss regarding how to conduct operations. There is really no substitute for experience in a small business.[7] Without it, the owner lacks practical knowledge of operating methods, procedures, and policies.

Another aspect of management ability is knowing when to step aside and let someone else do the job. This ability is shown in two ways. One is that of delegating authority to competent personnel. The other is by sharing ownership responsibility with one's heirs. Successful small business owners know the joy of running their own business. They also realize that if their children come into the business with them, the children want to share the responsibility and joy. (See Small Business Success: The Body Shop.)

ADEQUATE CAPITAL AND CREDIT

The third success factor is adequate capital and credit. **Capital** is the amount of money the owners have invested in the business. The greater the capital, the better the chances of survival. If the owners put only a small amount of capital into the business, it is likely that it will be quickly exhausted and either further investment or the borrowing of funds will be necessary. Since few banks will lend a small business more money than the owners themselves have invested, the ratio of loans to capital is seldom greater than 1:1. Successful businesses forecast their annual needs and

[6]A. B. Ibrahim and J. R. Goodwin, "Perceived Causes of Success in Small Business," *American Journal of Small Business,* Fall 1986, pp. 41–49.

[7]Robert W. Hornaday and Walter J. Wheatley, "Managerial Characteristics and the Financial Performance of Small Business," *Journal of Small Business Management,* April 1986, pp. 1–7.

■ SMALL BUSINESS SUCCESS ■

The Body Shop: Anita Roddick's Vision

 Anita Roddick believes a company can be ethical, socially responsible, and challenging for all the employees. In addition she believes customers should be given clear and complete information about products, not advertising hype. Does this sound too good to be true? It shouldn't, since Roddick created a business of her own to accomplish those very beliefs.

In 1976, at the age of 33, Roddick lived in England as a wife, homemaker, and mother of two young daughters. Armed only with her vision of a small store that would sell natural lotions for the skin and hair, Roddick borrowed $6,400 from a bank and launched The Body Shop.

Because she is a passionate environmentalist, Roddick incorporated her beliefs into her business and established her niche. The products in her store were biodegradable, and refillable containers were provided for customers. Even though her business sold only lotions and shampoos, Roddick believed it could serve as a symbol for environmental consciousness.

Product information was provided for customers in the form of pamphlets and a huge reference manual located in the store. Roddick believed that customer loyalty would grow as The Body Shop's credibility increased and that would come about through consumer education. Instead of hype and packaging she invested in product knowledge for all of her customers.

As for her employees, Roddick established a special training program that would emphasize the nature and uses of the product. The idea was to train employees to use the products more effectively, not just make a sale. Her goals were to elevate the employees' pride in their work, thereby encouraging them to do a thorough job, and to boost employee confidence by increasing their knowledge of the job.

Can such ideas really work in contemporary business? For over ten years The Body Shop has experienced sales and profit growth at an astounding 50 percent per year. By the end of 1990, The Body Shop had $23 million profit on $141 million in sales. There are franchises in 37 countries, including the U.S. and the possibility that more will be added is growing. In the U.S. alone for example, 2,500 people have requested franchises for The Body Shop.

One woman's vision caused a small business to soar to success in fourteen years. As for the future, Roddick's goal is to make The Body Shop a $1-billion company by 1995.

Source: Adapted from Bo Burlingham, "This Woman Has Changed Business Forever," *INC.,* June 1990, pp. 34–47.

ensure themselves that their capital (and accompanying loans) will be sufficient to maintain operations throughout the year.

Additionally, small businesses open lines of credit with their suppliers. In this way, if they lack the cash to pay for merchandise or supplies, the supplier will carry them for 30–60 days. Without credit, most small businesses would be unable to exist. Few have enough cash on hand to meet day-by-day bills. One of the problems faced by small businesses is **undercapitalization**—not enough money is invested in the firm to meet financial obligations. Most small firms get themselves into this bind by expanding too fast and allowing their money to be tied up in a slow-moving inventory. Successful firms sidestep these problems by forecasting demand, budgeting expenditures, and keeping available lines of credit. They are also careful about paying their bills promptly so that credit will be extended again in the future.

MODERN BUSINESS METHODS

The fourth success factor is modern business methods. The company must use the most efficient equipment and procedures available. Otherwise, the cost of doing business will rise and the competition will be able either to charge a lower price or to obtain a higher profit margin. For example, in a business where the good or service requires a high investment in machinery, such as a printing shop, the owner could find the competition squeezing out his or her enterprise if some new, more efficient printing machine was developed and every other firm bought one. Likewise, in many businesses today multiple copies of reports or letters are made with a copying machine rather than having the secretary type carbon copies. It is simply too expensive to use carbons. Additionally, successful firms are well organized so that everyone knows what he or she is supposed to be doing.

All of these factors relate to **intraorganizational efficiency.** If the business uses the latest methods, costs can be reduced and the firm's profit margin protected. Of course, the latest equipment will *not* produce cost savings if the new machinery is too expensive. For example, some small firms have learned to their dismay that even small computers can be too costly; there are cheaper ways of doing the same work. However, research reveals that successful small businesses are continually aware of the need to update their business methods.

A FINAL WORD

In this chapter the basic causes of small business failure have been examined and the factors that bring success have been reviewed. Quite obviously, small business managers must be aware of the failure factors so that they can avoid them, while working toward ensuring adequate attention to the success factors.

Many students believe that successfully managing a fledgling enterprise is not a great challenge. However, experience shows that most small business owners are not sufficiently analytical in their approach to operations. Marketing research is not carried out, little attention is paid to record keeping, budgets are either nonexistent or ignored, inventory levels are kept so high that there is not enough cash to pay bills as they come due, and modern business methods are not employed. Many of these managers simply use common sense, which is *not enough.* Small business success requires attention to so many factors that a formal, systematic approach must be used. The chapters that follow discuss methods used to ensure this approach.

■ SUMMARY

Every year many business firms cease operations. In recent years this failure rate has increased, although the rate varies according to the specific line of business or industry.

Why do businesses fail? There are two ways of answering this question. In terms of specific causes, there are seven underlying reasons. By degree of severity, they are incompetence, unbalanced experience, lack of experience in the line, lack of managerial experience, neglect, disaster, and fraud. In terms of management traps, 18 management-related causes account for most small business failures. The 18 relate to three major areas: poor financial planning, poor coordination between manufacturing and selling, and poor general administration. Some of the specific traps are inadequate records, cumulative losses, lack of product diversification, lack of marketing research, and lack of administrative coordination.

The latter part of the chapter examined those factors that help account for small business success. The primary factor is the existence of a real business opportunity. While the identification of such an opportunity can be determined with either a production or marketing orientation, the latter is preferred. This can be done with primary and/or secondary research, although most small businesses opt for the latter because it is less expensive. A second key factor is management ability. A third is adequate capital and credit. A fourth is modern business methods.

In comparing successful and unsuccessful small businesses, research shows that successful businesses tend to be analytical in their method of operations. The owner must develop a systematic approach, for small business management entails more than just "doing what comes naturally."

■ REVIEW AND DISCUSSION QUESTIONS

1. Describe the rates of business failure in the United States since 1970. Have failures increased or decreased? Explain.

2. Approximately 50 percent of small businesses do not survive the first five years. Is this statement accurate? Support your answer.

3. What is the major reason for small business failure?

4. In addition to your answer to question 3, what are some other major reasons why small businesses fail? Explain them.

5. The most common management traps are related to three major areas: poor financial planning, poor coordination between manufacturing and selling, and poor general administration. What is meant by this statement? Explain.

6. What is the primary factor in the success of any small business? Describe it.

7. How does a production orientation differ from a marketing orientation?

8. What is the difference between primary and secondary marketing research?

9. In addition to your answer to question 6, what are three other factors that account for small business success? Describe them.

10. What is meant by the statement, "Most small business owners are not sufficiently analytical in their approach to operations"?

It Was Fun While It Lasted

■ It took Charlsa Wyeth almost three years, but she finally managed to develop a synthetic fiber that looked like leather but was much more durable. "Many business executives," she told her banker, "like an attaché case made of rich leather. The major problem is that before long the leather begins to wear away. Put an attaché case under an airplane seat a half-dozen times and the finish becomes scuffed. Carry it with you on the road for a year and you're going to have to buy another one. It will be so beaten up that you will look like an executive whose business is on the rocks. And the worst part is that these attaché cases often cost over $200. My synthetic fiber keeps its finish despite rough handling."

Charlsa manufactured two kinds of attaché cases and began offering them through local retail chains. The first month she sold more than 1,000 of them, and during the first six months sales exceeded 4,500. The price to the retailer was $60, which was marked up to $125. This price was below the price for leather attaché cases and seemed to be well accepted by the market. Last month Charlsa brought out two new kinds of cases; one is a special, light-weight bag for carrying papers, and the other is for carrying heavier items. Both sell for $50 and retail for $100. Again, initial demand was strong.

Yesterday Charlsa learned some very unsettling news. A major attaché case manufacturer is introducing a new line of simulated leather cases. From the advertisement she read, it appears that the manufacturer is using a process similar to the one she discovered and that the competing cases have some features that are superior to those of her products. It costs Charlsa $35 to manufacture an attaché case. The competitor is offering its cases to the public at $50.

Charlsa has decided that her best course of action is to reduce her inventory as quickly as possible. Quite obviously, she is not going to be able to compete with the new attaché case. "It was fun while it lasted," she told her husband, "but in this market, if you can't compete you have to get out of the way. No matter. I'm working on another product that I think will be even better and it's going to take the competition a lot longer to catch up with me. For the moment, however, I've got to focus my attention on selling the product I have on hand."

1. Was Charlsa product-oriented or market-oriented? Defend your answer.

2. Why is Charlsa's new product line on the verge of failure? Was there anything she could have done about it?

3. Based on the information you have, what advice would you give Charlsa regarding a new product line? Be as helpful as possible.

Dance Studio for Sale

■ Calvin Horowitz is thinking about buying a dance studio. Calvin learned about the business opportunity from the owner himself. Calvin takes dancing lessons every Wednesday evening. One night, after finishing his lesson, he was in the hallway having a cup of coffee when the owner, Mr. Cecil, came by. Mr Cecil told Calvin that he had been talking to his accountant about selling the business. "I've owned this studio for 23 years," Mr. Cecil told Calvin, "and now I want to sell out and retire. I'm looking around right now for someone who would like to buy the business." Calvin was excited about the prospect and asked Mr. Cecil a lot of questions about the operation.

From what Calvin could determine from the conversation, Mr. Cecil has six full-time instructors and nine part-time instructors. Approximately 130 people take lessons each week. Some of these individuals are signed to 10- and 20-lesson contracts, while others walk in off the street and ask for a particular dance lesson.

Calvin does not know a great deal about owning a dance studio. He is in the insurance business. However, he did spend an evening looking over Mr. Cecil's operations earlier this week and found that it was very difficult to tell from the records exactly how much revenue Mr. Cecil has taken in this year. Some people pay by check and others with cash. Not all of these amounts have been entered in the books. Nor is it possible to pinpoint how many people actually come in for lessons because the instructors sometimes collect the money and, if it is in cash, give Mr. Cecil his share and pocket the rest. Additionally, Mr. Cecil has had three good years and two poor ones in the last five. Last year was one of the good ones.

Finally, Mr. Cecil does not seem to know (or at least he is not telling Calvin) a great deal about the customers who come in for lessons. However, he does run an ad every week in the Sunday edition of the local paper and believes that this is how people learn about his dance studio, in addition, of course, to the word-of-mouth advertising from his clientele. Mr. Cecil also believes that he, himself, helps account for some of this business because he arrives at the studio every day at midmorning and does not go home until after the last lesson. As a result, Mr. Cecil knows all of these people personally and encourages them to keep up their lessons and have their friends come along with them.

After thinking the matter over, Calvin is not sure whether this venture is a good one. There seems to be so much information that he does not have about the business that it will be very difficult to make a decision. However, he has told Mr. Cecil that he will let him know within two weeks.

1. From which of the specific causes of business failure does Mr. Cecil's operation suffer? List them.

2. Into which of the management traps discussed in this chapter has Mr. Cecil fallen? Explain.

3. What would you advise Calvin to do? Why?

■ ■ ▬▬▬▬▬▬▬▬▬▬▬▬▬▬▬▬▬▬▬▬▬▬▬▬ ■ ■

You Be the Consultant

HELP

Dolores Wexley was a successful dressmaker. In fact, she had so many orders that she was unable to keep up with all the business. There was always a 60-day waiting period for a dress. During her first five years as a dressmaker, Dolores increased her annual sales from $12,000 to over $50,000. However, she was not happy being just a dressmaker. She wanted to sell clothing through a retail outlet and make dresses as a sideline.

Taking the money she had saved, Dolores opened a store in a shopping mall on the other side of town. She purchased $11,000 worth of dresses and other ladies' wearing apparel and placed advertisements in the local newspaper. Each ad, which was approximately two inches square and ran in the bottom left-hand corner of the page, cost $425 per day. In addition, since she was forbidden by the terms of the lease to advertise in the store window, she sent letters to her old customers telling them where she was now located and encouraging them to visit her for handmade clothing as well as other apparel needs.

Six months after she opened in the shopping mall Dolores held a fashion show in the area outside her store. Over 500 people attended and looked at her merchandise. The cost of the show, including drinks and hors d'oeuvres, was $1,275. One person who attended the show bought a blouse for $22.50. Seven other people placed orders totaling $910 for handmade dresses.

Last month Dolores held another fashion show. This time 650 people attended. The cost of the show was $1,433. Three people bought merchandise totaling $87.50. Dolores also received nineteen orders totaling over $2,250 for handmade dresses.

This week Dolores sat down and looked at her financial records. Although she does not keep close tabs on her expenses, she estimates that she owes her creditors approximately $8,000 for dresses and other merchandise that they have sold her on credit. Additionally, her monthly rent is $875. Each of the last three months she has written to the owners of the mall, told them she has sold very little merchandise, and paid them $500 each time. There has been no response from them. Nor have they answered a letter her attorney wrote for her last month asking the owners to reduce her rent to $500 per month because she is unable to pay any more than this. The lease has one more year to run, and Dolores has been thinking about getting someone to assume it so she can move out and get another location. However, almost half the stores in the mall are currently unrented so there appears to be little hope that this will happen.

Dolores keeps her own books, but last month she had an accountant come by and examine them. The man told her that he was unable to figure out all of her transactions. Many of the receipts and other financial transactions have not been entered in the books. Dolores has simply stuffed them into a paper bag and kept them in the back of the store. The accountant has told her that if her sales do not increase dramatically within the next 90 days she will be in big financial trouble. She is unsure of what to do now.

■ **YOUR CONSULTATION** Assume that you are advising Dolores about what to do. What particular problems do you see facing her? How did she get into this mess in the first place? What would you recommend that she do now? Do you think her business will fail, or is there a chance to save it? Explain.

CHAPTER 3

The Family Business

Objectives

Many small business owners devote their lives to their enterprises. However, in order to keep the operation family-owned, sooner or later each of them must step aside and let someone else take the helm. Because the owner often feels that no one is as qualified as he or she, difficult questions arise when a successor is to be chosen before the owner leaves the business. Many family businesses delay making this decision only to find that when the owner dies the family becomes entangled in a squabble over who will head the operation and what direction it will take. The objective of this chapter is to examine these issues and to discuss how family succession should be handled. When you have finished studying the material in this chapter, you will be able to:

1. *Discuss the strengths inherent in many family-owned small businesses.*

2. *Describe the succession-related pressures on the business owner from both inside and outside sources.*

3. *Relate the nature of the succession issue.*

4. *Explain how an effective succession strategy can be formulated and implemented.*

FAMILY BUSINESS OPERATIONS

Throughout our economic history, family businesses have been the foundation of many giant corporations. John D. Rockefeller's South Improvement Oil Company eventually became Standard Oil of New Jersey. Richard Sears' Watch Company was the basis for Sears Roebuck. More recently, Sam Walton built his family-owned retail stores into Wal-Mart, the fastest growing retailer in America. Thus, the family business has long been the backbone of the American economy or as Randall Poe has put it, "If family business is not the backbone of the American economy, it is certainly the prime rib."[1]

In spite of their historical presence and success, family-owned businesses are being challenged today as never before. Unions, government regulation, inflation, increased competition, and management succession problems are some of the forces currently confronting family-owned businesses. At the same time there has been an

---

[1]Randall Poe, "The SOB's," *Across the Board*, May 5, 1980, p. 23.

emerging interest in the role and operations of these enterprises. Researchers, such as Neil Churchill and Kenneth Hatten, are now beginning to study their growth and development. Churchill and Hatten put it this way:

> The world and the United States are currently involved in rapid change and this requires businesses to develop strategies for facilitating change. Family businesses provide an environment where change is inevitable; where the transfer of decision making and power is certain and planned for; where one generation succeeds the other with biological inevitability. Understanding how this process is facilitated can, as with entrepreneurs and innovation, aid other sectors to respond appropriately to their environments. As this occurs, the study of owner-managed and family businesses can give the field of entrepreneurial research added legitimacy.[2]

MEETING THE CHALLENGES

Family businesses account for between 12.1 and 14.4 million of our nation's 15 million businesses, according to federal estimates. These family businesses also account for nearly 50 percent of the gross national product and employ approximately half of the private sector work force.[3] During the 1980s, over 600,000 new businesses began operations each year in this country.[4] Many of these were family firms that will help increase GNP and employment. However, small business survival is becoming increasingly more difficult.

Many family-owned companies succeed and grow in spite of the complex challenges they face. One reason for this success rate is that family businesses are not encumbered by demanding stockholders who want to dictate operating strategy. A second reason is that family members are willing to sacrifice short-term profits for long-term gains. Research shows that family members are more productive than other employees.[5] A third reason is their flexibility, a special trait that has allowed family firms to react and respond to various challenges and opportunities in an unrestricted manner. Many examples can be cited. The Stroh Brewery Company is a family-owned firm that has vaulted from seventh to third on the list of the largest U.S. breweries. This was accomplished by acquiring the Joseph Schlitz Brewing Company (a publicly traded corporation), an acquisition that was made possible because 27 family members were willing to accept lower dividends in order to finance the project. Another example is Lennox Industries (8 of 11 directors are related to the president, John W. Norris, Jr.), the heating and air conditioning concern that developed a "pulse combustion furnace" well ahead of all major competition. This was accomplished after family members agreed to shift operations from Iowa to Texas in order to take advantage of greater research capacities. Other examples of similar flexible approaches have been used by Hallmark Cards, the Mars Candy Bar Company,

---

[2]Neil C. Churchill and Kenneth J. Hatten, "Non-Market-Based Transfers of Wealth and Power: A Research Framework for Family Business," *American Journal of Small Business,* Winter 1987, pp. 51–64.

[3]John L. Ward, *Keeping the Family Business Healthy,* (San Francisco, CA: Jossey-Bass Publishers, 1987), p. xv.

[4]*The State of Small Business: A Report to the President,* 1989, p. 115.

[5]Bruce A. Kirchhoff and Judith J. Kirchhoff, "Family Contributions to Productivity and Profitability in Small Businesses," *Journal of Small Business Management,* October 1987, pp. 25–31.

Estee Lauder Perfumes,[6] and Motorola.[7] (See Small Business Success: Family Funeral Homes Face Mass Merchandising Strategies.)

These examples emphasize the importance of confronting new challenges. These efforts often spell the difference between success and failure, and many family enterprises fail. Research shows that most small firms go out of existence after ten years; only three out of ten survive into a second generation. More significantly, only 16 percent of all family enterprises make it to a third generation. One significant study demonstrated these facts by examining the life expectancy of 200 successful manufacturing firms.[8] The average life expectancy for a family business is 24 years (see Figure 3-1), which is ironically the average tenure for the founders of a business.[9]

Figure 3-1
Life Expectancy of 200 Successful Manufacturers, 1924–1984

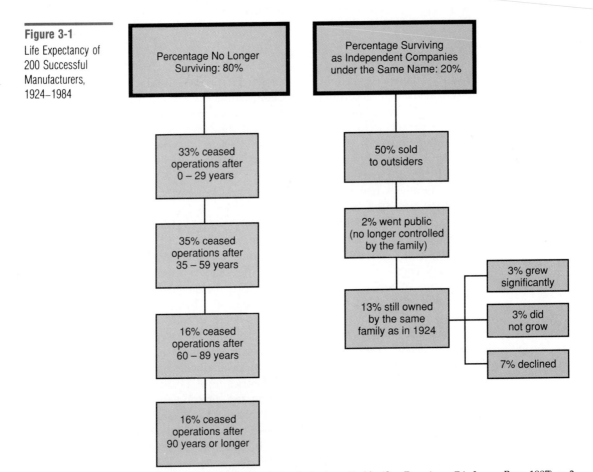

Source: John L. Ward, *Keeping the Family Business Healthy* (San Francisco, CA: Jossey Bass, 1987), p. 2.

---

[6]"The Silent Strengths of Family Business," *U.S. News and World Report,* April 25, 1983, p. 47; see also Sharon Nelton, "Strategies for Family Firms," *Nation's Business,* June 1986, p. 20.

[7]Norm Alster, "A Third-Generation Galven Moves Up," *Forbes,* April 30, 1990, pp. 57–62.

[8]Ward, *Keeping the Family Business Healthy.*

[9]Richard Beckhard and W. Gibb Dyer, Jr., "Managing Continuity in the Family-Owned Business," *Organizational Dynamics,* Summer 1983, pp. 7–8.

■ SMALL BUSINESS SUCCESS ■

Family Funeral Homes Face Mass Merchandising Strategies

 While many of the 22,000 funeral homes in North America are part of local or regional chains (the largest of which has 60 funeral homes), the great majority are small, family-owned operations. These homes are good illustrations of the traditional family business, and many of them survive through four and five generations.

The funeral service business is highly personalized. Families consider neighborhood, religion, and ethnicity, as well as economics, as they determine how to bury their deceased relatives. The same traditional influences have served as guidelines for the triumphant succession and transition of the majority of family funeral homes in the U.S. and Canada.

However, the funeral home industry of the 1990s is changing rapidly and family-owned firms must now face areas of competition that other industries have confronted for the last three decades: consolidation and mass merchandising. The major force behind this movement is Service Corporation International (SCI), a Houston-based corporation that owns 551 funeral homes, 122 cemeteries, and a funeral supply division valued at $62.5 million. SCI stock is publicly traded on the New York Stock Exchange and has revenues of $519 million. Although the company currently controls less than 5% of the $4.5-billion funeral market, SCI's open-armed approach to consolidation and its ability to use economies of scale in order to reduce expenses and increase efficiency has caused funeral homes across the continent to take note. SCI's mass merchandising strategy is becoming a formidable reality in the funeral home industry.

Family funeral homes are responding with two distinct strategies. Either they vigorously advertise that they are independent and family-owned in order to emphasize tradition, trust, and loyalty. Or they enter into cooperatives and franchise systems locally. This second alternative allows the funeral home to maintain its independence and family structure while enjoying the economic benefit that comes from purchasing supplies in large quantities.

Will mass merchandising strategies become dominant in the funeral industry or will family traditions and loyalty services persevere? The upcoming decade holds the answer, as family funeral homes of the 1990s prepare to face the challenges of "business" with the same vigor they have always shown when facing the challenges of "families."

Source: Adapted from Harvey D. Shapiro, "Funerals-R-Us," *Family Business,* June 1990, pp. 24–29.

As head of a family business, the entrepreneur judiciously spreads his or her hours over a variety of tasks in an environment that is unique, diverse, and challenging. Figure 3-2 illustrates the traditional roles of a business owner. However, these roles are carried out in an ever-changing environment. The challenges that confront the family managed business during its early years are markedly different from those faced later on. As Figure 3-3 illustrates, at *any* given time a family business may have *three* generations interacting.

Early concerns of survival and growth are supplemented by a need to delegate authority and plan for management succession. In progressing through an examination of these challenges, it is important to remember not only the roles of a family business owner but also the extreme and diverse pressures that the person faces.

FAMILY BUSINESS CHALLENGES

The challenges faced by family businesses extend from internal and external pressures to legal and survival issues.

Figure 3-2
The Business
Owner's World

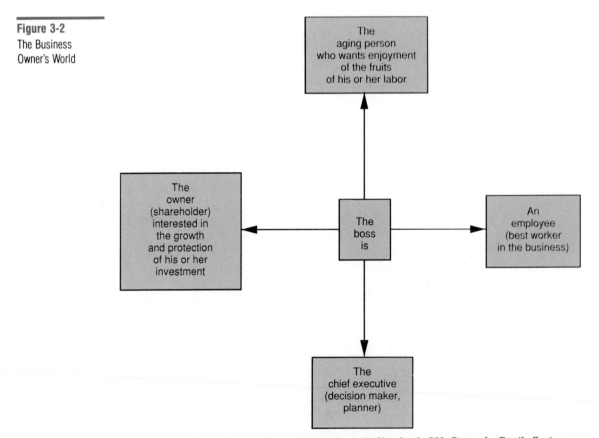

Source: Adapted from Leon A. Danco, *Beyond Survival* (Cleveland, OH: Center for Family Business, University Press, 1982) p. 22.

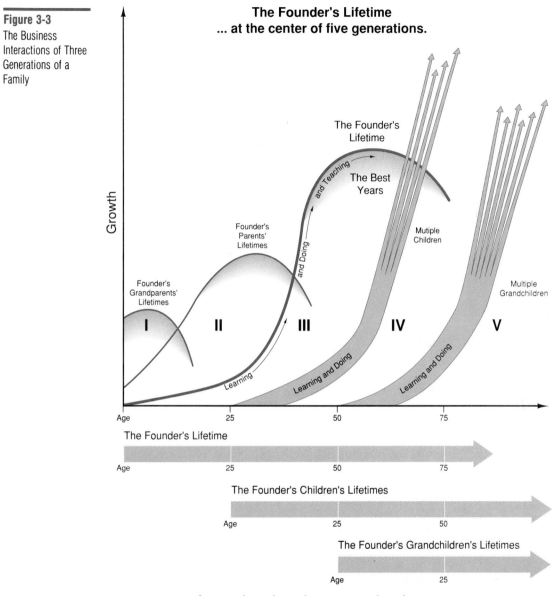

Figure 3-3
The Business Interactions of Three Generations of a Family

The Founder's Lifetime
... at the center of five generations.

Growth

The Founder's Lifetime

and Teaching

The Best Years

Founder's Parents' Lifetimes

and Doing

Mutiple Children

Founder's Grandparents' Lifetimes

Multiple Grandchildren

I   II   III   IV   V

Learning

Learning and Doing

Learning and Doing

Age   25   50   75

The Founder's Lifetime

Age   25   50   75

The Founder's Children's Lifetimes

Age   25   50

The Founder's Grandchildren's Lifetimes

Age   25

At any given time, three generations interact.
Source: Adapted from Leon A. Danco, *Inside the Family Business* (Cleveland, OH: Center for Family Business, University Press, 1985).

Figure 3-4

Pressures and Interests in a Family Business

		INSIDE THE FAMILY	OUTSIDE THE FAMILY
INSIDE THE BUSINESS		The family managers: Hanging onto or getting hold of company control Selection of family members as managers Continuity of family investment and involvement Building a dynasty Rivalry	The employees: Rewards for loyalty Sharing of equity, growth, and successes Professionalism Bridging family transitions Stake in the company
OUTSIDE THE BUSINESS		The relatives: Income and inheritance Family conflicts and alliances Degree of involvement in the business	The outsiders: Competition Market, product, supply, and technology influence Tax laws Regulatory agencies Trends in management practices

Source: Louis B. Barnes and Simon A. Hershon, "Transferring Power in the Family Business," *Harvard Business Review,* July/August 1976, p. 108.

INTERNAL AND EXTERNAL PRESSURES

The family business owner confronts pressures that arise from four distinct entities. As seen in Figure 3-4, there are pressures inside the family *and* inside the business. These often include issues such as maintaining or gaining control of the company, the continuity of family members as managers, and the rivalries among or between various family members.[10] At the same time there can be pressures arising from outside of the business but still within the structure of the family when other relatives question their own degree of involvement in the business and express concern about alliances that they are beginning to form.

Outside the family but inside the business, employees may demand such perquisites as a stake in the company, rewards for loyalty, and other means of sharing in the success of the venture. At the same time, "outsiders," such as competitors, government regulatory agencies, the IRS, suppliers, and customers, may introduce a whole new set of pressures for the small business manager to relieve.

LEGAL SUCCESSION ISSUES

Nepotism has always been a concern in family firms. However, beginning in 1984, a judicial challenge has confronted the long-existing and commonly accepted

---

[10]For example, see Ellen Wojohn, "Fathers and Sons," *Inc.,* April 1990, pp. 81–84; and Renee Edelman, "When Little Sister Means Business," *Working Woman,* February 1990, pp. 82–88.

practice. The results of the Oakland Scavenger case could change the employment practices of family firms forever.

This case questioned the legality of the practice in which family owners reserved for themselves and their relatives the most desirable and best paying positions in the firm. The suit arose when a group of black and Hispanic workers charged the California-based **Oakland Scavenger Company** with employment discrimination based on race. These employees believed that, since they were not related to the family that owned the operation, their prospects for moving ahead within the company were limited. The U.S. District Court in Northern California dismissed the suit, stating that it bore no relation to antidiscrimination laws. However, the U.S. Court of Appeals for the Ninth Circuit reviewed the decision and concluded that, "nepotistic concerns cannot supersede the nation's paramount goal of equal economic opportunity for all."[11]

The case was appealed to the Supreme Court. However, before there could be a ruling, the Oakland Scavenger Company was purchased by the Waste Management Corporation and the company agreed to an $8-million out-of-court settlement. The settlement allocated sums of at least $50,000 to 16 black and Hispanic plaintiffs, depending on their length of service, and also provided for payments to a class of more than 400 black and Hispanic workers who were employed by Oakland Scavenger after January 10, 1972.[12]

K. Peter Stalland, legal representative of the National Family Business Council, has stated that

> The effect this case can have on small business is tremendous. It means, conceivably, that almost any small business can be sued by an employee of a different ethnic origin than the owner, based upon not being accorded the same treatment as a son or daughter. The precedent is dangerous.[13]

This new legal question presents a challenge for future employment practices of family-owned businesses. With interpretations and further court cases sure to follow, legal experts in labor law are predicting statutory regulations from the federal government. Thus, the Oakland Scavenger case has started a movement that is sure to result in new guidelines and limitations for family employment. Family businesses must be aware of this contemporary challenge.

THE SURVIVAL ISSUE

George Abbott of the National Family Business Council has termed succession, ". . . the most important issue facing family business."[14] Succession of the business is continually acknowledged as important, yet **management succession plans** are absent from most family-owned businesses. Researchers cite three central reasons for this lapse:

---

[11]"Nepotism on Trial," *Inc. Magazine*, July 1984, p. 29.

[12]David Graulich, "You Can't Always Pay What You Want," *Family Business*, February 1990, pp. 16–19.

[13]"Nepotism on Trial."

[14]Poe, "The SOB's."

1. Owners are too busy keeping their business alive to plan for their own exit.

2. Owners do not have any confidence in the offspring who are supposed to replace them.

3. Owners do not see family perpetuity as a major concern.[15]

Leon A. Danco, founder of the Center for Family Business, states, "It is a daily miracle that there are any owner-managed businesses left in the world with so few making plans for their own continuity. The toughest thing for the business owner to realize is that time is running out on him."[16] (See Small Business Owner's Notebook: Family Business Succession.)

These facts of life—death or retirement—are inevitable but generally ignored. For a profitable succession of an entrepreneur's lifetime pursuit, the consideration of death or retirement must be part of a well conceived plan. The transition may be difficult, as it affects family members, bankers, employees, managers, competitors, lawyers, wives, and friends. However, as intertwined as the succession may appear, planning for succession with foresight creates a more favorable transition than does implementing it with hindsight.

STRATEGY AND STRUCTURE

The importance of succession has long been a topic of interest.[17] Yet the problem exists and continues to loom as a management challenge.

Effective management succession can reduce the legal problems associated not only with ownership, but with taxes and inheritance as well.[18] As with many of the challenges confronting family business, professional advice can be useful in effectuating proper succession plans. The use of financial institutions, insurance agents, accountants, and lawyers as well as management consultants and university professors have all been recommended.[19] Yet whatever the source, family business owners need to know how to carefully plan and structure the transition. Despite all the efforts to properly plan, finance, and manage a small family-owned business, many entrepreneurs stand by and watch their firms self-destruct because they have not properly confronted the challenge of succession.

Peter Davis has stated that the concept of "smooth succession" in a family firm is a contradiction of terms. This contradiction is due to the fact that succession is a

---

[15]W. Gibb Dyer, Jr., *Cultural Change in Family Firms*, (San Francisco: Jossey-Bass Publishers) 1986; Anthony J. Rutigliano, "When Worlds Collide," *Management Review*, February 1986.

[16]Leon A. Danco, *Beyond Survival*, (Reston, VA: Reston Publishing Company, 1975), p. 25.

[17]See, for example, Louis B. Barnes and Simon A. Hershon, "Transferring Power in the Family Business," *Harvard Business Review*, July/August 1976, p. 106; "CEO Profile, The Case for Succession Planning," *Small Business Report*, February 1985, pp. 79–85; Glenn R. Ayres, "Rough Family Justice: Equity in Family Business Succession Planning," *Family Business Review*, Spring 1990, pp. 3–22; and Ronald E. Berenbeim, "How Business Families Manage the Transition from Owner to Professional Management," *Family Business Review*, Spring 1990, pp. 69–110.

[18]Irving L. Blackman, "A Financial Guide to Turning Over the Helm," *Nation's Business*, January 1986, p. 40.

[19]Parks B. Dimsdale, "Management Succession—Facing the Future," *Journal of Small Business Management*, October 1974, pp. 42–46.

■ SMALL BUSINESS OWNER'S NOTEBOOK ■

Family Business Succession

It is not uncommon for family members who are supposed to take over the family business to be unqualified to do so. And since the people factor can be more critical in the family-owned business than in any other type of company, improper choices could lead to costly internal strife.

To deal with these problems, the best approach is to develop written policies for hiring, promoting, and compensating family members. Here are a few guidelines:

1. Require that children and other family members work outside the business for at least three years before joining the company. This gives them the opportunity to function independently, to build self-esteem, and to gain valuable experience that they can bring to the family business. For example, a family member may elect to work for a competitor or a consulting firm.

2. Require that family members entering the business satisfy the same entry requirements as nonfamily members. If a college degree has always been a requirement for entry, make sure this requirement also applies to family members. Salary should be treated in a similar fashion. Family members should earn the same pay as other employees serving in the same capacities. There are other ways to compensate family members if so desired.

3. Put limits on the number of family members allowed to join the business. Every aunt, nephew, and cousin will want a job in the family business, but that would leave no employment opportunities for other talented people who might then go to work for competitors.

4. Should children decide to leave the family business, refrain from using guilt or threats to keep them by your side. They may find out that they don't like the real world and want to come back.

Family members must be fashioned into a team working together to accomplish common interests. Fair policies on how relatives are hired, paid, and promoted goes a long way toward achieving this goal.

Source: Mark Stevens, "Putting the Family in the Family Business," *Small Business Reports*, November 1990, pp. 23–26.

highly charged emotional issue that requires not only structural changes but cultural changes as well.[20] Family business succession includes the transfer of ethics, values, and traditions along with the actual business itself.[21] The "family business" and the "business family" are two distinct components that must be dealt with and disentangled if progress towards succession is to be made.[22]

In attempting to provide some solutions to the succession issue, some researchers and theorists have offered advice regarding strategic plans. Jeffrey Barach believes that any attempt to keep all generations of a family under the same corporate roof is generally doomed. In order for a family business to grow and prosper, a "family of companies" may be appropriate. Barach contends that there are two major strategic goals that family firms must determine. First, if the family business is pursuing a goal of *expansion*, then leadership succession should be carefully structured. Second, if the family business is pursuing a goal of *separation*, then a family enterprise or a family of entrepreneurs may be the solution. Thus, Barach contends that a complete understanding of the family business's strategy *and* structuring is necessary in order to implement that strategic goal.[23]

Another strategy centers around the entry of the younger generation and the time when the "power" actually changes hands. Figure 3-5 illustrates the advantages and disadvantages of early entry of the younger generation versus delayed entry. The question centers around the ability of the successor to gain credibility with the firm's employees. The actual transfer of power is a critical issue in the implementation of any family strategic plan.[24]

In examining other literature, various researchers suggest the use of an attorney, accountant, or consultant in preparing a succession plan. However, the major requirements for successful management succession are the establishment of written policies and a willingness to confront the issues previously discussed. The following provides a strategic framework that can be used for this purpose.

DEVELOPING A SUCCESSION STRATEGY

A number of important issues must be considered when developing a succession strategy. These include (a) understanding the contextual aspects, (b) identifying successor qualities, and (c) carrying out the succession plan.[25]

---

[20]Peter Davis, "Realizing the Potential of the Family Business," *Organizational Dynamics*, Summer 1983, p. 47.

[21]Paul C. Rosenblatt, "Blood May Be Thicker, But in the Boardroom It Just Makes for Sticky Business," *Psychology Today*, July 1985, p. 55.

[22]Phyllis G. Holland and William R. Boulton, "Balancing the 'Family' and the 'Business' in the Family Business," *Business Horizons*, March/April 1984, p. 19.

[23]Jeffrey A. Barach, "Is There a Cure for the Paralyzed Family Board?" *Sloan Management Review*, Fall 1984, p. 3.

[24]T. Roger Peay and W. Gibb Dyer, "Power Orientations of Entrepreneurs and Succession Planning," *Journal of Small Business Management*, January 1989, pp. 47–52.

[25]Donald F. Kuratko and Richard M. Hodgetts, "Succession Strategies for Family Businesses," *Management Advisor*, Spring 1989, pp. 22–30.

Figure 3-5

Comparison of Entry
Strategies for
Succession in
Family Businesses

EARLY ENTRY STRATEGY

Advantages	Disadvantages
1. Intimate familiarity with the nature of the business and employees is acquired.	1. Conflict results when owner has difficulty in teaching or relinquishing control to successor.
2. Skills specifically required by the business are developed.	2. Normal mistakes tend to be viewed as incompetence in the successor.
3. Exposure to others in the business facilitates acceptance and the achievement of credibility.	3. Knowledge of the environment is limited and risks of inbreeding are incurred.
4. Strong relationships with constituents are readily established.	

DELAYED ENTRY STRATEGY

Advantages	Disadvantages
1. Successor's skills are judged with greater objectivity.	1. Specific expertise and understanding of organization's key success factors and culture may be lacking.
2. Development of self-confidence and growth independent of familial influence are achieved.	2. Set patterns of outside activity may conflict with those prevailing in the family firm.
3. Outside success establishes credibility and serves as a basis for accepting the successor as a competent executive.	3. Resentment may result when successors are advanced ahead of long-term employees.
4. Perspective of the business environment is broadened.	

Source: Jeffrey A. Barach, Joseph Gantisky, James A. Carlson, and Benjamin A. Doochin, "Entry of the Next Generation: Strategic Challenge for Family Business," *Journal of Small Business Management,* April 1988, p. 53.

UNDERSTANDING THE CONTEXTUAL ASPECTS

The five key aspects that contribute to an effective succession plan include time, type of venture, capabilities of the managers, the entrepreneur's vision, and environmental factors.

TIME   The earlier the entrepreneur begins to plan for a successor, the better the chances of finding the right person. The biggest problem the owner faces is the "forcing event" that requires immediate action. This type of situation invariably results in inadequate time to find the best replacement.

Forcing events are those happenings that cause the replacement of the owner-manager. These events require the entrepreneur to step aside and let someone else direct the operation. If an owner or manager experiences any of the following crises, a succession decision must be made:

☐ Death. The heirs must immediately find a successor to run the operation.

☐ Illness or some other form of nonterminal physical incapacitation.

☐ Mental or psychological breakdown that results in the individual having to withdraw from the business.

☐ Legal problems, such as being incarcerated for violation of the law.

☐ Financial difficulties that result in lenders demanding the removal of the owner-manager before lending the necessary funds to the enterprise.

These types of events are often unforeseen and there seldom is a contingency plan for dealing with them. As a result, such an occurrence creates a major problem for the business.

TYPE OF VENTURE Some entrepreneurs are easy to replace; some cannot be replaced. To a large degree, this is determined by the type of venture. An entrepreneur who is the idea person in a high-tech operation is going to be difficult to replace. The same is true for an entrepreneur whose personal business contacts throughout the industry are the key factors for success. On the other hand, a person running an operation that requires a minimum of knowledge or experience can usually be replaced without much trouble.

CAPABILITIES OF THE MANAGERS The skills, desires, and abilities of the replacement will dictate the future potential and direction of the enterprise. As the industry matures, the demands made on the entrepreneur may also change. Industries where high technology is the name of the game often realize that marketing has become increasingly important. A technologically skilled entrepreneur with an understanding of marketing, or the ability to develop an orientation in this direction, will be more valuable to the enterprise than will a scientific-technological entrepreneur.

ENTREPRENEUR'S VISION Most entrepreneurs have expectations, hopes, and desires for their organization. A successor, hopefully, will share this vision except, of course, in those cases where the entrepreneur's plans have gotten the organization in trouble and a new vision is needed.

ENVIRONMENTAL FACTORS Sometimes a successor is needed because the business environment changes and an accompanying change is needed at the top. In some cases owners have had to allow financial types to assume control of the venture because internal efficiency was more critical to short-run survival than was market effectiveness.

These contextual aspects influence the environment within which the successor will operate. Unless the individual and the environment has a "right fit," the successor will be less than maximally effective.

IDENTIFYING SUCCESSOR QUALITIES

There are many qualities or characteristics that successors should possess. Some will be more important than others, depending on the situation. However, in most cases, all will have some degree of importance. Some of the most common of these attributes include the following:

☐ sufficient knowledge of the business or a good position from which to acquire this knowledge (especially marketing or finance) within an acceptable time

☐ fundamental honesty and capability

☐ good health

☐ energy, alertness, and perceptiveness

☐ deep enthusiasm about the enterprise

☐ a personality compatible with the business

☐ a high degree of perseverance

☐ stability, maturity, and proper aggressiveness

☐ thoroughness; a proper respect for detail

☐ problem-solving ability and resourcefulness

☐ the ability to plan and organize

☐ a talent for developing people

☐ the personality of a starter and a finisher

☐ appropriate agreement with the owner's philosophy about the business

Locating an individual with the "right" traits can be difficult. If the ideal cannot be achieved, the emphasis should be placed on selecting a successor with the potential to develop the attributes listed above within an appropriate time frame. This choice must take into account (a) the business' concerns, (b) the owners' concerns, and (c) family member concerns. The specific areas within each will include the following:

The Business's Concerns:
☐ Type of business venture
☐ The business environment
☐ Stage of the firm's development
☐ The business's traditions and norms

Owner's Concerns:
☐ Relinquishing power and leadership
☐ Keeping the family functioning as a unit
☐ Defining family members' future roles in the business
☐ Keeping nonfamily resources in the firm

Family Members' Concerns:
☐ Gaining and losing control of family assets
☐ Having control over decisions made by business leadership
☐ Protecting interest when ownership is dispersed among family members
☐ Assurance that the business will continue[26]

---

[26]Adapted from Barnes and Hershon, "Transferring Power" Beckhard and Dyer, "Managing Continuity"; Churchill and Hatten, "Non-Market-Based Transfers"; Kuratko and Hodgetts, "Succession Strategies"; and Berenbeim, "How Business Families Manage."

These concerns prepare the advisor for establishing a management continuity strategy or policy. Examining these functions through the above framework allows written policies to be established in one of the following strategies:

1. The owner controls the management continuity strategy entirely. This is very common, yet legal advice is still needed and recommended.

2. The owner consults with selected family members. Here the legal advisor establishes a liaison between the family and the owner so as to facilitate the construction of the succession mechanism.

3. The owner works with professional advisors. This is an actual board of advisors from various professional disciplines and industries that works with the owner to establish the mechanism for succession.

4. The owner works with family involvement. This alternative allows the core family (blood members and spouses) to actively participate in and influence the decisions regarding succession.

Presuming that the owner still is reasonably healthy and the firm is in viable condition, the following additional actions should be considered:

5. Formulate buy-sell agreements at the outset of the company, or soon thereafter, and whenever a major change occurs. This is also the time to consider an appropriate insurance policy on key individuals who would provide the cash needed to acquire the equity of the departed.

6. Consider employee stock ownership plans (ESOPs). If the owner has no immediate successor in mind and respects the loyalty and competence of his employees, then an appropriate ESOP might be the best solution for passing control of the enterprise. Afterward, the employees could decide on the management hierarchy.

7. Sell or liquidate the business when the owner loses the zest for it but still is physically able to go on. This could provide the capital to launch another business. Whatever the owner's plans, the firm would be sold before it fails due to disinterest.

8. Sell or liquidate when the owner discovers a terminal illness, but still has time for the orderly transfer of management or ownership.[27]

In these cases, legal advice is beneficial, but the greater benefit is to have advisors (legal or otherwise) who understand the succession issues and are able to recommend a course of action.

Entrepreneurial founders of family firms often reject the thought of succession. Yet neither ignorance nor denial will change the inevitable. Therefore, it is crucial to pay careful attention to the importance of designing a plan for succession. Such a plan can prevent today's flourishing family businesses from becoming a statistic of diminishing family dynasties.

---

[27]Holland and Boulton, "Balancing"; "CEO Profile, The Case for Succession Planning," *Small Business Report,* February 1985, p. 79; Sue Birley, "Succession in the Family Firm: The Inheritor's View," *Journal of Small Business Management,* July 1986, pp. 36–43. See also Kevin McDermott, "Replacing the Old Man—A Guide to Succession," *D & B Reports,* July/August 1986, pp. 22–26; and Michael E. Trunko, "Managing the Family-Owned Business," *Entrepreneur,* February 1986, pp. 32–36.

CARRYING OUT THE SUCCESSION PLAN

While implementing a **succession plan** can be a problem, there are effective ways of dealing with it. The following presents a few important steps in doing so.

GROOM AN HEIR.   In some firms the entrepreneur will pick a successor and let it be known. However, many top managers hesitate when it comes to actually announcing a choice. There may be one person who appears to have the inside track or a small number (from 2 to 5) from whom the successor will be chosen, but no one knows for sure who will get the job. Even if the heir is designated, the founder may have difficulty relinquishing (or even sharing) the authority necessary for effective grooming.

AGREE ON A PLAN.   Effective succession requires a plan. Smaller organizations usually only need a detailed person-to-person discussion of how responsibilities will be transferred to the new president. No owner wants to step aside for a new person who will change things dramatically; no entrepreneur wants to see a lifetime of effort unraveled. Since these are concerns of family businesses, a detailed discussion of duties, obligations, and operations is imperative. At this point, it can be helpful to bring into the plan those who will be most affected by it. This participatory approach will often co-opt some critics and alleviate the fears of others. In any event, it is a useful management tactic for helping create unity behind the new person.

CONSIDER OUTSIDE HELP.   Promotion from within is a morale-building philosophy. Sometimes, however, it is a mistake. Does anyone in the firm *really* have the requisite skills for managing the operation? Sometimes the situation calls for an outside person. However, in small organizations there is the everpresent ego factor. Does the owner-manager have the wisdom to step aside and the courage to let someone else make strategic decisions? Or is the desire for control so great that the owner prefers to run the risks associated with personally managing the operation? The lesson is clear to the dispassionate observer; unfortunately, it is one that many owners have had to learn the hard way.

CONCLUSION

Table 3-1 provides a checklist of the many considerations presented in this chapter on succession. This checklist sets forth important steps that should be taken in addressing the family succession issue.

Family-owned small businesses present many unique and challenging problems that stymie the typical strategists. Recent legal challenges are illustrative of the diverse yet vital changes confronting family strategies of success.

In becoming aware of those challenges, family business owners should develop greater decision-making ability. Holland and Boulton referred to the owner-operator of a family firm as an "action manager," since he has significant freedom in decision making to turn thoughts into actions. "The commitment of action managers to their own objectives and their assessments of need for making adjustments determines what actions they will take.[28]

The purpose of this chapter has been to increase your awareness that assessments and adjustments must be implemented to confront these new legal challenges. It is hoped that confronting these challenges will lead to more effective strategies for family-owned small businesses to successfully survive and grow.

The health of our economy in upcoming decades depends heavily on the success of small business and the continual growth of family-owned firms. Their strategies

---

[28]Holland and Boulton, "Balancing."

Table 3-1 A Checklist For Succession: Some Important Steps

TO THE OWNERS OF FAMILY-RUN FIRMS:
_____ Learn to delegate; decentralize operations.
_____ Develop an organization chart—for real.
_____ Plan for more than one successor; increase the possibilities.
_____ Establish a personnel development program.
_____ Encourage the potential successor to gain experience outside of the business.
_____ Do not neglect daughters.
_____ Keep plans updated, continually review the progress of the business and successors.
_____ Strategically plan for the future—do not always focus on putting out daily fires.
_____ Establish family business meetings or forums to air issues.

TO THE CHILDREN OF FAMILY-RUN FIRMS:
_____ Announce interest in taking over the family firm.
_____ Take responsibility for your personal development.
_____ Get a mentor (someone from "outside" whom you respect).
_____ Gain experience outside the family business.
_____ Accountability training—hold positions that teach responsibility and offer opportunities for decision making.
_____ Learn to blend family traditions with future business goals.
_____ Avoid family feuds; work with the family not against it.
_____ Eliminate dad's or mom's "ghost"—prepare a clear takeover plan that eventually phases out older family leaders.

Source: Donald F. Kuratko and Richard M. Hodgetts, "Succession Strategies for Family Businesses," *Management Advisor,* Spring 1989, p. 30.

for innovation, invention, growth, and work must be enhanced with the future in mind. Wealth and business success in the United States have been rooted in the family business. The ability of contemporary family firms to confront new challenges—especially those that have been reviewed in this chapter—will serve as a gauge to the future development of that root in our economy.

■ SUMMARY

Family businesses account for between 12.1 and 14.4 million of the nation's 15 million businesses. Because there has been no well-designed succession plans, most of these operations are not passed on to others in the family, and when the owner dies the operation often dies with him or her. A number of different types of pressures impact the owner's succession plans. Figure 3-3 detailed some of these. In addition, legal issues, such as those raised by the Oakland Scavenger case, must be considered.

In dealing with family succession, it is best to have a well-formulated strategy. This plan will address three major areas: contextual aspects of the plan, successor qualities, and the way in which to implement the plan. The contextual aspects of the plan include (a) when the successor will be chosen; (b) the type of venture; (c) the capabilities of the person who will assume the helm; (d) the entrepreneur's vision; and (d) environmental factors, such as the economic business conditions. Successor qualities include those traits and behaviors that the successor should have. Examples include business knowledge, good health, problem-solving ability, a talent for developing others, and the ability to plan and organize. Implementing the plan requires grooming an heir, agreeing on a plan of action and, if necessary, going outside and bringing in new blood. Table 3-1 presents a checklist for carrying out these and other succession-related steps.

■ REVIEW AND DISCUSSION QUESTIONS

1. Many family-owned businesses have succeeded because they did not have to worry about pleasing stockholders and others more interested in short-run profit than in long-run gains. What does this statement mean?

2. What kinds of pressures do family businesses get from family members inside the business? From family members outside the business? Identify and describe three of each type of pressure.

3. What kinds of pressures do family businesses get from individuals who are inside the business but are not family members? Outsiders who are not employees of the business? Identify and describe three of each types of pressures.

4. In what way did the Oakland Scavenger case present a legal problem for family businesses seeking to pass the operation along to other members of the family?

5. When it comes to family businesses, some individuals say that "smooth succession" is a contradiction of terms. Why?

6. Explain how the following contextual issues are important in developing a succession strategy: time, the type of venture, and the capabilities of the successor.

7. In developing a succession strategy, in what way are the entrepreneur's vision and environmental factors important contextual issues?

8. Identify and describe four qualities that you feel are most important in a successor. Then identify three qualities that you believe are useful but of secondary importance. Defend your answers.

9. Why would it be useful for a family business to formulate a buy-sell agreement among the owners? When would such an agreement be of value?

10. When should a family business go outside the company to find a successor? What guidelines would you recommend that the business follow in this process?

■ ▬▬
Case Studies

All in Good Time

■ For the last 29 years George Withers has had a successful auto repair shop. The shop specializes in handling sports cars that require precision work. George and his crew of 22 mechanics are well known for the quality of their work, and customers have come from 100 miles away to have their cars repaired and tuned.

Because the business has done so well, George would like to keep it in the family. His son, Sam, has worked in the company as a mechanic for eight years, and his wife, Roberta, is the office manager. Sam would like to take over the reins when his father steps aside, but so far George, who is 68 years old, has given no sign of slowing down. Sam feels that if his father does not teach him how to run the business, he will be unprepared for the job should George suddenly fall ill and have to step down.

On two occasions both Roberta and Sam have talked to George about a succession plan, but George has simply waved them away by saying, "This will all be done in good time."

Earlier this month, George had an emergency appendectomy and was out of work for ten days. During this time Roberta and Sam scurried to keep things afloat. However, everything did not get back to normal until George returned. As a result, George's wife and son intend to talk to him about succession plans within the next month.

At the same time, a new issue has arisen. Tim Keating, who has worked at the garage since its founding, has told George that he would like the opportunity to take over the business when George retires. "I've been with you since we started," he said, "and when you got sick, I realized it was time for me to step forward. I think I've earned this right, and I'd like to talk to you about it."

1. Why has George not yet developed a succession plan?

2. Does the employee have any legal rights of succession, or can George teach the business to whomever he wants?

3. What should George do now? Explain.

Now What?

■ Nine years ago Maurice Anderson passed away, and his widow, Florence, took over the reins of the business. Anderson's is a men's specialty store that sells high-quality, custom-made suits. These suits sell for $750 to $1,500 and are very popular with top managers. The store's clientele consist of approximately 450 business people who buy an average of two suits per year.

Florence has a file on each of her customers. She knows the style and colors they like and, after reviewing their file, can discuss the outfits that would best fit their needs. Florence also stays abreast of the latest styles and fashions. So since she is aware of her customers' wardrobes, she can make suggestions regarding need changes and additions.

A great deal of Florence's ability is a result of her experience in the store. Before her husband's death, she was a homemaker and mother of two young children. Today the children, David, 27, and Kirsten, 25, have families of their own. David is an insurance agent and Kirsten as assistant branch manager for a local bank. Neither makes a great deal of money, so Florence has decided to ask them if they would like to join her in the business. She knows she could teach them all they need to know about running the store. Florence's informal plan is to continue managing the store for ten more years and then retire. She has been thinking of talking to David and Kirsten about this next week, when they get together to celebrate David's birthday. If her children decline the offer, Florence will then make plans to sell the operation and retire on the proceeds.

1. How much longer does Florence have for developing a succession plan? Explain.

2. What steps should she include in this plan?

3. How would you recommend she go about grooming an heir? Explain.

You Be the Consultant

FINDING THE RIGHT SUCCESSOR

Most people in Richard Gonzalez's home town know who he is because they have frequented his store, "Plants 'N Things." For the last 15 years Richard has sold plant materials, sod, garden equipment, and related supplies and materials. The store is located in a large shopping center near some of the most affluent neighborhoods in the town. Last year the store grossed $1.2 million and netted $320,000 before taxes. The operation employs 27 people and over the last five years the product offerings have been expanded to include a wider variety of plant materials and garden equipment. Richard is 59 years old and plans to work for approximately six more years. He has had three offers to sell the business, but he would prefer to turn it over to his children. The problem is that none of them agree with his way of running the operation.

The oldest is Martha, 31, who majored in history and for the last three years has worked in the store. Martha believes that Richard should expand the business and begin offering landscape services. "It's a natural growth area for us," she recently told her father, "and it would increase overall sales by about 25 percent." The problem in Richard's view is that a number of firms around town already offer this service, and there is nothing that he could do to make his service unique. In the final analysis, Richard believes that a move of this nature would result in a price war that would end with everyone either losing money or working on razor-thin margins.

The second oldest child is Robert, 29, who has been working with Richard for seven years. He joined the company immediately after graduating from the nearby university with a degree in biology. Robert believes that the company should continue expanding its line in the same general direction it has been following for the past five years. However, he would also like to see greater attention given to selling home plants and garden tools. "Home plants are easy to raise and the markup is phenomenal," he explains. "This would be a natural addition to our product line, given the number of people who come here every day and the high profit on garden tools." Richard basically agrees with this logic but feels that the investment in materials, facilities, and equipment would be extremely high and when this is factored into the profit formula, the strategy would be far less profitable than Robert believes.

Paul, 23, is the youngest and Richard's favorite. Richard would like to turn the company over to Paul because he feels that Paul has a better understanding of the business than his older siblings. Paul majored in marketing and spends most of his time working directly with customers and helping them choose the merchandise they need. The problem with designating Paul as the successor, in Richard's opinion, is that the two older children will not go along with the decision. There is likely to be a great deal of internal strife.

Richard understands that at some point in the near future he will have to decide whether the business will remain in the family or be sold to an outsider. Right now he believes that he needs to weigh the benefits and drawbacks associated with his various alternatives. He hopes to finalize a plan of action within the next six weeks.

■ **YOUR CONSULTATION** Help Richard decide on a plan of action. Tell him those steps he needs to implement in order to formulate an effective succession plan. Also help him resolve the problem of differences in vision between himself and his two oldest children. Additionally, what qualities do you think Richard should be looking for in the individual he chooses? Finally, whom should he choose? Give him your opinion and the reasoning behind your decision.

Part One Case Study

MEMORIAL FUNERAL HOME

HISTORY

The Memorial Funeral Home began as a small family business, founded in 1947 by Donald Kellen. Located in an upper-middle-class suburb of a large city, the business prospered and gained an excellent reputation. After 33 years as director of the business, Donald Kellen retired and was succeeded in 1980 by his son Kenneth.

Memorial is the only funeral home in the suburb. However, funeral homes in neighboring suburbs offer strong competition. Under the guidance of Kenneth Kellen, Memorial began diversifying its services. Currently, Memorial handles 65 funerals a year under its own name. In addition, Memorial supplies removal, embalming, directing, livery service, and rental of funeral vehicles to other funeral homes. While maintaining its primary function as a family-run, neighborhood business concentrating on personal service, Memorial has successfully diversified its operations.

Recognizing the rapidly changing ideas and expectations of society, Kenneth Kellen is adjusting. Economics is beginning to play a major role in funeral decisions. Clients are more sophisticated and informed, necessitating clear-cut definitions of services, costs, and available options.

FUNDAMENTAL COMPONENTS

A number of fundamental components are associated with the funeral home business:

☐ *PROPERTY.* Land and buildings must be large enough to meet the demands of visitations and funeral services. Owning such property—in a convenient and accessible location where the public can be properly served—constitutes one of the major, on-going costs of a funeral home operation.

☐ *FACILITIES.* A funeral home must be tastefully furnished to provide a homelike atmosphere and must be easily adaptable for visitations and for funeral services. Facilities also must be able to accommodate more than one funeral at a time.

☐ *AUTOMOTIVE EQUIPMENT.* Funeral directors must provide the latest in automobiles for transportation between the funeral home and the cemetery. Owning and maintaining this equipment, much of which is specially designed, is costly.

☐ *SELECTION ROOM.* Special facilities must be available to house the wide variety of merchandise (caskets, vaults, and clothing) made available by the funeral home

Source: This case was prepared by Dr. Donald F. Kuratko of the College of Business, Ball State University and is intended to be used as a basis for class discussion. Presented and accepted by the refereed Midwest Case Writers Association Workshop, 1985. All rights reserved to the author and to the Midwest Society of Case Research. Copyright © 1985 by Donald F. Kuratko. Reprinted by permission.

for burial purposes. This service requires considerable space and investment in inventory.

□ *PROFESSIONAL STAFF.*   Salaries make up the largest part of a funeral home's expense. Personnel must be carefully chosen so that families receive both expert and efficient service. To attract qualified personnel, funeral homes must compete with salaries paid by business, industry, and other professions.

□ *EDUCATIONAL REQUIREMENTS.*   Funeral directors and embalmers today are required by state law to meet certain college academic standards and pass state board examinations before they may be licensed to practice funeral directing and embalming. This highly specialized training prepares the funeral director to offer expert professional service to bereaved families, and the director must be paid a salary commensurate with his or her knowledge.

□ *DOCUMENTS.*   Funeral directors are required by law to complete a number of documents relating to each funeral.

□ *COUNSELING SKILL.*   An intangible factor in funeral cost is that of counseling. An effective funeral director helps families to better accept death, grief, and bereavement. The ability to take a traumatic situation and mold it into a meaningful and impressive service of remembrance for the surviving family is an important part of the funeral director's job and contributes to the survivors' mental and emotional health.

□ *TWENTY-FOUR-HOUR SERVICE.*   The typical funeral home is open continuously for service. This means the telephone must be attended, and personnel must be available to assist those who have experienced a death regardless of the day or the hour.

□ *COMMUNITY SERVICE.*   The funeral director must be a civic-spirited member of the community. He or she must be actively involved in business, civic, and religious organizations.

PUBLIC PERCEPTION

According to the National Funeral Directors Association (NFDA), there are approximately 22,000 funeral homes in the United States. A major concern of the industry is the new attitudes of the public regarding the disposition of the dead. The executive secretary of the NFDA has noted that

1. Many people believe that a funeral does meet many needs, including individual, family, religious, and community needs.

2. Some people believe that emotions can be intellectualized and the quickest possible disposition of the deceased is the best course of action.

3. There are those who as yet have formed no definite view. They have had little, if any, experience with death. They are honestly asking what needs arise when a death occurs, and whether the funeral helps to satisfy these needs.

Recent investigations of funeral homes by the Federal Trade Commission, as well as newspaper feature stories in exposé form, have not helped the image of the industry. The public, aroused by the sensational and emotional nature of the issue, is easily persuaded into the belief that some funeral homes are dishonest. A basic lack of understanding about death and the funeral home business lies at the root of the public mistrust.

Death is not the everyday experience it once was. Millions of Americans have never been present at the death of someone close to them. Millions of Americans have never been to a funeral, or even seen a funeral procession, except one that was televised. Millions of Americans have never seen a dead body except on television, in a movie, on a battlefield, or on a highway. Even where people have been directly involved in the arrangement of a funeral service, there is often confusion or doubt about the role of the funeral director and the cost of his services.

Often the place of the casket in the funeral service is unclear or undefined. Historically, the funeral director has been a provider of goods and some services. A casket was purchased, and all other services were provided "free." Today, according to the NFDA, on the average the merchandise amounts to only about 20 percent of the total cost of a funeral service.

FINANCIAL STRUCTURE

People are probably less knowledgeable about funeral costs than about any other aspect of funeral services. The following discussion provides a general description of pricing and payment in Memorial's section of the country.

METHODS   The surviving relatives accepting responsibility for payment may be charged under one of three methods or a combination thereof. The method used is chosen by the funeral director. The methods are (1) complete itemized pricing, which itemizes every detail; (2) functional pricing, which gives prices for major categories of costs; and (3) unit pricing, which gives only the complete price.

COMPLETE ITEMIZED PRICING.   For a typical funeral, the complete itemized pricing is detailed on a form similar to the one in Figure I-1. The following is a typical pricing structure:

Professional services	
Funeral director and staff	$400
Funeral home facilities	
Chapel and facilities (one night)	395
Embalming and preparation	215
Preparation room	95
Merchandise	
Casket	504
Cards and register book	135
Transportation	
Removal	95
Hearse	150
Total	**$1,989**

The range of services available, and therefore the costs, may vary (see Table I-1). In the foregoing example of itemized costs, the total of $1,989 minus the casket cost of $504 equals $1,485, which corresponds to Major Services—B in Table I-2.

Figure I-1

Memorial Funeral
Home Pricing Form

Services for:	Date:
1. Professional Services:	**Cash Advances:**
Professional Care of the Deceased, Staff Service Fee .... $_____	As a convenience to the family, we will advance payment for the following:
	Clergy Honorarium .... $_____
Professional Services of Funeral Director and Staff......... $_____	Beautician .... $_____
.... $_____	Chapel Organist .... $_____
.... $_____	Church Organist.............. $_____
	Death Notices .... $_____
	Certified Copies .... $_____
Total Professional Services .... $_____	.... $_____
	.... $_____
2. Funeral Home Facilities:	.... $_____
	.... $_____
Use of Chapel and Funeral Home for Visitation and Services .... $_____	.... $_____
	Total .... $_____
Preparation/Operating Room ...... $_____	**Summary:**
.... $_____	Our Charges .... $_____
.... $_____	Sales Tax.................... $_____
	Cash Advances .... $_____
Total Facilities .... $_____	Less Credits................. $_____
	TOTAL BALANCE DUE .... $_____
3. Merchandise:	
	The foregoing contract has been read by (to) me, and I (we) hereby acknowledge receipt of a copy of same and agree to pay the above funeral account and any such additional services or merchandise as ordered by me (us), on or before _____ 19 ____. The liability hereby assumed is in addition to the liability imposed by law upon the estate and others and shall not constitute a release thereof.
Casket.......................... $_____	
Burial Vault .... $_____	
Clothing .... $_____	
Printing, Clerical, and Sundry Business Expenses .... $_____	
.... $_____	
Total Merchandise .... $_____	Signature _____ Relationship
	Signature _____ Relationship
4. Transportation:	Signature _____ Relationship
	Funeral Director
Removal .... $_____	NET DUE ON/BEFORE _____ (30 Days). This account will become past due and delinquent if payment is not made on or before the above date. An Unanticipated Late Payment Fee of 3/4 of 1% per month (9% annual percentage rate) on the outstanding balance will be charged after that date on all accounts in default.
Funeral Coach .... $_____	
Limousines/Family Cars .... $_____	
Flower Cars .... $_____	
.... $_____	
Total Transportation .... $_____	

Table I-1 A Range of Funeral Services (Charges Listed by Categories)

MAJOR SERVICES PROVIDED	A	B	C	D	E
Use of chapel and funeral home for visitation and funeral services	2 nights and services next day	1 night and services next day	1 night and no services next day	Visitation on day of service (max. 4 hrs.)	No visitation or service
Removal of deceased from local home or hospital	Included	Included	Included	Included	Included
Professional care of the deceased, preparation room, and staff service fee	Included	Included	Included	Included	Not included
Transportation of deceased to local cemetery or crematory	Hearse included	Hearse included	Service vehicle	Hearse included	Service vehicle
Professional services of funeral director and staff, sundry business expenses	Included	Included	Included	Included	Included
Prayer cards/chapel folders, register book, donation envelopes, and acknowledgment cards	Included	Included	Included	Included	Not included
TOTAL PROFESSIONAL FEE	$1,685	$1,485	$1,260	$925	$425
Deceased transported to our funeral home from out of town	$1,175	$975	$750	$650	Direct to interment $195

Casket, vault, and other items of choice are left to the further discretion of the family and are added to the above service expenditures.

Table I-2 The Cost of Funerals

FUNERAL HOME COSTS	Average	Range
Overhead	$ 440	$ 169 to $ 943
Planning, management, supervision, embalming	237	137 to 422
Staff and salaries	523	276 to 798
Funeral vehicles	196	88 to 655
Casket	584	65 to 7,685
Outer receptacle (grave box or burial vault)	411	101 to 1,475
BURIAL COSTS		
Cemetery burial	582	345 to 1,065
Grave memorial	310	135 to 5,105
Mausoleum entombment	2,520	1,150 to 5,200
Cremation	147	110 to 150
Urn	159	30 to 1,100
Columbarium (place set aside in cemetery for ashes)	336	215 to 580
Funeral director profit	275	Not available
OPTIONAL ITEMS		
Death notices	69	31 to 113
Flowers	160	20 to 446
Clothes (for deceased)	72	27 to 104
Donation to church, rabbi, etc.	53	20 to 150
Music, organist, vocalist	38	15 to 220

Source: Funeral Directors Association of Greater Chicago.

The price of the casket will vary as well, ranging from approximately $65 to $7,685. Available at an extra charge are other services such as the following:

ITEM	Price Range
Burial vault	$105 to $1,200
Clergyman	$50 to $100
Beautician	$50
Chapel organist	$50
Cemetery charges:	
Grave opening	$295 to $535
Mausoleum	Varies greatly
Death notices (one day, one paper)	$75 (average)
Extra funeral cars:	
Flower car	$110
Limousine	$130
Copies of death certificate	$3 (first), $2 (each additional)
Burial garments	$75
Church soloist	$50

If cremation is desired, costs such as the casket and grave opening charges will be eliminated. Additional costs encountered would include the following:

ITEM	Price Range
Cremation	$ 95-$120
Cremation container (box)	$ 65-$ 75
Cremation urn	$116-$237

In the complete itemized pricing method, all costs are known. Included in some of the itemized costs are markups by the funeral director.

A comparison can be made between the costs of the Memorial Funeral Home and the average industry costs provided in Table I-2, which also lists the industry's range of costs for each item.

FUNCTIONAL PRICING A more compressed presentation of costs is provided under the functional pricing method. In contrast to the eight details provided under the complete itemized pricing method, the functional pricing method lists only three major categories:

Professional services	$1,105
Merchandise	639
Transportation	245
Total	$1,989

Functional pricing, like detailed pricing, adds all outside charges to the functional total. This method provides more detail than unit pricing but less than that provided by complete itemized pricing.

UNIT PRICING   Unit pricing is nothing more than providing the casket and all associated services under one lump sum. The unit total varies with the casket selected and with any increased services that are provided.

Years ago most funeral directors used a cost method known as the four-by-four method. It was based on the casket price with the funeral director's fixed costs and profit built into the calculation. For example, for a casket with a cost of $400, the calculation would be:

$$
\begin{array}{rl}
\text{Casket} & \$\ \ 400 \\
& \underline{\times\quad 4} \\
& \$1,600 \\
& \underline{+\ \ 400} \\
\text{Total} & \$2,000
\end{array}
$$

Subsequently, funeral directors used a five-by-six method: $400 \times 5 = \$2,000 + \$600 = \$2,600$. However, this method is no longer widely employed either. Rather it is common practice to simply determine all costs involved and add a percentage for profit. In the main, unit pricing is declining in popularity because more states are requiring itemized pricing.

FORM OF PAYMENT   So that there is no misunderstanding about who is to pay the bill, someone has to accept responsibility by signing a legal contract. This, along with the signing of an additional release form, allows removal of the body to take place. Full details are then documented on a comprehensive work sheet.

When services have been selected, certain cash payments must be made. A cash advance is also made to the funeral director to defray out-of-pocket costs. Finally, a direct payment must be made to the cemetery to pay all graveside costs in advance.

THE FUTURE

The emphasis today is on low-cost funerals and relatively inexpensive selections. Two kinds of funeral homes predominate in the industry: independent, family-run funeral homes with one location, and large corporate-run funeral homes with many locations, many employees, and many pieces of equipment.

Automobiles are a major capital outlay for the funeral director. In 1987 a new hearse cost from $34,000 to $52,000 (for deluxe models); a new limousine cost approximately $35,000. The initial outlay and future maintenance are major considerations for the independent funeral director.

As an alternative to owning vehicles independently, three or four noncompeting funeral homes sometimes pool their hearses, limousines, and flower cars, thus reducing the large capital expenditure. When necessary, professional services can be rendered by one director if another is busy. These developments are proving important to the survival of independent funeral homes.

THE CHALLENGE

Kenneth Kellen realizes that the economy and the environment pose problems for the survival and continued growth of his firm. He knows his expenses will remain high while a questioning public weighs its traditional obligations against current economic conditions. Kenneth's major concern is the direction that his firm must take in the years ahead. In his view, education of the public and adaptability of his business in meeting the changing demands of society are essential to the future of the Memorial Funeral Home.

In an interview with the case writers, Mr. Kellen provided the following information about his services and plans.

□ *GRIEF COUNSELING.*   Mr. Kellen has a master's degree and is completing his studies for a Ph.D. in guidance counseling and grief. He believes that his background will help the Memorial Funeral Home in the future because it enables him to provide professional counseling during the grief period.

□ *DIVERSIFIED OPERATIONS.*   Mr. Kellen has begun two service operations for other funeral homes. One provides professional services: embalming, directing, and removal. The other is a livery service that involves the use of his funeral vehicles by other funeral homes.

□ *COOPERATIVES.*   Mr. Kellen is not presently engaged in cooperatives with other funeral homes. He does, however, see cooperatives as a viable alternative to vast capital expenditures. Members of cooperatives share facilities, vehicles, and services. The formation of cooperatives allows the small, independent funeral home to compete favorably with the large funeral home that has many locations.

DISCUSSION QUESTIONS

1. Based on the information and background provided in this case, state whether you believe that the funeral business should be regulated by governmental (federal or state) agencies or whether you believe it should continue its traditional form of self-regulation through its own industry associations (e.g., National Funeral Directors Association). Why?

2. Which pricing method is best for the Memorial Funeral Home? Why?

3. What impact has the change of attitudes and beliefs in today's society had on the small funeral home?

4. What are the alternatives for succeeding in this ever-changing environment? Be complete in your answer. ■

Part One Entrepreneurial Simulation Program

CREATIVITY AND RISK

You have a unique decision-making style. This style is an inherent part of who you are. It has been developing since the day you were born, and has influenced every decision you have made. Each time you are called upon to make a decision, this style serves as a filter, influencing how you collect and interpret pertinent data and how you eventually arrive at a final determination.

As the owner of a new shoe store, you will have decisions to make each month regarding the types and quantities of shoes to order, pricing, advertising, decor, number of employees, and the amount of marketing information you wish to purchase. The success of your enterprise will depend on the appropriateness of your decisions. It is important that you identify and recognize your own personal style, and realize its impact on your ability to be a successful retail shoe store owner.

Creativity and risk are two important components of this style. Creativity determines the ability to recognize opportunities in the market. Risk determines the ability to do something about opportunities when they do arise. You are competing in a dynamic retail shoe environment. If you are not actively looking for new opportunities, or are not willing to try them out because you fear potential downside consequences, you may discover the other shoe stores will perform better than your store. In the world of business, once an opportunity is lost, there is no way to reclaim it.

Combinations of propensity towards creativity and risk can be organized into four distinct categories. People who are low in both creativity and risk are identified as "reproducers." People who are high in creativity and low in risk are identified as "dreamers." People who are low in creativity and high in risk are identified as "challengers." People who are high in both creativity and risk are identified as "innovators."

Reproducers are those store owners who look to see what the other store owners are doing and emulate the competitor's decisions. They feel safe being a member of the pack. After all, if other store owners make their decisions in this way, it must be safe. Reproducers are never leaders. They rarely entertain new or unconventional approaches to running their store. They will continue to use the same rationale for making their decisions, even if the retail shoe market has moved in a different direction. Reproducers, at best, tend to break even with their investment.

Dreamers are those store owners who have lots of good ideas but who never seem to put them into practice. They either lack the aggressiveness to do so, or they fear the possibility that they could be wrong. Dreamers are those who say "I wish I had" after it is too late to do something about it. Since dreamers had the idea first, they sometimes blame others for their own lack of action. Dreamers are usually average in their ability to be successful in the retail shoe business, but they seldom make it to the top.

Challengers are those store owners who like to take a lot of risks but who have few good new ideas of their own. They become discontent with the status quo and often make changes for the sake of making a change. Challengers may have few ideas of their own, but they are quick to act on any new idea that may come along. The challenger is someone who can make it happen and often does. The outcome, however, is not always a great success because the challenger does not always think through the idea before implementing it. Challengers usually do very well or very poorly in the retail shoe business, depending on the competitive business environment as defined by the other store owners.

Innovators are those store owners who are both creative and who are always ready to take a risk. They are full of alternatives and are willing to give any potential breakthrough idea a try. Innovators are motivated by their new ideas and by the expectation of implementing them. They sometimes risk more than they can afford to lose because they feel so strongly about their ideas that they will not, or cannot, consider potential problems. Innovators usually do well in the retail shoe business since they are always seeking new approaches and are proactive in implementing their programs while their competitors usually do not display such initiative in their management style.

As you operate your store, never lose sight of your own personal decision-making style when you make your monthly decisions. Be creative when developing your business strategy. Be open to opportunities and do not be afraid to take advantage of them. Remember that people who are not creative, or who are unwilling to implement new ideas, are usually not interested in starting their own small business.

DISCUSSION QUESTIONS

1. Identify which of the four creativity/risk categories you fall into, and relate specific instances in your recent past that confirm your selection for both creativity and risk.

2. Get together with someone who is not a classmate and whose creativity/risk style is the opposite of your own. Have that person describe how he or she would start and operate a retail shoe store. Picture yourself operating your store in the same way. How does it feel to have to use a decision-making style that is different from your own?

3. Select a retail merchant and observe him or her at work. Identify which of the four categories that person falls into. Discuss the dimensions of creativity and risk with the merchant, and see if that person agrees with your conclusions.

4. List four things a person from each category would do when making the monthly shoe store decisions in *ESP* that would typify their category characteristics. Share your list with the rest of the class. Come up with a class list for each category that the whole class agrees with.

5. Assume that you have an assistant in your shoe store that falls into a category that is opposite of yours. Describe how you would relate with that person when making the decisions that are required by *ESP.*

Part Two

Getting into Small Business

■ *There are three basic ways of getting into small business:*

□ *buying an ongoing concern*

□ *purchasing a franchise*

□ *starting from scratch*

The objective of Part Two is to examine these three approaches. Before entering the world of business, however, the prospective owner needs a plan of action that describes how the person proposes to get into business and how he or she will address the many operational and strategic problems to be encountered. Developing this plan is the first step in getting into small business. We will examine what such a plan contains and then apply it to the three ways of getting into small business.

In Chapter 4 we examine the nature of a business plan. We will give particular attention to the contents of each part of the plan. We also present a practical sample plan to illustrate what one should look like in final form.

In Chapter 5 we discuss how to go about buying an ongoing concern. We examine the advantages of getting into small business this way and point out a number of important questions to ask before buying. We will then set forth a formula for determining a reasonable purchase price.

Chapter 6 focuses on franchising. This is one of the most popular ways of getting into small business because the franchisor helps the prospective owner get started. We will discuss the nature and growth of franchising in the United States and examine the advantages and disadvantages of buying a franchise. We will then present the steps to take in evaluating franchise opportunities.

Chapter 7 examines the ways to go about starting a new business from scratch, the importance of uniqueness in the product or service, and the value of market analysis. We will also explain how to develop an "action plan."

When you have finished studying the material in Part Two you will know how a business plan is constructed. You will also be aware of the three basic ways of getting into small business and how to evaluate each. Finally, you will have a solid understanding of the advantages and disadvantages associated with each of the approaches to business ownership.

CHAPTER 4

Developing a Business Plan

Objectives

There are three basic ways of getting into small business: buying a current operation, buying a franchise, and starting one from scratch. There are many ways of raising the initial capital so vital for operations. In running a business on a day-to-day basis, hundreds of little things must be done. These are activities with which the small business owner has to be concerned. However, before any of them are carried out, the prospective owner needs a formal business plan. What is the business going to do? Where will it get the necessary starting capital? What kinds of management, marketing, and financial problems will it face? Rather than wait for these issues to arise, one should address them with a formal plan. Today more and more small firms are finding that a business plan is vital to their success. This chapter considers the nature and content of the business plan.

The first objective of this chapter is to examine the parts of a business plan. The second objective is to explain the way the plan is put together. The third objective is to provide a practical example of a small business plan. When you have completed Chapter 4 you will be able to:

1. *Explain the benefits of constructing a business plan.*

2. *Identify the specific issues that are addressed in the plan.*

3. *Discuss the value of projected income statements when using the plan for loan purposes.*

4. *Describe the appearance of a small business plan in finished form.*

5. *Explain how the content of the plan varies depending on whether it is used for operational or loan purposes.*

THE NATURE OF A BUSINESS PLAN

Most people who want to go into business for themselves need to borrow money. No bank will loan funds without a detailed **business plan** that shows what the company is going to do, its projected expenses and earnings, and its plans for repaying the loan. Even those who do not need to borrow money can profit from preparing a plan.[1]

---

[1]Robert Ackelsberg and Peter Arlow, "Small Businesses Do Plan, and It Pays Off," *Long-Range Planning,* October 1985, pp. 61–67; and Fred L. Fry and Charles R. Stoner, "Business Plans: Two Major Types," *Journal of Small Business Management,* January 1985, pp. 1–6.

The major advantage of such a plan is that it forces the owner-to-be to answer the questions, Where am I going and how will I get there? What opportunities and problems am I to run into along the way? and How will I deal with them? (See Small Business Success: Gift Baskets from the Heart.)

A business plan is a **road map** for the would-be entrepreneur. Like all plans, much of it may not happen as expected.[2] However, preparing the plan forces the individual to think about the conditions he or she will face. If the plan has to be changed, the person who prepared it can then modify the plan to fit reality.

Remember, it is *your* plan because it is *your* business. The emphasis of the business plan should always be final implementation of the venture. In other words, it is not enough to just write an effective plan; the entrepreneur must also see that the plan is executed in a way that will lead to a successful enterprise.

IMPORTANCE OF A BUSINESS PLAN

The entire business-planning process forces the entrepreneur to analyze all aspects of the venture and prepare an effective strategy to deal with the uncertainties that arise. Thus a business plan may help an entrepreneur avoid a project that is doomed to failure. As one researcher states, "If your proposed venture is marginal at best, the business plan will show you why and may help you avoid paying the high tuition of business failure. It is far cheaper not to begin an ill-fated business than to learn by experience what your business plan could have taught you at a cost of several hours of concentrated work."[3]

The need for the entrepreneur to prepare his or her *own* business plan extends to the entrepreneurial team as well. All of the key members should be involved in writing the plan. However, the lead entrepreneur must still understand each contribution of the team. In addition, consultants may be sought out to help prepare a business plan, yet the entrepreneur must remain the driving force behind the plan. Seeking the advice and assistance of outside professionals is always wise, but entrepreneurs need to understand every aspect since it is they who come under the scrutiny of financial sources. Thus, the business plan stands as the entrepreneur's description and prediction for his or her venture and it must be defended by the entrepreneur. Simply put, it is the entrepreneur's responsibility.

The business plan can provide a number of specific benefits for the entrepreneur who undertakes the challenge of developing this formal document. Listed below are some of these benefits:

1. The time, effort, research, and discipline needed to put together a formal business plan force the entrepreneur to view the venture critically and objectively.

2. The competitive, economic, and financial analyses included in the business plan subject the entrepreneur to close scrutiny of his or her assumptions about the success of the venture.

---

[2] Eric Larson, "The Best-Laid Plans," *Inc.*, February 1987, pp. 60–64.

[3] Joseph R. Mancuso, *How to Write a Winning Business Plan* (Englewood Cliffs, NJ: Prentice-Hall, 1985), p. 44.

■ SMALL BUSINESS SUCCESS ■

Gift Baskets from the Heart

 A new trend in gifts is the basket full of goodies. Gift Baskets from the Heart, a firm out of Fort Wayne, Indiana, that is specializing in this trend, is owned and operated by Karen Vaughn and her sister, Susan Augsburger. The gift basket business was Vaughn's idea.

"I became familiar with the idea while living in Raleigh, North Carolina," she said. "When I learned of the gift basket business, I knew it was the right time to go back to Fort Wayne and get started."

Vaughn earned her bachelor's degree in entrepreneurship and credits the program at Ball State University with giving her the tools she needed to launch the business successfully in December 1988.

Gift Baskets from the Heart specializes in gourmet food baskets, toiletries, newborn baby baskets, and some novelties. The company's clientele is mostly made up of women. "We have a wide range of specialty gourmet food baskets: Mexican, Italian, teas and breads. We are doing a lot in picnic baskets in the summer," she said.

The partners love shopping together for unique and, whenever possible, "homemade" products. They look for small gourmet food items such as jellies, jams, and sauces. For the toiletries they look for companies that will give them exclusives in the Fort Wayne area. "We like to coordinate scents, have the soaps, bath and shower lotion in the same scent. People like to pamper themselves with luxury bath items."

"Made from the Heart" is the name given to some of the unique handicrafts that go into the baskets, including handpainted baby mugs made by a Fort Wayne artist and other handmade items from Dallas.

According to Vaughn, some of the gourmet foods come from small family-owned businesses. "But it's a problem for us to find handcrafted products we can use because of the price points." The baskets start at $20 and go up, so the sisters have to make their purchases carefully. "We have sold baskets in excess of $100, but most are within the $20 to $30 range. It's similar to ordering flowers for special occasions."

Drawing upon her college training, Vaughn developed a complete business plan for the future. The next step is to break into the corporate market. It also looks likely that the partners will expand direct mail shipments; they already have an active network of friends in California who are buying baskets and referring the product to others.

Each basket is specifically designed for the prospective recipient according to information received from the giver. Although she describes the venture as "a challenge" and "very hard work," Vaughn adds, "But we feel it's good, and we enjoy it. And, we expect to be very successful."

Spoken like a true entrepreneur.

Source: *The Muncie Star,* August 28, 1989, and personal interview.

3. Since all aspects of the business venture must be addressed in the plan, the entrepreneur develops and examines operating strategies and expected results for outside evaluators.

4. The business plan quantifies goals and objectives, which provides measurable benchmarks for comparing forecasts with actual results.

5. The completed business plan provides the entrepreneur with a communication tool for outside financial sources as well as an operational tool for guiding the venture towards success.

WHAT IS A BUSINESS PLAN?

A **business plan** is the entrepreneur's road map for a successful enterprise. It is a written document that describes in detail a proposed venture, and its purpose is to illustrate the current status, expected needs, and projected results of a new or expanding business. Every characteristic of the project is described: marketing, research and development, manufacturing, management, risks, financing, and a timetable for accomplishing clearly identified goals. Each of these segments is necessary to show a clear picture of what the venture is, where it is going, and how the entrepreneur proposes to get it there.

Since planning is essential to the success of any undertaking, it must entail the formulation of objectives and directions for the future. Several critical factors must be addressed. There must be realistic goals that are specific, measurable, and set within time parameters. A commitment to success must be supported by everyone involved in the venture. Milestones must be established for continuous and timely evaluation of progress. Finally, there must be flexibility to allow for anticipation of the obstacles and formulation of alternative strategies.

New ventures and business plans go together. The reason is obvious—new ventures require capital, often substantial amounts of capital. Providers of capital, whether they are lending institutions, major investors in securities, or venture capitalists, require a great amount of information about the enterprise, and anything less than a business plan is insufficient to the task.

In summary, the business plan is the major tool used to guide the operation of the venture as well as the primary document used to manage it. Its major thrust is to compile the strategic development of the project into a comprehensive document for outside investors to read and understand. It allows the entrepreneur entrance into the investment process. A subsidiary benefit is that it enables the enterprise to avoid the common pitfalls that cause less organized efforts to fail.

THE COMPONENTS OF A BUSINESS PLAN

Readers of a business plan expect it to have two important qualities: It must be in order and it must be complete. With this in mind, the following list describes the ten segments that make up a complete and orderly business plan.

☐ EXECUTIVE SUMMARY   A short description of the venture should be the first information that the interested reader encounters. It should be written in an interesting way with proper emphasis placed on the more important aspects of the plan, such as the unique characteristics of the venture, the major marketing points, and the end result. Its purpose is to whet the reader's appetite for more information. A good summary will guarantee that the rest of the plan will be read.

☐ DESCRIPTION OF THE BUSINESS   This section contains a more comprehensive description of the venture. It should include a brief history of the company where applicable and some information about the industry of which it is a part. The product or service should be described in terms of its unique qualities and value to consumers. Finally, goals and milestones should be clarified.

☐ MARKETING   The marketing section is divided into two major parts. The first is research and analysis. The target market must be identified with emphasis on who will buy the product or service. Market size and trends must be measured and the market share must be estimated. In addition, the competition should be studied in considerable detail.

☐ The second focus is on the preparation of a marketing plan. This is perhaps the most important part of the business plan. It must discuss market strategy, sales and distribution, pricing, advertising, promotion, and public relations. Some businesses make the mistake of preparing only a marketing plan, but by itself and outside the structure of a business plan a marketing plan will not meet the needs of a new venture.

☐ RESEARCH, DEVELOPMENT AND DESIGN   This section includes developmental research leading to the design of the product. Industrial design is an art form that has successfully found its way into business, and it should not be neglected. Technical research results should be evaluated, and the cost structure of the newly designed product should be determined.

☐ MANUFACTURING   This section requires an investigation focused on identifying the optimal location for the venture. Proximity to suppliers, availability of transportation, and labor supply are of prime importance. The requirements and costs of production facilities and equipment must be determined in advance.

MANAGEMENT   The management team necessarily requires the presence of outstanding individuals to make the venture a success. Methods of compensation, such as salaries, employment agreements, stock purchase plans, levels of ownership, and other considerations, must be determined. The board of directors, advisers, and consultants are also part of the management team, and their selection should be based upon their potential contribution to the enterprise.

☐ CRITICAL RISKS   Risks must be analyzed to uncover potential problems before they materialize. Outside consultants can often be engaged to identify risks and recommend alternative courses of action. The important concept is that risk can be anticipated and controlled. Doing so will result in a more successful venture.

☐ FINANCIAL FORECASTING   Accountants can make a major contribution in this section. Obtaining financing has always depended upon fair and reasonable budgeting and forecasting. Beginning with the sales budget and projected inventory, material and labor requirements can be determined. Variable overhead can be scheduled for various levels of capacity, and when added to fixed overhead the manufacturing budget can be completed. A capital budget can then be prepared and, when coupled with debt service requirements, cash flow needs can be identified. The information thus developed can be summarized into pro forma financial statements, such as forecasted statements of earnings, financial position, and cash flows. If the work is done well, these projected statements should represent the actual financial achievements expected from the business plan. They also provide a standard with which to measure the actual results of operating the enterprise. These financial projections will serve as valuable tools for managing and controlling the business in the first few years.

☐ MILESTONE SCHEDULE   This segment of the business plan requires the determination of objectives and the timing of their accomplishment. Milestones and deadlines should be established and monitored while the venture is in progress. Each milestone is related to all the others and together they constitute a network of the entire project.

☐ APPENDIX   This section includes valuable information that is not contained in the other sections. It may include the names of references and advisers as well as drawings, documents, agreements, or other materials that support the plan. If deemed desirable, a bibliography may be presented.

PREPARING THE BUSINESS PLAN

Constructing a business plan is a challenge because of the great amount of work required to put together the ten components discussed above. After the requisite information is acquired, the package must be assembled in good form. Writing the plan is the most productive task considering its purpose. Vexing questions persist, such as "What should it look like?" and "How do I begin?" These questions deserve answers.

Remember that a business plan gives investors their first impression of a company. Therefore, the plan should present a professional image. Form as well as content is important. The document should be free of spelling, grammatical, or typographical errors. Perfection should be the norm; anything less is unacceptable. Binding and printing should have a professional appearance. The written plan should not exceed 40 pages. The cover page should be attractive, and it should contain the company name and address. A title page should contain the same information as that shown on the front cover as well as the company's telephone number and the month and year the plan is presented.

The first two pages should contain the executive summary, which should explain the company's current status, its products or services, the benefits to customers, financial forecasts summarized in paragraph form, the venture's objectives in the next few years, the amount of financing needed, and the benefits to investors. This is a lot of information for two pages, but if done well, the investor will get a good impression of the venture and will be enticed to read the rest of the plan.

A table of contents should follow the executive summary. Each section of the plan should be listed with the page numbers on which they are found.

Obviously, the remaining nine sections will follow the table of contents. If the tenth section, the appendix, is lengthy, it may be necessary to present it in a separate binder in order to keep the plan within the recommended 40 pages. Each of the sections should be written in a simple and straightforward manner. The purpose is to communicate, not dazzle.

An attractive appearance, proper length, an executive summary, a table of contents, and professionalism in grammar, spelling, and typing are important factors in putting together a comprehensive business plan. Believe it or not, these characteristics separate successful plans from failed ones. (See Small Business Owner's Notebook: Avoiding Business Plan Bloopers.)

The checklist that is provided in Table 4-1 offers entrepreneurs an opportunity to self-evaluate their business plans as they are developed. Each section is broken down into questions that examine the information needed in that particular segment of the business plan. Then the columns are used to evaluate (1) whether the information is in the plan; (2) whether the previous answer is clear or not; and (3) whether or not the answer is complete. This allows entrepreneurs the benefit of self-evaluating each segment of their plan *before* presenting it to financial and/or professional sources.

■ SMALL BUSINESS OWNER'S NOTEBOOK ■

Avoiding Business Plan Bloopers

 Financial sources have a limited amount of time and, therefore, they are sensitive to certain "turn offs" that entrepreneurs sometimes do. Here are some of the bloopers that potential small business owners in search of capital should try to avoid:

☐ a business plan that is handwritten

☐ misspellings and grammatical errors in the plan

☐ letters from friends saying how great the entrepreneur is

☐ a sample product that *doesn't* work

☐ feature articles about your venture with certain sections blacked out

☐ ignorance of the competition and a *claim* your business is unique

☐ financial reports that *do not* include the assumptions they are based upon

☐ failure to provide an *executive summary*

These are simple but important points that should be remembered when conducting business with financial institutions. Any or all of these bloopers can result in rejection for the prospective entrepreneur.

Source: Adapted from: Ellyn E. Spragins, "Venture Capital Express," *Inc.*, November 1990, pp. 159–160.

Table 4-1 A Business Plan Checklist (A Personal Step-by-Step Evaluation)

	Have you covered this in the plan?	Is the answer clear (yes or no)?	Is the answer complete (yes or no)?
I. Business Description Segment			
a. What type of business are you planning?			
b. What products or services will you sell?			
c. What type of opportunity is it (new, part-time, expansion, seasonal, year-round)?			
d. Why does it promise to be successful?			
e. What is the growth potential?			
f. How is it unique? *(Discuss strengths or weaknesses in this segment.)*			
II. Marketing Segment			
a. Who are your potential customers?			
b. How big is the market?			
c. Who are your competitors? How are their businesses prospering?			
d. How will you promote sales?			
e. What market share do you anticipate?			
f. How will you price your product or service?			
g. What advertising and promotional strategy are you using? *(Discuss strengths or weaknesses in this segment.)*			
III. Research, Design, and Development Segment			
a. Have you carefully described your design or development?			
b. Have you received any technical assistance?			

(continued)

	Have you covered this in the plan?	Is the answer clear (yes or no)?	Is the answer complete (yes or no)?
c. What research needs do you anticipate?			
d. Are the costs involved in research and design reasonable? *(Discuss strengths and weaknesses in this segment.)*			
IV. Manufacturing Segment			
a. Where will the business be?			
b. What influenced the choice of location?			
c. Have you described the needs for production (e.g., facilities and equipment)?			
d. Who will be your suppliers?			
e. What type of transportation is available?			
f. What is the supply of available labor?			
g. Have you discussed the manufacturing costs? *(Discuss strengths and weaknesses in this segment.)*			
V. Management Segment			
a. Who will manage the business?			
b. What qualifications do you have?			
c. How many employees will you need? What will they do?			
d. What are your plans for employee salaries or wages and benefits?			
e. What consultants or specialists will you need? Why will you need them?			
f. What legal form of ownership will you choose? Why?			
g. What licenses and permits will you need?			

(continued)

	Have you covered this in the plan?	Is the answer clear (yes or no)?	Is the answer complete (yes or no)?
h. What regulations will affect your business? *(Discuss strengths and weaknesses in this segment.)*			
VI. Critical Risks Segment			
a. What potential problems have you identified?			
b. What obstacles do you foresee?			
c. Have you calculated the risks?			
d. What alternative courses of action are there? *(Discuss strengths and weaknesses in this segment.)*			
VII. Financial Segment			
a. What is your total estimated business income for the first year? Monthly for the first year? Quarterly for the second and third years?			
b. What will it cost you to open the business?			
c. What will your monthly cash flow be during the first year?			
d. What will your personal monthly financial needs be?			
e. What sales volume will you need in order to make a profit during the first three years?			
f. What will be the break-even point?			
g. What will be your projected assets, liabilities, and net worth on the day before you expect to open?			
h. What will your total financial needs be?			
i. What will your potential funding sources be?			

(continued)

	Have you covered this in the plan?	Is the answer clear (yes or no)?	Is the answer complete (yes or no)?
j. How will you use the money from lenders or investors?			
k. How will the loans be secured? *(Discuss strengths and weaknesses in this segment.)*			
VIII. Milestone Schedule Segment			
a. What timing have you projected for this project?			
b. How have you set your objectives?			
c. Have you set up your deadlines for each stage of your venture?			
d. Is there a relationship between events in this venture? *(Discuss strengths and weaknesses in this segment.)*			
IX. Appendix Segment			
a. Have you included any documents, drawings, agreements, or other materials needed to support the plan?			
b. Are there any names of references, advisers, or technical sources you should include?			
c. Are there any other supporting documents? *(Discuss strengths and weaknesses in this segment.)*			

Source: Donald F. Kuratko and Ray V. Montagno, *The Entrepreneur's Guide to Venture Formation* (Muncie, Indiana: Center for Entrepreneurial Resources and Applied Research, Ball State University, 1987), pp. 28–34. Reprinted by permission.

HELPFUL HINTS FOR DEVELOPING THE BUSINESS PLAN

SUMMARY

- ☐ Confine to no more than three pages. This is the most crucial part of your plan because you must capture the reader's interest.
- ☐ Answer all fundamental questions. What, how, why, and where must be explained briefly.
- ☐ Complete this part after you have a finished business plan.

BUSINESS DESCRIPTION SEGMENT

☐ Identify your business by name.

☐ Provide a background of the industry along with a history of your company (if any exists).

☐ Clearly describe the potential of the new venture.

☐ Spell out any unique aspect or distinctive features of this venture.

MARKETING SEGMENT

☐ Convince investors that sales projections and competition can be met.

☐ Use and disclose market studies.

☐ Identify target market, market position, and market share.

☐ Evaluate all competition and specifically cover why and how you will be better than your competitors.

☐ Identify all market sources and assistance used for this segment.

☐ Demonstrate pricing strategy since your price must penetrate and maintain a market share to produce profits. (Thus the lowest price is not necessarily the best price.)

☐ Identify your advertising plans with cost estimates to validate the proposed strategy.

RESEARCH, DESIGN, AND DEVELOPMENT SEGMENT

☐ Cover the extent and costs involved in needed research, testing, and development.

☐ Explain carefully what has already been accomplished (prototype, lab testing, early development.)

☐ Mention any research or technical assistance that has been provided for you.

MANUFACTURING SEGMENT

☐ Describe the advantages of your location (zoning, tax laws, wage rates).

☐ List the production needs in terms of facilities (plant, storage, office space) and equipment (machinery, furnishings, supplies).

☐ Describe the access to transportation (for shipping and receiving).

☐ Indicate proximity to your suppliers.

☐ Mention the availability of labor in your location.

☐ Provide estimates of manufacturing costs. (Be careful; too many entrepreneurs underestimate their costs.)

MANAGEMENT SEGMENT

☐ Supply resumes of all key people in the management of your venture.

☐ Carefully describe the legal structure of your venture (sole proprietorship, partnership, or corporation).

☐ Cover the added assistance (if any) of advisers, consultants, and directors.

☐ Give information on how and how much everyone is to be compensated.

CRITICAL RISKS SEGMENT

☐ Discuss potential risks before investors point them out, for example,
price cutting by competitors
any potentially unfavorable industrywide trends
design or manufacturing costs in excess of estimates
sales projections not achieved
product development schedule not met
difficulties or long lead times encountered in the procurement of parts or
raw materials
greater than expected innovation and development costs to stay competitive

☐ Provide some alternative courses of action.

FINANCIAL SEGMENT

☐ Give actual estimated statements.

☐ Describe the needed sources for your funds and the uses you intend for the money.

☐ Develop and present a budget.

☐ Create stages of financing for purposes of allowing evaluation by investors at various points.

MILESTONE SCHEDULE SEGMENT

☐ Develop a timetable or chart to demonstrate when each phase of the venture is to be completed. This shows the relationship of events and provides a deadline for accomplishment.

REMEMBER, THE BUSINESS PLAN

☐ leads to a sound venture structure.

☐ includes a marketing plan.

☐ clarifies and outlines financial needs.

☐ identifies recognized obstacles and alternative solutions.

☐ serves as a communication tool for all financial and professional sources.

A PRACTICAL EXAMPLE

While every small business should have a plan, many people getting into business have no idea of the detail required for a complete business plan. This section provides an example of an actual business plan prepared for a nostalgia-style restaurant idea.

Each of the parts of a business plan discussed earlier in the chapter is illustrated in this detailed example. By carefully reviewing this business plan, you will gain a much better perspective of the final appearance that an entrepreneur's plan must have. This plan, prepared by Scott Voegele, illustrates his research for "YesterYears Diner" located in Batesville, Indiana.

Appendix

A COMPLETE BUSINESS PLAN

YesterYears Diner

STATEMENT OF PURPOSE

This financial proposal, presented by Scott Voegele, was prepared in pursuit of obtaining financing for YesterYears Diner, a restaurant to be located in Batesville, Indiana. YesterYears, Inc., is seeking a term loan in the amount of *$80,000.00*. The funding is essential for this start-up venture to successfully operate as a restaurant establishment. Through the profits generated by the business, Mr. Voegele calculates the full repayment of the term loan by the end of April 1993. A reserved loan of *$4,000.00* will be held by the bank as a line of credit to be used to cover any unanticipated costs. Mr. Voegele will invest *$16,000.00* of his own capital in this business venture.

Sources and Applications of Funding

SOURCES:

Bank Loans:

1. Term Loan	$ 80,000
2. Reserved Loan	4,000
3. Owner's Investment	16,000
TOTAL	$100,000

APPLICATIONS

Rent (sec. dep. + 1st and last mo.)	$2,550
Initial Inventory (opening + 10-day stock)	4,600
Equipment/Installation	80,000
Leasehold Improvement	3,250
Licenses/Tax Deposits	750
Grand Opening/Advertising	1,000
Utilities/Phone	750
Uniforms/Supplies	400
Insurance (1st quarter)	600
Owner/Operator Salary (pre-opening)	2,800
Working Capital	2,500
Reserve for Contingencies	800
TOTAL	$100,000

EXECUTIVE SUMMARY

Summary Description of the Business

YESTERYEARS WELCOMES YOU BACK TO THE FIVE-AND-DIME DINERS. Flashing neon lights and shiny chrome are making diners not just a thing of the past, but an opportunity of today. This full-service, diner-style restaurant will be located in Batesville, Indiana, midway between Cincinnati, Ohio, and Indianapolis, Indiana. YesterYears will be a place where the past comes alive in an atmosphere that blends the old with the new. The restaurant's unique atmosphere will appeal to all age groups. Everyone who comes to the diner will get a feel for what life was like in "yesteryears." The restaurant will serve "good old American" cuisine with a touch of "class." A sampling of the foods of the fifties and sixties will be offered, giving customers a *taste* of the old blended with the new. The menu will consist of speciality food items as well as the old reliable meat and potatoes dishes.

YesterYears will build a reputation as one of the better restaurants in the area. Mr. Voegele believes that by offering quality food, excellent service, and a unique atmosphere, YesterYears will be among the successful start-up's in the restaurant business today.

The restaurant will officially open for business on April 1, 1988. Mr. Voegele wants to have a month to work out any operational problems and train employees. The *Grand Opening* will be delayed until early May, due to more favorable conditions then (warmer weather, school year ending, more tourism, and so on). Restaurant hours will be 10:00 A.M. to midnight Monday through Saturday and 10:00 A.M. to 10:00 P.M. on Sunday fifty weeks of the year. Mr. Voegele understands the need for an excellent operational team and by hiring Mr. Thomas Buckley as master chef and kitchen manager, he has established the foundation for such an organization.

THE INDUSTRY, THE COMPANY, AND ITS PRODUCTS OR SERVICES

The Industry

Over the last few years, the restaurant industry has experienced tremendous growth. More people are eating out now than at any time in the past. In 1984, sales skyrocketed from a recession slump to $164.6 billion. That number grew by 5.9 percent to $174.3 billion in 1985 and exceeded $190 billion in 1986—a growth rate (in current dollars) of 8.4 percent for the year. Sales are expected to increase by almost 8 percent in 1987 (*U.S. Industrial Outlook: Eating and Drinking Places*, pp. 56–57). The National Restaurant Association (NRA) attributes the growth of the restaurant industry to the economy's recovery and the increase in the number of dual-income families. With both the wife and husband working, neither has time to prepare dinner. So more and more families are now eating dinner out. In fact, according to a survey by the NRA, the average consumer eats in some sort of restaurant at least four times a week and spends forty cents of every food dollar on meals prepared outside the home. Young adults between the ages of 18 and 24 and families with household incomes above $50,000 eat out the most—an average of almost five times a week.

Breaking the demographics down even further, men dine out 4.2 times a week, compared to 3.4 times a week for women. However, working women eat at restaurants more often than men—4.3 times a week, almost 50 percent more often than women who do not work outside the home. At the low end of the consumer spectrum are senior citizens, who dine out only 1.8 times a week.

While fast-food establishments are doing extremely well—their sales topped $47,129,314 in 1985—full-service restaurants and lunchrooms are still the kingpins of the food-service industry. In 1985, their sales exceeded $58,444,122.

As of 1982, there were 258,584 eating places in the United States and 6,213 eating places in Indiana (U.S. Department of Commerce figures). Currently there are 41 eating places in Franklin County and 58 in Ripley County; a total of 99 establishments were issued permits in the two counties in 1986.

The Company

YESTERYEARS WELCOMES YOU BACK TO THE FIVE-AND-DIME DINERS. With their flashing neon lights and shiny chrome, diners are back. After struggling through a few decades of near-extinction, Americans are once again literally eating them up. During the last year, the number of diners has grown by 8 percent, according to the National Restaurant Association (NRA).

YesterYears will be located in Batesville, Indiana, midway between Cincinnati, Ohio, and Indianapolis, Indiana. A sit-down diner, it will have a maximum seating capacity of sixty-eight persons.

Charged with memories of an era known for its simplicity, honesty, and security, YesterYears will offer both nostalgia and good old American cuisine in an atmosphere that blends the old with the new. The combination of fifties decor and memorabilia with the innovations of the eighties will capture the attention of the restaurant's targeted market. People will be able to look back to a period that was slower-paced and less complicated, to a time when they could relax and listen to the jukebox while enjoying simple, predictably good food.

YesterYears will cater not only to the people who lived during the 50s and 60s, but also to the teen community. The appeal of diners cuts across all age groups. Customers will come for the same reasons—entertainment, atmosphere, and the food.

Products and Services

YesterYears will offer a trendy and traditional diner menu; that is, food that is currently popular in many sit-down, casual restaurants. YesterYears will offer only a sampling of the foods that diners made famous. For instance, when customers visit YesterYears they will find not only contemporary dishes like trendy appetizers, soups, and salads, but also sandwiches such as tenderloin, chicken breast, club, fish, ham, and the traditional hamburgers. They will also find a number of "specialty" entrees such as steaks. Thus the management will be able to expand upon the menu to allow for changing customer preferences. A kids' menu also will be offered. (See Appendix A for complete menu.)

YesterYears will be designed so that if customer preferences change, which is not uncommon in today's fast-paced society, the restaurant also can change. With its unique atmosphere and its contemporary and specialty foods, YesterYears will be more than "just a passing fad."

MARKET RESEARCH AND ANALYSIS

Batesville, Indiana, the home of YesterYears diner-style restaurant, is located in both Ripley and Franklin Counties midway between Indianapolis, Indiana, and Cincinnati, Ohio, on Interstate 74, State Road 46, and State Road 229. The population of Batesville is 4,152 persons. The major employers of Batesville are the Hillenbrand Industry, the American Furniture Company, the Union Furniture Company, and the Weberding Custom Carving Shop.

Customers

YesterYears will be targeting a market consisting of persons between 18 and 24 years old and between 35 and 54 years old. These age ranges account for approximately 63% of the population of the two counties. Ripley County's current population is 24,481, and Franklin County's is 19,576. Populations of both counties are expected to grow. By 1990, persons in the two specified age ranges will account for approximately 81% of the population of the two counties. Population of the two counties is expected to reach 47,900 persons by then (Indiana Business Research Center, STATIS Machine and Affirmative Action Information, Indiana Employment Security Division).

Market Size and Trends

Ripley County consists of these cities or towns: Batesville, Milan, Versailles, Osgood, Sunman, Holton, and Napoleon. There was a total county population of 25,100 people in 1984. In 1984, the county's per capita personal income was $10,465. This was high compared to the average per capita personal income of Indiana, which was $8,545 (Indiana Labor Market Trends, Indiana Employment Security Division). The county's unemployment rate for 1984–1985 was 11.6%. The state average was 8.5 percent. Some of this relatively high unemployment can be attributed to the shutdown of the Marble Hill Nuclear construction site and to an increase in the number of employable age persons. By 1990, the county unemployment rate is expected to decrease to 7.6%. This will be below the state average, thus making employment opportunities favorable for individuals living in the area. (The Industrial/Business Assistance Study, 1986–87, Job Creation Program for Ripley Country.)

Franklin County consists of these cities or towns: Batesville, Brookville, Cedar Grove, Laurel, Mt. Carmel, and Oldenburg. There was a total county population of 20,332 people in 1984. The county's unemployment rate in 1984–85 was 8.3%, which was below the state average. According to Ralph Stewart, head of the Franklin County Planning Commission, unemployment rates in the area are expected to drop in the next few years due to much business growth within the county.

Batesville, Indiana, is a county-line town, having 3,469 people residing in Ripley County and 683 people residing in Franklin County. Businesses in county-line towns tend to draw a more favorable market share than businesses in other towns. (See Market Research and Analysis Appendix for further demographic information.)

A sample survey of 100 people was conducted by Mr. Voegele to see if his diner-style restaurant would indeed be accepted by the Batesville people. He used the information obtained from the survey to determine his menu prices and project his market share. (See Appendix B.)

Other factors to consider when looking at the market in Batesville are the major industries in the area. Individuals are constantly moving into the area for employment with Hillenbrand Industries. Currently, 2,300 individuals work for the company. A holding company headquartered in Batesville, Hillenbrand Industries has built its subsidiaries into several successful companies that enjoy leadership positions in the industries they serve. The subsidiaries include the Hill-Rom Company (health care), Batesville Casket Company (caskets), American Tourister (luggage), Medeco Security Locks (locks), and Fore-Thought Insurance Company (insurance). Three of the five subsidiaries are headquartered in Batesville. Some other businesses and industries that generate employment in the Batesville community are the American Furniture Company, the Union Furniture Company, and the Weberding Custom Carving Shop. These businesses and industries are growing rapidly, and bringing sophisticated, educated individuals to the Batesville community.

COMPETITION

A number of restaurants are located in Batesville that, if not taken seriously, could affect the sales and profit margin of YesterYears. The competition can be categorized as two types, primary and secondary.

PRIMARY COMPETITION

The Sherman House, located in downtown Batesville, is a century-old restaurant and inn that has been in business since 1852. The Sherman House draws its patrons from throughout the tri-state area and offers fine cuisine in an atmosphere of Old Vienna. The menu consists of a variety of entrees, from pizza to cracked crab, and they serve beer, wine, and liquor. The prices are high. The restaurant and inn are very well managed, partly due to the facts that the Hillenbrand family owns the business and money is available to hire professional people. YesterYears and the Sherman House will be the only restaurants in town that offer a unique atmosphere. Since YesterYears will serve the same quality of food at competitive prices, Mr. Voegele expects that a portion of the people who now patronize the Sherman House will come to YesterYears for its atmosphere and better prices. YesterYears will attempt to capture part of the Sherman House's market share.

The Hobo Hut, located on the edge of Batesville, has been in business for twelve years. They offer excellent food in a poor atmosphere. The building is old, and upkeep has been neglected. Seating is available for only thirty people, and they do a lot of carry-out business. YesterYears will compete strongly for their lunch crowd and their carry-out customers. YesterYear's atmosphere should be a definite advantage.

The Homestead, in downtown Batesville, has been in business for six years. They offer good food in a nice atmosphere. Service tends to be poor, and the restaurant is poorly managed. Prices are considered high for the quality of the food. Their main advantage over YesterYears will be their three-way liquor licenses—they serve beer, wine, and liquor. Otherwise, Mr. Voegele is certain that the food, service, price, and atmosphere of YesterYears will far exceed that of The Homestead.

Skyline Chili, in downtown Batesville, has been in business for just five months. They offer good food in a very nice atmosphere, their prices are competitive, and their service is adequate. Since the menu is limited (only chili, tacos, and salads), Mr. Voegele believes his diner can take away some of their lunch crowd by offering a more diverse product line at competitive prices in a more interesting atmosphere.

SECONDARY COMPETITION

Some of the secondary competitors for YesterYears are McDonald's, Hardee's, Dairy Queen, Kentucky Fried Chicken, Pizza King, Mama's Pizza, and Pizza Haus. All of these are either fast-food or short-order, limited menu, sit-down restaurants. In addition, some private clubs serve food. They include the Hillcrest Country Club, Eagle's, and the Elk's Club. These establishments offer nice atmosphere for dining, but their food is of low quality and their prices are high. (See Appendix C for a complete list of food establishments in the Batesville area.)

YesterYears's advantages over its competition will be sufficient to acquire a profitable market share. And its atmosphere—centered around a theme that everyone can enjoy—excellent food, good service, and competitive prices will help to ensure its continued success.

Estimated Market Share and Sales

Total sales for eating and drinking establishments in Ripley and Franklin Counties were $7,124,000 in 1982. YesterYears plans to capture approximately 3.0% of this total market, which will give sales of approximately $189,000 per year. This projection is based on dividing the total sales for eating and drinking establishments of the two counties by the sales volume obtained from the *Feasibility Projection Worksheet* (Appendix D). Since YesterYears will not serve alcoholic beverages, this estimated market share may be slightly off. Mr. Voegele will consider serving alcohol as a future expansion possibility.

Ongoing Market Evaluation

Recognizing the changing nature of customer preferences in food, style, taste, and so on, YesterYears is prepared to adapt to changes in demand. Mr. Voegele will constantly monitor the restaurant industry to see what changes are occurring, and he will watch closely for fluctuations in the Batesville market. Internally, he will use a suggestion box for customer complaints and suggestions. Response cards will be placed on every table, and customer comments will be encouraged.

MARKETING PLAN

Overall Marketing Strategy

YesterYears will be committed to offering quality food at reasonable prices. The location is such that it will draw clientele from people living in the surrounding areas and those traveling on Interstate 74. YesterYears will serve persons working, living, or passing through the city of Batesville.

Pricing will be "reasonable" in that the management will not attempt to undercut its secondary competition (such as McDonald's). The main concern will be with the primary competitors. Menu prices have been set so that the average check paid for a meal will not contradict the diner's reputation for serving quality food. People tend to associate quality with price, and prices that are too low decrease the profit margin and, as a result, the quality and quantity of the food that is served.

Advertising and Promotion

As the restaurant becomes known in the community and the surrounding areas, we expect our market to grow along with the market share. To attract the targeted market and expand the market, we will advertise in the weekly *Batesville Herald–Tribune* (circulation 5,000). We will have time slots on WRBI-FM and the area's TV stations. We will advertise in church bulletins and with fliers. Since we want to draw clientele off of Interstate 74, we will advertise on two 12′ × 25′ billboards, five miles east and west of Batesville. Owners of several restaurants located near Interstate 74 (McDonald's, Dairy Queen, and Hardee's) report that 50% of their business is generated off of Interstate 74. We plan to use mass advertising in the first few months of business, since YesterYears will be so different from other restaurants in the area.

YesterYears also will take advantage of opportunities for free advertising. Mayor Vic Kaiser will preside over a traditional ribbon-cutting ceremony at our Grand Opening, and we will invite representatives from all local news media. Afterward we will serve a complimentary brunch to a large number of the area's businesspeople, giving them a *taste* of what's in store for the people of Batesville at YesterYears. The goal is to generate the best advertising a new restaurant can have, enthusiastic word-of-mouth advertising.

MANAGEMENT TEAM

Organizational Chart

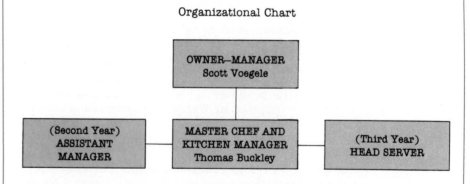

The key management roles in YesterYears, Inc., are those of the owner–manager and the master chef. The owner, Scott Voegele, currently has no experience in the restaurant business, but he has eight years' experience managing, training, planning, and selling.

(See his resume in Appendix E.) Mr. Voegele, a graduate from Ball State University in August 1987, believes that his Bachelor of Science Degree in Management with a specialty option in Small Business/Entrepreneurship will help him to make rational decisions concerning the success of his diner. Mr. Voegele will hire Mr. Thomas Buckley (age 34) before the venture is started as Master Chef and Kitchen Manager. Mr. Buckley has experience working in both of these areas. Mr. Voegele and Mr. Buckley understand that running a successful restaurant requires a great amount of logistics, planning, and coordination.

Key Management Personnel

Thomas Buckley will be the key person in the operations of YesterYears. He has sound food-service and management experience and is both people- and task-oriented. Mr. Voegele will oversee operations and assist wherever needed. His responsibilities as owner and manager will be numerous until the restaurant's operations begin to run smoothly. Sales and profits will determine whether Mr. Voegele can hire additional help. Mr. Voegele's rationale in hiring Mr. Buckley was to ensure that someone would always be at the restaurant—either himself or Mr. Buckley, or both—who could operate the business and take on responsibility. He will expect Mr. Buckley to make suggestions that will help to operate the restaurant efficiently. Mr. Voegele's aim is to delegate authority throughout the hierarchy so that his team of employees can make decisions while he is gone. This will increase the accountability of his staff's actions and boost employee morale. Mr. Buckley has ten years' experience in running and managing a restaurant. He has knowledge of produce buying, inventory control, staffing, and organization. Mr. Buckley and Mr. Voegele are healthy and energetic individuals. Their enthusiasm with this venture will be a driving force behind the success of YesterYears.

Mr. Buckley possesses considerable knowledge and experience in restaurant management and has agreed to assume much responsibility with YesterYears. Mr. Voegele believes that a starting salary of $26,000.00 a year will keep Mr. Buckley from seeking opportunities elsewhere. Also, Mr. Buckley will receive a 10% raise each year if he proves to be an asset to the restaurant. Mr. Buckley will sign a two-year employment contract with YesterYears. A profit-sharing arrangement can be worked out in several years if the venture has grown and profits are up.

Once business operations have shown growth, Mr. Voegele plans to hire an assistant manager and a head server. As an incentive to part-time employees, Mr. Voegele will hire these individuals from existing working staff. Each position will pay $1,000.00 per month and raises can be expected depending on job performance and profitability of the diner. Mr. Voegele will pay himself a starting salary of $12,000.00 per year. This, too, will increase as sales and profitability increase.

There are several personnel categories in the restaurant business: managers, cooks, servers, buspersons, dishwashers, and hosts/hostesses. In the opening stages of business, Mr. Voegele plans to combine some of the categories. For instance, the head server may double as the host or hostess, and servers may perform the busing functions. By combining duties, Mr. Voegele hopes to cut overhead. He wants to keep payroll at about 24 to 35 percent of total sales. Mr. Voegele and Mr. Buckley will have a lot to do with the development of excellent service and a spirit of teamwork. In demonstrating their attitudes toward the importance of competence and teamwork through their actions, both believe that actions speak louder than words. They believe their actions will be reflected down the line by the cooks, waiters and waitresses, hosts and hostesses, buspersons, and dishwashers. Mr. Voegele plans to train his personnel before giving them responsibility. He will hire bright, hard-working, neat individuals with good personalities. YesterYears customers will come to expect good service. Since service ranks high on most customers' priority lists, Mr. Voegele plans to train his staff extensively.

Supporting Professional Services

In order to ensure continued success, Mr. Voegele knows he will need a good accountant and a good lawyer. For this reason, he has enlisted the services of Mr. Greg Cooley, Certified Public Accountant, and Mr. John Kellerman, Attorney at Law. In addition, three competent advisors have agreed to hold conference meetings with Mr. Voegele whenever a problem concerning the restaurant arises. Advice concerning future business decisions will always be welcomed. Members of this Quasi board include Mr. Gilbert Young, Mr. George Brinkmoeller, and Mr. James Sturges. Mr. Young has owned and operated a Dairy Queen establishment in Batesville for fifteen years. In 1986, his business grossed over a million dollars in sales. His restaurant ranks 5th out of 5,400 Dairy Queens nationwide. Mr. Brinkmoeller holds the position of Vice-President of Corporate Services for Hillenbrand Industries. He is in charge of operations concerning the Sherman House Restaurant in Batesville. Mr. Sturges, who is president of the First Bank & Trust Company in Batesville, will be very helpful in financial decisions. All three men have agreed to donate their time to Mr. Voegele for professional business consulting during the first year of operation. After that, a fee will be negotiated for further consulting services. Mr. Voegele realizes that in order to ensure the success of YesterYears, he will occasionally need to call upon outside professionals.

OPERATIONS PLAN

YesterYears will be located at 112 Cross County Shopping Mall, Batesville, Indiana. The 1,800-square-foot area will be leased from Donald L. Leathery Company for $625.00 per month and 6% of sales in excess of $125,000 (See Lease Appendix for details.) The area surrounding this location includes such businesses as a Hallmark card shop, a Krogers supermarket, Ames Department Store, a McDonald's, and a Revco Drug Store. Known as "The Plaza," this newly developed area is just beginning to expand. The Plaza is located near Interstate 74, and many businesspeople and tourists stop there to shop, eat, fuel up, or relax.

YesterYears, Inc., will be a casual but sophisticated full-service restaurant. It will serve "good old American" cuisine specializing in half-pound hamburgers, steaks, and chicken. The diner-style restaurant will be successful because it will offer quality food and excellent service in an appealing atmosphere. In addition to all this, its management team will stress the importance of warmth and friendliness to ensuring customer satisfaction. Mr. Voegele wants to create an enjoyable eating experiences for all.

YesterYears will open its doors for business on April 1, 1988. A month later a Grand Opening will be held. This one-month delay will allow Mr. Voegele and his staff to work out any problems that might cause disruptions when business picks up. He explains his rationale: "If you advertise that YesterYears is going to have excellent service and quality food in a classy atmosphere, then that's what it better have. Bad word-of-mouth publicity about a newly opened restaurant is a sure killer."

Employees will arrive for work every day at 8:00 A.M. to start the food preparations before the doors open for business. Hours for customers will be 10:00 A.M. to midnight Monday through Saturday and 10 : 00 A.M. to 10:00 P.M. Sunday fifty weeks of the year. Reservations will be accepted if customers desire them. Since this is to be a full-service restaurant, a person will always be there to serve the customer. YesterYears's patrons will enjoy their meals in an atmosphere of the 50s and 60s. Some customers will come to the restaurant for an old-time soda or ice cream at the bar. Jukebox music will provide music of the 50s and 60s era.

Daily lunch specials will be offered, allowing the worker with the one-hour lunch break to get an excellent meal in an hour or less. Dinner entrees will be served from 5 : 00 P.M. until closing Monday through Sunday. Plenty of employees will be on hand at these busy times to allow for the fast service—and thus to deter potential customers from going to fast-food establishments. Frequent promotions, advertisements, and specials will help to ensure the continued success of YesterYears.

CRITICAL RISKS AND PROBLEMS

The biggest risk for YesterYears is the fact that the key person in the restaurant is the master chef and not the owner–manager. Mr. Buckley, having much experience in the restaurant business, will guide Mr. Voegele in making decisions for the diner. Such broad knowledge and experience as Mr. Buckley's is vital to YesterYears, and if he should decide to leave, the continued operations of the diner would be threatened. Mr. Voegele realizes that this is indeed a problem, and he has taken action to prevent this from happening. Mr. Voegele has provided for Mr. Buckley to be paid a $26,000 salary to start and increases each year as profits go up. He believes this will be sufficient incentive to keep Mr. Buckley from seeking employment elsewhere. With Mr. Voegele's educational backgound and his drive for success, his "hands-on" training should soon become *vital* experience.

Another potential problem in the restaurant business is the perennial threat of lawsuits. Mr. Voegele can be held liable for any accidental occurrences anywhere on the premises. If a customer falls on a slippery floor or cuts their lip on a chipped glass, the restaurant is liable, and a lawsuit could be brought upon the owner. Mr. Voegele will cover himself and the restaurant by having sufficient insurance. He will train his staff to be extremely cautious, and make them aware of possible trouble signs in and around the diner.

In the restaurant business, people preference is vital if the establishment is going to be a success. If someone is dissatisfied with the restaurant's food, service, or even the atmosphere, that person's "word-of-mouth" could make the difference between success and failure for the business. Management must always ensure customer satisfaction!

In any business, the owner–manager takes a risk, and there will always be problems that need attention. The difference between a good operations team and a bad one is that a good team is aware of potential problems and decides to take a *calculated* risk. Mr. Voegele has made such a decision!

Potential Problems

Surveys show that the primary reasons for small business failures lie in these areas:

1. inefficient control over costs and quality of product

2. bad stock control

3. underpricing of goods sold

4. bad customer relations

5. failure to promote and maintain a favorable public image

6. bad relations with suppliers

7. management's inability to reach decisions and act on them

8. failure to keep pace with management system

9. illness of key personnel

10. reluctance to seek professional assistance

11. failure to minimize taxation through tax planning

12. inadequate insurance
13. loss of impetus in sales
14. bad personnel relations
15. loss of key personnel
16. lack of staff training
17. lack of knowledge of merchandise
18. inability to cope adequately with competition
19. complacency toward competition
20. failure to anticipate market trends

OVERALL SCHEDULE

1/86 to 12/87

Market Research and Analysis; Marketing Plan, Design, and Development; Operations Plan

January 1988

* Contact city planning office to notify them of possible venture.
* Contact local banks about possible financing.
* Select location.
* Survey possible lease/buy facilities near the selected site.

February 1988

* Contact suppliers/distributors of equipment, food, beverages, etc.
* Review applicants for the position of chef and/or assistant manager.
* Advertise for part-time help; begin screening.

March 1988

* Obtain lease.
* Make leasehold improvements.
* Install equipment and fixtures.
* Contact supplier/distributors for shipments of goods.
* Obtain necessary licenses and permits.
* Contact utility companies for hook-up and installation.
* Hire full- and part-time employees.
* Train staff.
* Begin advertising.

April 1, 1988

- Open for business.
- Work out any operational problems.
- Hire and/or fire new and existing staff.

May 1, 1988

- GRAND OPENING
- Advertise extensively!!
- Serve the mayor a complimentary dinner. Afterwards hold the official ribbon-cutting ceremony. Invite the media.
- Ensure the continued success of YesterYears!

FINANCIAL STATEMENTS

Notes on the Income Projections

SALES

Sales figures are based on the average number of table turns daily, weekly, monthly, and yearly. With an average check per seat of $5.25 for lunch and/or $8.00 for dinner, the restaurant could serve a possible daily volume of approximately 136 customers. The *Feasibility Projection Worksheet* was used in calculating these sales. (See Appendix D for actual figures.)

COST OF MATERIAL

Inventory has an average cost of 40% of sales. This does not include a start-up spoilage rate. Based higher than the average (33%), the diner uses the excess percentage for any hidden variable labor costs.

COST OF LABOR

At 27% of sales, cost of labor was based on hiring 10 part-time employees and 1 salaried employee. Mr. Voegele's salary is not included. (See Appendix D for actual figures.)

PAYROLL TAXES

10% of wages and salaries.

UTILITIES

Based on a similar restuarant's costs. The figures were then rated by the utility companies to give an average cost per month. The cost of utilities may increase.

ADVERTISING

Newspaper, television, and radio spots; fliers; billboards; coupons.

DISCOUNTS, RETURNS, AND ALLOWANCES

4% of VISA and MasterCard purchases.

LICENSES AND PERMITS

Required by state and municipality; includes dues to the restaurant a retail owners' association, merchant's permit, sign permit, etc.

TELEPHONE

Deposit, installation, and monthly charge. Needed for sales, pricing, contacting both suppliers and market.

DEPRECIATION

Accountant's figures, based on straight-line method, with a zero salvage value placed on equipment and fixtures.

LEGAL AND ACCOUNTING

Retainers to John Kellerman, Attorney at Law, and Greg Cooley, CPA.

INSURANCE

Quote given by Barnum–Brown Insurance, Inc. Includes liability, key-man disability and life, workmen's compensation, and other coverages.

INTEREST (LOAN)

$80,000 at 10% amortized over 5 years.

GENERAL EXPENSES

Operating expenses too small to be itemized.

Explanation of Cash Flow Statements

The same explanations apply for the cash flow statements except for depreciation and interest on the term loan. Note that because cash flow was projected to be considerably high at the end of the second year, $50,000 was withdrawn for partial repayment of the loan.

Cash Budget—First Year: April 1, 1988, to March 31, 1989

Line item:	Pre-Startup	Apr-88	May-88	Jun-88	Jul-88	Aug-88	Sep-88	Oct-88	Nov-88	Dec-88	Jan-89	Feb-89	Mar-89
[CASH RECEIPTS]													
Net sales	0	$9,052	$23,289	$21,898	$18,204	$13,113	$14,453	$14,003	$13,603	$13,802	$15,245	$14,867	$15,621
Total cash receipts	0	9,052	23,289	21,898	18,204	13,113	14,453	14,003	13,603	13,802	15,245	14,867	15,621
[CASH DISBURSEMENTS]													
Cost of goods	2,760	3,641	9,396	8,799	7,322	5,285	5,821	5,641	5,481	5,561	6,138	5,987	6,288
Salary & wages	2,800	4,300	6,328	5,150	4,956	4,123	4,101	3,918	4,010	2,941	3,789	2,998	3,321
Payroll taxes—10%	280	430	633	515	496	413	410	392	401	294	379	300	332
Rent	2,550	650	650	650	650	650	650	650	858	1,484	1,571	1,548	1,593
Utilities & start-up deposits	500	492	652	439	442	481	398	329	467	605	608	608	569
Telephone & start-up deposit	250	85	85	85	85	85	85	85	85	85	85	85	85
Licenses & permits	750	456	0	0	65	0	0	65	0	0	65	0	0
Insurance	600	334	334	334	334	334	334	334	334	334	334	334	334
Advertising	1,000	1,020	1,020	1,020	1,020	1,020	1,020	1,020	1,020	1,020	1,020	1,020	1,020
Administrative—legal & CPA	0	775	225	225	225	225	225	225	225	225	225	225	225
General expenses	100	300	300	300	300	300	300	300	300	300	300	300	300
Loan principal payment + interest	0	1,700	1,700	1,700	1,700	1,700	1,700	1,700	1,700	1,700	1,700	1,700	1,700
Total cash disbursements	11,590	14,183	21,323	19,217	17,595	14,616	15,044	14,659	14,881	14,549	16,214	15,105	15,767
Net monthly cash flow	(11,590)	(5,131)	1,966	2,681	609	(1,503)	(591)	(656)	(1,278)	(747)	(969)	(238)	(146)
Opening cash balance	0	16,000	10,869	12,835	15,516	16,125	14,622	14,031	13,375	12,097	11,350	10,381	10,143
Reserved loan	0	0	0	0	0	0	0	0	0	0	0	0	0
Closing cash balance	0	10,869	12,835	15,516	16,125	14,622	14,031	13,375	12,097	11,350	10,381	10,143	9,997
Graph x-axis		4	5	6	7	8	9	10	11	12	1	2	3

Pro Forma Income Statement—First Year: April 1, 1988, to March 31, 1989

Line item:	Apr-88	May-88	Jun-88	Jul-88	Aug-88	Sep-88	Oct-88	Nov-88	Dec-88	Jan-89	Feb-89	Mar-89	Total	% of Net Sales
Gross sales	$9,102	$23,489	$21,998	$18,304	$13,213	$14,553	$14,103	$13,703	$13,902	$15,345	$14,967	$15,721	$188,400	101%
Discounts, returns, & allow.	50	200	100	100	100	100	100	100	100	100	100	100	$1,250	1%
Net sales	9,052	23,289	21,898	18,204	13,113	14,453	14,003	13,603	13,802	15,245	14,867	15,621	$187,150	100%
[COST OF GOODS SOLD]														
Food & preparation costs	3,641	9,396	8,799	7,322	5,285	5,821	5,641	5,481	5,561	6,138	5,987	6,288	$75,360	40%
Total cost of goods sold	3,641	9,396	8,799	7,322	5,285	5,821	5,641	5,481	5,561	6,138	5,987	6,288	$75,360	40%
Gross profit	5,411	13,893	13,099	10,882	7,828	8,632	8,362	8,122	8,241	9,107	8,880	9,333	$111,790	60%
[OPERATING EXPENSES]														
Salary & wages	4,300	6,328	5,150	4,956	4,123	4,101	3,918	4,010	2,941	3,789	2,998	3,321	$49,935	27%
Payroll taxes—10%	430	633	515	496	413	410	392	401	294	379	300	332	$4,995	3%
Rent	650	650	650	650	650	650	650	858	1,484	1,571	1,548	1,593	$11,604	6%
Utilities	492	652	439	442	481	398	329	467	605	608	608	569	$6,090	3%
Telephone	85	85	85	85	85	85	85	85	85	85	85	85	$1,020	1%
Licenses & permits	456	0	0	65	0	0	65	0	0	65	0	0	$651	0%
Insurance	334	334	334	334	334	334	334	334	334	334	334	334	$4,008	2%
Depreciation—equip. & fixtures	398	398	398	398	398	398	398	398	398	398	398	398	$4,776	3%
Interest on loan (10%)	667	658	649	641	632	623	614	605	596	587	577	568	$7,417	4%
Advertising	1,020	1,020	1,020	1,020	1,020	1,020	1,020	1,020	1,020	1,020	1,020	1,020	$12,240	7%
Administrative—legal & CPA	775	225	225	225	225	225	225	225	225	225	225	225	$3,250	2%
General expenses	300	300	300	300	300	300	300	300	300	300	300	300	$3,600	
Total operating expenses	9,907	11,283	9,765	9,612	8,661	8,544	8,330	8,703	8,282	9,361	8,393	8,745	$109,586	59%
Operating income/loss	(4,496)	2,610	3,334	1,270	(833)	88	32	(581)	(41)	(254)	487	588	$2,204	1%
Profit before taxes	(4,496)	2,610	3,334	1,270	(833)	88	32	(581)	(41)	(254)	487	588	2,204	1%
Provision for income tax	0	0	217	0	0	79	0	0	0	0	0	123	$419	0%
Net income/loss	(4,496)	2,610	3,117	1,270	(833)	9	32	(581)	(41)	(254)	487	465	$1,785	1%
Graph x-axis	4	5	6	7	8	9	10	11	12	1	2	3		

Cash Budget—Second Year: April 1, 1989, to March 31, 1990

Line item:	Month:	Apr-89	May-89	Jun-89	Jul-89	Aug-89	Sep-89	Oct-89	Nov-89	Dec-89	Jan-90	Feb-90	Mar-90	Total
[CASH RECEIPTS]														
Net sales		$37,888	$32,547	$34,228	$34,011	$33,996	$33,653	$31,212	$31,154	$28,077	$33,998	$32,486	$35,400	398,650
Total cash receipts		37,888	32,547	34,228	34,011	33,996	33,653	31,212	31,154	28,077	33,998	32,486	35,400	398,650
[CASH DISBURSEMENTS]														
Cost of goods		15,155	13,019	13,691	13,604	13,598	13,462	12,485	12,462	11,230	13,599	12,994	14,161	159,460
Salary & wages		7,138	5,964	6,997	6,854	6,043	6,382	5,567	6,410	5,805	6,884	5,762	6,589	76,395
Payroll taxes—10%		714	596	700	685	604	638	557	641	581	688	577	659	7,640
Rent		650	650	650	2,691	2,690	2,669	2,523	2,519	2,335	2,690	2,599	2,774	25,440
Utilities		593	652	654	683	679	682	674	662	652	608	598	587	7,724
Telephone		75	75	75	75	75	75	75	75	75	75	75	75	900
Licenses & permits		0	0	100	0	0	100	0	0	100	0	0	100	400
Insurance		700	700	700	700	700	700	700	700	700	700	700	700	8,400
Advertising		1,533	1,533	1,533	1,533	1,533	1,533	1,533	1,533	1,533	1,533	1,533	1,533	18,400
Administrative—legal & CPA		242	242	242	242	242	242	242	242	242	242	242	240	2,900
Income tax expense		0	0	6,673	0	0	4,711	0	0	2,878	0	0	4,514	18,776
General expenses		400	400	400	400	400	400	400	400	400	400	400	400	4,800
Loan principal payment + interest		1,700	1,700	1,700	1,700	1,700	1,700	1,700	1,700	1,700	1,700	1,700	1,700	20,400
Total cash disbursements		28,900	25,531	34,115	29,167	28,264	33,294	26,456	27,344	28,231	29,119	27,178	34,032	351,635
Net monthly cash flow		8,988	7,016	113	4,844	5,732	359	4,756	3,810	(154)	4,879	5,308	1,368	0
Opening cash balance		9,578	18,566	25,582	25,695	30,539	36,271	36,630	41,386	45,196	45,042	49,921	55,229	56,597
Reserved loan		0	0	0	0	0	0	0	0	0	0	0	0	0
Closing cash balance		18,566	25,582	25,695	30,539	36,271	36,630	41,386	45,196	45,042	49,921	55,229	56,597	56,597
Graph x-axis		4	5	6	7	8	9	10	11	12	1	2	3	

Note: Due to the large amount of excess cash on hand at year end, $50,000 will be used as an early repayment of term loan.

Pro Forma Income Statement—Second Year: April 1, 1989, to March 31, 1990

Line Item: Quarter:	1st	2nd	3rd	4th	Total	% of Net Sales
Gross sales	$104,663	$101,660	$90,443	$101,884	$398,650	101%
Discounts, returns, & allow.	750	750	750	750	3,000	1%
Net sales	103,913	100,910	89,693	101,134	395,650	100%
[COST OF GOODS SOLD]						
Food cost & preparation	41,865	40,664	36,177	40,754	159,460	40%
Total cost of goods sold	41,865	40,664	36,177	40,754	159,460	40%
Gross profit	62,048	60,246	53,516	60,380	236,190	60%
[OPERATING EXPENSES]						
Salaries & wages	20,099	19,205	17,992	19,099	76,395	19%
Payroll taxes—10%	2,010	1,921	1,799	1,910	7,640	2%
Rent	1,950	6,829	7,377	8,063	24,219	6%
Utilites	1,899	2,044	1,988	1,793	7,724	2%
Telephone	225	225	225	225	900	0%
Licenses & permits	100	100	100	100	400	0%
Insurance	2,100	2,100	2,100	2,100	8,400	2%
Depreciation—equip. & fixtures	1,194	1,194	1,194	1,194	4,776	1%
Interest on loan (10%)	1,647	1,560	1,471	1,379	6,057	2%
Advertising	4,600	4,600	4,600	4,600	18,400	5%
Administrative— legal & CPA	725	725	725	725	2,900	1%
General expenses	1,200	1,200	1,200	1,200	4,800	1%
Total operating expenses	37,749	41,703	40,771	42,388	162,611	41%
Operating income/loss	24,299	18,543	12,745	17,992	73,579	19%
Profit before taxes	19,066	13,460	8,223	12,898	53,647	14%
Provision for income tax	6,673	4,711	2,878	4,514	18,776	5%
Net income/loss	12,393	8,749	5,345	8,384	34,871	9%

Break-Even Worksheet

PART 1: CALCULATING THE BREAK-EVEN POINT

Fixed Expenses Breakdown

Salaries	$38,000
Payroll tax	$3,800
Rent	$7,800
Utilities	$6,090
Interest on loan	$7,417
Advertising	$12,240
Depreciation—equipment and fixtures	$4,776
Insurance	$4,008
Licenses & permits	$651
Total fixed expenses	$84,782

Break-Even Calculations

Fixed expenses (carried from cell F12)	$84,782
Gross margin (from pro forma income statement)	60%
The break-even point is:	$141,303

PART 2: GRAPHING THE BREAK-EVEN POINT

Enter starting sales:	$9,102
Enter sales increment:	$14,387

Net Sales [X & A]	Fixed exp. [B]	Variable exp. [C]	Total exp. [D]	Profit or loss [E]	Profit margin
$9,102	$84,782	$3,641	$88,423	($79,321)	−871%
$23,489	$84,782	$9,396	$94,178	($70,689)	−301%
$37,876	$84,782	$15,150	$99,932	($62,056)	−164%
$52,263	$84,782	$20,905	$105,687	($53,424)	−102%
$66,650	$84,782	$26,660	$111,442	($44,792)	−67%
$81,037	$84,782	$32,415	$117,197	($36,160)	−45%
$95,424	$84,782	$38,170	$122,952	($27,528)	−29%
$109,811	$84,782	$43,924	$128,706	($18,895)	−17%
$124,198	$84,782	$49,679	$134,461	($10,263)	−8%
$138,585	$84,782	$55,434	$140,216	($1,631)	−1%
$152,972	$84,782	$61,189	$145,971	$7,001	5%

Pro Forma Balance Sheet—Opening and First Two Years: Opening thru March 31, 1990

Line item:	Period: Opening	Mar-89	Mar-90
[CURRENT ASSETS]			
Cash	$18,500	$9,997	$56,597
Merchandise inventory	4,300	2,034	2,034
Supplies	200	200	200
Prepaid rent	0	650	0
Total current assets	23,000	12,881	58,831

(*continued*)

Pro Forma Balance Sheet—Opening and First Two Years: Opening thru March 31, 1990

Line item:	Period:	Opening	Mar-89	Mar-90
[FIXED ASSETS]				
Equipment & fixtures		74,600	74,600	74,600
Less depreciation		0	2,964	4,776
Leasehold improvements		0	3,250	0
Total fixed assets		74,600	74,886	69,824
Total assets		97,600	87,767	128,655
[LONG-TERM DEBT]				
Bank loan payable		80,000	67,018	52,678
[SHORT-TERM DEBT]				
Accumulated depreciation		0	2,964	4,776
Total liabilities		80,000	69,982	57,454
[OWNER EQUITY]				
Retained earnings		0	1,785	34,871
Stockholders' equity		16,000	16,00	16,000
Additional paid-in capital		1,600	0	0
Total owner equity		17,600	17,785	50,871
Total equity and liabilities		97,600	87,767	108,325

Note: Second year does not balance; it is off by $20,300. I cannot figure out why this is so.

Loan Amortization

Given: PV = 80000.00
I = 0.83333
N = 60

Then: PMT = 1,699.77

LOAN AMORTIZATION SCHEDULE

Period	Payment Size	Interest Due	Reduction of Principal	Principal Balance Remaining
1	1,699.77	666.67	1,033.10	78,966.90
2	1,699.77	658.06	1,041.71	77,925.19
3	1,699.77	649.38	1,050.39	76,874.80
4	1,699.77	640.62	1,059.15	75,815.65
5	1,699.77	631.80	1,067.97	74,747.68
6	1,699.77	622.90	1,076.87	73,670.80
7	1,699.77	613.92	1,085.85	72,584.96
8	1,699.77	604.87	1,094.89	71,490.06
9	1,699.77	595.75	1,104.02	70,386.05
10	1,699.77	586.55	1,113.22	69,272.83
11	1,699.77	577.27	1,122.50	68,150.33
12	1,699.77	567.92	1,131.85	67,018.48
13	1,699.77	558.49	1,141.28	65,877.20

LOAN AMORTIZATION SCHEDULE

Period	Payment Size	Interest Due	Reduction of Principal	Principal Balance Remaining
14	1,699.77	548.98	1,150.79	64,726.40
15	1,699.77	539.39	1,160.38	63,566.02
16	1,699.77	529.72	1,170.05	62,395.97
17	1,699.77	519.97	1,179.80	61,216.17
18	1,699.77	510.13	1,189.63	60,026.53
19	1,699.77	500.22	1,199.55	58,826.99
20	1,699.77	490.22	1,209.54	57,617.44
21	1,699.77	480.15	1,219.62	56,397.82
22	1,699.77	469.98	1,229.79	55,168.03
23	1,699.77	459.73	1,240.04	53,927.99
24	1,699.77	449.40	1,250.37	52,677.62
25	1,699.77	438.98	1,260.79	51,416.83
26	1,699.77	428.47	1,271.30	50,145.53
27	1,699.77	417.88	1,281.89	48,863.64
28	1,699.77	407.20	1,292.57	47,571.07
29	1,699.77	396.43	1,303.34	46,267.73
30	1,699.77	385.56	1,314.20	44,953.53
31	1,699.77	374.61	1,325.16	43,628.37
32	1,699.77	363.57	1,336.20	42,292.17
33	1,699.77	352.43	1,347.33	40,944.83
34	1,699.77	341.21	1,358.56	39,586.27
35	1,699.77	329.89	1,369.88	38,216.39
36	1,699.77	318.47	1,381.30	36,835.09
37	1,699.77	306.96	1,392.81	35,442.28
38	1,699.77	295.35	1,404.42	34,037.86
39	1,699.77	283.65	1,416.12	32,621.74
40	1,699.77	271.85	1,427.92	31,193.82
41	1,699.77	259.95	1,439.82	29,754.00
42	1,699.77	247.95	1,451.82	28,302.18
43	1,699.77	235.85	1,463.92	26,838.26
44	1,699.77	223.65	1,476.12	25,362.14
45	1,699.77	211.35	1,488.42	23,873.73
46	1,699.77	198.95	1,500.82	22,372.90
47	1,699.77	186.44	1,513.33	20,859.57
48	1,699.77	173.83	1,525.94	19,333.64
49	1,699.77	161.11	1,538.66	17,794.98
50	1,699.77	148.29	1,551.48	16,243.50
51	1,699.77	135.36	1,564.41	14,679.10
52	1,699.77	122.33	1,577.44	13,101.65
53	1,699.77	109.18	1,590.59	11,511.06
54	1,699.77	95.93	1,603.84	9,907.22
55	1,699.77	82.56	1,617.21	8,290.01
56	1,699.77	69.08	1,630.69	6,659.32
57	1,699.77	55.49	1,644.27	5,015.05
58	1,699.77	41.79	1,657.98	3,357.07
59	1,699.77	27.98	1,671.79	1,685.28
60	1,699.77	14.04	1,685.73	−0.45

Appendix A: Menu

Special Appetizers

crispy crinkle cut fries ... $1.75

fried cheese balls ... $1.95
Buttery cheddar cheese balls with
a crisp, Fried coating,
served with apple butter on the side.

beer batter onion rings ... $1.95

deep-fried mushrooms ... $1.95

deep-fried zucchini ... $1.95

combination fried vegetables ... $2.95
Mushrooms, Broccoli Cheese Melt
and Zucchini

potato skins
* Three to a serving
Plain...$1.95
Loaded...$2.95
* Cheddar cheese and bacon

Soups

--All of YesterYears Soups Are Home Made The Old Fashion Way--

onion soup
Bowl...$2.25   Cup...$1.65
* Covered with a thick layer of cheese

chicken noodle soup
Bowl...$2.25   Cup...$1.65

vegetable soup
Bowl...$2.25   Cup...$1.65

Salads

--Salads Are Made Up Freshly Every Day--

Dressings
French, Thousand Island, Creamy Bleu Cheese, Oil and Vinegar,
Low-Cal Italian

house salad ... $2.95
With cheddar cheese, bacon bits and chopped egg

YesterYears chef salad ... $3.75
* Topped with bacon, turkey breast, ham, cheddar and swiss
cheeses, hard-boiled egg, tomatoes, cucumber and black olives.
Served with garlic bread and your choice of dressing

creamy garden pasta salad ... $3.75
* A rainbow of rotelli pasta with cauliflower, broccoli,
carrots, zucchini and red onion in a creamy Italian dressing surrounded
by tossed greens and garnished with tomatoes, mushrooms, and black
olives. Served with garlic bread

Sandwiches

-- All of YesterYears Sandwiches are served with chips and a dill--

beer batter tenderloin... $4.25
* The biggest and best in Batesville; served deluxe

charbroiled chicken breast... $4.25
* With lettuce and tomato

classic club... $4.25
* Ham. turkey breast, cheese, bacon, lettuce, tomatoes, and mayonnaise-- served on toasted whole wheat or white bread

philly cheese steak... $4.25
* Thinly sliced roast beef sirloin, grilled and smothered with green peppers, onions, and mozzarella

grilled ham and cheese... $3.95
* Grilled the old-fashion way on a flat top

beer batter fish... $3.95
* Fresh Atlantic Cod   Cheese optional for...$ .30

Burgers

All of YesterYears Burgers are a full 1/2 pound, formed from the leanest of USDA choice chuck, charbroiled and served thick and juicy on your choice of a sesame seed, whole wheat, or white bun. Served with lettuce, tomatoes, onion, and pickle slices. Mayonnaise is available upon request. Served with chips & a dill.

50's and 60's burger... $4.25
* The old-fashioned burger, served deluxe, with an option of American or Swiss cheese topping on a sesame seed bun.

bleu cheese burger... $4.25
* The same deluxe burger served with melted bleu cheese crumbles

hickory smoked bbq burger... $4.25
* A tangy favorite-- served with American cheese

bacon 'n cheese burger... $4.25
* A traditional favorite, served with melted American or Swiss cheese and lean Indiana bacon

Dinner Specialties

All of YesterYears Dinners include a freshly tossed salad, choice of dressing, baked potato or crispy crinkle cut fries

Steaks

YesterYears steaks are USDA choice and are specially seasoned and charbroiled to perfection
* sauteed mushrooms with Burgundy wine sauce, if desired

10oz. new york strip dinner... $10.95   rib-eye dinner... $8.95

petite steak dinner... $6.95
* 6oz. sirloin for the lighter meal

marinated chicken dinner... $8.95
YesterYears chicken is 8 oz.'s of boneless breast marinated in our special teriyaki sauce and charbroiled to perfection
Served on a hot bed of rice

YesterYears diet plate... $4.95

* Sliced tomatoes, cottage cheese, served with a 6 oz. cut of broiled ground beef

Kids Menu

(12 years and under)

Hamburger Plate...$1.90
* includes Fries and Small Drink   Sandwich only...$.60

Grilled Cheese Plate...$1.90   Sandwich only...$.60
* includes Fries and Small Drink

Desserts

banana split pie... $1.95

* Mounded layers of chocolate, banana nut and strawberry ice cream, fresh bananas and salted peanuts. Prepared in a special crispy crust, topped with whipped cream, chocolate syrup and a cherry

fruit cobblers... $1.05   W/ ice cream... add $ .30
* Blackberry
* Peach
* Apple
* Cherry

YesterYears outrageous sundae... $1.95
* Your choice of ice cream topped with hot fudge and caramel
with nut and whipped cream, topped with a cherry

good old ice cream sodas... $1.75
* Comes with two straws

ice cream or sherbert... $1.25
* Your choice of thirteen flavors

Hot & Cold Beverages

Pot of Tea...$ .85
Coffee...$ .80   W / Free Refills
* Regular or decaffeinated, both freshly brewed
Cocoa...$ .95
* With whipped cream on top
Coke Classic, Diet Coke, Dr. Pepper, & Sprite...$ .95

Old Fashioned Fountain Style Flavored Cokes...$ .95
* Chocolate, Vanilla, or Cherry

Pot of Iced Tea...$ .85
Fruit Juices...$ .85
* Orange and Grapefruit (both freshly-squeezed), Pineapple,
Cranberry, Grape, Tomato,   Apple Cider
Lemonade, Limeade, Orangeade...$ .95
                    * Freshly-squeezed

Milk...$ .85
* White or Chocolate

Appendix B: Market Survey*

Sex: <u>58%</u> Male   <u>42%</u> Female

Age: <u>47%</u> Young   <u>38%</u> Middle-age   <u>15%</u> Elderly

1. What is your favorite restaurant in Batesville?

   <u>3%</u> Hardee's   <u>7%</u> Dairy Queen   <u>14%</u> Sherman House

   <u>38%</u> McDonald's   <u>2%</u> Pizza King   <u>5%</u> Homestead

   <u>13%</u> Kentucky Fried Chicken   <u>5%</u> Hobo Hut

   Other <u>8% Koch's; 3% Hillcrest Country Club; 2% Skyline Chili</u>

   Why?

   <u>31%</u> Food   <u>1%</u> Cleanliness   <u>8%</u> Atmosphere   <u>23%</u> Service

   <u>10%</u> Price   <u>1%</u> Location   <u>23%</u> Past experience

   Other <u>2% relative owns the restaurant</u>

2. Which meal do you eat out most often in Batesville?

   <u>68%</u> Lunch   <u>32%</u> Dinner

3. When you go out of town to eat, which meal is it for most often?

   <u>9%</u> Lunch   <u>91%</u> Dinner

   Distance traveled to the out-of-town restaurant?

   <u>42%</u> 0 to 20 miles   <u>51%</u> 20 to 60 miles   <u>7%</u> 60 + miles

   Why? <u>have a favorite restaurant; classy atmosphere; great food</u>

4. Would a 50s-and-60s-style diner appeal to you?   <u>92%</u> Yes   <u>8%</u> No

   If yes, when would you patronize the restaurant?   <u>74%</u> Lunch   <u>18%</u> Dinner

   If no, why not? <u>5% don't like diners; 3% prefer to continue going to their favorite restaurant</u>

5. How much are you willing to pay for lunch?

   <u>69%</u> 1 to 5 dollars   <u>31%</u> 6 to 10 dollars   <u>0%</u> 11 + dollars

6. How much are you willing to pay for dinner?

   <u>23%</u> 1 to 5 dollars   <u>66%</u> 6 to 10 dollars   <u>11%</u> 11 + dollars

7. If you could have good food at a sit-down, full-service restaurant, and you could have your meal in one-half hour or less, would this deter you from going to a fast-food establishment?

   <u>91%</u> Yes   <u>9%</u> No

*Based on a sample survey of 100 people.

Appendix C: Other Restaurants in Batesville

Restaurant	Address	How Long in Business
Sherman House Restaurant and Inn	35 S. Main Street	135 years
Young's Dairy Queen Restaurant	Highways 229 and 46	15 years
Pizza Haus, Inc.	104 E. Boehringer St.	13 years
Hobo Hut	Highway 46 East	12 years
Kentucky Fried Chicken	Highways 46 and 229	10 years
Hardee's	Highways I-74 and 229	9 years
The Homestead	100 E. Pearl Street	6 years
McDonald's	Cross Country Plaza	4 years
Mama's Pizza	E. George Street	1 year
Pizza King	801 Tekulve Road	1 year
Skyline Chili	211 E. Pearl Street	5 months

Appendix D: Feasibility Projection Worksheets

FEASIBILITY PROJECTION WORKSHEET

FIRST YEAR

SALES VOLUME

Meals	Number of Seats		Average Turnover per seat		Possible Daily Volume		Average Check per Seat		Highest Daily Sales		Vacant Seat Factor		Total Sales per Meal		Days Open Weekly		Weekly Sales		Weeks Open Yearly		Yearly Sales
Breakfast	n/a	×	n/a	=	n/a	×	n/a	=	n/a	×	2/3	=	n/a	×	n/a	=	n/a	×	n/a	=	n/a
Lunch	68	×	1.5	=	102	×	$5.25	=	535.50	×	2/3	=	357	×	7	=	2,499	×	50	=	129,950.00
Dinner	68	×	.5	=	34	×	$8.00	=	272.00	×	2/3	=	181	×	7	=	1,269	×	50	=	63,450.00

TOTAL SALES   DAILY $538   WEEKLY $3,768   YEARLY $188,400.00

FOOD COSTS

Total Daily Sales $538 × 1/3 = DAILY FOOD COSTS $179 × Days Open Weekly 7 = Weekly Food Costs $1,225 × Weeks Open Yearly 50 = Yearly Food Costs $62,767.00

PAYROLL

	Hire		Avg. No. Workers per Shift		Pay per Worker		Daily Payroll		Number of Shifts		Daily Payroll		Days per Week		Weekly Payroll		Weeks per Year		Yearly Payroll
Manager	2																		$12,000.00
Serving Staff																			
Waiters/ Waitresses	2		1	×	$3.00	=			2	=	$6.00	×	7	=	$42.00	×	50	=	$2,100.00
Busboys/ Busgirls	2		1	×	$3.35	=			2	=	$6.70	×	7	=	$46.90	×	50	=	$2,345.00
Kitchen Staff																			
Chef/Kitchen Mgr.	1																		$26,000.00
Other Cooks	2		1	×	$4.00	=			2	=	$8.00	×	7	=	$56.00	×	50	=	$2,800.00
Helpers	1		1	×	$3.35	=			2	=	$6.70	×	7	=	$46.90	×	50	=	$2,345.00
Other Employees																			
Bartenders			n/a	×	n/a	=			n/a	=	n/a	×	n/a	=	n/a	×	n/a	=	n/a
Cocktail Waitresses			n/a	×	n/a	=			n/a	=	n/a	×	n/a	=	n/a	×	n/a	=	n/a
Clean-up Staff	2		1	×	$3.35	=			2	=	$6.70	×	7	=	$46.90	×	50	=	$2,345.00
Others			n/a	×	n/a	=			n/a	=	n/a	×	n/a	=	n/a	×	n/a	=	n/a
TOTALS	10										DAILY				WEEKLY $11,935.00			YEARLY	$49,935.00

FEASIBILITY PROJECTION WORKSHEET

SECOND YEAR

SALES VOLUME

Number of Seats		Average Turnover per seat	Meals		Possible Daily Volume		Average Check per Seat		Highest Daily Sales		Vacant Seat Factor		Total Sales per Meal		Days Open Weekly		Weekly Sales		Weeks Open Yearly		Yearly Sales
n/a	×	n/a	Breakfast	=	n/a	×	n/a	=	n/a	×	2/3	=	n/a	×	n/a	=	n/a	×	n/a	=	n/a
68	×	2.5	Lunch	=	170	×	$5.25	=	893	×	2/3	=	595	×	7	=	4,165	×	50	=	208,250.00
68	×	1.5	Dinner	=	102	×	$8.00	=	816	×	2/3	=	544	×	7	=	3,808	×	50	=	190,400.00
TOTAL SALES													DAILY $1,139				WEEKLY $7,973			YEARLY	$398,650.00

FOOD COSTS

Total Daily Sales $1,139 × 1/3 = DAILY FOOD COSTS $380

	DAILY FOOD COSTS		Days Open Weekly		Weekly Food Costs		Weeks Open Yearly		Yearly Food Costs
	$380	×	7	=	$2,660	×	50	=	$133,000.00

PAYROLL

Hire		Avg. No. Workers per Shift		Pay per Worker		Number of Shifts		Daily Payroll		Days per Week		Weekly Payroll		Weeks per Year		Yearly Payroll
2	**Manager**														=	$17,000.00
	Assist. Manager														=	$12,000.00
	Serving Staff															
2	Waiters/Waitresses	1	×	$3.35	×	2	=	$6.70	×	7	=	$46.90	×	50	=	$2,345.00
2	Busboys/Busgirls	1	×	$3.70	×	2	=	$7.40	×	7	=	$51.80	×	50	=	$2,590.00
	Kitchen Staff															
1	Chef/Kitchen Mgr.														=	$28,600.00
4	Other Cooks	2	×	$4.35	×	2	=	$17.40	×	7	=	$121.80	×	50	=	$6,090.00
2	Helpers	1	×	$3.70	×	2	=	$7.40	×	7	=	$51.80	×	50	=	$2,590.00
	Other Employees															
	Bartenders	n/a	×	n/a	×	n/a	=	n/a	×	n/a	=	n/a	×	n/a	=	n/a
	Cocktail Waitresses	n/a	×	n/a	×	n/a	=	n/a	×	n/a	=	n/a	×	n/a	=	n/a
4	Clean-up Staff	2	×	$3.70	×	2	=	$14.80	×	7	=	$103.60	×	50	=	$5,180.00
	Others	n/a	×	n/a	×	n/a	=	n/a	×	n/a	=	n/a	×	n/a	=	n/a
TOTALS 15								DAILY				WEEKLY			YEARLY	$18,795.00 $76,395.00

FEASIBILITY PROJECTION WORKSHEET

SECOND YEAR, HIGH

SALES VOLUME

	Number of Seats		Average Turnover per seat		Possible Daily Volume		Average Check per Seat		Highest Daily Sales		Vacant Seat Factor		Total Sales per Meal		Days Open Weekly		Weekly Sales		Weeks Open Yearly		Yearly Sales
Breakfast =	n/a	×	n/a	=	n/a	×	n/a	=	n/a	×	2/3	=	n/a	×	n/a	=	n/a	×	n/a	=	n/a
Lunch =	68	×	3.5	=	238	×	$5.25	=	1,249.50	×	2/3	=	833	×	7	=	5,831	×	50	=	291,550.00
Dinner =	68	×	2.5	=	170	×	$8.00	=	1,360	×	2/3	=	907	×	7	=	6,349	×	50	=	317,450.00
TOTAL SALES												DAILY $1,740				WEEKLY $12,180			YEARLY	$609,000.00

FOOD COSTS

Total Daily Sales $1,740 × 1/3 = DAILY FOOD COSTS $580 ×

	Days Open Weekly		Weekly Food Costs		Weeks Open Yearly		Yearly Food Costs
	7	=	$4,060	×	50	=	$203,000.00

PAYROLL

	Hire		Avg. No. Workers per Shift		Pay per Worker		Number of Shifts		Daily Payroll		Days per Week		Weekly Payroll		Weeks per Year		Yearly Payroll
Manager	2																$17,000.00
Assist. Manager																	$12,000.00
Serving Staff																	
Waiters/Waitresses			1	×	$3.35	×	2	=	$6.70	×	7	=	$46.90	×	50	=	$2,345.00
Busboys/Busgirls			1	×	$3.70	×	2	=	$7.40	×	7	=	$51.80	×	50	=	$2,590.00
Kitchen Staff																	
Chef/Kitchen Mgr.	1																$28,600.00
Other Cooks	4		2	×	$4.35	×	2	=	$17.40	×	7	=	$121.80	×	50	=	$6,090.00
Helpers	2		1	×	$3.70	×	2	=	$7.40	×	7	=	$51.80	×	50	=	$2,590.00
Other Employees																	
Bartenders			n/a	×	n/a	×	n/a	=	n/a	×	n/a	=	n/a	×	n/a	=	n/a
Cocktail Waitresses			n/a	×	n/a	×	n/a	=	n/a	×	n/a	=	n/a	×	n/a	=	n/a
Clean-up Staff	4		2	×	$3.70	×	2	=	$14.80	×	7	=	$103.60	×	50	=	$5,180.00
Others			n/a	×	n/a	×	n/a	=	n/a	×	n/a	=	n/a	×	n/a	=	n/a
TOTALS	15								DAILY			WEEKLY			YEARLY		$18,795.00
																	$76,395.00

Appendix E: Management Team

SCOTT GEORGE VOEGELE

PERMANENT ADDRESS
54 Circle Lane
Batesville, IN   47006
(812)934-3394

TEMPORARY ADDRESS
208 North McKinley
Muncie, IN   47303
(317)282-8154

OCCUPATIONAL OBJECTIVE
To obtain an entry-level position in management with a growth-oriented company offering the opportunity for advancement

EDUCATION
Bachelor of Science degree in Management
Major: Small Business/Entrepreneurship
Ball State University, Muncie, IN   47306
Internship: Amoco Service Station, Batesville, IN
Graduation Date: August 1987
Cumulative GPA: 2.885 on a 4.0 scale
Management GPA: 3.225 on a 4.0 scale

WORK EXPERIENCE
Part-time summer employment financed 50 percent of my college education

5/86 to 9/87
Assistant Manager of Buckley's Amoco Service Station, Batesville, IN   47006
Responsibilities:
* Recorded daily business transactions
* Resolved customer problems and serviced customer needs and wants
* Hired, trained, and organized employees
* Assisted in the business planning

5/80 to 9/85
Retail Salesman of Buckley's Amoco Service Station
Responsibilities:
* Established good relations with customers and suppliers
* Sold petroleum products and automotive accessories
* Maintained control of inventory

5/84 to 9/85
Landscaper for J. P. Landscaping, Batesville, IN   47006
Responsibilities:
* Installed and maintained plants
* Trimmed trees and shrubbery
* Designed and planned layouts for customers

5/78 to 9/79
Gas Attendant for Hellmich's Amoco Service Station, Batesville, IN   47006
Note: Worked for the same Amoco company for eight years but under different management

HONORS
Dean's List—College Achievement and Recognition during Winter Quarter 1986–87 at Ball State University

COLLEGIATE INVOLVEMENT
Association of Collegiate Entrepreneurs (A.C.E.)
Represented Ball State University at the National A.C.E. Convention in Chicago, 1987

INTERESTS
Enjoy meeting people, traveling, and jogging

REFERENCES
Available upon request

Appendix F: Demographics Research

Demographic research included information on Batesville, Ripley County, Franklin County, the state of Indiana, and the food service industry in the U.S.

Batesville

Description of the City
Financial Data
Highways, Transportation, and Communications
Map

Ripley and Franklin Counties

Employment
Payroll
Number of Employees
Number of Business Establishments
Population Projections
Population Counts by Decade
Population by Age Group
Urban and Rural Populations
Mean Family Income
Persons by Place of Work
Families by Type, Income Level, Presence and Age of Children
Family Income Levels
Per Capita Money Income
Median Age of Population
Retail Trade—Number of Establishments and Sales

Indiana

Employment Distribution
Personal Income Distribution
Percent Change in Employment
Growth Rate

United States

Food Service Industry

SOURCES OF MARKET RESEARCH (DEMOGRAPHICS) DATA

Indiana Employment Security Division, *Indiana Work Force Summary and Establishment Employment*, 1984 summary.

U.S. Department of Labor, Bureau of Labor Statistics, *Employment and Earnings,* July 1984, p. 32; Indiana Employment Security Division, *Indiana Work Force Summary*.

U.S. Department of Commerce, *Survey of Current Business*, August 1985, Table 3.

Indiana Employment Security Division, *Indiana Work Force Summary and Establishment Employment*, 1974, 1979, and 1984 summaries.

U.S. Department of Labor, Bureau of Labor Statistics, *Employment and Earnings, States and Averages, 1939–1978; Supplement to Employment, Hours and Earnings, States and Areas, 1980–1983;* and *Employment and Earnings,* August 1984 and August 1985.

U.S. Department of Labor, Bureau of Labor Statistics, *Employment and Earnings,* Oct. 1981, Feb. 1974, and Mar. 1986, Table B-8.

Indiana Employment Security Division, *Labor Force Estimates,* 1974 and 1985 annual averages.

Indiana Employment and Security Division, *County Employment Patterns,* 1974 and 1984.

U.S. Department of Commerce, Bureau of the Census, *Statistical Abstract of the U.S.,* 1969–1985; U.S. Department of Labor, *Manpower Report of the President,* 1964–1969.

U.S. Department of Commerce, *Survey of Current Business,* August 1985, Table 3.

U.S. Department of Commerce, *State Personal Income 1929–1982,* Tables 1, 2, 7, and 8; *Survey of Current Business,* Aug. 1985, Table 3.

U.S. Department of Commerce, Bureau of Economic Analysis, *Economic Analysis Newsletter.*

U.S. Department of Commerce, *State Personal Income 1929–1982,* Table 2; *Survey of Current Business,* Aug. 1985, Table 3.

U.S. Department of Commerce, Bureau of the Census, *1980 Census of the Population,* Indiana Vol. 1, Part 16, Table 61.

U.S. Department of Commerce, Bureau of the Census, *Statistical Abstract of the U.S.,* 1960–1985.

U.S. Department of Commerce, Bureau of the Census, *1980 Census of the Population, General Social and Economic Characteristics,* Indiana, Tables 62 and 67; *1970 Census of the Population, Characteristics of the Population,* Indiana, Tables 17 and 165; *1960 Census of the Population,* Indiana, Table 53.

U.S. Department of Commerce, Bureau of the Census, *1980 Census of the Population, General Social and Economic Characteristics,* Indiana, Table 62; *1970 Census of the Population, Characteristics of the Population,* Table 21.

U.S. Department of Commerce, Bureau of the Census, *1980 Census of the Population, General Social and Economic Characteristics,* Indiana, Table 67; *1970 Census of the Population, Characteristics of the Population,* Indiana, Table 165.

Supplement to Employment, Hours and Earnings, States and Areas, 1980–1983; Employment and Earnings, August 1984, August 1985.

U.S. Department of Commerce, *State Personal Income, 1929–1982,* Tables 1, 2, 7, and 8; *Survey of Current Business,* August 1985, Table 3.

■ **SUMMARY**

A business plan is a road map for the would-be entrepreneur. The plan contains objectives, forecasts, and a description of the business—that is, what it will do and how it will operate.

Plans may vary in length. However, every plan must include detailed research that clearly illustrates the business concept, marketing element, management structure, critical risks involved, financial needs and projections, milestone objectives, and an appendix.

In each specific part of the plan the prospective owner describes operations and then addresses the major issues likely to be confronted. Many small business owners find it most helpful to begin their initial plan by describing how they will get into business and deal with start-up problems. Both of these areas relate to the financial side of operations. After putting dollar amounts on projected sales revenues, expenses, and profit, the new owner is in a position to develop the management and marketing parts of the plan. Those parts are easier to prepare when the financial calculations needed to support them have already been made.

No plan is complete and unchangeable. There is always a need for additions or deletions. Some things will not work out as expected. Others will have gone unnoticed in the original plan and will have to be added. In any event, the important point is that the plan provides initial direction for the owner. From there the individual can modify things as necessary.

The first consideration in an initial business plan should be that of getting into business. How will the individual attain ownership? One of the most common ways is by purchasing an ongoing concern. This topic is the subject of the next chapter.

■ **REVIEW AND DISCUSSION QUESTIONS**

1. What is the major advantage of a small business plan? Explain.

2. What is contained in the "getting into business" section of a small business plan? Be complete in your answer.

3. What are some of the start-up problems that should be addressed in a small business plan? Identify and describe three.

4. Of what value is a projected income statement to a small business plan? What parts of the plan does it support? Explain.

5. What kinds of issues or considerations would you address in the part of the plan that deals with purchasing and inventory control? Insurance? Be complete in your answer.

6. The specific parts of a business plan will vary, depending on the goods or services the firm is selling. Explain this statement.

7. Overall, what does a business plan look like? What are the main parts of such a plan? How would a plan for a small manufacturing firm differ from one for a small retailing firm? Compare and contrast them.

Case Studies

A Planning Matter

■ Jeffrey Fischer has been operating his small retail store for the last eighteen months. The first six months he grossed $100,000. During the next six months, he sold $180,000 worth of merchandise. During the last half-year he grossed $220,000. Jeffrey believes he will sell about $600,000 worth of goods during the next year.

Most of Jeff's time has been spent behind the cash register, helping customers with buying decisions, and directing the personnel. "I've been so busy with operating matters," he admitted recently, "that I have just not had time to figure out where the store is and where it's going. I just don't have time for planning. However, I am hoping that within the next two months I'll be able to delegate a lot of what I'm doing to others, and I'll have more time for planning operations. My banker says that if I want a line of credit, he'll get it for me. But if I'm going to grow as much as I want to, I've got to have a formal plan."

Although it appears that Jeff is prepared to draw up a business plan, he has admitted to Sue, his wife, that he worries about the writing of the plan. He does not know what is supposed to be in the plan and what he should leave out. The biggest problem appears to be his lack of experience. As Sue put it, "He's never done a business plan before, so he's concerned about how to do it. I've suggested that he talk to the banker or visit the SBA and just get some advice. It would help a lot if someone would show him a plan so that he'd have something to follow. In any event, he definitely needs some guidance. He's an operating entrepreneur, but that doesn't mean he knows much about formal planning."

1. What exactly is a business plan?

2. What belongs in a business plan? What specific parts should it contain? Explain.

3. How should Jeff go about putting together a business plan? Where should he begin?

Peruvian Rugs for Sale

■ When Barbara Kippler first opened her import store she was convinced that there was a market for Peruvian rugs and blankets. No store in the city sold imported merchandise of fine quality. In fact, during her first visit to Lima she was astounded at the low prices being asked for these handmade items. It was obvious to her that the price back in the States would be at least three times the amount.

After talking the matter over with her husband, she decided to open a Peruvian import store. She signed a one-year lease and flew back to Lima to negotiate the purchase of $80,000 worth of merchandise. To her surprise, she was able to buy a great deal more for that amount than planned because she was purchasing such a large quantity. By the time she got everything into the store and put in place, there was hardly any waiting room for the customers. Barbara was delighted. "The selection is so large, I should have no trouble helping people find something they like," she told her husband. That was six months ago. Since then Barbara has sold only five percent of the merchandise. This gross of $12,000 has been eaten up by monthly rental costs, utilities, and day-to-day expenses. Last month Barbara ran a special "1/3-off" sale. She spent $1,200 for the advertising, but took in only $700 for her marketing efforts.

Ten days ago Barbara admitted to herself that she needed some outside assistance. A friend who is also in the import business suggested she visit the local Small Business Administration office to see if they could help. The individual in the office put her in touch with a university professor who teaches small business. He, in turn, sent a group of students to talk to Barbara, look at her operation, and develop a plan of action to help her out. The first thing one of the students asked for was Barbara's business plan. She looked at the student and said, "I have a feeling there's more to operating this business than I thought." She then told the group that she had no such plan.

1. Based on the case information, what should Barbara have put in a business plan? Be as complete as you can.

2. If Barbara had worked up a business plan, what problems could she have avoided? Cite and explain three.

3. Can a business plan help her now, or is it too late? Defend your answer.

You Be the Consultant

A FAILURE TO PLAN

Dick Raskobb has been in business for nine months. When he first opened his lawn-care business, he had $13,000 in initial capital. Many of his friends thought he was crazy. They told him:

> The economy is in real bad shape right now. No one is going to buy lawn care products. They're too busy trying to make ends meet. Whenever things get bad, people stop spending money on frills. Look at how many houses in your neighborhood needed to be painted. The owners are waiting for things to improve so they can afford to pay for the paint job. The same is true for lawns. Except for watering the grass and giving it some fertilizer, most people are doing very little.

Dick listened politely, went ahead with his plans, and opened his store. He had five years of experience in selling lawn care products. He knew that there were many people around town who spent a great deal of time and money on their lawns, particularly in the upper-middle-income sections of town. Dick's store is located in a small shopping center in just such a section.

The store was officially opened on May 1. For the first couple of weeks business was moderately slow. By the end of the month, however, Dick was doing a booming business. His projected monthly sales were $13,000. In June he did $17,000 worth of business. July and August brought in $20,000 and $23,000, respectively. However, in September things began to slow down dramatically. Sales fell to $11,000. In the next three months they plummeted to $6,000, $5,000, and $2,200. Dick's total monthly expenses including rent, store mainte-nance, and finance charges on credit pur-chases of equipment come to $5,000. His gross margin on sales is 40%. So, on the $97,200 of revenue for June-December, he made $38,880. However, his monthly expenses claimed $35,000 of this, mean-ing that his profits were a mere $3,880 for seven months' work.

Dick is extremely upset with sales over the last four months. He is also con-cerned about the fact that his initial $13,000 of capital is almost all gone because of the $1,500 salary he has drawn each month.

Yesterday Dick dropped by to see a friend at the bank nearby. The friend listened quietly as Dick told his tale of woe. When he was finished the banker asked him, "Do you have a business plan that I can see?" Dick admitted to her that he did not. "When things started off so well, I didn't see any real need to draw one up." The banker nodded her head and said:

That's typical, although you *should* have put one together before you started the business. Did it ever occur to you that you were opening your store just as the lawn care business was entering its big season? You were starting off with your best months and should have planned for the down-turn. If you had done a business plan you would have picked this up. In any event, if you want a loan, I think we can arrange one. What I need from you is a business plan with some financial projections. In particular, I'd like a projected income statement for the next 12 to 18 months.

Dick agreed with everything the banker had told him. He also promised to draw up a plan. "I don't know how much money I'll need, but I hope to know when I've done the plan," he told her. "I'll be back to see you a week from today."

■ **YOUR CONSULTATION** Assume that you are advising Dick on how to draw up his business plan. Given the information in the case, be as complete as you can in relating what it should include. Where possible, make suggestions regarding financial requirements, paying attention to the seasonal nature of the business. Also be sure to help him gear his plan in such a way that it will impress the banker and help him get the loan.

CHAPTER 5

Buying an Ongoing Small Business

Objectives

One of the easiest ways of getting into small business for yourself is to buy an ongoing firm. A lot of headaches can be avoided with this approach. For example, the start-up problems will have been taken care of by the previous owners. Additionally, there is a track record you can examine in order to determine the types of products to sell, the prices to charge, and so on. On the other hand, there are also potential pitfalls. Examples include buying a company whose success has been due to the personality and charisma of the owner-manager, buying a company when the market for its product has peaked (as in the case of hula hoops), and paying too much for a company. Of these pitfalls perhaps the most common one is that of paying too much. Chapter 5 points out ways to avoid this.

The first objective of Chapter 5 is to examine the advantages associated with buying an ongoing business. The second objective is to explain a series of "right questions" that must be raised when considering the purchase of an ongoing business. The third objective is to examine a formula that can be used to determine the reasonable purchase price for an enterprise. When you are finished with Chapter 5 you will be able to:

1. *Explain three advantages of buying an ongoing small business.*

2. *List some questions that must be answered before deciding to buy an ongoing concern.*

3. *Define* book value, replacement value, *and* liquidation value.

4. *Discuss asset pricing.*

5. *Define* intangible asset.

6. *Determine a reasonable purchase price for an ongoing small business.*

ADVANTAGES OF BUYING AN ONGOING SMALL BUSINESS

Of the numerous advantages to buying an ongoing business, three of the most important are the following:

1. Since the enterprise is already in operation, there should be little doubt about its successful future operation.

2. The time and effort associated with starting a new enterprise are eliminated.

3. It is sometimes possible to buy an ongoing business at a bargain price.

Each of these three advantages is discussed below.

LITTLE OR NO CONCERN ABOUT SUCCESSFUL FUTURE OPERATION

Two great dangers face a new business: the possibility that it will not find a market for its goods or services and the chance that it will not be able to control its costs. If either event occurs, the new business will go bankrupt.

By buying an existing concern, however, most of these fears are alleviated. A successful business has already demonstrated the ability to attract customers, control costs, and make a profit. Additionally, many of the problems facing a newly formed firm are sidestepped. For example: Where should the company be located? How should it advertise? What type of plant or merchandise layout will be most effective? How much should be reordered every three months? What types of customers will this type of store attract? What pricing strategy should the firm use? Questions such as these have already been faced and answered. Thus, when buying an ongoing operation, the new owner is often purchasing a **known quantity.** Of course, it is important to check and see that there are no hidden problems in the operation. Barring something of this nature, however, the purchase of an existing successful small business can be a wise investment. (See Small Business Success: Due Diligence Pays Off.)

TIME AND EFFORT CAN BE REDUCED

An ongoing concern has already assembled the inventory, equipment, personnel, and facilities necessary to run the operation. In many cases this has taken the owners a long time to do. They have spent countless hours "working out the bugs" so that the business is as efficient as possible. Likewise, they have probably gone through a fair number of employees before getting the right type of personnel. Except for the top management in a small business, the personnel usually go with the sale. Therefore, if the new owners treat the workers fairly, they should not have to worry about hiring, placing, and training personnel. This has already been done.

In addition, the old owners have undoubtedly established relations with suppliers, bankers, and other businesspeople. These individuals can often be relied on to provide assistance to the new owners. The suppliers know the type of merchandise that the business orders and how often it needs to be replenished. They can be a source of advice in managing the operation, as can the bankers with whom the enterprise has been doing business. These individuals know the capital needs of the enterprise and often provide new owners with the same credit line and assistance that they gave the previous owners. The same holds true for the accountant the old owners used, the lawyer, and any other professionals that served the business in an advisory capacity. Naturally, the new owners may have their own bankers, accountant, and/or lawyer, but these old relationships are there if the new owners need them.

■ SMALL BUSINESS SUCCESS ■

Due Diligence Pays Off

 Hendrix F. C. Niemann was 37 years old, well educated, experienced in business, and out of work. He decided to use his severance pay and his savings to purchase a business of his own. For months Niemann analyzed numerous prospective businesses that were for sale: a hospital transcription service, a sandwich producer for vending machines, a sailboat dealership, and a food distribution company. None of these businesses seemed to offer the opportunity that Niemann wanted. He was married with three children and this business opportunity *had* to be right.

Finally, Niemann found an appropriate opportunity. Automatic Door Specialists, a manufacturer of security systems, had sales of $2 million, good cash flow, a purchase price just above book value, and a 65-year-old owner ready to retire. After going through 17 business brokers, dozens of business ads, and four months of unemployment, Niemann believed this was it. He signed a letter of agreement contingent upon a due diligence process (a careful inspection and analysis of the firm) accomplished by Niemann.

The due diligence inspection unearthed several interesting facts. For example, the company had sustained a $36,000 loss for the first half of the fiscal year; half of the account receivables were more than 90 days old and the majority dated back over a year; an inventory had been overstated causing a *true* year to date loss closer to $80,000; sales were down 50 percent; half of the company's net worth was gone; and once the debt from an acquisition was added to the books, there would be no money for Niemann to draw a salary! It got worse as Niemann met with the key employees to hear the "inside" story of Automatic Door Specialists. Key people had left the company to work for competitors, parts and tools were in short supply, promises had been made to customers and then forgotten, and the building was a firetrap with no hot water.

All of this bad news provided Niemann with enough facts to demand that either he receive a 50 percent reduction in the purchase price or the deal was off. The new purchase price was accepted by the seller and Automatic Door Specialists had a new owner. The due diligence process paid off for Hendrix Niemann.

Source: Adapted from Hendrix F. C. Niemann, "Buying a Business," *Inc.*, February 1990, pp. 28–38.

BUY AT A GOOD PRICE

Sometimes it is possible to buy an ongoing small business at a very good price. The owner may want to sell quickly because of a retirement decision or illness. Or the owner may be forced to sell the business in order to raise money for some emergency that has occurred. Or the owner may feel that there is greater opportunity in another type of business and is therefore willing to sell at a low price in order to take advantage of the new opportunity.

Ideally, when one is looking to buy an ongoing, successful small business, one of these three advantages (especially the last one) is present. However, there are very few times when someone in business is going to sell a successful firm at an extraordinarily low price. The owner of a successful small business built the enterprise through skillful business practices, knows how to deal with people, and has a good idea of the operation's fair-market value. He will seldom sell for much below the fair-market value. Therefore, the prospective owner must be careful about bidding high on a poor investment, or walking away from a good bargain because "it smells fishy." The way to avoid making the wrong decision is to evaluate the existing operation in a logical manner.

KEY QUESTIONS TO ASK

In deciding whether or not to buy, the astute prospective owner needs to ask and answer a series of "right questions."[1] The following section discusses these right questions and provides insights into the types of actions that should be taken in the case of each response.

WHY IS THE BUSINESS BEING SOLD?

One of the first questions that should be asked is *why* the owner is selling the business.[2] Quite often there is a difference between the reason given to prospective buyers and the real reason. Typical responses include, "I'm thinking about retiring"; "I've proven to myself that I can be successful in this line of business, so now I'm moving to another operation that will provide me with new challenges"; "I want to move to California and go into business with my brother-in-law there."

Any of these statements may be *accurate* and, if they can be *substantiated*, the buyer may find that the business is indeed worth purchasing. However, since there is little chance of substantiating this sort of personal information, the next best thing to do is to check around and gather business-related information. Is the owner in trouble with the suppliers? Is the lease on the building due for renewal and the landlord wishes to triple the rent? Worse yet, is the building about to be torn down? Other site-location problems may relate to competition in the nearby area or zoning changes. Is a new shopping mall about to be built nearby that will take much of the business away from this location? Has the city council passed a new ordinance that calls for the closing of business on Sunday, the day of the week on which this store does 25 percent of its business?

Financially, what is the owner going to do after selling the business? Is the owner planning to stay in town? What employment opportunities does he have? The reason for asking these questions is because the last thing a new owner wants is to find that the old owner has set up a similar business a block away and is drawing back all of the old customers. One way of preventing this from happening is to have an attorney

---

[1]See "Acquisition Strategies— Part I," *Small Business Report,* January 1987, pp. 30–35; and "Acquisition Strategies—Part II," *Small Business Report,* February 1987, pp. 26–31.

[2]Robert C. Ronstadt, "Exit, Stage Left: Why Entrepreneurs End Their Entrepreneurial Careers before Retirement," *Journal of Business Venturing,* Fall 1986, pp. 323–38.

write into the contract that the old owner will not operate any business in town that will compete with the current one for a period of at least five years. This is known as a **legal restraint of trade**—agreement not to compete. Doing this helps to retain the old customers.

WHAT IS THE PRESENT PHYSICAL CONDITION OF THE BUSINESS?

Even if the asking price for the operation appears to be fair, it is necessary to examine the *physical condition of the assets.* Does the company own the building? If it does, how much repair work needs to be done? If the building is leased, does the lease provide for the kinds of repairs that will enhance the successful operation of the business? For example, if it is a flower shop and it has a somewhat large refrigerator for keeping the flowers cool, who has to pay to expand the size of the refrigerator? If the landlord agrees to do so and to recover the investment through an increase in the lease price, the total cost of the additional refrigerated space must be compared to the expected increase in business. Meanwhile, if the landlord does not want to make this type of investment, the new owners must realize that *any permanent additions to the property remain with the property.* This means that if something cannot be simply carried out of the building, it stays. Pictures on the walls and chairs and desks bought by the business owner can be removed. However, new bookshelves nailed to the wall, carpeting attached to the floor, a new acoustic ceiling installed to cut down on noise in the shop, and the new refrigerated area all become the permanent property of the building owner. Therefore, the overriding question in examining the physical facilities is "How much will it cost to get things in order?"

WHAT IS THE CONDITION OF THE INVENTORY?

How much inventory does the owner show on the books? Does a physical check show that the inventory actually exists? Additionally, is the inventory **saleable,** or is it out-of-date or badly deteriorated?

WHAT IS THE STATE OF THE COMPANY'S OTHER ASSETS?

Most small businesses have assets in addition to the physical facilities and the inventory. In a machine shop, for example, there will be various types of presses and other machinery. In an office there will be typewriters, calculating machines, and addressing and duplicating equipment that may belong to the business. Additionally, there is probably a cash register. The question that must be asked about all of this equipment is "Is it still useful, or has it been replaced by more modern technology?" In short, are these assets obsolete?

Another asset that is often overlooked is the records of the firm. If the business has kept careful **credit records** it may be possible to determine who is a good credit risk and who is not. Additionally, these records make it easy for a new owner to decide how much credit to extend to the old customers.

Likewise, **sales records** can be very important because they show seasonal demands and peak periods. This can provide the new owner with information for inventory-control purposes and can greatly reduce the risks of over- or understocking.

Still another commonly overlooked asset is **past contracts.** What type of lease does the current owner have on the building? If the lease was signed three years ago and is a seven-year lease with a fixed rent, it may have been somewhat high when it came into effect but somewhat on the low side for comparable facilities today. Furthermore, over the next four years the rent should prove to be quite low considering what competitors will be paying. Of course, if the lease is about to expire that is a different story. Now the prospective owner has to talk to the landlord and find out what the terms of the new lease are going to be. Additionally, a prospective owner's lawyer should look at the old lease to determine if it can be passed on to a new owner and, regardless of the rent, how difficult it is to break the lease if the business should start to fail.

Finally, the prospective buyer must look at an intangible asset called **goodwill.** Goodwill is often defined as the value of a company over and above what is shown on the books. For example, if Charlie owns a restaurant and everyone in the neighborhood eats there regularly, Charlie has built up goodwill among the residents. If he were to sell his business, the buyer would have to pay not only for the physical assets in the restaurant (tables, chairs, ovens, dinnerware) but also for the goodwill that Charlie has accumulated over the years. The reputation of the business has a value.[3]

HOW MANY OF THE PERSONNEL WILL REMAIN?

It is often difficult to give customers the good service they have come to expect if seasoned employees decide that they do not want to remain with the new owner. The owner is certainly an important asset of the firm, but so are the employees; they play a role in making the business a success. Therefore, one question the prospective buyer must ask is "If some people will be leaving, will there be enough left to maintain the type of service the customer is used to getting?" In particular, the new owner must be concerned about key people who are not staying. If the new owner is buying an auto repair shop and the head of the repair unit is leaving, who will fill this position? Likewise, if the new owner is buying an appliance store and the star salesperson is leaving, how will sales be affected? If it is evident that these people will not be staying, the prospective buyer must subtract something from the purchase price by making some allowance for the decline in sales and the accompanying expense associated with replacing **key personnel.**

WHAT TYPE OF COMPETITION DOES THE BUSINESS FACE?

No matter what good or service the business provides, there is a limit to the number of people who will want it and the total amount of money they will spend for it. Thus, the greater the competition, the less the business's chance of earning large profits. As the **number of competitors** increases, the cost of fighting them usually goes up. More money must be spent on advertising. Price competition must be met with accompanying reductions in overall revenue. There are simply too many companies pursuing the same market.

Additionally, the **quality of the competition** must be considered. If there are nine competitors, the owner might estimate a market share of 10 percent. However, some of these competitors undoubtedly will be more effective than others. One or two may have very good advertising and know how to use it to capture 25 percent of the

---

[3]James M. Stancill, "Upgrade Your Company's Image—and Valuation," *Harvard Business Review,* January/February 1984, pp. 16–23.

market. A few others may offer outstanding service and use this advantage to capture 20 percent of the market. Meanwhile, the remaining six fight for what is left. Then, there is the **location of the competition.** In many instances a small business does not offer anything unique, so people buy on the basis of convenience. A service located on the corner may get most of the business of local residents. One located across town will get virtually none. Since the product is the same at each location, no one is going to drive across town. This analogy holds for groceries, notions, drugs, and hardware. If competitors are located near each other, each will take some of the business that the others could have expected, but none is going to maximize its income. On the other hand, if the merchandise is made up of items—such as furniture—that people shop for very carefully, a competitor in the immediate area can be a distinct advantage. For example, two furniture stores located near each other will tend to draw a total number of customers greater than they would if located ten blocks apart. When people shop for furniture, they go where there is a large selection available. In the case of two adjacent stores, customers will reason that if the furniture they are looking for is not in one, it might be in the other. Additionally, since they can step from one store to the next, they can easily compare prices and the terms of sale.

Finally, any analysis of competition should look for **unscrupulous practices.** How cutthroat are the competitors? If very cutthroat, the prospect buyer will have to be continually alert for such things as price fixing by some competitors as well as kickbacks to suppliers for special services. Usually, if the company has been around for a couple of years, it has been successful in dealing with these types of practices. However, if some competitors are getting bad reputations, the new owner will want to know this. After all, over time the customers are likely to form a stereotyped impression of enterprises in a given geographic area and simply refuse to do business with any of them. "There's no sense looking for clothing in the Eighth Street area. Most of the stores there sell low-quality merchandise at a high price. Let's go to a more reputable area." In this case the customers are retaliating against unethical business practices by boycotting the entire area where these firms are located. In short, an unethical business competitor can drag down other firms as well.

WHAT DOES THE FIRM'S FINANCIAL PICTURE LOOK LIKE?

It may be necessary for a prospective buyer to hire an accountant to look over the company's books. It is important to get an idea of how well the firm is doing financially. One of the primary areas of interest should be the **company's profitability.**[4] Are there any things the business is doing wrong that can be spotted from the statements? If so, can the prospective buyer eliminate these problems?

Individuals who are skilled in buying companies that are in trouble, straightening them out, and reselling them at a profit know what to look for when examining the books. So do good accountants. Both also know that the seller's books alone should not be taken as proof of sales or profits. One should insist on seeing records of bank deposits for the last two to three years. If the current owner has held the firm for

---

[4]For a discussion of the seller's point of view, see Charles W. O'Conor, "Packaging Your Business for Sale," *Harvard Business Review,* March/April 1985, pp. 52–58.

only a short time, the records of the previous owner should also be examined. In fact, it is not out of line to ask for the owner's income tax return. The astute buyer knows that the firm's records reflect its condition.

Another area of interest is the firm's **profit trend.** Is it making more money year after year? More importantly, are profits going up as fast as sales, or is more and more revenue necessary in order to attain the same profit? If the latter is true, this means that the business may have to increase sales 5–10 percent annually to net as much as it did the previous year. This spells trouble and is often a sign that the owner is selling because "there are easier ways to make a living."

Finally, even if the company is making money, the prospective buyer should compare the firm's performance to that of similar companies. For example, if a small shop is making 22 percent return on investment this year in contrast to 16 percent two years ago, is this good or bad? It certainly appears to be good, but what if competing stores are making a 32 percent return on investment. Given this information, the firm is not doing as well.

One way of comparing a company to the competition is to obtain comparative information put out by firms like Dun & Bradstreet, which gather data on retail and wholesale firms in various fields and provide businesspeople with an overall view of many key financial ratios. For example, one of the most important is the **comparison of current assets** (cash or those things that can be turned into cash in the short run) **to current liabilities** (those debts that will come due in the short run). This key ratio reflects the ability of a business to meet its current obligations. A second key ratio is the **comparison of net profits to net sales.** How much profit is the owner making for every dollar in sales? A third key ratio is **net profit to net worth.** How much profit is the individual making for every dollar invested in the firm? Table 5-1 shows the median or average figure for these three key ratios for several important types of business.

Note that grocery stores have a low amount of current assets compared to current liabilities when contrasted with furniture stores. Likewise, grocery stores have a lower profit margin on sales than do furniture stores. A close look at the table also

Table 5-1 Key Ratios by Business

LINE OF BUSINESS (number of concerns reporting)	Current Assets to Current Liabilities (times)	Net Profit on Net Sales (percent)	Net Profit on Net Worth (percent)
Auto and home supply stores (2,073)	2.3	3.2	11.6
Family clothing stores (1,373)	4.0	3.8	10.2
Department stores (1,032)	3.2	1.8	6.7
Furniture stores (2,226)	5.7	8.9	25.8
Service stations (1,673)	2.1	2.1	15.3
Grocery stores (2,295)	2.2	1.6	14.8
Jewelry stores (1,762)	3.4	5.4	12.2
Stationery stores (1,502)	2.8	3.5	14.5

Source: The Dun & Bradstreet Corp., *Key Business Ratios,* 1986.

reveals that businesses with slow-moving merchandise, such as furniture stores, often have high net profit on net sales and on net worth. They may not sell a great deal of merchandise every day, but they make a nice profit on what they do sell.

By comparing the accounting information obtained from a business's books to financial data such as that illustrated in Table 5-1, it is possible to determine how well the business is doing. If things look good, then the prospective buyer can turn to the question of how much to offer the seller.

DETERMINING THE PRICE

After the previously mentioned questions and issues have been resolved, the prospective owner must answer one final question, "How much are you willing to pay for the business?" This is not an easy question to answer. However, because the enterprise is small there are fewer factors to be considered than if a large corporation were being purchased. Additionally, some commonly accepted indicators can be used to establish the value of an enterprise.

ASSESSING VALUE

A number of indexes reflect a small business's value. Five of the most important are

1. book value
2. replacement value
3. liquidation value
4. past earnings
5. cash flow

BOOK VALUE   This term refers to the value of the company's assets from an accounting standpoint. For example, if the firm bought a new machine for $25,000 last year and it has been in operation for one year, its book value would be $20,000, assuming five-year, straight-line depreciation. Likewise, if the business has bought 1,000 shirts for $7 each, they would be carried on the books for $7,000. However, if something has lost value, its book value should be written down; assets should be carried at *cost* or *present* value, whichever is *lower.* For example, if the enterprise has just learned that the 1,000 shirts it bought are now out of style, it may be lucky to get $4 each for them. The shirts should be written down from $7,000 to $4,000.

REPLACEMENT VALUE   This refers to how much it would cost to buy the same machinery, materials, or merchandise on the market today. In many cases, the use of replacement value increases the asking price for a business. For example, land is seldom on the books at replacement value. If the land was bought ten years ago for $50,000 it may be worth double that today. Likewise, using the replacement value of machinery and equipment, given the recent inflation, would seriously inflate the value of these assets. In fact, most assets increase in value if replacement value is used.

LIQUIDATION VALUE   This reflects the worth of the business's assets if they were thrown on the market today and purchased by knowledgeable buyers. This value is usually the lowest of those discussed here, because most assets sell for far less than their original purchase price. Consider the fact, for example, that most people at an auction expect to buy things more cheaply there than anywhere else. **Auction value** is thus the liquidation value. It is what the owner can get for the assets in a competitive bidding situation.

PAST EARNINGS   These are important because the bottom-line reason for buying someone's business is to make money. Therefore, the prospective owner would be wise to choose a business that has been profitable in the past and, based on industry indicators, will continue to be profitable. Of course to obtain these earnings one also needs the **physical assets** (building, machinery, material, inventory) but, in the final analysis, the prospective owner must be concerned with what he or she can earn with these assets.

CASH FLOW   This is still another measure of value. Cash flow is equal to net profit after taxes plus any "noncash" expenses such as depreciation, depletion, or amortization. **Noncash expenses** are items that can be written off on the company's income tax, thus saving it money while not requiring a layout of cash. We will discuss these later, but for the moment keep in mind that these expenses help free up cash for the firm. The reason many people use cash flow as an index of value is that high cash flows are instrumental in reducing debt and helping the firm expand. A company with a high cash flow, therefore, is preferable to one whose cash flow is moderate or low.

None of these five indexes of value is likely to be used exclusively when determining a fair price for a small business. However, the liquidation value tends to be favored over book value or replacement value if the firm is going out of business. Likewise, in any computation of purchase price, past earnings will play a major role. Before looking at a formula for determining a fair purchase price, however, we must consider asset pricing.

ASSET PRICING

The first thing a prospective buyer needs to do is approach the purchase of a business from a rational standpoint. An analogy can be drawn between buying a business and buying a car. If a car salesperson tells a customer a particular auto can be purchased for $10,000 and convinces the individual to buy it, the price can often be raised $500 or $1,000 without losing the sale. The salesperson tells the customer, "I did the best I could, my sales manager refuses to agree. Could you go to $11,000?" This is, in effect, saying, "I've done the best I could, now it's up to you." In car-dealer terminology, this is called "low balling" the customer. The same thing can happen in buying a small business. The seller hooks the buyer on the business, and the buyer, in a rush to buy, pays too much.

With this in mind, the prospective buyer needs to look at what the owner is selling. Some of the common assets and the ways to evaluate them are discussed here.

☐ BUILDING   If the company owns it, what value does it have on the company books? Deduct the cost of any repairs or alterations that are needed to keep the facility in working shape.

☐ INVENTORY Adjust the purchase price to account for slow-moving or obsolete items.

☐ EQUIPMENT Deduct depreciation from the purchase price. If some of the equipment is not usable because of age or obsolescence, pay no more than liquidation value for it.

☐ PREPAID EXPENSES Buy them at face value. They include fire and theft insurance premiums that the owner pays annually and have coverage remaining.

☐ SUPPLIES If they are usable, buy them at the price the owner paid, unless the price has changed. In that case adjust upward or downward to reflect the change.

☐ ACCOUNTS RECEIVABLE Purchase these customer obligations after first deducting those so old that they are deemed uncollectible. Also, if it appears that it will take 60 days, on average, to collect the rest, deduct 2–3 percent from the total as an expense in the investment in these receivables, unless there is a monthly charge on outstanding accounts. Remember: time is money, and unless the business charges the customer a monthly interest charge, the new owner is buying accounts receivable that will not be turned into cash for 60 days. Since most retail credit cards charge $1-1\frac{1}{2}$ percent a month, the buyer should make a similar charge to the seller.

☐ GOODWILL This is the excess of the selling price over the value of the physical assets. Goodwill depends on such things as (1) how long it would take to set up a similar business and the expense and risk associated with such a venture; (2) the amount of income to be made by purchasing an ongoing concern rather than starting a new one; (3) the price the owner of this business is asking for goodwill compared to that asked by owners of similar businesses; and (4) the value associated with the old owner's agreement to remain out of the same business within the competitive area.

Of these assets, goodwill is the only **intangible** one. The buyer cannot *see* goodwill; the individual can only try to assess its presence and assign a value to it. Before illustrating how this can be done, one final point merits discussion: the buyer should not pay more for goodwill than can be recovered from profits within a reasonable period of time. Usually this period is three to five years, although if one were purchasing a major corporation such as Coca-Cola, the goodwill price might take twenty years to recover because the product line is good for an indefinite period of time.

ONE ACCEPTABLE FORMULA

No one has a surefire way of attaching a price to the value of an ongoing small business. However, one formula is so uncomplicated and straightforward that it warrants our attention.[5] The seven steps of the formula are described here and illustrated with a real-life situation. Refer to Table 5-2 as you read the steps.

---

[5]"How to Buy or Sell a Business," *Small Business Reporter,* Vol. 8, No. 11 (San Francisco: Bank of America National Trust and Savings Association, 1969), p. 11.

Table 5-2 Determining a Purchase Price

STEP		AMOUNT
1. Liabilities or market value of all assets, minus liabilities		$100,000
2. Earning power at 10%	$10,000	
3. Salary for the owner-manager	15,000	
	$25,000	
4. Average annual earnings before subtracting the owner-manager's salary	30,000	
5. Extra earning power of the business (step 4 minus step 3)	5,000	
6. Value of intangibles using a 5-year profit figure (5 times step 5)		25,000
7. Final price (step 1 plus step 6)		$125,000

Step 1: Determine the value of the business by identifying the liquidation or market value of all the assets and then subtracting the debts or liabilities of the business. This has been determined to be $100,000 for the sake of our example.

Step 2: Determine how much the buyer could earn with this money if it were invested somewhere else. If the risk in the current business is very high, this percentage should be set at perhaps 15–25 percent. If the risk is not very great, 10 percent would be a fair figure. In our example the earning power has been set at 10 percent.

Step 3: To that figure must be added a salary for the owner-manager. This figure has been set at $15,000. The sum of steps 2 and 3 represents the total that the prospective buyer could expect to earn if the investment were placed elsewhere and the efforts involved in working in the business are taken into account.

Step 4: Determine the average net profit before taxes and the salary the owner-manager can obtain from this business over the next few years. This is a key calculation because it forces the buyer to answer the question, How long will it take to recoup the investment? This figure has been determined to be $30,000.

Step 5: Subtract the earning power and the salary (steps 2 and 3) from the average net earnings figure in step 4. This represents the "extra earning power" the buyer will obtain by owning this business.

Step 6: Take this extra earning power and estimate the number of years it will exist. This, in effect, represents what the buyer is willing to pay for the firm's goodwill. In our example, a five-year profit figure has been used. This means that the buyer is willing to pay $25,000 for the firm's intangible assets. If the firm is well established, 5 is a reasonable multiplier. If it is a new company, it is common to find the multiplier varying between 1 and 3. Obviously, the better-established the business, the more the buyer should be willing to pay for goodwill.

Step 7: This is the final price. It is equal to the net market value of the assets plus the value of the intangibles. In this case the buyer has set a purchase price of $125,000 as fair and reasonable.

An advantage of this formula is that it helps the buyer arrive at a fair price for the intangible assets, specifically goodwill. In our example (Table 5-2), the total of the earning power and the owner-manager's salary was less than the average annual net earnings. This can be easily verified by comparing the total of steps 2 and 3 with that in step 4: the latter is larger. However, if the latter is *not* larger, the seller should not assign *any* value to goodwill, because the earning power of the investment and the amount the buyer can earn from personal effort are *greater* than can be obtained from running the business. How then does the buyer decide on a final selling price?

In this case the buyer needs to recalculate the price by determining the average annual profit and capitalizing it by the desired rate of return. For example, assume that the initial data in Table 5-2 are the same except that the average annual net earnings before subtracting the earning power and owner-manager's salary is only $20,000. In this case there is no extra earning power from the business (step 5), and the value of the intangibles (step 6) will be zero. Additionally, since the buyer wants to obtain an earning power of 10 percent (step 2), it is necessary to take the average annual net earnings and subtract the owner-manager's salary:

$$\$20,000 - \$15,000 = \$5,000 \text{ profit}$$

After the new owner takes a salary of $15,000, only $5,000 will be left as a return on the original investment. Since the individual wants to secure a 10 percent return on the original investment, the purchase price must be 10 times the profit, or

$$\$5,000 \div 0.10 = \$50,000 \text{ purchase price}$$

Since this may be difficult to grasp without practice, another example is in order. This time, still using the data in Table 5-2, assume that the average net earnings before the owner-manager's salary is subtracted is $23,000. In this case, then, the buyer's profit after salary is deducted will be

$$\$23,000 - \$15,000 = \$8,000 \text{ profit}$$

Since the individual wishes to make a 10 percent return on the investment, the purchase price is equal to 10 times the profit, or

$$\$8,000 \div 0.10 = \$80,000 \text{ purchase price}$$

Finally, consider an example for which the basic data in Table 5-2 still apply but the average annual net earnings before the owner-manager's salary is $25,000. How much should the individual now pay for the business? The answer is $100,000 because there will be no extra earning power. The person will just clear the desired 10 percent on investment if there is a profit of $25,000 before taxes and salary, and $10,000 after the salary is deducted. This leaves a return of 10 percent, which, as seen in step 2 of the table, is the desired earning power.

Before closing this discussion about buying an ongoing concern, a final point is in order. The formula we've presented provides a reasonable estimate of what to pay for a small business. However, this price must be tempered by how badly a seller wants to get rid of the business and how much the buyer wants to acquire it. Quite often the *desire* of either or both parties dictates the final selling price, and a mathematical formula is just the beginning. Thus, in the first example where a final selling price of

$125,000 was reached, the buyer would have to compare this price with the asking price. If the seller wants $130,000, the buyer might offer $120,000 and then negotiate up to $125,000. This does not mean, however, that the final price will always be the midpoint between the original asking price and the original bid. If the seller refuses to accept less than $130,000, the buyer should either walk away from the deal or agree to pay a premium for the business. In this case the individual's return will be reduced slightly because more is being paid for the business. Would such a purchase be wise? This question can be answered only by the prospective purchaser, for in the final analysis "fair price" is whatever the buyer is willing to pay.[6]

BE PREPARED TO ASSUME CONTROL

By the time the price is agreed upon, the new owner ought to have an **action plan** already outlined. This plan should have two parts. First, financing of the business should be arranged. How is the money to be raised? If some of the funds are to be borrowed, the individual should already have discussed the matter with a banker and know how much money the bank is willing to lend. Otherwise, personal sources of capital should be investigated.

Second, will business continue as before, or must some specific changes be made in the operation? If the new owner has decided to change some things, the plan for implementing these changes should be operational so that it can be put into effect immediately.

Buying a business is somewhat like bidding on a house: if the seller accepts, the buyer must be prepared to pay the asking price and move in. Thus, the question the prospective buyer should be asking when bidding for a small business is not "Will the seller accept this price?" but "What will I do if the seller accepts my offer?" Unless the potential owner can answer this question satisfactorily, more planning is necessary.

The Small Business Owner's Notebook provides an interesting look at the "other side" of buying a business. The tips for selling a business are presented in order to better realize the maximum price a seller is attempting to negotiate. (See Small Business Owner's Notebook: Tips for Selling a Business.)

■ SUMMARY

There are a number of advantages to buying an ongoing business. Three of the most important are that there need be little or no concern about its successful future operation, the time and effort associated with starting a new enterprise are eliminated, and a bargain price may be possible.

Before deciding whether to buy, however, the prospective owner needs to be concerned with asking and answering a series of *right questions*. These include: Why is the business being sold? What is the physical condition of the business? What is the condition of the inventory? What is the state of the company's other assets? How

---

[6]For a thorough analysis on valuation of a business see "Valuing a Closely Held Business," *The Small Business Report,* November 1986, pp. 30–34; and "Buying a Business: What to Watch Out For," *Financial Enterprise,* Summer 1987, pp. 13–14.

■ SMALL BUSINESS OWNER'S NOTEBOOK ■

Tips for Selling a Business

Regardless of the reason you are selling your business, keeping the following ten suggestions in mind can help to maximize the amount of money you make on the deal.

1. When negotiations concerning the sale of the business occur, allow professionals in the merger and acquisitions field to handle all the talking. This will prevent the owner's personal feelings and ego from preventing a sound business deal.

2. Try to find a buyer that sees the potential of your business in the long run. This type of client, known as a "strategic buyer," will be willing to pay more for the business.

3. Be sure to carefully consider the net after-tax effect of the sale. Each type of sale may have different tax consequences.

4. Consider a flexible payment schedule. The buyer may be willing to pay more if the payments are deferred over time.

5. Remember that an attractive selling price can be obtained, even if there is an asset that you wish to keep (such as real estate, patents, or an automobile).

6. Try to get the buyer to assume both balance sheet and "off balance sheet" liabilities.

7. Request an employment contract that states your availability to work or consult for a fee.

8. As part of the sale, seek reimbursement of all legal and other fees.

9. If the long-term future of the business looks good, you may earn more money by accepting contingent payments if they are offered by the buyer.

10. Since state income rates vary widely, consider relocating your home. A new location may be more beneficial to you before selling your business.

Before making the decision to sell, be sure to check all avenues so that you can maximize the money you receive for the hard work you have put into your business.

Source: Ira D. Cohen, "Ten Tips When Selling Your Firm," *Small Business Reports*, August 1990, pp. 42–45.

many of the employees will remain? What competition does the business face? What is the firm's financial picture?

After all of these questions have been answered satisfactorily, the prospective buyer must determine how much he or she is willing to pay for the business. Some of the indexes of a small business's value are book value, replacement value, liquidation value, past earnings, and cash flow. In the final analysis, however, the prospective owner should be concerned with buying the company's assets at *market value,* and then paying something for *goodwill* if it is deemed to be an asset.

■ REVIEW AND DISCUSSION QUESTIONS

1. What are the advantages of buying an ongoing business? Explain them.

2. What "right questions" need to be answered in deciding whether to buy a business?

3. Which is the most important in item 2 above? Why?

4 How can Dun & Bradstreet help a prospective small business owner evaluate an ongoing firm and decide whether or not to buy it?

5. What is book value? Replacement value? Liquidation value? Past earnings? Cash flow?

6. How should a prospective buyer go about pricing the assets of a company? Explain.

7. What are the seven steps involved in pricing a small business?

8. A prospective buyer is thinking about purchasing a small business. The following facts have been gathered: liquidation value of all assets minus liabilities is $200,000; earning power desired is 20 percent; the prospective buyer needs a yearly salary of $20,000; average annual earnings before subtracting the owner-manager's salary are $40,000; any extra earning power is estimated to be of value for 5 years. How much should the buyer be willing to pay for the business?

9. If the price is agreed to, the buyer should be prepared to take control. What does "taking control" involve?

Case Studies

For Sale—The Mirror Shop

■ The Mirror Shop, located on the corner of Seventh and Main, is the best-known mirror store in a city of 400,000 people. Phyllis and Peter Schmidt have owned and managed the operation for over twenty years.

The shop specializes in the design and installation of mirrors but also does picture framing. For example, last month a local restaurant and bar wanted the mirror behind its bar replaced. This can be quite a job, but Phyllis, Peter, and their staff of five designed and installed the mirror within three days. Another typical job is the installation of wall mirrors in homes. One of their recent jobs was installing a large plate-glass mirror in the foyer and another large mirror with an etched design on a stairway wall in a home. Not all of their jobs are this complex. Quite a few of them simply require the mounting of pictures behind glass.

The Schmidts rent their store. They currently have a favorable five-year lease with three years left to run. They have $12,000 worth of inventory consisting mostly of mirrors, frames, glass, and equipment needed to cut glass and mount pictures. There are also some samples of their work located in the front window. Finally, they have a truck that contains equipment needed for on-site installation. The book value of their assets is $20,000. With total annual sales of $150,000, the Schmidts have been able to clear $35,000 annually after all expenses, except federal taxes.

Last month Mr. Schmidt went for his annual physical. The doctor diagnosed a heart problem and strongly urged him to consider retirement. Although he is only 58 years old, Mr. Schmidt has decided to follow the doctor's advice. Through a mutual friend he has been in touch with Stanley Casey, who has worked in the mirror business for twenty years. Stanley has looked over Mr. Schmidt's operation and thinks it would be a good buy. However, Stanley has never owned an enterprise of his own; he has always worked for someone else. The Schmidts are asking $100,000 for their operation. Stanley is uncertain about whether this is a fair price.

1. What types of questions should Stanley be able to answer before deciding whether or not to buy the Schmidts' business?

2. Would a firm like this have any goodwill? Explain.

3. How should Stanley compute a purchase price? Explain.

Deciding What to Pay

■ Cynthia Smith is thinking about buying a small manufacturing firm. The company has been in business for 35 years and has a national reputation for precision machine tooling. The founder and owner, Paul Prentiss, would like to turn the firm over to his two children, but neither of them wants it. So he has decided to sell the firm and set up trust funds for his grandchildren.

Cynthia has talked to Paul on three occasions and knows that he has an offer of $650,000 for the firm. Apparently Paul believes that the company is worth more than this and is going to hold out for a higher price. Based on her review of Paul's books, Cynthia has arrived at the following conclusions:

  □ The market value of all assets is $625,000.

  □ Paul is drawing a salary of $50,000 annually.

  □ All of the personnel, including Paul, will stay on.

  □ A fair earning rate on the investment is 15%.

  □ Average annual net earnings before subtracting the owner's salary is $200,000.

  □ Because of the firm's reputation, the years-of-profit multiplier should be 6.

1. Given the above data, how much would you recommend that Cynthia pay for the firm?

2. What would you recommend she pay for it if the average annual earnings before subtracting the owner's salary were $175,000?

3. How much would you recommend if the average annual earnings before subtracting the owner's salary were $150,000?

You Be the Consultant

A POTENTIAL BUSINESS

Bob Whitney and his wife Angie are both physical education instructors at an urban high school. Last year Bob's grandparents died and left him an inheritance of $150,000. Not sure of what to do with the money, Bob and Angie decided to put it into a savings account at 5 percent interest. By the end of the year they had accumulated $7,500 in interest, all of which was taxable. Their next-door neighbor, an accountant, advised they get into something that would shelter some of their taxes. "Look into a business," he suggested.

Bob and Angie do not know very much about business. They have never had a course in any aspect of either management or finance. However, they do feel they understand something about the need for physical fitness and would be comfortable in a business in this field. Last week Bob learned about an indoor racquetball club that was built three years ago. The original cost for the 20 racquetball courts, dressing rooms, sauna, and lounge was $500,000. The owner told his banker that he would like to sell this investment and get into something else. The banker just happens to be the Whitneys' banker as well, and that is how Bob and Angie learned about the venture.

The banker set up a telephone meeting with the owner, Karl Coopersmith. Karl suggested that the three of them meet at the club and tour the facilities. During the tour the Whitneys noticed that the facilities were in good shape. They saw a lot of people coming and going, and all of the courts were in use the entire time they were there. Karl told them that he would like to sell and is in the process of contacting a number of local bankers and accountants he knows to see if any of their clients would be interested in buying the club, either individually or in partnership. Karl told the Whitneys that the membership dues are $175 per year, which entitles the member to use the exercise room and the saunas. The cost for playing racquetball is $7 an hour and up to four people can play at once. Due to the great demand in the area, members have to call at least five days in advance to reserve a court. Karl also told them that there are currently 1,211 members and that unless more courts are built the club cannot support more than another 89 members. "As it is," he said, "it is getting difficult to get a court on the weekend or in the evening. I've got just about all the members I can handle."

Bob and Angie admitted to Karl that they do not know a lot about business. He encouraged them to have their accountant come by and look at his books and advise them on the profitability of the venture. "I won't throw numbers at you," he said, "because I know you are not trained in accounting. Let's let your accountant decide if this is the right type of business for you to buy. However, let me give you the bottom line. It cost me $500,000 to build the club and I won't sell it for less than $600,000. I have an outstanding loan at the bank for just under $450,000, so I want $150,000 cash and the owners can assume my loan at the rate I got last year, which is 1 percent lower than loans today." Bob and Angie told Karl that they would be in touch.

■ **YOUR CONSULTATION** Assume that you are advising Bob and Angie on whether or not to buy the racquetball club. What would you tell them? Be specific in your recommendations. In particular, would you suggest that they go it alone or seek other partners? Have they asked the right questions? What further questions do you feel should be asked? What stipulations should they require of Karl?

CHAPTER 6

Operating a Franchise

Objectives

In some cases a prospective small business owner-manager will neither want to start a business from scratch nor buy an existing one. In this case a prospective owner may want to take a middle-of-the-road approach by purchasing a franchise such as a McDonald's, a Subway sandwich shop, or a TCBY Yogurt shop. Many of these units are owned and managed by individual investors but operate under the franchisor's rules and regulations.

The first objective of Chapter 6 is to look at the nature and growth of franchising. We will then examine the advantages and disadvantages of franchising and explain the steps to follow in evaluating franchise opportunities. The final objective is to discuss the future of franchising. When you have completed Chapter 6 you will be able to:

1. *Define the term* franchise.

2. *Describe the difference between the franchising of a product or service and the franchising of an entire business operation.*

3. *Discuss the growth of franchising in the last decade.*

4. *State four advantages of franchising.*

5. *Identify and discuss three disadvantages of franchising.*

6. *Prepare an action plan for evaluating a franchise operation to determine if it is a good deal.*

7. *Answer the question "What is the future of franchising?"*

THE NATURE OF FRANCHISING

A **franchise** is a system of distribution that enables a supplier (the *franchisor*) to arrange for a dealer (the *franchisee*) to handle a specific product or service under certain mutually agreed upon conditions. In most cases the franchisee is given the right to distribute and sell goods or services within a specific area. The business itself is owned by the franchisee and the franchisor is paid a fee and/or a commission on sales. In essence, there are two types of franchising arrangements: the franchising of a product or service and the franchising of an entire business enterprise.

PRODUCT OR SERVICE FRANCHISE

When a *product* is franchised, the franchisee receives the goods from the franchisor and sells them through a wholesale or retail outlet. An auto dealership provides an illustration. The owner receives cars from an auto manufacturer and has an exclusive right to sell them. Retail purchasers cannot buy directly from the factory. They must go through a dealer who has a franchise. Another illustration of product franchising is the local General Electric dealer. This individual receives the product from the company and, in turn, sells it to the consumer. Retail firms that sell a wide variety of goods will have franchise agreements with many different manufacturers for all kinds of products: General Electric for air conditioners, RCA for radios, Magnavox for televisions, Whirlpool for washers and dryers, and so forth. In all of these cases, the control that is exerted over the retailer by the supplier is small and it is limited to the particular franchised product. The franchisor does not attempt to control the operation of the business itself.

When a *service* is franchised, the franchisee receives a license for a trade name and the particular services to be sold. Again, the franchisor does not attempt to control the operation of the business itself. The franchisee directs daily activities—hiring and firing of employees, operational business decisions, and budgeting concerns—whereas the franchisor maintains control over certain standardization features expected of all franchisees.

BUSINESS FRANCHISE

When the word franchise is used today, however, it often refers to the *franchising of an entire business enterprise.*[1] Common examples include McDonald's, Pizza Hut, and Burger King. In these cases, the franchisee operates the unit under a common trade name. The business operation, the establishment's appearance, the merchandise, and even the operating procedures are standardized to a high degree. In an effort to maintain this standardized image and marketing approach to the general buying public, the franchisor usually maintains a strong, formalized system of control over the business operation. In this type of a franchise arrangement the responsibilities of both parties, the franchisor and the franchisee, are spelled out in the franchise contract and are usually considered to be of mutual advantage to both parties. The remainder of this chapter focuses on the franchising of an entire enterprise as opposed to the franchising of a particular product, product line, or service. (See Small Business Success: Franchisor and Franchisee.)

HOW A SMALL BUSINESS FRANCHISE WORKS

Franchise systems for goods and services generally work the same way. The franchisee, an independent business person, contracts for a complete business package. This usually requires the individual to do one or more of the following:

---

[1] J. Donald Weinrauch, "Franchising an Established Business," *Journal of Small Business Management,* July 1986, pp. 1–7.

■ **SMALL BUSINESS SUCCESS** ■

Franchisor and Franchisee

Since the mid-sixties, the Rosati family in Chicago has developed and expanded its pizza operations very successfully. Using primarily family members, the company established 30 different locations throughout the Chicago metropolitan area.

In 1988 Rosati's Pizza ventured into franchising by offering its business to people outside the family organization for the first time. As the company changed from a family-run business to a franchise, the owners faced the challenges of setting up a support system, developing a collective buying program, and creating an advertising program for a nationwide franchise.

Just as the Rosati family owners began to achieve success with their franchise system in 1989, they decided to expand their entree selections to include pasta. Rather than create a new set of manuals and menus of their own, the Rosatis purchased the rights to five Pasta Lovers Trattoria franchises. Today they are both franchisors *and* franchisees. In an effort to avoid expenses and gain efficiency, the Rosatis sacrificed some of the control and independence they had come to know over the years. Yet, they believe that the experience gained from each role (franchisor and franchisee) improves their overall performance.

The Rosati experience is relatively new in the franchise industry, but it is one that will become more popular as this combination proves successful.

Source: Adapted from Frances Huffman, "Switch Hitters," *Entrepreneur*, January 1991, pp. 235–40.

1. Make a financial investment in the operation.
2. Obtain and maintain a standardized inventory and/or equipment package that is usually purchased from the franchisor.
3. Maintain a specified quality of performance.
4. Follow the specific operating procedures and promotional efforts of the franchisor.
5. Pay a franchise fee as well as a percentage of the gross revenues.
6. Engage in a continuing business relationship.

In turn, the franchisor provides the following types of benefits and assistance:

1. The company name. For example, if someone bought a Burger King franchise, they could use this name outside the unit. This would provide the business with drawing power. A well-known name, such as Burger King, ensures higher sales than an unknown name, such as Ralph's Big Burgers.

2. Identifying symbols, logos, designs, and facilities. For example, all McDonald's units have the same identifying golden arches outside. Likewise, the facilities are similar inside.

3. Professional management training for each independent unit's staff.

4. Sale of specific merchandise necessary for the unit's operation at wholesale prices. Usually provided are all of the equipment to run the operation as well as the food or materials needed for the final product.

5. Financial assistance, if needed, to help the unit in any way possible.

6. Continuing aid and guidance to ensure that everything is being done in accordance with the contract.[2]

THE GROWTH OF SMALL BUSINESS FRANCHISING

Franchising has proved to be a very popular vehicle for becoming a small business owner. As Figure 6-1 shows, more than 509,000 franchises were establishments by 1988. The federal government estimates that franchise business accounted for approximately $640 billion in sales that year.[3] The number of franchised businesses in various industries and their 1988 estimated sales are listed in Table 6-1. Of these, a number have become household words: McDonald's, Kentucky Fried Chicken, and Burger King, to name but three.

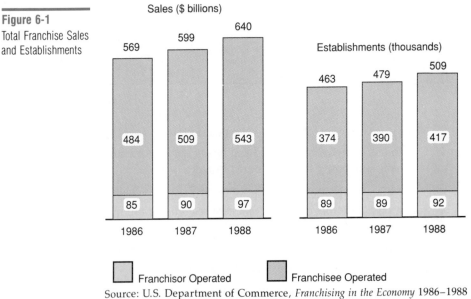

Figure 6-1
Total Franchise Sales and Establishments

Source: U.S. Department of Commerce, *Franchising in the Economy* 1986–1988 (Washington, D.C.: U.S. Government Printing Office, 1988), p.2.

[2]For a complete resources book, see Robert Justis and Richard Judd, *Franchising* (Cincinnati, OH: Southwestern Publishing Company, 1989).

[3]U.S. Department of Commerce, *Franchising in the Economy: 1986–1988* (Washington, D.C.: U.S. Government Printing Office, 1988) Chart 1, p. 2.

Table 6-1 Franchising in the Economy: 1988

Kinds of Franchised Business	Establishments (Number)			Sales ($000)			Percent Change 1987–1988		Percent Change 1986–1988	
	Total	Company-owned	Franchisee-owned	Total	Company-owned	Franchisee-owned	Estab.	Sales	Estab.	Sales
Total: All Franchising	**509,278**	**92,400**	**416,878**	**639,607,533**	**97,042,320**	**542,565,213**	**6.3**	**6.7**	**10.2**	**12.4**
Automobile and Truck Dealers	27,750	0	27,750	335,445,000	0	335,445,000	0.5	4.9	0.5	9.2
Automotive Products and Services	41,467	5,190	36,277	13,739,965	4,542,359	9,197,606	5.5	11.8	12.8	21.6
Business Aids and Services	62,977	7,021	55,956	16,840,651	2,900,195	13,940,456	11.0	14.9	19.5	26.7
Accounting, Credit, Collection Agencies and General Business Systems	2,215	21	2,194	189,489	5,365	184,124	11.1	10.6	15.7	17.1
Employment Services	6,881	2,489	4,392	4,235,061	1,949,130	2,285,931	12.8	15.5	22.8	31.5
Printing and Copying Services	6,361	114	6,247	1,361,280	35,600	1,325,680	14.4	16.0	29.7	32.3
Tax Preparation	8,640	3,533	5,107	521,815	279,357	242,458	2.2	2.5	4.4	13.1
Real Estate	16,916	144	16,772	6,402,447	60,750	6,341,697	11.5	13.6	20.7	24.7
Miscellaneous Business Services	21,964	720	21,244	4,130,559	569,993	3,560,566	13.0	18.0	22.0	25.8
Construction, Home Improvements, Maintenance and Cleaning Services	25,473	838	24,635	6,245,914	1,624,194	4,621,720	17.5	19.6	34.8	35.3
Convenience Stores	17,211	9,598	7,613	13,561,555	7,857,425	5,704,130	5.6	10.0	10.9	20.2
Educational Products and Services	10,620	611	10,009	1,181,480	292,588	888,892	10.5	15.2	23.1	26.3
Restaurants (all types)	90,789	27,027	63,762	63,231,119	21,927,963	41,303,156	8.9	11.2	16.1	21.0
Gasoline Service Stations	112,000	20,160	91,840	91,894,000	16,541,000	75,353,000	– 3.3	3.0	– 7.1	6.1
Hotels, Motels and Campgrounds	10,358	1,351	9,007	19,700,444	5,713,869	13,986,575	11.6	11.0	26.3	23.3
Laundry and Drycleaning Services	2,570	227	2,343	405,872	58,342	347,530	17.4	26.9	11.9	39.1
Recreation, Entertainment and Travel	8,926	441	8,485	4,990,490	779,785	4,210,705	9.1	24.2	13.0	40.6
Rental Services (Auto-Truck)	10,554	2,515	8,039	6,977,735	3,958,710	3,019,025	5.6	6.8	10.8	13.4
Rental Services (Equipment)	3,332	667	2,665	766,835	227,985	538,850	17.1	17.8	22.6	7.1
Retailing (Non-Food)	52,842	12,121	40,721	28,469,458	8,665,905	19,803,553	10.4	12.0	16.2	23.2
Retailing (Food other than Convenience Stores)	23,647	3,477	20,170	12,088,630	3,034,349	9,054,281	15.4	9.2	19.1	12.5
Soft Drink Bottlers	1,070	589	481	22,134,000	18,593,000	3,541,000	– 2.8	6.0	– 11.1	12.6
Miscellaneous	7,692	567	7,125	1,934,385	324,651	1,609,734	13.9	28.4	25.6	48.1

Source: U.S. Department of Commerce, *Franchising in the Economy* (Washington, D.C.: U.S. Government Printing Office, 1988), p. 28.

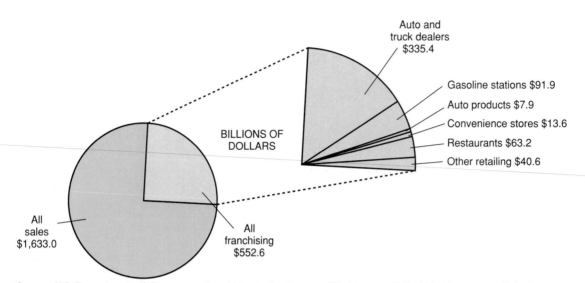

Source: U.S. Department of Commerce, *Franchising in the Economy* (Washington, D.C.: U.S. Government Printing Office, 1988), p. 15.

Figure 6-2
Franchising
Encompasses 34%
of Retail Sales

One example of the dominance of franchises can be seen in the retail industry. Thirty-four percent of all U.S. retail sales were attributed to franchises accounting for a total of $552.6 billion. (See Figure 6-2.)

Despite the growing popularity of franchises, the potential franchisee needs to be aware that many franchise operations fail. Table 6-2 lists the most common reasons for failure and tells how these major pitfalls can be avoided.

Franchising has also opened up **opportunities for minorities.** For example, of the 2,177 franchisors the federal government recently surveyed, 572 reported a total of 10,142 units owned by minority businesspersons. Included in this group were 3,615 African Americans; 2,808 persons with Spanish surnames; 3,616 Asian Americans;

Table 6-2 Reasons for Failure and Success in Franchising

REASON FOR FAILURE	PRESCRIPTION FOR SUCCESS
Bad location	Excellent physical location
Stiff competition	Prosperous on-going small business
Inadequate capital	Financial strength
Management "spread too thin"	Solid management team
Inappropriate business concept	A unique and protected process or marketable idea
Weak organizational structure	Simple, well-defined concept that franchisees can easily implement
Poor legal/contractual framework	Appropriate legal structure
Poor quality control	Quality control for products and services
Selling franchise outlets too quickly	Strong financial backing
Unexpected operating expenditures	Healthy gross margins
Changing consumer tastes	Long-term market prospects

Source: J. Donald Weinrauch, "Franchising an Established Business," *Journal of Small Business Management,* July 1986, p. 3. Reprinted by permission.

Franchising companies: 354
Number of franchising outlets: 31,626

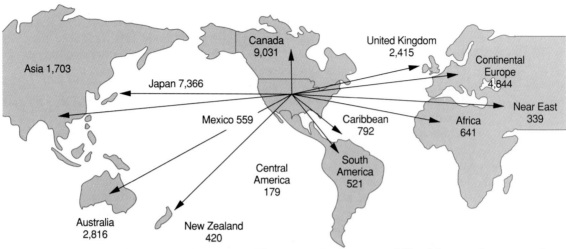

Figure 6-3
International
Franchising

and 103 native Americans. The most minority-owned franchises are in auto products and service businesses, restaurants, food stores, and convenience stores.[4]

Expansion into **foreign markets** by U.S. franchisors has continued to increase. In 1971 there were 156 companies with a total of 3,365 units in overseas locations. In 1986 there were 354 franchisors with a total of 31,626 overseas units.[5] In most cases the franchisor has sold the outlets to the franchisee either directly or through a master licensee who holds the right to develop the franchisor's system in a specific country or region of the world. In a small percentage of cases the franchisor has run the unit directly or engaged in a joint venture with local operating partners. Figure 6-3 shows the general distribution of international franchises.

ADVANTAGES OF FRANCHISING

A number of advantages are associated with franchising.[6] Some of the most important advantages are listed below:

1. Training and guidance are provided by the franchisor.
2. The franchise provides brand-name appeal.
3. The track record of other franchisees provides proof of success.
4. Financial assistance can be secured from the franchisor.

The following sections examine each of these advantages.

---

[4]U.S. Department of Commerce, *Franchising in the Economy,* p. 11.

[5]U.S. Department of Commerce, *Franchising in the Economy,* p.9.

[6]See Alden Peterson and Rajiv P. Dant, "Perceived Advantages of the Franchise Option From the Franchisee Perspective: Empirical Insights From A Service Franchise,"*Journal of Small Business Management*, July 1990, pp. 46–61.

TRAINING AND GUIDANCE

Perhaps the greatest advantage of buying a franchise, as compared to starting a new business or buying an existing one, is that the franchisor will usually provide both training and guidance to the franchisee. As a result, the likelihood of success is much greater for national franchisees who have received this assistance than for small-business owners in general. For example, it has been reported that the ratio of failure for small enterprises in general to franchised businesses, may be as high as 4 or 5 to 1.

Some of the best-known training programs are those offered by McDonald's and Holiday Inn. At McDonald's the owner is sent to "Hamburger U" before starting the business. There the individual learns how to make the hamburgers, manage the unit, control inventory, keep records, and deal with personnel problems. Other national franchisors provide the same kind of training. For example, the Mister Donut franchise requires each owner to attend an eight-week training course in which they cover topics such as doughnut making, merchandising, production scheduling, labor scheduling, advertising, and accounting. One of the greatest advantages of these training programs is that they provide an individual who has only a limited amount of training in business the opportunity to pick up a great deal of practical information that can spell the difference between success and failure.

Another benefit is that of **continuing assistance.** A well-operated franchise system stays in continual contact with the franchises, providing them with practical business tips, follow-up training, and pamphlets and manuals designed to make the overall operation more efficient.

BRAND-NAME APPEAL

An individual who buys a well-known national franchise, especially a big-name one, has a good chance to succeed. The franchisor's name is a drawing card for the establishment. Commenting on this point, the chairman of the board of Horn & Hardart summed up the importance of having the Burger King franchise in Manhattan by noting, "I could walk down there today, take down the Burger King sign, and put one up that read Fred's Burgers, and volume would drop 60 percent before the end of the day."[7]

People are often more aware of the product or service offered by a national franchise and prefer it to those offered by lesser-known outlets. One way the large franchisors accomplish this brand-name appeal is through advertising. Consider the television commercials you see and hear every day from Burger King, McDonald's, Pizza Hut, Subway, Kentucky Fried Chicken, Denny's, and a host of other national franchises. They all have catchy jingles that help create that all-important brand-name appeal.

A PROVEN TRACK RECORD

Another benefit of buying a franchise is that the franchisor has already proved that the operation can be successful. Of course, if someone is the first individual to buy a franchise, this is not the case. However, if the organization has been around for five

---

[7]"Fast-Food Franchisors Squeeze Out the Little Guy," *Business Week,* May 31, 1976, p. 42.

to ten years and has fifty or more units, it should not be difficult to check to see how successful the operations have been. If all of the units are still in operation and the owners report that they are doing well financially, one thing is certain: the franchisor has proved that the layout and location of the store, the pricing policy, the quality of the goods or service, and the overall management system are successful. If a person buys a successful business from another individual, it may be difficult to determine how much of its success is a function of the old owner's personality or drive. However, when one buys into a franchise organization in which there have been many successes, it is likely that the franchising concept accounts for success rather than the managerial skills or drive of one individual. (Table 6-3 provides some information on selected franchise opportunities.)

FINANCIAL ASSISTANCE

Another reason a franchise can be a good investment is that the franchisor may be able to help the new owner secure the financial assistance needed to run the operation. For example, many bankers will think twice about lending an owner money to open an automobile-transmission-repair operation. However, if it is an AAMCO transmission, this might be a different story. The banker knows that if the prospective businessperson is going to be associated with a national chain, the chances of going bankrupt will be greatly reduced because the franchisor will stand behind the individual and try to help in every way possible. In fact, in some cases franchisors have personally helped the franchisee get started by lending the individual money and not requiring any repayment until the operation is up and running smoothly. In short, buying a franchise is often an ideal way to ensure assistance from the financial community.

DISADVANTAGES OF FRANCHISING

The prospective franchisee must weigh the advantages of franchising against the accompanying disadvantages. Some of the most important drawbacks are

1. franchise fees
2. the control exercised by the franchisor
3. awareness of some of the unfulfilled promises from franchisors

The following sections examine each of these disadvantages.

FRANCHISE FEES

In business, no one gets something for nothing. The larger and more successful the franchisor, the greater the franchise fee that is usually charged. In order to get a franchise from a national chain it is not uncommon to be faced with a fee of $5,000 to $100,000. Smaller franchisors or those who have not had great success charge less. Nevertheless, when deciding whether or not to take the franchise route into small business, it is necessary to weigh the return you could get by putting the money into another type of business. Also, remember that this fee covers only the benefits discussed in the previous section. The prospective franchisee must also pay for building the unit and stocking it, although the franchisor may help out here by providing assistance in securing a bank loan. Additionally, there is usually a fee tied to gross

Table 6-3 Franchise Opportunities

THE 25 FASTEST-GROWING FRANCHISES

1. Subway/*Submarine Sandwiches*/1,174
2. Jani-King/*Commercial Cleaning*/562
3. Coverall North America Inc./*Commercial Cleaning*/510
4. Intelligent Electronics Inc./*Computer-Related Products & Services*/497
5. Chem-Dry/*Carpet, Upholstery & Drapery Cleaning/Dyeing*/372
6. Little Caesars Pizza/*Pizza*/322
7. Mail Boxes Etc. USA/*Packing, Mailing & Shipping Services*/320
8. Jazzercise Inc./*Fitness Centers*/307
9. Choice Hotels & Motels Int'l./*Hotels & Motels*/271
10. Hardee's/*Misc. Fast Foods*/253
11. Electronic Realty Associates/*Real Estate Services*/246
12. Heel/Sew Quik/*Shoe Repair*/240
13. Sport It/*Sports Equipment*/237
14. Nutri System/*Diet & Weight-Control Centers*/215
15. Worldwide Refinishing Systems Inc./*Porcelain/Marble Restoration*/197
16. Arby's Inc./*Misc. Fast Foods*/190
17. ServiceMaster/*Commercial Cleaning*/176
18. Decorating Den/*Misc. Decorative Products & Services*/175
19. Days Inns of America Franchising Inc./*Hotels & Motels*/172
20. ABC Seamless Inc./*Siding*/150
21. Help U-Sell Real Estate/*Real Estate Services*/148
22. Handle With Care Packaging Store/*Packing, Mailing & Shipping Services*/146
23. Jackson Hewitt Tax Service/*Income Tax Services*/134
24. Fax-9/*Business Add-On Services*/124
24. I Can't Believe It's Yogurt/*Frozen Yogurt*/124
25. Floor Coverings Int'l./*Floor & Wall-Coverings Stores*/122

THE TOP 25 LOW-INVESTMENT FRANCHISES

1. Jazzercise Inc./*Fitness Centers*
2. H & R Block/*Income Tax Services*
3. Packy The Shipper/*Business Add-On Services*
4. Novus Windshield Repair/*Auto Glass Services*
5. Duraclean/*Carpet, Upholstery & Drapery Cleaning/Dyeing*
6. Sport It/*Sports Equipment*
7. Homes & Land Magazine/*Publishing Businesses*
8. Fax-9/*Business Add-On Services*
9. Triple Check Income Tax Service/*Income Tax Services*
10. Uniclean Systems Inc./*Commercial Cleaning*
11. Floor Coverings Int'l./*Floor & Wall-Coverings Stores*
12. American Poolplayers Association/*Sports Activities*
13. Stork News/*Announcement Services*
14. Bighorn Sheepskin Co./*Misc. Retail Products*
15. Spotless Office Services/*Commercial Cleaning*
16. Rug Doctor Pro/*Carpet, Upholstery & Drapery Cleaning/Dyeing*
17. Computerized Travel Service Network/*Travel Services*
18. Rental Guide Magazine/*Publishing Businesses*
19. Aerowest/Westair Washroom Sanitation Service/*Misc. Maintenance Products & Services*
20. Liqui-Green Lawn Care Corp./*Lawn Care & Landscaping Services*
21. Add-Ventures/*Construction & Remodeling Services*
22. Interclean Service System Inc./*Commercial Cleaning*
23. Pressed 4 Time Inc./*Dry Cleaning*
24. Pee Wee Workout/*Children's Fitness Centers*
25. Novus Plate Glass Repair/*Window Tinting/Glass Installation & Repair Services*

Table 6-3 *(continued)*

THE TOP 25 NEW FRANCHISES	
1. General Nutrition Franchising/*Misc. Specialty Foods*	15. Valvoline Instant Oil Change/*Oil Change & Lubrication-Specialty Services*
2. O.P.E.N. Cleaning Systems/*Commercial Cleaning*	16. AmeriSpec Home Inspection Service/*Property Inspection Services*
3. Jackson Hewitt Tax Service/*Income Tax Services*	17. WOW Inc. of Orlando/*Exterior Power Washing*
4. Fax-9/*Business Add-On Services*	18. Pet Valu/*Pet Stores & Services*
5. Freshens Premium Yogurt/*Frozen Yogurt*	19. Postal Annex + /*Packing, Mailing & Shipping Services*
6. Rally's Hamburgers/*Hamburgers*	20. Cinnabon/*Cinnamon Rolls*
7. Floor Coverings Int'l./*Floor & Wall-Coverings Stores*	21. Avis Lube/*Oil Change & Lubrication-Specialty Services*
8. Speedy Sign-A-Rama, USA/*Signs*	22. Discount Realty Int'l./*Real Estate Services*
9. Fastsigns/*Signs*	23. Gloria Jean's Coffee Bean Franchising Corp./*Coffees & Teas*
10. Sterling Optical/*Optical Products & Services*	24. Kitchen Tune Up/*Kitchen/Cabinet Improvements*
11. Signs Now/*Signs*	25. Monograms Plus/*Personal Services*
12. TV Facts Magazine/*Television Magazines*	
13. Yogen Fruz/*Frozen Yogurt*	
14. Sensible Car Rental Inc./*Used-Auto Rentals*	

Source: "The Annual Franchise 500," *Entrepreneur*, January 1991, p. 202. Reprinted by permission of *Entrepreneur* Magazine, August 1991.

sales. Typically, the franchise buyer pays an initial franchise fee, spends his own money to build a store, buys his own equipment and inventory, then pays a continuing royalty based on sales, usually between 5 and 12 percent. Most franchisors require buyers to have 25–50 percent of the initial costs in cash. The rest can be borrowed—in some cases, from the franchising organization itself.[8] Table 6-4 presents a list of the costs involved in buying a franchise.

FRANCHISOR CONTROL

When one works in a large corporation, the company controls the employee's activities. If an individual has a personal business, he or she controls his or her own activities. A franchise operator is somewhere between these two extremes. The franchisor generally exercises a fair degree of control over the operation. For example, if one were to visit a McDonald's in New York City, Chicago, and San Francisco, it would be difficult to tell them apart. The building, decor, and interior of the rooms would all look identical because of the uniformity of design. The same is true in the case of Burger King and Pizza Hut.

Likewise, operations of the various units would be the same. One can expect to eat an identically tasting hamburger regardless of which McDonald's franchise unit

---

[8]Bryce Webster, *The Insider's Guide to Franchising* (New York: NY: Macmillan, 1986); and Lloyd T. Tarbutton, *Franchising: The How-to Book* (Englewood Cliffs, NJ: Prentice-Hall, 1986).

Table 6-4 The Cost of Franchising

Don't let the advantages of franchising cloud the fact that significant costs are involved. Although the franchise fee may be $75,000, the actual cost of "opening your doors for business" can be more than $200,000! Depending upon the type of franchise, the following expenditures are possible:

1. **The Basic Franchise Fee**
   For this, you may receive a wide range of services: personnel training, licenses, operations manuals, training materials, site selection and location preparation assistance, etc. Or you may receive none of these.

2. **Insurance**
   You will need coverage for a variety of things such as plate glass, office contents, vehicles, and others. You should also obtain so-called umbrella insurance. It is inexpensive and is meant to help out in the event of crippling million- or multimillion-dollar lawsuits.

3. **Opening Product Inventory**
   If initial inventory is not included in your franchise fee, you will have to obtain enough to open your franchise.

4. **Remodeling and Leasehold Improvements**
   In most commercial leases, you are responsible for these costs.

5. **Utility Charges**
   Deposits to cover the first month or two are usually required for electricity, gas, oil, telephone, and water.

6. **Payroll**
   This should include the costs of training employees before the store opens. You should also include a reasonable salary for yourself.

7. **Debt Service**
   This includes principal and interest payments.

8. **Bookkeeping and Accounting Fees**
   In addition to the services the franchisor may supply in this area, it is always wise to use your own CPA.

9. **Legal and Professional Fees**
   The cost of hiring an attorney to review the franchise contract, file for and obtain any necessary zoning or planning ordinances, and handle any unforeseen conflicts must be factored into your opening-costs projections.

10. **State and Local Licenses, Permits, and Certificates**
    These run the gamut from liquor licenses to building permits for renovations.

Source: Donald F. Kuratko, "Achieving the American Dream as a Franchisee," *Small Business Network,* July 1987, p. 2.

cooked it. In order to achieve this degree of uniformity, the franchisor keeps a very close eye on the unit's operation. If the entrepreneur does not follow franchisor directions and starts raising prices or changing the menu, the entrepreneur may not have the franchise license renewed when the contract expires.

UNFULFILLED PROMISES

In some cases, especially among lesser-known franchisors, the franchisees have not received all they were promised.[9] For example, many franchisees have found

---

[9]Russell M. Knight, "Franchising from the Franchisor's and Franchisee's Points of View," *Journal of Small Business Management,* July 1986, pp. 8–15.

themselves with trade names that have no drawing power. In other cases the franchise system was associated with a prominent sports figure or entertainment star, who had simply loaned his name to the organizers of the system but had little to do with the management of the chain. Most of these "celebrity" franchise chains have folded, after absorbing the savings of many franchisees.

Many franchisees have found that the promised assistance from the franchisor has not been forthcoming. For example, instead of being able to purchase supplies more cheaply through the franchisor, many operators have found themselves paying exorbitant prices for supplies. The Select Committee on Small Business of the U.S. Congress found a large restaurant chain buying maraschino cherries for $1.50 a gallon and selling them to franchisees for $4.50 a gallon. Furthermore, a pizza chain was buying spices at $3 and reselling them to franchisees for $21.50. If franchisees complain, however, they risk having their agreement with the franchisor terminated or not renewed. This can be done by simply finding some problem with the complainers' operations, since in most franchise contracts this is a specified cause for termination.

EVALUATING THE OPPORTUNITIES

How can the average businessperson evaluate a franchise operation and decide if it is a good deal? Unfortunately, there is no mathematical formula like there is for evaluating the purchase of an ongoing business (Chapter 5). Nor is it possible simply to ask a friend, because the most popular franchises, which are probably the only ones with which the individual is familiar, are not giving franchises to people seeking to enter the field. This leaves only the smaller, lesser-known, and more risky franchise operations. Therefore, in order to ensure that one's investment is adequately protected, an evaluation of franchise opportunities must be undertaken.[10] Figure 6-4 provides an illustration of a complete flow chart for the franchising process.

LEARN OF OPPORTUNITIES

One of the first things a prospective franchisee must do is to find a reliable source of information about franchising opportunities. Some of the most readily available sources are newspapers and **trade publications.** *Entrepreneur* magazine carries advertisements of franchise opportunities, and exhibitions and trade shows are held by franchisors from time to time in various cities. Finally, one can turn to **franchisors themselves** to get information on specific opportunities, although in this case one needs to beware of being promised more than what will be delivered.

INVESTIGATE THE FRANCHISOR

The prospective investor should get as much information as possible on the franchisor. So many people have lost their life savings in franchise schemes that, except in dealing with a long-established franchisor, one is best advised to go into the investigation prepared for the worst. In particular, if the franchisor seems too eager to sell

---

[10]For additional guidelines, see *Franchise Opportunities Handbook* (Washington, D.C.: U.S. Department of Commerce, 1986), pp. xxix–xxx.

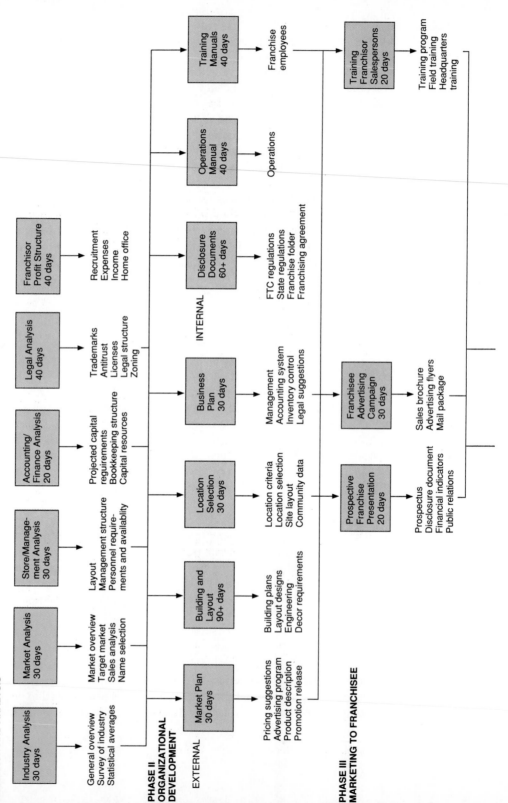

Figure 6-4 The Franchise PERT Chart

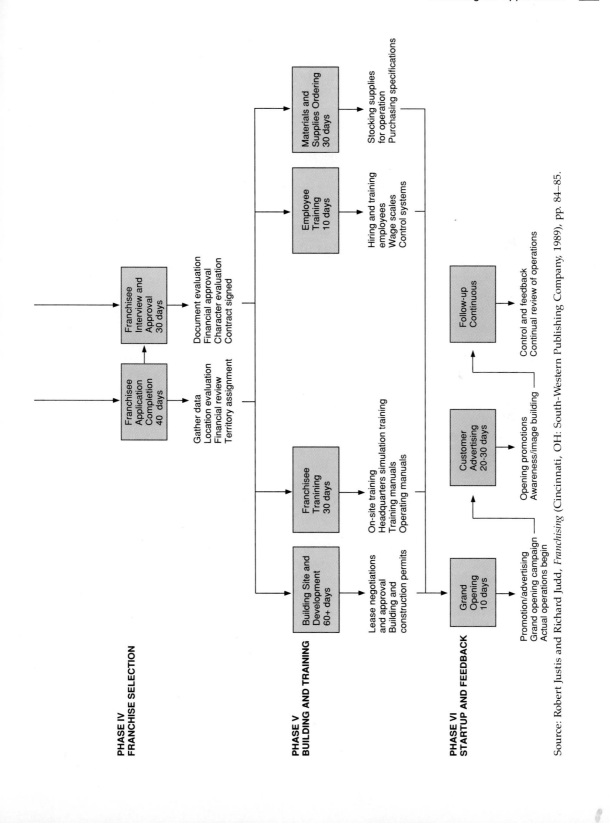

PHASE IV
FRANCHISE SELECTION

Franchisee Application Completion 40 days

Gather data
Location evaluation
Financial review
Territory assignment

Franchisee Interview and Approval 30 days

Document evaluation
Financial approval
Character evaluation
Contract signed

PHASE V
BUILDING AND TRAINING

Building Site and Development 60+ days

Lease negotiations and approval
Building and construction permits

Franchisee Training 30 days

On-site training
Headquarters simulation training
Training manuals
Operating manuals

Employee Training 10 days

Hiring and training employees
Wage scales
Control systems

Materials and Supplies Ordering 30 days

Stocking supplies for operation
Purchasing specifications

PHASE VI
STARTUP AND FEEDBACK

Grand Opening 10 days

Promotion/advertising
Grand opening campaign
Actual operations begin

Customer Advertising 20–30 days

Opening promotions
Awareness/image building

Follow-up Continuous

Control and feedback
Continual review of operations

Source: Robert Justis and Richard Judd, *Franchising* (Cincinnati, OH: South-Western Publishing Company, 1989), pp. 84–85.

dealerships or units, it is cause for alarm. Likewise, if the franchisor does not make a vigorous effort to check out the prospective investors, it is usually a sign that the seller does not think the operation will last long and is probably interested in just taking the franchise fees and absconding with them. Remember: no reputable franchisor is going to sell a franchise without ensuring that the buyer is capable of operating it successfully. McDonald's, one of the most careful of all franchisors, carefully screens all applicants and it claims it has never had a unit go bankrupt. Table 6-5 provides a franchise evaluation checklist form to assist your analysis.

SEEK PROFESSIONAL HELP

If the franchisor passes the initial investigation and offers a franchise contract, the first thing to do is take it to a **qualified attorney.** The attorney will understand the terms of the agreement and can explain any penalties or restrictive clauses that limit what the franchisee can do. Of major importance are contract provisions related to cancellation and/or renewal of the franchise. Can the franchisor take away the franchise for some minor rule infraction? More importantly, if the agreement is canceled, how much of the initial franchise fee will be refunded to the individual? If the franchise can be purchased back by the franchisor at 20 percent of the initial fee, the lawyer will need to carefully examine the ease with which the franchisor can terminate the agreement.

Other considerations include the franchise fee, the percentage of gross revenues to be paid to the franchisor, the type and extent of training to be provided, the territorial limits of the franchise, and the provisions for supplying materials to the unit. In addition, the lawyer needs to examine the degree of control the franchisor will have over operations, including price requirements, performance standards, and the required days and hours of operation.

Additionally, the individual should seek financial counsel. A good **banker** should be able to look over the franchisor's prospectus and give an opinion regarding its feasibility. Is the projected revenue too high for a new unit? Is the return on investment overly optimistic? Would the bank be prepared to advance a loan on this type of business undertaking?

The investor should also talk to a **certified public accountant** (CPA) who can review the data and construct a projected income statement for the first few years. Does the investment look promising? What are some things that might go wrong and jeopardize the investment? How likely are these developments? Is this the type of investment that constitutes an acceptable risk for the prospective buyer, or should the individual walk away from the deal?

Legal and financial professionals will help the prospective franchisee answer some very important questions. In particular, they will force the individual to face the risks inherent in a franchise and answer the question "Am I willing to take this type of risk?"

THE DECISION: IT'S UP TO YOU

At this point, the prospective investor has gathered all of the information that is needed. It is now up to the investor to make the final decision on the matter. As in

Table 6-5 Franchise Checklist Evaluation

NAME OF FRANCHISOR _____ DATE _____

ADDRESS _____

Directions: Mark the square which most accurately represents the franchise position.

RATING: 5 = Excellent; 4 = High; 3 = Average; 2 = Low; 1 = Poor

EXISTING FRANCHISEE		5	4	3	2	1
Average Profitability (5 units)	$ _____					
Investment Startup	$ _____					
Favorable Relations with Franchisor						
Strength of Operations						
Reliability of Franchisor's Promises						
Required Sales Quotas						
Training Programs						
Favorable Contract						
Favorable Territory						
Promotion/Advertising						

Subtotal = _____

FRANCHISOR		5	4	3	2	1
Fees						
Initial Franchise Fee	$ _____					
Royalty Fees	_____ %					
Advertising Fees	_____ %					
Other Fees	_____ %					
Values						
Value of Product or Service						
Value of Training						
Value of Trademark						
Activities						
Franchisor's Experience						
Franchisor's Litigation						
Exclusive Territory						
Renewal/Termination Rights						
Contract Length						
Disclosure Document (U.F.O.C.)						
Restrictions						
Market Potential and Acceptance						

Subtotal = _____
TOTAL   = _____

Score: 110–125 Superior; 100–109 Excellent; 90–99 Very Good; 80–89 Good; 70–79 Average; Below 70 Substandard

Source: Robert Justis and Richard Judd, *Franchising* (Cincinnati, OH: South-Western Publishing Company, 1989), p. 418. Reproduced from *Franchising* with the permission of South-Western Publishing Company. Copyright 1989 by South-Western Publishing Company. All rights reserved.

Table 6-6 Asking the Right Questions

THE FRANCHISOR

1. For how many years has the firm offering the franchise been in business?
   ☐ 1–2   ☐ 3–5   ☐ 6–10   ☐ 10 +
2. Has the franchisor a reputation for honesty and fair dealing among those who currently hold franchises?
   ☐ yes   ☐ no
3. With which of the following will the franchisor help you?
   ☐ management training program   ☐ capital
   ☐ employee training program   ☐ credit
   ☐ public relations program   ☐ merchandising ideas
4. Will the franchisor help you find a location for the new business?
   ☐ yes   ☐ no
5. Is the franchising firm adequately financed so that it can carry out its stated plan of financial assistance and expansion?
   ☐ yes   ☐ no
6. Has the franchisor shown you certified figures indicating the net profits of one or more units that you have personally checked?
   ☐ yes   ☐ no
7. Is the franchisor a one-person company ☐ or a corporation with experienced, well-trained management ☐?
8. What can the franchisor do for you that you cannot do for yourself?
   _____
   _____
   _____
9. Has the franchisor investigated you carefully enough to assure itself that you can successfully operate one of their franchises at a profit to them and to you?
   ☐ yes   ☐ no

THE FRANCHISE

1. Did your lawyer approve the franchise contract after studying it paragraph by paragraph?
   ☐ yes   ☐ no
2. Does the franchise call on you to take any steps that, according to your lawyer, are illegal?
   ☐ yes   ☐ no
3. Does the franchise give you an exclusive territory for the length of the franchise ☐ , or can the franchisor sell a second or third franchise in your territory ☐?
4. Is the franchisor connected in any way with any other franchise company handling similar merchandise or services?
   ☐ yes   ☐ no
5. If your answer to the above question is yes, what is your protection against the other franchising organization?
   _____
6. Under what circumstances can you terminate the franchise contract and at what cost to you?
   _____
   _____
7. If you sell your franchise will you be compensated for your goodwill?
   _____
   _____

Table 6-6 *(continued)*

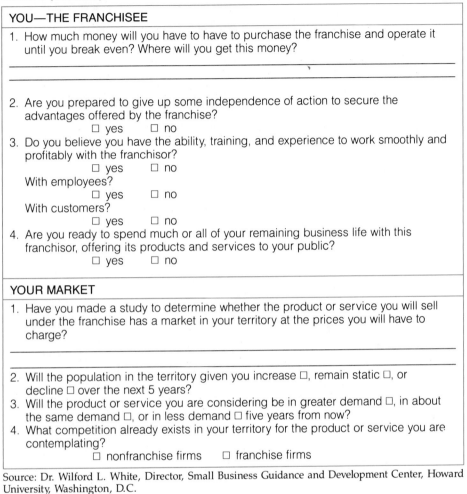

YOU—THE FRANCHISEE

1. How much money will you have to have to purchase the franchise and operate it until you break even? Where will you get this money?

_____

2. Are you prepared to give up some independence of action to secure the advantages offered by the franchise?
　　　　　☐ yes　　☐ no
3. Do you believe you have the ability, training, and experience to work smoothly and profitably with the franchisor?
　　　　　☐ yes　　☐ no
　With employees?
　　　　　☐ yes　　☐ no
　With customers?
　　　　　☐ yes　　☐ no
4. Are you ready to spend much or all of your remaining business life with this franchisor, offering its products and services to your public?
　　　　　☐ yes　　☐ no

YOUR MARKET

1. Have you made a study to determine whether the product or service you will sell under the franchise has a market in your territory at the prices you will have to charge?

_____

2. Will the population in the territory given you increase ☐, remain static ☐, or decline ☐ over the next 5 years?
3. Will the product or service you are considering be in greater demand ☐, in about the same demand ☐, or in less demand ☐ five years from now?
4. What competition already exists in your territory for the product or service you are contemplating?
　　　　　☐ nonfranchise firms　　☐ franchise firms

Source: Dr. Wilford L. White, Director, Small Business Guidance and Development Center, Howard University, Washington, D.C.

the case of buying an ongoing business, however, there are a series of "right questions" that can help. Table 6-6 lists the questions a prospective investor should ask before investing in a franchise.

TRENDS IN FRANCHISING

The future of franchising promises to be an exciting one. In particular, some interesting franchise trends are emerging. One is the testing of different products under the same roof, such as ice cream and pizza. At the present time, these new "combinations" are in food-related areas, but other combinations have been emerging in the early 1990s.

A second emerging trend is the movement of new and small companies into the franchise system of distribution. The area is proving attractive for more than just small or established enterprises.

■ SMALL BUSINESS OWNER'S NOTEBOOK ■

The Uniform Franchise Offering Circular

In 1979 the Federal Trade Commission established a Franchise Disclosure Rule requiring franchisors to make full presale disclosure nationwide. To comply with this ruling, the Uniform Franchise Offering Circular (UFOC) was developed.

The UFOC is divided into 23 items, which provide different segments of information for prospective franchisees. In summary form, here are the major sections:

Sections I-IV:	Covers the franchisor, the franchisor's background, and the franchise being offered.
Sections V-VI:	Delineates the franchise fees, both initial and ongoing.
Section VII:	Sets forth all of the initial expenses involved to establish the entire franchise.
Sections VIII-IX:	Details the franchise's obligation to purchase specific goods, supplies, services, and so forth from the franchisor.
Section X:	Provides information on any financing arrangements available to franchisees.
Section XI:	Describes in detail the contractual obligations of the franchisor to the franchisee.
Section XII:	Clearly outlines the geographic market within which the franchisee must operate.
Section XIII-XIV:	Discloses all pertinent information regarding trademarks, tradenames, patents, and so forth.
Section XV:	Outlines the franchisor's expectations of the franchisee (day to day operations).
Section XVI:	Explains any restrictions or limitations.
Section XVII:	Sets forth the conditions for renewal, termination, or sale of the franchise.
Section XVIII:	Discloses the *actual* relationship between the franchise and any celebrity figure used in advertising for the franchise.
Section XIX:	Provides a factual description of any potential "earnings claims," including their assumptions and actual figures.
Section XX:	Lists the names and addresses of *all* existing franchises in the state where the proposed franchise is to be located.
Section XXI-XXIII:	Provides certified financial statements for the previous three fiscal years and a copy of the actual franchise contract.

The UFOC must be given to a prospective franchisee at least 10 days prior to the payment of any fees or contracts signed. It is the responsibility of the franchisee to read and understand the various sections delineated in this document.

Source: Adapted from David J. Kaufmann and David E. Robbins, "Now Read This," *Entrepreneur,* January 1991, pp. 100–105.

Another trend is the acquisition of additional franchises by franchisees. Many franchisors like this multiunit approach because it means that their successful franchisees are expanding and adding vitality to their overall franchise system.

A fourth trend is the growth of franchising in the service sector. This is particularly evident in areas such as maid services, home repair and remodeling, carpet cleaning, and various other maintenance and cleaning services. Another growing area is that of business aids, as reflected by the rise of franchising services in accounting, collection services, message taking, mail processing, advertising services, package wrapping and shipping, business consulting, security, business record keeping, tax preparation, and personnel services. A third major area of development in the service sector is auto repairs and services. Franchised growth during the 1990s is likely to be particularly strong in the large automotive aftermarket including auto centers that provide services such as tune-ups, quick lubes, mufflers, transmissions, brakes, painting, tires, electric repairs, and general car care. Other areas that are expected to advance rapidly include weight-control centers, hair salons, temporary help services, printing and copying services, medical centers, and clothing stores.[11]

Over the next ten years there will also be more legislation regulating franchising. (See Small Business Owner's Notebook: The Uniform Franchise Offering Circular.) Franchisors themselves admit that it is one of the major problems they will have to face. Pending legislation and court rulings all promise to make the franchising area a confusing one. Additionally, the retail environment throughout the United States is becoming increasingly complex. However, this merely means that the franchisee will have to be a better businessperson than his or her predecessors. Many of the laws will not injure but rather will protect the franchisee from unfair practices by unscrupulous franchisors.[12] Aside from this, retailing will undoubtedly change in terms of product mix and store design and layout. For example, some supermarkets are fighting fast-food outlets by putting in fast-food departments of their own. In short, survival in the retail environment will require creative marketing. Franchising will play an important role in this environment. What are needed are entrepreneurs with the ability and daring to assume the challenges and risks that will be inherent in franchise operations of the 1990s.

■ SUMMARY

A franchise is a system of distribution that enables a supplier (the franchisor) to arrange for a dealer (the franchisee) to handle a specific product or service under certain mutually agreed upon conditions. In essence, there are two types of franchising arrangements: those involving the franchising of a product or service and those involving the franchising of an entire business enterprise.

---

[11]*Franchise Opportunities Handbook* (Washington, D.C.: U.S. Department of Commerce), pp. 5–6; and Robert T. Justis and Richard Judd, "Master Franchising: A New Look," *Journal of Small Business Management,* July 1986, pp. 16–21.

[12]For a legal discussion on the law of franchising, see Kenneth W. Clarkson, Roger L. Miller, Gaylord A. Jentz, and Frank B. Cross, *West's Business Law,* 4th ed. (St. Paul, MN: West Publishing Company, 1989), pp. 770–80.

Franchising has proved to be a very popular vehicle for getting into business. In the 1970s there were almost 400,000 franchise establishments. Today that number is over 500,000.

A number of advantages are associated with franchising. Some of the most important are the training and guidance provided by the franchisor, brand-name appeal of the franchise, track record of other franchisees as proof of success, and the financial assistance—direct or indirect—the franchisee can obtain from the franchisor.

A number of disadvantages are also associated with franchising. These include franchise fees, the control exercised by the franchisor, and awareness of the unfulfilled promises of some franchisors.

How can the average businessperson evaluate a franchise operation in order to decide if it is a good deal? One of the first things a prospective franchisee must do is find a source of information about franchising opportunities. Then the individual should get as much information about the franchisor and the franchise contract as possible. Next, professionals such as a lawyer, banker, and CPA should look over the deal and offer their candid opinion. After this, it is up to the prospective investor. The type of checklist provided in this chapter will help the prospective investor make the decision.

The last part of the chapter examined future trends in franchising. Some of these are (a) multiproduct offerings; (b) the entrance of young and small companies;

(c) multiunit franchisees; (d) the growth of service-related franchises in areas such as maid services, home remodeling, auto repair, weight control, medical services, and clothing stores; and (e) the eventual increase in regulating legislation.

■ REVIEW AND DISCUSSION QUESTIONS

1. What is meant by the term *franchise?*

2. In a franchising agreement, what is the franchisee often called upon to do? What responsibilities does the franchisor assume?

3. How fast has franchising grown since 1986? What are the reasons for this growth?

4. What are some of the major advantages of franchising? Cite and explain three.

5. What are some of the major disadvantages of franchising? Cite and explain at least two.

6. How can a prospective franchisee go about evaluating a franchise opportunity? Explain.

7. In making an evaluation of whether or not to get into a franchise operation, the potential investor should ask a series of questions. What questions should the potential investor ask about the franchisor; the franchise; the market; the potential investor (himself or herself)?

8. Discuss the future of franchising. Explain the trends being forecast and their potential impact on investors.

■ ▬▬▬▬▬▬▬▬▬▬▬▬▬▬▬▬▬▬▬▬▬▬▬▬▬
Case Studies

Checking It Out

■ When Arlene Ryan inherited $50,000 from her grandfather, she decided to use the money to start her own business. Arlene has been a legal secretary for fourteen years and feels she knows quite a bit about business. "Every day I take depositions and type legal memoranda," she noted to a friend. "And I've seen lots of businesses fail because they didn't have adequate capital or proper management. Believe me, when you work for a law firm, you see—and learn—plenty."

It was almost six months before Arlene decided on a business to pursue. A franchise ad in a business magazine caught her attention. Arlene called and found out that the franchisor was selling fast-food franchises in her area. "We are in the process of moving into your section of the country," the spokesperson told her. "We have 111 franchisees throughout the nation and want to sell twenty-six in your state." Arlene went to a meeting the franchisor held at a local hotel and, along with a large number of other potential investors, listened to the sales pitch. It all sounded very good. The cost of the franchise was $10,000 plus 4% of gross revenues. The franchisor promised assistance with site location and personnel training and encouraged the prospective franchisees to ask questions and investigate the organization. "If you don't feel this is a good deal for you, it's not a good deal for us either; good business is a two-way street," the spokesperson pointed out. "We are going to be looking very carefully at all franchisee applications, and you ought to be giving us the same degree of scrutiny."

Arlene liked what she heard but felt it would be prudent to do some checking on her own. Before leaving the meeting, she asked the spokesperson for the names and addresses of some current franchisees. "I don't have a list with me," he said, "but I can write down some that I know of and you can get their numbers from the operator." He then scribbled four names and locations on a piece of paper and handed it to her.

Arlene called information operators for the four locations and was able to get telephone numbers for only two of the franchises. The other addresses apparently were wrong. She then placed calls to the two franchisees. The first person said that she had owned her franchise for one year and felt it was too early to judge the success of the operation. When she found out that Arlene was thinking about buying a franchise, she asked if Arlene would consider buying hers. The price the woman quoted was $3,000 below what the company was currently quoting. The second person told Arlene that he simply did not give out information over the phone. He seemed somewhat edgy about talking to her and continually sidestepped Arlene's requests for specific financial information. Finally he told her, "Look, if you really want this information, I think you should talk to my attorney. If he says it's okay to tell you, I will." He then gave Arlene the attorney's number. Before she could call the lawyer, Arlene left for lunch. When she returned one of the partners of her firm was standing beside her desk. "Hey, Arlene, what are you doing calling this guy?" he asked, holding up the telephone number of the franchisee's attorney. "Are you planning to sue someone? That's his specialty, you know." Arlene smiled. "As a matter of fact, I am. I'm thinking of suing you guys for back wages." The attorney laughed along with her and then walked back into his office.

1. What is your appraisal of the situation? Does it look good or bad?

2. Would you recommend that Arlene buy the franchise from the woman who has offered to sell? Why or why not?

3. What would you recommend that Arlene do now? Be complete in your answer.

A New Opportunity

■ Gary Charles has been an auto mechanic for ten years. He and his wife Nancy have a small but comfortable home in a Chicago suburb. Thanks to a strict budget, they can afford to send their two children to a private school and still bank a reasonable amount of money.

However, Gary realized that inflation was eroding his earning power. He decided to go into business for himself in hopes of expanding his income. After checking out a number of sources, Gary learned that one of the country's largest automatic transmission repair services was looking for a franchisee in his area. After talking to the franchisor, he was encouraged. His experience as an auto mechanic would be invaluable to him. At the franchisor's suggestion, Gary selected five names at random from a list of the company's franchisees located within a fifty-mile radius. He called three and went to visit the other two personally. Each was very enthusiastic about their business, said the franchisor was very helpful to them, and encouraged Gary to seek his own franchise.

After going back to the franchisor and expressing further interest, Gary learned that the franchise fee was $20,000 and $7\frac{1}{2}$ percent of the business's gross revenue. From a phone call to one of the franchisees, Gary learned that these were standard terms. He then decided to look seriously into the matter. He hired an accountant and a lawyer and sat down with a representative of the franchisor. The latter indicated that they would help Gary get financing, select a location, and get the operation started. In particular, they offered monthly conferences for all franchise operators to review various phases of operations, weekly parts deliveries from their warehouse, weekly reviews of sales progress and business proficiency, and guaranteed weekly newspaper and TV ads encouraging the public to use their outlets for handling transmission problems.

Gary's lawyer and accountant have both told him that the franchise offer looks good. Now it is up to him.

1. What are the advantages of buying this franchise?

2. What are the disadvantages of buying this franchise?

3. What would you recommend that Gary do? Why?

You Be the Consultant

PAUL'S PROBLEM

Paul Robert is tired of working for a large retail chain. He has been there twenty years and would like to go into business for himself. A bachelor, Paul has saved more than $100,000 and has been making inquiries about buying a franchise from a national fast-food chain. The franchise will cost $35,000 but the organization will help Paul choose a site, arrange financing for the building and the equipment, and provide technical and managerial assistance in running the operation.

Paul is favorably impressed by the support that will be forthcoming from the franchisor. However, he realizes that if he leaves the retail chain he will give up his pension plan and his annual bonus. He is currently making $27,000 a year with a 10 percent bonus. His pension plan (Paul is currently 39) would pay him 50 percent of the average of his last five years' salary. If the chances for personal gain are better in a franchise, he would like to leave. However, if there is a good chance of bankruptcy, he would rather remain with his current job.

In the metropolitan area (population 500,000) there are already four of these franchises, but none is located in the southwest section of the city, the fastest-growing area. Paul's unit would be located there. Additionally, the franchisor has promised that there will be no other unit in this area for at least five years, and then it will be located at least ten blocks from Paul's location.

■ **YOUR CONSULTATION** Assume that you are Paul's best friend. He has asked you for advice regarding whether or not he should buy the franchise. In particular, he wants you to tell him the benefits and drawbacks associated with franchising and give him your opinion on whether he should buy a franchise. Be as specific as possible in your consultation.

CHAPTER 7

Starting a New Small Business

Objectives

Sometimes the best way of getting into small business is to start from the ground up. In fact, most people use this approach. The purpose of this chapter is to examine the steps involved in starting a new small business. First we will focus on the importance of uniqueness in any new business venture. Then we will examine market analysis, focusing primarily on the gathering and the analyzing of key types of information. Finally we will discuss the importance of an action plan and the three segments of such a plan. When you have studied Chapter 7 you will be able to:

1. *Explain how a "new-new" approach to small business differs from a "new-old" approach.*
2. *Identify and discuss the six steps in the scientific method.*
3. *List the key questions a prospective business owner should be able to answer personally.*
4. *Describe how to go about evaluating the financial picture of an enterprise.*
5. *Explain other key factors with which the new owner should be concerned.*

UNIQUENESS IS THE KEY

The most effective way to approach a new small business venture is by creating a product or service that is unique: one that is not being offered today but, if it were, it would be in great demand. The next-best way is to adapt something that is currently on the market or extend the offering into an area where it is not presently available. The first approach is often referred to as *new-new;* the second, as *new-old.*

NEW-NEW APPROACH

The best approach to getting into small business is that of developing a totally new product or service.[1] Of course, we are always hearing about new products entering the market, and they at least seem new to us. Typical illustrations include a new

---

[1]See Frances Huffman, "21 Hottest Businesses for 1991," *Entrepreneur,* December 1990, pp. 75–87.

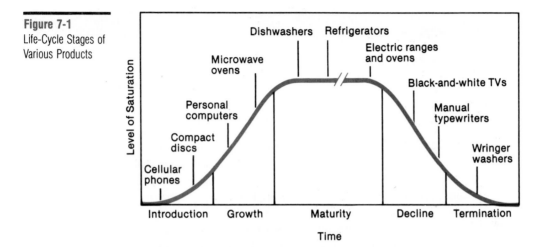

Figure 7-1
Life-Cycle Stages of Various Products

hand drill with a lifetime guarantee against defective performance, a house paint that will not peel or chip for three years, a car tire that will last 50,000 miles, and the video recorder. All of these products, and more, have been introduced as a result of research and development (R&D) efforts by major corporations.

What we must realize, however, is that unique ideas are not produced only by large companies. Moreover, the rate at which new products come onto the market has caused the public to expect to replace many of their household goods continually. Figure 7-1 presents the life-cycle stages of some common products. Note that some are beginning to be accepted, some are in the maturity stage, and others are no longer in demand.

How does one discover or invent new products? One of the easiest ways is to make a list of annoying experiences or hazards encountered during a given period of time with various products or services. Common examples include objects that fall out of one's hand, household chores that are difficult to do, and items that are hard to store. Is there some way to alleviate these problems? This is how most businesspeople get ideas for new products; history is full of examples.

James Ritty once observed the mechanism for recording the revolutions of a ship's propeller. As he watched the device tally the propeller's revolutions, he realized that the idea could be adapted to the recording of sales transactions, a problem he had been trying to solve for some time. The result led eventually to development of the modern cash register.

In more modern times there is the case of the Iowa auto dealer who invented a snow removal blade that could be attached to the rear of any car in three minutes. In one test the blade removed snow almost a foot deep, an important breakthrough for people in states where snow is a winter hazard. The product is now being produced and sold. Another example of a new idea is wearable art. (See Small Business Success: Spin Art.)

NEW-OLD APPROACH

Most small businesses do not start with a totally unique idea. Instead, an individual "piggybacks" on someone else's idea by either improving a product or offering a

■ SMALL BUSINESS SUCCESS ■

Spin Art

Fresh, innovative ideas are needed to make a successful start-up business. A radical new product or idea may take the public by storm and either become a short-lived fad or a relatively lasting item. An entrepreneur with some insight is able to get into these early start-ups and make them profitable. One such new idea that has recently become quite popular is "spin art."

"Wearable art" has been a buzzword for several years now. The idea of being able to turn an artistic creation into an item of clothing has really caught on. One form of wearable art has been the new spin art. Spin art involves placing an ink or paint on a shirt, fastening the shirt in a horizontal position on a "spinner," and letting centrifugal force do the rest. The splattered effect that occurs from the spinning motion creates a unique design. The shirt is then placed in a special drier and is immediately ready to wear.

The ability to watch their own designs form before their eyes is what makes spin art especially appealing to children. For adults, however, the creating is not as important as the final product. Some spin art stores rectify that dilemma by displaying various finished designs so that the customer has some idea of what his or her shirt will look like after it has been in the spinner.

The owner of a spin art store must be willing to spend a lot of time working with the customers. Many people are reluctant to try something new, especially if it means attempting to be creative and unique. The owner and employees must be able to jump in and help the customer get started.

One of the advantages of a spin art store is the limited number of supplies required to complete a design. The only items needed are shirts and paint, which eliminates the necessity to deal with a multitude of vendors when buying supplies and increases the opportunity for turning a profit. For example, Splatters Ink, located in Salt Lake City, opened in May of 1989. In its first nine months of operation the store grossed $230,000.

The quality that makes spin art stores easy to operate can become a disadvantage when it comes to attracting customers. A limited selection of clothing items may not be enough to attract potential customers. For this reason many stores use the spin art idea simply to enhance their product lines. A store's ability to outfit a customer with socks, hats, jewelry, and so forth is what may attract more customers.

Although many spin art stores may be successful, there are probably just as many failures. Perhaps the one premise that can lead to success is a commitment to creativity. Says one store owner, "You've got to keep changing your ideas."

Source: Adapted from Kenneth Rosenberg, "The Big Spin," *Entrepreneur,* August 1990, pp. 121–25.

service in an area where it is not currently available.[2] Some of the most common examples are restaurants, clothing stores, or similar outlets that are set up in sprawling suburban areas that do not have an abundance of these stores. Of course, these kinds of operations can be risky because of the ease with which competitors can move in. If you are considering this kind of enterprise, try to offer a good or a service that is difficult to copy. For example, a computerized billing and accounting service for medical doctors can be successful if the business has a sufficient number of doctors (18–25) to cover the cost of computer operators and administrative expenses in order to turn an adequate profit. Or consider another type of enterprise that is likely to be overlooked by other would-be entrepreneurs.

Regardless of whether the business is based on a new-new or a new-old idea, the prospective owner cannot rely exclusively on gut feeling or intuition in order to get started. Market analysis is the key to a successful venture.

MARKET ANALYSIS

Market analysis can help a prospective small business owner determine whether there is a demand for a particular good or service and whether this demand is sufficient to justify starting a small business operation. Large firms do a great deal of market analysis, but such efforts are not restricted to large companies. Small enterprises can, and do, benefit from this activity. And it need not cost a great deal of money, for much of the data gathering and analysis can be performed by the prospective owner-manager personally.[3] All the prospective owner-manager needs to do is accurately formulate the questions that need to be answered and then objectively analyze the data received in response to the questions. In essence, **market analysis** is simply the application of the scientific method to business problems. These steps make up the **scientific method:**

1. State the problem or question in as clear a manner as possible.
2. Gather all the necessary facts about the problem or question.
3. Organize and analyze the facts.
4. Develop one or more courses of action, keeping in mind the pros and cons of each.
5. Select the best alternative and implement it.
6. Observe the progress of this alternative and adjust it as required.

This method can be used not only by people entering a small business for the first time, but by businesspeople who are already conducting operations and looking at the possibilities of expanding their business into new lines or products. However, our attention here is confined to new ventures. The prospective entrepreneur can analyze a business opportunity by breaking the scientific method into four basic steps:

---

[2] See "The Most Fascinating Ideas for 1991," *Fortune,* January 14, 1991, pp. 30–62.

[3] Alan R. Andreasen, "Cost-Conscious Marketing Research,"*Harvard Business Review,* July/August 1983, pp. 74–75.

- fact gathering
- organization of the facts
- analysis of the facts
- implementation of an action plan

FACT GATHERING

The first step is to gather information about the proposed venture. Who would be attracted to this product or service? How many people in the area would buy it? What sales volume would be needed to break even? Are there any competitors in the area? How well established are they? What does the future of the business look like? Answers to these types of questions can be obtained by reading industry journals, getting data from the Small Business Administration, and talking to a local banker who is knowledgeable about the area.

ORGANIZATION OF THE FACTS

After all the facts have been gathered they must be organized in a logical fashion. Facts related to costs and revenues should be put together, because this information will help the individual compute the break-even point for operations. Competition and projected sales in the local area go together because from this information an estimate of market share can be projected. Facts related to industry growth can be used to make projections regarding future sales and profit potential. Organizing the facts in this fashion allows for a more thorough analysis of the information at hand.

ANALYSIS OF THE FACTS

In the analysis stage, the prospective owner-manager answers the question "What does it all mean?" In some cases this question is not difficult because the information speaks for itself. For example, is the return on investment in this business high enough to justify the risk? Does the future of the operation look promising? Answers to such questions provide the individual with insights about the future potential of certain businesses.

Analysis of **sales and cost data** will provide the person with an idea of the profit margin. This can be compared with data on typical profit margins in the industry, which can be obtained in any business college library or from the Small Business Administration.

Another common analysis is that of determining the **number of competing firms** in the area and the number of total customers. Is there a large enough population to support another business? Table 7-1 illustrates the relationship between population and certain types of retail establishments. This approach can be used in estimating the potential sales volume of the proposed store.

Still another way to analyze data, which is similar to the one examined in Table 7-1, is to use an index of sales potential such as an index of consumer purchasing power. For example, *Sales and Marketing Management* magazine publishes a "Buying Power Index" each year. The magazine also contains information useful in setting sales quotas, planning distribution, and studying sales potential. Information on

Table 7-1 Population Needed to Support Selected Kinds of Businesses

KIND OF BUSINESS	PERSONS PER OUTLET
Luggage, leather goods stores	140,684
Bicycle shops	100,083
Pet shops	82,455
Bookstores	59,815
Camera, photographic supply stores	57,030
Fish (seafood) markets	51,971
Department stores	44,379
Hobby, toy stores	44,099
Heating, plumbing equipment dealers	40,589
Stationery stores	33,290
Aircraft, boat, motorcycle dealers	30,497
Dairy products stores	29,728
Music, records, musical instruments stores	23,363
Fruit, vegetable markets	21,259
Sporting goods stores	17,270
Gift, novelty, souvenir stores	14,965
Bakery products stores	10,126
Men's and boys' wear stores	8,403
Shoe stores	7,679
Hardware stores	6,374
Household appliances, radio, TV stores	6,148
Drugstores	3,749
Furniture, home furnishings stores	3,437
Eating places	842
Grocery stores, including delicatessens	770

Source: "Census of Retail Trade: Geographic Area Series Report," Bureau of the Census, U.S. Department of Commerce, 1983.

population and income are provided for every state by county and city. This type of information can help the prospective owner-manager predict sales in the area and determine whether the business would be an acceptable risk.

Still another type of analysis is that of **consumer surveys.** These surveys attempt to learn what consumers want. They do not have to be conducted by the prospective owner; consumer surveys are often conducted by colleges and universities or Chambers of Commerce and are generally available for the asking. These surveys provide important information about local consumer demand, often revealing data that contradicts national norms. For instance, although there may be twice as many outlets in an area as the national average, local consumer demand is such that there is still room for another outlet.

IMPLEMENTATION OF AN ACTION PLAN

If the analysis reveals that the business venture is a wise one, the owner can go ahead and begin operations. The specific procedures that should be followed during this action phase will be discussed in the next section. For the moment, however, it is imperative to remember that the plan may not work perfectly. Some modification may be necessary. Thus, the owner has to be flexible in planning. If something does not work out, a contingency or backup plan should be available. The last thing the owner should do is adopt an "all or nothing" strategy.

THE ACTION PLAN

After the analysis is complete and the owner is ready to proceed, there should be an action plan. What will be done and how will it be done? This plan should cover three areas:

1. the owner as a person
2. the financial picture
3. other factors

THE OWNER AS A PERSON

Before making the final decision about going into business, the owner needs to ask a number of personal questions. Ten of the most important ones are listed here. As you read, mark the response that best describes you.

1. ARE YOU A SELF-STARTER?
   - ☐ I can get going without help from others.
   - ☐ Once someone gets me going, I am just fine.
   - ☐ I take things easy and do not move until I have to.

2. HOW DO YOU FEEL ABOUT OTHERS?
   - ☐ I can get along with just about anyone.
   - ☐ I do not need anyone else.
   - ☐ People irritate me.

3. CAN YOU LEAD PEOPLE?
   - ☐ I can get most people to go along with me once I start something.
   - ☐ I can give the orders if someone tells me what should be done.
   - ☐ I let someone else get things done and go along if I like it.

4. CAN YOU TAKE RESPONSIBILITY?
   - ☐ I take charge and see things through.
   - ☐ I'll take over if necessary, but would rather let someone else be responsible.
   - ☐ If there is someone around who wants to do it, I let them.

5. ARE YOU AN ORGANIZER?
   - ☐ I like to have a plan before I begin.
   - ☐ I do all right unless things get too confusing, in which case I quit.
   - ☐ Whenever I have things all set up something always comes along to disrupt the plan, so I take things as they come.

6. ARE YOU A HARD WORKER?
   - ☐ I can keep going as long as necessary.
   - ☐ I work hard for a while, but then that's it.
   - ☐ I cannot see that hard work gets you anywhere.

7. CAN YOU MAKE DECISIONS?
   - ☐ I can make decisions, and they usually turn out pretty well.
   - ☐ I can make decisions if I have plenty of time, but fast decision making upsets me.
   - ☐ I do not like to be the one who has to decide things.

8. CAN PEOPLE RELY ON YOUR WORD?
   - ☐ Yes, I do not say things I do not mean.
   - ☐ I try to level with people, but sometimes I say what is easiest.
   - ☐ Why bother? The other person does not know the difference.

9. CAN YOU STICK WITH IT?
   - ☐ When I make up my mind to do something, nothing stops me.
   - ☐ I usually finish what I start.
   - ☐ If things start to go awry, I usually quit.

10. HOW GOOD IS YOUR HEALTH?
    - ☐ Excellent.
    - ☐ Pretty good.
    - ☐ Okay, but it has been better.

Now count the number of checks you have made next to the first responses and multiply this number by three. Count those next to the second responses and multiply by two. Count the number of times you checked the third answer. Total these three numbers. Out of a total possible 30 points, a successful small business person will have at least 25 points. If not, the prospective owner-manager should consider bringing in a partner or abandoning the idea of going into business alone.

THE FINANCIAL PICTURE

The next thing the prospective owner-manager must do is evaluate the financial picture of the enterprise. How much will it cost to stay in business for the first year? How much revenue will the firm generate during this time period? If the outflow is greater than the inflow, how long will it take before the business turns the corner?

In answering these questions, two kinds of expenses must be considered: start-up and monthly. Table 7-2 illustrates a typical worksheet for making the necessary calculations. Notice that this worksheet is based on the assumption that no money will flow in for about three months. Also, all start-up costs are totally covered. If the firm is in the manufacturing business, however, it will be three to four months before any goods are produced and sold, so the factors in Column 3 have to be doubled and the amount of cash needed for start-up will be greater.

Much of the information needed to fill in this worksheet should already have been gathered and at least partially analyzed. Now, however, it can be put into a format that allows the owner to look at the overall financial picture.

To this point the individual should be concerned with what is called **upside gain and downside loss.** This term refers to the profits the business can make and the losses it can suffer. How much money will the operation take in if everything goes well? How much will it gross if things are "as expected"? How much will it lose if things do not work out well? Answers to these questions provide a composite picture

Table 7-2 Checklist for Estimating Start-up Expenses

MONTHLY EXPENSES		CASH NEEDED TO START THE BUSINESS (see column 3)	WHAT TO PUT IN COLUMN 2 (These figures are estimates. The owner-manager decides how many months to allow, depending on the type of business.)
Item	Estimate based on sales of $ _____ per year		
	Column 1	Column 2	Column 3
Salary of owner—manager	$	$	3 times Column 1
Other salaries and wages			3 times Column 1
Rent			3 times Column 1
Advertising			3 times Column 1
Delivery expense			3 times Column 1
Supplies			3 times Column 1
Telephone and telegraph			3 times Column 1
Other utilities			3 times Column 1
Insurance			6 times Column 1
Taxes, Social Security			4 times Column 1
Interest			3 times Column 1
Maintenance			3 times Column 1
Legal and other professional assistance			3 times Column 1
Miscellaneous			3 times Column 1

START-UP COSTS		TO ARRIVE AT ESTIMATE
Item	Estimate	
Fixtures and equipment	$	Determine what is typical for this kind of business; talk to suppliers.
Decorating and remodeling		Talk to a contractor.
Installation of fixtures, equipment		Talk to suppliers.
Starting inventory		Talk to suppliers.
Deposits with public utilities		Contact utility companies.
Legal and other professional fees		Talk to lawyer, accountant, etc.
Licenses and permits		Contact appropriate city offices.
Advertising and promotion		Decide what will be used; talk to media.
Accounts receivable		Estimate how much will be tied up in receivables by credit customers and for how long.
Cash		Allow for unexpected expenses and losses, special purchases, etc.
Other expenses		List them and estimate costs.
TOTAL CASH NEEDED TO START	$ _____	Add all estimated amounts.

of the most optimistic, the most likely, *and* the most pessimistic results. The thing the owner has to keep in mind is that the upside profit may be minimal while the downside loss is great.

It is necessary to examine overall gains and losses. This kind of analysis is referred to as **risk versus reward** and points out the importance of getting an adequate return on the amount of money risked.

OTHER FACTORS

The third set of factors with which the prospective owner-manager must be concerned consists of operational areas that will be examined throughout the remainder of this book. However, they warrant attention here because of their importance in start-up activities. Some of the major considerations, put in the form of questions, include the following:

☐ THE BUILDING
  Is it currently adequate?
  Can it be fixed up without spending too much money?
  Is there room for expansion?
  Can people get to it easily from parking spaces, bus stops, or their homes?
  Has a lawyer checked the lease agreement and zoning ordinances?

☐ MERCHANDISE AND EQUIPMENT
  Have suppliers who will sell at reasonable prices been located?
  Have prices and credit terms of suppliers been compared?
  Have all the equipment and supplies needed for operation been purchased?

☐ RECORDKEEPING
  Is there a recordkeeping system for income and expense; inventory; payroll; taxes?
  Is there an accountant to help with records and financial statements?
  Have all the financial statements needed for control purposes been identified?
    Do you know how to use them?

☐ INSURANCE AND LEGAL CONCERNS
  Have plans been made for protecting the store against insurable losses?
  Have all licenses and permits been obtained?
  Has a lawyer been hired to assist with the legal aspects of the operation?

☐ MARKETING AND PERSONNEL
  Have prices for all goods been determined?
  Has a buying plan been worked out?
  Is an advertising program or some form of promotion ready to go?
  Will credit be given to customers? On what basis?
  Will salespeople be used? If so, how will they be recruited? Is there a training program for them? How much will they be paid?

If questions like these can be answered, the owner-manager is in a good position to begin. However, in most cases it is necessary for the individual to look more closely into one or more of these operational areas. (See Small Business Owner's Notebook: Strategic Planning.) There are some aspects of the operation that the

■ **SMALL BUSINESS OWNER'S NOTEBOOK** ■

Strategic Planning

 Strategic planning is often considered to be one of the most important roles of upper management. However, one aspect of strategic planning that is often overlooked is implementation. How does a business stop spinning its wheels and start to realize a successful business strategy?

The planning process must be designed to lead naturally and logically into the implementation of specific projects. Action can then be accomplished by breaking the plan down into projects, each defined by the following factors:

Purpose: What is the project designed to achieve?

Scope: What department levels of management will be involved?

Contribution to overall objectives: How will the project interrelate with other projects and the strategic plan as a whole?

Resource requirements: What human and financial resources are needed to complete the project?

Timing: What schedules and deadlines are necessary for project completion?

These projects should then be ranked in order of their contribution to the strategic plan as a whole. This will allow the prime consideration, in resources and funding, to go to those projects that are considered most important.

These projects will then need to be closely monitored. It is vital that the managers of each project make regular progress reports. These reports should include

1. any problems or anticipated delays

2. plans and schedules to overcome such delays

3. a reevaluation of the likelihood of reaching the project goals

The strategic plan should not only be divided into specific projects, but it should also allow for the development of operational plans that take into consideration

1. annual objectives

2. annual budgets

3. financial implications

4. potential cash surplus and deficit

5. the need for outside financing

Source: Kenneth G. Koehler, "Turning Strategic Vision into Reality," *Small Business Reports,* August 1989, pp. 15–17.

individual does not fully understand. We will direct our attention to these key areas in the chapters that follow, beginning with the primary problem confronting most small businesses—obtaining initial capital and credit.

■ SUMMARY

The easiest and best way to approach a new business venture is by coming up with a product or service that is unique. Sometimes this can be done by using what is called a new-new approach; that is, the development of an entirely new idea for a product or service, as was the case with the first Polaroid camera. In most instances, however, the prospective owner-manager must be content to use a new-old approach by "piggybacking" on someone else's ideas. This is done either by expanding upon what the competition is doing or by offering a good or service in an area where it is not presently available.

In either event, market analysis can help a prospective owner-manager determine whether there is a demand for a particular good or service and, if so, whether this demand is sufficient to justify starting operations. The way in which market analysis is carried out is through the use of the scientific method. The steps in this method are to state the problem or question in a clear manner, to gather all the necessary facts about the problem or question, to organize and analyze these facts, to develop one or more courses of action, to select the best alternative and implement it, and to observe the progress of this alternative and adjust it as required. These steps can be

broken down into four more basic ones: fact gathering, organization of the facts, analysis of the facts, and implementation of an action plan. They were discussed in this chapter, with particular attention given to the action plan.

In particular, the action plan should cover three primary areas: the owner's personality, the financial picture, and other major factors vital to the action plan. In dealing with the first of these, the owner needs to assess his or her strengths and work habits. On the financial side, the prospective owner-manager needs to examine the financial picture of the enterprise and to determine the costs of setting up the operation and the amount of revenue that will be generated during the initial period. Finally, the prospective owner-manager must review a series of other operational considerations ranging from the building, merchandise, and equipment needed for operations to record keeping, insurance, legal, marketing, and personnel matters. The next section will examine these operational areas in greater detail.

■ REVIEW AND DISCUSSION QUESTIONS

1. What is the new-new approach to starting a small business? How does this approach differ from a new-old approach?

2. What are the six steps in the scientific method?

3. Of the six steps in the scientific method, which is the most important for the prospective small business owner-manager? Support your answer.

4. Market analysis can help a prospective small business owner-manager determine if there is a demand for a particular good or service. What does this statement mean?

5. What kinds of questions should the small business owner be able to answer when developing an action plan? List at least five.

6. How can an individual thinking of going into business go about evaluating the financial picture of the enterprise? Use the methodology of Table 7-2 in preparing your answer.

7. In addition to personal and financial issues, with what other factors should the prospective owner be concerned? Describe at least four.

Case Studies

It's for the Dogs

■ Chris Wasserberg is a salesperson for a Fortune 500 firm. He has a bachelor's degree in marketing and is one of the firm's best salespeople. It is likely that Chris will one day become a sales manager if he stays with the firm. However, this is doubtful, given the fact that he hopes to start his own business.

Since he was hired seven years ago, Chris has managed to build a nest egg of $60,000. He is now looking for a business that would require no more than $20,000 to $30,000 to get started. The rest would be used for operating capital and to keep him going until the company turns profitable. In the past Chris has gathered ideas by reading magazines such as *Business Week* and *Venture*, which report the new types of businesses that are being opened.

Last week Chris read a story that intrigued him. A man on the West Coast has been building custom doghouses that are built of expensive materials and sell for $5,000 to $15,000 each. Chris realizes that few people can afford to pay this much for a doghouse. On the other hand, most doghouses are not distinctive, and owners simply pay $50 to $150 for basic doghouses. Chris believes there may be a market for doghouses between these two extremes, in the range of $250 to $500.

Chris has done research and believes that it would not be too difficult to differentiate his product from the standard doghouse. In particular, he is considering building a house that is slightly larger than the typical one, well insulated, and floored with washable vinyl; he would put the dog's name above the door and shingle the roof. Additionally, he believes that if the house had the same basic design as the owner's, it would be more appealing. The two biggest obstacles will be marketing and production; that is, getting people to order houses for their dogs and then getting the houses built. Chris believes that with his marketing background, he can handle the marketing, and it should not be too difficult to find someone to handle the construction. Moreover, until the business takes off, he believes he can continue with his sales job.

1. Is there anything unique about Chris's idea? Explain.
2. What is the first thing he should do in following up on his idea? Explain.
3. When this is done, what else should Chris do? Outline a general course of action for him.

Now What?

■ Selling men's clothing is something Paul Ramirez knows a great deal about, since he has been doing it for almost twenty-five years. However, last month Paul and his boss had a serious argument and Paul is thinking about quitting. Since he really does not know any other line of work, he has been looking around for a similar business opportunity and he believes he has found one. A new shopping mall is opening in the western part of town, but many of the local merchants are hesitant about opening stores there. However, a study by Paul's current employer shows that the number of potential shoppers and the per capita income in this section of town is much greater than is commonly thought.

Paul has known the individual who built the shopping center since they went to school together. The developer has been urging Paul to go into business for himself for years, most recently last week. He has quoted Paul a monthly rental charge for a men's store in the mall. "I have two of these stores already signed up and I'd like to get four in all. The competition will draw customers to the mall, and your business would do very well indeed."

Ever since the conversation Paul has been thinking about the offer. He has enough money saved to open such a store and keep it afloat for six months, even if things go badly; if sales were good, the store would be able to make money within a few months. Furthermore, Paul is certain that he can get a sufficient line of credit from manufacturers to stock the store, and knows enough about the business to be able to hire and train the necessary personnel. However, he does not know much about the financial side of business, and is not sure about how to proceed from here. All he knows is that he would like to go into business for himself.

1. What types of questions does Paul need to ask himself at this point? List at least five.

2. What does Paul need to do in gathering financial information about the operation? Outline your recommendations.

3. In addition to your answers to questions 1 and 2, what else does Paul need to do? Explain.

You Be the Consultant

IN OVER HIS HEAD

Later this year Ed Graham will graduate from college with a bachelor's degree in hotel and restaurant management. Throughout his undergraduate career, Ed has been thinking seriously of going into business for himself. He has taken a number of courses directly related to the operation of hotels and motels and believes that he knows quite a bit about this business.

His uncle Ted is a banker in Florida and has been urging Ed, ever since he learned about his nephew's area of study, to get into a hotel business down there. Ed has always expressed an interest in doing so, and his uncle continually sends him information on small hotels and motels that are for sale throughout the state.

Last week Ted sent his nephew an announcement about a bankrupt motel going on the selling block. The motel has forty units and is located on the west side of Florida near a retirement community. Although this is not an ideal location, with a lot of hard work and some effective advertising, Ted believes it could be made into a successful operation.

During his spring break Ed flew down to Florida and, with his uncle, went over and looked at the property. There is definitely work that needs to be done, and back taxes must be paid. However, Ed believes the basic structure is sound and that with the right management, the operation could indeed be a good investment. His uncle has told him that he will lend him the necessary money to get everything in order. "You've studied all about hotel management so you know what to look for and how to determine what needs to be done. Work up an action plan and give it to me. I'll have my people go over it, draw up the papers, and you'll be in business."

Now Ed is really nervous. After serious reflection, he feels he does not know as much about hotel-motel management as his uncle believes he does. His experience has been in the form of college-sponsored field trips through restaurant and hotel operations and talks by operating managers—that is all. Additionally, Ed has a basic understanding of accounting, but he does not know how to keep books for an actual enterprise. Nor does he know for certain how to go about constructing the action plan his uncle has requested. He is now beginning to think that he knows a lot more about small business *theory* than about small business *practice*. On the other hand, he does not want to disappoint his uncle by backing out of the deal. "What I need to do," he has told himself, "is talk to someone who can give me a big-picture approach to this problem, showing me the things that need to be done, the right kinds of questions to ask, and the places to go to find the answers."

■ **YOUR CONSULTATION** Assume that Ed has called on you and asked for your help. What would you tell him to do? Outline an action plan and fill it in by telling him how he can get the information you have suggested. Also, help him identify some of the questions he should ask *himself* before deciding whether to go into this particular business.

Part Two Case Study

THE QUIET HUT

Ray and Ruthie Stonecipher retired a few years ago. They're enjoying the solitude of northern Wisconsin and the many outdoor activities which have long been a central part of their lives. Among a variety of interests, careers, and avocations the Stoneciphers pursued was a business they started in the early 1970s. Recently, they reflected on the beginnings of this business, the reasons for starting it, the philosophy that guided it, and the thinking that went into decisions about location, products, and related issues.

THE FOUNDING

The Stoneciphers explain that their motives in starting the business were "multiple and partially involved the social environment of the early 70s." In Ray's own words:

We had an opportunity to purchase a piece of property consisting of two large metal buildings and an older house at a very attractive price and we could purchase it on very attractive land contract terms. The buildings, the land, and the house had been let go very badly for a number of years and thus required a lot of work to put back into good condition, but they were all structurally sound. We proceeded to start work on the property during the summer and by the following fall everything was starting to look better. It then occurred to us that we needed to do something with the metal buildings. Lots of ideas were thought of and rejected for one reason or another until we hit on the idea of a retail outlet that would specialize in certain types of sporting goods. The specialization would be centered on people-powered recreational equipment.

The reason for this special focus was that Ray and Ruthie had been involved for several years in several conservation organizations and realized that people-powered equipment used essentially no fuels, and was quiet and compatible with the environment. It was also consistent with the trend toward physical fitness. Ray explains further:

Ruthie and I had been involved for a number of years prior to this in backpacking, cross-country skiing, etc. We therefore felt we had some expertise in these areas. In addition, at that particular time there were almost no sources of this equipment or expertise available in the whole area (Wisconsin, Illinois, etc.).

Source: This case was prepared by Cyril C. Ling, University of Wisconsin, Whitewater, with the assistance of Michael R. Hansen and Paul Klein and is intended to be used as a basis for class discussion. Presented and accepted by the refereed Midwest Society for Case Research. All rights reserved to the author and the Midwest Society Case Research. Copyrighted © 1989 by Cyril C. Ling.

Ray was a professor of physics and astronomy at the University of Wisconsin, Whitewater, and Ruthie had a masters degree in home economics. They certainly didn't consider themselves to be experts in business. Their assessment:

> We had absolutely no experience at running a retail business, but we figured that if we used our heads, stayed out of debt and worked our "rears off" we could make it work. We assumed that it would take at least three years to make it profitable and we decided we would build it and finance it out of our own pocket with only the occasional use of short term bank loans (usually three month loans). We also decided that we would only carry top line equipment and depend on our expertise to show people why they were better off purchasing the best rather than second rate equipment.

In addition to these business and personal factors, the university setting in the early 1970s was another complex and complicating ingredient. Across America, university campuses were embroiled in protests and Wisconsin's experience was not much different than that of other states. But, in Wisconsin there was an added reality. In 1971, the University of Wisconsin and the Wisconsin State University system merged to create the University of Wisconsin System. It is not surprising that considerable uncertainty would accompany such a large scale undertaking. Plans were being developed, promises were made, realities were faced, protests continued, campus security issues mounted, and the people involved confronted substantial discomfort. With all these problems accompanied by program cuts and faculty terminations, the Stoneciphers nurtured their new business to help provide some stability, independence, and peace of mind in the face of turbulence. Finally, the business was a component in their retirement planning, providing flexibility in the timing of and transition to retirement.

The name of the business has seemed intriguing. Ray's explanation of their choice is interesting.

> We do not like to see or hear snowmobiles, A.T.V.'s, dirt motorcycles, or motor boats in our environment. We believe it is far too noisy in almost everyone's environment, and our need to cut our use of fossil fuels is very dominant in our thinking. We see the lack of a national commitment to reduce the burning of fossil fuels as among the most serious threats facing this nation and the biota itself . . . . The name "Quiet Hut" expressed our philosophy.

EARLY TRANSITIONS

The Quiet Hut was established outside of Whitewater, a community of 11,000 in south-central Wisconsin, in 1972. The product line was predictable, given the founders' philosophy—canoes, kayaks, some bicycles, backpacks, cross-country skis, and assorted camping gear. In 1975, a customer came in for repair work on his bicycle. Ruthie explained that they had no repair capability, but that he was welcome to use the tools they had and work on his bike there. Dave Saalsaa worked on his bike for three days and when he finished, Ray offered him a job repairing customers' bicycles.

Ray expanded the bicycle business with Dave's help, converting a connecting back room to a cycle repair shop and showroom. The expanded venture proved successful enough that the next step was taken—acquisition of the Raleigh franchise. They sought a Schwinn franchise also, but the bike maker's restrictions on store layout, and shared space with a competing brand (Raleigh) initially prevented this. Somewhat later, Schwinn's policies changed and that franchise was acquired. The bicycle business became the dominant part of the Quiet Hut's product line, and Dave's responsibilities continued to grow; he became general manager of the business by the early 1980s. The Trek bicycle line was added, strengthening that part of the business even more.

After a decade of building the business and giving increasing operating authority to Dave, Ray and Ruthie Stonecipher decided it was time for them to step away from the business. Dave, now married and finished with his degree, faced a difficult choice: either go look for a new job or buy the business. By the end of 1983, Dave and Grace Saalsaa were the new owners of the Quiet Hut, and like their mentors, performed all of the business functions themselves, except for the work done by their outside accountant.

The new owner's first year was a difficult one. Like many small businesses, the Saalsaa's venture lacked cash, a condition made more serious by a winter of light snow and a rainy summer. Their response to these difficult conditions was an analysis of the shortcomings of their location. The result was a move from their semi-rural site to one near downtown Whitewater.

DEVELOPMENT AND FOCUS

From its inception, the Quiet Hut had concentrated on high quality products accompanied by personal service, in areas about which the owners were knowledgeable and expert. The process of passing product knowledge to the customer enables customers to differentiate among products and make informed buying decisions. This approach is vital to the kind of product/market segmentation the Quiet Hut seeks. Competing with large volume discounters on a price basis is generally not a viable strategy for small businesses and the Quiet Hut is no exception. The business began with the founders, then Dave, having substantial knowledge about the products they elected to sell. This forms the base on which they chose to compete.

Products and accessories were developed around the bicycle and ski lines to produce business stability. The franchises for two lines of skis, Fischer and Landsem, had to be reacquired following transfer of the business to the Saalsaas, as did the Schwinn franchise. Not only were these products important to the business, but so was instruction which had been part of the service provided since the start.

The initial move from the semi-rural location on SR 59 to near downtown, one block off Main Street (US12), contained both positives and negatives. The new location, on Fremont Street, provided greater visibility to the business, had more than twice the vehicle traffic passing it daily, and put the business closer to its customers. Fremont Street was at the western edge of the downtown stopping area and within walking distance of the university campus. The new facility, a converted house, was not as well suited to business as the previous space. In the house, all three levels needed to be used for merchandise and their inventory had to be cut due to the space limitations. Shopping in a house was somewhat awkward, and even uncomfortable for some customers, and the visibility the location provided, though improved, was still not ideal. An unexpected problem was vandalism; the house was in the general path trod between the campus and downtown taverns. Fence repairs and general cleanup were regularly needed.

COMPETITORS

Over the decade and one-half that the business has existed, competition has grown from nearly nothing to considerable. Dave sees the Yellow Jersey in Madison as the most aggressive competitor. The Madison area is 40 miles from Whitewater and Yellow Jersey has four stores there, offering only bicycles and cycle repair. Wheel and Sprocket in Milwaukee (55 miles east) offers essentially the same type of product line as the Saalsaa's store and nearly the same services. Haack's in Madison and Janesville (30 miles southwest) offers both skis and cycles with comparable quality and prices. There is no direct competitor in Whitewater.

GROWTH

While growth is one of the positive and attractive goals a business seeks, it brings new problems and challenges. One of the early signs and problems of growth is the need for additional staffing. The Saalsaas found they could no longer accomplish all of the work themselves; new part-time and full-time employees were needed. Over the past five years, two full-time and four part-time people were hired. Also, a full-time cycle repairman was added to free Dave for other functions. Training, also, has had to receive attention. The Quiet Hut's reputation has always been associated with product knowledge, customer information and education, and service. When customers are turned over to employees, training becomes the critical factor that assures the business philosophy is executed as the owners wish. Dave and Grace have generally made employment decisions jointly, with Grace handling most of the employment and training functions and Dave doing training in cycle repair.

Growth brings changes, too, in the product line. Over the past few years, Trek has become the shop's best selling bike and the Raleigh line has been dropped. Fischer skis, now offered in both touring and racing cross-country models, are the store's best selling skis. Other product areas have been expanded to further complement the main lines. Saddle bags, water bottles, bicycle helmets, ski totes, ski clothing, gloves and most recently athletic clothing have been added. This increase in inventory has only been possible due to a second change in location which solved the space constraints of the Fremont Street house. The summer of 1986 was also one of very heavy rainfall again followed by a winter of less than normal snowfall. And, 1987 brought another new location, to the heart of the downtown area. But, this relocation would not likely have occurred if prime space on Main Street had not been available. The new site is a corner facility in one of the two main business blocks in the downtown portion of Main (US12). The location offers numerous advantages including substantial product display space, high visibility, the highest traffic count of any Whitewater street, and greater proximity to the campus as well as downtown shoppers. The building affords three times the space of the Fremont Street house, so greater product expansion is possible. A name change accompanied the new location; Quiet Hut Sports, the owners believe, is more descriptive of the real nature of the business.

The Main Street location had immediate effects. Business volume recovered from 1986, product line expansion has been achieved, and Quiet Hut Sports has been able to pay its bills when competitors have not. Further, the customer radius has continued to grow. Both bike and ski customers come from distances of 100 miles, suggesting that the strategies initiated at the founding, and developed over more than 15 years, are being validated by customers. While the early years were difficult, learning was gradual, weather was often terrible, and capital was short, Quiet Hut Sports survived these critical forces.

CRITICAL FORCES

Businesses in recreational types of products and services generally feel the impacts of changing economic conditions, especially shifts in disposable personal income. While these trends have had some effects on Quiet Hut Sports, Dave Saalsaa believes the business is buffered by two factors: the area economy is a mixed, stable economy and the university presence is a direct stabilizer for his product-markets. But, neither products nor markets are static. Quiet Hut has had to be responsive to customer needs and demands and it has had to maintain its quality image. It has added the technology represented by BMX and other specialized types of bikes and given up the Raleigh line. Repair service, too, has had to adjust to the changing technology from manufacturers.

A trend toward increased bicycling has been especially important to the business. In the 70s, the growth was partly due to the substantial rise in fuel prices, but more recently has resulted from several factors. The physical fitness trend has spilled over to cycling and public exposure through Olympic television coverage and movies has also tended to expand cycling. The National Sporting Goods Association claims cycling is exceeded only by swimming in number of participants.[1] Also significant is that cyclists are spending as much on clothing as they do on bikes.[2] Cross-country skiing shows a similar sales pattern.[3] Also important to Quiet Hut is the proximity to the Kettle Moraine recreation area bike trail.

Seasonality is another fact of life that Quiet Hut Sports faces. In addition to the changing weather of the seasons, each business seems to have its own peak period of activity. The peak sales period in bicycling is generally from April through June. Cross-country ski sales tend to be highest in December through February. Inventory decisions must obviously be made well in advance, with marketing and promotion efforts timed to maximize sales.

INTERNAL CHARACTERISTICS

Dave and Grace Saalsaa are the greatest resource Quiet Hut has. When they purchased the business in 1983, they had no experience owning, operating, or managing a business. Dave's degree is in geography and Grace's is in instrumental music. Their approach to business decisions tends to be complementary; Dave advocates risk-taking, Grace takes a conservative posture. The result tends to a middle ground that has made for some stability. They see their strengths as knowledge of the product, of the customer, and of the competition. They do not perceive themselves as particularly

[1] Claire Walter, "Selling America's No. 2 Sport: Bicycling," *Stores*, December, 1986, p. 36. See also, David DiBello, "Cycle Mania," *S&MM*, November 11, 1985, p. 42.

[2] Stephen Ready, "Cycle Mania," *S&MM*, November 11, 1985, p. 30.

[3] Claire Walter, "Skiing Sophistication," *Stores*, December 1985, p. 33.

strong or knowledgeable managers nor, they admit, do they conceptualize their business. Little is written down about how they manage the business and they find it difficult to explain their success. Survival is still a very high priority value.

Finance is probably the weakest area of the business, but recognizing that fact, they engaged an accountant shortly after taking over the firm. That decision has helped in day-to-day financial activity, but has not addressed the chronic capital problem. Profits are being reinvested to finance growth on a fairly slow basis.

Marketing is much stronger in the owner's view. They believe they have a good grasp of their customer profile—an active person interested in physical fitness, upwardly mobile, with a high education level, in the 18–35 age range currently. Generally, 7 percent of sales is deployed to advertising and promotion, most of which is in print ads in the six area newspapers, and a statewide magazine. Downtown retail promotions and preferred customer events are also used. Promotional leaflets have been distributed at the university and the yellow pages are utilized. The owners believe radio advertising has not been cost-effective. No formal market research has been done, but the Saalsaas think more of their business comes from the general area than from the student population. More attention to marketing to students is being undertaken. Pricing is consistent with the product/market segment long ago chosen for the Quiet Hut—in general, high quality, enduring products competitively priced in the upper segment of their markets.

THE FUTURE

The Saalsaas see no reason to alter the fabric of their business developed over a 17-year period. They plan to remain with a high-quality product line, high-priced end of the market, with strength in product knowledge and customer service and information. The recent additions of a larger clothing inventory and mountain bikes have yet to fully develop in the marketplace. Recent national trends have shown expenditure growth for sports equipment and sports clothing at about 4 percent annually and for sports footwear, 7 percent annually.[4]

Dave and Grace have discussed the addition of downhill skis, but feel they currently lack experience in this area. Also under consideration is an expansion into business clothing. A new Wal-Mart has opened in Whitewater, a new large K-Mart has recently opened in Delavan, about 15 miles away, and a new sporting goods store has opened next door to the Quiet Hut.

DISCUSSION QUESTIONS

1. What are the internal strengths of Quiet Hut Sports?
2. What are the external *internal* weaknesses?
3. What are the firm's external opportunities?
4. What external threats face the business?
5. What is the firm's current strategy?
6. What are the company's objectives? ■

---

[4]Standard and Poor's Industry Surveys, "Leisure Time," March 26, 1987, p. 139.

Part Two Entrepreneurial Simulation Program

DEVELOPING A PLAN OF ACTION

Whether it's a shoe store or a computer repair shop, to be successful you must develop a plan detailing how you will operate your enterprise. You do not just open a retail store with the idea that you will handle problems as they arise. There are too many variables to consider and too many decisions that need to be made in a timely manner. Before you begin any entrepreneurial operation, you must have a plan of action.

ESP provides you with an opportunity to set up such a plan of action. You now know all about financial plans for borrowing money, marketing plans for selling your product, and operational plans for the day-to-day operation of your business. These are very important, but can be somewhat awkward to develop for a simulated retail operation. The simulated environment is more limiting than if you were opening an actual shoe store. Still there are approaches you can take that will result in an effective plan of action for your store.

The first step is to identify what kind of store yours will be. This is known as a mission statement. The mission statement should be a paragraph or two in which you formally state your plan of action in the broadest terms. What kind of store do you want to operate in this simulated retail environment? Your store can be one that specializes in quality shoes. Your store might cater only to children. Perhaps your store will sell only women's shoes. You can make your store whatever you want it to be, only you have to formally state your intentions.

The second step is to lay out your goals. Goals are something that you will constantly strive to attain, but will never reach. With these goals you will state how you plan to achieve what you have stated in your mission statement. Goals have to do with such things as market share, pricing strategy, growth, and inventory control. These goals should be operationally specific, but not time specific, in their attainment. As the simulation continues, you will be dealing with different sets of circumstances, but your goals should constantly guide you to success in your business venture. Remember to keep the goals consistent with the reality of the simulated environment. Between three and eight goals should be sufficient in the development of your plan.

The third step is to develop the specific objectives that you will strive to attain as part of your commitment to reaching your goals. Objectives differ from goals in that they are designed to be reached by a specified point in time. Also, objectives are specific to the goals. An example of an objective, under an inventory control goal, would be to never have more than twice the number of shoes at the beginning of a new month than you plan to sell that month. Each objective should be time specific. Each objective should be measurable. Each objective should, if and when attained, bring you closer to reaching the overall goal. Make your goals meaningful and realistic in the limitations of the simulated environment. Have anywhere from two to six objectives under each goal, and consider adding others if and when appropriate throughout the simulated year.

The fourth step is to lay out any equations, charts, spreadsheets, pro forma statements, or whatever else you may need to make your decisions or to evaluate your goals. These can be operational procedures that you could use every month when making your decisions. Or they can be projections that could be compared to actual performance on a monthly basis. Take, for example, the objective identified in the previous paragraph. How will you decide how many shoes to order each month to keep the inventory level at the start of a new month under twice the number you plan to sell? Is there an equation that will formulate a working relationship between existing inventory, new purchases, and sales that could help you decide how many lots to order each month? Is there a chart or a table that you can put together to help you with that kind of decision? Such tools will not only help you make your monthly decisions, but will also keep you aware and on track of your goals and objectives.

This four-step process will help you plan and carry out a successful year in the retail shoe business. The time you spend developing your plan will be time well spent, and will launch you on the road to becoming a successful retail merchant. This is only the beginning of an effective overall business plan. It may only be the first step, but you will find it will help you focus on success as a retail shoe store owner.

DISCUSSION QUESTIONS

1. Put together a mission statement for your store. You may be several months into the simulation, but use this occasion to state who you are and what your perceived image should be to your customers.

2. Document one goal that follows from your mission statement. Describe how that goal relates to your mission statement, and how it will help in your ambition to be as successful in the retail shoe business as possible.

3. Put together one objective that relates to your goal. Be specific as to when you will achieve this objective and how you will be able to measure whether or not you were successful in its attainment.

4. Design some model or instrument that will help you achieve your objective and/or measure your success. Describe how to apply the technique so that someone else could use it in your absence.

Part Three

Start-up Problems

■ *The purpose of Part Three is to examine the problems that face new small businesses as they begin operations. In particular, we will focus our study on the financial, location, layout, and legal issues involved in the start-up of operations.*

In Chapter 8 we will examine how small businesses go about raising the necessary capital for their operations. Particular attention will be devoted to the various types of capital that can be raised and to the sources of such capital.

Next, in Chapter 9, we will analyze how small businesses go about determining their location and layout. We will pose the question "Is it better to lease or to buy?" and provide examples of cases that illustrate when each approach is a wise strategy. The last part of Chapter 9 presents key information about the importance of layout in various types of small business: retail, wholesale, service, and manufacturing.

Chapter 10, the last chapter in Part Three, examines the three legal forms of organization: the proprietorship, the partnership, and the corporation. We will present the advantages and disadvantages associated with each and discuss what an "S" corporation is and how it works.

When you have finished studying the material in Part Three, you will be familiar with the major operating problems that face a fledgling small business and the methods for dealing with these problems.

CHAPTER 8

Sources of
Start-up Capital

Objectives

One of the first questions the small business person must confront is "Where will the money to start the business be obtained?" If the individual can answer this, a follow-up question is "After those initial funds are exhausted, where will more be raised?" Remember, it is not enough for a small business to get started; it must be able to survive at least 90 days without further inflows of funds. Until that much capital is available, the business owner is not yet ready to launch the venture.

Some experts recommend that a new enterprise be able to operate for up to six months without any inflow of funds from operations. Only if the company has raised this amount of money should the owner begin business. In many cases, this amount may be more than adequate. However, it does help make the point that few businesses have ever been started with too much initial funding. Most of those that go insolvent or cease operations during their first year do so because they have simply run out of money.

In Chapter 8 we are going to study the various ways of obtaining initial capital funding. The first objective is to examine the various types of capital that are available to the small business. The second objective is to study the various sources of capital that the owner should investigate. Particular attention will be given to the role of the Small Business Administration in this process. When you have finished studying Chapter 8 you will be able to:

1. Distinguish among short-term, intermediate-term, and long-term loans.

2. Describe what is meant by equity capital.

3. Discuss these sources of capital: internal funds, trade credit, equity sources, banks, and other private sources.

4. Explain the role of the Small Business Administration in helping small businesses secure funding, as well as the part played by the Small Business Investment Corporation.

TYPES OF CAPITAL

Every business needs capital in order to begin and maintain operations. Basically there are four types of capital:

1. short-term loans

2. intermediate-term loans

3. long-term loans

4. equity capital

SHORT-TERM LOANS

A **short-term loan** is one that is scheduled to be repaid within a period of one year. The most common forms of short-term loans are **trade credit**—which is created when the seller allows the buyer to take the merchandise immediately and pay for it later—and short-term bank loans. Short-term loans are particularly helpful when there is a temporary need for more capital, as in the case of a retailer who builds up a seasonal inventory and pays for it when it is sold. For example, it is typical to find businesses that sell swimwear increasing their inventory during the late spring, while those that sell skiwear will begin building up their inventory in the early to mid fall. Without trade credit or a short-term bank loan, the owner would have to have a large amount of capital on hand to handle peak buying periods.

Most trade credit and short-term bank loans are **self-liquidating;** that is, the money obtained from the sale of the inventory is used to pay off the loan. In the case of bank financing, most of these loans are unsecured, which means that they are not backed by collateral. However, if the business does not have a good credit rating or a lot of money is involved, the bank will insist that the loan be secured by some of the business's assets.[1]

INTERMEDIATE-TERM LOANS

Intermediate-term loans provide capital for periods from one to ten years. Such loans are usually paid back in a series of installments. For example, if a business borrows $10,000 with principle and interest due once a year and the rate of interest is 10 percent, the loan would be repaid as shown in Table 8-1.

Table 8-1 Loan Repayment Schedule

END OF YEAR	BALANCE	DUE Principal	DUE Interest	DUE Total
1	$10,000	$1,000	$1,000	$2,000
2	9,000	1,000	900	1,900
3	8,000	1,000	800	1,800
4	7,000	1,000	700	1,700
5	6,000	1,000	600	1,600
6	5,000	1,000	500	1,500
7	4,000	1,000	400	1,400
8	3,000	1,000	300	1,300
9	2,000	1,000	200	1,200
10	1,000	1,000	100	1,100

[1] Jerry A. Viscione, "How Long Should You Borrow Short Term?" *Harvard Business Review,* March/April 1986, pp. 20–34.

Intermediate-term loans fill the gap in the financial requirements of many small- and moderate-size businesses. They make capital available for other than temporary needs, helping the owner who needs funds to expand the operation but lacks the capital resources. Thanks to this type of loan, owners are able to purchase machinery, equipment, and other fixed assets immediately and pay for them over the life of the loan.

In return, most banks and other lenders impose certain conditions. Primary among them is usually the right of the lender to control major expenditures during the life of the loan and the requirement that the borrower furnish the lender with annual financial statements. In this way the business is prevented from doing anything that might seriously endanger its chances of repaying the loan. Furthermore, it is common for the loan to be backed by collateral, such as the plant and equipment that the business has purchased with the proceeds of the loan.

LONG-TERM LOANS

Long-term loans have a duration of ten or more years. Only businesses that have been in existence for an extended period of time can get loans of this duration. Thus, they are usually reserved for large, stable corporations. Additionally, it is common for the lender to insist on collateral. When collateral is given in the form of a mortgage, however, long-term loans can also be secured by small- and intermediate-size businesses. After all, if the business goes bankrupt, the bank can always step in, take the property and sell it, thereby recovering at least part of the loan. Aside from this method of securing long-term funds, however, the small business must often turn to equity capital to meet its needs.

EQUITY CAPITAL

Equity capital is not a loan in the strict sense of the word. It is an investment in the business, and there is no promise on the part of the firm to repay this capital. The investment, which usually comes about through the sale of common stock, is a permanent part of the firm's capital structure. This structure can be increased by either investing profits back into the business or selling additional stock to investors.

In many cases, equity capital is the only way in which a small business can increase its capital base. Banks and other financial institutions may not be willing to assume the risk associated with lending the firm money. Or the company may have borrowed so much already that the bank is unwilling to go any further. In financial terms, the company is **overextended;** it has nothing more to borrow against. When this happens, the business must either sell stock, plow back earnings, or pass up growth opportunities because there are no additional sources of capital to tap in taking advantage of these opportunities.

SOURCES OF CAPITAL

Choosing a source of capital is not an easy decision. There are numerous alternatives, depending on the business, how much funding is needed, its credit rating, prior sales records, and the economy in general.[2] The following sections examine

---

[2]James McNeill Stancill, "How Much Money Does Your Venture Need?" *Harvard Business Review,* May/June 1986, pp. 122–39.

some of the major sources of capital that are available to the small business firm and their relative merits and drawbacks.[3]

INTERNAL FUNDS

One of the most basic sources of capital, often overlooked by small business people, is **internal funds.** These are monies that have been kept in the firm in the form of retained earnings. Of course, few businesspeople forget what they have earned in profits the previous year and reinvested in the business; but many of them fail to consider that what they will make this year can be invested in the business to help meet expansion needs. Instead they rush outside looking for bank loans. *The first place to look for funding is internally.* With careful budgeting, many small firms can raise part or all of the money they need. (See Small Business Success: Club Sportswear, Inc.)

TRADE CREDIT

Another commonly overlooked source of capital is **trade credit,** by which suppliers, in effect, help finance operations. For example, in most credit transactions there

Club Sportswear, which began with the sale of cleverly designed T-shirts, now boasts 30 in-house employees and 1,600 accounts.

---

[3]Bill Liebtag, "Capital Formation by Small Business," *Journal of Accounting,* June 1987, pp. 82–92. Also, for a complete analysis of sources of finance for small businesses see "Financing Patterns of Small Business," *The State of Small Business: A Report of the President* (Washington, D. C.: U.S. Government Printing Office, 1990), pp. 65–89.

■ SMALL BUSINESS SUCCESS ■

Club Sportswear, Inc.

In 1984 a 19-year-old junior at the University of Southern California named Tom Knapp decided to earn extra money by designing T-shirts with clever logos and then selling the shirts to students. He bought 120 T-shirts at $4 each and inscribed the logo "Club USC" on a design of a spilling martini. Knapp priced the shirts at $9 each and sold every one within a week earning himself revenues of $1,080 on the original purchase of $480.

Knapp's instant success motivated him to develop a distinctive line of sportswear that would be marketed nationally. He selected volleyball beachwear as the targeted niche since the U.S. men's volleyball team had captured the gold medal in the 1984 Olympics. In his $2\frac{1}{2}$-room apartment, Knapp developed Club Sportswear and designed a logo of a yacht club flag in green, pink, and blue with a backward "C" and a backward "S".

Knapp first produced volleyball shorts and sweatshirts but in order to compete with established companies he had to attend trade shows and sponsor volleyball tournaments. Knapp's agreement to sponsor tournaments successfully increased his company's name recognition.

The hard work began to pay off. By the end of 1985 sales totaled $100,000 and Club Sportswear was growing. Knapp rented an office, hired four employees, and put four commissioned sales representatives on the road. By the end of 1986 sales had grown by 700 percent reaching $800,000. Sales have doubled every year since that time and Tom Knapp, now 25 years old, has expanded Club Sportswear, Inc., to include 30 in-house employees, 23 sales representatives covering the U.S., and 1,600 accounts.

Source: Adapted from Bob Weinstein, "The Beach Boy," *Entrepreneur*, August 1990, pp. 82–86.

are terms of 30, 60, or 90 days. The most common trade-credit terms are **2/10, net 30** **("two ten, net thirty")**: if the buyer pays the bill within 10 days there is a 2 percent discount, and regardless of the buyer's position on payment schedules, the entire bill must be paid within 30 days.

Consider the effects of this approach in the case of a business that buys $10,000 worth of merchandise on the first day of every month. If paid for on delivery the owner needs to have $10,000 available. Like most owners of small businesses, however, he does not have this much on hand, so he arranges for a bank loan. Borrowing the money on the first of every month and repaying it by the thirtieth, for all practical purposes, results in his business having a $10,000 loan outstanding at all times. Assuming a 10 percent interest rate, his annual loan cost is $1,000.

Trade credit is the third approach that can be used to finance the inventory. By taking delivery on the first of the month and not paying until the tenth, the small business owner will need a loan for only twenty days per month, so the interest paid for the year will be only $667 ($10,000 × 0.1 × 20/30). Furthermore, the owner gets his 2 percent discount, or $200 per month off his bill. In a year's time the use of trade credit is saving the business $2,400. After subtracting the loan cost of $667, the owner is ahead $1,733. Thus, trade discounts can be very profitable.

Another way of using trade credit is to get the supplier to provide the goods on **consignment.** Under this type of arrangement the buyer does not pay for the goods until they are sold. Auto dealers, large appliance retailers, and farm equipment dealers, for example, often pay for the goods only after they are sold.

EQUITY SOURCES

One of the most preferable methods of obtaining permanent capital is through equity sources.[4] In tapping these sources, the small business owner should first look at his or her own financial resources. Are there any personal funds that could be invested in the business? Some small business owners find that they have cash surrender value in their life insurance policies that can be invested in the business. Or they have some property against which they can borrow money for use in the company.

Next the owner should turn to personal friends who might be interested in investing in the business. Tempering one's efforts in this area with the cliche "don't mix business and friendship," the owner can examine this avenue of investment.

Finally, in just about every community in the country there are people with idle funds to invest in a worthwhile venture. If the small business owner does not know these people personally, an accountant or banker might be able to refer them to one in this category.

BANKS

Banks offer many types of loan services. Some of the most common are straight commercial loans, term loans, accounts receivable loans, warehouse receipt loans, and collateral loans. The following sections examine each.

STRAIGHT COMMERCIAL LOANS   These loans are usually made for a period of 30 to 90 days. They are generally based on the financial statements of the borrower and are self-liquidating. It is common to find these loans being used for seasonal financing and for building up inventories.

TERM LOANS   Term loans have a maturity of between one and ten years. Most are short-term (one to four years) and unsecured. Longer-term loans, however, are generally backed by some of the firm's assets. In either event, small loan repayments are made throughout the life of the loan—monthly, quarterly, every six months, or annually. Depending on the specific terms of the agreement, it is not uncommon for a large payment to be made at the end of the loan. This is referred to as a **balloon loan,** in which case the periodic repayments are rather small with the large bulk of the loan paid off at the end of the term. This, of course, can be very beneficial to a small business because it means that on a loan of $25,000 for five years, perhaps as much as $20,000 can be paid at the end. This gives the company time to build up its business before having to make the large, final payment. Furthermore, today's dollars will be inflated in five years, so the business is able to borrow "hard" dollars now and repay the loan with "soft" dollars later on.

---

[4]John B. Maier II and David A. Walker, "The Role of Venture Capital in Financing Small Business," *Journal of Business Venturing,* Summer 1987, pp. 207–14; and W. Keith Schilt, "How to Obtain Venture Capital," *Business Horizons,* May/June 1987, pp. 76–81.

ACCOUNTS RECEIVABLE LOANS   Accounts receivable loans are made by many large banks. In this case, the loan is made against the company's receivables; when they are collected, the bank is repaid. In some instances, the bank becomes actively involved by notifying the business's customers that payments on their accounts are to be made directly to the bank. These collections are then credited to the account of the borrower, after service and interest charges are deducted, of course. In other instances, the bank does not get directly involved, and the small business simply collects the receivables and sends the proceeds to the bank to repay the loan. The disadvantages of this type of loan arrangement are that the cost is high and considerable record keeping is required. As a result, a business has to have a large amount of accounts receivable for this method of raising capital to be feasible.

WAREHOUSE RECEIPT LOANS   Under this form of financing, inventory is stored in warehouses and a receipt for the inventory is given to the bank as security for a loan that is used to pay off the supplier. As the business sells the merchandise, the business owner buys back portions of the loan. This kind of borrowing enables the business to get along with a smaller investment in working capital. However, loans of this type are used only for nonperishable items that are readily marketable. Thus if the business owner cannot sell the goods, the bank can assume ownership and seek a buyer of its own. Such an approach ensures that the bank will, at worst, suffer only a partial loss of the loan.

COLLATERAL LOANS   These loans are made by banks on the basis of such security as real estate mortgages, life insurance policies (the cash surrender value), stocks, and bonds. The borrower puts up the collateral, and the bank advances the money. As the loan is repaid, the collateral is returned to the borrower. (See Small Business Owner's Notebook: The Bank and the Small Business Owner.)

OTHER PRIVATE SOURCES OF CAPITAL

In addition to the capital sources discussed in the preceding sections, there are other private sources of capital. The following sections examine some of these sources.

INSURANCE COMPANIES   Insurance companies collect billions of dollars every year. Some of these funds are used to pay claims, but a large portion is invested. This is particularly true in the case of life insurance. Few people who buy a life insurance policy will die this year; however, the insurance company has to invest the monies paid for premiums in order to pay the face value of the policy when the policyholder does die. One of the primary ways the company accrues money is by investing in real estate loans or mortgages, particularly in new construction. Therefore, insurance companies may be especially interested in lending the small business owner money if he or she has a construction firm. Also, if the owner has an insurance policy that has built up some cash surrender value, he or she can borrow that money at a relatively low interest rate. For example, while most banks today are charging 10 percent annual interest for loans, the typical insurance policy allows the policyholder to borrow the cash surrender value at 5 to 6 percent.

FINANCE COMPANIES   Some finance companies specialize in lending money to businesses. These firms are not to be confused with personal finance companies, which loan small sums to individual consumers. These finance companies deal mostly in

■ **SMALL BUSINESS OWNER'S NOTEBOOK** ■

The Bank and the Small Business Owner

Most small business owners realize the various services that a good bank should provide. Loans, lines of credit, competent financial advice, and willingness to handle special projects are some of the usual bank services. As they acquire these services, many small business owners feel dominated by the bank. However, small business owners have certain rights when dealing with banks. The following legal reminders underscore the fact that the banker-customer relationship is a *mutual* one.

1. FIDUCIARY RELATIONSHIP   The law views the bank-customer relationship as "fiduciary," that is, one of extreme trust and confidence. Therefore, when dispensing financial advice a bank must put the customer's interests ahead of its own.

2. ULTIMATUMS   Banks must avoid demands that put a business in poor situations, such as demanding a loan payment that the bank knows would result in failure of the business.

3. MISREPRESENTATION   Banks must not suppress facts or policies. If penalties or fees are required, then the bank must clearly specify them in agreements with the customer.

4. ARM'S LENGTH   Banks must maintain an "arm's-length" distance from business operations. They cannot interfere with the management of the company.

5. FAIR AND HONEST   The law requires fair treatment of all customers. The size of a business makes no difference—all customers are to be given fair arrangements.

Source: Adapted from A. Barry Cappello, "Finding a New Bank," *Small Business Reports,* June 1989, pp. 52–57.

secured loans, usually with interest rates much higher than those charged by banks. Finance companies often provide loans in cases where a bank has reviewed the situation and decided against granting the business a loan. Since the potential risk to the finance company is higher, the interest charge is also higher.

FACTORS   Another source of capital, especially short-term funds, is **accounts receivable factoring. Factors** (which are similar to brokers) advance companies money on the basis of accounts receivable. They differ from other financial sources in that they *buy* the accounts receivable. This means they purchase them **without recourse**—if a person who owes an account receivable does not pay, the factor is the one who loses money. By contrast, when a bank finances accounts receivable, the business that borrowed the funds must make good on a failure to pay. Since the factor takes a greater risk, the cost of factoring is much higher than that of accounts receivable financing. Additionally, the factor is unlikely to buy all of a business's accounts receivable.

Rather, the individual will determine which ones offer the best chance for payment and buy their accounts. The remainder will be left for the business to collect. Some businesspeople object to the high cost of factoring and to the factor dealing directly with their customers. However, in those cases where the small business needs money, factoring may be the only possible way to raise the necessary capital.

SMALL BUSINESS ADMINISTRATION

The Small Business Administration (SBA) is an independent agency of the federal government. It was established by Congress for the purpose of advising and assisting the nation's small businesses. One of the primary areas in which it helps small firms is by guaranteeing loans.

In past years the SBA had monies for direct loans. However, these funds have all but dried up. The only two groups that currently can obtain direct SBA loans are Vietnam veterans and handicapped individuals. All others who qualify for assistance must settle for SBA-guaranteed loans. These loans are negotiated by the small business owner and the bank with repayment guaranteed by the SBA.

Direct SBA loans currently have a maximum of $150,000, whereas the loan-guarantee program allows the SBA to go to a maximum of $750,000. Small business people, negotiating the best rate they can with their local banker, are paying approximately $2\frac{1}{4}$ percent over the prime rate for loans of seven years or less and $2\frac{3}{4}$ percent over the prime rate for loans of longer than seven years.[5]

In order to qualify for a direct or guaranteed SBA loan, a company must qualify as a small business and meet the agency's credit requirements. In order to be a small business (as explained in Chapter 1) the company must

1. be independently owned and operated

2. not be dominant in its field

3. meet certain standards of size in terms of employment or annual receipts

In order to meet SBA credit requirements, the applicant must[6]

1. be of good character

2. show the ability to operate a business successfully

3. have enough capital in an existing firm so that, with an SBA loan, the business can operate on a sound financial basis

4. show that the proposed loan is of such sound value or is so secured as to reasonably ensure repayment

5. show that the past earnings record and future prospects of the firm indicate ability to repay the loan and other fixed debts, if any, out of profits

6. be able to provide, from personal resources, sufficient funds to have a reasonable amount at hand to withstand possible losses, particularly during the early stages of a new venture

---

[5]"Fact Sheet—SBA Loan Program" (Washington, D.C.: U.S. Small Business Administration, 1987).

[6]"Fact Sheet—SBA Loan Program" (Washington, D.C.: U.S. Small Business Administration, 1987).

An individual or business that meets these requirements can then formally apply for a loan. The SBA recommends that those already in business follow seven steps:

1. Prepare a current financial statement (balance sheet) listing all assets and all liabilities of the business.

2. Prepare an earnings (profit and loss) statement for the current period to the date of the balance sheet.

3. Prepare a current personal financial statement of the owner, or of each partner or stockholder that owns 20 percent or more of the corporate stock.

4. List the collateral to be offered as security for the loan and estimate the present market value of each item.

5. State the amount of the loan being requested and the exact purposes for which it will be used.

6. Take all of this material to your banker and ask for a direct bank loan. If you are turned down, ask the bank to make the loan under the SBA's Loan Guarantee Plan or Immediate Participation Plan. If the bank is interested in an SBA guaranteed or participation loan, ask the banker to contact the SBA and discuss the application. In most such cases, the SBA deals directly with the bank.

7. If a guaranteed loan or a participation loan is not available, write or visit the nearest SBA office.

Individuals who need a loan in order to start a business should follow eight steps:

1. Describe the type of business to be established.

2. Describe your experience and management capabilities.

3. Prepare an estimate of how much you or others have to invest in the business and how much you will need to borrow.

4. Prepare a current financial statement, listing all personal assets and liabilities.

5. Prepare a detailed projection of earnings for the first year the business will be in operation.

6. List the collateral to be offered as security for the loan and estimate the present market value of each item.

7. Take all of this material to your banker and ask for a direct bank loan. If you are turned down, ask the bank to make the loan under the SBA's Loan Guarantee Plan or Immediate Participation Plan. If the bank is interested in an SBA guaranteed or participation loan, ask the banker to contact the SBA and discuss the application. In most such cases, the SBA deals directly with the bank.

8. If a guaranteed loan or a participation loan is not available, write or visit the nearest SBA office.[7]

---

[7]The information in this section can be found in "Fact Sheet—SBA Loan Program" (Washington, D.C.: U.S. Small Business Administration, 1987).

STATE AND LOCAL DEVELOPMENT COMPANIES

The SBA is also authorized to lend funds to state and local development companies for use in financing specific small businesses. An increasing number of states and local communities are organizing development corporations, or industrial foundations, to promote the establishment or expansion of business in their areas. Some of the services offered by these organizations are listed below:

- □ BUYING, DEVELOPING, AND SELLING INDUSTRIAL SITES   This usually results in less delay and more reasonable prices for the small manufacturer seeking a site than negotiations through regular business channels.

- □ BUYING AND BUILDING PLANTS FOR LEASE OR SALE   Here, too, a purchase price may be lower than would have been available otherwise. If the plant is leased, less investment in fixed assets by the small business will be necessary and more money can be available for working capital.

- □ PROVIDING FUNDS BY DIRECT INTERMEDIATE- OR LONG-TERM LOANS OR BY PURCHASE OF STOCK IN THE BUSINESS   In some cases, development companies will lend larger amounts in proportion to the value of the security for longer periods than is customary for banks.

- □ GIVING MANAGEMENT, ENGINEERING, AND OTHER COUNSELING SERVICES TO SMALL BUSINESSES   By pooling the knowledge of the businesspeople of the community, an industrial foundation is often able to provide expert advice.

The SBA's role has diminished in recent years. During the 1970s it participated directly and actually loaned some of the funds to development companies. Today its role is that of guaranteeing part of the monies that are being raised. In a typical arrangement, the state or local development company will put up 10 percent of the total funds, borrow 50 percent from the bank, and float **debentures** (unsecured bonds) for the remainder. The SBA guarantees the debentures.

As an example, Table 8-2 provides the description of the Certified Development Company Program (503).

SMALL BUSINESS INVESTMENT COMPANIES

Another avenue for securing funding is through small business investment companies (SBICs), which are licensed by and operate under the responsibility of the SBA. The purpose of SBICs is to provide venture capital to small businesses. This capital can take various forms from secured to unsecured loans, debt security with equity characteristics, or simply pure equity as represented by common and preferred stock.

Venture capital is characterized as high risk and tends to be responsive to the needs of the small business rather than the requirements of those who are investing the funds. More importantly, there tends to be a very active and continuing relationship between the small business and the venture capitalist. At present, there are about 307 SBICs with total capital resources of about 2.4 billion dollars, including both private and government capital. These SBICs have a portfolio of approximately 2,000 small businesses with active financing balances of over 1 billion dollars.[8]

---

[8]For further information on SBICs, see John R. Wilmeth's article in *SBIC Digest*, April 1988; and *The Directory of Operating Small Business Investment Companies* (Small Business Administration: Investment Division), 1988.

Table 8-2 U.S. Small Business Administration
Certified Development Company Program (503)

GENERAL PROGRAM DESCRIPTION
The Certified Development Company Program was started in order to alleviate a perceived shortage of long-term credit for existing, healthy small businesses needing to expand operations. CDCs work with financial institutions to package long-term loans for small businesses. Loan proceeds may be used for fixed asset acquisition. This includes land acquisition/construction of business buildings, land improvements, purchase of an existing business building, purchase of long-life equipment, and leasehold improvements under certain conditions. In addition, loan proceeds may be used for certain costs associated with a project, such as surveying, engineering, and architectural fees. CDCs may not provide working capital.
In a typical loan package, 50% of the funds comes from a private lender, 40% comes from the issue of a 100% SBA-guaranteed debenture, and 10% comes from the borrowing firm.
The maximum SBA debenture/loan amount per small business is $500,000. The interest rate on the portion of the loan derived from the debenture issue is fixed and will equal approximately $\frac{3}{4}$% over the interest rate on treasury bonds of a comparable maturity. The financial institution will determine the interest rate charged on its portion of the loan, and this rate may be either fixed or variable.

ELIGIBILITY CRITERIA
CDCs can package loans for new-business start-ups and for existing businesses seeking to expand. However, most CDC assistance goes to existing businesses. In order to qualify for assistance, a firm must be independently owned and operated, be for profit, have been turned down by at least one financial institution for financing of the entire project, and have a net income not exceeding $2 million over the last two years. Other requirements may also apply.
Some types of businesses are explicitly excluded from eligibility under this program. These include lending institutions, passive investment companies, real estate investment companies, and unregulated media firms.

APPLICATION PROCEDURE
Preliminary information can be obtained directly from the appropriate CDC. If your project meets eligibility criteria, you will have to work with a financial institution to prepare an application. Several pieces of information will be required during the application. Among these are a description of the business; current and past financial statements; a description of the project to be financed; personal history and financial statements from all officers, directors, and owners of 20% or more of the firm's stock; resumes of the principals; a projected operating statement for two years; and a statement from a bank explaining why it will not finance the entire project.

Source: "Certified Development Company Program (503)," pamphlet published by the U.S. Small Business Administration, U.S. Government Printing Office, Washington, D.C.: 1990.

The SBICs are able to borrow $4 for every $1 of private capital through a line of credit established by the SBA for SBICs with the Federal Financing Bank. This practice of borrowing a lot more than is being put up by an investor is called **leveraging.** These funds are available for eligible SBICs on a monthly basis.[9]

In the past, many SBICs preferred to lend money to firms that were already in business. During the 1980s, however, they invested into start-ups, especially among firms in high-tech fields. Because of the gains made by some of these firms with

---

[9]See "Capital Crunch for SBICs," *Nation's Business*, September 1986, pp. 14–16.

their technological breakthroughs, SBICs realized that they were passing up a very high potential profit by excluding them from investment consideration. Today, most SBICs look for a modest but steady return on their investments.

Minority-enterprise SBICs (MESBICs) have been formed for the purpose of providing venture capital and equity financing to small businesses owned by people who are economically or socially disadvantaged. African Americans, Puerto Ricans, Mexican Americans, Native Americans, and Eskimos are included within this group. The MESBICs have an organizational structure similar to SBICs except that the nature of the SBA leverage is different. Certain rules and regulations have been liberalized to enable the MESBICs to overcome financing problems unique to businesses owned by members of minority groups. It is common to find MESBICs investing in tandem with commercial banks with funds 90 percent guaranteed under other SBA programs. In 1988 there were 128 minority-enterprise SBICs with total capital resources of 424 million dollars. They have a combined portfolio of more than 1,350 minority firms.[10]

SMALL BUSINESS INNOVATION RESEARCH PROGRAM

The Small Business Innovation Research (SBIR) Program was established in 1982 under the Small Business Innovation Development Act. While the SBIR solicitation process and award authority was assigned to participating federal agencies, the legislation authorizes SBA to

☐ implement the program government-wide

☐ set the governing program policy

☐ monitor the performance of the federal agencies participating in the program

☐ analyze the annual reports of each of these agencies on the progress of the SBIR program

☐ report SBA findings to Congress

The functions required of SBA under the Act are implemented through the Office of Innovation, Research, and Technology. Specifically, the Act requires each federal agency having an extramural research and development budget in excess of $100 million per fiscal year to establish an SBIR Program. The program is funded by setting aside a graduated percentage of R&D dollars specified by the legislation. The maximum level is 1.25 percent.

The SBIR Program has three phases:

☐ The majority of Phase I awards are $50,000 for a six-month period or less and are designed to evaluate the scientific and technical merit and feasibility of an idea.

☐ In Phase II, projects from Phase I with the most potential are funded for two years to proceed with product development. The majority of these awards are funded for $500,000 or less.

---

[10]John R. Wilmeth, *SBIC Digest,* April 1988.

☐ In Phase III, private investment is involved and aimed to bring an innovation to the marketplace. This phase also may involve production contracts with a federal agency for future use by the federal government. No SBIR funds may be utilized during Phase III.[11]

MINORITY BUSINESS DEVELOPMENT AGENCY

The Minority Business Development Agency (MBDA) was started with SBA seed money and operates under SBA guidelines. The MBDA provides special assistance to minority individuals, partnerships, and corporations. It helps them to acquire and control medium- and large-size firms and divisions and established product lines. The qualification of a minority business owner as disadvantaged is the same as that for MESBIC-assisted businesses.

The MBDA also makes grants to professional consulting firms to assist minority buyers in the entire process from analyzing and negotiating for a business to actually acquiring it. These consulting firms also help identify the best source of financing and prepare the applications, documentation (other than legal), and other information required by lenders and/or investors.

Minorities interested in obtaining MBDA help must demonstrate: (1) financial ability by providing at least 5 percent of the total cost of the purchase of the business being acquired in cash or tangible assets; and (2) a sound knowledge of the particular business and industry. The business to be acquired must: show a sound potential for profits based on products and markets; demonstrate a high growth rate in sales, earnings, and similar measures; and exhibit technological and capital requirements consistent with entry by the new owners. Finally, the business should have net assets in excess of $1 million or gross revenues in excess of $3 million during the preceding twelve months. If all of these requirements are met, the MBDA will assist in identifying sources of capital for purchasing the company.

■ SUMMARY

One of the first questions a prospective small business owner must be able to answer is "What kind of capital do I need and where can it be obtained?" Basically, there are four types of capital: short-term loans, intermediate-term loans, long-term loans, and equity capital. Each was discussed in this chapter.

After determining the type of capital needed, the prospective owner must follow through and determine the source from which this type of capital can be obtained. Of the large number of capital sources, those discussed in this chapter include internal funds, trade credit, equity sources, banks, other private sources of capital, the Small Business Administration, state and local development companies, small business investment companies, and the Minority Business Development Agency. In each instance, we examined the types of capital and services typically provided. Some of these capital sources are of more value to one kind of business than another, as in the case of factoring, which would be used by a business that has a large amount of accounts receivable but not by a business that deals basically for cash.

---

[11]Kathleen C. Brannen and Joel C. Gard, "Grantsmanship and Entrepreneurship: A Partnership Opportunity under the Small Business Innovation Development Act," *Journal of Small Business Management,* July 1985, pp. 44–49.

In the latter part of the chapter we examined the role of the SBA in helping the small business owner obtain capital despite being turned down by his or her local bank. In any event, regardless of the type of business, there are capital sources that can be helpful in raising the all-important initial funding. Despite the potential risk to the investor, the business may find a venture capitalist who feels that the firm is promising and will return a large profit. The most important thing for the small business person to do is to investigate these capital sources before plunging headlong into the venture.

■ REVIEW AND DISCUSSION QUESTIONS

1. What are the two most common forms of short-term loans? Explain them.

2. What are intermediate-term loans, and when do small businesses use them? How about long-term loans?

3. What is equity capital?

4. Explain how the following capital sources are used by small businesses: internal funds, trade credit, equity sources.

5. What kinds of loan services do banks provide for small businesses? Describe four of them.

6. Discuss how the following can be of value to small businesses that want to raise capital: insurance companies, finance companies, factors.

7. In what way(s) does the SBA help small businesses raise capital? Be specific.

8. Explain how each of the following helps small businesses meet their capital needs: state and local development companies, small business investment companies, the Minority Business Development Agency.

■ Case Studies

Just in Time

■ When the Kwik Kar garage opened last year, Jeffrey and Linda Wheeler believed they had identified a market niche that would be very profitable. Kwik Kar is designed to provide general auto maintenance in less than thirty minutes. The most common service is an oil change and lubrication of the auto. This can generally be done in ten to fifteen minutes.

When the garage first opened, the Wheelers were amazed at the demand. While they advertised that they could provide an "oil and lube" job in fifteen minutes, their claim was based on no more than five cars being serviced at the same time. Demand was so strong, however, that they had to encourage some people to come back later in the day or at a prearranged time so that they could guarantee fifteen-minute service. Most individuals were happy to comply, and the garage proved to be highly profitable.

The Wheelers invested $80,000 in equipment and another $20,000 in inventory including oil supplies, belts, batteries, and mufflers. They were also thinking about adding tires, but something happened six months ago that had a radical effect on their business. Three competitors opened up in the same neighborhood. As a result, the Wheelers' business dropped dramatically and in each of the last four months they have lost more than $8,500. At the present time they have $12,500 in cash and $23,500 in inventory. Their accountant has estimated that they will be able to survive only two more months unless there is a turnaround in business.

In an effort to create more demand, Jeffrey went to see the head of the transportation department of a very large company in the area. This firm has over 500 salespeople and 1,350 other employees who drive company-owned cars. These cars are currently being serviced in-house, but the firm has decided it would be more economical to have routine maintenance performed by an outside company. Yesterday Jeffrey received a call from the company and learned that Kwik Kar has been awarded a one-year contract for this general maintenance. The firm wants each car serviced an average of six times a year and will pay Kwik Kar $20 per service, for a total annual payment of $220,000 ($20 × 6 × 1,850). Regardless of how many cars are serviced each month, the firm will pay $18,333 ($220,000/12) on the first of every month. Jeffrey was delighted with the news. As he told Linda, "This contract arrived just in time."

The contract will go into effect in forty-five days. In the interim, Jeffrey and Linda plan to get the necessary funds to tide them over and to purchase additional supplies so that they are ready to begin servicing the firm's autos.

1. Should a bank be willing to advance Jeffrey and Linda funds based on their contract with the firm? Explain. Yes because of known income in the contract

2. What type of loan would a bank be most likely to consider: short-, intermediate-, or long-term? Why? Short term, because it can be quickly be paid back Credit line

3. If no bank will lend them money, what would you recommend that the Wheelers do? Explain. Invest their own cash. If there not willing to do that, they shouldn't be borrowing from anyone.

An Answer to Prayer

■ Eric and Joanne Jackson are a minority couple who live in the inner city of a large metropolitan area. They run a small printing shop (total sales last year: $1.1 million) that caters mostly to specialized jobs. Six months ago the economy in the city suffered a downturn, and the Jacksons' business revenues dropped substantially. They have been forced to lay off three of their sales force of seven people.

Realizing that friends, relatives, and the local banker had all loaned them as much money as they could, the Jacksons have been looking for fresh sources of capital. They intend to use the money to buy some machinery that will enable them to diversify their services. In this way, they believe they will stand a much better chance of surviving economic fluctuations.

The Jacksons have just discovered that an SBA loan could help them out in this new venture. They have also heard that there are firms called small business investment companies (SBICs) that are licensed and financed by the SBA for the purpose of providing venture capital to small business concerns.

Early tomorrow morning the Jacksons will visit their local SBA office to learn about these SBICs, how much money they lend, and what requirements and restrictions are associated with borrowing from them. As Eric said to Joanne last night, "This just might be the answer to our prayers."

1. What is a small business investment company? What does it do?

2. Why would an SBIC, especially a minority-enterprise SBIC, want to lend money to the Jacksons?

3. What requirements and restrictions would accompany a loan from a minority-enterprise SBIC? Explain.

You Be the Consultant

THE CHARTER BUSINESS

Joe Miller wants to go into business for himself. He has skippered his own small private yacht for over ten years and he knows that many tourists come to Florida every year between October and March. Some of them like to travel to the Bahamas or down toward South America by renting a boat, a skipper, and a crew and just taking off. Naturally there are not too many people who can afford the high fees associated with this type of vacationing, but Joe believes there are enough to justify his going into this charter business.

After shopping around for six months, Joe has found a new, large sailboat that can sleep ten people. It retails for $400,000 and, according to a friend who owns one, is very popular with people who want to rent a boat and go sailing for a couple of weeks. Joe has saved $75,000 in the last five years and believes that with a loan from a bank, he can buy the boat and go into the charter business.

During the last month, however, Joe has been very disappointed. He has applied at five banks and they have all told him the same thing: "We think your idea has a great deal of merit. Undoubtedly there are many people who want to charter sailboats and spend their vacation on the high seas. However, we are not set up for that type of business. We prefer to lend money for houses or automobiles, and sailboats are really out of our bailiwick. Perhaps another bank would be interested in such a loan, but, at least for the time being, we do not feel qualified to get into this line."

Joe is disappointed because he was counting on using the boat as collateral for the loan. Since it costs $400,000 and is expected to increase in value each year (because of inflation) by 8%–10%, the bank's loan would be very safe. Furthermore, Joe cannot understand the logic of the banks. Not one of them told him that the business venture was a bad idea. In fact, after he explained his anticipated costs and revenues to one of the bankers the banker told him his presentation was well thought out and made good business sense. Nevertheless, no one is willing to lend him the money.

However, Joe has not given up. He has learned that sometimes the Small Business Administration will guarantee loans that banks have turned down. He has decided to go down to the nearby SBA field office and talk to someone there. If it looks feasible, he intends to fill out the papers and submit his application immediately.

■ **YOUR CONSULTATION**   Help Joe out by providing him advice and assistance. What types of loans does the SBA guarantee? What are some of the prerequisites for borrowing with SBA assistance? How should Joe prepare for his visit? Should he take any materials with him? What are his chances for success? Explain.

Determining Location and Layout

Objectives

Another start-up problem for a new business is that of choosing a location and a layout. The requirements for both are heavily influenced by the type of operation. Throughout Chapter 9 attention will be directed to the four common forms of small business: retailer, wholesaler, service enterprise, and manufacturer.

The first objective of Chapter 9 is to examine factors involved in selecting a location, including personal factors, economics, competition, geographic considerations, and local laws and regulations. Then we will relate these factors to retail, wholesale, service, and manufacturing businesses. The second objective is to examine the issue of leasing versus buying facilities and equipment. The third objective is to study some of the factors involved in adapting facilities to the specific needs of a business. The fourth and last objective is to examine the layout of a small business. When you have finished studying the material in this chapter you will be able to:

1. Identify and discuss the general factors involved in determining the location of a business.

2. Discuss some of the typical problems and issues confronting specific types of small business and tell some of the ways they can be alleviated.

3. Compare and contrast the advantages of leasing and buying facilities and equipment.

4. Explain the four major considerations in adapting facilities for business operations.

5. Identify the five major factors that must be kept in mind when laying out a business.

6. Discuss some of the layout problems that confront small businesses.

7. State some guidelines for dealing with typical layout problems.

GENERAL FACTORS IN SELECTING A LOCATION

Regardless of the type of business, some general factors will influence where the operation is located. The most important are

☐ personal factors

☐ economics

☐ competition

☐ geographic considerations

☐ local laws and regulations

PERSONAL FACTORS

One of the most important factors in choosing a small business location is the personal values of the owner. Where does the owner *want* to locate? A preference for a small town or a large city, near one's relatives or far from them, a warm climate or a cold one—all will affect the decision.

ECONOMICS AND COMPETITION

The economic base of the local area is another important factor. This determines the **purchasing power** of the community (its ability to buy goods and services) and is reflected by such things as the number of people employed, total family income, bank deposits, per capita retail sales, and the number and value of homes in the area. These statistics relate whether the locale is thriving economically or just getting by. Obviously the owner will want to set up a business in an area that has an increasing amount of purchasing power for the goods and services it is offering.

Competition can be good or bad, depending on whether the business thrives on it or is destroyed by it. Retail stores, for example, that are located in shopping malls often do quite well if there is competition because people who shop competitively will go there to compare and buy. Since there is a large volume of traffic, all the retailer needs to do is get a "fair share" of this business. Retailers handling shopping goods or general merchandise, and wholesalers or manufacturers who are not dependent on the local market, do well in a healthy competitive environment. However, not everyone does. For example, small grocery wholesalers can be severely hurt by competition.

Also, one must take into account the competence of the owner-manager. Is the owner hard-working, ambitious, and experienced? If so, the owner will have a much easier time of it than if he or she does not possess these traits.

GEOGRAPHIC CONSIDERATIONS

A third area of concern in locating a business is geographic considerations. This is particularly important in the marketing of goods and services that are restricted geographically. For example, a ski lodge can be located only in a region where there are skiers, and a boat repair shop must be located near the water.

Another such consideration is "nearness to market." Some goods must be located near where they are to be sold. For example, bricks require production close to the market because they are very heavy and it is quite costly to ship them long distances. Likewise, processing plants for weight-losing materials will be located near the source of these materials so that, for example, dirt and ore can be separated and only the ore needs to be shipped.

Still another important geographic consideration is the labor supply. Sometimes the specific location of a business is determined by where adequate labor can be found. If people with a particular skill live only in the Northeast, that is where the business must be established.[1] (See Small Business Owner's Notebook: Entrepreneurial Locations.)

STATE AND LOCAL LAWS AND REGULATIONS

Various codes, ordinances, and deed restrictions should be researched carefully. The establishment and operation of a business is usually restricted by state and local laws and private deed restrictions. The entrepreneur needs to analyze them and determine their potential effects on his or her business. For example, the zoning ordinances and subdivision regulations determine where and under what conditions a business may operate. And building, electrical, plumbing, fire, health, and other codes require that construction and operation of a business meet certain standards in order to protect the public's health and safety. Various permits and licenses are

---

■ SMALL BUSINESS OWNER'S NOTEBOOK ■

Entrepreneurial Locations

 Each year *Inc.* magazine surveys cities across the U.S. in terms of growth, employment, business start-ups, available financing, and small business support. The following lists provide some interesting results of the 1990 rankings:

Most Fast-Growth Companies

1. Lincoln, NE
2. Washington, D.C.
3. Sioux Falls, SD
4. Reading, PA

Most Start-Up Businesses

1. Las Vegas, NV
2. Orlando, FL
3. Charleston, SC

Overall Top Ten Locations

1. Las Vegas, NV
2. Washington, D.C.
3. Orlando, FL
4. Tallahassee, FL
5. San Jose, CA
6. Atlanta, GA
7. Charleston, SC
8. Lincoln, NE
9. Raleigh-Durham, NC
10. Anaheim, CA

Source: John Case, "The Most Entrepreneurial Cities in America," *Inc.*, March 1990, pp. 41–50, and Cognetics, Inc., Cambridge, MA.

---

[1] Jose DeCordoba, "Location, Location, Location: The Right Sites for New Businesses are Sometimes in Unexpected Places," *Wall Street Journal*, May 15, 1987, p. 200.

needed for certifying compliance. In addition, licenses for sales and other taxes have to be obtained. Often, a new small business owner will need the advice and help of an attorney and contractors in dealing with these matters.

SPECIFIC FACTORS IN SELECTING A LOCATION

In addition to the general factors in selecting a location, some specific factors relate to the particular type of business: retail, wholesale, service, or manufacturing. We will examine each of these specific factors.

RETAIL LOCATIONS

Retail stores have location problems different from those of other small enterprises. For this reason, greater attention will be paid to retail stores than to the other kinds of small businesses.

SMALL TOWNS ARE OFTEN A GOOD BET   Small towns often live up to their reputation; that is, they are friendly, and everyone has a sincere interest in seeing the community grow and expand. As a result, service is often better and the quality of work superior to that found in large cities. This positive image spills over to new small businesses in town, often making it unnecessary for the owners to spend two or three years earning a good reputation. Research shows that certain types of businesses are heavily represented in small towns, including general stores, feed and seed stores, farm implement stores, service stations, and hardware stores. Small retailers in these lines would do well to consider locating in small towns.

Furthermore, many large chains have a minimum size limit for towns in which they locate. As a result, businesses in these smaller towns need not be concerned about competition from those retail giants.

This does not mean that small businesses cannot survive in large cities. For example, variety stores, lunch counters and stands, drugstores, and liquor stores appear to do equally well in both small and big communities. However, some types of businesses require a large number of customers and are thus not likely to do well in small towns. Examples include delicatessens, optical shops, and specialty stores for the sale of such things as office and school supplies, cameras, books, and cigars.

BUSINESS DISTRICTS   Depending on the size of the city or town, there may be one or more business districts. Usually one is downtown, and if the city has expanded in recent years, another is in the general location of this expansion. If expansion has occurred in several directions or over a wide geographic area in one direction, it is not uncommon to find a business district for each, if only in the form of a giant mall or shopping center.

Large cities have more than one downtown shopping location. Sometimes these are some distance from each other; in other instances they are adjacent to one another so that there is an area for business equipment, another for general merchandise, and a third for clothing, for example. Then leading from this central district are main arteries that may have specialized stores and shops along them. In recent years many downtown areas have been renovated with federal assistance, and medium-sized cities are experiencing a rebirth of business in their downtown areas. In large metropolises, however, access to downtown is largely dependent on public transportation, and many of these cities have found that their transportation systems are not adequate. In such cases, small business owners are wise to think about locating elsewhere.

Large cities also have neighborhood shopping areas. In a manner of speaking, these neighborhoods are very much like small towns, and the number, type, and size of the retail stores in them reflect the areas they serve. And then there are outlying shopping centers. These serve suburban communities, and to a large degree, have been built by industrial real estate promoters, department stores, discount chains, or corporate chains. Whether one can obtain a lease in these shopping centers is heavily dependent on who owns them. For example, if real estate promoters or department stores do, they tend to exclude discount houses and, in some cases, supermarkets. On the other hand, the latter attract a great deal of traffic and, as a result, when they own the shopping center they tend to rent to smaller stores that capitalize on the presence of supermarket shoppers. In deciding whether to set up in a shopping center, the owner should know the types of businesses that will be there and the kinds of customers they are likely to draw. It is best if customers shop at more than one store, for then there is a spillover or multiple effect, which is important to businesses located in the shopping center.[2]

KEY AREAS OF CONCERN   A number of key concerns factor into making a final site-selection decision. One of these is the rent-paying capacity. Some businesses are able to locate in high-rent areas, whereas others must stay in low-rent areas. For example, drugstores, restaurants, and men's and women's apparel stores can usually afford high-rent locations, while furniture and food stores, which require a lot of space, are more likely to be located in low-rent locations.

Another prime consideration is the terms of the lease. A typical retail lease is one of two types: fixed-rate or percentage. With a **fixed-rate lease,** the rent is set and does not vary. With a **percentage lease** the rent is often less, but the lessor gets a percentage of sales. For example, a fixed-rate lease might be $600 a month, while a percentage arrangement calls for $300 a month plus 3 percent of gross revenues. Leases can be secured for varying time periods, but for the beginning retailer it is wise to get a one- or two-year lease with an option to renew. Also, the individual should negotiate with the landlord regarding any remodeling that needs to be done and who will pay for it. In this way, all of the expenses of setting up the operation are considered and the owner knows how much of the financial burden the business will have to assume.

A third basic area of concern is the type of merchandise being sold. For example, convenience-goods stores usually locate where a sufficient number of customers have quick and easy access to the store. Thus, they are found in well-populated neighborhoods, in industrial or business areas, and in downtown shopping centers. The same is true for variety stores and small drugstores. Retailers selling specialized merchandise, however, tend to do better if they are located in the central district. The ultimate choice, of course, depends on the type of customer the store is trying to attract, the

---

[2]Tim Falconer, "How Business Centers Give Small Companies Large Clout," *Canadian Business*, November 1986, pp. 159–160.

sales volume it must have to break even, and the ease with which customers can get to the store.

A fourth area of concern is the proximity to other businesses. Some retail stores do well if they are located near competition, whereas others are most successful if they are located away from competition. Likewise, some retail stores do well when they are located near certain other types of retail stores. The following are examples:

- □ Men's and women's apparel and variety stores are commonly located near department stores.

- □ Restaurants, barber shops, and candy, tobacco, and jewelry stores are often found near theaters.

- □ Florists are often grouped with shoe stores, clothing stores, and other retail shops.

- □ Drugstores may be found with any of the above groupings.

- □ Paint, home furnishings, and furniture stores are generally in close proximity to each other.

WHOLESALE LOCATIONS

Wholesalers have problems similar to those of retailers. In addition, however, the wholesaler must realize that the success of the business usually depends most heavily on economic conditions in the local market. The business will be supplying retailers in the community, and if the retailers have problems, so will the wholesaler.

Many small wholesalers are established retailers who have experimented with quantity buying for the purpose of reselling to retailers. When this happens the individual will set up business in the same town, and location is really not a major issue. Other wholesalers get into the business after breaking away from a wholesale house and starting their own operation. These two approaches account for almost 90 percent of all small wholesale houses.

In most large cities there are wholesale districts, and within those areas there are usually multistoried plants (because of the high warehousing costs and ground rents). However, because these locations are limited, new wholesalers are unlikely to be able to secure that type of location. In this case, the new wholesaler can choose a site outside the city and use truck delivery to meet the needs of the city customers, or can join with other small wholesalers and build wholesale outlets on the edge of town. Such a location enables the wholesaler to serve both the city and the suburban retailer.

SERVICE LOCATIONS

Service establishments have location requirements similar to those of retail stores. And to the extent it engages in retail trade, a service operation will be affected by the same considerations. However, the most important factor in location is the type of service the business offers. For example, a professional or personal service for which clients come to the place of business needs to be highly accessible. This often requires an office location in the financial district or a shop location in one of the better retail areas. On the other hand, if customers do not come to the site, the location can be selected primarily in terms of the owner's preferences, space requirements, and rent cost. And if the business has a reputation for very high quality workmanship, it is likely to attract customers in spite of poor location, something that is not true of other types of small businesses. However, since a reputation is built on performance, this fact is useful to the small business owner only after the first location has been established.

Finally, it should be noted that there is currently a trend toward drive-in services. Dry-cleaning and laundry establishments have used the concept for a long time and other service businesses have picked it up. Fast-food chains selling everything from hamburgers and soft drinks to milk and bread are employing this idea. Also, some service businesses are finding that people are willing to buy if they go to the customer rather than having the customer come to the store. Home furnishings like custom-made window treatments are sold this way, and mobile pet-grooming businesses are found in many cities. (See Small Business Success: Growing More Than Corn in Iowa.)

■ SMALL BUSINESS SUCCESS ■

Growing More Than Corn in Iowa

In 1979 Clark McLeod, a former Iowa junior high school teacher, convinced a friend to invest $100,000 in a new business that would install and repair telephone systems. By 1981 Teleconnect had revenues of $2 million but its real growth was yet to come.

McLeod's original business plan outlined a strategy for Teleconnect to become a regional long-distance carrier by leasing the microwave transmission lines from other companies.

While Teleconnect was somewhat successful in Iowa and Illinois, the mid-1980s posed greater challenges for McLeod's company. AT&T was increasing its leasing rates, thus causing Teleconnect to raise its prices. By 1985 McLeod put together a plan to build his own transmission facility using a fiber optics network. However, before construction began on the proposed $30-million facility, McLeod discovered an Oklahoma-based pipeline company (Wil-Tel) that had a network of decommissioned pipelines. Teleconnect and Wil-Tel signed an agreement to have Wil-Tel install fiber optics through its pipelines and then lease the lines to Teleconnect. Through this network, McLeod's company had access to Des Moines, Dallas, Cleveland, Miami, and Los Angeles without building their own transmission facility. Now, the real growth started.

With the company growing at an average of 60 percent annually, McLeod took the company public in 1987, raising over $40 million in stock, and in December of 1988 Teleconnect merged with Southern-Net (out of Atlanta) to become Telecom USA. Revenues for 1989 were in excess of $712 million with the expectation of $1 billion in revenues for 1990. Today, Telecom USA is the fourth largest long-distance carrier in the United States.

Source: Adapted from Michael Fitzpatrick, "Going the Distance," *Entrepreneur,* April 1990, pp. 78–82.

MANUFACTURING LOCATIONS

The big problem facing the owner-manager of a small manufacturing plant is that once the building is built and the equipment placed within it, the cost of moving to another location can be prohibitive. Thus, it often makes sense to rent facilities instead of building them. It also supports the use of general, rather than specialized, machinery because less-specialized machinery is easier to sell should it be necessary to liquidate some assets. Keeping these things in mind, the owner needs to seek a location at which the combined cost of production and distribution are minimized. Some of the factors that will influence the overall decision include

- □ nearness to markets
- □ nearness to suppliers
- □ adequacy and cost of the labor supply
- □ adequacy and cost of the power supply
- □ state and local regulations and taxes
- □ transportation services and costs

When a rural site and an urban site seem to offer the same benefits, small plant owners tend to favor the rural site. The reasons include less traffic congestion, ample parking, lower land cost, lower taxes, and fewer problems with local regulations. Others include room for expansion and the likelihood of efficient transportation systems for both shipping and receiving goods.[3]

POINTS TO REMEMBER ABOUT LOCATION

To summarize, the following points should be considered when selecting a site for a small business:

- □ Study and evaluate the selected area carefully.
- □ Check for parking availability.
- □ Avoid areas of traffic congestion.
- □ Make sure the location is easily accessible and noticeable.
- □ Note any incompatible businesses nearby (for example, factories and warehouses near a potential jewelry store).
- □ Check on the ownership of vacant lots and attempt to determine future building plans. The image of the area may be a key factor.
- □ Check the success and failure record of nearby businesses; they provide a track record of that area.

---

[3]See Craig Galbraith and Alex F. DeNoble, "Location Decisions by High Technology Firms: A Comparison of Firm Size, Industry Type, and Institutional Form," *Entrepreneurship Theory and Practice*, Winter 1988, pp. 31–48.

Table 9-1 Site Selection Evaluation Chart

FACTOR	RATING*			POINTS†		
	Site 1	Site 2	Site 3	Site 1	Site 2	Site 3
Demographics of customers						
Labor supply						
Zoning and other regulations						
Cost (rent/buy)						
Taxes (property, excise)						
Labor supply						
Neighborhood image						
Business climate—success rate						
Proximity to suppliers						
Proximity to market						
Transportation						
Parking						
Accessibility						
Pollution						
Traffic patterns						
Types of businesses in area						
Future value of area						
Expansion capabilities						
TOTAL POINTS				—	—	—

*Rating Scale: A = Extremely important, a vital factor—10 points.
　　　　　　　 B = Important, usually considered a factor—7 points.
　　　　　　　 C = Should consider, but not very important—4 points.
　　　　　　　 D = Slightly concerned, may or may not be a factor—1 point.
†Multiply the rating-scale by 10 if the site is excellent, by 7 if it is good, by 4 if it is fair, and by 1 if it is poor.

☐ Evaluate daily, weekend, and evening traffic patterns in the area (for example, high or low levels of activity).

☐ Watch for high-pollution areas.

The prospective owner should note and compare the sites being considered. This can be done easily with the aid of an evaluation chart like the one in Table 9-1.

LEASING VERSUS BUYING

Many small manufacturers decide to lease their facilities, as do many retailers, wholesalers, and service enterprises. The same is true for equipment. The following sections examine the advantages of leasing and buying, a key area of concern to the owner-manager.

ADVANTAGES OF LEASING

The major benefit of leasing is that the initial outlay is much less than if the building or equipment is bought outright. Additionally, the cost of maintaining these assets, in particular the equipment, is borne by the lessor. Both of these advantages can be very important to the owner who is just starting out and needs to hold onto working capital. It should also be noted that leasing expenses represent costs of doing business and are thus tax-deductible. Finally, in the case of leased equipment, when the lease contract is up, the owner is free to lease other equipment. Thus, the individual need not worry about being saddled with outmoded equipment, which can happen if it is purchased outright.

How common is leasing? Research shows that in recent years it has increased dramatically, and that half of all plants, stores, and offices in the United States now lease some of their equipment. Likewise, most small stores are leased, since the owners lack the financial resources to buy.

ADVANTAGES OF BUYING

Sometimes, especially with equipment, buying has more advantages than leasing. This is particularly so if the businessperson needs to gain a tax advantage of depreciation write-offs on an accelerated basis. However, keep in mind that investment tax credits—which allow direct deductions in taxes—have been *removed* from the tax codes. Thus, the tax benefit of buying is focused on depreciation only. Also, certain assets should be purchased initially, rather than leased with an option to buy later. The initial purchase price may be far less than the total cost of leasing and then buying. The owner-manager would have to consult an accountant in order to determine the overall tax saving. A comparison of the financial benefits of leasing and buying could be made at the same time.

ADAPTING THE FACILITIES

Depending on the type of business, some changes may have to be made in the building. The four major considerations are

- ☐ the construction
- ☐ the function
- ☐ the appearance
- ☐ the lighting, color, and air-conditioning

In terms of construction and design, the general condition of the building is of major importance. How old is it? Will it withstand the rigors of everyday business? Also, how well designed is it in terms of the business's needs? Many old buildings have less functional designs that call for remodeling, an expense that increases the overall cost of the facilities. Also, the owner must check to see if these necessary alterations *can* be made; that is, if they are physically possible and economically feasible. When changes are not possible, the cost of doing business is sometimes increased dramatically. For example, in a production operation, easy receipt of raw materials and shipment of finished products are dominant considerations. Meanwhile, in service industries customers must have accessibility to the merchandise. In the case of a retail store, the customers must be able to enter and leave the store easily. The same is true of service industries. And then there is the matter of deliveries. Is there a back door through which goods can be delivered? All of these questions must be answered in ensuring that the facilities meet the needs of the business.

Another important consideration is the appearance of the building. A bank will look very different from a retail store. Thus, in locating a bank, one must be certain that the external appearance is "proper." Furthermore, if the owner-manager is considering buying the building, it is necessary to evaluate its resale potential. Finally, it should be noted that some attempt should be made to make the building's appearance distinctive so that people will remember the outside appearance even if they do not remember the particular name of the store.

A third consideration is the matter of lighting, color, and air-conditioning. Lighting should be decorative as well as functional. In some instances, as in clothing stores, the lighting must allow the customer to see the true color of garments. In other businesses indirect, soft-colored light can be used because it is pleasing to the eye. Color is also important on walls and ceilings. Light, pastel colors are more pleasing and more economical because they reflect light. Likewise, colors help create certain moods. For example, yellow is very pleasing and is commonly referred to as a "happy" color. The next time you are in a well-designed doctor's or dentist's office, look at the color of the room. It has been deliberately chosen to put you at ease.

Finally, there is the air-conditioning, a virtual necessity in most businesses. This machinery not only keeps the customers cool; it helps to make the work environment comfortable for the employees. Without air-conditioning, efficiency in most small businesses would drop dramatically.

LAYOUT

The **layout** of a business is the physical arrangement of its fixtures, equipment, and machinery. If it is effective, it follows a predetermined plan and blends the people and the physical surroundings in such a way as to produce maximum efficiency.[4] In examining the overall layout, certain factors must be kept in mind:

1. A logical and optimum arrangement of the equipment and merchandise in regard to the flow of production or the buying habits of the customers should be identified.

2. The layout should take full advantage of natural conditions resulting from the building construction.

3. The layout should allow for the maximum efficiency of the machinery.

4. Materials and merchandise should be placed in such a way as to make them readily accessible to the worker or the customer.

5. A clear view of the facilities should be available to the management, worker, or customer so that the individual is able to observe (depending on who it is) the workers, the materials, or the merchandise.

RETAIL STORE LAYOUT

Retail store layout should be designed with three things in mind: customer satisfaction as attained through convenience, service, and attractiveness; maximum sales,

---

[4]See Dale M. Lewis and M. Wayne DeLozier, *Retailing* (Columbus, Ohio: Merrill Publishing Company, 1986), pp. 298–307.

which can be accomplished with the proper selection of fixtures and arrangement of the merchandise; and economy of operation.

There are many ways of attaining these objectives, and some general guidelines are obvious. Most stores can profit from what are almost universal suggestions.[5]

One of the basic rules of layout is that those goods that generate the greatest profit volume should be given preference over those that sell slowly. What the retailer needs to do is place the goods that generate the most profit in the *best* selling areas and the others in the *poorer* selling areas. Which area of the store is the "best one"? This depends on the customers' reasons for being there. Research shows that if people come to the store for a specific item and know where the item is located, they are likely to take a different route toward the goods than if they are simply browsing. Most people in a typical retail store are browsers; when they enter a store they are most likely to move toward those things that catch their eye. Although these customers think they are walking in a random manner, they are actually much more likely to turn to the right than to the left. Therefore, goods with high gross margins and low replacement costs should be located to the right of the entrance. Individuals who know where they are going are more likely to go to the left upon entering the store, wishing to get away from the crowd so that they can get to the merchandise they are seeking faster. Therefore, low-gross-margin merchandise should be placed to the left of the entrance. Furthermore, the farther one goes into the store (assuming that there is no exit on the other end), the lower the potential sales volume of that area. Merchandise in the front of the store is likely to sell better than merchandise placed in the middle or the back of the store. Finally, while the goods on the right are high-gross-margin items and those on the left are lower-gross-margin ones, the goods in the middle of the store fall in between. A retail store layout in terms of sales percentage by area is illustrated in Figure 9-1.

The first thing to do in designing a store layout is make a drawing of the floor space to scale and divide it into areas such as in Figure 9-1. Then the goods should be strategically placed in the store. In making decisions regarding the location of merchandise, several factors should be considered.

Figure 9-1

Retail Store Layout with Percent of Sales by Area

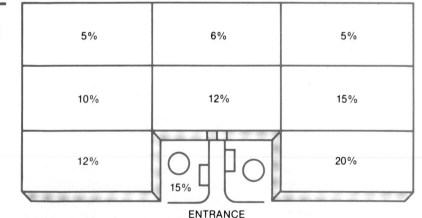

[5]See Gerald Pintel and Jay Diamond, *Retailing*, (Englewood Cliffs, N.J.: Prentice-Hall, Inc., 1987), pp. 174–83.

One factor is the location of essential nonselling functions, such as the manager's office. Others include where displays will be located throughout the store, where goods will be received and stored, and where telephones and package checking will be placed.

A second factor is the location of **impulse goods.** These are goods that people buy on the spur of the moment, in contrast to **demand items,** specific items that the customer comes to the store to purchase. As an example, an individual may go to the drugstore to buy some cough medicine, a demand good. But to get to it (if the store is laid out properly), the individual has to walk past aisles of impulse items, because the medicines, hospital supplies, and prescription department are at the back of the store. The same logic is used by many other retail establishments, including shoe stores. The shoes are located in the back of the store, and the hosiery, shoe polish, and other sundries are located up front. In a supermarket many of these impulse items are located near the cash register; as the customer stands in line waiting to check out, he or she encounters such items as *TV Guide*, gum, *Reader's Digest*, and razor blades.

A third important location factor is employee convenience. It is important that the worker be able to serve the customer quickly and efficiently. Part of this problem can be solved through careful layout. For example, in a men's store, it is typical to arrange suits by size rather than by color. This makes it easy for the salesperson to help the customer choose a suit. Home furnishings are arranged the same way, with electrical appliances located in one area, furniture in another, and garden equipment in still another. Finally, the layout should be arranged in such a way that it does not cause large crowds of people to gather in one area. For example, some stores place the cash register and the gift-wrapping facilities in the same spot. However, this can cause a delay in service since some people may simply want to pay for their purchases and leave the store, while other customers are waiting around to have their purchases wrapped. In order to avoid these problems, some stores place cash registers throughout the store and keep the wrapping department in the rear. In this way, the only individuals going to that area are those needing gifts wrapped. Another way of preventing crowds from gathering in some areas of the store is to break them up by placing obstacles in their path. A layout, display, or sizable showcase requires customers to walk around it. Because of the human tendency to choose the path of least resistance, people are going to walk in the direction that seems to have the clearest path. Using this logic, the owner can lay out the store so that people will walk in one direction rather than another.

WHOLESALE OPERATIONS LAYOUT

The ideal layouts for wholesale operations are different from those of retailers because the basic function of the business is different. The retailer's main objective is to keep the customer satisfied, while the wholesaler's job is to fill orders as quickly as possible. About 60 percent of a wholesaler's cost of operations is for payroll, so the wholesaler needs to get as much work as possible out of the personnel. One way of doing this is by having adequate materials-handling equipment.

Most wholesale-warehouse activities lend themselves to a type of production-line operation in which the employee works as quickly as possible to fill each order. Layout is very helpful in the process because some goods are ordered more often than

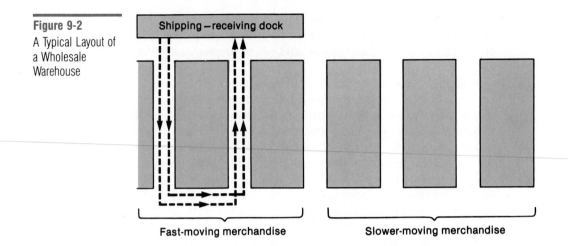

Figure 9-2
A Typical Layout of a Wholesale Warehouse

Shipping — receiving dock

Fast-moving merchandise   Slower-moving merchandise

others. Therefore, what most wholesalers do is place the fast-moving items in one area and the slower-moving ones in an area farther away. When an order is received, the employee—using some form of materials-handling equipment—goes down the various warehouse aisles, picking up the items. In order to make it even easier, the individual may pick up items from one side of the aisle only. This is illustrated in Figure 9-2 in which the employee travels down the first aisle, taking goods only from the racks on the right, and then travels up the second aisle, taking goods only from racks on the left. When the individual has finished, he or she is at the shipping-receiving dock. If there are more items on the order, someone else will go down the first aisle taking items from the racks on the left and then turn around and come up the next aisle, taking goods only from the racks on the right. This approach reduces the amount of time needed to fill orders.

SERVICE ENTERPRISES

Service enterprises are diverse in nature, and it would be impossible to discuss all of the layout considerations in just a few pages. The specific layout will be dictated by the needs of the operation. However, service enterprises tend to be of two types: those that deal in merchandise and those that process goods.

Merchandising service enterprises include motels, hotels, restaurants, and personal service establishments. In these cases it is most important that customer convenience and pleasing appearance be taken into account in the layout plan.

A cafeteria provides a good example. In a cafeteria two areas merit attention: the dining room and the kitchen. In choosing tables and chairs for a cafeteria, a general rule is that at least half of the tables should seat a minimum of four people. Tables that seat just two people should be placed along the walls or near windows so that the patrons can look out. Or the owner can place booths along the walls, especially if there is no outside view. Many customers today prefer booths to tables. However, the owner should be sure to leave enough aisle space so that the patrons can easily reach the tables and booths and there is no danger of tripping over other people or bumping into them. Furthermore, the cafeteria should be arranged in such a way that when the customers enter there is a small reception space that funnels them into a corridor leading to the serving line. This type of arrangement separates those waiting for service from those who are eating. Diners tend to like this because they are not bothered by people shuffling through a line, talking to each other as they go. Finally, there is the question of how the foods should be laid out. Which should come first and which should come last? After the trays, napkins, and silverware, many cafeterias like to place salads and rolls and then the main course and, finally, the desserts. However, some have reversed the latter categories and offer the desserts before the main course in an effort to get the person to buy dessert first since this is a higher-markup item than the main course. Finally, there is the question of where to put the cash register. In small cafeterias it is common for people to pay when they come to the end of the line. However, many large cafeterias use two cash registers. The first, located at the end of the food line, is used to total the individual's bill. This ticket is placed on the person's tray and taken to the table. After eating, the customer goes to a cash register located near the door and pays the bill. This approach allows people to move through the serving line faster because there is not the inevitable delay caused by those who are looking for their money or counting their change.

The kitchen requires just as much attention to layout. Six principles are often recommended. The first is that there be adequate working space. At least four linear feet of work space should be allowed for each person actively preparing food. There also has to be space for laying out the foods both before and after they are cooked. Second, these worktables should be reasonably close to the cooking equipment, thereby reducing the time and effort needed to move the food from the table to the cooking area and back again. Third, the aisles must be adequate to permit people to move around the kitchen easily. Fourth, different types of cooking and preparation functions should be separated. For example, there should be separate tables for salads, meats, and pastries. Fifth, the equipment and materials should be placed as close to the point of use as possible. For example, mixers, flour, sugar, and utensils should be located near those who will need them. Finally, major equipment should also be located in such a way as to maximize convenience and minimize interference among the kitchen help. Some of the typical arrangements of the equipment are all-in-a-row, L-shaped, parallel-back-to-back, and parallel-facing arrangements. These will be discussed in the following section.

In considering all of these layout problems, the owner-manager does not have to rely on a trial-and-error approach, changing things that do not work and leaving the rest alone. Many equipment manufacturers have engineering or service divisions that can assist in this work. After all, who should know more about layout than the people who sell the machines that are going to have to be placed in the business? They have seen numerous layout problems and can recommend not only the best type of equipment for the job but the layout(s) that will work best, given the physical dimensions of the space available.

Processing service enterprises are more like factories. Illustrations include dry-cleaning establishments, repair shops, and stores that alter garments. In these cases the customer usually does not see the work being done. The article is simply dropped off and then picked up later. Most small process-type service businesses profit from the same principles that apply to manufacturing layout.

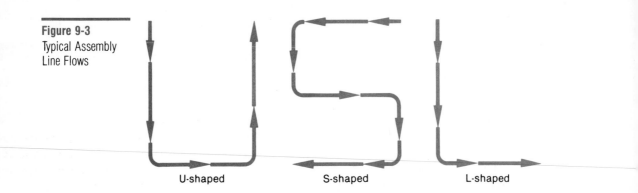

Figure 9-3
Typical Assembly
Line Flows

U-shaped   S-shaped   L-shaped

MANUFACTURING

Layout in a manufacturing establishment depends heavily on the specific process in which the factory is engaged. For example, if there is an assembly line, the arrangement should be such that as the product flows down the line it comes closer and closer to completion. However, this does not mean that the company has to have a narrow, rectangular building to accommodate a long assembly line. If the building is square in shape, the line can double back in a U-shape or an S-shape. Still other buildings allow for an L-shaped assembly line; see Figure 9-3. The important thing is to use all of the space available for the operations and not buy or rent any more space than is needed.

If the operation is not an assembly line, there are only two other possibilities. The company either makes products to customers' specifications (such a business is commonly referred to as a **job shop**) or it manufactures products in limited batches such as in lots of 1,000 units. In both of these cases it is typical to find a separate department performing each of the important processes for the job. Then there is an **expediter** who keeps track of the various jobs being worked on and sees that all of the parts for each unit are produced and assembled as required. When some parts have not been produced or have been lost, the expediter may remove parts from completed orders that do not have to be finished right away, and give them to jobs ahead of them on the schedule. In these types of operations it is important to prepare a route sheet for each standardized product being manufactured and/or for every job order processed, indicating the sequence of the factory operations to be performed. The sequence of operations will suggest the best layout to use. But rather than get into an involved discussion of specific manufacturing layouts, we will simply summarize some of the basic principles of plan layout:

1. Materials and semifinished products should follow the shortest and fastest route from entrance to exit.

2. A minimum of physical handling is essential, so as many operations as possible should be performed at each stop.

3. Bottlenecks that can slow down the production process should be identified and steps taken to ensure that they do not develop.

4. Misused space is as wasteful as underutilized machinery and equipment.

5. Backtracking, overlapping of work, and unnecessary inspections can be eliminated by continually seeking new sequences and combinations of steps in processing or fabrication.

■ SUMMARY

In choosing a location for a business some general factors play a key role. These include personal factors, economics, competition, and geographic considerations. There are also some specific factors that have a direct effect on the location of each of the four common types of small business: retail, wholesale, service, and manufacturing. Some of these factors were discussed in the chapter, with considerable attention given to retail locations since they are the most common type.

Then the matter of leasing versus buying was examined. There are advantages to each. The major benefit of leasing is that the initial outlay is much less than if the building or equipment is bought outright. Also, the rental cost is tax-deductible. The major benefit of buying is that both tax credits and depreciation write-offs are available to the owner. However, since the rules affecting these credits and depreciation write-offs change, the small business owner is well-advised to have an accountant help in determining whether it is better to lease or buy.

Next, some of the changes that must be considered in making the facilities ready for use were considered. Particular consideration was given to the construction, function, appearance, lighting, color, and air-conditioning of the building.

Finally, the matter of layout was studied. How should the fixtures, equipment, and machinery be arranged? Attention was given to each major type of small business, particularly that of the retail outlet. Problems were identified and guidelines were provided.

■ REVIEW AND DISCUSSION QUESTIONS

1. What are three general factors with which the small business owner must be concerned when determining the location of the business? Describe each.

2. Many retailers find that small towns are a good place to locate. Why is this so?

3. What are three of the key factors with which retailers must be concerned when making a final decision on site selection? Explain each.

4. When it comes to site selection, what does a retail-establishment owner need to know? A wholesaler? A service-establishment owner? A small manufacturer?

5. What are the advantages associated with leasing facilities and equipment rather than buying them?

6. What are the advantages of buying facilities and equipment rather than leasing them? Explain your answer.

7. What types of issues should the owner-manager be concerned with in adapting facilities to meet the needs of the specific business? Explain.

8. What is meant by the term *layout?* What functions or activities does it involve?

9. If you were giving a retailer general advice on store layout, what would you tell him or her? Be complete in your answer. What if you were talking to the owner of a wholesale operation? A service enterprise? A factory?

Decisions, Decisions

■ A new shopping mall is being built on the north side of town, and Samuel Simpson has rented space near the main entrance for his cafeteria. His reasoning is quite simple: the owners of the mall intend to allow only one cafeteria or restaurant and three small fast-food outlets. With all of the traffic passing through the mall and the number of office buildings within a short distance, a cafeteria should be able to draw people every day of the week.

The terms of the lease call for rent of $500 a month plus 5 percent of gross sales. The agreement is for 36 months, at the end of which time a new lease will be written. The owners of the mall have offered to buy all of the fixtures and equipment needed in the cafeteria and incorporate these expenses into the price of the lease, or he can arrange his own financing. In any event, if he decides to vacate the premises when the original lease is up, he can do so and take all of his equipment and fixtures with him. The only condition is that he leave the area in its original shape; that is, all walls, holes in the walls, and damaged floors must be repaired.

Samuel is quite happy with the lease arrangement and believes he would be able to operate a profitable business there. At the moment, however, he is not sure whether to buy the necessary equipment or lease it. Nor does he know exactly what kind of equipment and fixtures he will need or how they should be laid out in the eating and cooking areas. However, he believes that he can get outside assistance, and if worse comes to worse, he intends to copy the layout of a successful cafeteria in the downtown area. "If their layout works for them," he has reasoned, "it should work for me."

1. Has Samuel made a good choice in regard to location? Support your answer.

2. What are the respective advantages of leasing and buying? Which would you recommend to Samuel? Why?

3. What do you think of his ideas regarding layout? Is he on the right track? Are there any things you would want to tell him? Explain.

Randy's Findings

■ Roberta Wilson owns a small boutique in an upscale shopping center. Roberta's store is on the second level, immediately opposite the elevator and the stairs. Although the rent is 15 percent more for this location than others on that level, Roberta feels that it is money well spent. "The minute people arrive on the second level, the first thing they see is my store. When they leave the second level, the last thing they see is my store. So I get them coming and going. And since sales are a function of foot traffic, it really pays to be located where I am."

Although she does not know the sales of the other boutiques on the second level, Roberta believes that she sells more than they do. "It's all a matter of location and merchandise selection," she explained to her younger brother Randy, who is in the process of writing a paper for his small business class. Randy wants to use Roberta's store for his research, and she has agreed to provide him with whatever information he needs.

One of the things Randy decided to do was to make a comparison of the store's layout and the percent of sales made by area in the store. This was not as difficult as it seemed, given the fact that Roberta's accountant had provided her with a breakdown of sales on the basis of merchandise. All Randy had to do to complete this part of the paper was determine what percentage of sales was made in each area of the store.

When he completed this portion of the research, Randy found this layout:

18%	17%	15%
10%	10%	8%
9%	7%	6%

Entrance

1. Based on Randy's diagram, what conclusions can you draw regarding Roberta's store layout? (Consult Figure 9-1 in drawing your conclusions.)

2. What store layout mistake(s) might Roberta be making? Explain.

3. What recommendations would you make to help Roberta increase her sales? Be complete in your answer.

You Be the Consultant

A FAMILY PROBLEM

Four brothers have decided to enter into a partnership arrangement and open their own discount store. After giving the matter of location a great deal of thought, they have decided that they want to stay within the city, which has a population in excess of 1.5 million. The Yellow Pages directory shows that a large number of discount stores are already located in the metropolitan area, so the competition will be stronger than if they chose a rural location. Nevertheless, they have made up their minds.

The brothers intend to buy their goods in sufficiently large quantities so they can pass on savings to their customers in the form of reduced prices. In particular they have already entered into tentative agreements with suppliers for televisions, radios, typewriters, calculators, home appliances, books, clothing, and furniture. In the case of furniture, they intend to have samples on the floor from which customers can choose. The merchandise will then be shipped from a factory outlet. In this way the store will simply be the middleman between the manufacturer and the buyer.

At the present time the brothers are looking for a store site. They believe that they need at least four floors. In all likelihood, this will call for the rental (or purchase) of an entire building. They will meet with their accountant later in the week to discuss the benefits and drawbacks associated with leasing and buying. They realize that they are going to have to put out a great deal of money during the first ninety days of operation, but they believe that after then they can begin to recoup some of this large initial investment. Also, when the business is running, they hope to increase their use of credit and thus keep the amount of personal funds in the business to a minimum.

Then there is the issue of layout. The brothers are unsure of how to place the merchandise throughout the building. One of them feels that the highest-demand items should be on the first floor because that location will get the most traffic. More people are going to look at the goods located there than in any other part of the store. One of the other brothers feels that the highest-demand items should be placed on the second or third floor because in order to get to them the customers will have to walk past a lot of other merchandise, and they will be likely to buy more than just the high-demand items. The two other brothers believe the high-demand items should be spread throughout the store so as to attract customers to all levels of the building. All, however, agree on one thing—they need to find out more about layout. They also feel that they need to know more about the general location of the store. Should it be by itself on the edge of the city, or should it be located in the

downtown area? They prefer the downtown area, but they know the rents there are much higher than those in the outskirts. Also, they are afraid that people would have greater difficulty getting to a downtown store since there are limited parking facilities and the public transportation system is not considered very good. On the other hand, if they move to the edge of town there is the problem of attracting people. After all, with the competition firmly entrenched, the customers might just as easily go to one of the other stores.

The brothers hope to make a final decision regarding the steps to take in handling their location and layout problems before the month is out. For the moment, however, they feel overwhelmed by the large number of questions still facing them. "If we had known there would be this many problems, we might have decided against going into business on our own," one of them said. "But since we have come this far, we are determined not to turn back now. We'll just have to go out and find answers to these problems. We're not going to let location and layout be our undoing."

■ **YOUR CONSULTATION** Should the brothers locate their store downtown or on the edge of the city? Why? Would they be better off buying or leasing the building and the fixtures and equipment they will need? Be specific in your responses. How would you solve the layout problem? What types of goods should they place on the first floor and which should they put on the upper levels?

CHAPTER 10

Selecting the Legal Form for an Organization

Objectives

There are numerous legal forms for business organizations, the major ones being the proprietorship, the partnership, and the corporation. The objectives of Chapter 10 are to examine each of these forms and discuss their advantages and disadvantages. Each has some benefits and some shortcomings of which the prospective owner should be aware. When you have studied this chapter you will be able to:

1. *Define the term* proprietorship.
2. *Identify four advantages of the proprietorship.*
3. *Describe three major drawbacks of the proprietorship.*
4. *Define the term* partnership.
5. *Compare and contrast general, limited, and other partners.*
6. *Point out the advantages and disadvantages of partnerships.*
7. *Explain how corporations are organized.*
8. *Describe the major advantages and disadvantages of the corporate form of ownership.*
9. *Explain some of the benefits of the "S" corporation.*

THE PROPRIETORSHIP

A **proprietorship** is a business that is owned and controlled by only one person. This is the most common form of ownership in the United States by far; see Table 10-1.[1] Why is this form of ownership so popular? The answer is found in the many advantages it offers.

---

[1] For further discussion on the legal aspects of proprietorships see Rate A. Howell, John R. Allison, and Robert A. Prentice, *Business Law* (Chicago, IL: The Dryden Press, 1989), pp. 721–28.

Table 10-1 Nonfarm Business Ownership

FORM OF OWNERSHIP	NUMBER
Proprietorship	12,115,000
Partnership	1,807,000
Corporation	3,577,000

Source: *The State of Small Business: Report to the President,* 1987, p. 15.

ADVANTAGES OF THE PROPRIETORSHIP

Numerous advantages are associated with the proprietorship, but four are particularly important:

1. financial advantages

2. lack of restrictions

3. secrecy

4. personal satisfaction

FINANCIAL ADVANTAGES   Perhaps the major advantage of the proprietorship is that the owner-manager owns the entire business, and all of the profits belong to him or her. Of course, it is necessary to pay taxes on these earnings, but these are just regular taxes, the same as you and I pay. For example, if Mr. Jones is a proprietor and earns $20,500 this year and has deductions of $4,500—leaving a net of $16,000—he will pay the same amount of taxes as an office worker who earns the same amount of money and has identical deductions. Additionally, proprietors sometimes have higher credit ratings than owners of partnerships or corporations, because their personal assets as well as their business assets stand behind them.

LACK OF RESTRICTIONS   Another advantage of the proprietorship is the lack of restrictions. The individual has a great deal of freedom in deciding how the firm will be run. There are no partners or stockholders that must be consulted. Additionally, because the operation is usually much smaller than that of other business forms, a proprietorship is often much easier to manage. There are fewer people to worry about and fewer complicated business dealings with which to be concerned. Finally, although in some cases a license must be obtained from the state (such as in the operation of a bar or a barbershop), there are no serious restrictions on either starting or terminating operations. Thus, an individual can form a proprietorship and then close the business without having to get permission from a state or federal agency.

SECRECY   A third advantage of the proprietorship is secrecy. Sometimes the less the competition knows about one's business, the better. A sole proprietor needs to reveal very few things about his or her operation. Of course, the owner must file federal and state income tax returns. For the most part, however, the proprietor can keep operations secret, and the competition can only make "guesstimates" regarding its sales, profit margins, and overall financial strength.

PERSONAL SATISFACTION   Many proprietors report that the best thing about owning their own business is the personal satisfaction they derive from it. The individual can work as many, or as few, hours a week as he or she wants. Additionally, the goals that are pursued are the proprietor's own. If the business is a success, the owner knows it is due to his or her own contributions.

DISADVANTAGES OF THE PROPRIETORSHIP

Despite its many advantages, there are also some drawbacks associated with the proprietorship. In determining whether this type of operation will be best for the business, the owner needs to consider such things as

1. unlimited liability
2. limited size
3. limited life

UNLIMITED LIABILITY   Perhaps the greatest drawback of the sole proprietorship is that of unlimited liability; the individual is responsible for all debts incurred. Creditors have a claim for these debts and can exercise it against both the business assets and personal assets of the proprietor. As a result, if the owner's operation is worth $80,000 and the individual has debts of $125,000, the creditors can sue the proprietor and force him or her to liquidate personal assets to pay the financial obligations. This explains why a sole proprietor may have a higher credit rating than other business owners. For example, the president of a corporation may find that the bank will lend the corporation up to 75 percent of the firm's value. If the company suffers a financial setback, the only things the bank has a claim against are the assets of the corporation. In the case of a proprietor, however, the bank can also claim the owner's personal assets. When the bank determines a fair line of credit for the business it will add together the owner's business and personal assets.

LIMITED SIZE   Since there is only one owner of the business, there is a limit to the amount of capital that can be raised for operations. For example, assume that a bank has a policy of lending up to 50 percent of the value of a business and that a sole proprietorship has personal and business assets worth $150,000. The bank will lend the company up to $75,000. However, this is as far as the bank is willing to go. If the owner needs an additional $25,000 to take advantage of a business opportunity, one of the few ways to get the money is to take in another partner who has personal assets of $50,000.

To a large degree the growth of a proprietorship is dependent on reinvested profits. Financially speaking, the business's growth is limited. In particular, sole proprietorships are virtually excluded from entering areas where large capital expenditures are required, such as mass-production operations and large manufacturing plants.

An additional problem arises from the fact that there is only one owner. That individual is responsible for doing everything: buying, selling, extending credit, advertising, hiring, firing, and handling all other business-related matters. This can be quite a burden, and as the business increases in size, the owner may find that he or she is weighted down with all these duties. One way of dealing with them is to delegate authority to subordinates, but the major decisions must still be made by the owner. When all of these things are considered, it becomes evident that the proprietorship is indeed limited in size. Any attempt to grow beyond this limit will result in uncontrollable operations.

LIMITED LIFE   The life of the proprietorship depends entirely on the proprietor. If the individual dies, is imprisoned, goes bankrupt, or simply chooses to cease operations, the business dies. This presents a risk to the people who work for the firm and to the creditors. In order to offset some of these risks, it is common for creditors to require the proprietor to carry life insurance sufficient to cover all financial obligations. Then, if the owner should die unexpectedly, the face value of the policy can be used to pay all of the firm's debts. If the size of the policy is sufficiently large, it may even be possible for someone else to continue operating the business, but this is unlikely. The major reason is that a proprietor usually leaves the estate to his or her spouse. In most cases the spouse does not know enough about the business to keep it going or does not care to. Thus, it is fair to say that when the sole proprietor dies the business ends. It has a limited life.

THE PARTNERSHIP

A **partnership,** as defined by the Uniform Partnership Act, is "an association of two or more persons to carry on as co-owners of a business for profit."[2] In recent years the partnership has declined in popularity. At present only about 10 percent of all business firms in this country are partnerships. Nevertheless, there are currently more than a million of them, and they account for billions of dollars in sales. See Figure 10-1.

In most cases, partnerships consist of two owners, although there can be any number of partners. For example, advertising agencies, stock brokerages, and public accounting firms often have five or more partners. In addition, **master limited part-**

Figure 10-1
Relative Predominance of Proprietorships, Partnerships, and Corporations in U.S. Business

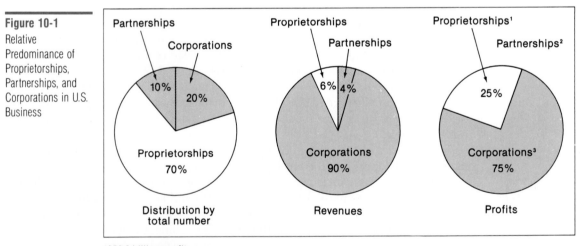

[1]$50.6 billion profit.
[2]$7.3 billion *loss*
[3]$154.3 billion profit.

Source: *Statistical Abstract of the United States: 1990* (Washington, D.C.: U.S. Government Printing Office, 1990), Table 858, p. 521.

[2]For the complete Uniform Partnership Act see Kenneth W. Clarkson, Roger L. Miller, Gaylord A. Jentz and Frank B. Cross, *West's Business Law,* 4th edition (St. Paul, Minnesota: West Publishing Co., 1989), pp. A-159–A-186.

nerships have evolved, which blend the interests of several private partnerships into one, larger "master" partnership.[3]

A partnership can be formed by people simply getting together and agreeing to operate a business. However, such an informal arrangement is unlikely. If only to protect themselves in case one of the partners dies, most partners prefer to have a formal partnership contract drawn up. An example of a simple partnership contract is provided in Figure 10-2. More specific terms are usually spelled out after item 5. These typically cover such areas as

1. how the profits and losses will be divided
2. the method to be followed if original partners withdraw from the firm or new ones enter the business
3. how the assets will be divided in case the partnership is dissolved
4. the duties of the partners
5. the manner in which any controversies arising out of the contract will be settled (a typical approach is arbitration)

At the bottom of the agreement, after all of the provisions are listed, the partners sign their names. The document is then a legally binding contract for all of the parties involved.

TYPES OF PARTNERSHIPS

In a partnership there can be various types of partners. Members of the general public tend to think of all partners as equally responsible for the debts of the business and as equally entitled to the profits. However, this is a simplistic view. Actually, the rights, duties, and obligations of the partners are usually determined by such factors as how much money each has invested in the partnership, how much liability each is willing to assume, and whether each partner wants his or her membership known to the general public. In all, there are three categories of partners: general partners, limited partners, and other types of partners.

GENERAL PARTNERS   General partners have unlimited liability and are usually very active in the operation of the business. Each partnership must have at least one general partner. In this way there is someone who assumes ultimate responsibility for all of the firm's obligations and is authorized to enter into contracts for the firm. If all of the partners fall into this category, the organization is commonly known as a **general partnership.**

LIMITED PARTNERS   Under the provisions of the Uniform Limited Partnership Act, which has been enacted by most states, individuals who want to invest in a partnership but do not want to risk all of their assets can do so as **limited partners.** Their liability is limited to the amount of money they have invested in the company. For example, if Bob puts $5,000 into his uncle's firm and is a limited partner, the most that Bob can lose in case of bankruptcy is the $5,000. On the other hand, his uncle, assuming he is the general partner, can lose all of his business and personal assets.

---

[3]Keith Wishon and Robert P. Roche, "Making the Switch: Corporation to Partnership," *Journal of Accountancy,* March 1987, pp. 90–95.

This agreement is executed on this _____ day of _____ 19___ between _____

_____ and _____, all of _____.

1. The name of the partnership will be _____.

2. The principal place of business of the partnership will be at _____.

3. The partnership will engage in the business of _____
and in such other related business as agreed upon by the partners.

4. The partnership will begin operations _____, 19___, and continue until terminated as herein provided.

5. The initial capital of the partnership shall be $_____. Each person agrees to contribute cash or
property at agreed upon valuation as follows:

PARTNER	AMOUNT	PERCENT
_____	$_____	_____
_____	_____	_____
_____	_____	_____
_____	_____	_____

Figure 10-2

Example of a
Partnership Contract

OTHER TYPES OF PARTNERS   While the most common types of partners are general and limited, there are other categories including silent, secret, dormant, and nominal. A **silent partner** is one who is known as a partner by the general public but does not play an active role in the operation of the business. A **secret partner** is just the opposite; he or she is not known as a partner by the general public but does play an active role in the operation of the business. A **dormant partner** is not known as a partner by the general public and does not play an active role in the operation of the business. A **nominal partner** is a partner in name only. This typically occurs when a well-known person allows his or her name to be used by a partnership. The individual invests no money in the firm and plays no role in its management.

Before continuing, it is important to remember that some people may have limited liability according to the partnership contract but end up with unlimited liability because of some action they take. For example, a limited partner is not empowered to act in the name of the firm; he or she plays no active role in the operation. However, if a limited partner enters into a contract for the partnership by passing himself or herself off as a general partner, the individual can become liable for any losses resulting from this action.

Likewise, a nominal partner can get into the same bind. For example, Mrs. White has been asked for a loan by the general partner, Mr. Smith. Mrs. White would not ordinarily lend money to a partnership but in this case she is willing to do so because she knows that Mr. Adams, a local millionaire, is a partner and if the business gets into trouble she believes Mr. Adams will bail it out. Mr. Smith has told her that although Mr. Adams is a general partner, some of his funds are tied up in a big European deal and thus he is unable to come up with the money right now.

Unbeknownst to Mrs. White, she is being told a lie. Mr. Adams is Mr. Smith's cousin and, in an effort to help him out in his business, has allowed the Adams name to be used. The business is called "Adams Hardware." However, Mr. Adams does not have a financial interest in the store; he is a limited partner. Given this information, can Mr. Adams be held responsible if Mrs. White lends Mr. Smith the money and the store goes bankrupt? Without getting into the legal ramifications of the problem, let us introduce one final fact. Mr. Adams *knows* that Mr. Smith has passed him off as a general partner. Because of this, Mr. Adams *can* be held liable for the firm's obligations and he will lose his right to limited liability. If a nominal partner knows that he (or she) is being passed off as a general partner and does not step forward and reveal himself to be a nominal partner, he loses his limited liability. In short, if a limited partner passes himself or herself off as a general partner, the courts will rule that the limited partner is now a general partner and can be held responsible for any debts that arise because of the misrepresentation.

ADVANTAGES OF THE PARTNERSHIP

Numerous advantages are associated with the partnership. The most important ones are

1. increased sources of capital and credit
2. improved decision-making potential
3. improved chances for expansion and growth
4. definite legal status

INCREASED SOURCES OF CAPITAL AND CREDIT   The proprietor relies on his or her own personal funds to provide the capital the business needs. This capital also backs any credit that is extended to the firm by others. However, since there is only one person in the proprietorship, the individual's capital and credit is limited. A partnership can overcome this problem, at least partially, by bringing in more people with capital to invest and personal assets that can be used as collateral for bank loans and credit. Banks and creditors often feel that there is less risk in lending to a partnership than to a proprietorship because there are more people to pay the outstanding debts should the business suffer a financial setback.

IMPROVED DECISION-MAKING POTENTIAL   The saying "two heads are better than one" has particular application to partnerships. If there are three or four partners, the chances are increased that the individuals will be able to make better decisions collectively than the proprietor operating alone. This is particularly true if each partner is a specialist in some area. For example, if one is a salesperson, another is an accountant, and a third is the "idea" person, the partnership may be able to outperform any competitive proprietorship.

IMPROVED CHANCES FOR EXPANSION AND GROWTH   Thanks to the increased sources of capital and credit, and the improved decision-making potential, the partnership is usually in a much better position to expand and grow than is the proprietorship. In particular, the partnership has the money and managerial expertise to supervise more employees and manage larger facilities. Therefore, as the operations

■ SMALL BUSINESS SUCCESS ■

Seltzer in the Family

Alan Miller and his son Randy started the original New York Seltzer Company in 1982 using an old bottling plant in Brooklyn that was once used by Alan's grandfather Jake. Prior to starting the seltzer company, Alan and his son were headed in diverse directions. Alan worked as an aerospace engineer for TRW and continued to do so until 1985. Randy had various "other" activities at the time, such as working as a stuntman. Alan did not see stuntwork as a positive career choice and decided to keep his son alive by putting him to work in a business.

Once the bottling began, Randy tried to sell the products out of a 1968 Mustang. He put in many long hours and drove as much as 200 miles a day as he tried to generate accounts. Within the first few months he did get 30 accounts, and when he reached 50 accounts the business really began to take off. Randy became an excellent salesperson and marketer, while his father concentrated on product development. Through the process the two became close friends.

In 1984 the company moved its bottling to California. This saved a great deal on distribution costs and allowed the Millers to have better control over the process. In addition, the Millers began to dispense New York Seltzer through beer distributors and opened the company up to a national market.

Since 1988 sales have remained stable at $100 million, but the Millers believe they can reach $300 million once they introduce some new products and work out some minor distribution problems. Considering that the company has only been in operation for eight years, the Millers have done an incredible job of building. Although their company has grown, the father and son still see New York Seltzer as a two-man operation as Randy continues to concentrate on sales while his father focuses on product development.

Source: Adapted from Bob Weinstein, "The FizzBiz," *Entrepreneur,* October 1990, pp. 95–99.

increase in size, the owners are able to maintain control of operations. (See Small Business Success: Seltzer in the Family.)

DEFINITE LEGAL STATUS   Because partnerships have been in existence for centuries, many court decisions have been rendered in regard to all sorts of legal problems. Thus, a good lawyer will be able to answer virtually any question that might arise about partner ownership, liability, or continuity of operations.

DISADVANTAGES OF THE PARTNERSHIP

While it has many advantages, the partnership also has some disadvantages. There are four in particular:

1. unlimited liability
2. problem of continuity

3. managerial problems

4. size limitations

UNLIMITED LIABILITY   As noted earlier, some partners are limited partners and as long as they do nothing to jeopardize this status, they can lose only their investment should the business suffer a financial setback. The other partners are general partners, and they must assume unlimited liability for all obligations. However, it is important to remember that profits and losses are not always shared equally. It is common for everything to be shared in relation to capital contribution. For example, the individual who puts up half the money gets half of the profits and, of course must take responsibility for half of the losses. On the other hand, this is *not* always the way profits and losses are divided, because the general partners are considered to be *both individually and collectively liable* for the debts of the partnership. This means that if one of the general partners cannot come up with his or her share of the losses, the others must make it up. The latter, of course, can sue the delinquent partner, but for the moment it is they who must pay. Keeping this in mind, it should be obvious why wealthy persons do not like to be general partners in businesses where everyone else has only moderate wealth. They can end up carrying their poorer partners.

PROBLEM OF CONTINUITY   If one of the partners dies, goes to jail, is judged insane, or simply wants to withdraw from the business, the partnership is terminated. As the number of partners increases, the likelihood that one of these events will occur becomes increasingly greater. For example, consider the case of five partners where one of them dies. In order to reorganize the partnership, it is necessary for the remaining partners to buy out the individual's share, the value of which may be difficult to determine. And if the partners do not have the necessary assets, such action is impossible. In this case, the only alternative may be to bring in a partner with the money to buy out the share of the deceased. Yet it is often difficult to find a person who is acceptable to all of the partners—a requirement for any new partner. Such problems affect the continuity of partnerships.

MANAGERIAL PROBLEMS   While all of the general partners have the right to contract in the name of the business, the firm may find that "too many cooks spoil the broth." One way of overcoming this problem is having each partner restrict his or her activities to one area of operations. For example, one works exclusively in purchasing, another takes responsibility for handling the books, and a third is responsible for selling. Yet even when these agreements are spelled out in writing, it is common for problems to arise and for partners to interfere in each other's areas of responsibilities.

SIZE LIMITATIONS   Although a partnership can usually raise more money than a proprietorship, there is a limit to the amount of capital and credit that bankers and suppliers will provide. Sooner or later the firm will have reached its limit. Thus, the partnership can grow larger than the proprietorship, but it cannot reach the size of the large corporations because its financial assets will not permit it to do so.

THE CORPORATION

Most large businesses in the United States today are corporations—for example, American Telephone & Telegraph, General Motors, DuPont, Sears Roebuck, IBM, Goodyear Tire, and Westinghouse Electric. Although they constitute only about 20 percent of all business firms, corporations account for over 90 percent of all business receipts and the largest percentage of wages paid. Figure 10-3 shows the percentage of proprietorships, partnerships, and corporations in selected business areas today.

What makes the corporation such a popular form of organization? One reason is that, legally, a corporation is an artificial being that has the right to conduct business affairs in its own name, sue and be sued, and exist indefinitely.

ORGANIZING THE CORPORATION

In contrast to the proprietorship and partnership, it is necessary to get permission from the state to create a corporation. The first step in this process is usually that of filing the necessary application form with the appropriate state official. Most states require at least three incorporators, each of whom must be an adult, and the payment of the necessary fees at filing time. Aside from this, there is usually little other paper work that has to be done.

Figure 10-4 shows the basic form of an application for incorporation. Usually the form is written in such a way that the activities and objectives of the firm are not very limited. Additionally, since the incorporators often want to minimize taxes, they will check the incorporation fees and taxes levied by the various states. Because of their tax rates, Delaware, Maryland, and New Jersey are very popular states in which to incorporate.

Once the filing is complete and the approval to incorporate has been given, the secretary of the state will issue the corporation a **corporate charter.** This charter relates such things as the type of business the firm is in and the number of shares of stock it intends to issue. The business must operate within the confines of this charter, and any changes have to come from either the stockholders or new government regulations.

THE CORPORATE STRUCTURE

The corporate charter provides the basis for the corporate structure. According to the charter, the stockholders own the firm and have the right to elect the board of directors. These individuals in turn choose the president, who appoints the top corporate officers. This process continues down the line, all the way down to the workers' level.

The people who own the stock, the **stockholders,** are permitted to elect the members of the board of directors. For example, if Alice owns ten shares of stock in the Jones Corporation and a total of 10,000 are issued, she is the owner of 1/1,000th of the firm and can cast her ten votes for any director she wants. The same is true for those who hold the other 9,990 shares of stock. Under this procedure, the largest stockholders have the greatest amount to say about the management of the corporation.

The **board of directors,** meanwhile, is responsible for seeing that the business is managed properly. In this capacity, they are charged with formulating long-range

Figure 10-3
Percentage of
Proprietorships,
Partnerships, and
Corporations in
Various Business
Areas

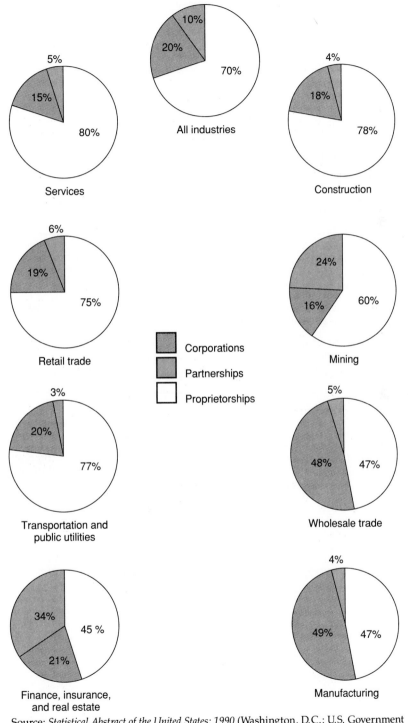

Services

All industries

Construction

Retail trade

Mining

Corporations
Partnerships
Proprietorships

Transportation and
public utilities

Wholesale trade

Finance, insurance,
and real estate

Manufacturing

Source: *Statistical Abstract of the United States: 1990* (Washington, D.C.: U.S. Government Printing Office, 1990), Table 860, p. 522.

Figure 10-4

Application for
Incorporation

ARTICLES OF INCORPORATION OF

_____

We the undersigned natural persons of the age of 21 years or more, acting as incorporators of a corporation under the _____ Business Corporation Act, adopt the following Articles of Incorporation for such corporation:

FIRST: The name of the corporation is: _____.

SECOND: The period of its duration is _____.

THIRD: The purpose or purposes for which the corporation is organized are: _____
_____.

FOURTH: The total number of shares that the corporation shall have authority to issue is: _____.

FIFTH: The corporation will not commence business until at least one thousand dollars has been received by it as consideration for the issuance of the shares.

SIXTH: Provisions limiting or denying to shareholders the preemptive right to acquire additional or treasury shares of the corporation are: _____.

SEVENTH: Provisions for the regulation of the internal affairs of the corporation are: _____
_____.

EIGHTH: The address of the initial registered office of the corporation is: _____
_____ and the name of its initial registered agent at such address is:
_____.

NINTH: The number of directors constituting the initial board of directors of the corporation is _____, and the names and addresses of the persons who are to serve as directors until the first annual meeting of shareholders or until their successors are elected and shall qualify are:

Name	Address
_____	_____
_____	_____
_____	_____
_____	_____
_____	_____

TENTH: The name and address of each incorporator is:

_____	_____
_____	_____
_____	_____

Dated _____, 19___   Incorporators

direction, approving plans of top management, and seeing that overall policy is carried out. If there is some problem with the management and the company is not doing well, the board of directors may decide to change the president and hire a new one. Thus, the board of directors, voted into office by the stockholders, are ultimately responsible for the overall management of the business.[4]

ADVANTAGES OF THE CORPORATION

The corporate form of ownership offers some very important advantages. Five of the major ones are

1. limited liability
2. indefinite life
3. growth potential
4. managerial efficiency
5. transfer of ownership

LIMITED LIABILITY   Stockholders in the corporation are like limited partners in that they can lose no more than they have invested in the business. For example, Andy and Sue buy 100 shares of stock for $1,000 in their cousin Bob's corporation. A year later the business goes bankrupt. How much do Andy and Sue lose as a result? Only $1,000. Keep in mind, however, that *Bob* may lose a lot more, because he *may* be personally responsible for debts of the corporation. Earlier we noted that some people in a partnership may be limited partners while others are general partners. Lenders are aware that the liability of the investors in a small corporation is limited. Therefore, in order to secure a large loan, banks or other lending institutions will require the owner to sign *both* personally and in the name of the business. This individual does *not* have limited liability. Yet this is only reasonable, for no bank would be foolish enough to lend a small corporation a great deal of money and then find in the case of financial failure that their ability to collect is restricted to the assets of the business. Lenders want to ensure that the owner is as careful as possible with the money, and what better way to do this than to make the person personally liable for the obligation?

INDEFINITE LIFE   Unlike a proprietorship or partnership, a corporation can exist indefinitely. If a major stockholder dies, the ownership is simply transferred to the heirs. If these people do not want the stock, they can sell it. In short, as long as there is a market for the stock—and there should be if the corporation is doing well—the ownership of the business may change hands but the corporation remains in existence. A look at some of the major corporations in the United States bears this out: Standard Oil of Indiana (1889), General Electric (1892), IBM (1911), General Motors (1916), and Ford Motor Company (1919).

---

[4]For a detailed discussion of corporate laws and regulations see Lawrence S. Clark and Peter D. Kinder, *Law and Business* (New York: McGraw-Hill, 1986), pp. 395–486; or Frederick G. Kempin, Jr., Jeremy L. Wiesen, and John W. Bagby, *Legal Aspects of the Management Process* (St. Paul, MN: West Publishing Company, 1990), pp. 501–721.

GROWTH POTENTIAL   In contrast to the proprietorship or partnership, the corporation generally has greater growth potential because it is able to raise more capital. By selling shares of stock, the company can often raise large amounts of money. Of course each stockholder may buy only ten or twenty shares, but if enough people are willing to invest, the corporation can raise a great deal of capital. (See Small Business Owner's Notebook: Restructuring a Growing Company.)

MANAGERIAL EFFICIENCY   As a business grows in size, it requires greater managerial expertise. The proprietorship is heavily dependent on the skills and abilities of the proprietor; the partnership relies greatly on the capabilities of the general partners. However, the corporation often separates ownership from management so that the people who own the company do not manage it. Even when they do, they still tend to bring in specialists such as sales managers, accountants, and lawyers. In short, as the size of the firm increases, so does the reliance on professional management.

TRANSFER OF OWNERSHIP   When an individual buys stock in a corporation, the person is given a **stock certificate.** This certificate can be sold if the individual is not happy with the investment, as long as there is a market for the stock. Small corporations have limited markets; it may be difficult for them to sell stock immediately. Large firms have ready markets for their stock, and there is usually no problem in making an immediate sale. The financial section of any newspaper gives the latest prices of many corporations' stock, from AT&T to General Motors to Exxon. Regardless of the corporation's size, however, if the company is in good financial shape the investor is generally able to sell the stock easily.

DISADVANTAGES OF THE CORPORATION

There are also some disadvantages associated with the corporate form of ownership. Four of them are

1. heavy taxation

2. high organizing expenses

3. government restrictions

4. lack of secrecy

HEAVY TAXATION   Corporations are subject to heavier taxes on their earnings than either proprietorships or partnerships. In recent years this has been 15 percent on the first $50,000, 25 percent on the next $25,000, 34 percent on the next $25,000, 39 percent on income over $100,000 up to $335,000, and 34 percent on everything above this amount. Then they are subject to a state tax by the state in which they are incorporated. Finally, if the company gives a dividend to stockholders, these individuals must pay a personal income tax on all dividends of more than $100. Those corporate earnings are subject to *double taxation.*[5]

---

[5]See Kent Royalty, Robert Calhoun, Radie Bunn, and Wayne Wells, "The Impact of Tax Reform on the Choice of Small Business Legal Form," *Journal of Small Business Management,* January 1988, pp. 9–17.

■ SMALL BUSINESS OWNER'S NOTEBOOK ■

Restructuring a Growing Company

 The challenge of managing a growing venture is sometimes more difficult than starting up the company. This is due to the fact that the symptoms of growth problems seem insignificant at first. However, problems of increasing bureaucracy and delays begin to affect the flexibility and excitement that usually characterize an entrepreneurial venture. It is imperative that owners recognize and deal with these issues.

CMP Publications, Inc., has successfully handled its remarkable growth. Founded in 1971 by Gerard G. Leeds and his wife, Lilo, the company specializes in publishing magazines and newspapers for industries such as computers, communications, travel, and health care. CMP Publications grew at an astounding 30 percent per year, but lost good executives who had become frustrated by the stagnation inside of the company.

In 1986 Gerry Leeds decided to reorganize the company in order to handle the growth. He appointed group managers to supervise the various areas of the corporation and gave the managers the authority and responsibility to make key decisions. In addition, the groups were to be run like companies within a company with specific strategies differentiating each.

Today, the reorganizing has already proved successful. CMP has 14 publications, and in 1990 sales climbed 11 percent to $174 million. More importantly, the owners feel that additional growth is not only possible but also welcome. CMP Publications three-step restructuring plan entails:

1. The creation of subgroups for better organization and relief of centralized control.

2. The assignment of grant managers who are given the authority and responsibility to make decisions for their groups.

3. The removal of administrative roadblocks that slow information and resources flow.

Source: Adapted from Tom Richman, "Reorganizing for Growth," *Inc.*, January 1991, pp. 110–11.

HIGH ORGANIZING EXPENSES   In order to incorporate, a business must pay certain fees. These include a charter fee to the state in which the business incorporates and corporate fees in all of the states in which it operates. (These fees are sometimes in the form of a tax for the right to conduct business in the particular state.) Additionally, because of all the legal procedures and red tape, the company usually has to have an attorney. All of this can add up to a sizable incorporation bill.

GOVERNMENT RESTRICTIONS   As opposed to the proprietorship and the partnership, the corporation faces a tremendous number of government restrictions. Its stock sales are regulated by federal and state governments, and the organization must maintain records and reports for examination by government agencies. Additionally, if it tries to merge or consolidate with another organization, it is required to comply with certain laws.

LACK OF SECRECY   Since the corporation has to make various records available to the government, its operations are much less confidential than those of other organizational forms. Additionally, the corporation must provide an annual report to each stockholder so that as the firm gets bigger the degree of secrecy declines. Everyone, including the competition, can find out the firm's sales revenues, gross profit, total assets, net profit, and other financial data. Virtually nothing is secret.

THE "S" CORPORATION

In an effort to help small businesses, Congress has provided for Subchapter-S corporations, named after the subchapter of the Internal Revenue Code that permits their existence. These corporations are now called **S corporations.** The tax code allows the earnings of these small corporations to be taxed as partnership income to stockholders. In this way the double taxation on dividends is avoided.

In order to exercise this tax option, a number of conditions must be met. Two of the most important, based on the latest legislative changes, are that there can be no more than thirty-five stockholders, and no more than 25 percent of the corporate income can come from such passive investments as dividends, rent, and capital gains.

There are other advantages to being an S corporation, as well. The full explanation of the impact and value of this option for a small corporation is best left to the firm's accountant or an outside certified public accountant. The option is available and it should be considered. However, it is neither a tax dodge nor a panacea for tax problems. This is obvious in the fact that only 20 percent of small business corporations have chosen the S corporation option. Its specific advantages are simply not of value to every small corporation.[6]

■ SUMMARY

A proprietorship is owned and controlled by one person. It is currently the most common form of ownership in the United States. Some of the advantages it offers are certain financial advantages, lack of restrictions, secrecy, and personal satisfaction. Its disadvantages include unlimited liability, limited size, and limited life.

A partnership is an association of two or more persons to carry on as co-owners of a business for profit. There are two major types of partners, general and limited, and there are several less common types. General partners have unlimited liability. Limited partners' financial responsibility is restricted to their investment. Other partners tend to have limited liability. However, this can change if they represent themselves to the public as general partners and, as a result of their action, cause the partnership some financial loss. The advantages of the partnership include greater

---

[6]See Steven J. Appel, "S Corporation Benefits for Small Business," *Business Forum,* Fall 1987, pp. 18–21. Also see Kenneth W. Clarkson, Roger L. Miller, Gaylord A. Jentz, and Frank B. Cross, *West's Business Law,* 4th ed. (St. Paul, MN: West Publishing Company, 1989), pp. 689–90.

capital and credit, improved decision-making potential, improved chances for expansion and growth, and definite legal status. On the other hand, the drawbacks include unlimited liability, continuity problems, management problems, and size limitations.

Most large businesses in this country are corporations. As a small business increases in size, this legal form of organization warrants attention. While permission from the state is necessary for a corporation to come into existence, this legal form provides some very important advantages, including limited liability, indefinite life, growth potential, managerial efficiency, and transfer of ownership. On the other hand, the disadvantages associated with the corporate form of ownership include heavy taxation, high organizing expenses, government restrictions, and lack of secrecy. Additionally the owner should have a certified public accountant examine the company's books and help it decide whether or not to exercise the Subchapter-S option (become an S corporation).

■ REVIEW AND DISCUSSION QUESTIONS

1. What is a proprietorship?
2. What are some of the advantages and disadvantages of a proprietorship? List and describe three of each.
3. In contrast to the proprietorship, how popular is the partnership? Explain.
4. How does a general partner differ from a limited partner?
5. What is each of the following: silent partner, secret partner, dormant partner, nominal partner?
6. What are some of the advantages and disadvantages of a partnership? List and describe three of each.
7. Explain how a business goes about incorporating.
8. What are some of the advantages and disadvantages of incorporating? Discuss four of each.
9. Why would a small corporation exercise the Subchapter-S option? Explain.

Case Studies

Getting Bigger

■ The cost of student meals at Public School 41 has increased so much over the last five years that the school board decided to look into using a catering service. The board asked for bids and, after receiving and analyzing them, gave the contract to William Judson.

Bill's small catering service had been providing hot lunches to three factories in the local area. The Public School 41 contract increased his sales revenue by almost 35 percent, and when the contract came up for renewal at the end of last year, Bill successfully bid again. At the same time he won contracts to cater meals for three other schools.

This year Bill would like to bid on catering contracts at seven more schools and five more companies. However, he is worried about how to manage the entire operation. At present he has eight workers in addition to his wife and three grown children. He operates as a sole proprietorship and feels that he may not be able to expand the business any further. A friend has told him that he should consider taking on a partner, but Bill has never worked with a partner and does not know anything about the advantages and disadvantages of a partnership. However, he intends to look into it.

1. What would be the advantages of a partnership for Bill? The disadvantages? Explain each. *Financial + share the work load. Shared Profits, Control of the business*

2. Would a partnership form of organization be helpful to Bill, or is he better off as he is? Support your answer. *Yes, it will help financial Same as above*

Going Public

■ When Harvey, Eugene, and William Carruthers started their retail company ten years ago, they formed a partnership. "All for one and one for all," is the way Harvey put it. "We each put $10,000 into the business and agreed to share all profits and losses equally." When it came to expanding the operation, they used the same approach: each put up one-third of the necessary capital.

The business grew slowly for the first five years. Sales were $495,000 by the end of that time period. The last five years, however, have seen rapid growth, and sales have now hit the $3 million mark. The brothers would like to again expand the operation, but it appears that it will cost approximately $500,000 to carry out their plan to increase inventory, add more floor space, and open a second store across town. "We just don't have the $500,000," Harvey explained, "and we are reluctant to borrow that much money. After all, we started as a small partnership. We never thought we'd get this big, and we don't have the internal funds to support big expansion."

The firm's accountant has suggested that they consider incorporating and selling stock to raise the money. This idea sounds good to the brothers, but they are concerned about losing control. The accountant explained that they could keep half of the stock for themselves, so they would never have to worry about being forced out. This was welcome news, but it has not dispelled all of their fears. In particular, the brothers are concerned about three things: (a) their tax rate would be higher as a corporation than it is as a partnership; (b) there would be large organizing expenses; and (c) there would be more governmental restrictions. Of the three, the tax rate is the most important to them. Nevertheless, they realize that unless they incorporate, they will be unable to finance their expansion.

1. What are the benefits of incorporating? Briefly identify and describe three of the most important. *large amount of Investment capital, Continual life of Co. Continual growth*

2. How serious are the drawbacks about which the partners are concerned? Explain. *Very, because profits may go down for the brothers + Control of the Co*

3. Is incorporation a wise decision for the Carruthers brothers? Why or why not? *Yes see above*

You Be the Consultant

IT ALL DEPENDS

The Harlow family opened its first motel in 1952. At first things were slow. It was almost eleven months before they broke even and three years before they felt that the operation was going to be a success. However, they stayed with it, and by 1957 they were able to increase the size of the motel from twenty-eight to fifty rooms. Again in 1959 they expanded, this time to one hundred rooms. In each case their occupancy rate was so high that they had to turn people away during the months of April to September, and they were 85 percent occupied during the other months. By industry standards, they were one of the most successful motels in the country.

As they entered the 1960s Harold and Becky decided that, rather than expanding, they would be better off buying another motel, perhaps in a locale close by. They would hire someone to run their current operation, and spend most of their time at the new location until they got it running properly. This they did in 1962, and, like their first motel, it was an overwhelming success within a few years. From then on they bought a new motel every five years, so that by 1980 they had five motels with an average of one hundred rooms per unit.

During all of this time Becky and Harold kept their own financial records and brought in a certified public accountant once a year to close the books and prepare their income tax returns. Last week the new accountant they just hired asked them how long they intended to go on running five motels. They told him that they enjoyed the operation and

hoped to keep at it for about another ten years, at which time they would sell out and retire.

Harold admitted to the accountant that trying to keep all of the motels going at the same time was difficult, but that he had some excellent managers working for him. The accountant asked him why he did not buy a new motel every year and really expand the business. Harold explained that he did not want to borrow money for expansion. That was when the accountant asked him if he would consider incorporating. "If you incorporate," he said, "you could sell stock and use the money to buy more motels. Additionally, you could keep some of the stock for yourself so you would maintain control of the operation, sell some for expansion purposes, and sell the rest to raise some money that you can put aside into a savings account or some conservative investment. This way if things go bad, you will still have a nest egg built up." The accountant also explained to Harold and Becky that, as a partnership, they are currently responsible for all debts of the business. As a corporation, they would have limited liability; if the corporation were to fail, the creditors could not sue them for their personal assets. Their assets would be protected. So the money Harold would get for selling the stock would be safely tucked away.

The Harlows admit that they have never really considered looking at another form of organization. They have assumed that a partnership was the best form for them. They are willing to examine the benefits of a corporation, and they will go ahead and incorporate if it promises them greater advantages. "It all depends," said Harold, "on the advantages and disadvantages."

■ **YOUR CONSULTATION** Help Becky and Harold out by advising them. First, tell them what the advantages and disadvantages of a partnership are. Then contrast these with those of the corporation. Finally, give them your opinion on whether or not they should incorporate.

Part Three Case Study

WORSHAM & COMPANY: MISSION IMPOSSIBLE

INTRODUCTION

Worsham's Masterfuel, Worsham & Company, and Nifty Auto Parts are three separate entities related to automobile repair, service, and replacement parts that are owned and controlled by Robert and Jill Worsham.

Worsham's Masterfuel service station was opened by Robert's father, Bill, in 1940. Robert started Worsham & Company in 1967 to sell tubeless tire accessories, then diversified and expanded into wholesale distribution of small replacement auto parts. The wholesale division was profitable through the mid 1980s. The Nifty Auto Parts division was opened in 1988 as a retail extension of Worsham & Company.

The local populace, meanwhile, was being slowly but inexorably drawn towards the metropolitan area for employment and trade. In the 1980s, retail and wholesale chain operations extending from the metropolitan area began encroaching on Worsham's sales territory. By the fall of 1988 changes in customer buying habits, fierce competition, loss of sales, and high debt had forced the Worshams to scale down operations and to reduce employment to immediate family members.

BACKGROUND

Worsham's Masterfuel service station was opened in the early 1940s by Robert's father, Bill Worsham. The station has continued operations in its original location in the center of the quaint Midwestern town of Shortsburg. The original 1940s-style concrete block building has been expanded to house all three divisions.

Shortsburg, population of 3,900, retains a small town atmosphere. It was once the central marketplace for a fifteen- to twenty-mile radius. Local businesses were patronized and the community prospered. Worsham's is located less than a half mile from a major expressway, now only ten minutes from a growing metropolitan area that has a population approaching one million. The easy access to the interstate and the changing attitudes and lifestyles of the community have gradually reduced their patronage of local business. To add further to the dismay of local businesses, shopping malls have opened between Shortsburg and the metropolitan area, and resale and wholesale chains have been locating outlets along access points to the freeway.

Shortsburg's status has changed within a decade from a self-sufficient area market center to an outlying suburb. Many of Shortsburg's residents are employed in the metropolitan area and are accustomed to traveling freeways to shop. Local businesses are losing these customers because of the availability of lower cost alternatives.

Source: This case was prepared by R.F. Reimer of Indiana University Southeast and is intended to be used as a basis for class discussion. Presented and accepted by the refereed Midwest Society for Case Research. All rights reserved to the author and to the Midwest Society for Case Research. Copyright © 1988 by R.F. Reimer.

MANAGEMENT

All of Worsham's enterprises are managed by Robert Worsham who, with his wife, Jill, and his father, Bill, are all involved in the daily operations.

Shortsburg has always been Robert and Jill's hometown. Robert was always near his father's gas station while he was growing up, providing him with extensive knowledge of automobile repair and service. Robert has demonstrated the ambition and dedication to run a small business. He has considerable hands-on knowledge and has taken sixty hours of college business courses to develop his managerial knowledge.

Robert is active in his church and community and continues to support the volunteer fire department from which he resigned after 15 years to devote more time to his business. Robert is considered by the community to be one of Shortsburg's successful, local entrepreneurs.

Jill has an outgoing personality. She is involved in the church and has repeatedly held various positions including Lay Leader, a public relations position generally held by men. Jill is an active member of a national sorority, holding offices at various times in her 23 years as a member. She attended college for two years until her marriage to Robert. Robert and Jill have two children: James, 13 and Robin, 18.

Bill Worsham, although still active, is in his 80s and limits his interest only to the service station. He has humorously mentioned looking forward to the day when he will walk across the street to Grout's Funeral Home and lie down for a long nap.

Sam the Mechanic is in his 60s and is indispensable to the station. His mechanical skills are considerable and his loyalty unquestionable. Sam the Mechanic has been with Bill Worsham since the early 1960s.

WORSHAM'S MASTERFUEL SERVICE STATION

The station offers full-service gasoline islands and always has a mechanic on duty in its two-bay garage facility. The owners are community-minded and rely on local repeat customers for 95% of their business. The remaining 5% comes from interstate travelers in need of fuel or repairs.

Bill Worsham is operating the station on a daily basis with the aid of his long-time crony, Sam the Mechanic. The two work as a team and have earned local loyalty because of their longstanding experience in the community of Shortsburg.

Quality service, small-town friendliness, and convenience have helped Worsham's Masterfuel acquire and retain customers throughout the years. They do not advertise, but rely on word-of-mouth from satisfied customers. The building is well maintained, clean, and neatly painted in keeping with the community of Shortsburg. It is located on a one-acre corner lot. Figure III-1 shows the design layout of the service station. The service station revenue is divided between 60% gasoline sales and 40% repair work service depending on the season. All repair parts and chemicals are purchased from Worsham & Company. Bill says the markup on these products is 60%. Half of the markup is allocated to the service station and half to Worsham & Company.

The major competition for Worsham's, a full-service station, are the area's self-service stations and convenience stores that offer gasoline. Worsham's is the only full-service station in Shortsburg and maintains prices well above their competitors.

Bill Worsham sold the goodwill of the service station to Robert and Jill Worsham in 1985, for $29,500. The land and building are still owned by Bill Worsham.

Figure III-1
Layout of Worsham's
Masterfuel

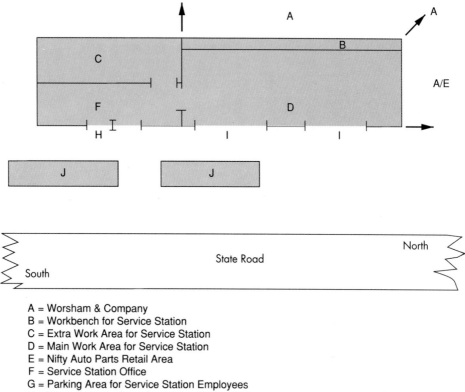

A = Worsham & Company
B = Workbench for Service Station
C = Extra Work Area for Service Station
D = Main Work Area for Service Station
E = Nifty Auto Parts Retail Area
F = Service Station Office
G = Parking Area for Service Station Employees
H = Glass Entrance Door for Service Station Office
I = 12' x 12' Overhead Door for Service Station
J = Gasoline Pumps

An EPA investigation of foreign substances in the drainage ditch at the rear of the property prompted the installation of new underground tanks in 1987 at a cost of $30,000. The newly-installed tanks were paid for by Bill Worsham. The financial data, in Table III-1, are yearly revenues and expenses as kept for the service station. The Worsham Gasoline Account represents gasoline used by Worsham & Company and in personal vehicles owned by the Worshams.

WORSHAM & COMPANY

In 1960, Robert Worsham, just out of the Army, started working for Barnes Stop Fast Corporation selling tubeless tire repair equipment. Growing up near his father's station and working at Barnes Stop Fast for seven years, Robert developed an extensive knowledge of automobile repairs.

In 1967, Robert terminated his relationship with Barnes Stop Fast and founded Worsham & Company. Worsham & Company originally began selling tubeless tire repair equipment, then diversified by selling starter motor repair kits. Robert was operating out of his 200 square foot garage at his Shortsburg home.

Table III-1 Worsham's Masterfuel Income Statements

INCOME	1986	1987	1988
Gasoline	$60,854.33	$ 79,954.82	$79,511.76
Accessories	10,439.62	10,854.64	9,258.49
Labor	6,235.98	7,227.85	6,965.58
Tires & Batteries	357.17	885.09	1,088.19
Oil	4,643.64	3,856.73	3,959.23
ATF	436.75	352.30	392.00
Vending	3,664.31	2,934.03	1,630.55
Gross Income	$86,633.80	$106,067.46	$102,805.80
EXPENSES			
Gasoline	$39,682.95	$66,993.64	$35,244.78
Payroll	15,929.51	20,330.00	11,696.77
Rent	4,229.76	0.00	7,218.39
Advertising	825.15	600.79	673.50
Resale Items	9,283.13	10,295.46	10,162.49
Insurance	0.00	0.00	2,907.32
Licenses and Permits	0.00	0.00	430.00
Utilities	3,202.97	1,337.65	3,008.55
Security	0.00	0.00	588.49
Sales Tax	4,466.01	4,724.85	2,502.76
Supplies	2,089.82	1,424.47	1,877.24
Testing	0.00	0.00	215.00
Equipment	226.65	1,010.97	219.01
Donations	41.50	0.00	89.05
Vending Resale	1,541.06	1,448.96	1,347.61
Interest	0.00	0.00	4,340.10
Vehicle Service	385.56	1,492.38	4,550.91
Worsham Gasoline Account	0.00	0.00	28,962.70
Bank Charges	156.56	285.76	369.96
Professional and legal	0.00	0.00	613.33
Miscellaneous	0.00	0.00	1,621.08
Total Expenses	$82,019.13	$109,944.93	$118,639.04
Gross Profit	$4,614.67	(3,877.47)	(15,833.24)

In 1978, Robert decided to expand his company by stocking and distributing small replacement automobile parts. In the early 1980s, the company became a distributor for Acme-Portland Wholesale. Worsham & Company distributes small auto parts such as spark plugs, hoses, fuses, and light bulbs. The company also distributes such various chemicals as carburetor cleaners, antifreeze, and windshield cleaner solvent.

Because warehouse space with access to the interstate was at a premium, a new warehouse was built in 1984 to accommodate business expansion. The warehouse is 4,800 square feet, concrete block, fully-heated with twenty-foot ceilings and is attached to Worsham's Marathon for a total of 5,200 square feet of floor space. Local warehouse space presently commands upwards of $2.00 per square foot in long-term rentals. A diagram of the Worsham Complex is shown in Figure III-2.

The business was built on a reputation for customer service and competitive pricing. In 1984, Worsham & Company had approximately 360 customers in the southern part of the state. These were mainly garages, service stations, and independent

Figure III-2
Diagram of Worsham
& Company

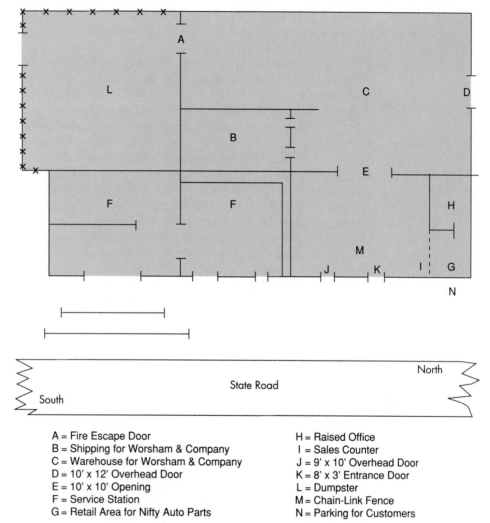

A = Fire Escape Door
B = Shipping for Worsham & Company
C = Warehouse for Worsham & Company
D = 10' x 12' Overhead Door
E = 10' x 10' Opening
F = Service Station
G = Retail Area for Nifty Auto Parts

H = Raised Office
I = Sales Counter
J = 9' x 10' Overhead Door
K = 8' x 3' Entrance Door
L = Dumpster
M = Chain-Link Fence
N = Parking for Customers

mechanics. Although many of these customers remain loyal because of their long-standing relationship with Robert, he believes that fully 75% of his customers are sensitive to price.

Worsham & Company continued to grow with sales reaching $130,000 in 1986. Additional employees were hired. The customers were serviced and orders were taken by two salesmen working on salary and commission. These two salesmen called on larger customers every other week. Orders were packed and invoiced from the warehouse. Two weeks later, on the salesmen's return trip, the orders were delivered and shelved. New orders were also taken for the next trip.

An independent contractor was hired to call on small customers who stocked a minimum inventory. This third salesman was paid commission only and sold items directly off a supply truck. A higher price was charged to these customers to compensate for the commission paid to the salesman. The salesman was not an employee of

Worsham & Company and assumed all expenses in selling the merchandise while earning the commission from the sale. Three support people were employed for the warehouse and office.

In 1984, sales began decreasing. Because of falling commissions, both full-time salesmen left and were not replaced to save salaries. Jill began working part-time in 1985 to compensate for the released employees. Jill delivered products and acquired a working knowledge of the business. By 1986, the company employed only four people: Robert, an office manager, and two warehouse employees. Both warehouse personnel were released in the summer of 1988. Although the warehouse contains 4,800 square feet, less than one-fourth of the space was ever utilized. They use space heaters in small scattered areas of the warehouse where they work and the main heating unit to the warehouse has never been used. The last full-time employee, the office manager, left voluntarily in the fall of 1988, leaving only family members working for Worsham & Company. Even though Robert works 9 a.m. to 5 p.m. daily at Worsham's, answering technical questions, maintaining inventory, and setting prices, he also calls on approximately 25 customers that are outside of the company's 30-mile delivery area. Orders are shipped to these customers via UPS. Robert obtained additional employment as a night security guard in nearby Campbellsville in 1986.

In August 1988, Jill Worsham became the company's only outside sales representative. She is available to the business three days a week and makes sales calls on approximately 150 customers. Increased competition has forced Worsham's to cut delivery time to two days. The orders are packed, invoiced, and delivered by James Worsham, the son, the day following order placement. Jill is continually trying to expand the customer base. She receives leads from present customers and also looks for new garages or service stations opening in the area.

Jill has acquired several new customers for Worsham & Company, including two car dealers that purchase chemicals and wiper blades. With continued service, Jill expects to gain additional customers for the business.

NIFTY AUTO PARTS Nifty Auto Parts was opened in 1988, as a retail division of Worsham & Company to prop up falling sales. Presently, the counter is covered by warehouse/office personnel with Robert, James or Jill filling in as needed. Nifty carries no inventory on its books, but is billed from Worsham & Company as items are sold. No significant costs were involved in opening or maintaining this business.

The only advertising is in the yellow pages of the local telephone directory. The telephone and all other expenses are paid through Worsham & Company.

PRODUCTS

The products distributed by Worsham & Company are small packaged auto parts. The products are ordered from vendors and are received by Worsham & Company in two days. Products are purchased and kept in inventory for resale and delivery to customers. The items are purchased based on past working knowledge of parts sold. No usable written inventory records were kept. The average time for a product to remain in inventory is estimated at 135 days.

The products have an extended shelf life. The inventory maintains its value because of a lenient return policy from vendors. Slow selling or outdated items, if kept in original cartons and in good condition, may be returned to the vendor for full credit in most cases. A few vendors do charge a ten percent restocking fee on returned merchandise. During early 1988, over $10,000 of slow moving inventory was returned to the vendors.

Some vendors offer discounts for cash payments on purchases, and the company often pays cash on smaller purchases. By mid 1988, however, because of slow payment, the company's largest vendor, Atlantic-Portland, required all orders to be paid C.O.D.

COMPETITION

Worsham & Company's sales leveled off as competition from larger wholesale auto parts distributors, convenience stores, and large chain retailers located less than ten minutes away by the freeway became more numerous and intense. Hundreds of retail outlets, such as Nationwise, are located in the nearby metropolitan area. Worsham's strongest competition is George's Auto, which is located in the same block as Worsham's, and has five outlets in the area. George's Auto and Hacker Brothers recently added outside salesmen to distribute auto parts and supplies in Worsham's business area.

Worsham & Company must also compete in the same territory with national distributors such as NAPA and Mighty Man. Mighty Man distributes auto parts from a route truck driven by salesmen.

Worsham & Company cannot compete in price with their larger competitors because of economies of scale in buying by the larger companies. Robert and Jill rely on knowledgeable, personal service to create customer loyalty. Despite the service and knowledge, customers continue to fall away, opting instead for lower prices on what are perceived to be commodity items. In addition, as older customers retire and move or expire, the loyalty factor becomes less and less important.

FINANCIAL POSITION

The data in Tables III-2 and III-3 were taken directly from the financial statements kept by Worsham & Company. A computer was purchased along with some commercial software which was modified by a local person for Worsham's use. The computer generates a lot of paper and lists the inventory by description and selling price, but does not yield information as to quantities sold or on-hand costs.

There are no cumulative data and the owners order by "feel" and familiarity. There is some attempt at financial control, but money is essentially handled by Jill from shoe boxes containing cash, invoices, incoming checks and bills due. Borrowing is done from a local bank, whenever bills pile up or operating cash is needed.

BUSINESS PHILOSOPHY

Robert Worsham's business policy is that all customers should be treated equally. To accomplish this, he insists that all items will carry the same 30% markup. This policy is used in all three of Worsham's companies.

It is also a company policy that all extra discounts from vendors be passed on to the customers. These extra discounts may be the result of buying in large volume or a special offer from the vendors. Having the same profit margin on all products does not take into consideration the sales volume or turnover of any particular item.

Table III-2 Worsham & Company and Nifty Auto Parts
Consolidated Balance Sheet

ASSETS	1985	1986	1987	1988
Current Assets:				
Cash	$ 0.00	$ 0.00	$ 0.00	$ 0.00
Accts. Receivable	5,728.07	10,553.55	7,556.05	5,643.64
Notes Receivable	0.00	0.00	2,392.13	2,392.13
Inventory	66,432.03	49,103.89	36,327.32	37,749.81
Consigned Invent.	4,755.95	3,041.83	3,041.83	2,803.41
Prepaid Expense	1,153.28	549.93	(3,306.88)	0.00
Total Current Assets	$ 78,069.33	$ 63,249.20	$ 46,010.45	$ 48,589.09
Fixed Assets:				
Worsham's Marathon	$ 23,808.31	$ 22,482.40	$ 22,074.65	$ 20,702.02
Equipment	24,768.37	36,768.37	36,768.37	33,118.37
Vehicles	28,551.24	28,551.24	28,511.24	31,015.98
Fixed Assets	$ 77,127.92	$ 87,802.01	$ 87,354.26	$ 84,837.17
Depreciation	36,837.39	44,090.90	45,299.90	49,929.90
Total Fixed Assets	$ 40,290.53	$ 43,711.11	$ 42,054.36	$ 34,907.27
TOTAL ASSETS	$118,359.86	$106,960.31	$ 88,064.81	$ 83,496.36
LIABILITIES AND OWNER'S EQUITY				
Current Liabilities:				
Accounts Payable	$ 8,549.52	$ 14,566.55	$ 16,213.17	$ 12,213.65
Accrued Liab.	2,288.58	1,284.53	1,674.85	1,271.42
Total Current Liabilities	$ 10,838.10	$ 22,478.42	$ 26,613.39	$ 18,711.51
NonCurrent Liabilities:				
Notes Payable	$253,264.47	$238,470.57	$227,721.98	$252,148.23
Total NonCurrent Liabilities	$253,264.47	$238,470.57	$227,721.98	$252,148.23
Owner's Equity:				
Capital	$ 81,674.10	$ 35,898.87	$ 15,919.18	$ 15,919.18
Retained Earnings	(227,416.81)	(189,887.55)	(182,189.74)	(203,282.56)
Total Liabilities & Owner's Equity	$118,359.86	$106,960.31	$ 88,064.81	$ 83,496.36

Robert and Jill do not have any long-term business plan, except "to be profitable and to meet the needs of the community." They and their family are under considerable stress and face a potential reduction in living standards. Because they are well known and Robert is owner of his father's business, they are loathe to abandon any part of the business and are frantically working to save everything.

A major concern to the Worshams is the company's debt. Purchase of the service station, increased operating expenses, and growing inventory were all financed by debt. As sales fall and costs increase, it is unlikely that the outstanding debt can be retired under present operation conditions. The debt is not related to the addition of the land or warehouse which are owned by Bill Worsham.

Robert and Jill are desperately looking for solutions that will permit them to retain their community standing, keep the family business and to remain a "profitable community-minded company."

Table III-3 Worsham & Company and Nifty Auto Parts
Consolidated Income Statement

	1985	1986	1987	1988
Interest Income	$ 492.39	$ 356.86	$ 565.03	$ 681.40
Net Sales	93,460.27	127,563.89	112,760.72	109,559.46
Cost of Goods Sold	58,912.13	78,340.07	70,541.66	66,069.49
Gross Profit on Sales	$ 35,040.53	$ 49,580.68	$ 42,784.09	$ 44,171.37
Expenses:**				
Advertising	$ 1,131.09	$ 594.43	$ 680.67	$ 222.79
Profess. Fees	2,386.81	2,928.45	1,484.30	2,882.51
Vehicle	10,264.66	7,628.50	5,015.92	3,972.06
Insurance	3,984.24	4,357.35	1,211.18	4,140.38
Salaries	42,020.04	40,453.21	37,170.89	19,975.30
Commissions	18,904.65	7,541.61	4,925.64	2,096.81
Emp.s' Benefit	1,181.90	632.90	21.76	3,711.10
Travel	5,633.88	5,767.70	1,650.03	67.92
Bank Charges	919.45	287.33	320.26	325.89
Interest	22,197.47	22,328.00	8,326.69	11,698.61
Depreciation	9,313.45	7,253.51	8,290.30	9,681.12
Office Supplies	3,686.09	2,521.46	1,405.37	1,885.32
Utilities	2,342.15	1,927.66	1,746.05	2,101.81
Telephone	2,372.98	998.20	758.12	1,490.77
Gen. Repair	1,809.99	2,274.62	1,279.23	1,108.54
Charity Contribs.	127.10	40.50	2.00	127.20
Taxes	7,059.47	4,657.69	3,709.38	3,540.28
Equip. Lease	5,177.40	2,588.70	0.00	0.00
Total Expenses	$ 64,206.94	$114,781.84	$ 77,997.79	$ 69,028.41
Income Before Tax	($ 30,151.19)	($ 65,914.88)	($ 36,343.76)	($ 26,219.84)
Income Tax	0.00	0.00	0.00	0.00
NET INCOME (LOSS)	($ 30,151.19)	($ 65,914.88)	($ 36,343.76)	($ 26,219.84)

**Some expenses are combined with other related expenses. Tax expense consists of Property Tax and Employees' Salary Taxes.

DISCUSSION QUESTIONS

1. What external factors have contributed to Worshams' declining sales?

2. What internal factors have contributed to Worshams' declining position?

3. What are the most serious threats facing the Worshams?

4. How do companies get in this condition? ∎

Part Three Entrepreneurial Simulation Program

IT'S YOUR BUSINESS

You began the shoe store simulation with a business development grant of $50,000. This aspect of the simulation may have given you the impression that getting money to start a small business is a simple proposition. In reality grants, especially to start a new business, are not easy to come by. You don't just ask a government agency or financial institution for $50,000. Those who have been fortunate enough to obtain start-up money had to first develop a detailed business plan and then show some reason why they should be allocated the funds. In order to get you going as soon as possible, however, the simulation took one of the hardest aspects of starting your own business, raising the necessary capital, and made it a foregone conclusion.

You have been awarded a $50,000 grant and given everything you need to go into business. By this time you probably also have several months of experience as a shoe store owner. Your store is open for business, and you have an inventory of shoes to sell. Whether or not you still have any of the original $50,000 left in the bank depends on the success of your strategy and how well you are doing in the retail shoe industry.

You selected the site of your store from a choice of five potential locations, which ranged from a building in one of the older parts of town to a spot in one of the fanciest malls in the area. Your selection was based on the potential of the location to attract customers. By now you should be aware that there are other important considerations, like advertising and the prices you are charging, that affect the likelihood of customers buying shoes at your store.

Some store owners open for business with a solid business strategy, only to panic several months into the simulation when they see what their competitors are doing. They then want to change their whole retail business strategy. However, once you start the simulation, there are some adjustments that you can make and others that you cannot. For instance, you cannot select a new location for your store. Store location is an uncontrollable variable. Changes, however, can be made with respect to such variables as the types of shoes carried, pricing, and how much you spend on advertising.

When making decisions about your inventory and advertising, keep in mind where your store is located. There is less of a demand for quality men's and woman's shoes in the more economically depressed parts of town than there is in other areas. Shoppers usually do not go to fancy malls to purchase discount shoes. Don't forget the uncontrollable variables when making decisions regarding the controllable variables. The total decision package that you put together for your store must be consistent.

Another factor you can control is the decor of your store. Each month you have an opportunity to spend some money improving the look of your store. Store decor is as important to the shoe buyer as location and advertising. Also once you spend one dollar on your store, the effect on the shoe customer continues for many months after that dollar is spent. When you purchase specific advertising, its impact on the customer lasts for just one month. When you put money into fixing up your store, the impact continues from month to month at 50 percent of the value in the prior month until the amount spent has been fully depreciated.

As a retail store owner, it is important to know which variables are under your control and which are not. It is also important to always keep in mind the effect of each variable on the success of the business. The first $50,000 was no problem but, as you have seen by now, retained earnings from store operation are not easy to come by. Although you have to be diligent about how you spend your money each month, a balance in expenditures must be maintained to insure you the greatest volume of sales and the largest profit. There is no sense wishing you could start over and, say, place your store in some other part of town. You have to focus on those variables within your control and do your best to make as much money as you can each month. When making your monthly decisions, don't lose sight of those variables and the impact that each has on the decision of customers to choose your store for their footwear needs.

DISCUSSION QUESTIONS

1. Analyze the market research data and determine how much competition there is in your market niche and in your sector of the community. What does this data tell you? What must you do to take advantage of this situation?

2. Go through the Participant's Instructions for the simulation and identify which variables are controllable and which are uncontrollable from month to month. Do you take into consideration all the variables you have control over when you make your monthly decisions? Could your strategy be based on changing something that you have no control over?

3. Assume that you put $1,000 into store decor. What would be the value of that improvement to your store in attracting customers each month over the next five months?

4. Assume that you put $100 each month into store decor, starting in January, for ten consecutive months. What would be the value of that improvement to your store each month in attracting customers over twelve months of operation?

Part Four

Managing Operations

■ The primary objective of Part Four is to explain how a small business is managed. We focus particular attention on the nature of the managerial process, human resource management in small business, and management of the growing small business.

Chapter 11 concentrates on the nature of the managerial process. We explain how small businesses should go about planning, organizing, directing, and controlling their operations. We review the key points in each managerial function, including the planning process, structure and delegation, communication, leadership, budgeting, and the break-even point.

Chapter 12 examines the human resource management functions in small business. We review assessment, recruitment, screening applicants, selection, and training. In addition, compensation of employees and the regulations concerning personnel policies are covered. Finally, the most critical human resource issues for the 1990s are identified.

Chapter 13 describes some of the unique challenges that an entrepreneur must face when managing a growing small business. Special emphasis is placed on the ways in which those challenges affect small business managers, international expansion, and the use of outside advisors.

CHAPTER 11

The Nature of the Managerial Process

Objectives

While many owner-managers have substantial investments in their businesses, few of them are managers in the full sense of the word. They usually know far more about the technical side of their business than about the managerial side. The first objective of Chapter 11 is to examine what management should mean to the small business entrepreneur. The second objective is to look closely at each step in the planning process and explain how the small business manager can implement these steps. The next objective is to review the organizing process, focusing on structure and delegation. The key elements in the directing function are then examined with an emphasis on communication and leadership. The last objective is to examine the control process with particular attention placed on the control techniques of budgets and break-even analysis. When you have finished studying the material in this chapter, you will be able to:

1. Define the term management.

2. Describe the first law of operating priority and discuss its relevance to effective small business management.

3. Define the term planning *and discuss the steps in this process.*

4. List some of the major principles of planning.

5. Define the term organizing *and discuss the four factors of the process.*

6. Explain what communication is, how it can break down, and how effective communication can be achieved.

7. Explain the three most common types of leaders and tell when each tends to be most effective.

8. Describe the control process.

9. Explain what a budget is and tell how comprehensive and flexible budgets work.

10. Compute the break-even point.

WHAT IS MANAGEMENT?

Before examining the planning and organizing functions, it is important to understand what is meant by the term *management,* for planning and organizing are functions of management.[1]

Management is the process of getting things done through people. By definition, it presents the small business owner with a major problem, namely relying on *others* to do work. Why is this a problem? Because many owner-managers have gotten where they are by relying on *themselves.* Unfortunately, there is a limit as to how much work any one person can do. And as a small business begins to grow, the amount of time required for making sure that everything is being done properly, and on time, increases dramatically. The result is that owner-managers, if they are not careful, soon find themselves severely overworked. To avoid this, they must be prepared to do those tasks for which they are best fitted and delegate the rest to their employees.

DOING VERSUS THINKING

Management activities can be divided into two groups: doing activities and thinking activities. **Doing activities** are often busy-work things such as answering the telephone, opening the mail, setting up shelves and displays, and taking care of minor things around the store. **Thinking activities** are those time-consuming tasks that require the manager to sit down and carefully formulate solutions to problems. Planning overall operations, organizing the structure and the job so that everyone knows what he or she is supposed to be doing, leading the personnel with a well-thought-out, motivational approach, and controlling operations so as to prevent major problems from occurring are all examples of thinking work.

Research shows that most managers tend to spend far too much time *doing* things. However, as seen in Figure 11-1, effective owner-managers spend more time thinking. Why do owner-managers, in particular, have a problem in this area? The answer

Figure 11-1
Effective Use of
Work Time

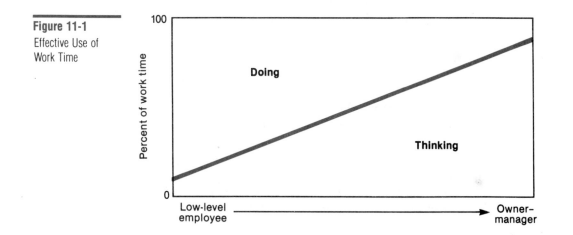

---

[1]For a thorough discussion of the management functions see Richard M. Hodgetts and Donald F. Kuratko, *Management,* 3rd. ed. (San Diego: Harcourt Brace Jovanovich, 1991).

is that they are accustomed to doing things themselves. As the business gets larger, they fall prey to what is called the **first law of operating priority,** which holds that when a manager is confronted with doing work and thinking work, he or she will opt for the former.

The dual principles of getting things done through people and giving priority to *thinking* work influence the **basic management functions** including

- planning
- organizing
- directing
- controlling

PLANNING

Planning is the process of setting objectives and then determining the steps that have to be carried out in order to attain them.[2] In all there are eight steps in the planning process, and the owner-manager should be familiar with them. Additionally, the individual should apply the principles of planning. We will examine both of these areas now.

THE PLANNING PROCESS

The planning process has eight basic steps:

1. Become aware of opportunity.
2. Set objectives.
3. Forecast the environment.
4. Determine alternative courses of action.
5. Evaluate the alternative courses of action.
6. Select one of the courses and implement it.
7. Formulate support plans.
8. Budget the plan.

BE AWARE OF OPPORTUNITY   The first step in the planning process is becoming aware of opportunity. Remember that small businesses succeed or fail based on how well they are able to supply the customer with needed goods and services. These demands are continually changing. For example, if you were to compare a list of the twenty largest-selling products in America of five years ago with the list for today, you would see that the lists are indeed different. In fact, some things people bought five years ago are no longer being sold. While this indicates that the needs of con-

---

[2]Christopher Orpen, "The Effects of Long-Range Planning on Small Business Performance: A Further Examination," *Journal of Small Business Management,* January 1985, pp. 16–23.

sumers change and that the market is very competitive, it also shows that opportunities are waiting to be exploited.

In the first phase of the planning process, the small business manager must ask the following questions: What goods or services will my customers want five years from now? What about two years from now? Next year? By seeking to answer these questions, the individual can begin to focus on potential opportunities.[3]

SET OBJECTIVES   The owner then needs to set objectives for the business on the basis of current and projected opportunities. These objectives should give direction to the firm. For example, the owner might decide that during the next year the business should gross $150,000 and net $15,000 before taxes. How can this be done? Obviously, strategies must be formulated, procedures designed, and a budget drawn up, all directed toward helping attain the objectives. Without the formulation of such overall objectives, the owner does not know where the business should be going.

FORECAST THE ENVIRONMENT   Now the owner needs to get more specific and identify those changes most likely to occur in the environment. "What kinds of markets will there be?" "What volume of sales are we likely to attain?" "How much will we be able to charge for our goods?" "How much will it cost us to manufacture these goods?" To a large degree the specifics of the plan are determined at this point, because this is when the owner decides what is most likely to happen during the next year or two.

DETERMINE ALTERNATIVE COURSES OF ACTION   The next step in the planning process is to search for and examine alternative courses of action. For example, suppose a small business owner learns that he can purchase all of the suits he wants at a 25 percent discount, but the manufacturer's sale will last only one week. In deciding whether to take advantage of this sale, the owner would want to determine the alternative courses of action available should he decide to buy the merchandise. For example, the owner might have a giant discount sale and try to move all of the clothing as quickly as possible. On the other hand, if the store is a high-quality retail outlet, and its customers are unaccustomed to buying things on sale, it might lose some of the customers with such a marketing strategy. In this case the only thing to do would be to store the suits, advertise heavily, and try to generate more demand. In resolving the dilemma, the manager should list the most likely alternative courses of action.

EVALUATE THE ALTERNATIVE COURSES OF ACTION   At this point, the manager needs to determine the benefits and drawbacks associated with each course of action. He or she asks, "Which alternative offers the best combination of success *and* payoff?" One alternative may secure the firm total sales of $250,000, but its probability of success may be very remote, as low as 10 percent. Conversely, another alternative may result in sales of only $175,000 but have a success probability of 60 percent. For example, consider the small business owner who has identified four alternative courses of action, each of which has a different sales potential and likelihood of success:

---

[3]Jeffrey C. Shuman and John A. Seeger, "The Theory and Practice of Strategic Management in Smaller Rapid-Growth Firms," *American Journal of Small Business,* Summer 1986, pp. 7–18.

ALTERNATIVE	PROBABILITY OF SUCCESS	POTENTIAL TOTAL SALES
1	10%	$250,000
2	15%	200,000
3	15%	190,000
4	60%	175,000

Having this information, the owner is in a position to select a course of action.[4]

SELECT A COURSE OF ACTION AND IMPLEMENT IT   At this stage of the planning process, the owner determines the best "expected payoff"—given the probability of success and the potential sales associated with each alternative—and then implements it. The expected payoff can be determined in this way:

ALTERNATIVE	POTENTIAL TOTAL SALES	PROBABILITY OF SUCCESS	EXPECTED PAYOFF
1	$250,000	10%	$ 25,000
2	200,000	15%	30,000
3	190,000	15%	28,500
4	175,000	60%	105,000

Alternative 4 is the best one. It provides the greatest *combination* of success probability and potential sales. Now all the owner needs to do is to implement this alternative.

In some cases, unfortunately, the owner may feel at a loss in identifying total sales and/or assigning probabilities of success. In these cases a more qualitative approach can be utilized. One of the simplest, yet most direct, ways of doing so is by using the **"go-wait-stop"** decision-making matrix. First popularized by General Electric when it needed an easy-to-use method for evaluating its numerous product lines, the matrix allows an entrepreneur to analyze the firm's goods and services and make a decision regarding whether to invest more money and push the line, wait and get more information, or reduce investment in the line and begin phasing it out. The matrix can be adjusted to meet the needs of any operation. In most cases, the two most important dimensions are the sales potential of each product line or service and the company's capabilities in producing the line or offering the service. The matrix is shown in Figure 11-2.

When using the matrix to select a course of action, the manager merely evaluates the potential of each good or service and determines the firm's capability to produce it. Where the two dimensions intersect on the matrix determines what should be done. For example, consider the situations in the box following Figure 11-2:

---

[4]For an interesting study on planning, see Donald L. Sexton and Philip van Auken, "A Longitudinal Study of Small Business Strategic Planning," *Journal of Small Business Management,* January 1985, pp. 7–15.

Figure 11-2
The Go–Wait–Stop
Strategy Matrix

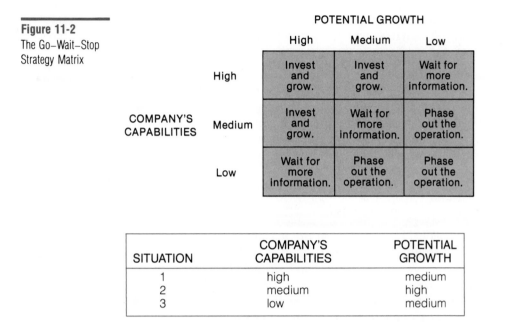

SITUATION	COMPANY'S CAPABILITIES	POTENTIAL GROWTH
1	high	medium
2	medium	high
3	low	medium

What should the manager do in each case? These questions can be easily answered by placing the three situations on the grid shown in Figure 11-3. Reference to Figure 11-2 provides the answer. What should the company do in situation 1? It should invest more money in the good or service and expand its operations there. The same answer holds for situation 2. However, the firm should disinvest in situation 3. Why? Because its low capability is not offset by the medium potential growth of the good or service.

The go-wait-stop strategy is similar to the expected probability method we examined earlier. The major difference, however, is that the go-wait-stop approach does not require mathematical calculations. These are taken into account in the analysis, making it easier for many people to use.

FORMULATE SUPPORT PLANS   Once the course of action has been determined, the manager needs to formulate support plans. "How can the business implement its chosen course of action?" "What things still need to be done?" For example, if the owner-manager of the men's store intends to introduce a new advertising campaign and try to sell all of the suits he has purchased at a discount, will he have enough salespeople to handle the increased business? Additionally, while waiting for the suits to be sold, will he have room to store the merchandise, or will he have to rent some facilities? Finally, how is he going to pay for the suits? Is there sufficient money

Figure 11-3
From Strategy to
Structure

From Strategy to Structure

on hand or will a short-term bank loan be necessary? All of these questions must be asked and then dealt with in support plans.[5] (See Small Business Success: A Strategy to Retain Customers.)

BUDGET THE PLAN   Finally, the owner must take a look at how much money implementation of the plan will cost week-by-week or month-by-month. In this way, the individual can work out a budget to support the implementation. Quite often a large initial outlay is followed by smaller expenditures. Regardless of how it occurs, however, the manager must know the required outflows and be prepared to meet them. Careful budgeting can help in this process.

ORGANIZING

Organizing is the process of assigning duties and coordinating efforts among all organizational personnel to ensure maximum efficiency in the attainment of objectives. Organizing naturally follows planning, since it involves the determination of what everyone is going to do in reaching the predetermined objectives. In fact, research reveals that successful firms follow the adage "from strategy to structure," as diagrammed in Figure 11-3. Note that planning comes before organizing. In general terms, planning helps the firm to interact with its environment, while structure helps it to carry out operations efficiently. In so doing, the owner-manager should be concerned about four things:

1. job definitions
2. departmentalization
3. span of control
4. delegation of authority

The following sections examine each of these and then look at some principles of organizing.

JOB DEFINITIONS

Job definitions are descriptions of people's jobs. In small businesses it is common to find the owner simply giving people directions and letting them take it from there. For example, the owner might say, "Barney, go out and help with sales at the front counter." Although we may not understand what the owner is telling Barney, it is undoubtedly clear to Barney.

As a small business begins to grow, however, this type of informality must decline and jobs need to be better defined, although they may never be written down. This process usually takes the form of job specialization, in which each worker handles one or two primary tasks.

DEPARTMENTALIZATION

Departmentalization is the process of arranging personnel into various groups on the basis of the activities and functions that must be performed. This can be done in

---

[5]Cass Bettinger, "The Need for Strategic Planning," *Small Business Report*, September 1986, p. 10.

■ SMALL BUSINESS SUCCESS ■

A Strategy to Retain Customers

 Barry Steinberg is the owner and sales president of Direct Tire in Watertown, Massachusetts, and because of his extreme attention to customers, his company's margins are twice the industry average. What does Steinberg offer that his competition does not? Superior customer service. For Steinberg, service is not just a way to distinguish his shop from other tire stores. It's the most profitable way to run his business. His goal is to turn everyone who enters his store into a repeat customer.

Steinberg keeps his customers satisfied by providing them with a host of conveniences. First, if a customer wants his or her tires in one hour, Steinberg will schedule an appointment at the customer's convenience. Any client who has to go to work may either be driven to work by one of Steinberg's employees or may just borrow one of the company's seven loaners and pick up his or her own car on the way home. Steinberg figures each car costs him about $400 per month, for a total of $28,800 per year. And that's in addition to the $8 per hour he spends having someone there to drive customers around while their cars are in the shop.

Another one of Steinberg's strategies for maintaining high-quality service is to keep the store fully stocked. Direct Tires could get by with $200,000 worth of inventory, but that would mean occasionally disappointing a customer. By increasing his inventory 20 percent, Steinberg almost always has what customers want. At 11 percent interest, the annual cost on the extra inventory is $4,400, which represents an investment in customer service.

To further guarantee customer service, Steinberg hires a headhunter to recruit the best mechanics and alignment specialists around, then he pays his 27 employees 15 percent to 25 percent over scale. Since labor amounts to 28 percent of sales, Steinberg could cut expenses at least $168,000 just by paying the industry standard. He could also save the money he spends on headhunters' commissions—about $4,000 per year—by taking the usual approach to hiring. But he is committed to employing reliable, well-qualified technicians—a commitment that costs him more than $172,000 per year. Steinberg recently bought a $24,000 machine that helps mechanics pinpoint a car's brake problems. Not only does it improve the level of service, but it helps him attract the best technicians. His customers benefit both ways.

In addition to all this, Steinberg helps his employees look professional by buying their work clothes at a cost of $21,000 per year. Finally, he spends $900 per year on magazines for the waiting room and another $2,500 per year on fresh coffee.

Small wonder that, despite generally flat sales for the industry as a whole, Direct Tire's revenues continue to increase steadily, as they have every year since its founding in 1974.

Source: Adapted from Paul B. Brown, "The Real Cost of Customer Service," *Inc.*, September 1990, pp. 49–60.

Figure 11-4
A Functional
Departmentalization
Arrangement

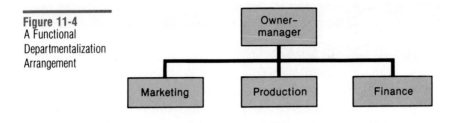

a number of ways. Two of the most common are functional departmentalization and product departmentalization.

FUNCTIONAL DEPARTMENTALIZATION   The most common way of organizing a small business is by function. That is, everyone is placed in a department on the basis of the activity they perform. This has some pronounced advantages. One is that all people doing the same thing are grouped together, thereby promoting specialization. A second is the ease with which the people can be organized. All the owner needs to do is determine the functions around which to organize. In a manufacturing firm, for example, the functions are marketing, production, and finance (see Figure 11-4). The business must have a customer (marketing), turn out a good or service (production), and have enough money to maintain operations (finance). Analogies can be drawn for nonmanufacturing firms. For example, in a bank the primary functions are auditing, banking comptroller, operations, legal affairs, and public relations. In an insurance firm they are actuarial services, underwriting, agency business, and claims adjustment.

PRODUCT DEPARTMENTALIZATION   Another way to departmentalize is by product line. This arrangement is used widely in retailing. Manufacturing firms with diverse product lines also use it. Figure 11-5 illustrates retail departmentalization.

A primary advantage of product departmentalization is that it allows the business to establish profit centers. All activities associated with each line can be identified, and revenues and expenses can be determined. In this way the owner can measure each line's profitability for the purpose of pruning the losing or marginal lines and pushing the winners. As small businesses grow, many owner-managers find it useful to change from a functional departmentalization to product departmentalization.

Figure 11-5
A Product
Departmentalization
Arrangement for a
Department Store

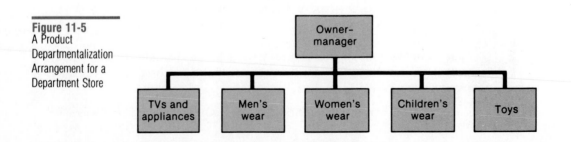

SPAN OF CONTROL

Another element of a business's internal organization is **span of control,** which is the number of people who report to a superior. If a business is quite small, the owner-manager is usually the only boss. He or she gives all the orders, and everyone reports directly to him or her. This is referred to as a **wide span of control.** If there are seven employees, the business's organization chart looks like this:

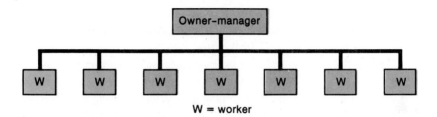

W = worker

As the company grows, it is likely that the owner will hire more people. This is where span of control becomes an important issue. At some point the owner-manager will have to decide how many subordinates he or she can personally supervise. Although a number of factors will influence the span of control decision, in general there are narrow spans and wide spans. A **narrow span of control** for a business with twelve employees might look like this:

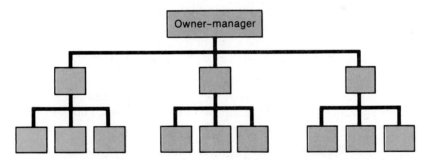

The owner directly manages three people, each of whom also manages three. In a functional setting where there is a marketing, production, and finance department, this approach can be used efficiently. However, there need not be three different departments in order to use it. Everyone may be doing the same thing, but the owner-manager does not have to direct all of their efforts personally.

Which of these arrangements is best for a small business? There is no right answer. However, research reveals that owner-managers tend to have too wide a span of control. They fail to delegate sufficient authority and rely too much on their own abilities. The effective entrepreneur determines what span will promote the highest degree of efficiency, and uses it.

DELEGATION OF AUTHORITY

The effective owner-manager delegates authority to his or her subordinates. The ineffective one retains all of the authority and, in the process, ends up losing subordinates who feel they are not trusted or believe there are no opportunities to advance and grow in their jobs.

The key issue, of course, is how much authority an owner-manager should delegate. Earlier we noted the importance of assigning "doing" tasks to subordinates while hanging on to "thinking" tasks. In order to be more specific regarding delegation, let us look at the criteria that affect this process.[6]

SIZE   As an organization grows, it becomes more difficult for the owner-manager to make all the decisions. There are simply too many matters that need to be addressed. Thus, the person must either delegate authority or suffer a loss of efficiency.

COST   If a decision is relatively minor—involving little money—it is usually best to delegate it to a subordinate. On the other hand, if a lot of money is involved, the owner-manager will want to play a very active role in the decision. After all, it is his or her money that is at stake. In many small businesses, decisions involving matters of less than $100 are best delegated to subordinates. Since this often encompasses a large percentage of the expenditures, the owner-manager's time is freed up for more important matters.

ENERGY OF THE OWNER-MANAGER   Some individuals are very energetic and enjoy getting involved in as many decisions as possible. It may not be very efficient, but it is what they want, and as long as they have the energy to do so they intend to remain as involved as possible. Thus, decision making is centralized in some businesses and it will remain so until the owner-manager feels it is time to slow up. On the other hand, some owner-managers do not have the energy to make all the decisions that fall within the scope of their responsibility. In some of these cases the individual delegates more authority than he or she should.

NATURE OF THE WORK   Some jobs are very simple, while others are quite complex. In the case of simple tasks, the owner-manager can delegate authority because the workers should easily be capable of handling them. With tasks that are more difficult, the entrepreneur may have to help out; the amount of delegation must be less.

COMPETITION   If there is a lot of competition, the owner-manager will find it beneficial to delegate authority so that faster, on-the-spot decisions can be made. If the competition reduces its prices by 10 percent and the owner is out of town, the personnel do not have to wait before responding to the threat; an immediate response can be made. Thus, the more the competition, the greater the amount of delegation that is needed.

TRUST IN SUBORDINATES   Some owners have a great deal of trust in their people, while other owners do not. Trusting owners are more likely to delegate authority. Of course, there are times when the owner-manager may be wise not to entrust decisions to subordinates. For example, if a great deal of money is involved the individual may prefer to make the decision personally. However, many times a lack of trust is nothing more than a belief that the subordinate is not qualified to make the decision. This can be corrected through careful, systematic employee training.

---

[6]Timothy W. Firnstahl, "Letting Go," *Harvard Business Review*, September/October 1986: pp. 15–22.

DESIRE FOR INDEPENDENCE   Regardless of the owner-manager's feelings, the desire of subordinates for independence or decision-making authority will influence the degree of delegation. If the subordinates want more authority, the entrepreneur will have to accommodate them or risk losing their services. If the subordinates do not want more authority, the entrepreneur must assume more authority or determine how to replace the workers with ones who do.

These are not the only criteria that affect delegation of authority. However, they do spell out some of the general factors that help determine the amount of delegation that will provide the greatest efficiency.

DIRECTING

Directing, another management function, involves two basic subfunctions: communicating and leading. Communicating is important because the owner-manager needs to give directions and get feedback from subordinates. Leading is important because the individual must know how to influence workers in order to direct their efforts toward the achievement of company goals.

COMMUNICATION

Communication is the process of conveying meanings from sender to receiver. In a small business, the owner-manager's greatest concern needs to be that of preventing communication breakdown, which can prove very costly to the business.[7]

COMMUNICATION BREAKDOWN   One of the biggest communication problems is that of differing perceptions. **Perception** is a person's view of reality. Sometimes what is conveyed and what a person perceives are different.

A second communication problem arises out of incorrect **inference,** which occurs when a person makes a wrong assumption about what is being communicated.

A third common communication barrier is **semantics.** Sometimes the specific words people use get them in trouble.

ACHIEVING COMMUNICATION EFFECTIVENESS   How can these communication barriers be overcome and communication effectiveness be developed? The best way is by understanding the steps in the communication process:

ATTENTION   The first step in the communication process is attention. The individual must stop what he or she is doing and direct attention to the speaker. The listener is often preoccupied with many things he or she has to do, and if the speaker is not very interesting, the listener's mind will begin to wander. The other things the listener has on his or her mind constitute what is called **message competition.** In order to get the person's attention, this competition must be overcome.

UNDERSTANDING   Even when the individual pays attention there is the likelihood that he or she will not know what is being communicated; the person may not understand. How can understanding be achieved? Owner-managers commonly try to attain it by asking their people, "Do you understand what I have just said?" However, this is the wrong question to ask, because it puts pressure on the person to say

[7]See S.D. Malik and Kenneth N. Wexley, "Improving the Owner/Manager's Handling of Subordinate Resistance to Unpopular Decisions," *Journal of Small Business Management,* July 1986, pp. 22–28.

yes. Rather, the owner-manager should ask, "What have I just told you?" In this way, the listener is forced to reformulate the message. If there is a lack of understanding, the owner-manager should be able to pick it up at this point.

ACCEPTANCE   Some people understand the message but are not willing to go along with it; there is no acceptance. The manager can often tell if someone is going to go along with the message just by the way the person responds. The manager must remain sensitive to the feedback the subordinate gives.

ACTION   The last step in the communication process is action. The person must follow through and do what is expected of him or her. Sometimes people try very hard to do what is expected but, because of unforeseen difficulties, they are unable to do so. Other times they need further assistance from their boss. In either event, the communication process does not end until the message is carried out as expected. The effective owner-manager realizes that telling people to do something and then sending them off to do it does not end the communication process. There needs to be a **completed feedback cycle,** in which the action is checked and it is determined that things were done as required.

LEADERSHIP

Leadership is the process of influencing people to direct their efforts toward the achievement of some particular goal(s). For example, in a small business the owner-manager must encourage people to be as efficient as possible so that the enterprise will be profitable, the workers will get to keep their jobs, and everyone will earn more money. In practice, we find different types of leaders. Some are easygoing, while others are intense. Some are greatly interested in the personnel; others appear most concerned with getting the work out. Some are extroverted; others are introverted. Figure 11-6 provides an illustration of leadership behaviors. As can be seen, there are many ways a leader can behave. However, if we take all of these behaviors and synthesize them, we can come up with a composite leadership behavior. For example, we can categorize some leaders as high authoritarian while others are highly democratic. And as seen in Figure 11-6, leadership behavior can be described in terms of the amount of authority held by managers and the amount given to subordinates. Progressing across this continuum from left to right, the authoritarian, or boss-centered, leader gives way to a democratic, or subordinate-centered, leader. If we were to continue on even farther, we would go off the figure. This would occur in the case of the laissez-faire leader who allows the people to do just about whatever they want. In one sense of the word, this individual is not a true leader, although there are some rare situations in which this type of leader is the most effective of all. The following sections examine the types of leaders—authoritarian, participative, and laissez-faire—in greater detail.

AUTHORITARIAN LEADERS   These leaders tend to be work-centered. Their major emphasis is on the task to be accomplished. As a result, they tend to give little attention to the human element. In some cases, these leaders can be very effective. For example, in a crisis situation authoritarian leaders have been found to be superior. Attention is focused on accomplishing an objective in the fastest, most efficient way possible. Authoritarian leaders can do just this.

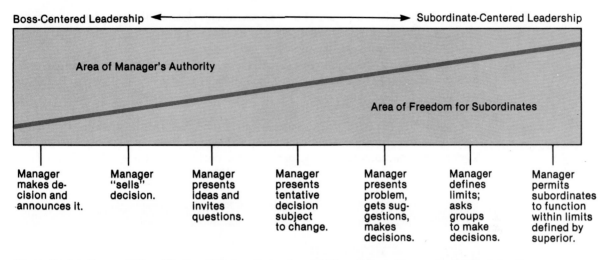

Boss-Centered Leadership ◄─────────────────────────────► Subordinate-Centered Leadership

Area of Manager's Authority

Area of Freedom for Subordinates

| Manager makes decision and announces it. | Manager "sells" decision. | Manager presents ideas and invites questions. | Manager presents tentative decision subject to change. | Manager presents problem, gets suggestions, makes decisions. | Manager defines limits; asks groups to make decisions. | Manager permits subordinates to function within limits defined by superior. |

Figure 11-6
A Continuum of
Leadership Behavior

The drawback to this type of leadership behavior is that it is not effective in very many instances. Most subordinates feel that this type of leader is too pushy and work-oriented and does not care about them as human beings.

PARTICIPATIVE LEADERS   These leaders are concerned with both the work and the people doing it. They encourage their subordinates to take an active role in helping manage the enterprise, although they reserve the right to make the final decision on matters of major importance. They are willing to share decision-making authority but do not abdicate their role as leader by allowing the subordinates to make all the decisions; they reserve the important matters for themselves. Many people like this style of leadership because it is more democratic. As a result, it is common to find high *espirit de corps* among groups operating under a participative leader. Advantages that have been cited for participative leadership include the following:

1. It results in improved decision making, since the participants get an opportunity to critique and provide input to the leader's decisions.

2. Personnel are usually much more willing to accept any changes needed to implement these decisions, since they had a hand in fashioning them.

3. It fosters strong identification between the leader and followers. When workers feel they are trusted, defensiveness declines and a positive relationship can develop between the leader and followers.

4. It fosters the development of high achievement drive. When subordinates know what they are supposed to be doing and they have the freedom to achieve it, they are goal-oriented and they derive satisfaction from getting things done.

On the other hand, one must be careful about assuming that participative leadership is always the most effective. It is not—unless certain conditions are present. For example, it is more time-consuming to be a participative leader than an authoritarian leader. The participative leader must sit down with people, discuss what needs to be done, examine their particular skills and needs, and then decide what responsibilities to assign them. Additionally, both the leader and subordinates have to believe that this type of leadership behavior will be beneficial. If either feels it is inappropriate, it will not be effective. (See Small Business Owner's Notebook: Employee Motivation.)

LAISSEZ-FAIRE LEADERS   These leaders are uninvolved in the affairs of their business. One way to illustrate this is with a diagram that contrasts the laissez-faire leader with the authoritarian leader and the participative leader. See Figure 11-7.

■   SMALL BUSINESS OWNER'S NOTEBOOK   ■

Employee Motivation

 It is very easy for a small business owner to be excited and motivated when he or she first starts a business. The dream of turning a start-up into a thriving, growing venture is enough to stimulate any true entrepreneur. But as the business grows and more employees are needed to maintain the operations, the problems begin to arise. Employees may not share the same goals and dreams as the owner, which can lead to a lack of motivation.

The way to excite employees is not necessarily by providing the usual motivators (incentives, awards, bonuses), but rather by getting rid of factors that de-motivate them. Motivators usually only inspire employees for a short time. However, by eliminating "roadblocks" that decrease employee motivation, the manager may encourage the employees to have a more positive feeling toward their jobs.

Various steps can be taken to rid a company of de-motivators. Many of the steps focus on improving the "boss/subordinate" relationship. If the manager is more accessible to the employees and if his or her decisions reflect a consideration of the employees' ideas, then many of the de-motivating factors that arise when employees feel disregarded can be eliminated. Another factor that may help to boost employee motivation is the clear definition of each person's job or role. An employee who receives conflicting orders from various supervisors is quickly discouraged. By allowing employees to expand and become flexible within their jobs, a company sends out a message that each employee's insights and on-the-job knowledge is important to the operations of the firm.

By simply reevaluating the way a company is run, management can eliminate the various factors that lead to low motivation. Employees are then more likely to provide the kind of exceptional service that can prove satisfying to the employees and customers alike.

Source: Dr. John Persico, Jr., "Employee Motivation: Is It Necessary?" *Small Business Reports*, March 1990, pp. 33–37.

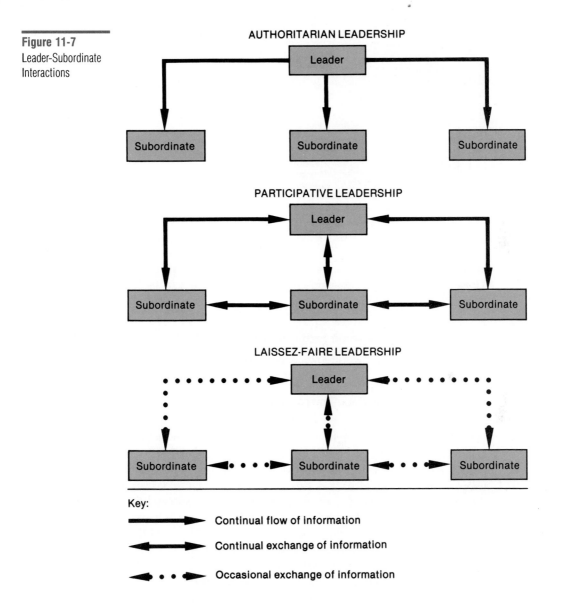

Figure 11-7
Leader-Subordinate
Interactions

AUTHORITARIAN LEADERSHIP

PARTICIPATIVE LEADERSHIP

LAISSEZ-FAIRE LEADERSHIP

Key:

Continual flow of information

Continual exchange of information

Occasional exchange of information

Note in the figure that there are only occasional exchanges of information between the laissez-faire leader and subordinates. While this leadership style is not often successful, it can be very effective when used with highly motivated, highly skilled subordinates. For example, the owner-manager of a research and development laboratory who manages scientists is often most effective when he or she leaves them alone to do their work. They do not need either direction or encouragement from the boss.

LEADERSHIP DIMENSIONS   Which type of leadership style is best in what type of situation? The answer to this question can be answered only by the individual owner-manager. However, research reveals that every leader exercises two basic

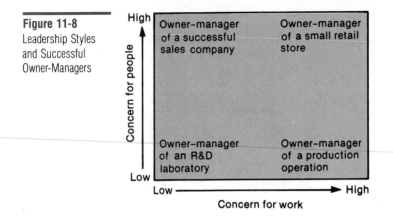

Figure 11-8
Leadership Styles
and Successful
Owner-Managers

leadership dimensions to some degree: concern for work and concern for people. These dimensions are independent; that is, someone can be high on one without being low on the other. Thus, four combinations of leadership behavior are seen:

- high concern for work; high concern for people
- high concern for work; low concern for people
- low concern for work; high concern for people
- low concern for work; low concern for people

When can a leader be effective by exercising high concern for both dimensions? How about high concern for work, low concern for people? What about the reverse? Finally, when can a leader be effective with a low concern for both the work and the people? The answer, of course, *depends on the situation.* However, Figure 11-8 relates the four combinations of leadership concern to four successful owner-managers to illustrate typical leadership styles. Keep in mind that *any* of these styles may be effective in any particular situation. All we have done in Figure 11-8 is identify managers who are *often* effective with each of these combinations.

The owner-manager in manufacturing often finds that work is so highly structured that the most effective style is a work-oriented one. There is little that the individual can do to create a more friendly environment, so the person is best off concentrating on the work.

The typical retail owner-manager often needs to have a high concern for both people and work. The job requires interest in both dimensions.

A typical sales group does not need to be told to "go out and sell." Therefore, concern for work is not a problem for the owner-manager. The leader is best off maintaining a friendly environment and letting the salespeople take care of the work.

Finally, as noted earlier, the owner-manager of a R&D laboratory often has highly motivated scientists who rely on the manager simply to take care of office procedures and see that they have the equipment they need. As a result, this leader is often very successful showing a low concern for both people and work.

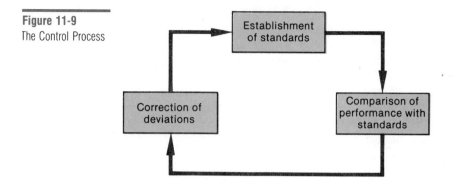

Figure 11-9
The Control Process

THE CONTROL PROCESS

Regardless of whether the owner-manager is monitoring the sales results of product lines or the performance of personnel, the approach is the same. Known as the **control process,** it entails establishing standards, comparing performance against these standards, and correcting deviations. See Figure 11-9.

The performance standards should have been set by the owner-manager in the planning process. In this regard, controlling really begins with the formulation of objectives. However, the process comes into its own when performance is compared against the standards. As we will see later in this chapter, this comparison can be made in terms of profit, cash, accounts receivable, or any of the typical items found on the balance sheet. It can also be used for income statement items such as revenues or expenses.[8]

After this comparison is made, it is determined if corrective action is required. Were some objectives not met? If so, what should be done about it? In some cases, general economic conditions may have brought about a decline in consumer purchasing. In other instances, the company may have spent too much on advertising and been unable to generate sufficient demand. In any event, the most important thing for the small business owner-manager to realize is that making excuses is a waste of time. The owner-manager must now work to solve problems in order to get things back to where they should be. Before examining this idea in greater depth, however, let us look at some of the basic ideas that will help the owner-manager to control the overall operations.

BASIC IDEAS IN CONTROLLING

The most important part of a control system is **timely feedback.** The system must provide information that is useful for decision making. For example, if the business is running low on cash, this should be known in sufficient time to borrow money from the bank or arrange for a line of credit with a supplier.

Second, the information the owner-manager receives for control purposes should be *easily understood.* This allows the owner-manager to see what action is required and start taking appropriate steps.

[8]For example, see "Controlling Office Supplies: Systems for Better Cost Management," *Small Business Report,* October 1987, pp. 56–59.

Third, a good control system, whether it is a series of budgets or a purchasing-inventory system, should be *worth its cost.* It would not make sense to institute a system that costs $2,000 if the overall savings to the business will be only $300.

Finally, when something goes wrong, the control system should help the owner-manager *identify the problem* and see how it can be prevented in the future. Sometimes, of course, a problem is no one's fault and the chance of its happening again is very slim. For example, an owner-manager may increase the firm's insurance deductible from $250 to $500 and suffer a major fire the next week. The change in the deductible would cost the owner-manager another $250. No one can be blamed for this problem. Who could have anticipated fire? In a case such as this, the owner-manager should just accept it as a cost of doing business and move on to other matters.

BUDGETING

The most commonly used control technique in small businesses is the budget. A **budget** is a type of plan that specifies anticipated results in numerical terms and serves as a control device for feedback, evaluation, and follow up. Budgets are often created on the basis of past experience; that is, how much did it cost to get this job done last time? Even if the undertaking is a new one for the firm, it is possible to gather general operating-cost statistics. As will be seen in Chapter 19, there are a number of specific types of budgets that can be used by small business managers, depending on the needs of their organizations. Two of the most common are the *sales budget* and the *cash budget.* In businesses like manufacturing there will also be a *manufacturing budget* and a *purchasing budget,* because they, too, are of primary importance to those operations. In any event, budgets help the owner-manager tie together all parts of the business. Particularly, this can be done through the use of comprehensive and flexible budgeting.

COMPREHENSIVE AND FLEXIBLE BUDGETING

When a small business uses **comprehensive budgeting,** all phases of the operation are covered by budgets. The best way to do this is to begin with the sales forecast. Then, based on the amount of goods the firm anticipates selling, expenses can be determined and profit objectives set.

Many small business owners spend too much time constructing budgets and following up to see how well things have gone. Few businesses need more than two or three major budgets.

Of course, these budgets must be flexible. For example, the sales budget and expense budget should relate to each other. If sales increase by 18 percent in a three-month period and only 10 percent was forecasted, how much will expenses increase? The answer might be 14 percent. In this case, the owner-manager should allocate more money for expenses. And, this in turn may necessitate a bank loan or an extension of the business's credit line. By maintaining flexibility, the firm can adjust to these changing conditions.

When budgets are increased (or decreased) based on changes in the level of business activity, the firm uses what are called **flexible budgets.** These budgets are constructed for a given level of activity and then adjusted upward or downward.

Another way of achieving this flexibility is to use what is called a **supplemental monthly budget.** At the beginning of each month the owner-manager forecasts operations and determines whether the initial budget will be sufficient or will need adjustments because volume is expected to be higher or lower than usual during the month. As long as the owner-manager has the time and ability to forecast the needs of the coming month and make the necessary sales projection, this approach can be very effective.

However, in many cases the owner-manager waits until the month is over and then learns that sales were much higher than expected. The business had to purchase more units than it anticipated, and although sales were high, a very large number of accounts payable are due to creditors for materials the business needed. In this instance, the owner-manager must sit down, determine how much revenue was taken in, pay the outstanding bills, and see what the profit for the period was. When this happens, the individual is engaged in a game of "catch up" because things are only brought back to an even keel after the month is over. To avoid this monthly problem, the owner-manager should use the previous year's sales as a gauge in determining what to expect. If December is a big month for the retail store, it is foolish to assume that only one-twelfth of its annual sales will be made during this month. It is better to stock up and be ready for the increased demand. In fact, many retailers find that if they run out of goods during the December holiday season, potential sales are lost forever. There is simply no time to reorder, and suppliers have already exhausted their own inventories. (After all, who wants to produce 500,000 units, sell 350,000 of them to retailers, and hold on to the rest to help out retailers who have run out by December 15?) Thus, the retailer must order the right amount in advance. Basing their orders on sales of previous years helps retailers to do this.

Of course, budgets are not the only tools for helping the manager control operations. There are many others, one of the most popular being the break-even point.

BREAK-EVEN POINT

The **break-even point** is the point where a company's sales revenue is equal to its cost of production. By definition, the company will lose money if sales are less than this amount and make a profit if sales are greater than this amount.[9]

Two types of costs must be understood in computing the break-even point: fixed and variable. A **fixed cost** is one that remains constant, at least in the short run, regardless of operations. Property insurance, property taxes, and administrative salaries are examples. The company's property insurance rates do not change with the level of production. If the company has a good year or a bad year, it pays the same amount of property tax.

A **variable cost** changes in relation to output. When production is low, variable costs are low; when production goes up, so do these costs. An example is the cost of

---

[9]See "Break-even Analysis: Analyzing the Relationship between Costs and Revenue," *Small Business Report,* August 1986, pp. 22–24.

materials. The more the firm manufactures, the higher is this cost. Another example is the cost of labor. As a firm hires more and more workers and adds a second shift, production costs rise. As the company reduces production, lays off workers, and drops back to one shift, these costs decline.

COMPUTING THE BREAK-EVEN POINT

In computing the break-even point, there are three major cost-revenue components:

1. total fixed cost
2. selling price per unit
3. variable cost per unit

After these have been determined, the variable cost per unit can be subtracted from the selling price to determine the **margin above cost.** This margin can then be applied to the fixed cost. Break-even occurs where total fixed cost is equal to the total of these margins above cost. The mathematical formula for computing the break-even point (BEP) in units is

$$BEP = \frac{\text{Total fixed costs}}{\text{Selling price minus variable cost}}$$

For example, assume that Company A has fixed costs of $50,000, a selling price per unit of $150, and a variable cost per unit of $60. The computation of the BEP would be

$$BEP = \frac{\$50,000}{\$150 - \$60}$$

$$= \frac{50,000}{90}$$

$$= 555.55$$

$$= 556 \text{ units}$$

The firm needs to sell 556 units to break even. At a selling price of $150 per unit, the break-even point in revenue is $83,400. If the firm sells less than 556 units, it will lose money. If it sells more, it will make a profit. Figure 11-10 shows a graphic solution to the problem.

A DOUBLE BREAK-EVEN POINT

In Figure 11-10, variable costs per unit are shown to have remained the same. However, research shows that it sometimes costs more per unit to manufacture 10,000 units than to manufacture 2,000 because variable costs rise. When this happens, the small business must ask itself two questions: How many units will we have to make (and, of course, sell) to break even? and At what point will we maximize profits? Remember, profit is not always maximized by producing as many units as possible and selling them at a fixed price. If variable costs rise and selling price

Figure 11-10
Graphing the
Break-even Point

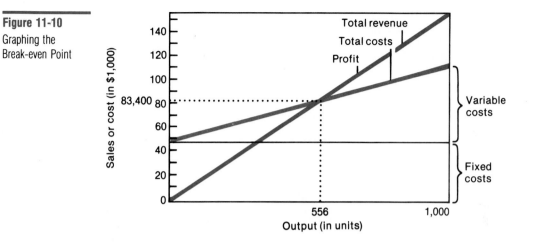

remains the same, there is a point at which the company will lose money. For example, the business may break even at 2,000 units, become increasingly profitable up to 7,000 units, see variable expenses rise dramatically after 8,000 units, and finally break even again at 10,000 units. In this case, there are two break-even points and the firm must operate between them. Before looking at an example of this, let us consider two other concepts: marginal cost and marginal revenue.

Marginal cost is the expense associated with producing the next unit. For example, if it costs $1.00 to produce the first 1,000 units and 96¢ to produce the second 1,000 units, there is what is called a **return to scale.** That is, as the scale of production increases, the cost per unit decreases.

Marginal revenue is the amount of money the business will get from *selling* one more unit. Oftentimes, this number is fixed so that if the business sells one unit it will make $5, and if it sells 100 units it will make $500.

Drawing upon the marginal cost and marginal revenue concepts, it is possible to determine total revenue, total cost, and total profit. **Total revenue,** as noted earlier, is the selling price multiplied by the number of units sold. Thus, while marginal revenue refers to one specific sale, total revenue is a running total of all the marginal revenues. Likewise, **total profit** is the difference between total revenue and total cost. The small business owner-manager who is interested in the break-even point needs to know not only total revenue, cost, and profit, but also the marginal cost and revenue. The marginal cost and revenue allow a unit-by-unit analysis. In order to make this clear and bring the double break-even point back into the discussion, let us look at a specific example.

AN EXAMPLE   Consider the case of small business that has been offered a sub-contract to manufacture twelve subsystems for a large aerospace firm. For each one delivered to the aerospace firm, the small business will be paid $10,000. Should the business take the contract? To answer this question, the company must determine the profitability of the undertaking. In particular, the business needs to estimate its tool-up costs and the marginal cost for manufacturing each subsystem.

Table 11-1 Cost and Revenue Data for the Aerospace Contract

NUMBER MANUFACTURED	TOTAL REVENUE	TOTAL COST	TOTAL PROFIT	MARGINAL COST	MARGINAL REVENUE
1	$ 10,000	$ 20,000	($10,000)	$20,000	$10,000
2	20,000	28,000	(8,000)	8,000	10,000
3	30,000	34,000	(4,000)	6,000	10,000
4	40,000	34,000	1,000	5,000	10,000
5	50,000	43,000	7,000	4,000	10,000
6	60,000	48,000	12,000	5,000	10,000
7	70,000	54,000	16,000	6,000	10,000
8	80,000	62,000	18,000	8,000	10,000
9	90,000	72,000	18,000	10,000	10,000
10	100,000	100,000	0	28,000	10,000
11	110,000	140,000	(3,000)	40,000	10,000
12	120,000	180,000	(60,000)	40,000	16,000

After examining the situation very carefully, the small business has determined the total revenue, total cost, and total profit for the entire undertaking. These data are provided in Table 11-1. Note in the table that if the firm manufactured only one subsystem it would lose $10,000; the total cost of producing the first one would be $20,000. A large number of start-up costs would be associated with the undertaking, and the business could not break even with just one unit. Unit number 2 would cost $8,000 to manufacture. This means that the firm would make a profit of $2,000 on the second one (since the selling price is $10,000), but it would still not be able to break even. Remember, it would be down $10,000 after unit number 1, so now it would be down $8,000. Continuing on down Table 11-1, it is evident that it must sell four units in order to break even. Given the information in Table 11-1, should the firm accept the contract? No. The reason is quite simple. If the business manufactures all twelve units it will lose $60,000. This is because the marginal cost associated with units 10, 11, and 12 are $28,000, $40,000, and $40,000, respectively. In short, to manufacture any more than nine units would result in a serious loss. What causes the marginal cost to suddenly shoot upward? From the data in the table alone, we cannot know the answer. However, it may be that the subsystems require some special material that is in short supply and getting it in time to meet the contract demands would cost an exceptionally large amount of money. What should the small business do? It should either ask that the contract be reduced to nine units or refuse the contract.

Figure 11-11 provides a graphic illustration of this example. Note that there are two break-even points. The first occurs after the third unit, and the second occurs after the ninth unit. How does the firm know when to stop manufacturing? The answer is when its profit is maximized. When does this occur? A simple rule of thumb is *when marginal cost equals marginal revenue*. In our example, the company breaks even on the tenth unit and should attempt no further production. Keep in mind, of course, that we are talking about a situation in which the firm has already broken even for the first time. A look at Figure 11-11 shows that the marginal cost and marginal revenue are equal at nine units, so this is the most the firm can manufacture and still hope to maximize profit.

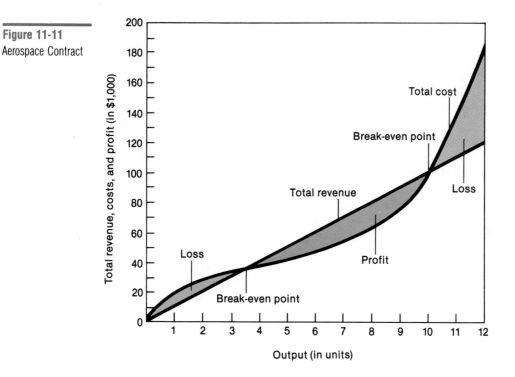

Figure 11-11
Aerospace Contract

■ SUMMARY

Management is the process of getting things done through people. For the small business owner-manager it means relying on others for assistance. This can be quite a chore because many owner-managers fall prey to the first law of operating priority; they tend to give first consideration to "doing" tasks and let many "thinking" tasks go unattended. Additionally, the individual needs to be concerned with planning and organizing.

Planning is the process of setting objectives and then determining the steps that must be carried out to implement them. The steps of this process include becoming aware of the opportunity, setting objectives, forecasting the environment, determining alternative courses of action, evaluating the alternative courses of action, selecting a course of action and implementing it, formulating support plans, and budgeting the plan.

Organizing is the process of assigning duties and coordinating efforts to ensure maximum efficiency in the attainment of objectives. In carrying out the organizing process, the owner-manager needs to be concerned with job definitions, departmentalization, span of control, and delegation of authority.

Another important management function is directing, which involves communicating and leading. Communication is the process of conveying meanings from sender to receiver. The barriers that prevent meanings from getting to the receiver include errors in perception, inference, and semantics. Such barriers can be overcome if the owner-manager ensures that a message goes through all four steps in the communication process: attention, understanding, acceptance, and action.

Leadership is the process of influencing people to direct their effort toward the achievement of particular goals. The basic types of leadership are authoritarian, participative, and laissez-faire. The first is work-centered; the second balances a concern for both people and work; the third is basically uninvolved in the affairs of the business. Depending on the situation, any of these types can be effective.

The controlling process consists of three steps: establishing standards, comparing performance against these standards, and correcting deviations. Because of its wide-ranging scope, this process really begins when the initial objectives are set. However, the heart of control is comparing results against standards and then making decisions about what should be done. An effective control system incorporates concern for timely feedback, easily understandable information, and economy.

Two of the most useful control techniques for small businesses are budgeting and computing the break-even point. A budget is a plan that specifies anticipated results in numerical terms and serves as a control device for feedback, evaluation, and follow-up. In particular, budgets should be both comprehensive and flexible.

The break-even point occurs when a company's total sales revenue is equal to its total costs. In determining this point, the owner-manager needs to understand the difference between fixed and variable costs. Then the individual can use the rather simple formula for the break-even point (BEP): selling price minus variable cost divided into total fixed cost. In some cases, it is necessary to compute two break-even points and operate between them.

■ REVIEW AND DISCUSSION QUESTIONS

1. What is meant by the term *management?*

2. Why do many owner-managers fall prey to the first law of operating priority? Explain, incorporating into your answer a description of this law.

3. List the eight steps in the planning process and briefly describe each one.

4. Explain how a go-wait-stop strategy matrix is useful to an owner-manager in selecting a course of action.

5. What is meant by the term *organizing?*

6. Of what importance are job descriptions in the organizing process?

7. What are the two most common forms of departmentalization? What should an owner-manager know about each?

8. How does a wide span of control differ from a narrow one? What should an owner-manager know about span of control? Explain.

9. How can an owner-manager improve his or her communication? Incorporate the four steps of the communication process into your answer.

10. What is meant by the term *leadership?*

11. Explain how each type of leader goes about managing his or her subordinates: authoritarian, participative, laissez-faire.

12. Describe the three steps in the control process.

13. What is a comprehensive budget; a flexible budget?

14. What does the term *break even* mean?

15. How does a small business compute its break-even point? Be sure to include a discussion of fixed expenses and variable expenses in your answer.

Case Studies

No Time for Planning

■ "I'm in a very competitive business," Joel Agee told his accountant Sam Freeling. "That's why I haven't been able to make much money in the last three years. However, I think that things are going to get better this year and I'm certain that profits will rise dramatically." This argument did not sit well with Sam. He has been Joe's accountant for two years, and every time they have sat down to go over the end-of-the-year books they have found that things were not as rosy as they had believed they would be the prior January. Although several important reasons could be cited for Joel's business's poor performance, Sam is convinced that the major cause is a failure to plan. Sam's argument with his client was as follows:

> You have no objectives, Joel, that's why you don't do very well in this business. You operate on a day-to-day basis. For example, I have continually urged you to set a profit objective and then work backward in determining how much you have to sell and with what markup. This is the logical way of doing things. However, you prefer to just go along on a day-to-day basis without any real plan of action. I don't understand how you stay in business.

Joel was not upset with his accountant's suggestions. However, he did not agree with them either. His counterargument was as follows:

> If I did what you want me to do, I'd be spending all of my time planning, reviewing the plan, and determining what is going wrong and why. If I did that, how would I have any time to actually run the business? You really don't understand this operation. If I want to sell anything, I have to be out on the floor, talking to customers, showing them the merchandise, and trying to close the sale. I don't have time for planning. When I get to be a big business, of course, I know I'll have to do some planning; but by then I'll have the help I need and I'll be able to devote time for it. For right now, however, planning has to wait.

1. Is Joel more interested in the doing or the thinking side of management?

2. With whose arguments do you agree more, Sam's or Joel's? Explain.

3. If you were asked to advise Joel, what would you say? Be specific.

The Friendly Offer

■ When Frank Hargrove was graduated from State University, he said goodbye to his friends and headed back east to take a position in his father's small business. Over the last seven years the Hargrove's business has grown at an average annual rate of 22 percent. A large portion of the growth has resulted from government subcontracts.

Last week Frank received a call from one of his former classmates, Tim Reardon. Tim's company has just received a large government contract and he is looking for subcontractors. Tim wanted to know if Frank's firm would be interested in building some precision navigation systems, an area in which Frank's firm has been quite active in recent years. When Frank expressed some interest, Tim immediately sent him the necessary information related to costs. Frank's analysis of the data reveals that the contract would call for this company to build fifteen navigation systems. The cost and revenue data for the contract are given in the table.

NUMBER MANUFACTURED	TOTAL REVENUE	TOTAL COST	MARGINAL COST	MARGINAL REVENUE
1	$12,000	$40,000	$40,000	$12,000
2	24,000	52,000	12,000	12,000
3	36,000	62,000	10,000	12,000
4	48,000	69,000	7,000	12,000
5	60,000	73,000	4,000	12,000
6	72,000	77,000	4,000	12,000
7	84,000	81,000	4,000	12,000
8	96,000	86,000	5,000	12,000
9	108,000	93,000	7,000	12,000
10	120,000	106,000	12,000	12,000
11	132,000	120,000	15,000	12,000
12	144,000	140,000	20,000	12,000
13	156,000	165,000	25,000	12,000
14	168,000	195,000	30,000	12,000
15	180,000	225,000	30,000	12,000

1. How profitable would the contract be to Frank's firm? Show your calculations.

2. If the contract is negotiable, what do you believe Frank should do? Explain.

3. If the contract is not negotiable, what do you believe Frank should do? Explain.

You Be the Consultant

THE BIG DISCREPANCY

The Gowland Company, a firm with twenty-five workers, has been having efficiency problems. Paul Gowland, the president, decided to call in a consultant to study the situation and make recommendations. The consultant decided to concentrate on communication. In an effort to determine if any communication problems might be causing the inefficiencies, the consultant asked the personnel a number of questions about such things as trust, loyalty, and openness. Table 11-2 provides a breakdown of the questions and responses.

Table 11-2 Communication Survey Responses

	TOP STAFF SAYS OF ITSELF (%)	LOWER MANAGEMENT SAYS OF TOP STAFF (%)	LOWER MANAGEMENT SAYS OF ITSELF (%)	WORKERS SAY OF LOWER MANAGEMENT (%)
Do you communicate with your people frequently on important matters? Yes?	93	60	96	27
Do you keep your people informed on what is going on? Yes?	90	58	95	25
What level of trust do you have in your people? (a) high, (b) fairly high, (c) somewhat low, (d) low	a = 91 b = 9 c = 0 d = 0	a = 15 b = 45 c = 40 d = 0	a = 99 b = 5 c = 4 d = 1	a = 0 b = 4 c = 65 d = 31
Do you consult with your people on matters that affect their work and the working conditions? Yes?	96	70	98	33
Do your subordinates feel free to discuss job-related problems with you? Yes?	100	75	99	22
Do you use the communication process more: (a) for gathering information and passing it on, or (b) as a means of controlling output and performance?	a = 100 b = 0	a = 70 b = 30	a = 98 b = 2	a = 26 b = 74

After gathering and tabulating the data, the consultant showed it to Paul. Paul was surprised. He called in his assistant and showed the results to him. The assistant said that the results could not be correct. "Look at the difference between the responses at the upper and lower parts of the hierarchy. There has to be a tremendous amount of bias in the answers. There's too much discrepancy."

■ **YOUR CONSULTATION** As a new management consultant brought in to review these results, how would you interpret the data? What would you recommend?

CHAPTER 12

Human Resource Management in Small Business

Objectives

The human resource management process is, perhaps, one of the most critical functions for small business owners to deal with. The first objective of Chapter 12 is to examine the staffing function by reviewing the ways in which small business owners should assess their personnel needs, recruit and select competent people, indoctrinate and train the personnel, and, finally, compensate the personnel. A second major objective is to examine the current state of personnel practices in small business as well as to reveal the critical human resource issues for the 1990s. The final objective of the chapter is to discuss employee morale and review methods for improving job satisfaction and employee performance. When you have finished studying the material in this chapter, you will be able to:

1. Define the staffing function in the human resource management process.

2. Explain how small businesses should assess personnel needs.

3. Describe the ways to recruit and select competent employees for small firms.

4. Explain the indoctrination and training methods for personnel.

5. Identify the compensation and benefits needed for personnel.

6. Describe the current state of personnel practices in small business.

7. Explain the critical personnel issues confronting small business in the future.

8. Discuss the importance of job satisfaction and employee performance.

9. Define the term management by objectives *and explain its usefulness to small business.*

STAFFING

One of the most important parts of the human resource process is that of staffing. This function involves not only recruiting new employees but selecting, indoctrinating, training, and compensating them as well.[1] We will examine each of these areas and then present some staffing principles for small business owners.

ASSESSING STAFFING NEEDS

The first step in staffing is to determine how many new employees will be needed over the next six to twelve months. The owner-manager begins this task by examining the current operations and foreseeable work requirements and predicting the probable turnover rate. The individual should be able to answer the following key questions:

- ☐ Will any additional manpower be needed, or can all the work be done by the present work force?
- ☐ Can any jobs be eliminated, thereby freeing people for other work?
- ☐ If more people are needed, should they be full-time or part-time?

On the basis of the answers to these questions, the owner-manager can begin recruiting the necessary personnel.

RECRUITING PERSONNEL

In recruiting personnel, four steps should be taken:

1. Assess short-run and long-run needs.
2. Write a job description and job specifications for each vacancy.[2]
3. Organize a recruiting campaign.
4. Be aware of government regulations regarding discrimination in employment.

With these in mind, the owner-manager can begin formal recruiting. Several sources of personnel are available for small business recruiting.

PRESENT EMPLOYEES   Is a new person really needed, or is there a current employee who would fill the bill? If the latter is the case, recruit this person. Remember: promotion is good for employee morale.

FORMER EMPLOYEES   Sometimes past employees who have left of their own accord can be rehired. Also, these people may refer applicants. If someone is being rehired, the thing the owner-manager should look at is *why* the person left initially. Regardless of how well the individual performed in the past, however, the owner should be wary of hiring people who tend to move from job to job. The owner should look for those who are likely to stay with the business for the indefinite future.

COMMERCIAL EMPLOYMENT AGENCIES   A reliable employment agency can be very helpful in locating applicants. These agencies, if used properly, will do the initial screening of the candidates and send over only those who appear to have the qualifications set by the owner-manager. These agencies charge a fee for their services.

---

[1]See "The Human Resource Manager: A New Force at the Top," *Small Business Report,* July 1987, pp. 28–33.

[2]For a thorough explanation see Roger J. Plachy, "Writing Job Descriptions that Get Results," *Personnel,* October 1987, pp. 56–63.

CLASSIFIED ADVERTISEMENTS Classified newspaper ads are a fruitful means of attracting recruits. Many people who are out of work look in the help-wanted section of the newspaper. In the ad the owner-manager can give a short description of the job, the needed qualifications, and the starting salary. In some cases, however, it is preferable to give a salary range or simply say that salary is "competitive."

SCHOOLS AND TEACHERS Many trade schools, business schools, and universities have employment services for their students and alumni. By spending an afternoon interviewing there, the small business owner may be able to recruit some highly qualified applicants.

As the business taps the available labor supply, it may find there are more applicants than available positions. At this point, the owner must decide whom to select. (See Small Business Owner's Notebook: Employee Leasing.)

SCREENING POTENTIAL EMPLOYEES

In screening job applicants, the place to start is with an employment **application form.** This provides information on the person's background and training. Is the business looking for a salesperson? If so, someone with selling experience may be preferable to someone without it. Is a mechanic being sought? If so, the person should have some training and experience in this area. The application form helps screen out those who are least likely to be successful in the job.

In addition, the applicant should be **interviewed.** A lot can be learned about a person in the interview. Does the individual have the right temperament and personality for the job? Has the person written anything on the application form that warrants discussion? Are there questions that were not on the application form that need to be answered?

Finally, in some cases a **test** is in order. For example, if the person will be required to carry heavy material the individual should be asked to demonstrate this ability. If there is some question about the applicant's physical health, a medical exam should be required. Meanwhile, if the person is going to be typing or operating a machine, these skills should be checked out. Is the individual sufficiently fast and accurate? Keep in mind, however, that the test should measure skills actually used on the job. If the company gives a math test but the job requires no math, the business can be accused of discrimination or of using an improper testing instrument. In short, tie the test to the job, and if this is not possible, do not use tests in screening applicants.[3]

SELECTING AND INDOCTRINATING EMPLOYEES

If the screening process is carried out properly, the owner-manager should be in a position to select those applicants who are most fit for the job. In making the final cut, attention should be directed toward applicants' **references;** they should be checked for both accuracy and input. Has the individual actually worked as a mechanic for this other company? Why did the person leave the job? Does the applicant have any shortcomings that have not yet been identified but could be determined through a phone call to the previous employer?[4]

---

[3]Steven D. Maurer and Charles H. Fay, "Legally Fair Hiring Practices for Small Business," *Journal of Small Business Management,* January 1986, pp. 47–53.

[4]See Robert D. Gatewood and Hubert S. Feild, "A Personnel Selection Program for Small Business," *Journal of Small Business Management,* October 1987, pp. 16–24.

■ **SMALL BUSINESS OWNER'S NOTEBOOK** ■

Employee Leasing

When the headaches of payroll taxes, health insurance, and other government regulations become too burdensome for small business owners, it may be time to seek an alternative: employee leasing. Today 300 to 400 leasing companies represent approximately 700,000 workers. The leasing company operates almost like an offsite personnel department in that it assumes the responsibilities for payroll taxes, employee benefits, worker's compensation, and unemployment insurance. And, because the leasing company represents a large number of workers, it can offer choice benefits packages.

The small business is charged a monthly fee per employee in addition to its payroll compensation. This fee can range from $20 to $50, depending upon the benefits desired for the employees. One company in Rhode Island found that it saved approximately $7,000 by using the health care benefits package provided by the leasing company as compared to the cost of supplying coverage on its own.

However, retaining an employee leasing firm to perform personnel duties does involve some risks. The following key points should be kept in mind when considering an employee leasing firm:

■ Request and check references on the leasing firm before signing any contract.

■ Be sure to read and understand the contract. (Have an attorney read it over.)

■ Review the financial statements of the leasing firm. (If the firm refuses to provide these records, there may be a problem.)

■ Check with the National Staff Leasing Association (15910 Ventura Blvd., Suite 731, Encino, California 91436) for answers to any additional questions you may have.

Source: Adapted from Bruce G. Posner, "The Joy of Leasing," *Inc.*, May 1990, pp. 119–22.

If the individual checks out and is hired, the next step is **indoctrination** or job orientation. The person should be made to feel at home in the organization. Many new employees feel lost or nervous during their first few days on the job. To help them overcome this, the new person should be shown around, introduced to the people with whom he or she will be working, and shown how his or her job fits into the overall scheme of things. (See Small Business Success: Bringing In the Right Person.)

TRAINING PERSONNEL

In order to get the greatest efficiency from employees, it is helpful to develop a training program. Such a program should be based on careful planning that includes

■   **SMALL BUSINESS SUCCESS**   ■

Bring in the Right Person

Luck is sometimes described as opportunity meeting preparation. In an extension of that concept, Laney Thornton thinks of business as hard work coupled with a series of lucky breaks. For Thornton, one of those breaks came when he hired the right person at the right time. Forty-five-year-old Thornton never wanted to work for someone else. He was working as a consultant when a couple of industry contacts provided him with an opportunity to start his own fashion import business. Luckily, his "nonplanner" way of thinking fit the fashion industry, a field where planning is about as popular as last year's styles and where a company's fate can hang on the fickle taste of an unpredictable public.

Soon, Thornton was busy setting up contacts in India to import footwear, brass, and apparel. But, even as he became busier, it seemed as if his company was going nowhere fast. In 1976 he took the advice of a friend and hired his daughter-in-law, Eileen West, a self-taught clothing designer. West instantly became a focal point of Thornton's company. In the beginning she only worked part-time, but even then her fashion savvy became evident when she put together an all-cotton, coordinated line of women's clothes. In addition to her great fashion sense, West displayed a terrific knowledge of retail stores, such as knowing where to buy supplies. She also showed a good eye for detail and an excellent sense of design, an area in which the company would have to make advancements if it were going to succeed. West brought a sense of accomplishment to the company.

After three years, West's keen insight into the fashion industry brought on the attention of companies who were interested in licensing the Eileen West name and look. Today, the Eileen West Company has thirteen such licenses, and Eileen West serves as the company president. Obviously, this former part-timer proved to be a major contributor to the company's success.

Source: Adapted from Charles Fuller, "West Side Story," *Entrepreneur,* July 1990, pp. 192–97.

1. establishing training needs and goals
2. choosing the most practical training methods
3. evaluating the results[5]

In a very small business operation, the owner-manager usually does the training. In a slightly larger operation, it is possible to get the foreman to train production and maintenance people, the office manager to train clerical workers, and the sales manager to perform this function with salespeople.

---

[5]For a good discussion see James W. Fairfield-Sonn, "A Strategic Model for Small Business Training and Development," *Journal of Small Business Management,* January 1987, pp. 11–18.

The method of training will depend greatly on the type of job and the skill requirements necessary to carry out this work. However, in broad terms, five training methods are available:

☐ CONFERENCE OR STRUCTURED DISCUSSION   This is usually guided by a leader and is an excellent method for training supervisors. It is a guided discussion of important ideas. For example, human relations training is typically handled this way.

☐ LECTURE   This is ideal for providing certain kinds of information to trainees.

☐ ROLE PLAYING   This consists of acting out particular scenarios. It is particularly useful when trying to teach salespeople how to sell or supervisors how to discipline subordinates. It is learning by seeing and doing.

☐ PROGRAMMED INSTRUCTION   This consists of a "canned" presentation in which the individual learns at his or her own pace. These programs can be used to support the training effort and do not cost very much.

☐ ON-THE-JOB TRAINING   This is the most practical of all methods in small business. It is used for specific job training, such as showing someone how to run a machine.

On-the-job training is the most common training method in small business. The first step is to break the job down into its various parts. This can be done in writing with a job breakdown sheet kept for future reference as a training aid. It is not advisable to try to do a job breakdown off the top of your head; even the most skilled trainers fail to remember each step in carrying out a job. In working out the various job steps that need to be explained to the trainee, many trainers like to actually do the job and write down each step as they complete it. They then know that they have a complete list for instructional purposes.

ON-THE-JOB TRAINING STEPS   While the foregoing provides some general information and guidelines for training people, the owner-manager should know a number of specific things about training.[6] For example, when using on-the-job training, which may vary from a few hours to several full days, depending on the complexity of the work, four distinct steps should be followed:

1. preparation
2. demonstration
3. application
4. inspection

In the **preparation** step, the trainer should find out what the trainee already knows about the job. The trainer can then proceed to cover what the individual still needs to learn. In the **demonstration** step, the trainee should be shown how the job is done. As each step in this process is completed the trainer should encourage the trainee to ask questions. If there are none, the trainer should take the initiative and ask some.

---

[6]See McRae C. Banks, Allen L. Bures, and Donald L. Champion, "Decision-Making Factors in Small Business Training and Development," *Journal of Small Business Management*, January 1987, pp. 19–25.

"What have I just told you about how to do that step?" "What would you do if this particular problem developed?" "How would you handle the situation?" If questions alone are insufficient, the trainer can also ask the trainee to carry out the step. "Show me how you would do it. You do it and I'll watch." Next, the trainer should allow the trainee to carry out the whole process. In this **application** step the trainer should not oversee the operation too closely because this may make the trainee nervous. The trainer should stand off to one side and watch. When the trainee does something right, praise should be given. If the trainee runs into trouble, the trainer should step in and show how to correct the situation. Finally, there is the **inspection** step. This is where the trainer looks over what has been done and evaluates it. The evaluation should be a positive one. If the trainee has done the job wrong, it should be pointed out and advice should be given as to how the error can be avoided. The trainee should close on a *positive* note, indicating support and confidence in the trainee.

COMPENSATION

Another important aspect of staffing is compensation, which takes two forms: wages and salaries, and benefits. The former is the money people are paid on a weekly or biweekly basis, while the latter consists of retirement benefits, insurance programs, sick leave, and paid vacations.

WAGE AND SALARY SYSTEMS Most small business owners have essentially two choices when it comes to wage and salary compensation. Employees can be paid either on the basis of *time* (by the hour, day, week, or month) or on the basis of *output* (an incentive piece-rate plan). In either case, the compensation must be within the guidelines of the Equal Employment Opportunity regulations in order to avoid discriminatory inequalities. This means that there must be equal pay for substantially equal work. Therefore, once a job has been established and a pay rate set, anyone who performs this job should be paid the same rate. The only exception is if the person has been doing the job for a number of years and has received annual pay increases. In such a case, any new incoming employee need only be paid the current *starting* wage.

Straight salary is a pretty clearcut compensation method, so let us concentrate on **incentive compensation systems.** Under these systems, an individual's pay is based on how much work is done. For example, in some instances the worker is paid a straight piece rate; he or she receives money for each item produced or processed, such as 25¢ per widget. In other cases, the person is given a guaranteed day rate such as $25 per day regardless of how much work is done as well as an incentive per item, such as 10¢ per piece.

There is no universal agreement among the experts as to which method of wage payment is best, straight salary or incentive.[7] However, generally speaking, incentive wages are both practical and effective *only* when the following conditions exist:

1. The units of output are measurable and readily distinguishable. In this way, it is possible to tell how much work the individual has actually done.

---

[7]See Sita C. Amba-Rao and Dilip Pendse, "Human Resource Compensation and Maintenance Practice," *American Journal of Small Business,* Fall 1985, pp. 19–29.

2. A clear relationship exists between output and the worker's effort. The individual should be directly rewarded for what he or she does.

3. Quality is less important than quantity. (If the work is highly technical, the output is likely to be shoddy and to fail inspection.)

4. Supervisors do not have sufficient time to devote much attention to individual performance. If the work requires a lot of supervision, it probably cannot be done quickly and easily, so the workers will not like the incentive payment plan.

5. There is advance knowledge regarding the cost per unit. In this way, the owner-manager can estimate how high the incentive rate can go.

BENEFITS   Many types of employee benefits are currently provided by small businesses. Some are required by law, while others are voluntary.

One required benefit is **unemployment compensation,** which is designed to provide subsistence payments for employees who are between jobs. The fund for these payments is supported by contributions from the employer. Depending on the state and the amount of unemployment the firm has had in recent years, these contributions will vary.

Another required benefit is **Social Security.** Most firms are required to contribute to this fund and, along with employee contributions, serve to finance the system. Upon retirement, workers are entitled to a monthly pension.

A third is **workers' compensation,** which is designed to help employees who have job-related illnesses or injuries and cannot work. The employer pays the entire cost of workers' compensation. Usually this is done by participating in a private or state-run insurance plan.

Voluntary programs take many forms. Some of the most common include: paid holidays, paid vacations, health insurance, life insurance, disability insurance, educational programs, and recreational programs. The number of programs and degree of employer participation vary, depending on how financially successful the firm is, the types of benefits most desired by the employees, and other factors.

One employee benefit for small businesses to develop is pension coverage. Less than 20 percent of employees in smaller firms have any type of pension compared with 80 percent of employees in large businesses. A **Simplified Employee Pension (SEP),** which operates like an individual retirement account and a corporate profit sharing plan, may be one solution for small business owners. The paperwork and administrative fees are minimal, since any brokerage house or mutual fund company will set up a prototype SEP plan at no cost to the employer. The administrative fees, which range from $35 to $100 per account, are charged to the participating employees. Because the SEP forms are standardized, all the business owner needs to provide is a list of qualified employees.

Annual contributions to the plan for each employee can range from zero and 15 percent up to $30,000. The law requires that all employees receive the *same* percentage if they have worked for the company three of the past five years and earned at least $342 per year. Small business owners do not even fill out separate tax forms. Once deposited into the account the money belongs to the employee who pays the brokerage house to invest it. The money builds a retirement fund for the employee,

Table 12-1 Compensation and Benefits Practices in Small Business

PERCENTAGE OF COMPANIES USING THE FOLLOWING JOB EVALUATION (PRICING) METHODS							
	Formal Job Evaluation	Market Rate	Performance Appraisal	Job Requirement	Experience/ Seniority	Minimum Wage	Union Contract	Incentive
Small	3%	30%	18%	21%	34%	19%	2%	9%
Medium	15%	40%	22%	38%	33%	20%	6%	2%
Large	12%	44%	18%	12%	28%	5%	12%	10%

PERCENTAGE OF COMPANIES OFFERING THE FOLLOWING INCENTIVE PLANS						
	Commission	Bonuses	Profit Sharing	ESOP	Piecerate	Standard Hour	Gainsharing Plan
Small	31%	48%	17%	3%	4%	3%	12%
Medium	36%	55%	31%	9%	16%	16%	12%
Large	39%	54%	26%	6%	5%	15%	13%

PERCENTAGE OF COMPANIES OFFERING THE FOLLOWING BENEFITS					
	Health Insurance	Dental Insurance	Vision Insurance	Life Insurance	Disability	Pension Plan
Small	68%	15%	5%	54%	37%	19%
Medium	95%	33%	22%	85%	73%	53%
Large	100%	34%	9%	97%	87%	67%

PERCENTAGE OF COMPANIES WITH A VACATION PLAN AND THE AVERAGE NUMBER OF DAYS ALLOWED PER YEAR FOR MANAGERS AND NON-MANAGERS			
	Percentage	Days for Managers	Days for Non-managers
Small	72%	10.12	7.68
Medium	98%	14.00	7.00
Large	100%	13.50	10.00

Source: Jeffrey S. Hornsby and Donald F. Kuratko, "Human Resource Management as Small Businesses Grow," *Mid-American Journal of Business*, Spring 1990, p. 35.

tax free, until the money is withdrawn. For companies with fewer than 100 employees the SEP may provide a competitive advantage toward attracting quality personnel.[8]

In an effort to examine the various types of compensation and benefits practices that smaller firms utilize, two researchers, Hornsby and Kuratko, conducted a study of small businesses ranging from very small (1–50 employees) to larger firms (over 150 employees).[9] Their results indicate that the compensation and benefits practices used by small businesses are more sophisticated than generally believed. Table 12-1 presents the complete results of the study. It is interesting to realize that small firms now utilize more sophisticated incentive plans, such as gainsharing, commissions, and bonuses. In addition, benefits such as health insurance, dental insurance, life insurance, disability and pension plans are now being offered by small businesses with more regularity than ever before.

---

[8]Jill Andresky Fraser, "The Big Easy," *Inc.*, January 1991, pp. 113–14.

[9]Jeffrey S. Hornsby and Donald F. Kuratko, "Human Resource Management as Small Businesses Grow," *Mid-American Journal of Business*, Spring 1990, pp. 31–38.

PRINCIPLES OF STAFFING

The owner-manager should be aware of a number of staffing principles. Among the most important are

☐ PRINCIPLE OF STAFFING OBJECTIVE   The owner-manager should fill all positions with personnel who are both willing and able to occupy them.

☐ PRINCIPLE OF STAFFING   The more adequately the owner-manager defines the jobs to be done, the personnel requirements for these jobs, and the kinds of training and development that are required, the more likely it is that workers will be competent in their jobs.

☐ PRINCIPLE OF JOB DEFINITION   The more clearly each job is defined, the more likely it is that personnel will know what is expected of them.

☐ PRINCIPLE OF OPEN COMPETITION   The owner-manager who fills job openings on the basis of the "best available candidate" is more likely to hire effective people than is the individual who recruits on the basis of friendship or expediency.

☐ PRINCIPLE OF EMPLOYEE APPRAISAL   If job requirements are clearly spelled out and used as a basis for evaluating personnel, motivation will remain high and tardiness, absenteeism, and turnover will be minimized.

☐ PRINCIPLE OF EMPLOYEE TRAINING   The more effectively personnel are trained, the better job they will do.

☐ PRINCIPLE OF OWNER-MANAGER TRAINING   As the owner-manager obtains on-the-job training and attends outside workshops and clinics designed to improve his or her performance, overall company efficiency and profit should increase.

THE CURRENT STATE OF PERSONNEL PRACTICES

There has been a generalization that small businesses are too small to employ any sophisticated personnel practices. However, current research demonstrates that small businesses do use many of the latest practices. Table 12-2 illustrates the current personnel practices being utilized by small business. The particular study from which Table 12-2 was excerpted analyzed small firms in three different size categories (1–50 employees, 51–100 employees, and over 150 employees) in order to establish the types of practices employed by various sizes of small businesses.[10]

As illustrated in Table 12-2, small businesses do employ more sophisticated practices as the firms grow in size. (Although small businesses of all sizes are more aware of the importance of attracting and retaining quality workers.) In the categories of benefits and compensation the increase in company size affects the particular practice that is used. However, in the categories of job analysis (assessment), recruitment, and selection, the sophistication level of the different practices does not vary too much. For example, size does not determine the use of observation and

---

[10]Jeffrey S. Hornsby and Donald F. Kuratko, "Human Resource Management in Small Business: Critical Issues for the 1990's," *Journal of Small Business Management*, July 1990, pp. 9–18.

Table 12-2 Current Personnel Practices in Small Business

Personnel Practice	1–50 employees Use (%)	51–100 Use (%)	101–150 Use (%)
Job Analysis (Assessment)			
Observation	50	63	69
Questionnaires	10	21	46
Interviews	31	42	50
Recruitment			
Newspaper	50	62	63
Government Employment Agency	27	38	50
Private Employment Agency	23	38	25
Referrals	67	75	69
Walk-ins	58	67	66
Radio	2	0	0
Selection			
Application Blanks	88	100	100
Reference Checks	90	100	98
Interviews	100	100	100
Drug Tests	3	9	24
Psychological Tests	25	25	30
Aptitude Tests	25	23	43
Compensation			
Market Rate	30	40	44
Performance Appraisals	18	22	18
Job Requirements	21	38	12
Experience/Seniority	34	33	28
Minimum Wage	19	20	5
Union Contracts	2	6	12
Incentives	9	2	10

interviews as methods of job analysis, although larger small businesses do seem more inclined to use questionnaires as a job analysis method. Size does appear to be a factor as to whether or not the business has written job descriptions.

For recruitment and selection, newspaper advertisements, government employment agencies, private employment agencies, employee referrals, and walk-ins are used extensively as recruiting tools by small businesses. However, as expected, smaller firms are more likely to rely on the less expensive newspaper advertisements, referrals, and walk-ins. Larger firms use application forms, reference checks, and interviews in addition to the less expensive newspaper ads, referrals, and walk-ins. In fact, companies in all three size categories responded that they use these methods nearly 100 percent of the time. Yet, larger firms will use drug testing, personality tests, and aptitude tests more frequently than the smaller firms.

This indicates that small business owners are responding to the need for improved personnel practices in order to gain a competitive edge in hiring the best possible employees.

Table 12-2 *(continued)*

Personnel Practice	1–50 employees Use (%)	51–100 Use (%)	101–150 Use (%)
Benefits			
Health Insurance	68	95	100
Dental Insurance	15	33	34
Vision Insurance	5	22	9
Life Insurance	54	85	97
Disability	37	73	87
Pension	19	53	67
Sick Leave	27	55	70
Vacation Plans	72	98	100
Incentive Plans			
Commissions	31	36	39
Bonuses	48	55	54
Profit Sharing	17	31	26
ESOP	3	9	6
Piecework	4	16	5
Standard Hour	3	16	15
Gainsharing	12	12	13
Performance Appraisal			
Rating Scale	35	49	59
Narrative Essay	29	50	68
Goal Setting	32	49	59
Training			
On-The-Job	96	100	100
Apprenticeships	24	43	33
Coaching	79	85	69
Seminars	50	60	59
Computer-Aided Instruction	16	25	21

Source: Jeffrey S. Hornsby and Donald F. Kuratko, "Human Resource Management in Small Business: Critical Issues for the 1990's," *Journal of Small Business Management*, July 1990, pp. 14.

CRITICAL ISSUES FOR THE 1990s

The entire function of effective human resource management is one that small business owners need to develop and improve as they expand and grow.[11] In many firms the owner must personally handle all of the personnel practices and, thus, inefficiencies may occur due to the amount of other activities the owner will perform. Thus, many people believe that small business owners fail to recognize or understand the critical issues that face businesses regarding personnel.

However, regardless of the size of a small business (larger firms may hire personnel managers), owners of small firms do recognize the most critical factors in human resource management that confront them in the 1990s.[12] The concern focuses on the

[11]Robert D. Gatewood and Hubert S. Feild, "A Personnel Selection Program for Small Business," *Journal of Small Business Management*, October 1987, pp. 16–24.

[12]See Hornsby and Kuratko, "Human Resource Management as Small Businesses Grow."

need to obtain and retain a quality work force. Wages, benefits, job security, and/or training are all perceived as critical issues in the 1990s. The size of a small business does not appear to be related to the type of concerns that small business owners recognize in personnel issues. In all size categories—from very small businesses (under 50 employees) to larger small businesses (over 150 employees)—the issues of quality workers, wages, benefits, and training are faced by all small businesses. (See Table 12-3 for a complete breakdown of the issues by the size of the firm.) Thus, it is apparent that small business owners recognize the issues that must be continually improved upon if a more quality work force is desired.

Table 12-3 Issues Perceived to be Important for the Future of Small Business Personnel Management

Ranking	Issues
	Company Size 1–50
1	Wages
2	Availability of Quality Workers
3	Benefits
4	Government Regulations
5	Training
6	Employee Attitudes
7	Job Security
8	Employee Turnover
9	Competition
10	Customer Service
	Company Size 51–100
1	Availability of Quality Workers
2	Wages
3	Government Regulations
4	Benefits
5	Job Security
6	Training
7	Employee Turnover
8	Competition
9	Quality Work Life
10	Technology
11	Cost of Product
	Company Size 101–150
1	Benefits
2	Wages
3	Availability of Quality Workers
4	Job Security
5	Training
6	Government Regulations
7	Employee Turnover
8	Expansion
9	Quality of Work Life
10	Employee Motivation

Source: Jeffrey S. Hornsby and Donald F. Kuratko, "Human Resource Management in Small Business: Critical Issues for the 1990's," *Journal of Small Business Management,* July 1990, p. 16.

Excellent Selection

Children's Book Room

Special Orders

Books Shipped

Complimentary Gift Wrap

Gift Certificates

Readers' Club

Recommendations

A Book Lover's Bookstore

EMPLOYEE MORALE

Even though the human resource management issues are recognized and being improved upon, certain questions about the employees must be addressed. Are the workers doing what they should be doing? Is morale good? Are the personnel content? Do they feel that they are being treated properly?

In answering these questions, the owner-manager often finds his or her attention turning toward such behavioral topics as communication, motivation, and leadership. These concerns fall within the control process because they affect a company's overall performance. The major reason for employee problems can be traced to lack of job satisfaction.

JOB SATISFACTION

Job satisfaction determines how employees view their work. When they view it favorably, there is a much greater likelihood of high productivity, although the two are not directly related. For example, in some organizations workers are very satisfied but their output is no higher than those in firms where average satisfaction is reported.

Nevertheless, by remaining alert for signs of dissatisfaction, it is possible for the owner-manager to know when job satisfaction is within acceptable bounds. Keeping in mind that "acceptable" varies depending on the type of business and industry, the following indicators suggest job satisfaction:

- ☐ LABOR TURNOVER   Is the number of people leaving the organization for jobs elsewhere increasing?
- ☐ PRODUCTIVITY   Is the cost per unit rising because of worker inefficiency?
- ☐ WASTE AND SCRAP   Is the amount of material being discarded higher than it should be?
- ☐ PRODUCT QUALITY   Are customers returning goods because they have been made improperly or do not perform as expected?
- ☐ SERVICE QUALITY   Are customers complaining about the service they receive?
- ☐ TARDINESS AND ABSENTEEISM   Are employees coming to work late or staying home more frequently than before?
- ☐ ACCIDENTS   Have there been more accidents or injuries in the workplace than usual?
- ☐ COMPLAINTS OR GRIEVANCES   Is the owner-manager hearing more worker complaints, especially about minor things? If there is a union, are more grievances being filed?
- ☐ SUGGESTIONS   If there is a suggestion box, is the number of suggestions for improving morale or working conditions beginning to increase?
- ☐ EXIT INTERVIEWS   When individuals who are quitting are asked why, do they indicate dissatisfaction with the work environment?

These are not the only indexes of employee morale, but they are some of the primary ones. When poor morale is indicated, the owner-manager needs to take appropriate action.

IMPROVING EMPLOYEE PERFORMANCE

Two control-related areas warrant the owner-manager's special attention because they are related to employee morale. The first is the link between pay and performance. The second is the spirit of teamwork.

EXAMINE THE PAY-PERFORMANCE LINK   One of the most common causes of poor morale can be tied to the pay-performance link.[13] Do those who do the best work receive the highest salaries? In many small businesses, the minimum wage is paid to beginning personnel, and all salaries are kept secret. Only the owner and the respective employee knows how much each employee makes.

Over time, however, raises are given to those who stay and they are not uniform; some people get more money than others. This can create a morale problem when employees feel that raises are arbitrary and not tied to performance. When this is the case, two things can happen. First, those who can make more money by going elsewhere will take advantage of such employment opportunities. Second, those who stay will do less work, reasoning that "I may not be paid what I'm worth, but I'm not putting forth as much effort as I used to, either."

How should this problem be handled? First, the manager should try to tie raises to performance whenever possible. Not everyone's job is quantifiable. It may be easy to evaluate a salesperson's performance by simply looking at how much the person sold, but a stock clerk's performance may call for a highly subjective evaluation. This is why, as we will see in the next section on management by objectives, some kind of evaluation system should be used.

Second, the owner-manager should remain alert to locally competitive salaries. What are other firms paying? Some businesses are unable to match the salaries of other employers, but they must come close or risk losing their key personnel.

Overall, however, few people leave their jobs just because of dissatisfaction with their pay. In many cases, that is just one of the reasons. Another is the dissatisfaction with the work environment. The personnel simply do not like it there; there is no feeling of teamwork.

DEVELOP TEAMWORK   Teamwork occurs when everyone in the organization acts in a cooperative way. Individuals pitch in to help each other out, and any competition is of a friendly, constructive nature.

Although some owner-managers believe that they encourage teamwork, they actually promote competition. For example, the owner who goes overboard in praising and rewarding the best salesperson will soon find the other salespeople working to undermine that individual. After all, if only the best salesperson receives attention, the others on the sales force will become upset and figure out ways to "get" him or her. And they may get help from other employees. For example, the secretary may be slow in doing the paperwork for this star salesperson's orders. Other salespeople will probably stop passing leads to the person for fear that they might increase his or her sales even more. The result is in-fighting among the personnel.

---

[13]See Sita C. Amba-Rao and Dilip Pendse, "Human Resource Compensation and Maintenance Practices," *American Journal of Small Business*, Fall 1985, pp. 19–29.

How can the owner-manager ensure that teamwork develops? The best way is by rewarding those who are team players and, most important of all, reprimanding (and in some cases firing) those who refuse to cooperate for the overall good.

Remember that money is an important work variable. An employee will not continue to work for the small business owner-manager who pays extremely low salaries when a higher-paying job is available. However, the work climate is also important. People want to be happy in their jobs. Research shows that the psychological side of the work environment—including such things as a feeling of importance, the opportunity to do meaningful work, and the belief that they are contributing to the business—is often more important to employees than salary and working conditions. When these good feelings are present, morale tends to be high and performance good.

MANAGEMENT BY OBJECTIVES

How can a small business systematically maintain high morale? One way is through the use of an overall integrative system like management by objectives (MBO). The MBO process is really a simple one, consisting of but six steps. These steps are illustrated in Figure 12-1.

First, the owner-manager identifies the goals of the business. What are our sales and profit objectives? What things would we like to accomplish?

Next, the owner-manager needs to look over the current organizational structure and see what everyone is doing. This helps him or her determine whether personnel

Figure 12-1
The Basic Management-by-Objectives (MBO) Cycle

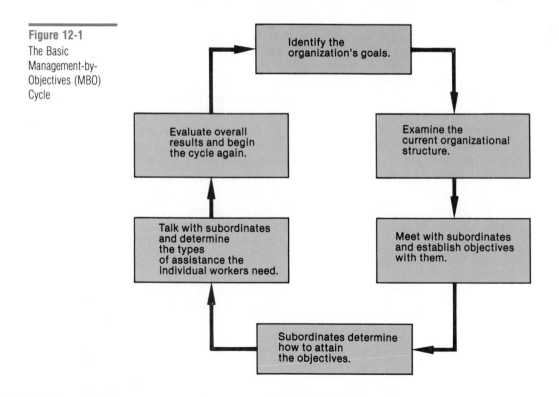

Employee's Name: _____			Date: _____	
FACTOR	**UNSATISFACTORY** Totally inadequate	**FAIR** Meets minimal requirements	**GOOD** Exceeds minimal requirements	**SUPERIOR** Does an excellent job	**EXCEPTIONAL** Is consistently outstanding
QUANTITY The volume of work produced					
QUALITY The accuracy and thor- oughness of the work					
SUPERVISION The need for direction, correction, and/or advice					
ATTENDANCE Dependability, regularity, and promptness					

Figure 12-2

Employee Evaluation
Rating Form

activities are helping achieve the goals. Can the goals be attained if everyone keeps doing what they are doing currently? Or should work assignments be changed so that there is a better blending between goals and activities?

Third, the owner-manager needs to sit down with each subordinate and review his or her objectives for the year. This need not be highly formal. However, the subordinate should know exactly what job(s) he or she is to perform. In the case of a salesperson, this is usually quite simple. For example, the owner-manager and subordinate may agree that the latter will "sell $75,000 worth of merchandise this year." With the office worker, purchasing manager, or sales clerk it is more difficult to set specific, measurable performance objectives. Nevertheless, some attempt should be made, for only in this way can the owner-manager help to ensure that the biggest rewards go to the most productive workers. In any event, the subordinate and the owner-manager must agree on what the subordinate is to do. In this way, work assignments are made clear, and the worker has had input in the decision.

Fourth, the subordinate decides how the objectives that have been assigned can be attained efficiently. What shortcuts can be used to improve productivity? How can sales be increased? What steps can be taken to become more efficient? In this stage of the process, the subordinate answers such key questions as What must be done, How will it be done, and How will I know when I've done a good job?

Fifth, during the year the owner-manager has a basis for evaluating each worker's performance. Additionally, he or she can identify those workers who are having problems and can determine how to help out.

Finally, results are measured against objectives. This is the last stage of the controlling process, and for many owner-managers it is an arbitrary evaluation in which he or she concludes that the employee has done a poor, average, or good job. A better way to carry out this evaluation, however, is to use a rating form that is simple and to the point. Figure 12-2 provides an example. This example is not an elaborate instrument; it summarizes the worker's entire performance by using only a handful of factors. However, a small business owner-manager does not need an elaborate or detailed system. He or she knows all of the workers and merely needs a form that will help review their annual performance.

BENEFITS OF MBO

MBO is very popular because it is both comprehensive and easy to understand. In particular, managers like it because it helps them to identify important business objectives and the people who are responsible for attaining them.

A second benefit is that, whenever possible, these objectives are quantified and a time dimension is applied. Thus, the worker knows what is expected and by when particular objectives are to be attained.

Third, MBO helps the manager to identify the organization's key objectives. There are many goals the business can pursue, but some are more important than others. These are the ones that merit consideration. Additionally, minor objectives are often accomplished in the attainment of major ones.

Fourth, the number of objectives pursued by the workers is limited to four or five. In this way, individuals know what is expected of them and can work toward these ends. When people have too many objectives, they tend to become confused and try to do everything at once.

Fifth, MBO helps the owner-manager to coordinate the activities of various departments or groups in the business. By identifying what each is doing, the owner knows how all of the pieces of the puzzle fit together. Thus, MBO provides a basis for teamwork and cooperation.

Finally, MBO frees the owner-manager for more important activities. By encouraging the individual to delegate time-consuming jobs and devote his or her energies to major planning and control matters, the owner-manager is not inundated with busy work to the overall detriment of the business.

■ SUMMARY

Human resource management is one of the most important management functions. The complete personnel process has several subfunctions including assessing staffing needs, recruiting personnel, screening potential employees, selecting and indoctrinating employees, training employees, compensation, and providing adequate benefits. The current practices in human resource management used by small businesses vary according to the size category of the firms (from companies under 50 employees to those employing more than 150 people). The critical issues in human resource management confronting small business owners in the 1990s include wages, benefits, job security, and training.

In most cases, employee morale problems can be traced to lack of job satisfaction. Job-satisfaction indicators include labor turnover, productivity, product quality, employee complaints or grievances, and exit interview information. Two of the most effective ways to deal with these problems are to improve the pay-performance link and to develop teamwork within the organization.

One way to control performance is to adopt a systematic approach that covers all key aspects of the business. Management by objective (MBO) can do this. Not only is the approach comprehensive, but it also helps the owner-manager to identify everyone's objectives.

■ REVIEW AND DISCUSSION QUESTIONS

1. What are some of the questions an owner-manager must ask to assess the firm's personnel needs?

2. How should the small business owner go about recruiting personnel? Include in your answer the four steps discussed in this chapter.

3. How should the owner-manager screen and select new employees? Explain.

4. List some of the current personnel practices being utilized by small firms in all size categories.

5. What are the differences in personnel practices currently used by small businesses?

6. Identify four critical personnel issues confronting small business owners in the 1990s.

7. How can the owner-manager tell when employee job satisfaction is declining? What are some typical job-satisfaction indicators? List and describe at least five.

8. What is the relationship between pay, performance, and morale?

9. What does MBO mean? How does it work? What are some of its benefits? How can it benefit small business?

Case Studies

The Ineffective Employees

■ When Joanne Addams opened her retail store she had only three employees: herself, her aunt, and her niece. Sales were slow, and the three women were more than able to handle all of the chores. However, as the store's reputation grew and sales increased, Joanne realized that she would have to hire more people. After giving the matter a great deal of thought, she concluded that it would be best to hire people to help with the selling and allow her aunt and niece to handle the nonselling activities. Joanne explained the reasoning to her husband this way, "It's easier to train someone to sell than it is to train them to handle inventory, payroll, and administrative work. If I lose one of the new people and am short a salesperson, I can always call on Aunt Kay or Kim to help out. However, if I hire a woman to take care of inventory or purchasing and she leaves, the burden will fall directly on my shoulders."

So two months ago Joanne started hiring some new personnel. Four people have been brought on board in eight weeks. Unfortunately, things have not worked out as well as Joanne had hoped. The new hires do not seem to know how to sell. Additionally, one of them has already asked for a raise. When Joanne told her she would have to think about it, the woman pointed out that all other retail stores in the area are paying 20 percent more than she is.

These developments have Joanne concerned. "Maybe I don't know how to hire people," she told her husband. "I seemed to be doing fine when there were just three of us, but since I've begun adding new people, things have taken a turn for the worse. Maybe I should get some advice on staffing."

1. What should Joanne do to improve the sales abilities of her new people? Explain.

2. If her people are indeed underpaid, what could Joanne do to improve the situation other than give them raises?

3. Do you believe Joanne needs outside help in handling the staffing function, or should she take care of it herself? Explain.

Bud's New Plan

■ The Arlen Sales Company sells industrial equipment to factories and manufacturing firms. The company has been in operation for almost ten years and during this time, its sales have increased fourfold. Recently, however, the firm has been encountering problems. In particular, three of sixteen salespeople have left and it appears that at least three more will be leaving before the end of the month. All have taken jobs with competing firms. If the company does not replace these people and correct the problem immediately, Arlen could be out of business before the end of the year.

After studying the situation, the owner, Bud Arlen, cannot determine exactly what the problem is. However, he thinks it might be the new incentive pay plan he established three months ago. Before then, everyone in the firm was given a specific sales territory in the United States. Furthermore, in addition to a guaranteed salary, each person was paid a commission of 12 percent on sales. Any sales made in a territory because of a lead from a salesperson in another territory were shared between the two salespeople. Bud changed all of this by announcing that under his new plan, there would no longer be sales territories. Everyone was free to sell anywhere in the United States. However, commissions were reduced to 9 percent of sales, and the monthly guaranteed salary was cut by 20 percent. Bud felt he had to do this because costs in the industry were rising faster than prices and savings had to be made somewhere.

The first salespeople to quit were those who had been the most successful, having developed the most lucrative territories in the country. When they went to work for the competition they took many of their customers with them. Since products in this industry are similar in nature, there is a tremendous amount of loyalty between businesses and the salespeople.

Bud feels that the only way to offset these developments is to counterraid the competition—hire away some of their people and, in the process, pick up new accounts. He is not sure what else he can do to straighten out the situation.

1. What caused the current problem at the Arlen Sales Company?

2. What has happened to employee morale? Why? Explain.

3. What should Bud do to bring the situation under control? Be specific.

You Be the Consultant

A QUALITY WORKFORCE

For the last five years Kendon Associates, Inc., has attempted to build its work force into a productive, competitive group. As a medical laboratory that processes blood samples that help doctors in their diagnoses, efficiency, effectiveness, and quality performance is mandatory. In addition, the turnaround time must be as short as possible (within hours) so the doctors can effectively make their diagnoses. Also, three shifts of workers are needed because the laboratory operates on a 24-hour basis.

Eighty-five people are employed by Kendon and turnover is high. Also, employee morale is very low since the workers have no benefits other than five sick days, five vacation days, and a life insurance policy. The hourly wages are competitive, yet the workers believe they should move elsewhere once they gain some experience.

Dr. Richard Kenwork is the president and owner of the laboratory. He believes that his operation is too small to offer any sophisticated benefits. He also believes that turnover and poor morale are impossible to deal with in his type of business. Since his understanding of human resource management is limited, Dr. Kenwork has sought the assistance of a consultant.

■ **YOUR CONSULTATION** As the consultant to Kendon Associates, explain to Dr. Kenwork the various personnel practices that could be utilized by his business, even though it is small. Also, relate the importance of employee morale and outline some specific steps that could be used to improve the situation at Kendon.

CHAPTER 13

Managing the Growing Small Business

Objectives The traditional management functions examined in Chapters 11 and 12 apply to small business. However, entrepreneurs should be aware of the various challenges that are unique to managing a growing small business. The first objective of Chapter 13 is to examine these unique managerial concerns. The second objective is to highlight some of the key elements involved in the growth stage of a firm. In addition, the transition from entrepreneur to manager is discussed in order to illustrate the differences in each role. The final objective of Chapter 13 is to study the international opportunities for growing firms. The expanding global marketplace is presented as well as specific considerations for small firms in international business. When you have finished studying the material in this chapter, you will be able to:

1. Describe the unique managerial concerns that confront small businesses.

2. Discuss the advantages and disadvantages of the distinctive size of a small business.

3. Define the one-man-band syndrome.

4. Identify the challenges presented through the community obligations of small firms.

5. Recognize the key elements involved in the growth stage of firms.

6. Explain the differences in style between an entrepreneur and a manager.

7. List some sources of outside managerial assistance for small business owners.

8. Identify the international opportunities available to small business.

9. Describe five major international business considerations for small businesses.

10. Define key international trade terms.

UNIQUE MANAGERIAL CONCERNS OF SMALL BUSINESS

Small business differs in many ways from larger, more structured business. Chapter 11 explored the traditional managerial functions that should be followed by all business—large and small. However, several unique managerial concerns confront small business in particular. These concerns may seem insignificant to the operation of a large business, but they do become important to many small business managers.

THE DISTINCTION OF SMALL SIZE

The distinction of being *small* presents small businesses with certain disadvantages. The limited market, for example, restricts a small firm. Because a small firm's size limits its ability to geographically extend throughout a region or state, it must recognize and service its available market. Another disadvantage is the higher ordering costs that burden many small firms. Since they are small and do not order large lots of inventory from suppliers, small businesses usually do not receive quantity discounts and must pay higher prices. Finally, a smaller staff forces small firms to accept less specialization of labor. Thus, employees and managers are expected to perform numerous functions.

However, the distinction of small size is not all bad, and the advantages to being small should be recognized and capitalized upon. One advantage is greater flexibility. In small firms, decisions can be made and implemented immediately, without the input of committees and the delay of bureaucratic layers. Production, marketing, and service are all areas that can be adjusted quickly for a competitive advantage over larger businesses in the same field. A second advantage is constant communication with the community. A small business owner lives in the community and is personally involved in community affairs. The special insight offered by this involvement allows the small business owner to adjust products or services to suit the specific needs or desires of the particular community. This leads to the third and probably most important advantage of closeness to the customer: the ability to offer personal service. The personal service that a small business owner can provide is one of the key elements to success today. Major corporations work feverishly to duplicate or imitate the idea of personal service. Since the opportunity to provide personal service is an advantage that small firms possess by nature of their size, it *must* be capitalized upon.

THE ONE-MAN-BAND SYNDROME

Most small business owners start their businesses alone or with a few family members or close associates. In effect, the business *is* the entrepreneur and the entrepreneur is the business.[1] However, a danger arises if the owner refuses to relinquish any authority as the small business grows. Some owners fail to delegate responsibility to employees, thereby retaining *all* decision-making authority. One study revealed that most planning in small firms is done by the owner alone, as are other operational activities.[2] This "syndrome" is often derived from the same pattern of independence that helped start the business in the first place. However, the owner who continues to perform as a one-man or one-woman band can restrict the growth of the firm because the owner's ability is limited. How can proper planning for the business be accomplished if the owner is immersed in daily operations? Thus, the small business owner must recognize the importance of delegation. If the owner can

---

[1]David E. Gumpert and David P. Boyd, "The Loneliness of the Small Business Owner," *Harvard Business Review,* November/December 1984, pp. 19–24.

[2]Charles B. Shrader, Charles L. Mumford, and Virginia L. Blackburn, "Strategic and Operational Planning, Uncertainty, and Performance in Small Firms" *Journal of Small Business Management,* October 1989, pp. 45–60.

break away from the natural tendency to "do everything," then the business will benefit from a wider array of the manager's abilities.

TIME MANAGEMENT

Effective time management is not exclusively a small business challenge. However, a limited size and staff forces the small business owner to face this challenge most diligently. It has been said that a person will never *find* time to do anything but must, in fact, *make* the time. In other words, small business owners should learn to use time as a resource and not allow time to use them.[3] There are numerous suggestions for the effective use of time, but in order to perform daily managerial activities in the most time-efficient manner, managers should follow four critical steps:

1. ASSESSMENT   The business owner should analyze his or her daily activities and rank them in order of importance. (A written list on a note pad is recommended.)

2. PRIORITIZATION   The owner should divide and categorize activities based upon his or her ability to devote time to their accomplishment that day. In other words, the owner should avoid a procrastination of duties.

3. CREATING PROCEDURES   Repetitive daily activities could easily be handled by an employee if instructions were provided. This could become a major time saver since the owner would have a system that allows the fourth and last step to be put into effect.

4. DELEGATION   Delegation can be accomplished after procedures have been created for various jobs. As mentioned in the one-man-band syndrome, delegation is a critical skill that small business owners need to develop.

All of these steps in effective time management require self-discipline on the part of the small business owner.

COMMUNITY OBLIGATIONS

Proximity to the community was mentioned earlier as an advantage for the size of the small business. However, unlike major corporations that have public relations departments, the small business owner is involved with community activities directly. The community presents unique challenges to small business in three ways: participation, leadership, and donations.

Each of these expectations from the community requires careful planning and budgeting by the small business owner. Many community members believe the small business owner has "excess" time since he or she owns the business. They also believe that the owner has the leadership abilities needed for various community activities. Although it may be true that the owner possesses leadership ability, the owner usually does not have excess time. Therefore, small business owners need to plan carefully the activities that they believe would be most beneficial. One consideration is the amount of advertising or recognition the business will receive for the

---

[3]Charles R. Hobbs, "Time Power," *Small Business Reports*, January 1990, pp. 46–55; and also Jack Falvey, "New and Improved Time Management," *Small Business Reports*, July 1990, pp. 14–17.

owner's participation. When the owner can justify his or her community involvement, both the business and the community benefit.

Financial donations also require careful analysis and budgeting. Again, because consumers have access to the small business owner (as opposed to never reaching the chief executive officer of major corporations), he or she may be inundated with requests for donations to charitable and community organizations. While each organization may have a worthy cause, the small business owner cannot support every one and remain financially healthy. Thus, the owner needs to decide which of the organizations to assist and budget a predetermined amount for annual donations. Any other solicitations for money must be placed in writing and submitted to the small business owner for consideration. This is the only means by which small business owners can avoid constant cash donations without careful budget consideration.

The critical fact to remember is that time and money are extremely valuable resources for a small business owner. They should be budgeted in a meaningful way. Therefore, small business owners need to analyze their community involvement and continuously reassess the costs versus the benefits.

CONTINUING MANAGEMENT EDUCATION

A final unique concern for the small business owner is that of continuing management education. All of the previously mentioned concerns provide very little time left for an owner to maintain or improve his or her managerial knowledge. However, the environment of the 1990s has produced dramatic changes that can affect the procedures, processes, programs, philosophy, or even the product of a small business. The ancient Greek philosopher Epictetus once said, "It is impossible for a man to learn what he thinks he already knows." This quote illustrates the need for small business people to dedicate time to learning new techniques and principles for their business. Trade associations, seminars, conferences, publications, and college courses all provide opportunities for small business owners to continue their management education. Staying abreast of industry changes is another way for small business people to maintain a competitive edge.

OTHER ISSUES IN THE FORMATIVE YEARS

Many other managerial issues confront small business owners in the formative years of the business. Table 13-1 provides a list of the ten most crucial issues identified by small business managers.[4] As illustrated in the table, those issues focus on internal problems that require traditional managerial skills. Marketing, human resource planning, finance, and legal concerns summarize the issues most often cited. Chapters 11 and 12, as well as other discussions of finance and marketing in this textbook, are valuable in gaining information on the critical issues confronting small business.

The unique managerial concerns of small business that were presented in this section directly impact the growth period through which many small businesses evolve. The next section examines some of the key elements of the growth stage.

---

[4]Guvenc G. Alpander, Kent D. Carter, and Roderick A. Forsgren, "Managerial Issues and Problem-Solving in the Formative Years," *Journal of Small Business Management*, April 1990, pp. 9–18.

Table 13-1 The Most Critical Problems Encountered
by Firms in Their Formative Years

1. Finding new customers
2. Obtaining financing
3. Recruiting and hiring new employees
4. Recruiting and hiring new managers
5. Dealing with current employee problems
6. Product pricing
7. Planning for market expansion
8. Handling legal problems
9. Determining and maintaining product quality
10. Dealing with various government agencies

Source: Adapted from Guvenc G. Alpander, Kent D. Carter,
and Roderick A. Forsgren, "Managerial Issues and Problem-Solving in the Formative Years," *Journal of Small Business Management*, April 1990, p. 12.

KEY ELEMENTS OF GROWTH

Five key managerial actions come into play during the growth stage: control, responsibility, tolerance of failure, change, and flexibility.

CONTROL

Growth brings about problems in command and control. In order to solve these
problems, management must answer three critical questions: Does the control system
imply trust? Does the resource allocation system imply trust? Is it easier to ask for
permission than to ask for forgiveness? These questions reveal a great deal about the
control of a venture. If answered yes, the venture is moving toward a good blend of
control and participation. If answered no, the reasons for the negative response
should be closely examined.

RESPONSIBILITY

As the small business grows, the distinction between authority and responsibility
becomes more apparent. This is because authority can always be delegated, but it is
also important to create a sense of responsibility. It is through responsibility that flexibility, innovation, and a supportive environment are established. Since people tend
to look beyond the ordinary limits of their job if a sense of responsibility is developed, the growth stage is better served by the innovative activity and shared responsibility of all of the business's members.

TOLERANCE OF FAILURE

Even if a small business has avoided the initial start-up pitfalls and expanded to
the growth stage, it is still important to maintain a tolerance for failure. The level of
failure that the entrepreneur experienced and learned from at the start of the venture
should be the same level expected, tolerated, and learned from in this stage.
Although no business should seek failure, to continually innovate and grow will
require a degree of tolerance for failure as opposed to punishment for failure.

Three distinct forms of failure should be distinguished:

☐ MORAL FAILURE   This form of failure is a violation of internal trust. Since the firm is based on mutual expectations and trust, this violation can result in serious negative consequences.

☐ PERSONAL FAILURE   This form of failure is brought about by a lack of skill or application. Usually responsibility for this form of failure is shared by the firm and the individual. Normally, therefore, there is an attempt to remedy the situation in a mutually beneficial way.

☐ UNCONTROLLABLE FAILURE.   This form of failure is caused by external factors and is the most difficult to prepare for or deal with. Resource limitations, strategic direction, and market changes are examples of forces outside the control of employees. Top management must carefully analyze the context of this form of failure and work to prevent its recurrence.

CHANGE

Planning, operations, and implementation are all subject to continual changes as the venture moves through the growth stage and beyond. Retaining an innovative and opportunistic posture during growth requires a sense of variation from the norm. It should be realized, however, that change holds many implications for the enterprise in terms of resources, people, and structure. It is therefore important that flexibility regarding change be preserved during growth. This allows for faster managerial response to environmental conditions.

FLEXIBILITY

One of the most powerful assets that a small business possesses is flexibility. During the growth stage the ability to access and accumulate resources is needed. "Networking" is a method of using external resources that are not owned by the small business.[5] It is only through the ability to remain flexible that entrepreneurs can establish the network of relationships needed for assistance during periods of growth.

THE TRANSITION FROM ENTREPRENEUR TO MANAGER

The transitions between the various stages of a venture are complemented (or in some cases retarded) by the ability of the entrepreneur to make a transition in style. The entrepreneurial style relates to the creativity, innovation, and risk-taking ability needed to start up a venture, whereas the managerial style emphasizes the planning and organizational ability needed to operate the business. A key transition occurs during the growth stage when the entrepreneur shifts into a managerial style. This is not easy to do. As Hofer and Charan have noted, "Among the different transitions that are possible, probably the most difficult to achieve and also perhaps the most

---

[5]J. Carlos Jarillo, "Entrepreneurship and Growth: The Strategic Use of External Resources," *Journal of Business Venturing*, Vol. 4, 1989, pp. 133–47.

important for organizational development is that of moving from a one-person, entrepreneurial managed firm to one run by a functionally organized, professional management team."[6]

A number of problems arise when making this transition, especially if the enterprise is characterized by factors such as (1) a highly centralized decision-making system, (2) an overdependence on one or two key individuals, (3) an inadequate repertoire of managerial skills and training, and (4) a paternalistic atmosphere.[7] These characteristics, while often effective in the start-up and survival of a new venture, pose a threat to the development of the firm during the growth stage. Quite often these characteristics inhibit the development of the venture by detracting from the entrepreneur's ability to manage the growth stage successfully.

In order to bring about the necessary transition, the entrepreneur must carefully plan and then gradually implement the transition process. Hofer and Charan have suggested a seven-step process (see Figure 13-1):

1. The entrepreneur must want to make the change, and must want it strongly enough to undertake major modifications in his or her own task behavior.

2. The day-to-day decision-making procedures of the organization must be changed. Specifically, participation in this process must be expanded. Greater emphasis should also be placed on the use of formal decision techniques.

3. The two or three key operating tasks that are primarily responsible for the organization's success must be institutionalized. This may involve the selection of new people to supplement or replace those "indispensable" individuals who have performed these tasks in the past.

4. Middle-level management must be developed. Specialists must learn to become functional managers, while functional managers must learn to become general managers.

5. The firm's strategy should be evaluated and modified, if necessary, to achieve growth.

6. The organizational structure and its management systems and procedures must be slowly modified to fit the company's new strategy and senior managers.

7. The firm must develop a professional board of directors.[8]

The key factor in this process is found in the first step—the entrepreneur. Entrepreneurial self-management is the major area of concern.

BALANCING THE FOCUS (ENTREPRENEUR AND MANAGER)

In managing the growth stage, two important points must be remembered. First, an adaptive firm needs to retain certain entrepreneurial characteristics in order to encourage innovation and creativity from its personnel while making a transition

---

[6]Charles W. Hofer and Ram Charan, "The Transition to Professional Management: Mission Impossible?" *American Journal of Small Business,* Summer 1984, p. 3.

[7]Hofer and Charan, p. 4.

[8]Hofer and Charan, p. 6.

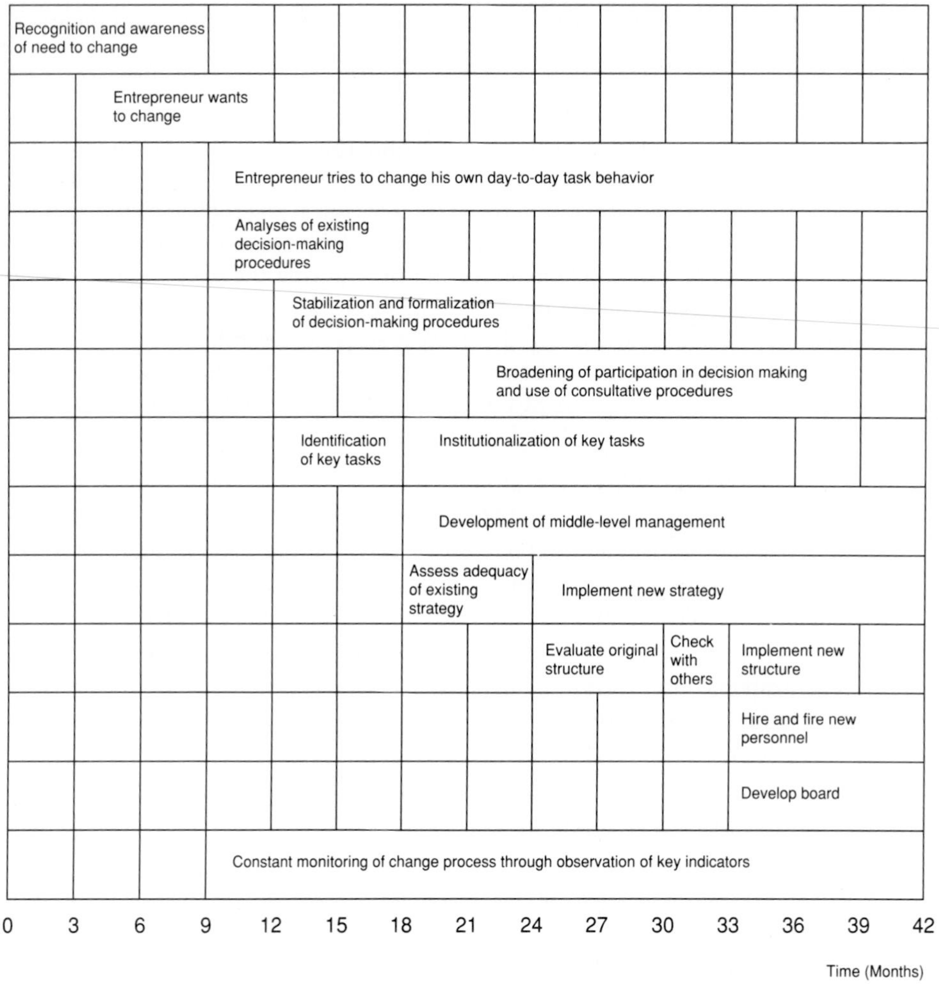

Recognition and awareness of need to change

Entrepreneur wants to change

Entrepreneur tries to change his own day-to-day task behavior

Analyses of existing decision-making procedures

Stabilization and formalization of decision-making procedures

Broadening of participation in decision making and use of consultative procedures

Identification of key tasks | Institutionalization of key tasks

Development of middle-level management

Assess adequacy of existing strategy | Implement new strategy

Evaluate original structure | Check with others | Implement new structure

Hire and fire new personnel

Develop board

Constant monitoring of change process through observation of key indicators

0　3　6　9　12　15　18　21　24　27　30　33　36　39　42

Time (Months)

Source: Charles W. Hofer and Ram Charan, "The Transition to Professional Management: Mission Impossible?" *American Journal of Small Business,* Summer 1984, p. 11. Reprinted with permission.

Figure 13-1

A Schematic Representation of the Transition Process Showing the Relative Time Dimensions Involved in the Change

toward a more managerial style. This critical entrepreneur/manager balance is extremely difficult to achieve. As Stevenson and Gumpert have noted, "Everybody wants to be innovative, flexible, and creative. But for every Apple, Domino's, and Lotus, there are thousands of new restaurants, clothing stores, and consulting firms that presumably have tried to be innovative, to grow, and to show other characteristics that are entrepreneurial in the dynamic sense—but have failed."[9]

The ability to remain entrepreneurial while adopting some of the more administrative traits is vital to the successful growth of a venture. Table 13-2 compares the characteristics and pressures of five major factors: strategic orientation, commitment to seize opportunities, commitment of resources, control of resources, and

---

[9]Howard H. Stevenson and David E. Gumpert, "The Heart of Entrepreneurship," *Harvard Business Review,* March/April 1985, p. 85.

Table 13-2 The Entrepreneurial Culture versus the Administrative Culture

	ENTREPRENEURIAL FOCUS		ADMINISTRATIVE FOCUS	
	Characteristics	Pressures	Characteristics	Pressures
STRATEGIC ORIENTATION	Driven by perception of opportunity	Diminishing opportunities Rapidly changing technology, consumer economics, social values, and political rules	Driven by controlled resources	Social contracts Performance measurement criteria Planning systems and cycles
COMMITMENT TO SEIZE OPPORTUNITIES	Revolutionary, with short duration	Action orientation Narrow decision windows Acceptance of reasonable risks Few decision constituencies	Evolutionary, with long duration	Acknowledgment of multiple constituencies Negotiation about strategic course Risk reduction Coordination with existing resource base
COMMITMENT OF RESOURCES	Many stages, with minimal exposure at each stage	Lack of predictable resource needs Lack of control over the environment Social demands for appropriate use of resources Foreign competition Demands for more efficient use	A single stage, with complete commitment out of decision	Need to reduce risk Incentive compensation Turnover in managers Capital budgeting systems Formal planning systems
CONTROL OF RESOURCES	Episodic use or rent of required resources	Increased resource specialization Long resource life compared with need Risk of obsolescence Risk inherent in the identified opportunity Inflexibility of permanent commitment to resources	Ownership or employment of required resources	Power, status, and financial rewards Coordination of activity Efficiency measures Inertia and cost of change Industry structures
MANAGEMENT STRUCTURE	Flat, with multiple informal networks	Coordination of key noncontrolled resources Challenge to hierarchy Employees' desire for independence	Hierarchy	Need for clearly defined authority and responsibility Organizational culture Reward systems Management theory

management structure. Each of these five areas is critical to the balance needed for entrepreneurial managing. At the two ends of the continuum (entrepreneurial focus versus administrative focus) are specific points of view. Stevenson and Gumpert have characterized these in question format:

The administrative point of view:

☐ What sources do I control?

☐ What structure determines our organization's relationship to its market?

☐ How can I minimize the impact of others on my ability to perform?

☐ What opportunity is appropriate?

The entrepreneur's point of view:

☐ Where is the opportunity?

☐ How do I capitalize on it?

☐ What resources do I need?

☐ How do I gain control over them?

☐ What structure is best?[10]

OUTSIDE MANAGERIAL ASSISTANCE

Since the small business is limited in size and personnel, the use of assistance outside of the small business can be utilized. One study identified the impact of outside assistance on the performance of small firms.[11] Their findings supported the fact that small businesses benefit from outside assistance, especially in administration and operating areas.

Chapter 24 of our text is devoted to the sources of government assistance for small businesses. Small Business Development Centers (SBDSs), Small Business Institutes (SBIs), and Small Business Incubators are all examined as potential sources of assistance especially in managerial areas.

Another suggested source of assistance is a board of advisors. "Quasi-boards" are comprised of volunteers who serve in an advisory capacity to the owner.[12] This group could be made up of professionals, such as accountants, lawyers, or consultants, that the small business owner is familiar with. The board would provide an outside view of the business and make recommendations for the small business owner. The quasi-board avoids some of the legal responsibilities associated with formal boards of directors.[13]

---

[10]Stevenson and Gumpert, p. 86–87.

[11]James J. Chrisman and John Leslie, "Strategic, Administrative, and Operating Problems: The Impact of Outsiders on Small Business Performance," *Entrepreneurship Theory and Practice*, Spring 1989, pp. 37–49.

[12]Harold W. Fox, "Quasi-Boards—Useful Small Business Confidants," *Harvard Business Review*, January/February 1982, pp. 64–72.

[13]Fred A. Tillman, "Commentary on Legal Liability: Organizing the Advisory Council," *Family Business Review*, Fall 1988, pp. 287–88.

INTERNATIONAL EXPANSION: THE GLOBAL OPPORTUNITIES FOR GROWING FIRMS

As a small business grows, one of the best avenues for opportunity is the global marketplace. Doing business internationally has become more favorable for smaller firms. For example, 25% of all exporting businesses in the United States are small businesses. More importantly, a survey of small exporters found that in 41 percent of the cases, international sales growth exceeded domestic sales growth.[14]

The Small Business Administration reported the following exporting facts:

☐ Businesses with fewer than 500 employees account for more than 12 percent of the value of U.S. goods exported directly by manufacturers or through their sales offices.

☐ Of 23,732 companies exporting directly, an impressive 88 percent were small businesses.

☐ An additional 9 percent of the value of U.S. exports were handled indirectly through wholesalers and brokers. By including these indirect exporters, the share of overall small business exports rises to about 21 percent.

☐ Small manufacturers account for about the same share of total U.S. manufacturing output, an indication they may export about as much of their manufactured output as larger businesses.[15]

In order to encourage small businesses to increase their efforts toward international expansion, the federal government has developed programs in the last few years that focus on the emergence of the unified European market. For example, in 1989 the Commerce Department and the European Commission cosponsored the first international show exclusively for small businesses. The "Export 89" show provided small companies with a new opportunity to develop exports and make key business contacts. Likewise, the Small Business Administration sharply increased its staff and budget for exports in 1988. The SBA held a series of export conferences, culminating with a world-trade meeting in Seattle in March of 1990. Small businesses are responding to these efforts. In 1989, 67 percent more companies participated in the Commerce Department's export-related events than in 1987.

Diversification abroad can offer potential for new markets in growing economies and provide an opportunity to capitalize on new trends developing for the domestic markets. In addition, international expansion can help hedge against a recession or changes in domestic demand, extend the life of certain successful products, and, overall, create a more competitive atmosphere within a small firm.[16] (See Small Business Success: Used Parts—International.)

---

[14]Gene R. Barrett, "Where Small and Mid-Sized Companies Can Find Export Help," *Journal of Accounting,* September 1990, pp. 46–50.

[15]Jack G. Kaikati, "Opportunities for Smaller U.S. Industrial Firms in Europe," *Industrial Marketing Management,* Vol. 19, 1990, pp. 339–48.

[16]Nobuaki Namiki, "Export Strategy for Small Business," *Journal of Small Business Management,* April 1988, pp. 32–37.

■ **SMALL BUSINESS SUCCESS** ■

Used Engine Parts—International

 Bill Rucker, 32, has realized the potential for small business export. Rucker is the founder and CEO of Tracom, Inc., a company that sells used truck engine parts. It all started in 1982 when Rucker gave up the ownership of his gas station to form a new business that bought and sold used school bus engines. Somehow a copy of a magazine that featured one of Rucker's ads wound up in Australia. Rucker received a call from the owner of a Ford truck salvage company in Australia who was interested in purchasing steering boxes. Rucker found the steering boxes for $5 each, then he called the client back and asked for $25 a piece. In the end, $10,000 worth of Ford parts were shipped. Rucker's next turning point came in 1986 when an Allisons dealer from California wanted to purchase several of the larger transmissions used in trucks and industrial equipment. Within a week, Rucker had found four of the transmissions, bought them for $6,000, and sold them that same day for $10,000, thus gaining more profit in one day than he did in an average month. Rucker then formally established Tracom, which supplied used truck transmission and engine parts.

Rucker came to realize that, unlike wealthier Americans who usually replace old engines, foreign customers tend to rebuild engines over and over. It was then that he decided to concentrate on the overseas market. By simply using an industry directory, Rucker contacted Detco, one of Australia's largest rebuilders of Detroit Diesel engines, and sold the company $50,000 worth of engines at a markup of 100 percent. In 1986 Rucker took his first trip to Australia where he secured a deal to become Detco's only U.S. supplier of Detroit Diesel engines. One year later, Rucker visited England where he garnered $75,000 worth of orders from one company.

Bill Rucker's ability to identify a lucrative foreign market greatly improved his profitability and sales. The small size of domestic orders were replaced by large single orders from foreign companies. Today, Tracom derives 40 percent of its $3 million total sales from exports and stands as a perfect example of the expanding opportunities for entrepreneurs overseas.

Source: Stephen D. Solomon, "The Accidental Trader," *Inc.*, March 1990, pp. 84–89.

The development of the European Community in 1992 is one of the most important events to occur in the entire international marketplace. As the trade barriers between the European countries are removed, a single continent-scale market of 320 million people is being established that will be observed through the free movement of goods, people, and capital.[17]

---

[17]See Robert M. Bryan, "Europe 1992," *Small Business Reports*, January 1990, pp. 30–38.

Since the European Community currently produces a gross domestic product of $4.7 trillion in goods and services, the expectation of a 4.5 percent increase by the year 2000 certainly provides a special international opportunity for U.S. small businesses.

Another major development is the *privatization* of government-owned businesses in many nations that were once completely socialist. Eastern Europe and the Soviet Union have demonstrated a credible movement towards free enterprise during the 1990s.[18]

Also, many state-owned operations are being sold to private investors, and still others are on the sales block. Here are some examples:

☐ Great Britain sold British Gas for $7.9 billion, British Airways went on the block for $1.4 billion, and the British government intends to sell additional government-owned businesses with a total value of several billion dollars.

☐ Spain sold its automaker SEAT to Volkswagen for $600 million.

☐ Sweden sold 30 percent of SSAB, the nationalized steel company, to private Swedish insurance companies.

☐ Italy's state holding company, IRI, sold more than 20 companies, including Alfa Romeo, and raised $3.6 billion by selling minority stakes in subsidiaries, including Alitalia, the state airline.

☐ France sold $1.9 billion of shares in glass manufacturer Saint-Gobain and plans to sell as many as 65 more companies for $45 billion within the next couple of years.

These privatization developments point to the increase in competitiveness that is occurring in Europe as more and more countries abandon their drift toward socialism and start turning toward free enterprise to solve their economic woes. They also indicate that competitiveness within the EC will increase during the years ahead, and those U.S. firms that hope to compete successfully will have to have a fundamental understanding of international management.[19]

INTERNATIONAL BUSINESS CONSIDERATIONS

A small business owner must consider several important questions when deciding whether or not to expand into international markets. First, is the company's product or service unique? There should be a special niche which can be filled by the firm's product or service. Uniqueness coupled with high quality will establish a clear demand for the small business. Second, is the company flexible? A small firm needs to adapt to the differences in language, culture, and methods of doing business if it hopes to be successful in global markets. Third, is the small business owner committed to international expansion? Preparations for overseas expansion could take six to eight months so it is imperative that the owner of a small firm be willing to devote

---

[18]Christopher Farrell and Gail Shares, "Blueprints for a Free Market in Eastern Europe," *Business Week*, February 5, 1990, pp. 88–89; and Mark Stevens, "Big Russian Market for Small U.S. Business," *Small Business Reports*, September 1990, pp. 24–27.

[19]Richard M. Hodgetts and Fred Luthans, *International Management* (New York: McGraw-Hill, Inc., 1991), p. 10.

■ **SMALL BUSINESS OWNER'S NOTEBOOK** ■

Sources of International Assistance

 Intermediaries are available to service small and midsized companies that are new to exporting. Several types of export service companies offer assistance in the United States. Brokers and agents set up specific deals with international buyers using small staffs and industry contacts in one or two countries. Export management companies (EMCs) have larger staffs to handle the financing and shipping details as well as to arrange export deals. Export trading companies, which are large companies that work with a variety of products, actually take title to the goods, unlike brokers and EMCs.

Two types of overseas marketing representatives can assist the exporter. Agents are similar to manufacturers' representatives in this country in that they work on commission. Distributors may buy the goods outright from the exporter or place them in inventory to sell on commission. Either way, the distributor extends credit and handles customer service.

Export financing help is available from several sources. The Export-Import Bank (Eximbank) offers a working capital guarantee program that guarantees loans made to support pre-export expenses. It also offers direct loans and loan guarantees to finance U.S. export sales and extends loans to foreign buyers of U.S. exports. The SBA has an export revolving line of credit program that guarantees credit lines of up to $750,000 for export-related activities. The Overseas Private Investment Company (OPIC) finances private investment for projects in developing nations through loan guarantees and direct loans to small and midsized companies.

Export credit insurance is available through the Foreign Credit Insurance Association, an association of U.S. insurance companies acting as an agent of Eximbank. Policies are available for companies new to exporting and for those with limited export experience.

Export counseling is available from many sources, including the Commerce Department, the SBA, state programs, and several private agencies.

Source: Gene R. Barrett, "Where Small and Midsized Companies Can Find Export Help," *Journal of Accountancy*, September 1990, p. 48.

the time and energy needed to establish international opportunities. (See Small Business Owner's Notebook: Sources of International Assistance.) Fourth, is the small business willing to commit the money and resources? Modifications in production, translation services, overseas telephone bills, visits to foreign countries, transportation expenses, and so on, are all examples of possible costs in terms of money and resources that a small business owner should be aware of. Fifth, can the small business compete with foreign and domestic firms? It takes time to establish the foreign markets and a small business must be prepared to handle competitive challenges in price and costs in order to survive the start-up period for international operations.[20]

These questions illustrate the type of preparations that are needed for international expansion. Figure 13-2 provides a complete listing of the trade development services available in each state. This assistance may be essential for a small business owner considering international expansion. Whether the entrepreneur wants to attend a conference, find a local expert service, or research financing alternatives, each state has developed a wealth of resources that can assist the small business owner with international expansion.

Table 13-3 defines some key international terms that may be useful for a small business owner attempting to learn international business. While the list is not complete, it does provide a good foundation toward understanding some of the new terms and phrases associated with doing business internationally. A small business owner needs to become familiar with the "language" of the international marketplace in order to better understand its environment.

This discussion of international business is intended to assist small business owners as they begin their expansion into the global marketplace. However, there is a great deal more to be learned about international business, depending upon the type of product or service and the depth of international involvement. Further research in the specific area of international interest is always recommended for any small business owner seeking international expansion.

FORMS OF INTERNATIONAL INVOLVEMENT[21]

When entering a foreign market, a small business must decide on the amount of involvement it wishes to make. Figure 13-3 depicts the five most common forms of international involvement.

The simplest form of international involvement is **exporting or importing.** In the case of exporting, for example, a company will find someone in a foreign country to either purchase its goods directly or act as a selling agent. In the first case, the company has very little responsibility—it merely produces the goods and ships them to the foreign customer. In the second case, the company typically is responsible for the costs of warehousing the goods until they are sold and paying all the costs associated with insuring the goods, shipping them to the customer, and so on. While this arrangement is more costly than merely selling directly to a foreign customer, it can be more profitable if the market for the product is good. This is because the company will pay the agent only a salary (and perhaps commission) and can keep the rest of the sales revenue.

A **licensing arrangement** is an agreement in which one firm (the licensor) agrees to allow another firm (the licensee) to use its patents, production processes, trademarks, or company name in return for the payment of an agreed-upon fee. The licensor typically controls the agreement very closely. For example, in the case of an

---

[20]See Ronaleen A. Roha, "Taking Your Small Business Global," *Changing Times,* December 1989, pp. 103–109.

[21]Adapted from Richard M. Hodgetts and Donald F. Kuratko, *Management,* 3rd ed. (San Diego: Harcourt Brace Jovanovich, 1991), pp. 97–99.

Figure 13-2
State Trade
Development
Services. Sources of
assistance by state

	Alabama	Alaska	Arizona	Arkansas	California	Colorado	Connecticut	Delaware	Florida	Georgia	Hawaii	Idaho	Illinois	Indiana	Iowa	Kansas	Kentucky
Seminars-conferences																	
One-on-one counseling																	
Market studies prepared																	
Language bank																	
Referrals to local export services																	
Newsletter					(a)												
How-to handbook					(b)												
Sales leads disseminated																	
Trade shows																	
Trade missions																	
Foreign offices-representatives											(c)						
Operational finance program																	

Explanations

Seminars-conferences – State sponsors seminars for exporters, either basic, specific function or specific market.

One-on-one counseling – State staff provides actual export counseling to individual businesses in addition to making appropriate referrals.

Market studies prepared – State staff prepares specific market studies for individual companies.

Language bank – State program matches foreign-speaking visitors with bilingual local residents who provide volunteer translation services.

Referrals to local export services – State matches exporters with exporter services, for example, matchmaker fair, export service directory, individual referrals, etc.

Newsletter– State publishes an international trade newsletter.

How-to handbook – State publishes a basic how-to-export handbook.

Sales leads disseminated – State collects and distributes sales leads to in-state businesses.

Trade shows – State assists with and accompanies or represents businesses at trade shows.

American licensor that allows an overseas firm to produce and market its products in Europe, the licensee will be required to manufacture the product to precise specifications. The licensee cannot make changes in the production process or modify the product without specific approval. The licensor receives either a fixed fee or a percentage of the gross revenues from the sale of the product. In most cases, the latter arrangement is used. If the agreement gives the licensee the exclusive right to produce and sell the product in a geographic area, such as Europe, the percentage of gross revenues is usually larger (often 10 percent) than in the case where there are three to four licensees and they are restricted in terms of geographic area. For example, one company may have the exclusive rights to Great Britain only, while another

The table shows states (columns) with shaded cells indicating program participation. Columns left to right: Louisiana (d), Maine, Maryland, Massachusetts, Michigan, Minnesota, Mississippi, Missouri, Montana, Nebraska, Nevada, New Hampshire, New Jersey, New Mexico, New York, North Carolina, North Dakota, Ohio, Oklahoma, Oregon, Pennsylvania, Rhode Island, South Carolina, South Dakota, Tennessee, Texas, Utah, Vermont, Virginia, Washington, West Virginia, Wisconsin, Wyoming.

	Louisiana (d)	Maine	Maryland	Massachusetts	Michigan	Minnesota	Mississippi	Missouri	Montana	Nebraska	Nevada	New Hampshire	New Jersey	New Mexico	New York	North Carolina	North Dakota	Ohio	Oklahoma	Oregon	Pennsylvania	Rhode Island	South Carolina	South Dakota	Tennessee	Texas	Utah	Vermont	Virginia	Washington	West Virginia	Wisconsin	Wyoming
1		■	■	■	■	■	■	■	■	■	■	■	■	■	■	■	■	■	■	■	■	■	■		■	■	■	■	■	■	■	■	■
2			■	■	■	■	■	■	■	■		■	■	■	■	■	■	■	■	■	■	■	■	■	■	■	■	■	■	■	■	■	■
3			■	■	■	■		■	■	■		■	■	■	■		■	■	■		■	■	■		■	■	■	■	■	■	■	■	
4			■	■		■		■	■	■	■	■	■	■	■		■		■	■	■		■	■		■	■	■	■	■		■	
5			■	■		■	■	■		■		■		■		■	■		■	■	■	■	■		■	■	■	■	■		■		
6			■	■	■		■		■		■		■	■	■	■		■	■		■		■	■		■		■	■	■		■	
7			■	■		■		■	■		■		■		■	■		■		■	■		■		■	■		■		■	■		
8			■	■		■		■		■		■			■	■		■		■		■	■		■	■		■		■		■	
9			■	■		■		■		■		■		■		■		■		■	■		■		■	■		■		■	■		
10			■	■		■		■		■				■		■		■			■		■		■	■		■		■			

Notes

Trade missions – State assists with and accompanies business on trade missions.

Foreign offices-representatives – State office or contractual representative located abroad.

Operational financing program – State has an export financing assistance program that is currently operational.

(a) California issues a bimonthly column to local chambers and trade groups for publication in their newsletters.

(b) California produces a "road map" to low-cost and free trade services.

(c) Georgia's foreign offices are only active in attracting reverse investment.

(d) Louisiana has recently established a new Office of International Trade, Finance and Development within the Department of Commerce and Industry. The office is expected to offer a full range of trade promotion services.

Source: Gary L. Keefe, "Helping Clients Prepare for Global Markets," *Journal of Accountancy*, July 1989, pp. 58–59.

may have France, and so on. Most licensing agreements are for the production of manufactured goods such as industrial motors or equipment.

A **joint venture** is a partnership agreement in which two or more firms or investors undertake a project for a specific length of time. Many joint ventures are a matter of necessity. Quite often, neither firm has enough capital, or is willing to risk this total amount, to undertake the project alone. In some cases, a joint venture is used because the overseas partner wants to get a foothold in a foreign market and realizes that by teaming up with a company in that geographic locale, a great deal of time and effort can be saved. For example, when doing business in Japan, many firms have found it profitable to get a Japanese partner who knows the customs and culture of the country and is aware of how business should be transacted.

Table 13-3 Key International Trade Terms

acceptance: This term has several related meanings: (1) A time draft (or bill of exchange) the drawee (the payer) has accepted and is unconditionally obligated to pay at maturity. The draft must be presented first for acceptance—the drawee becomes the "acceptor"—then for payment. The word "accepted" and the date and place of payment must be written on the face of the draft. (2) The drawee's act of receiving a draft and thus entering into the obligation to pay its value at maturity. (3) Broadly speaking, any agreement to purchase goods under specified terms.

ad valorem rate: A tariff calculated as a percentage of the value of goods clearing customs (for example, 15 percent ad valorem means 15 percent of the value). See also **tariff.**

bill of lading: A document that establishes the terms of a contract between a shipper and a transportation company under which freight is to be moved between specified points for a specified charge. Usually prepared by the shipper on forms issued by the carrier, it serves as a document of title, a contract of carriage, and a receipt for goods.

carnet: A customs document permitting the holder to carry or send merchandise temporarily into certain foreign countries (for display demonstration of similar purposes) without paying duties or posting bonds.

CIF (Cost-Insurance-Freight): A system of valuing imports that includes all costs, insurance, and freight involved in shipping the goods from their port of embarkation to their destination. In contrast, a system of FOB (free on board) valuation includes inland transportation costs involved in delivery of goods to a port in the exporting country and the cost of loading the merchandise on the vessel but excludes the cost of ocean shipping and insurance. Another system of valuation, FAS (free along side), differs from FOB only in that cost of loading the merchandise on the vessel is not included.

consignment: Delivery of merchandise from an exporter (the consignor) to an agent (the consignee) under an agreement that the agent sell the merchandise for the exporter's account. The consignor retains the title to the goods until the consignee has sold them. The consignee sells the goods for commission and remits the net proceeds to the consignor.

customhouse broker: A person or company licensed by the Treasury Department and engaged in entering and clearing goods through customs. A broker's duties include preparing the entry blank and filing it, advising the importer on duties to be paid, advancing duties and other costs, and arranging for delivery to clients, their trucking company, or other carrier.

customs: The authorities designated to collect duties levied by a country on imports and exports. The term also applies to the procedures involved in such collection.

Table 13-3 *(continued)*

duty: A tax imposed on imports by a country's customs authority. Duties are generally based on the value of the goods (ad valorem duties), some other factor, such as weight or quantity (specific duties), or a combination of value and other factors (compounded duties). See also **tariff.**

Eximbank: The Export-Import Bank of the United States that facilitates and aids in financing exports of U.S. goods and services. Eximbank has implemented a variety of programs to meet the needs of the U.S. exporting community according to the size of the transaction. These programs can involve direct lending or the issuance of guarantees and insurance so that exporters and private banks can extend appropriate financing without taking undue risks. Eximbank's direct lending program is limited to larger sales of U.S. products and services around the world. The guarantees, insurance and discount programs, have been designed to assist exporters in smaller sales of products and services.

FOB (free on board): A pricing term indicating the quoted price includes the cost of loading the goods into transport vessels at the specified place. The price quoted applies only at inland shipping points, and the seller arranges for loading of the goods on or in railway cars, trucks, lighters, barges, aircraft, or other conveyances furnished for transportation.

General Agreement on Tariffs and Trade (GATT): A multilateral treaty subscribed to by 85 governments that together account for more than four-fifths of world trade. Its primary objective is to liberalize world trade and place it on a secure basis, thereby contributing to global economic growth and development. The GATT is the only principal multilateral agreement that delineates rules for international trade.

L/C or LOC (letter of credit): A document issued by a bank per instructions from a buyer of goods authorizing the seller to draw a specified sum of money under specified terms, usually the receipt by the bank of certain documents within a given time.

open account: A trade arrangement under which goods are shipped to a foreign buyer without guarantee of payment. The obvious risk this method poses to the supplier makes it essential that the buyer's integrity be unquestionable.

sight draft: A draft payable on presentation to the drawee. A sight draft is used when the seller wishes to retain control of the shipment, either for credit reasons or for title retention. Money is payable "at sight" or upon presentation of the completed documents.

tariff: A tax on imports; the rate at which imported goods are taxed. The term "tariff" usually refers to a list or schedule of articles of merchandise with the rate of duty to be paid to the government for their importation.

Source: Gary L. Keefe, "Helping Clients Prepare for Global Markets," *Journal of Accountancy,* July 1989, pp. 64–65.

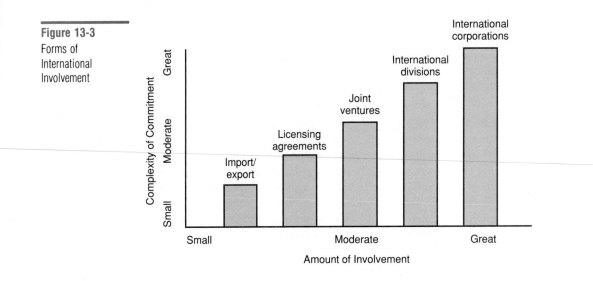

Figure 13-3
Forms of
International
Involvement

When a company decides to set up an **international division,** it accepts a large amount of involvement in the overseas market. This typically involves the establishment of manufacturing plants in one or more countries. These plants may range from assembly plants to full-scale operations. When this happens, the company's domestic operations are often separated from the overseas operations and an international division is established.

The last step in international involvement is the emergence of an **international corporation.** Under this form of involvement, the overseas operation is viewed as a full-fledged part of the business rather than just an overseas branch or foreign sales arm. The company's strategic plan reflects this change in thinking by viewing the firm's markets as worldwide. It is also common to find international corporations with boards of directors whose members come from many different nations. This helps the company develop and maintain an international focus.

As can be seen from these descriptions, small businesses have a number of options to choose from in the international arena. Careful preparation by the small business owner is a key factor in launching a successful international expansion.

■ SUMMARY

Managing a growing small business presents unique managerial challenges for owners to consider. Understanding the disadvantages as well as the advantages of their small size helps small business managers gain a better focus on their strategies for success. The one-man-band syndrome occurs when a small business begins to grow and the entrepreneur is accustomed to doing everything alone. Learning to delegate and share responsibilities are keys to assisting small business expansion. Effective time management through assessment, prioritization, and delegation will help the small business owner avoid wasting valuable time on needless activities and concentrate more on critical areas. Community involvement by small business owners is a distinctive advantage in one sense, but it must be handled carefully. Participation, leadership, and financial donations are all types of expectations the community may have for small business owners. Time as well as money are valuable resources that must be meaningfully budgeted. Finally, continuing management education is essential if the owner wants to remain current in both knowledge and abilities.

The key elements of the growth stage are control, responsibility, tolerance of failure, change, and flexibility. These elements need to be considered as small firms begin to expand. The evolution during this stage also requires a transition in the owner's style from that of an entrepreneur to that of a manager. The differences can be understood by reviewing the five major factors in Table 13-2.

Outside assistance is recommended for growing firms. "Quasi-boards" can be developed, in which professionals volunteer to assist in an advisory capacity.

The final section of Chapter 13 is devoted to the international opportunities for small growing firms. The development of the European Community in 1992 and the increased development of capitalism throughout Eastern Europe and the Soviet Union offer support for a new global marketplace. Preparations must be made by small business owners if they wish to expand their business internationally. Figure 13-2 and Table 13-3 present valuable assistance for international preparation. There are five major forms of international involvement for small business owners to consider: export/import, licensing, joint venture, international division, and international corporation. It is only through careful preparation that small firms can determine their involvement.

■ REVIEW AND DISCUSSION QUESTIONS

1. Identify five unique managerial concerns of small businesses.

2. What are some of the advantages and disadvantages associated with the distinction of small size?

3. Define the one-man-band syndrome.

4. How can a small business owner improve his or her time management?

5. Explain three forms of community obligations that small business owners encounter.

6. Describe the five key elements involved in the growth stage of a business.

7. Explain the transition that a small business owner must make from entrepreneur to manager.

8. How can a "quasi-board" help a small business?

9. Why have the international opportunities increased for growing small businesses?

10. Identify five major questions that a small business owner should consider when deciding to expand into international markets.

11. List four types of international trade assistance that can be found in many states.

12. Define the following key international business terms: CIF; FOB; GATT; LOC.

13. Identify the five major forms of international involvement.

■
Case Studies

Making the Transition

■ Bill Maher is the founder and owner of American Clean Services, an industrial cleaning company. Bill started the business five years ago by himself. At that time, he hired part-time workers as he needed them based on the job that was contracted. However, the business has grown steadily as larger contracts have been established with major factories and warehouses. This growth has forced Bill to expand his work force to 25 full-time employees and, at times, an additional 20 part-time helpers.

Many of the full-time employees are unhappy with the way Bill is handling operations. He makes *all* of the decisions on every project and refuses to assign authority to anyone else. This causes numerous delays since Bill must visit all of the job sites each day. One employee claimed Bill spent more time in his truck than he did on any project, so how could he understand the problems on every job site? Bill simply believes that he must run the business as he always has, that is, by keeping complete control of his projects. Says Bill, "If it's been good enough to get my company this far, why shouldn't I continue the same way?"

1. What should Bill understand about entrepreneurs and small business growth?

2. How would you approach Bill concerning his style of operating the business?

3. Identify the key elements of growth that directly affect Bill's business.

Expanding Globally

■ Mary Higgins and Brenda Jacobs are partners in a small electronics firm, Electronic Specialties (Es, Inc.), that has developed and patented some state-of-the-art computer components. Es, Inc. has had moderate success selling these components to large U.S.-based computer manufacturers. The biggest problem is that in recent months the computer market has begun to turn soft, and many of the manufacturers are offering substantial discounts in order to generate sales. So although Es, Inc. has found an increasing demand for its product, it is now grossing less money than it did a year ago.

In an effort to increase both sales and profit, the partners have decided to expand into Europe. The partners believe that Europe will soon have more lucrative markets because the European Community will encourage these countries to open their doors for imported goods. If trade barriers are removed, the partners are convinced that they can export the goods at very competitive prices. In addition, the partners intend to find a partner in the European Community so that they have someone to help with the marketing and financing of the product. Of course, if the components can be produced more cheaply with local labor, the partnership is willing to forgo exporting and have everything produced locally.

At the present time, the partners are trying to answer three questions: First, what is the best entry strategy to use in reaching the European market? Second, what type of marketing strategy will be most effective? Third, if production has to be coordinated between the United States and an overseas country, what is the best way to handle this? The partners believe that over the next six months they will have a very good idea of what is going to happen regarding the opening up of foreign markets. In the interim, they intend to work up a preliminary strategic plan to use as a guide.

1. What recommendations would you suggest regarding expansion into Europe?
2. What five major questions should they consider before expanding internationally?
3. What specific trade services offered by most states should the partners seek out?

You Be the Consultant

IT USED TO BE FUN

When he first opened his own business, Dick Anzar loved it. He went to work early in the morning and did not leave until after 9:00 PM. In order to spend time with his family, he would take off a few hours in the afternoon and then return to the store after supper and stay until closing time. While he was gone from the store in the late afternoon, part-time personnel handled the operation.

That was five years ago. Since then, Dick's business has grown tremendously. Now he employs eight full-time people and sells seven times as much as he did originally. With this increase in business, however, have come a lot of headaches. In particular, Dick has to make many more decisions than he did before. Additionally, while he wants to get his people involved in the decision-making process and not do all the work himself, he feels that there are many things he must do on his own. He does not believe he can delegate much authority. For example, Dick still makes all decisions regarding purchasing, pricing, advertising, hiring, firing, and merchandise display, and he still sells goods in the store.

Recently, Dick went to the doctor for his annual physical. The doctor told Dick he was working too hard and had to start slowing down. "You've been running that store single-handed for as long as I can remember," he told Dick. "You've got lots of help in the store. Start relying on them to help you out."

Dick does not disagree. The doctor is offering good advice, and Dick knows that he is going to have to start delegating more authority and getting out of the actual hustle-bustle of daily activity. However, this worries him. A few months ago, he tried turning over more work to his employees and staying in the background. During that time he concerned himself with the overall operation of the store and left the minor, day-to-day business to the staff. But Dick was bored with this side of the operation. He wants to be actively involved for two reasons. First, he believes the owner-manager's job is to play an active role in the business, not just sit on the sidelines. Second, he wants to be in the forefront of the action, like he always has been.

Dick does not know how to resolve this dilemma. He would like to maintain his level of involvement at the shop but realizes that, for health reasons, this is inadvisable. On the other hand, to be a manager, in the true sense of the word, seems boring to him.

■ **YOUR CONSULTATION** Help Dick out. First, explain the exciting aspects of planning and organizing and how important delegation is for growth. Second, explain the key elements in the growth stage that Dick should understand. Finally, recommend a way that Dick can avoid the one-man-band syndrome.

Part Four Case Study

INNER-CITY PAINT CORPORATION

HISTORY

Stanley Walsh began Inner-City Paint Corporation in a run-down warehouse, which he rented, on the fringe of Chicago's "downtown" business area. The company is still located at the original 1976 site.

Inner-City is a small company that manufactures wall paint. It does not compete with giants such as Glidden and DuPont. There are small paint manufacturers in Chicago that supply the immediate area. The proliferation of paint manufacturers is due to the fact that the weight of the product (fifty-two and one-half pounds per five-gallon container) makes the cost of shipping great distances prohibitive. Inner-City's chief product is flat white wall paint sold in five-gallon plastic cans. It also produces colors on request in fifty-five-gallon containers.

The primary market of Inner-City is the small to medium-sized decorating company. Pricing must be competitive; and until recently, Inner-City had shown steady growth in this market. The slowdown in the housing market combined with a slowdown in the overall economy caused financial difficulty for Inner-City Plant Corporation. Inner-City's reputation had been built on fast service: it frequently supplied paint to contractors within twenty-four hours. Speedy delivery to customers became difficult when Inner-City was required to pay cash on delivery (C.O.D.) for its raw materials.

Inner-City had been operating without management controls or financial controls. It had grown from a very small two-person company with sales of $60,000 annually in 1976, to sales of $1,800,000 and thirty-eight employees in 1981. Stanley Walsh realized that tighter controls within his organization would be necessary if the company was to survive.

EQUIPMENT

Five mixers are used in the manufacturing process. Three large mixers can produce a maximum of 400 gallons, per batch, per mixer. The two smaller mixers can produce a maximum of 100 gallons, per batch, per mixer.

Two lift trucks are used for moving raw materials. The materials are packed in 100-pound bags. The lift trucks also move finished goods, which are stacked on pallets.

A small testing lab ensures the quality of materials received and the consistent quality of their finished product. The equipment in the lab is sufficient to handle the current volume of product manufactured.

Source: This case was prepared by Dr. Donald F. Kuratko from the College of Business, Ball State University, and Dr. Norman J. Gierlasinski from the School of Business, Central Washington University. It was presented at the 1984 Workshop of the Midwest Society for Case Research. It also appears in *Annual Advances in Business Cases, 1984*, pp. 243–251, edited by Charles Douds. Reprinted by permission.

Transportation equipment consists of two 24-foot delivery trucks and two vans. This small fleet is more than sufficient because many customers pick up their orders to save delivery costs.

FACILITIES

Inner-City performs all operations from one building consisting of 16,400 square feet. The majority of the space is devoted to manufacturing and storage; only 850 square feet is assigned as office space. The building is forty-five years old and in disrepair. It is being leased in three-year increments. The current monthly rent on this lease is $2,700. The rent is low in consideration of the poor condition of the building and its undesirable location in a run-down neighborhood (south side of Chicago). These conditions are suitable to Inner-City because of the dusty, dirty nature of the manufacturing process and the small contribution of the rent to overhead costs.

PRODUCT

Flat white paint is made with pigment (titanium dioxide and silicates), vehicle (resin), and water. The water makes up 72% of the contents of the product. To produce a color, the necessary pigment is added to the flat white paint. The pigment used to produce the color has been previously tested in the lab to ensure consistent quality of texture. Essentially, the process is the mixing of powders with water, then tapping off the result into five- or fifty-five-gallon containers. Color overruns are tapped off into two-gallon containers.

Inventory records are not kept. The warehouse manager keeps a mental count of what is in stock. He documents (on a lined yellow pad) what has been shipped for the day and to whom. That list is given to the billing clerk at the end of each day.

The cost of the materials to produce flat white paint is $2.40 per gallon. The cost for colors is approximately 40%-50% higher. Five-gallon covered plastic pails cost Inner-City $1.72 each. Fifty-five-gallon drums (with lids) are $8.35 each.

Selling price varies with the quantity purchased. To the average customer, flat white sells at $27.45 for five gallons and $182.75 for 55 gallons. Colors vary in selling price, because of the variety in pigment cost and quantity ordered. Customers purchase on credit and usually pay their invoices in 30 to 60 days. Inner-City telephones the customer after 60 days of nonpayment and inquires when payment will be made.

MANAGEMENT

The president and majority stockholder is Stanley Walsh. He began his career as a house painter and advanced to become a painter for a large decorating company. Mr. Walsh painted mostly walls in large commercial buildings and hospitals. Eventually, he came to believe that he could produce a paint that was less expensive and of higher quality than what was being used. A keen desire to open his own business resulted in the creation of Inner-City Paint Corporation.

Mr. Walsh manages the corporation today in much the same way that he did when the business began. He personally must open *all* the mail, approve *all* payments, and inspect *all* customer billings before they are mailed. He has been unable to detach himself from any detail of the operation and cannot properly delegate authority. As the company has grown, the time element alone has aggravated the situation. Frequently, these tasks are performed days after transactions occur and mail is received.

The office is managed by Mrs. Walsh (Mr. Walsh's mother). Two part-time clerks assist her, and all records are processed manually.

The plant is managed by a man in his twenties, whom Mr. Walsh hired from one of his customers. Mr. Walsh became acquainted with him when the man picked up paint from Inner-City for his previous employer. Prior to the eight months he has been employed by Mr. Walsh as plant manager, his only other experience has been that of painter.

EMPLOYEES

Thirty-five employees (twenty workers are part-time) work in various phases of the manufacturing process. The employees are nonunion, and most are unskilled laborers. They take turns making paint and driving the delivery trucks.

Stanley Walsh does all of the sales and public relations work. He spends approximately one half of every day making sales calls and answering complaints about defective paint. He is the only salesman. Other salesmen had been employed in the past, but Mr. Walsh felt that they "could not be trusted."

CUSTOMER PERCEPTION

Customers view Inner-City as a company that provides fast service and negotiates on price and payment out of desperation. Mr. Walsh is seen as a disorganized man who may not be able to keep Inner-City afloat much longer. Paint contractors are reluctant to give Inner-City large orders out of fear that the paint may not be ready on a continuous, reliable basis. Larger orders usually go to larger companies that have demonstrated their reliability and solvency.

Rumors abound that Inner-City is in difficult financial straits, that it is unable to pay suppliers, and that it owes a considerable sum for payment on back taxes. All of the above contribute to the customers' serious lack of confidence in the corporation.

FINANCIAL STRUCTURE

Tables IV-1 and IV-2 are the most current financial statements of Inner-City Paint Corporation. They have been prepared by the company's accounting service. No audit has been performed, because Mr. Walsh did not want to incur the expense it would have required.

FUTURE

Stanley Walsh wishes to improve the financial situation and reputation of Inner-City Paint Corporation. He is considering the purchase of a computer to organize the business and reduce needless paperwork. He has read about consultants who are able to quickly spot problems in businesses, but he will not spend more than $300 on such a consultant.

The solution that Mr. Walsh favors most is one that requires him to borrow money from the bank, which he will then use to pay his current bills. He feels that as soon as business conditions improve, he will be able to pay back the loans. He believes that the problems Inner-City is experiencing are due to the overall poor economy and are only temporary.

Table IV-1 Balance Sheet for the Year Ended June 30

CURRENT ASSETS		
Cash	$ 1,535	
Accounts receivable (net of allowance for bad debts of $63,400)	242,320	
Inventory	18,660	
Total current assets		$262,515
Machinery and transportation equipment	47,550	
Less: accumulated depreciation	15,500	
Net fixed assets		32,050
Total assets		$294,565
CURRENT LIABILITIES		
Accounts payable	$217,820	
Salaries payable	22,480	
Notes payable	6,220	
Taxes payable	38,510	
Total current liabilities		$285,030
Long-term notes payable		15,000
OWNERS' EQUITY		
Common stock, no par, 1,824 shares outstanding		12,400
Deficit		(17,865)
Total liabilities & owners' equity		$294,565

Table IV-2 Income Statement for the Year Ended June 30

Sales		$1,784,080
Cost of goods sold		1,428,730
Gross margin		$ 355,350
Selling expenses	$ 72,460	
Administrative expenses	67,280	
President's salary	132,000	
Office manager's salary	66,000	
Total expenses		337,740
Net income		$ 17,610

DISCUSSION QUESTIONS

1. What is the role of strategic management in Inner-City Paint? What impact, if any, is this having on the present company's performance?

2. What are the strengths of Inner-City Paint?

3. What are the weaknesses of Inner-City Paint?

4. What are the strategic factors facing Inner-City Paint?

5. How should Mr. Walsh deal with the negative rumors about his company?

6. What type of documentation should Mr. Walsh prepare before asking the bank for a loan? ■

Part Four Entrepreneurial Simulation Program

EVALUATING CRITICAL SUCCESS FACTORS

Each month you obtain feedback as to how you did the prior month. This feedback comes in the form of such variables as sales by type and size of shoe, missed sales, a listing of your expenses, and a synopsis of your assets as you enter the next month. You also have marketing research data available to you and can purchase as much data as you wish each month. All in all, you have access to a wide variety of facts. The question is, which elements of this data do you pay attention to and use when you make each set of monthly decisions?

Critical success factors are defined as those elements of data that are given special attention because of their significance in the decision-making process. They can be either positive or negative, and their essential character is their proven ability to provide a special awareness, or an early warning, of any potential unpleasant surprise or missed opportunity.

Critical success factors are the first items of data that a store owner looks for at the end of each monthly cycle. If satisfactory, these factors suggest a successful month of operation. If unsatisfactory, they signal the need for a change in strategy. Because these critical success factors are strongly correlated with success in the mind of the owner, they usually provide the first indication that there are problems that need to be addressed.

Critical success factors can only be related to controllable variables. It would be totally useless, as well as frustrating, to depend on feedback from variables that are out of the scope of the store owner's control. These variables may act independently, or in concert with other variables, to provide the first line of feedback on the success of the store.

The establishment of critical success factors depends on two things: the objective accuracy of the data elements and the subjective feeling of the store owner that the particular elements of data are important. Two store owners, provided with the same data, may select two completely different sets of critical success factors with which to measure their store's success. The subjective difference depends on each owner's management style and his or her past experience in using the selected data elements for feedback regarding the store's operation.

Critical success factors should bring significant threats and business opportunities into clearer focus. They provide a formal review of the prior month's operation so that it can be compared to the specific goals and objectives of the store. They can also be used to evaluate tactics designed to improve the competitive position of the store.

The business plan you developed earlier is incomplete without a formal process by which to evaluate the plan against the monthly operation of the store. The use of critical success factors allows the business plan to become a viable work plan for the store owner. It also provides a vehicle by which to communicate the success of the operation to other interested parties, such as investors or bankers.

Critical-success-factor methodology is business driven. Its use helps store owners determine which data factors should receive their primary attention each month. It also indicates those elements of data that would be the best candidates for use in more detailed reports or for doing further analysis. Finally, it eliminates the time spent going through less valuable data by focusing on those of primary importance to the operation of the store and the performance of the competition.

Store owners who are strong risk takers, or who like to be more heuristic in making their monthly decisions, may fear that the use of critical success factors will restrict their decision-making style. However, the use of critical success factors provides the store owner with an internally consistent way of evaluating the ongoing success of the store. Such information may prove invaluable when approaching another party for additional funds to help in hard times or to expand the operation of the store.

DISCUSSION QUESTIONS

1. Identify three to five critical success factors for your store. Describe why each element of data is important to your operation.

2. Using the critical success factors identified in question one above, formally describe how you would process the data to obtain the desired information about your store and the other stores in the simulated community. Develop a scenario using the data and describe what actions you would take if you were to see such data at the end of a month.

3. Compare your set of critical success factors with the set identified by other store owners in the simulation. What can you say regarding why each person selected that particular set of critical success factors to evaluate the success of their store? How does this correlate with the risk style of the individual store owners?

4. Assume that you were operating a real shoe store. What other critical success factors could you identify and use to evaluate the operation of your store each month? Why would these be important to you?

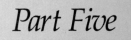

Part Five

Marketing Goods
and Services

■ *The success of every small business depends on its ability to sell its goods and/or services. The objective of Part Five is to study the ways in which the marketing function is carried out.*

Chapter 14 provides comprehensive understandings about the concepts of market and market niche. We then focus attention on marketing research: what it is, how it is carried out, and the value it has for the small business.

Chapter 15 is concerned with pricing, advertising, and selling. We begin with a review of pricing considerations and present a strategy of pricing for profit. We then direct attention toward the way in which small businesses actually set prices. The next part of the chapter examines the role of advertising in small business marketing. You will learn how small firms build appeal for their goods and services. Many small businesses depend on the selling capabilities of their people. In this chapter we also examine the subject of selling. We focus on setting the stage for selling, sales training, sales psychology, and the selling process.

Chapter 16, the last chapter in Part Five, deals with customer credit. Many people today do not pay cash; they purchase only on credit. Thus, the small business owner-manager needs to be familiar with the kinds of credit that are commonly available and how to use credit in fashioning a marketing strategy. We also discuss regulations related to consumer credit and the ways small businesses themselves use credit.

When you have finished studying the material in Part Five, you will have a solid understanding of the marketing function and the role it plays in small business. You will also know how small businesses go about pricing, advertising, selling, and granting credit to customers.

Understanding the Market

Objectives

One of the most important things the owner-manager needs to understand about the marketing of goods and services is the market itself. This knowledge is fundamental to pricing, advertising, selling, and the granting of credit—topics that are studied later in Part Five.

The first objective of Chapter 14 is to examine what a market is and how customers in particular markets behave. We will focus attention on relevant price range and competition. The second objective is to study how market niche analysis is carried out. The third objective is to examine marketing research. You will learn how it is conducted and how the research data is used. When you have finished studying the material in Chapter 14, you will be able to:

1. Explain the terms market *and* market niche.

2. Describe the relevant price range and discuss its importance in market analysis.

3. Identify and describe the four types of markets: monopoly, oligopoly, monopolistic competition, and pure competition.

4. Explain how to construct a customer profile that will show a business's current market niche.

5. Tell how marketing research data is gathered.

6. List the six steps of the marketing survey research process.

7. Explain how to use marketing research data.

WHAT IS A MARKET?

A **market** is a group of consumers that behave in a similar way. For example, after Christmas many stores have sales to clear out merchandise left over from the holiday shopping season. In particular, they offer holiday cards and wrapping paper at large discounts. Some people start shopping for the next year's holidays on December 26. Those people constitute a market. So do those who buy suits that cost between $100 and $200, those who purchase only Oldsmobiles, and those who buy best-selling novels as soon as they come out. In each instance, there is a classification or **market niche** into which these people can be placed.

MANY CUSTOMERS, MANY MARKET NICHES

People buy all sorts of goods and services. Thus, they fall into *many* market niches. For example, using just price as the determinant of demand, consider the following individuals and the price ranges within which they buy goods:

	MR. A	MS. B	MR. C
Suits	$ 200–300	$ 125–225	$ 70–150
Books	5–50	3–20	3–10
Automobiles	9,000–22,000	7,000–14,000	4,000–10,000
Homes	125,000–195,000	80,000–120,000	45,000–85,000
Restaurant meals			
(for one)	20–35	15–25	12–20
Watches	125–300	50–150	30–60

Mr. A appears to be the most affluent. Certainly, he is willing to spend more money for the goods and services he buys. Mr. C appears to be the least affluent. He buys much less expensive things than Mr. A and is more likely than Mr. A to be a bargain shopper. Ms. B falls somewhere between. In all, three different market niches for goods are described in this example: high price, medium price, and low price.[1] (See Small Business Success: Finding a Niche.)

RELEVANT PRICE RANGE

In analyzing market niches, the small business owner-manager needs to be concerned with both relevant price range and competition. The price range is important because there are levels *above* which current customers will not buy, as well as levels *below* which these people will not purchase. Additionally, there are levels below which the business owner cannot sell at a profit. These three factors help determine the **relevant price range.** If the current price is above the minimum level for customer acceptance and owner's profit and below the level customers judge as "too high," the price is within the relevant range. How high or low can the owner set a price? It depends on the customers in the market niche. For example, using the graph in Figure 14-1 as an illustration, any price higher than "A" is too high; the current customers will not buy the suits for that much money. Meanwhile, any price below point "B" is too low; the customers will consider the suits to be of inferior quality. Note in the graph that point "B" is above the acceptable profit level. In this example, the customers are willing to pay high prices, and unless the owner wants to lose this market niche, price should remain within the relevant range. Other stores can cater to those who want to pay more and less than this range. Note in the graph that the relevant price range is $275–$350. Although this price is relatively high, there is a strong demand for suits in this range; that is, the high price does not scare away the customers. The reason is undoubtedly the high quality of the suits. They are regarded by these buyers as **specialty items,** and the customers will seek them out and pay whatever is being asked (within the range of relevance) by the seller.

---

[1] See Paula Munier Lee, "The Micro-Marketing Revolution," *Small Business Reports,* February 1990, pp. 71–82.

■ SMALL BUSINESS SUCCESS ■

Finding a Niche

At a time when six of Canada's largest investment firms had merged or been sold and the trend seemed to be moving towards big companies doing all of the trading, Rusty Goepel and Ken Shields decided to head out on their own and fight the big guys.

In March 1989, Goepel approached Shields and proposed that they join forces and start their own investment firm. By September of the same year, they had opened their doors for business with offices in Vancouver, Calgary, and Toronto.

The partners of Goepel, Shields & Partners, Inc., had three things in common. They had sunk a large amount of their own money into the firm to get it started, they had taken quite sizable pay cuts, and they were betting everything that there was a big enough niche in the marketplace for them to survive. However, forming Goepel, Shields wasn't just a spur-of-the-moment decision. The partners had realized that as banks moved into the investment business, a need had arisen for a "western-oriented, research-driven institutional boutique."

In May the future partners sat down to discuss what type of investment firm they would start and how it would be set up. Within one week lawyers had drafted an agreement that divided about 50 percent of the equity between Goepel, Shields, and two other founding partners. (It might be interesting to note that Goepel invested $350,000 for a return of 18 percent of the stock, Shields put up $300,000 in return for 15 percent, and the two other partners, Yue and Roberts, each contributed $250,000 to retain 12.5 percent each.)

In mid-June the founders started spreading the word around that they needed partners to join their firm, and they enticed interested parties with the opportunity to purchase left-over stock. For many senior investors whose big companies were being hit hard, the offer sounded too good to pass up. With the fear of big pay cuts or even job loss, many of them decided to join Goepel and Shields.

The investment company has been able to remain successful despite the fact that many of the investment deals are still being handled by the larger firms in Canada. However, this isn't to say that the firm has not had to make some cutbacks. Nixon, one of the partners, observed after a recent business trip that in the old days of working for Loewen he would have taken a limo to and from the airport, and the trip would have cost around $700. However, this trip was taken by riding the bus to and from the airport, cost about $79, and they still got the deal.

Source: Adapted from Desmond Smith, "Niche Players," *Canadian Business*, April 1990, pp. 46–54.

Figure 14-1
Suit Purchases

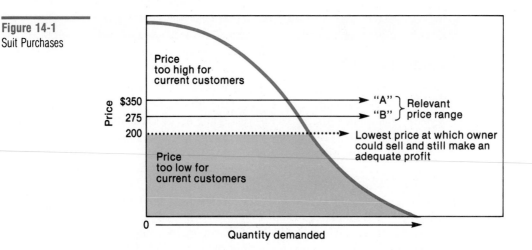

However, not all products fit into this category. In many cases, customers will substitute one good for another. For example, if the price of belts triples, suspenders might come back in style; if hardcover books cost too much, readers will wait for paperback editions. Food is another example. Hamburger, for instance, will be substituted for steaks if the cost of steaks rises too much. Likewise, if the price of hamburger rises, people will stop buying it and substitute something else, such as hot dogs. Meanwhile, if the price of hamburger drops while the price of other meats remains the same, people are likely to increase their purchases of hamburger. This is illustrated in Figure 14-2.

In the case of hamburger demand, the relevant price range is much broader. People will pay more for a pound of hamburger than they are currently paying, but if the price declines, they will buy *more*. Nonetheless, even here there is a price that is too high and a price below which the store owner could not afford to stock the product. Additionally, keep in mind that as the price of hamburger drops, it is likely that the price of other meats will also drop. As the hamburger price approaches the bottom of the relevant price range (see Figure 14-2), some customers will buy less hamburger and purchase more steaks. They will trade off the lower-priced meats for more

Figure 14-2
Hamburger Demand

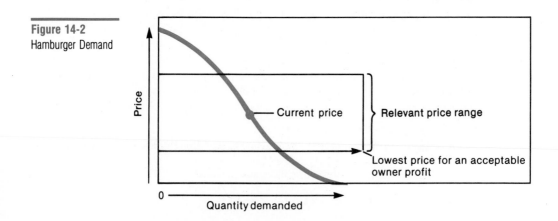

expensive ones because, if they can afford all of these products, they will prefer T-bone and filet mignon at least as often as hamburger. In short, there is a price below which people will not buy, preferring to buy a substitute.

COMPETITION

In looking at markets, it is important to examine not only the relevant price ranges but the presence of competition.[2] People usually base their buying decisions on need, the price charged by competing firms, and the availability of substitute products. The more competition there is for a particular product, the more likely it is that there will be a range of prices and numerous similar goods that can be substituted for it. In putting this into perspective, it is useful to look at the four possible economic conditions within which small businesses operate. Most businesses operate in a competitive environment. However, the *degree of competition* tells the story. The natural gas utility has no competition, whereas the furniture store on Mulberry Street may be fighting for its life. The different types of market situations are

1. monopoly

2. oligopoly

3. monopolistic competition

4. pure competition

MONOPOLY   In a **monopoly** there is *only one* seller or producer, and there are no substitutes. One must either do business with this firm or forego the good or service. There are various ways of developing a monopoly, from having it given to the business through legislation—as in the case of the public utility that has the exclusive right to sell electricity in an area—to obtaining a monopoly through a patent right—as in the case of a firm like Polaroid, which dominates the instant-picture market. A small business seldom has a monopoly, although if a restaurant has such a loyal following that there is always a waiting line, it has a monopoly for all practical purposes; the customers are unwilling to accept another restaurant as a substitute.

OLIGOPOLY   An **oligopoly** is a market in which there are *a few* dominant firms. Often, these companies account for 70–80 percent of industry sales. For the purchase of American-made autos, General Motors, Ford, and Chrysler, the "Big Three," fit into this category. Obviously there are no small businesses in oligopolies, at least not at the national level. However, if there are a few that dominate a local market, they can be thought of as an oligopoly in that they will follow the same basic strategies as those of their giant counterparts. For example, while the businesses in an oligopoly do not have a unique good or service for sale, they know that the strategies of each will affect the other. As a result, there tends to be a philosophy of "live and let live." They often do not compete on the basis of price, but they use advertising and personal selling to draw customers into their establishments. Like the monopoly, few small businesses fit well into this category.

---

[2]See "Market Share and Profitability," *Small Business Report,* October 1987, pp. 20–22.

Table 14-1 Comparison of the Four Market Models

	MONOPOLY	OLIGOPOLY	MONOPOLISTIC COMPETITION	PURE COMPETITION
Number of firms	one	a few	many	very many
Control over price	much	depends on what the others do	some	none
Type of product	unique	unique or standardized	unique or standardized	standardized
Access to the industry	impossible	difficult	fairly easy	very easy
Use of nonprice competition	public relations advertising	much	much	none

MONOPOLISTIC COMPETITION **Monopolistic competition** exists when there are *many* firms in an industry, each producing only a small share of the output that is demanded. In order to capture as large a share of this market as possible, each firm attempts to distinguish its goods and services from those of the competition. Advertising, credit, personal selling, and reputation are all used to draw people away from other products and businesses. Competition is vigorous. Common illustrations of monopolistic competition include restaurants, cleaning establishments, service stations, shoe stores, and grocery stores. *Most small businesses fall into this category.*

PURE COMPETITION **Pure competition** exists when *many independent sellers* offer products in the same basic way. The products are standardized—they are almost identical—and buyers are indifferent to which one they purchase. In addition, no firm can exercise significant control over the product's price because none supplies more than a small fraction of the total output being demanded. The most common example of this is in agriculture. Farmers who sell corn, wheat, or barley find that sellers buy their produce on the basis of weight (bushels) because there is very little difference, if any, between corn grown in one field and corn grown in the next.

These market models are contrasted in Table 14-1. As noted earlier, the market within which most small businesses fall is monopolistic competition. A business survives in this type of a market by examining the current needs of the customers, determining which goods and services appeal to the customers, and then giving them what they want. This is done by examining one's market niche and continually conducting marketing research.

EXAMINING THE CURRENT MARKET NICHE

Once the small business owner-manager understands a market and how it is affected by both price and competition, he or she is in a position to examine the business's current market niche.[3] Who are the customers? Do they pay for their purchases with cash or credit? Who are the bargain shoppers? What do they buy? How

---

[3]"Marketing Planning," *Small Business Report*, April 1986, pp. 68–72.

often do they buy? Answers to questions such as these provide a **customer profile.** Based on the results, the owner-manager can determine what to stock, how to price, where to advertise, and what services to provide.[4]

MARKET NICHE ANALYSIS: AN EXAMPLE

One of the first ways to examine a business's market niche is by breaking down the types of customers and their shopping habits. For example, consider the case of a drugstore owner who gathered age data on customers who frequented the store during a recent two-week period. A breakdown of customers' ages revealed the following information:

Adolescents and children	960
Males age 20–40	1,140
Males age 40–60	940
Males age 60 +	830
Females age 20–40	1,250
Females age 40–60	1,440
Females age 60 +	1,600

In addition, a breakdown of their buying habits, based on information gathered by store employees and the owner, reveals the profile shown in Table 14-2.

From this information, the owner knows that many of the customers like to charge things and that traffic is much heavier on weekends than during the week.

Table 14-2 Breakdown of Drugstore Customers' Buying Habits

TYPE OF CUSTOMER	CASH PURCHASES	CHARGE PURCHASES	BARGAIN SHOPPERS	DAYTIME SHOPPERS	EVENING SHOPPERS	WEEKEND SHOPPERS	BUY FAD ITEMS	BUY STAPLES (newspapers, gum, candy, etc.)	EAT AT LUNCH COUNTER	BUY HEALTH AND COSMETIC PRODUCTS
Adolescents and children	X			X		X	X	X	X	X
Males, 20–40		X			X	X	X	X		X
Males, 40–60		X			X	X	X	X		X
Males, 60 +	X			X		X		X		X
Females, 20–40		X	X	X	X	X	X	X		X
Females, 40–60	X	X	X		X	X		X		X
Females, 60 +	X		X	X			X	X	X	X

---

[4]See Jack Harms, "Are You a Marketing-Oriented Company?" *Small Business Reports,* March 1990, pp. 20–24.

Additionally, whereas everyone buys some product lines (staples and cosmetics), only about one-third of the customers eat at the lunch counter.

Data like these are useful in examining customer purchasing habits. By collecting more such data at a later time, the owner can find out a great many things—in particular, *changes* in customer buying habits that indicate *trends.* For example, the drugstore in our example has a lunch counter. However, most drugstores today do not have them because the return on investment is too low—people tend to prefer to eat at restaurants and fast-food chains today. As a result, many drugstore owners have taken out the lunch counters and put in records, books, and other fast-moving merchandise. Will this trend affect the drugstore in our example? This is difficult to say, but one thing is certain: it is a development that the owner should monitor by periodically comparing the cost of running the lunch counter with the revenue it generates. Is the return on this investment as high as in other areas of the store? This is referred to as **return-on-investment (ROI) control,** and it is one of the most effective control procedures. In essence, it says to the owner-manager, do not keep any product line that does not provide at least a minimum return on investment. The owner must establish what this minimum is, but let us assume that the drugstore offers ten major product lines and wants a return of at least 12 percent from each. At the end of the year, the accountant closes the books and then makes the calculations, which reveal the following:

MAJOR LINE	RETURN ON INVESTMENT
1	17
2	13
3	21
4	29
5	11
6	14
7	28
8	6
9	12
10	2

From the data it is obvious that items 5, 8, and 10 are not producing the desired return. From this information, the owner must decide whether or not to drop them. If the lines are not new and do not hold some promise for the future, they should be dropped. The only exception to this is if they are **complementary products,** bought by people who come into the store to buy something else. If that is the case, it may be wise for the store to carry both lines, since the customer may go elsewhere if he or she cannot obtain both kinds of products at this location.

MARKET NICHE DANGER SIGNALS

In addition to the financial analysis, the owner should use some qualitative criteria in judging whether the store is meeting the needs of its customers. This can often be determined by observing the behavior of customers and employees. Some danger signals are the following:

1. Many customers leave the store without buying anything.

2. Many former customers no longer shop here.

3. Customers are not urged to buy additional items or trade up to more expensive items.

4. Traffic (pedestrian and vehicular) in front of the store has fallen off.

5. Customers are returning more merchandise than they used to.

6. This month's sales are down from last year, and sales for the year to date are down from last year.

7. Employees are slow in greeting customers.

8. Employees appear indifferent and make customers wait unnecessarily.

9. Employees' personal appearance is not neat.

10. Salespeople lack knowledge of the store's merchandise.

11. The number of employee errors is increasing.

12. Because of high prices, the store has a reputation of being greedy.

13. The better-qualified employees are leaving for jobs with competitors.

Although knowledge of current market niche and customer buying habits is very important, a more vital consideration is those changes that will occur in the next three to five years. How will the market change? Remember, today's successful products will eventually become marginal winners and then losers. New goods and services must be in the wings ready to replace the current ones. These can be identified and cultivated through marketing research. (See Small Business Owner's Notebook: Competing with Giants.)

MARKETING RESEARCH

Marketing research is the systematic study of those factors that affect a business's sales. If the small business owner-manager is astute, he or she has been conducting some kind of marketing research from the first day the business opened.[5] Location, customer needs, competition, and product lines have long been recognized as areas of concern. The problem with most businesses, however, is that conditions change over time, and owners may not be aware of them.

In particular, *marketing habits* change. For example, in metropolitan areas many people used to use public transportation to shop downtown. However, the massive movement of people to the suburbs and increasing automobile ownership have led to the emergence of the suburban shopping center as the dominant retail outlet in most parts of the country. This same mobility, in conjunction with the advent of larger and better refrigerators and freezers, has changed the food-buying habits of many people. Instead of making a few purchases at the neighborhood grocery each day, most people now do large-scale food shopping at a supermarket, at lower prices, once or twice a week.

Likewise, trends toward shorter working hours and greater interest in convenience products, do-it-yourself goods, and sports equipment have been noted. The rising purchasing power of Americans has increased the demand for luxury

[5]Stephen W. McDaniel and A. Parasuraman, "Practical Guidelines for Small Business Marketing Research," *Journal of Small Business Management*, January 1986, pp. 1–8.

■   **SMALL BUSINESS OWNER'S NOTEBOOK**   ■

Competing with Giants

 How can a small retailer compete against the power, size, prices, and selection offered by giant mass merchandisers? Walmart, for example, currently operates in 1,465 locations and adds a new store *every other day!* While a new Walmart can expect sales in excess of $15 million annually, specialty stores will lose an estimated 9.9 percent in sales, building materials stores will lose 10.4 percent, apparel stores will lose 11.5 percent, service businesses will lose 14.2 percent, and home furnishings will lose 18.9 percent.

In order to survive such competition, and remain distinctive in the eyes of customers, small businesses need to apply the following strategies:

1. Offer products unavailable in the larger stores.

2. Develop a reputation for better product knowledge.

3. Offer personalized service/delivery, repair, installation, and so on.

4. Emphasize high-grade products (counter to the low-end goods that are sometimes sold by the "giants").

5. Stock different product lines than the larger store carries.

6. Help promote the community to attract new customers from surrounding areas.

7. Constantly stress the "family" part of the family business by using expressions such as "locally-owned," "family-owned," "our family serving you" when promoting or advertising the company.

These strategies may be critical for competing with giant stores such as Walmart. If they are applied with the same determination that the entrepreneurs used to start their businesses, then these strategies will initiate a new level of competition for small businesses.

Source: Adapted from David Diamond, "When Walmart Comes to Town," *Family Business,* December 1990, pp. 36–41.

---

products and services. All of these changes have a tremendous effect on buying habits. These changes add up to the need for a business to remain flexible. This is where marketing research enters the picture.[6]

HOW TO CONDUCT MARKETING RESEARCH

How can the small business owner obtain the necessary marketing research? Three broad sources should be considered. First, there are trade associations, regular

---

[6]See Robin T. Peterson, "Small Business Adoption of the Marketing Concept vs. Other Business Strategies," *Journal of Small Business Management,* January 1989, pp. 38–46.

business advisors, business agencies, and, to a limited extent, suppliers that can offer factual information. Second, the owner-manager can acquire the services of an independent marketing research service. Third, the owner-manager can organize a marketing research effort within the firm itself. The best method for a particular business depends on the resources of the business, the availability of the needed information, the complexity and size of the problem, and most important of all, the costs involved.[7]

SECONDARY SOURCES

Regardless of who conducts the research, a good place to begin is with data from currently available **secondary sources.** These documents present statistics that have been compiled on the industry, the competition, and the local area, as well as information gleaned from business publications. This is fundamental in marketing research and often yields the greatest value for the investment. However, they should *never* be the *only* sources tapped because they seldom provide all of the information needed by the owner-manager. Two of the most important secondary sources are local statistics and sales analysis.

LOCAL STATISTICS   One way to begin a marketing research effort is by getting statistics on the local community. These can often be obtained from the Chamber of Commerce, the city government, and census data. These data can help in compiling a profile of the local population by age distribution, average income, family size, automobile ownership, home ownership, and number of school-age children. By analyzing these data, it is often possible to come up with some helpful facts.

Another important area of consideration is changing population. Currently over half the population of the United States is under 45 years of age. These people have different buying habits than older people. The geographic breakdown of this population can tell the small business owner-manager where people are moving to and from. For example, in recent years Arizona, Florida, California, and Colorado have been increasing in population. Some that have been either losing population or growing very slowly are North Dakota, South Dakota, Virginia, and Wyoming. By studying population changes, the business owner can determine whether the firm is located in a growing area or one that is likely to become economically stagnant in the next five to ten years.

A third way to get local statistics without expending a lot of time and effort is to read the local newspaper and subscribe to trade journals and business publications. The local newspaper often carries reports of income levels for the community and the region, and its financial section is another ready source of important statistical information. Additionally, publications such as *Business Week,* the *Wall Street Journal,* and *Fortune* offer a wealth of information that can prove useful in making marketing decisions. The astute business owner-manager will cut out and file statistics that directly affect his or her business. In this way, the individual can compile a **market fact file** for use in marketing research.

---

[7]For a detailed discussion of marketing research data sources see Michael F. d'Amico, "Marketing Research for Small Business," *Journal of Small Business Management,* January 1978, pp. 41–49.

SALES ANALYSIS   A type of marketing research that can be conducted within the place of business is sales analysis. By analyzing sales data the owner-manager can answer many questions—questions such as: How many dishwashers did we sell last year? How many freezers did we sell? What is our most profitable product line? What is our biggest seller? Did most people pay cash or charge it? Do most of our customers live close by or more than ten miles away? These questions are easily answered by examining sales slips on which the customer's name and address, the date, the item sold, and the amount paid for the item are recorded.

PRIMARY SOURCES

Statistics and sales analysis can provide very important information, but the data are limited in that they are *historical*. No "new" facts are considered; it is just old information that is being studied. In order to collect current data, some form of survey research is necessary. This can be done by the small business itself, or an outside survey research firm can be hired. In either case, the steps in the research are the same.

SURVEY RESEARCH   There are six steps in conducting **marketing survey research.**

1. ANALYZE THE SITUATION.   What are the conditions in the industry and in the local area? For example, assume that the small business owner provides rug cleaning services. The first thing the owner-manager, or the marketing survey organization, would want to do is get background information. This could be done by asking the trade association or national industry group to which the business owners belong if any national or area surveys have been conducted. Then the Chamber of Commerce and other local sources of data could be consulted. During this background research, the investigators should get information that will help in the second step.

2. FORMULATE A STATEMENT OF THE PROBLEM.   Obviously there must be some problem or the owner-manager would not be having the research conducted in the first place. Sometimes this problem is nothing more than a desire to know whether to expand services by moving into another geographic area.

3. DESIGN THE RESEARCH.   How will further information be collected so that the problem can be analyzed in sufficient depth?

4. CARRY OUT THE SURVEY.   Numerous methods can be used. One of the most common ways is the use of interviews and/or questionnaires. Regardless of who carries them out, however, the issue of bias must be addressed. Sometimes, the way a person asks a question generates a particular response. The same is true for the way a question is written in a questionnaire. For example, if the owner of the rug cleaning firm decides to interview 100 people in the local area and ask them questions about rug cleaning, the owner will get different answers depending on how the questions are phrased. If the owner asks, "Would you consider using my firm to clean your rugs?" the respondent will probably answer yes. However, the person is not saying that he or she *will* do so, merely that he or she will *consider* it. A better way to gather marketing research data is to ask **open-ended questions** such as "How do you clean your rugs?" The answer will tell the owner how many people hire professionals and how many do it themselves. Then the questioner can ask, "Why do you hire a professional (or do it yourself)?" This answer will indicate something about how the homeowner values his or her time. This, in turn, will provide some basis for distinguishing potential customers from people who will do it themselves.

5. TABULATE, ANALYZE, AND REPORT THE INFORMATION. At this stage the information is put into some meaningful form. Sometimes the person collecting the information will believe that the answers point to one conclusion overall, because he or she remembers several of the interviewees very well and those people all said the same thing. However, by analyzing *all* of the responses, it may turn out that just the opposite answer was given by most people.

6. APPLY THE DATA TO SOLVE THE PROBLEM. What percentage of the interviewees said that they hire professionals for rug cleaning services? How many potential homes will use this service every year? How many competing firms offer rug cleaning? What percentage of this market can the firm capture? By answering these questions, the small business owner is in a position to determine whether it is a good idea to expand the business into another geographic area.

OTHER METHODS OF DATA COLLECTION In our example of the steps in survey research, one of the most common methods of data collection—home interviews— was used. Another method of gathering data—probably the simplest method of all—is the **store interview** or **questionnaire.** Retail stores, in particular, can use this approach with very little trouble. A common way of doing so is to have a personable, pleasant interviewer approach customers and ask them to answer a few simple questions. Usually these questions are limited in number so that it takes only a few moments. The information is recorded on an easily marked interview card so that there is a permanent record of the comments. Typical questions include: "How often do you visit this store?" "Where do you live?" "How many times a week do you shop?" "What kinds of products do you come to this store to buy?" "Why do you like shopping at this store?" If the owner believes there may be some resistance to answering such questions, there are ways of overcoming it. For example, instead of asking shoppers a series of questions, point-of-sale survey cards that shoppers fill out and drop in a box can be used. On the survey card is a place for the person's name and answers to a few questions. Then the owner can draw a predetermined number of responses from the box, with these respondents receiving a prize. In this case, the survey instrument is used both to gather information and as a contest entry blank.

Another method often used by small business is the **mail survey.** This type of questionnaire is sent to the respondent with a request to fill it out and return it in a stamped or postage-guaranteed envelope. Such surveys are usually cheaper than personal interviews and easier to tabulate. The Small Business Administration reports that many people do indeed respond to mail questionnaires. In fact, some companies have found them to be more reliable than interviews. For example, one large consumer goods firm discovered that the results it obtained from interview surveys were different from those it obtained from a mail survey. After analyzing the eventual buying habits of the consumers, the mail survey was found to be more accurate.

A third common form of survey is the **telephone interview.** In using this method, the owner-manager should ensure that the respondents know they are being asked to participate in a survey. Prepared questions are asked and the answers are recorded. The obvious advantages of telephone interviews are that a single interviewer can handle a large number of respondents and the overall cost is relatively low. Of course, the person carrying out the interview must have a pleasant voice and the questionnaire the person reads should be simple, direct, and brief. If the call takes too long, the respondent is likely to terminate it.

Finally, one should not overlook **specialized surveys** for collecting consumer data, some of which lend themselves to **demonstration approaches.** New products or product prototypes are often researched this way. A place is created where consumers can examine the products and ask questions about them. Supermarkets often set up demonstration tables at which new food items are cooked and shoppers are urged to sample the products. Department stores also do this. A salesperson shows how a new product works and encourages the shopper to buy one before leaving the store.[8]

HOW TO USE THE RESEARCH DATA

Having collected the data, the business owner must decide how to use the information. Until now, all the owner has done is collect a mass of facts and figures.

First, the *data must be tabulated and arranged in some useful form.* For example, if a small business owner believes that most shoppers in his toy store are children or young parents, he might be interested in the number of people in this section of town who are in the age ranges 0–9 (children) and 20–39 (the most common ages for the parents), and whether the numbers are increasing or decreasing. Assume that the owner has collected census data for the metropolitan area for ten years ago and for today and finds the data presented in Table 14-3.

Note that the percentage breakdowns are about the same today as they were ten years ago. Approximately 26 percent of the group is children below the age of 10, while almost 30 percent of the group is between the ages of 20 and 39. Thus, there have been no significant population shifts. Additionally, to the owner's advantage, the number of people in the local area has increased by 45 percent.

Table 14-3 Age Distribution in the Local Area

AGE (YEARS)	10 YEARS AGO		TODAY	
	NUMBER	PERCENT OF POPULATION	NUMBER	PERCENT OF POPULATION
0–9	88,617	26.4	125,768	25.8
10–19	76,212	22.6	112,386	23.0
20–29	51,007	15.2	82,087	16.8
30–39	42,839	12.7	55,320	11.5
40–49	36,793	11.0	42,107	8.6
50–59	25,107	7.5	40,567	8.2
60 +	15,361	4.6	29,138	6.1
TOTAL	335,936	100.0	487,373	100.0

---

[8]For examples of various approaches, see Alan R. Andreasen, "Cost-Conscious Marketing Research," *Harvard Business Review,* July/August 1983, pp. 74–75.

The foregoing leads to the other important step in using research data: the owner must *interpret the statistics.* What do they tell the owner that can help in making decisions? This is often the most difficult part of the research. The owner must evaluate the data objectively, not twist or distort their meaning.

Finally, the business owner must *proceed with caution.* Marketing research can never predict the future. What it can do, if properly used, is to forecast probable events based on trends and current consumer behavior. How well it forecasts the future depends on the accuracy of the data and the objectivity of the interpretation of the data.

■ SUMMARY

A market is a group of consumers who behave in a similar way. However, since people buy all sorts of goods and services many market niches exist. In analyzing market niches, the owner-manager needs to consider relevant price range and competition. The former is the price within which the customers will buy. The latter represents the threat to this niche. In studying the competition, the degree of competitiveness tells the story. Thus, of the four types of markets—monopoly, oligopoly, monopolistic competition, and pure competition—it is monopolistic competition and its high degree of competitiveness with which the small business owner-manager is most concerned.

In addition to understanding price and competition, the small business owner needs to understand the firm's current market niche. The development of a customer profile is one of the best ways to do this.

Marketing research is the systematic study of the factors that affect a business's sales. Analyzing these factors is important because customer buying habits are continually changing. In conducting marketing research, secondary sources such as local statistics and sales analysis are good places to begin. These can then be supplemented with primary sources such as market survey research, in which new, previously unavailable data are gathered. When these new data are available, the owner-manager must know how to use them. By objectively arranging, analyzing, and interpreting the data, valuable conclusions can be drawn. The owner-manager must now allow personal biases or opinions to alter an objective evaluation of the data. If the owner-manager can do this, maximum value can be derived from the survey.

■ REVIEW AND DISCUSSION QUESTIONS

1. What is meant by the term *market; market niche?*

2. Explain what a small business owner-manager needs to know about relevant price range.

3. How do each of the following differ from the others: monopoly, oligopoly, monopolistic competition, pure competition?

4. Explain how a customer profile can be useful to an owner-manager who is interested in examining a market niche.

5. What is meant by the term *marketing research?*

6. How can local statistics and sales analyses help an owner-manager gather research data?

7. How is market survey research carried out? Explain the six steps.

8. What are the most common data-collection methods small businesses use in their marketing research? Describe at least two.

9. Specifically, what should a small business owner know about using research data? How can the information be useful? Explain.

Case Studies

They're Getting to Be the Biggest

■ When Paula and Fred Monturk opened their appliance store they knew they would have to cater to a specific niche if they hoped to survive. They decided to go after the top end of the market, although they would offer some appliances at the middle and lower ends as well.

The Monturks carry an assortment of appliances including such large-ticket items as washers, dryers, refrigerators, and freezers and such small-ticket items as blenders, coffee makers, mixers, can openers, and toasters. Their big-ticket items are name-brand merchandise that is not available in many other stores. "We stock major appliances that are retailed only through selective outlets," Paula explains. "This gives us an advantage in terms of market differentiation and helps justify our higher prices. If all stores sold what we did, customers would have no reason to come to us. And if our products were sold in discount houses, there'd be little we could do to survive. Exclusivity is the name of our game."

A review of the Monturk's sales shows that they do very well selling high-price appliances. However, they also make a great deal of money selling moderate- and low-priced goods. In fact, in the last year and a half 50 percent of their sales were accounted for by appliances priced less than $50. These goods are sold in many retail stores, but customers have been willing to purchase them from the Monturks at prices about 10 percent above the competition. Although the Monturks have been unable to explain why customers purchase lower-priced merchandise from them, a brief review of their customers' addresses shows that most of them live within a mile of the store.

The Monturks are very pleased with their sales record and intend to expand their offerings next year. They are now negotiating exclusive franchise agreements with four manufacturers for a wide array of big-ticket home appliances. "This should increase our sales 40 percent," says Paula, "and make us the biggest name-brand appliance retailer in the region."

1. Do the Monturks really know who their customers are?

2. Based on the case data, what mistakes do the Monturks appear to be making? Explain.

3. What changes should the Monturks make in their approach? Explain.

The Inquisitive Nephew

■   The Grant Building, located in a large metropolitan area, is a 55-story office building. On the ground floor and the one immediately below, there are many shops, including a luggage store owned and managed by Margie and Hank Brandon. Suitcases and attaché cases are their specialty, although they sell supplemental merchandise as well.

A few weeks ago, Margie's nephew Gerald dropped by. He works for a marketing research firm across town and had come by to take them out to lunch. During the visit, the three of them began talking about the store's business. Margie said they feel very lucky to be located in the Grant Building because "our customers are located in the same building. Every time one of the big executives needs a new attache case or has his suitcase damaged during a business trip, we can expect a visit from him."

The statement intrigued Gerald. "How do you know that all of your customers are located in the Grant Building?" he asked. Hank explained that the store does no advertising and that "most of the people who come into the store are people I see coming into the building every day."

Gerald then asked them how they generate sales to people that do not work in their building. "Don't you do *any* type of advertising *at all?*" What Gerald learned was that they had moved into the Grant Building six years ago when they heard about a shop vacancy. They had been selling suitcases and other leather goods in a small store across town. The business was doing all right, but they were convinced that they could do much better by catering to businesspeople.

Gerald was very impressed, especially over the fact that Margie and Hank had been able to survive in business through common sense and, perhaps, some luck. Nevertheless, he suggested that they conduct some marketing research to see what they could learn about their customers and, in the process, increase both their sales and profits.

Both Margie and Hank said that they would be happy to have him come by and design a marketing research study for them—especially after Gerald told them he would not charge them for it. "I just want to see if I can help you do even better," he said.

Gerald is scheduled to visit them tomorrow. In the interim, he has asked them to have their records for the last two years available and be prepared to give him about two hours of their time. "I think I can design a program that will collect all of the information you need without taking too much of your time. All I'll need from you will be some initial assistance and the promise that you will ask each customer to fill out the form I have made up for you, since this will give us some background on who shops at your store and why."

1. What is marketing research? How can it help small business owner-managers like Hank and Margie?

2. What kind of marketing research survey do you think Gerald will put together for them? Explain.

3. Can a survey of this kind be of any value to the owners? How?

You Be the Consultant

JACK'S PROBLEM

When Jack Holden opened his independent service station fifteen years ago, he gave his customers more than just a place to buy gas. He hired his two younger brothers, both of whom were mechanics, and offered a wide range of services as well.

As word of the service station's quality work and fair prices spread, Jack brought in a third mechanic. Meanwhile, the amount of gas pumped at the station rose by almost 40 percent in the first year. Jack kept the station open eighteen hours a day seven days a week, and within three years the station was prospering beyond his wildest dreams.

However, things then began to turn around due to a number of significant developments. First, the neighborhood began to change. The middle- and upper-middle-income residents started to move farther south; they were replaced by upper-lower- and lower-middle-income groups that had different purchasing habits. Second, the new residents did most of their own auto repair and let minor things go unattended. They did not have money to spend for auto maintenance. Third, many of them were more concerned with the price of gas than with keeping their cars in top-notch shape. They bought only regular gas and were likely to bring their cars in for service only when there was a special sale.

During the last few years, Jack has attempted to increase his business by offering a slightly lower price on gasoline at the self-service pumps. At the same time he has been thinking about ways to supplement his income. Apparently he has been relying too heavily on the auto maintenance part of the business. He has to find other solutions. A friend has recommended that he put in new pumps that can be operated by the car owner while the station owner or manager oversees everything from a small booth. The owner or manager can turn on the pump and collect the money from the customer after the gas has been pumped. In this way, the business can maximize its income by keeping expenses to a minimum. Another recommendation is that Jack sell non-auto-related items. In particular, the people who come in to buy gas might be interested in fast-moving, convenience items such as milk, beer, cigarettes, and candy.

Jack is not sure that this is a very good idea. However, he has driven around town and found that four large oil companies are taking down their stations and putting in automatic pumps and service-related products. Jack has also checked into the amount of financing that would be necessary to copy this approach, and it is within the financial reach of the station. However, he is not sure if it is a good idea.

■ **YOUR CONSULTATION** Help Jack out. Tell why he has been losing business in recent years. Describe the type of business environment in which he currently operates. Then tell him what you think he should do now. Be specific in your consultation.

Pricing, Advertising, and Selling

Objectives

If the small business owner-manager understands the fundamentals of marketing, as discussed in Chapter 14, he or she also knows something about pricing and advertising. However, pricing, advertising, and selling are so important to small businesses that they warrant more attention. The first objective of Chapter 15 is to study the concepts of pricing with which the owner-manager should be familiar. Then some of the ideas vital to pricing for profit will be reviewed. Our discussion of pricing will finish with an analysis of how small businesses set price. The second objective is to look at advertising in small business. We will focus attention on the advantages of advertising, advertising appeals, and how to decide which advertising medium is best for the business. The third objective of the chapter is to review some ideas about selling and the selling process. We discuss some research in sales psychology that helps to explain consumer buying motivations. When you have finished the material in Chapter 15, you will be able to:

1. Identify and describe the four pricing considerations.

2. Explain the four factors to consider in pricing for profit.

3. Describe how small businesses set price.

4. Discuss the advantages of advertising and how to develop advertising appeals.

5. Explain how small business owners should go about selecting the best media for their advertising.

6. Recognize advertising and promotion issues that are important to small businesses.

7. Explain the five fundamental steps of the selling process.

8. Discuss the role of sales psychology in the selling process.

PRICING CONSIDERATIONS

The owner-manager's primary consideration in pricing must be cost. No one can afford to sell below this level—at least not for very long. However, since this point is obvious, we won't spend much time on it here. Rather, let us turn to other considerations in pricing. These include

1. the nature of the product
2. the competition
3. marketing strategy
4. general business conditions

THE NATURE OF THE PRODUCT

The demand for some products seems to be little affected by a change in price. For example, whether the price of salt is raised or lowered has little effect on the quantity sold. However, the demand for many products *does* respond to price, and this demand can be stimulated with prices changes. Demand can be stimulated in two ways. First, some goods will sell better if the price is *lowered*, that is, demand increases. However, the opposite approach is to *raise* the price and manage to maintain approximately the same demand as before. If this occurs it must be because buyers believe that the product or service is still a good value at the higher price.

THE COMPETITION

A second pricing consideration is the competition. The way competing firms price similar goods affects what the small business owner-manager can charge. This is particularly so when customers cannot distinguish the product sold by one store from that sold by another. For example, for most people milk is milk, so it really does not matter where they buy it, as long as the store is conveniently located. As a result, if two stores are across the street from each other and the price of milk is 5¢ a gallon less at one of them, customers will flock to that one. The same is true in the case of bread, shoelaces, socks, and gasolines.

Few products are bought *solely* on the basis of price, however. Many times people will pay *more* money for a particular good because it has a quality image. Television sets are an example. If a set has problems, the average consumer will not know how to repair it. Therefore, when that person buys, quality will be a major criterion and price will rank farther down the list. Of course, the small business owner-manager cannot guarantee quality in TVs, appliances, or similar goods, but the owner-manager can try to secure franchise agreements from well-known major manufacturers—GE, RCA, DuPont—so that he or she can carry their products. This will provide a competitive edge over other stores.

Finally, regardless of quality, most goods eventually wear out or break down. Sooner or later, a car needs an oil change. A TV will require picture adjustment. A washing machine will need a new belt. This is where service comes in. Few small businesses can compete with large companies on a head-to-head price basis. However, they can distinguish their goods and services from those of the competition through personal service. For example, many people who go to a service station for car maintenance will return if the service is satisfactory. They will also buy their gasoline and other auto-related products there. Similarly, services such as haircuts, dental work, and medical health care are all greatly influenced by the quality of the service. Thus, price in and of itself will not always determine demand. In fact, businesses that offer high quality often can raise their prices without suffering any decline in demand.

MARKETING STRATEGY

A third pricing consideration is marketing strategy. Some small firms prefer to be price leaders even if this means lower over-all volume. Others prefer to simply meet the competition and price their merchandise between the highest and lowest sellers. Still others like to price low and make their money through increased volume.[1]

The owner must decide whether he or she wants to make a lot of profit in the short-run or aim for long-run profit in the form of repeat business. If the owner sells fad items, prices will probably be high because the owner knows that there is little chance of repeat business for any particular line. Additionally, if the fad suddenly fades, the owner may wind up with a lot of unsalable inventory. For this reason, the owner will want to recover the investment as soon as possible. On the other hand, many small businesses sell the same types of goods and services all the time. If they are of high quality, the owner will probably have high prices and develop a reputation for being "expensive but good." Conversely, owners who sell items of average quality usually price them competitively and work on securing repeat business.

Marketing strategy helps the public identify a firm. When people want to buy something at the lowest possible price, they go to companies they have come to know as discounters. On the other hand, when they want to buy something of high quality that, if not satisfactory, can be returned, they go to stores that have a reputation for handling these kinds of transactions. In short, marketing strategy helps the business establish an **image.**

GENERAL BUSINESS CONDITIONS

Most businesses are affected by general business conditions. This is particularly so for small enterprises. When economic conditions are poor it is common for them to keep inventories at a minimum and price goods to move fast. The impact of the environment is most noticeable at the wholesale level, because wholesalers tend to sell large quantities of goods on a very narrow profit margin. Changes in their cost of doing business must often be passed along immediately so as to protect this narrow margin. At the retail level, price changes are slower in coming because most stores price their goods high enough to absorb minor variations in the cost of doing business. Nevertheless, all costs are eventually passed along to the consumer.

PRICING FOR PROFIT

All pricing methods are based on a cost-plus-profit markup. Only if this strategy proves unworkable will the owner-manager reduce price and try to cut his or her losses on a particular line. The factors to consider in setting price are

---

[1]Tyzoon T. Tyebjee, Albert V. Bruno, and Shelby H. McIntyre, "Growing Ventures Can Anticipate Marketing Stages," *Harvard Business Review,* January/February 1983, pp. 62–66.

1. the cost of goods
2. competitive prices
3. market demand

COST OF GOODS

The primary objective in pricing for profit is to set a price that is high enough to cover the cost of the goods and the expenses incurred in selling them and to generate some profit. A simple formula for this is

$$\text{Selling price} = \text{Purchase price} + \text{Operating expenses} + \text{Profit}$$

Note in this formula that operating expenses fall into two categories: **production costs** (materials and labor) and the **overhead** (the rent for the building, the utility bills, and other general costs that are not directly covered when the production costs are determined). Profit is then a percentage of the total.

COMPETITIVE PRICES

We have already discussed this topic in some depth. Most small business owner-managers keep an eye on what their competitors are charging for similar goods and services. Unless there is some good reason not to, most small firms price with the competition. (See Small Business Success: Pricing for Revenge.)

MARKET DEMAND

Although this topic also has been examined in some detail, we need to consider profit versus volume. Research reveals that many sellers try to hold the line on price so as to maintain market share. Sometimes, however, demand is so strong that the owner will raise the price as high as market conditions allow. This can usually be done only when a new product or service is in short supply and when there is a strong market demand. Additionally, it is important to remember that there may be an "ideal" price. This can be illustrated with a **demand schedule,** a graph that plots varying prices against anticipated demand; see Figure 15-1. Note that four points are designated on this schedule. Computing the total revenue at each point, we get

2,500 units @ $45 each = $112,500

5,000 units @ $35 each = $175,000

7,500 units @ $25 each = $187,500

10,000 units @ $15 each = $150,000

In this case the owner should price at $25, since revenue would be maximized at that point. Anything higher or lower than $25 will result in less revenue. According to the schedule, if the owner is willing to give up $37,500, he or she could sell another 2,500 units by pricing at $15. Typically, however, the owner prices for profit, the $25 price would be preferred over the $15 price.[2]

---

[2]See Eric Mitchell, "How Not to Raise Prices," *Small Business Reports,* November 1990, pp. 64–67.

■ **SMALL BUSINESS SUCCESS** ■

Pricing for Revenge

 Ninety-seven-year-old Rose Blumkin, affectionately known as Mrs. B, emigrated from Russia with her husband in 1917 by walking through Siberia and China to Japan. They eventually migrated to and wound up in the United States, and Mrs. B remembers being so poor that they were happy when the family had bread. When she was six years old, she swore to her mother she would not be poor forever. Her father was a rabbi, and her family had suffered through planned persecutions and massacres of Jews.

By 1919, Mrs. B and her husband had moved to Omaha, Nebraska, in order to improve their English by living among other Russian immigrants. It was in Omaha that they opened a secondhand clothing store. When sales slackened during the Great Depression, they added secondhand furniture to the items they carried. She and her husband worked side by side until he died at the age of 57.

By 1989 the Nebraska Furniture Mart could boast $160-million in sales. Two grandsons were president and vice president. However, in May of 1989, Mrs. B and the grandsons locked horns over how to run the carpet department. "They wanted to be big shots," she said, "I made my family too rich." So in December of the same year, she opened the 360,000-square-foot Mrs. B's Warehouse across the street from her grandsons' business. Mrs. B was starting over at 95 years of age. As to why she opened her new establishment directly across from her former furniture store, Mrs. B stated that she wanted to have a front row seat when she ran the grandsons' store right down to the ground.

Mrs. B has achieved legendary status among the locals. "They remember you by what you do for them. You're giving them prices they can't get from nobody else. You're honest with them." People seem to believe her. She is reportedly notorious for undercutting her salespeople's lowest quoted price.

Mrs. B spends her evenings driving around Omaha to check out the competition. She knows furniture, she knows her competition, and she "loves the middle class." Apparently, this is her formula for success.

Source: Adapted from Dennis Rodkin, "Give 'Em Hell, Granny," *Entrepreneur,* December 1990, pp. 139–144.

HOW SMALL BUSINESSES SET PRICES

In Chapter 1 we noted that there are three major groups of small businesses: merchandisers, service establishments, and manufacturers. We now examine how prices are set by small businesses in each of these categories, considering merchandisers, first of all, as either wholesalers or retailers.

WHOLESALERS

Wholesale prices are generally based on an established markup or gross profit for each line. At the wholesale level price is very important because most retailers base

Figure 15-1
Price and Demand

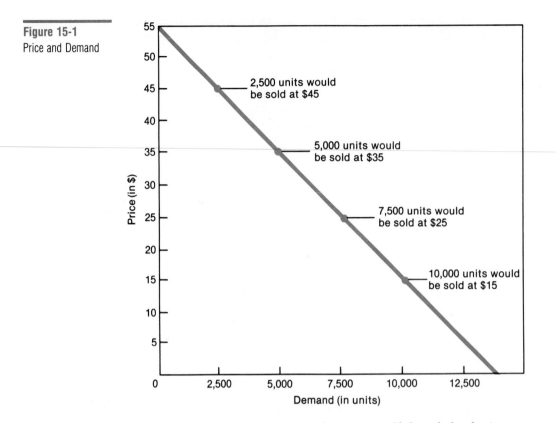

their purchase decisions very heavily on price. If the wholesaler is not competitive the retailers will buy from a different wholesaler. Additionally, since wholesalers purchase in large quantities and cannot always pass along price increases immediately, they can lose money if prices fluctuate greatly. In particular, the wholesaler can get squeezed between the manufacturer and the retailer. If the manufacturer raises prices and the retailer resists increased costs, the wholesaler may have to absorb a large reduction in profit or even a loss. Since wholesalers have small profit margins, they monitor price movements carefully.

One way they do this is by keeping abreast of competitive prices. A second is by charging different retailers different prices for the same merchandise. This price differentiation is determined by such factors as the size of the order (larger orders get lower prices per unit), the individual retailer's bargaining ability, and the services—such as credit and delivery—being extended to the retailer. Wholesalers commonly use a discount or price schedule for each group of goods or services, with maximum and minimum prices for different quantities.

RETAILERS

Retailers offer the most interesting example of small business pricing. Except in those cases where the store uses manufacturers' suggested prices, the owner needs to be concerned with many of the concepts we have already discussed, including the nature of the product, competition, and general business conditions. Of these, the nature of the product is usually the most significant, because different types of products are priced in different ways.

Staple convenience goods such as candy bars, chewing gum, newspapers, magazines, and other items that are standardized tend to carry customary prices or be priced according to the going market price. These goods usually carry low prices, and any price cutting will be met quickly by the competition. Also, in the case of such items as candy and gum, prices tend to be set, for example, at 20¢ or 25¢, not in between. Research has shown that consumers would rather pay 25¢ than 22¢ to avoid digging out two pennies—an inconvenience for them.

Fashion goods tend to be priced high and, if they do not sell, they are marked down. Novelty or specialty goods also carry a high markup and, once the novelty wears off or the selling season is over, the price is lowered.

Groceries, on average, tend to be purchased by people who shop for the best buys. Many supermarkets have adopted unit pricing to help in this process. In fact, many places require it by law. **Unit pricing** calls for the listing of the product's price in terms of some unit of measurement such as an ounce, a pint, or a yard. For example, by listing the price per ounce for sugar, the consumer is able to comparison shop and determine which product offers the most for the money. Competitive pressures will likely force the small, independent grocer to do the same eventually.

How do retailers, in particular, go about determining price? Except in those cases where this decision is made for them, as with manufacturers' suggested retail prices, they tend to use a system of markup and/or markon.

MARKUP   **Markup** is the difference between selling price and the cost of the good being sold. Sometimes the term **gross margin** is used; it means the same thing. Some business owners mark up each item individually, but an average markup for the various lines of goods carried is more common. For example, watches may be marked up 100 percent, television sets 35 percent, and dairy products 16 percent. By using this approach, the time devoted to marking up goods can be greatly reduced.

There are two basic ways of marking up goods. One is to use a *percentage of the retail selling price.* The other is to use a *percentage of the cost* of the good. For example, if a pair of socks costs 80¢ and is sold for $1.00, the markup (20¢) on selling price is 20 percent (20¢/$1.00) while the markup on cost is 25 percent (20¢/80¢). The markup on the selling price is *always a smaller percentage,* because the denominator in the calculation is larger ($1.00 as opposed to 80¢ in this case). Today most businesses base markups on the retail price, because this tells them how much of their sales dollar can be used to pay bills and how much will be left over for profit.

The computation of markup is not difficult, especially if the owner has a markup table such as the one shown in Table 15-1. A **markup table** allows the businessperson to quickly determine the retail price. The following examples illustrate how this is done.

EXAMPLE 1   A retailer who sells radios and TVs uses a standard 50 percent markup on retail on all portable radios. How much should the retailer charge for a portable radio that costs $20? In answering this question five steps should be taken:

1. Determine the cost of the good, which in this case is $20.

2. Find the required gross profit figure (50%) in the *Markup as Percentage of Retail Price* column in Table 15-1.

Table 15-1 A Markup Table

MARKUP AS PERCENTAGE OF RETAIL PRICE	MARKUP AS PERCENTAGE OF COST	MARKUP AS PERCENTAGE OF RETAIL PRICE	MARKUP AS PERCENTAGE OF COST
10	11.11	31	44.93
11	12.36	32	47.06
12	13.64	33	49.25
13	14.94	34	51.52
14	16.28	35	53.85
15	17.65	36	56.25
16	19.05	37	58.73
17	20.48	38	61.29
18	21.95	39	63.93
19	23.46	40	66.67
20	25.00	41	69.49
21	26.58	42	72.41
22	28.21	43	75.44
23	29.87	44	78.57
24	31.58	45	81.82
25	33.33	46	85.19
26	35.14	47	88.68
27	36.99	48	92.31
28	38.89	49	96.08
29	40.85	50	100.00
30	42.86		

3. Find the corresponding figure opposite 50% in the *Markup as Percentage of Cost* column in the table, which is 100%.

4. Multiply the cost of the good ($20) by that figure to get the dollars and cents markup on cost. In this case: $20 × 1.00 = $20.

5. Add the markup on cost result ($20) to the cost of the good ($20) to arrive at the selling price: $20 + $20 = $40 selling price.

The solution can be checked by determining the results of selling 100 radios.

Sales revenue (100 radios × $40)	$4,000
Less: Cost of goods (100 radios × $20)	$2,000
Gross profit	$2,000

Gross profit as a percent of sales:

$$\frac{2,000}{4,000} \times 100\% = 50\%$$

Thus a markup of 100% on the cost of goods will produce a 50 percent gross profit.

EXAMPLE 2   A college bookstore is about to receive the books it has ordered for the fall semester. A quick scan of the sales reports shows that many of the hardcover business texts cost the store $24. The markup on retail is 25 percent. How much does the owner need to charge in order to attain his markup? In answering this question, the same five steps are used.

1. Determine the cost of the good, which in this case is $24.

2. Find the required gross profit figure (25%) in the *Markup as Percentage of Retail Price* column in Table 15-1.

3. Find the corresponding figure opposite 25% in the *Markup as Percentage of Cost* column in the table, which is 33.33%.

4. Multiply the cost of the good ($24) by that figure to get the dollars-and-cents markup on cost. In this case: $24 × .33 = $8.00.

5. Add the markup on cost result ($8) to the cost of the good ($24) to arrive at the selling price: $24 + $8 = $32 selling price.

These calculations can be checked by determining the results of selling 100 textbooks.

Sales revenue (100 texts × $32)	$3,200
Less: cost of goods (100 books × $24)	2,400
Gross profit	$ 800

Gross profit as a percent of sales:

$$\frac{800}{3,200} = 25\%$$

Thus a markup of 33.33 percent on the cost of goods will produce a 25 percent gross profit.

In these two examples the selling price after markup was $40 and $32, respectively. However, the selling price is usually adjusted up or down to make the price more appealing, especially in the case of the portable radio, which the consumer does not *have* to buy. The student, of course, may feel that he or she cannot get through the course without the textbook. In any event, instead of charging $40 for the radio the retailer may price it at $39.95 or $41.95. The bookstore may do the same, opting for a final price of $31.95. This **psychological pricing** attracts people better than a price that has been rounded to the nearest dollar.

MARKON   In addition to the initial markup, many retailers also compute a markon. Simply stated, a **markon** is an increase over and above the initial markup on goods that will be reduced in price later on or that can be easily damaged or stolen. For example, high-fashion goods tend to have a limited market. Therefore, while a blouse may be priced at $29.95 initially, if it does not sell it may be marked down to $24.95 and then to $19.95. Realizing the unpredictability of the market, the retailer will add a sufficient markon to ensure that after markdowns the desired gross margin is maintained.

As an example, consider the case of the retailer who estimates that of the 300 blouses purchased last week, it will be possible to sell 100 at $29.95, another 100 at $24.95, and the last 100 at $19.95. Additionally, assume that the owner wants a gross margin on sales of 40% and that the cost of each blouse is $15. Using Table 15-1, it is obvious that a 40 percent markup on retail price requires the owner to add 66.67% to the cost. This results in a retail price of $25 ($15 × .667 = $10 markup plus the original cost of $15). Thus, the retailer must sell each blouse at an *average* price of $25. The retailer must add a markon to this price so that it can be reduced later on. Without going into the specific mathematical computations, the owner will average (just about) $25 if the three prices—$29.95, $24.95, and $19.95—are used and 100 blouses are sold at each price level. This is illustrated in the table below:

PRICE	BLOUSES SOLD	TOTAL
$29.95	100	$2,995
24.95	100	2,495
19.95	100	1,995
		$7,485

Dividing $7,485 by 300 gives an average selling price of $24.95.

SERVICE ENTERPRISES

There are many types of service enterprises, and their methods of pricing vary widely.[3] However, some general concepts apply. Most importantly, the enterprise must keep accurate records so that it can price for profit. Sometimes established prices are fixed by state boards, competing firms, or prevailing price schedules. In these cases the owner-manager needs simply to maintain costs at or below the accepted price.

Sometimes the owner-manager offers a new good or service and is unsure of what to charge. This requires the person to set what appears to be a fair price, analyze the results, and then adjust the price if necessary.

Still other times, as in service stations or businesses where the time of the job will vary, a **multiplier approach** is used. For example, assume that it costs a service station $10 an hour for one of its mechanics to service an auto. Additionally, the business must add in a cost for equipment and parts, the building itself, administrative overhead, and profit. This is the multiplier. Assuming that the multiplier is 2.8, the owner will charge the mechanic's wage rate times 2.8, the latter covering all other costs associated with the job. In the case of a four-hour job, then, the price is $10 \times 4 \times 2.8 = \$112$. So long as the multiplier is based on accurate cost accounting, it is a simple way to ensure pricing for profit in a service enterprise.

MANUFACTURERS

Small manufacturers set prices in accordance with the cost of production. If only one product is manufactured, it is usually not very difficult to determine the unit price. Production costs, distribution and selling costs, and a margin for profit are all added together to arrive at the final price. If competition is weak or demand is strong, the producer may raise this price. However, most manufacturers are not in a position to greatly alter prices. It is usually safest merely to meet the competition. (See Small Business Owner's Notebook: Pricing for the Product Life Cycle.)

---

[3]See Joe F. Goetz, Jr., "The Pricing Decision: A Service Industry's Experience," *Journal of Small Business Management*, April 1985, pp. 61–67.

■ SMALL BUSINESS OWNER'S NOTEBOOK ■

Pricing for the Product Life Cycle

 Customer demand and volume of sales will vary with the development of a product. Thus, pricing for new products needs to be adjusted at each stage of the product life cycle. The following outline provides some suggested pricing methods that relate to the different stages in the product life cycle.

PRODUCT LIFE CYCLE STAGE	PRICING STRATEGY	REASONS/EFFECTS
Introductory Stage Unique product	"Skimming"— deliberately setting a high price to maximize short-term profits.	If a product is truly one of a kind then the initial price is set high to establish a quality image, provide capital to offset development costs, and allow for future price reductions to handle competition.
Nonunique product	"Penetration"— setting prices at such a low level that products are sold at a loss.	Allows quick gains in market share by setting price below the competitors' prices.
Growth Stage	"Consumer Pricing"— combination of penetration or competitive pricing in order to gain market share. Depends upon the consumer's perceived value of product.	Pricing depends upon the number of potential competitors, size of total market, and distribution of that market.
Maturity Stage	"Demand-oriented" Pricing—flexible strategy that bases pricing decisions on the level of demand for the product.	Sales growth declines and customers are very price sensitive at this stage.
Decline Stage	"Loss Leader" Pricing—pricing the product below cost in an attempt to attract customers to other products.	Product possesses little or no attraction to customers. Idea is to have low prices bring customers to the newer product lines.

Source: Adapted from Colleen Green, "Strategic Pricing," *Small Business Reports,* August 1989, pp. 27–33.

ADVERTISING AND SMALL BUSINESS

The average individual is subjected to hundreds of advertisements every day. Some are radio and television messages, others are in newspapers and magazines and on billboards. In many cases, the ads have been purchased by large businesses, but small firms also advertise because they, too, know that advertising can pay off.

In fact, it is virtually impossible for a small business person to sidestep the use of advertising. When a salesperson greets a customer who enters the store the salesperson is, if only indirectly, advertising the establishment. Likewise, whenever the small business owner-manager displays an item of merchandise in the showroom, this is advertising. In the South, particularly, it is common for the businessperson to urge the customer to "come back and see us again"; this is another form of advertising. When a satisfied customer tells a friend about how good the store is, this, too, is advertising. However, while point-of-sale and word-of-mouth advertising will help a small business, they are not enough. To truly generate sales it is necessary to advertise on a larger scale. As a result, for the modern small business owner-manager, the question is no longer *if* advertising should be done, but *how much* should be done?[4]

ADVANTAGES OF ADVERTISING

Numerous advantages can be gained from effective advertising. One of these is drawing power. Good advertising is like a magnet. It will pull people into the store, and this is the first thing the small business needs.

Second, advertising can hold people as customers, which is important because many other firms out there want to take these customers away. Quite simply put, a business is either growing or contracting. For example, the National Retail Merchants Association has estimated that if the average store stopped advertising it would go out of business in three to four years because, on average, the store would lose 20–25 percent of its customers each year. A store with 1,200 regular customers must add one each day in order to replace the one it can count on losing.

In addition to attracting and holding customers, a variety of other advantages can be obtained through advertising. For example, advertising can help to identify a business with the goods or services it offers. This is often done through the use of a trademark or symbol. For example, if you were to see a Coke bottle without any writing on it, you would still recognize it as a Coca-Cola bottle. The shape of the bottle is distinctive. Likewise, the trademarks for many other large corporations are easily identified. Small businesses can do the same thing by getting their customers to identify their businesses with the services they offer. This is done by creating a distinctive piece of advertising or a logo that people will immediately associate with the particular business.

Other advantages of advertising include the ability to create goodwill, build confidence in the business, increase sales, speed turnover, and spread fixed expenses over a larger volume. In regard to the latter advantage, for example, if a store has a property tax of $1,000 and sells 10,000 units a year, then 10¢ from each unit must be put

---

[4]Regnor Seglund, "How to Reduce Advertising Costs," *Journal of Small Business Management*, July 1985, pp. 66–70.

aside to pay the property tax. However, if through effective advertising the store can raise its volume to 20,000 units a year, then only 5¢ from each unit need be put aside to pay the property tax.

KEEPING THINGS IN PERSPECTIVE

On the other hand, it is also important for the small business owner to keep things in perspective. There are a number of things advertising cannot do. For example, advertising is *not* a substitute or an aid for an inferior product or service. All advertising will do in such a case is call to the attention of the buying public that the business has a shoddy product.

Second, advertising will not lead to sales if there is poor followup in the store itself. The ad may get people to come into the store, but they will not buy or come back again if they are ignored or treated poorly.

Third, advertising cannot create overnight traffic, and a single ad is not likely to increase sales. Advertising must be continual.

DEVELOPING ADVERTISING APPEALS

With all of this in mind, the small business owner-manager is ready to develop an advertising appeal.[5] In so doing, he or she must remember that people do not simply buy *things;* they purchase goods and services that *will satisfy their wants.* They do not buy a car but, rather, a machine that will get them to work and take them on vacation. They do not buy a toothbrush, but an instrument that will help them clean their teeth and prevent cavities. People buy *value.* Thus an advertisement must communicate: "Buy at our store; we have the value you want." In more explicit terms, people want

- □ convenience and comfort
- □ love and friendship
- □ security
- □ social approval and status
- □ life, health, and well-being
- □ profit, savings, and economy
- □ stylishness

Of course, in trying to project the message that the store's products offer one or more of these things, the owner-manager must also keep in mind that there are three types of customers: those who are thrifty (bargain appeal); those who seek service (convenience appeal); and those who look for quality (snob appeal). By interpreting products or services in terms of these appeals, the small business owner-manager can begin to focus on the market niche the store is trying to capture.

---

[5]See "Advertising Strategy: Precise Objectives Optimize Investment," *Small Business Report,* October 1986, pp. 71–75.

SOME MORE THINGS TO KEEP IN MIND

One thing the owner-manager should know is that women tend to read advertising more than men. Additionally, women buy almost 80 percent of all necessities and they greatly influence most other purchases. Research shows that only at the lowest income levels do men exert greater influence than do women. Consequently, advertising should appeal to women.

Another thing the owner-manager needs to keep in mind is that a good advertisement has certain qualities. An effective ad

- ☐ IS SIMPLE   People can understand the message easily.

- ☐ IS INFORMATIVE   The message tells people something valuable or useful.

- ☐ IS ENTHUSIASTIC   The message is optimistic, showing that the company believes in its product or service.

- ☐ IS TRUTHFUL   The information is factual and honest.

- ☐ PROVIDES ESSENTIAL ANSWERS   The message tells *who* is providing *what, when, where, how,* and *why.* This makes the nature and purpose of the advertisement clear to people.

Additionally, the business should use the ad to present an image to the customer. People often buy on the basis of image. Where do we go to shop for furniture? Why, everyone knows that Store A has the best reputation (image) for furniture. Let's go there. Where do we go to buy suits? To Store B, of course; everyone knows that it has the best quality for the money. In cases like these a store is chosen because of its image. Advertising can help to create this image in the minds of the buying public.

DOING IT YOURSELF OR GETTING OUTSIDE HELP

Should the owner-manager write advertisements personally or use outside help? There is no "right" answer to this question, because of the number of variables involved. One of the first things to consider, however, is the cost of outside help. The cost of having an advertising agency write ads may be too high for a particular business. Additionally, there is the cost of transmitting them. For example, how much does one minute of radio time cost? One minute of television time? Or, if direct mailing is being considered, how much will it cost to direct mail to 1,000 people, including the cost of the mailing list? Many small businesses feel that until they can afford to spend a great deal on advertising, they are better off doing it themselves.

If this is the case, the owner-manager's next decision is what to include in the ad and what to omit. In short, he or she is concerned with what the advertisement should look like. The place to start is with what belongs in the ad. Then the owner-manager should see how competing firms are advertising, especially those known to be successful. Next, the individual should be able to get some useful ideas from suppliers, trade associations, and trade publications. Additionally, if the store is going to use radio or television advertising, these media will provide some aid. Finally, the individual could test the ad on some customers and employees to see whether they like it.

SELECTING THE RIGHT MEDIA

Owner-managers select forms of advertising, including newspapers, television, direct mail, and outdoor advertising. The following sections examine each of these.

NEWSPAPERS Newspapers are the favorite medium of retailers, because they reach the greatest number of consumers. They also receive the greatest percentage of the money spent on advertising in the country. Given the research data that a single newspaper is read by 2.7 people, the owner can multiply the paper's circulation by 2.5 to get a rough idea of how many people will see the ad. Of these, perhaps one-fourth will actually read the ad.

Before deciding to place a **display ad** in the local newspaper, however, the small business owner-manager must know something about the business's potential customers. If the enterprise is located in a large city, the individual may be paying for an ad that will be seen by a million people, of whom only 5 percent would shop at the store, if only because of travel distance. This owner-manager would be better off looking for a limited-circulation paper or a shopping paper that carries ads for local businesses.

Another thing to know about newspaper advertising is the importance of getting a good spot for the ad. While it is not always possible to obtain a guarantee for a specific location, it is usually possible to arrange to have the ad appear on a certain page or in a certain section. Occasionally, the owner-manager may find his or her ad at the bottom of the page, tucked between more imposing ads, or right next to an ad of a competitor. While these things cannot always be avoided, they can be minimized by preparing an ad that is well-designed, appealing, and interesting. In this way, it is less likely to get lost in the maze of an advertising page. Additionally, the owner-manager should be aware of some things that can help him or her get better space treatment:

1. Do not quibble with the newspaper's advertising department about insignificant details.

2. Write or type the copy plainly and without mistakes. This ensures that it will be typeset correctly.

3. Submit the copy well before publication deadline.

4. Except in rare emergencies, do not ask for any last-minute changes.

5. Pay the bill promptly. This keeps the business in good standing with the newspaper, and there is sometimes a discount for immediate payment.

We also need to consider newspaper **classified ads.** People typically use classified ads to look for specific items or services at low prices. Discounted lines of old models of major and minor household appliances are readily sold through these ads, as are used cars, antiques, scarce items, and distress merchandise, all of which can be inexpensively advertised in classified sections.

Telephone book yellow pages and classified sections in city directories are based on similar appeals, but they have somewhat greater prestige and give an impression of stability. They are particularly effective for service businesses where there is little opportunity for bargain sales or seasonal promotions. Directory advertising stresses availability, reliability, permanence, prestige, and economy.

RADIO–TELEVISION ADVERTISING Until recently radio and television advertising was so expensive that the average small business could not afford it. However, broadcasting stations now make significant efforts to bring costs within the budget of small advertisers. "Spot" advertisements, if worded properly and timed correctly, can get good results inexpensively. During the day, many people listen to the radio and this can be a very effective medium. During the evening, more people's attention is turned to TV, which makes it the preferable medium then. The following guidelines are useful when advertising on radio or television:

1. Small stations or stations in small towns are less expensive and can be very efficient in reaching a target audience.

2. Where possible, the owner-manager should choose the station that projects the strongest listener appeal. If several stations are available, the owner-manager should test them over a period of time to determine whether their usual programs are appealing to the store's potential customers.

3. Check the number of commercials that are broadcast. If there are a lot, the business's commercial could get crowded in with scores of others and not get much listener attention.

4. Study the station's programming schedule. Try to get time just before or during a program that has significant listener appeal. Sports events, for example, are excellent time periods for advertising male-appeal merchandise, sports equipment, and cars.

5. Make the commercial short and interesting. State the message efficiently. Catch the listener with the content and the sales pitch for action, and then stop.

DIRECT MAIL   Direct-mail advertising is more selective than newspaper or radio and television advertising. To ensure adequate but controlled coverage, it is important to use a selective mailing list compiled from the business's records or from various sources in the community. Telephone and city directories are also useful for this purpose.

There are many examples of direct-mail advertisements. Examples include the circulars sent to people's homes announcing weekly grocery specials and a letter from a store offering a special discount to those bringing the letter to the store with them. Many small businesses like this approach because it helps them to direct their ad at a particular market, especially when the business is mailing the ads to past customers. Other advantages of direct-mail advertising include the following:

1. The firm can say more than it can in newspaper or radio-television advertising.

2. It is possible to try novel ideas on selected clients.

3. There is a better chance to get across the "personality" of the business.

4. The firm can use a more personal approach and appeal.[6]

OUTDOOR ADS   Outdoor ads include painted signs, billboards, and electrical displays. These ads are directed at passersby. As such, they must be simple and to the point. Additionally, they must be strategically placed so that people can see them and act on them. For example, to locate a sign saying "Eat Here" 100 feet from a diner may be of little value; by the time people can read the sign, they have already driven past the diner. It is much better to place the billboard 200–300 feet down the road. Likewise, since the driver only has four to five seconds to read the message, it needs to elicit the desired action almost immediately. The message cannot encourage the individual to think about the matter; it must stimulate the person to slow down and turn into the diner's parking lot.

DOES ADVERTISING REALLY PAY OFF?

Many small businesses are reluctant to advertise because they are concerned about whether advertising really pays off. Obviously, effective advertising should increase sales volume, and this in turn can be used to pay for the advertising and provide a greater profit to the owner. To ensure that it does pay off, the owner-manager needs to include the expense of advertising in markup calculations. Additionally, a specific amount of money should be put into the operating budget for advertising. One way of determining "how much" is to find out the national average of advertising percentages to sales ratios for the type of business and then adjust this figure for local conditions.

A number of tests can be used to measure response to an ad. They vary by the type of ad and the medium that was used. For example, if it is a newspaper ad with a coupon, the small business owner can easily determine the number of coupons that were redeemed in the store. However, this will not tell the whole story, because some of the people who came into the store may have purchased more merchandise

---

[6]See Erika Kotite, "Opportunity Knocks with Mail Order: Who Will Buy?" *Entrepreneur,* February 1991, pp. 90–99.

than what was advertised. Others may have decided not to take advantage of the coupon but bought something else. So the number of coupons only provides general feedback on the ad's effectiveness. To determine the full impact of the ad the owner has to compare daily or weekly sales against the same time the year before to determine whether any significant sales increases can be attributed to the increased flow of traffic in the store.

A second way of testing an ad's effectiveness is to include a hidden offer or a special phrase such as "When you come in tell us 'Big Bob' sent you." People who ask for the hidden offer or use the special phrase quite obviously have heard or read the ad and are acting on the message. If more than one ad is being run, the owner can compare the number of people responding to each. In this way, the owner may find that, for example, radio ads are more effective than TV ads.

A third way of testing the effectiveness of an ad is to simply examine actual sales of the product(s) being advertised. If there is a special sale on an item and the store sells twice as many as it has in recent weeks, quite obviously the ad worked. If sales remain the same as always, the ad was ineffective.

Of course, except in the case of coupons or other items that people bring into the store with them, it cannot be said that *every* new sale is a result of the advertising program. Conversely, if business starts to drop off it might be argued that the drop off would have been ever greater if there had been no advertising program. All of these measurement methods are basically *indirect.* The owner is using the best possible judgment, but there is no direct proof that the person is right. Yet this is the best the owner can do, for even large corporations measure the effectiveness of their advertising indirectly by gauging how many people hear or see their ads and then act on them. The estimates provide only general feedback on the effectiveness of the program. In summarizing tests of advertising effectiveness, Luthans and Hodgetts wrote:

> All of these tests provide only an indirect measure of advertising effectiveness. We do not know for sure that ads that are read and/or remembered will produce sales. However, until someone designs a more direct type of test for evaluating advertising effectiveness, current procedures will have to do.[7]

SELLING: SETTING THE STAGE

The art and science of selling is important to the survival of every small business. Obviously the owner-manager cannot do all of the selling; he or she must have help. Therefore, in setting the stage for an effective sales force, the owner-manager must organize the firm appropriately, obtain prospective salespeople, screen them, and select those that seem to have the greatest promise.

STEP ONE: ORGANIZE FOR SALES

The first consideration of the owner-manager, who often ends up being the sales manager as well, is to organize the sales force. This begins with a determination of what everyone in the enterprise is supposed to be doing. If the business has more

---

[7]Fred Luthans and Richard M. Hodgetts, *Business* (Hinsdale, IL: The Dryden Press, 1989), p. 365.

Table 15-2 Outline for a General Sales Job Description

SALES
Sell the line, demonstrate. Handle questions and objections. Check stock—discover new product uses. Interpret sales points of the line to customers. Assess customers' needs. Emphasize quality. Explain company policies on price, delivery, and credit. Get the order.
SALES PROMOTION
Develop new prospects and new accounts. Distribute literature, catalogs, desk pieces. Know and use company's advertisements and promotions. Evaluate effectiveness of company's advertising programs.
GOODWILL
Counsel customers on their problems. Demonstrate loyalty and respect for the company.

Source: *Managing to Sell* (Washington, D.C.: Small Business Administration, 1976), p. 43.

than one office, attention will also have to be given to territorial assignments. Additionally, if special knowledge of the merchandise is required or if the owner-manager has a wide offering of merchandise, it may be necessary to divide the selling work by line. For example, in hardware stores one salesperson may sell power tools, while another sells garden supplies. If the business has only a few product lines, however, all of the salespeople may sell any of the goods to customers.

One way of determining what everyone should be doing is to develop job descriptions for the salespeople. Job descriptions specify each person's job. As a business grows, more types of marketing jobs, ranging from advertising and sales promotion to purchasing and selling, may be needed. Table 15-2 lists some duties to consider in putting together general sales job descriptions.

STEP TWO: IDENTIFY POTENTIAL SALESPEOPLE

Once the organization's sales structure is established, it is time for the owner-manager to turn to the identification of potential salespeople. Before deciding on the specific type of individual that is needed, the owner-manager must examine the needs of the business. Of course, all salespeople need a number of general characteristics. For example, they should be in good health, have some experience in selling, and, most important of all, have a pleasing personality.

After determining the type of person that will fit the bill, the owner-manager must find the individual. Good salespeople are hard to get.[8] They have no trouble finding jobs; there is strong demand for them. Nevertheless, a number of sources can

---

[8]See Charlene Herried, Mark Peterson, and Donna Chang, "Type A, Occupational Stress, and Salesperson Performance," *Journal of Small Business Management*, July 1985, pp. 59–65.

be tapped. First, some of the present employees who are not currently selling may fit the bill. Another source is people who sell for other companies. Institutions are another source of prospective salespeople; colleges and universities, high schools, trade schools, and correspondence schools have placement offices that can serve the small business owner-manager. Newspapers, school papers, and trade journals have also proved effective in attracting qualified prospects. Other sources include voluntary applicants, employment agencies, and recommendations from employees or customers.

STEP THREE: EVALUATE THE PROSPECTS AND DECIDE ON THEM

From among the prospective salespeople, the owner-manager must choose those that are most likely to do the best job. One way of screening out the least desirable ones is to gather information on each with an application form. This form should provide background information that will help the owner-manager compare the candidates.

Then there is the interview. During this stage of the screening process the owner-manager can evaluate the prospective candidates' personality, attitudes, and character. Many owner-managers prepare a checklist of questions to ask during the interview. This helps to ensure that they do not omit an important question and helps them evaluate all the applicants in a consistent manner.[9]

SALES TRAINING

Regardless of how much time, effort, and money is spent selecting good salespeople, it will be wasted if the firm does not follow through with an effective training program. Sales training can be the single most important factor in a successful selling operation.

Sales training is vital to the small business owner-manager.[10] Most small businesses are engaged in retail sales, and it is in this field that the poorest selling job is being done today. Part of this poor showing is the result of low pay. Many salespeople are paid a straight salary—one that is insufficient to attract highly competent personnel. An equally important reason for poor sales performance is the lack of training and guidance.

How does a small business train employees for selling? By emphasizing *service*. The salesperson's job is to carry out a transaction that is mutually profitable and satisfactory to both the store and the purchaser, and in the process gain a permanent customer. In so doing, the salesperson must know four fundamental areas of knowledge, often referred to as the **four knows:**

1. Know yourself.

2. Know your company.

3. Know your product or merchandise.

4. Know your customer.

---

[9]See "Building a Sales Force—The Key: Effective Hiring Program," *Small Business Report*, November 1986, pp. 71–77.

[10]"Sales Training Methods," *Small Business Report*, June 1986, pp. 32–33.

KNOW YOURSELF

The first thing a good salesperson must know is himself or herself, specifically, the image he or she projects to others. What type of physical impression does the person make? Are the individual's clothes appropriate? Is the person clean and well-groomed? Does he or she stand erect and assume a posture that inspires confidence?

Additionally, a good salesperson should have a well-modulated voice, and always speak in terms of the customer's needs. For example, instead of trying to sell someone a shirt by saying, "I like this one," the person would be better off saying, "This shirt is very durable and will withstand a great deal of washing and ironing." In the first instance the salesperson put himself or herself first. In the second instance the salesperson tried to explain how the shirt would be a good buy for the money. Remember, an effective salesperson sells *value*—the product's value to the customer.

Finally, to be successful as a salesperson, the individual must have **social intelligence.** The person must exhibit tact, diplomacy, judgment, and a knack for knowing the right thing to say and do at the right time. A good salesperson, for example, never loses his or her temper or argues with the customer. All this does is scare off or aggravate a prospective buyer. If the customer does not feel that a particular product or service provides the value he or she is seeking, the salesperson should not push it any further. The customer may return in the future and buy. Therefore, once the salesperson realizes that the store does not have what the customer needs, the salesperson should switch from selling to maintaining goodwill. "I'm sorry we don't have what you need today. However, do come by again soon if we can be of service."

KNOW YOUR COMPANY

A good salesperson knows something about the history, policies, and procedures of the firm. In particular, the salesperson should be aware of the business's present goals and objectives, its organizational framework, and its management. The salesperson should also be well versed on various company policies, such as those related to customer service, sales, and advertising. He or she should know the rules and regulations that apply to work schedules, uniforms, equipment, credit, collection, and inventory control. Finally, the salesperson should have some knowledge of the particular industry or trade and of the competition within the field.

KNOW YOUR PRODUCT

A knowledge of the product line is essential to selling. A salesperson cannot sell a good or service unless he or she is familiar with the product. Of course, if there are 10,000 items being sold, no salesperson is going to know all there is to know about each item. However, the salesperson should have a general knowledge of the various lines. Additionally, if the product is expensive, complicated, or technical, it is even more important that the salesperson know about it.

Consider the case of hardware salespeople. From which of these salespersons would you buy a hammer?

▶ *Salesperson 1*
"Here are our hammers right here. This is a quality hammer. Yes, sir, we sell a lot of these hammers . . ."

▶ *Salesperson 2*

"Let me show you our best-quality hammer. It is made of crucible-case steel and is fully chrome-plated. This means the head will last a lifetime and it will not rust. The face and claws are tempered just right so the hammer will not crack or break. The claws are split to a fine point, which means that you can easily pull even the smallest nail with it. Look at this handle. It is made of selected second-growth hickory for extra strength; and the handle has a quality mahogany finish. Notice that the handle is put in with an iron wedge so it will not come loose . . ."[11]

Most people would prefer to buy from the second salesperson. This individual knows the product and is aware of its value to the customer.

KNOW YOUR CUSTOMER

The salesperson must know the customer, and it helps to know the customer's name. If people introduce themselves at the beginning of the conversation, the seller should continually refer to them by name. This boosts the buyer's ego and shows that the salesperson has an interest in pleasing them. People appreciate this personal approach.

Why do people buy at one store and not another? The most commonly cited buying motives are

- status
- emulation (imitation)
- social needs
- physical and mental health
- avoidance of effort
- cost savings

In order to understand the *why* of consumer behavior, the salesperson needs to know some things about sales psychology.[12]

SALES PSYCHOLOGY

People acquire particular goods and services for a variety of reasons. One is to satisfy such *physical needs* as food, clothing, and shelter. For example, why do people eat? Because if they do not they will die.

Another reason people buy things is because of *psychological desires.* Why do a lot of people eat at Joe's Restaurant? Because they feel it is the "in" place to eat. In this case, they satisfy a physical need while at the same time satisfying a psychological desire: the desire for status. Another reason is *imitation.* Since the "in" people in town eat at Joe's, other people feel that they gain status by imitating this pattern.

Regardless of the type of buying decision examiner, all of them are based on **buying motives.** In order to determine what a person's buying motives are, we have to

---

[11]*Managing to Sell* (Washington, D.C.: Small Business Administration, 1976), p. 20.

[12]See Rick Barrera, "A Direct Approach to Sales Prospecting," *Small Business Reports,* October 1990, pp. 33–38.

determine the underlying wants that are served by them. This is the focus of motivation research.

MOTIVATION RESEARCH

Motivation research, MR as it is often called, is carried out by specialists with backgrounds in the social sciences—mainly psychology and sociology. These specialists have learned that buying habits, like all actions, exist on three levels:

- ☐ **conscious motives,** the reasons people give for buying something
- ☐ **suppressed motives,** the underlying reasons, of which people are aware but unwilling to either admit or think about
- ☐ **unconscious motives,** some of the very real reasons people do things but of which they are unaware

Buying motives can be represented in the form of an iceberg; see Figure 15-2.

Until the MR people came along, most sales research was concerned with *what* consumers bought rather than *why* they bought it. By investigating the wrong things, some companies made very big mistakes. For example, prior to MR it was believed that farm machinery was purchased on the basis of profit and efficiency motives. How much did the equipment cost and how efficient was it when compared with competitive machinery? Through MR it was learned that farm machinery sells better when it is painted in eye-attracting colors; and the brighter the color, the better the farmers like it. Since farmers are unwilling to admit their preference for color, however, the manufacturers appealed to their conscious motives by pointing out the controls were made of different colors so as to allow for more effective handling, while other parts of the machine were color-coded for safety. When this explanation was given to the farmers, they consciously accepted what they unconsciously wanted.

MR has also shown that consumers are more often influenced by attitudes than by objective facts. For example, if a product comes in the shape, size, or color that the buyer believes is *appropriate* for this type of a product, it may be purchased regardless of the fact that there is a more efficient product on the shelf.

Figure 15-2
The Buying Motives
Iceberg

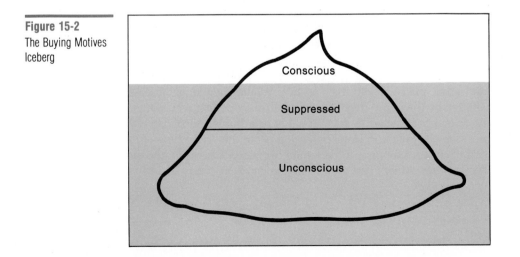

BUYING MOTIVES

What the salesperson needs to be concerned about is the buying motives of the individual. For example, why do people buy new automobiles? Many individuals say they purchase a new car on the basis of economy. Which model will be the least expensive to run? Research, however, shows that the cost of fuel and maintenance tends to be secondary to the cost of the automobile itself. In short, the reason people give for buying a car and the *real* reason are not always the same. Quite a few automobiles are sold on the basis of design and styling. If the person likes the car's looks and visualizes himself or herself behind the wheel, the person may well buy the auto.

Consumer products purchased at the supermarket also are purchased, in many instances, on the basis of appealing design; in this case we call it **packaging.** Then there is the matter of **image.** An executive on the way up may buy a Buick because he believes that this is the appropriate car for him. A surgeon may drive a Cadillac because she feels this is the right car for her. Bringing together these two ideas of packaging and image, buyers often have an image of what is contained in a package and buy on the basis of that unconscious image.

> If you don't believe the importance of packaging, consider what has happened in countless preferences tests where the same product was sent out in different packages but were said to be different. In one, involving coffee, a specially designed container was preferred by more than 80 percent of those tested. As a reward for their participation, the people taking the test were offered free samples of their preference of the three labels. But when asked if they cared if it was in a different container, almost all said no, as long as it was the same blend they had preferred in the test. Although they weren't conscious of it, they had imbued the coffee in the special jar with superior qualities. Consider, too, what happened when a major facial tissue company changed its package design to what they thought would be recognized as a handsomer package. Same name and same product, but almost overnight that company lost 25 percent of their former market. There was obviously some unconscious image that affected sales.[13]

Another factor influencing purchases is the product's brand name. Certain goods have a "right-sounding" name that triggers favorable associations or images when heard. Thus, small businesses often find that brand-name products sell much better than products with private labels.

And then there is the location of the store, which many MR specialists tend to feel is part of the packaging concept. There are places where people buy certain goods and other places where they do not. Where individuals choose to shop is largely affected by the image they have of the firm. A person who wants a cup of coffee may be favorably attracted to a McDonald's or a Burger King. However, the person may not stop at a Sheraton Hotel because it is not the "right type of place" to buy a quick cup of coffee. Likewise, if the family car needs a tune-up, the individual may take it back to the dealer. The gravity of the problem tends to influence where the car gets serviced.

---

[13]*Why Customers Buy (And Why They Don't)* (Washington, D.C.: Small Business Administration, 1967), p. 17.

A buying motive that cannot be overlooked is that of price. The price of the product can influence people to buy or not to buy. For example, a certain product may sell extremely well between $1.25 and $1.75 but not below or above this range. Of particular interest to MR specialists is why people will buy something for $1.25 but not for $1.20. The answer must be that there is a *right price.* Many women, for example, will not buy inexpensive cosmetics because they feel these products are cheap and will not enhance their image. Men are the same way. Many will buy an after-shave cologne for $10 but would walk away if the product were marked down to $5.

On the other hand, in the case of necessities or essential goods, people do tend to buy lower-priced merchandise. This is illustrated by the popularity of generic and "house-brand" food items. In fact, many shoppers pride themselves on getting the most for their food dollar.

As a result, it is necessary to examine the type of good that is being sold when considering the impact of price on buying habits. Keep in mind, however, that on an *overall* basis, price tends to be of secondary importance. In most cases, quality, suitability, and general satisfaction rank ahead of price.

THE SELLING PROCESS

If a salesperson understands sales psychology and buying motives, he or she should be reasonably effective in selling. However, the person should also understand the **selling process.** The "art of selling" marks the difference between a salesperson and an order taker. The sales process can be broken down into five steps:

1. Attract the prospect's attention.
2. Gain the prospect's interest with the sales pitch.
3. Create a desire in the individual for the product.
4. Establish confidence or conviction in the mind of the individual.
5. Secure action by the customer.

In accomplishing a sale, the seller must make the preapproach, the approach, and the presentation or demonstration, handle objections, and then close the sale. These things fit into the sales process in this way:

1. Attract attention through the **preapproach.**
2. Gain interest with the **approach.**
3. Create a desire with the **presentation.**
4. Establish confidence by **answering objections.**
5. Secure action by **closing** the sale.

■ SUMMARY

In this chapter pricing, advertising, and sales—all of them major marketing topics—were examined. The owner-manager's primary consideration in pricing must be cost. The owner cannot afford to sell below this level. In addition to cost the owner considers the nature of the product, the competition, marketing strategy, and general business conditions. Pricing for profit requires an understanding of the cost of goods, competitive prices, and market demand. Drawing on such considerations, small business people set their prices.

Competition is often keen among wholesalers, and retailers buy elsewhere if the prices are too high. As a result, the wholesaler sometimes cannot readily pass along manufacturers' price increases to the retailer. For this reason, the owner-manager spends a good deal of time watching wholesale prices to ensure that the business is not caught in a price-squeeze.

Retailers often price on the basis of a predetermined markup. For example, on certain goods it is typical to add on 50 percent. The markup table in Table 15-1 illustrates how these markups can be computed both as a percentage of cost and as a percentage of retail price. In addition to the initial markup, many retailers also compute a markon.

Service enterprises typically use a multiplier in arriving at their price. They determine how much it will cost to provide a particular service and then multiply the figure by the multiplier. For example, a service with a cost of $10 and a multiplier of 2.0 will be priced at $20.

Manufacturers set their prices in accordance with the cost of production. If they produce more than one product, some method is used for allocating costs. Then a margin of profit is determined and a final selling price set.

Advertising is important to a small business in creating drawing power and goodwill, building confidence in the business, increasing sales, speeding turnover, and spreading fixed expenses over a larger volume. The advertising of the small business should appeal to women and be simple, informative, enthusiastic, and truthful. Most small businesses write their own ads, rather than use an ad agency.

There are many advertising media, including newspapers, radio and television, direct mail, and outdoor advertising, each with advantages and limitations. The owner-manager, personally, must decide how much advertising will benefit the business and what medium should be used. Without effective advertising it is difficult for most small businesses to survive.

The success of every small business depends on its ability to sell goods and services. Thus, selling and the selling process must be understood to implement an effective sales program. Motivation research helps to explain consumers' behavior in purchasing goods and services. Knowing the findings of this type of research improves the entrepreneur's chances for business success.

■ REVIEW AND DISCUSSION QUESTIONS

1. What should an owner-manager know about the following price considerations: the nature of the product, the competition, marketing strategy, and general business conditions?

2. Explain how the following factors influence the owner-manager's objective of pricing for profit: cost of goods, competitive prices, and market demands.

3. How do wholesalers set their prices? Do they change these prices frequently? Explain.

4. One of the most important retail pricing concepts is that of markup. How does a markup work? Incorporate these terms in your answer: *cost, markup as a percentage of retail selling price, markup as a percentage of cost,* and *selling price.*

5. When would a retailer use a markon? Give an example, being sure to define the term *markon.*

6. Explain how manufacturers set their prices. Use an example in your answer.

7. In your own words, what are some of the advantages of using advertising?

8. Many suggestions have been made for improving advertising effectiveness. Some of them relate to the qualities of a good ad. Identify and describe at least four of these qualities.

9. Why are newspapers the most popular form of advertising for the small business owner? Also, what are some of the rules of thumb that can help the entrepreneur get better space treatment in newspapers? Explain.

10. How can a small business owner decide if radio or television advertising would be more beneficial? Cite and explain at least four guidelines he or she should follow.

11. When is direct mail an effective form of promotion? What about outdoor ads? Be specific.

12. What are the three steps the owner-manager should follow in setting the stage for selling? Describe each.

13. Explain the "four knows" of sales training.

14. Explain conscious, suppressed, and unconscious motives. Which best describes the buying motives of individuals?

15. There are five steps in the selling process. What takes place in each? Explain.

Case Studies

She's in the Driver's Seat

■ Wanda Hersey is confused. During the three years she has owned her jewelry store, she has spent all of her promotional money for radio advertising. Yesterday she was visited by a salesperson from the local newspaper. The man discussed the benefits of newspaper advertising and tried to show her that newspaper advertising provides much more coverage for the money. Wanda listened carefully and was very impressed with some of the things he said. She had not known about the advantages of newspaper advertising and was surprised with some of the data he cited.

On the other hand, Wanda is not yet ready to switch her advertising from radio to newspaper. "The salesperson was certainly convincing, and I don't doubt that his statistics were correct," she told Tom. "However, there are two sides to every story. There have to be some very good reasons for so many people using radio to advertise. And unless I'm mistaken, over half of my competitors advertise on the radio. After thinking it over, I called the marketing director at the radio station with some questions. She told me I had been given a very strong sales pitch by the newspaper sales person and invited me to lunch tomorrow. She wants to show me some research on the benefits of radio advertising. I'm looking forward to hearing what she has to say."

Tom listened quietly. Then he asked, "What are you going to do? Have you given it any preliminary thought?"

Wanda smiled. "I'm going to listen closely and take notes. Then I'm going to call up the newspaper salesperson, tell him what happened, and give him a chance to take me to lunch and counter the radio salesperson's pitch. Then I'll think it over and make a decision. Who knows? I may call up the TV stations and ask them to talk to me, too. After all, I'm the customer and I'm in the driver's seat. If they want my business, they're going to have to sell me."

1. What are the benefits of newspaper advertising? Identify and describe two.

2. What are the benefits of radio advertising? Identify and describe two.

3. How should Wanda determine which advertising medium is best for her firm? Be complete in your answer.

Harry's Problem

■ Frances Conway is a new salesperson at Pushling Home Appliances. The store has seven salespeople on the floor at all times. Additionally, Harry Pushling, the owner, is always in the store and he spends a great deal of his time either selling or supervising the salespeople.

Frances has been working at Pushling's for three months and her performance has been poor. Harry knows from past records how much a new person should be able to sell and Frances is doing about 60 percent of the amount, so he decided to keep an eye on her for a couple of weeks.

During this time he saw a number of problems in her sales approach, delivery, and close. For example, with one customer Harry noted that she rushed her sales delivery and seemed more interested in getting the person to buy something than in trying to determine what would be best for the individual. Another time Frances explained the benefits of a product to a prospective buyer and acted hurt when the person asked some questions that revealed he did not understand all of her explanation. In a third instance Harry noticed that Frances was rude to a customer who seemed unable to make up her mind about a purchase. In still another case Frances tried to hurry a sale, and the customer told her off. After this happened Frances sulked and refused to wait on customers for almost an hour.

Harry does not have a formal training program, although he does have weekly sales meetings where selling techniques are discussed. However, he does not feel this approach is sufficient to improve Frances's selling effectiveness. He believes she needs more direct training, but he is unsure of what form this should take.

1. What type of training does Frances need in order to be a more effective salesperson?

2. How should Harry go about improving her sales effectiveness?

3. Does Harry need a formal training program? Could you give him any other recommendations regarding selling? Explain.

You Be the Consultant

GAMES FOR SALE

The "Toy Store" is a retail outlet that caters to adults as well as to children and teenagers. The store carries the types of items found in most other toy stores as well as unique games that appeal to teenagers and adults. Included in the latter category are mechanical games of skill. The "Toy Store" has an agreement with a large manufacturer, by which it serves as the only retail outlet for its games within a 50-mile radius. Because of patent rights, the manufacturer is the only firm currently producing these games. His typical toys are priced in line with the competition. The unique games, however, are not. In fact, the owner of the store, who has total control over the pricing of the games, is determined to charge what the market will bear. Unfortunately, he does not know how to go about setting the *best* price because he does not have any guidelines to follow. He has looked for similar games in some of the large department stores in the hope that he could charge 20 percent over this amount. However, he has found nothing.

One of the things he has been considering lately is that of putting a 50 percent markup on the games, in contrast to the 33 percent he gets on the typical toys. With a 33 percent markup on the games, he is unable to keep enough in stock. Demand is so high that he continually runs out. On the other hand, he is concerned about pricing too high and losing customers.

One of his friends has told him that a number of factors must be taken into consideration when pricing. Some of these are the nature of the product, the type of competition, the marketing strategy that the business has typically used, and the state of the economy. However, the owner is unsure of how these particular factors affect the pricing decision.

Actually, what the owner wants to do is simply determine an ideal markup for the goods, price them at this level, and be done with the matter. He wishes he knew more about pricing. Not having had any real training in setting prices, however, he believes that the best thing he can do now is price the games extremely high and, if they do not sell, then start reducing the price downward to the point where supply and demand balance out. He realizes that this is a trial-and-error approach, but it is the best he can think of under the circumstances.

Additionally, the owner does not know very much about advertising. He tends to run the same basic ad week after week. It shows the picture of a couple of the store's toys, usually one of the typical toys and one of the games, and relates the prices of each. The purpose of the ad is to attract people to the store. Although the store is doing quite well, the owner believes that his ads could be improved. The problem is that he lacks the inspiration for improving them. He simply writes the ads on the basis of instinct.

■ **YOUR CONSULTATION** Assume that the owner is a personal friend of yours and has related the above information to you. As best you can, give him your recommendations regarding the pricing of the unique games. Also, explain to him how he can change prices in order to maximize his profits without losing customers. Finally, give him some suggestions for improving his advertising. Be as specific as possible.

Customer Credit

Objectives

Customer credit is another important marketing tool. It can stimulate sales, help the owner-manager analyze customer buying habits, and serve as a basis for advertising and promotion campaigns. Our first objective in Chapter 16 is to examine the link between sales and credit. Then we discuss the various kinds of credit—charge account credit, installment credit, and trade credit. Our second objective is to look at the Truth-in-Lending Act and note the ways it regulates credit sales. The third objective is to study how credit is used by retailers, wholesalers, service establishments, and small manufacturing firms. When you have finished studying the material in Chapter 16 you will be able to:

1. *Discuss the relationship between credit and sales.*
2. *Describe how the following kinds of credit work: 30-day charge accounts, revolving charge accounts, installment credit, and trade credit.*
3. *List the things a business must tell the customer before a revolving charge account is opened.*
4. *List the things a customer must be told on his or her monthly credit statement.*
5. *Identify the things a buyer must be told when an installment contract is used.*
6. *Explain how to set up a retail credit system.*
7. *Tell how wholesalers and service businesses go about extending credit to their customers.*
8. *Describe how a manufacturer gathers credit information on its customers and explain the various credit terms it extends to them.*

CREDIT AND SALES

The decision to offer credit to customers is a wise one for many small business owner-managers. Sales are often made because customers know they can "charge it." Furthermore, credit records allow the owner-manager to analyze customer buying habits, discover opportunities for sales promotions, and detect declines in purchases that indicate trouble spots for the firm.

Most importantly, credit is a sales tool. Many customers are accustomed to charging purchases, especially large ones, and paying for them later. This is not only a convenient method of buying things, it also allows the individual who does not have sufficient funds on hand to take possession of the goods and make payment at a future date. Also, by delaying payment the buyer is able to use tomorrow's "soft dollars" instead of today's "hard dollars." The longer one puts off paying, the easier it should be to meet old bills.

Another major reason why small businesses need to consider the use of credit is to meet the competition. Large retail stores such as Sears, Penney, and Ward all offer credit. And so does just about everyone else. Competition demands that the small business consider it.

Finally, and often overlooked by small business, credit records are an excellent source of customer information. Who buys what, when, and why? Questions like these can often be answered by analyzing credit sales records, and the answers can serve as a basis for advertising or promotion strategies. For example, a business that services autos might put its credit customers on a twelve-month list and send them a card to remind them that it is time to get their car serviced again. A toy store that sells a birthday toy to a parent can use a mail ad the next year to remind the parents to come in again and look at the new games that have just arrived. Charge customers tend to be more loyal than cash customers. A credit agreement creates a bond between the buyer and the business, and this relationship can be cultivated.

KINDS OF CREDIT

There are two kinds of credit: consumer credit and trade credit. Consumer credit is used by individuals for purchasing at the retail level. Trade credit is extended by one business firm to another to facilitate the sale of commercial or production goods.

CONSUMER CREDIT

The many types of consumer credit can be categorized as either charge account credit or installment credit.

CHARGE ACCOUNT CREDIT　One kind of charge account credit is the **30-day charge account,** which allows the customer to buy merchandise on credit and pay for it at the end of the month. Some customers simply tell the proprietor to "charge it," although most businesses prefer to have the individual sign for the goods. In any event, the owner sends a bill at the end of the month, and the customer is expected to pay immediately. In recent years, because of the large number of 30-day accounts, some firms have put their customers on different 30-day cycles. For example, a store with 2,500 30-day accounts will bill 100 of their customers every work day. In this way, the typical end-of-the-month billing charge is reduced, and the business has a steady flow of income rather than a large amount of money at the beginning of the month followed by very little until the end of the next 30-day cycle.

The other kind of charge account is the **revolving charge.** In this case, the individual does not have to pay the entire bill at the end of the month, but a minimum payment is required. The rest of the bill is carried on the books, and the individual can charge up to a predetermined credit level, say, $500.00. For this amount of credit, the typical finance charge is 1.5 percent monthly with the charge based on the average daily balance. This is usually calculated by adding the balance outstanding for each day of the month and dividing by the number of days in the billing period. Table 16-1 provides an example of a customer's revolving charge account for a year's time.

Table 16-1 A Revolving Charge Account

	PURCHASES	PAYMENT	INTEREST CHARGE	BALANCE
				$500.00
January	$200.00	$300.00	$6.00	406.00
February	125.00	75.00	6.84	462.84
March	50.00	300.00	3.19	216.03
April	110.00	85.00	3.62	244.65
May	300.00	200.00	5.17	349.82
June	135.00	275.00	3.15	212.97
July	150.00	150.00	3.19	216.16
August	225.00	150.00	4.37	295.53
September	90.00	150.00	3.53	239.06
October	50.00	50.00	3.59	242.65
November	100.00	190.00	2.29	154.94
December	400.00	200.00	5.32	360.26

Few stores, unless they are quite large, issue their own credit cards or directly provide a revolving charge. However, they do honor the credit cards of other organizations that offer such credit. The most common are VISA and MasterCard, which are almost universally accepted by merchants. Others include Diners Club and American Express, which are very popular among businesspeople.

The credit card companies pay the business and, in turn, collect the bill from the customer. For this service most charge the business a fee of about 5 percent. Thus, for every $10 of merchandise the business sells, it might receive $9.50. Why would a small business be interested in honoring those credit cards? Two big reasons are that the credit card company guarantees payment of the account and that many customers shop only where they can use a credit card.

INSTALLMENT CREDIT   Installment credit is used when customers buy merchandise that is fairly expensive and they want to finance it over time. Typical installment purchases include appliances, autos, and boats. When the small business owner sells something on an installment contract, the good serves as collateral for the loan. (In fact, if the merchandise cannot be repossessed, installment credit is out of the question.) In this way, if there is a default, the refrigerator, car, or boat can be repossessed.

Few small firms can afford to carry an installment contract; they need to get their money back into the business. As a result, they often sell the contract to a bank or finance company. The bank or finance company receives the price of the merchandise and the credit charges over the life of the contract, while the small business receives a net settlement from the transaction.

Banks tend to pay more than finance companies for installment contracts, because they purchase them, **"with recourse,"** meaning that if the customer does not pay, they get their money back from the small business. Since their risk is limited, they are willing to pay a higher percentage of the contract price. Finance companies pay less because they purchased **without recourse;** if the customer does not pay, any loss is theirs.

TRADE CREDIT

Trade credit is extended by business firms to other business firms. For example, manufacturers often extend it to their wholesalers, and wholesalers to their retailers.

Trade credit is important to businesses for two reasons. First, it is a means of simplifying payment. Rather than writing a check every time something is bought, the account is settled at the end of a specific time period, such as 30 days. Second, credit serves as a financing device, providing a free or low-cost loan, depending on how quickly the bill is paid.

In most cases, trade credit is given on an open account. At the end of a particular time, such as 30 days after the customer receives the statement, the bill is due. However, there are variations of this. For example, in some cases a 2 percent discount is given if the invoice is paid within the first 10 days of receipt. In other instances, 60-, 90-, or 120-day billing periods are permitted because this is the normal turnover period for that business's inventory. At the end of this time, the entire bill is due, and if it is not paid, a finance charge can be assessed. Realistically, however, manufacturers know that these finance charges will not be paid unless it is standard in the industry. Otherwise, the purchasers simply ignore them. Furthermore, although discounts are only supposed to be taken for early payment, in some industries buyers take them regardless of when they render their payment. Thus, actual terms of payment are often dictated more by industry practice than by the firm issuing the credit. In most industries, however, the seller determines the credit collection.

REGULATION OF CONSUMER CREDIT

Whenever people buy things on credit there is the possibility of confusion. Two of the most frequent consumer questions are How much is it costing me to use credit? and What is the total price of the product including finance charges? In an effort to help consumers, the **Truth-in-Lending Act** was passed by Congress. The purpose of this law is to ensure a meaningful disclosure of credit terms so that the buyer is able to compare the various types of credit available and choose the one that is best. The buyer is entitled to know all of the finance costs associated with the transaction. In particular, the law requires specific disclosure for revolving charge accounts and installment contracts.

REVOLVING CHARGES

The Truth-in-Lending Act provides that before an individual opens a revolving charge account, he or she must be given the following information:

1. The conditions under which a finance charge can be made and the period within which, if payment is made, there is no finance charge.

2. How the balance on which a finance charge can be imposed will be determined.

3. How the actual finance charge will be calculated.

4. The periodic rates used and the range of balances to which each rate applies, as well as the corresponding annual percentage rate calculation to the nearest quarter of one percent (0.25 percent). For example, the rate will be 1.5 percent monthly on all charges up to $500 and 1 percent on everything above this amount.

5. The way in which additional charges for new purchases are calculated.

6. A description of any lien the creditor can acquire on the customer's property, such as the right to repossess the boat or household appliance for failure to pay.

7. The minimum amount of money that must be paid on the bill for the time period under discussion. For example, each month the buyer must pay 10 percent of the outstanding bill or $10, whichever is greater.[1]

Periodic statements must be sent to every customer with an outstanding balance of $1 or more. Information must be provided on the current state of the account and any activity that has taken place since the last billing period. Specifically, the following information must be provided:

1. The unpaid balance at the beginning of the current billing period.

2. The amount and date of each new transaction during the billing period as well as a brief description of the item, unless this was previously given to the customer.

3. Any payments or returns of merchandise made by the customer.

4. The finance charge expressed in dollars and cents, as well as in terms of the annual percentage rate.

5. The periodic rates used in calculating the finance charge and the range of balances, if any, to which they apply.

6. The closing date of the billing cycle and the unpaid balance as of that date, which will be the beginning balance for the next period.[2]

INSTALLMENT CONTRACTS

Installment contract credit terms must also be communicated to the buyer. As with revolving charges, there are a series of things that must be told to the customer. Among the most important of these are

1. the selling price of the product

2. the down payment and the trade-in allowance

3. the amount financed

4. all prepaid finance charges

5. the number, amount, and dates of payments

6. the total dollar amount of finance charge

7. a description of any penalty charge for prepayment of the principal.[3]

In those cases where the installment contract involves the installation of merchandise in the home, the Truth-in-Lending Act grants the customer the **right of recession.** This is the right to change one's mind and cancel the contract. If exercised in

---

[1]*Understanding Truth-in-Lending* (Washington, D.C.: Small Business Administration), 1989.

[2]*Understanding Truth-in-Lending.*

[3]*Understanding Truth-in-Lending.*

writing within three business days following the date of sale or the date required disclosures were made, whichever is later, the buyer need not go through with the sale.

RETAILING CREDIT

In recent years, many customers have begun using retail credit. Numerous reasons can be cited, including the facts that it is a quick, easy way to pay for purchases, the retailer provides a complete record of charges and payments, and finance charges are tax-deductible. However, this explains only why customers use credit. Why do small businesses make it available? Some of the reasons they do are that they can

1. secure additional business from current customers at little or no extra cost
2. attract new customers who will buy only on credit
3. expand sales and thereby increase profits
4. compete with other stores that offer credit to their customers
5. get an edge on competitors who do not offer credit

ESTABLISHING A CREDIT SYSTEM

There are a number of important steps in establishing a retail credit system. Prime among these are

1. the credit application
2. the credit check
3. establishment of a line of credit
4. setting forth of the terms of payment
5. controlling the account
6. taking appropriate action to settle the account

THE CREDIT APPLICATION Depending on the size of the store and its philosophy of management, there are a number of ways of getting credit applications. In small stores, the salespeople or owner may personally solicit applications, or all regular customers may be sent an application and urged to apply. Most stores, however, have a sign urging people to ask for a credit application. Exhibit 16-1 provides an example of a typical application.

CREDIT CHECK If the customer is known to the store, a credit check may not be deemed necessary. However, if the person is new to the area or the personnel do not know the applicant, the services of a credit bureau are in order. **Credit bureaus** are service agencies that gather, compile, and distribute information on the assets and financial obligations of consumers. These bureaus are supported by merchants and businesses that are interested in obtaining credit checks on people. When one considers that most adults have had credit in one form or another—a charge account with a local merchant, an oil company credit card, a VISA card—it is obvious that a credit history can be compiled. More than 2,200 retail credit bureaus nationwide

Exhibit 16-1 Sample Charge Account Application

Charge Account Application

NAME _____
     MR., MRS., MS.

ADDRESS _____

SPOUSE'S NAME _____

OWN HOME OR RENT? _____ TELEPHONE _____

HOW LONG AT ABOVE ADDRESS? _____

PREVIOUS ADDRESS _____

EMPLOYED BY _____ HOW LONG _____

POSITION _____ INCOME PER MONTH _____

BUSINESS PHONE _____

PREVIOUS EMPLOYER _____

IF SELF-EMPLOYED, NAME OF BUSINESS _____

DRIVERS LICENSE # _____ EXP. DATE _____

ACTIVE CHARGE ACCOUNTS:

1. _____ # _____

2. _____ # _____

3. _____ # _____

VISA # _____ EXP. DATE _____

MASTERCARD # _____ EXP. DATE _____

AMERICAN EXPRESS # _____ EXP. DATE _____

MAJOR OIL CO. CREDIT CARD # _____ EXP. DATE _____

BANK _____ SAVINGS _____ CHECKING _____

CHARACTER REFERENCES:

1. _____

2. _____

3. _____

ALL OF THE ABOVE QUESTIONS MUST BE ANSWERED BEFORE APPLICATION CAN BE CONSIDERED.
I UNDERSTAND THAT THIS IS A 30-DAY ACCOUNT AND MUST BE PAID UPON RECEIPT OF STATEMENT.

SIGNED _____
                 APPLICANT'S SIGNATURE

belong to a national trade association, the Associated Credit Bureaus, so no matter where people move in the country a retail merchant should be able to get information on them.

When requested, the credit bureau provides the prospect's credit record, but it does not give an opinion on whether the individual is a good credit risk. This decision is left to the business owner. When the credit report indicates that the application should not be given credit, the person can be turned down. However, under the **Fair Credit Reporting Act,** the business must tell the applicant the name and the address of the credit bureau supplying the report. In this way, if the report is incorrect the individual can take steps to have it corrected.

ESTABLISHMENT OF A LINE OF CREDIT   If the customer is judged to be a good credit risk, the owner-manager must then decide on a line of credit. On 30-day charges, the buyer is usually allowed to purchase without restrictions. In most cases, the outstanding bill is less than $100. However, on revolving charges, where the business can lose quite a bit of money if the customer cannot pay, a credit limit is established. Depending on the individual's income (which should be obtained on the credit application and then verified in the credit check), this amount typically ranges between $500 and $1,000. If a customer requests a larger line of credit, the owner determines whether an increase is justified. The manager has a dual responsibility to the customer: to give credit where it is justified and to refuse it when the buyer seems to be overextended.

SETTING FORTH THE TERMS OF PAYMENT   The owner-manager should be sure that the customer understands the method of payment and the credit terms. If the customer is expected to pay off the 30-day charge within 30 days and fails to do so, there may be a $1\frac{1}{2}$ percent finance charge. Additionally, the owner-manager may refuse to allow further charge purchases until the bill is paid. The customer should understand all of these conditions before using the credit. This way, there are no hard feelings if problems develop.

CONTROLLING THE ACCOUNT   From time to time, every retail store that offers credit has trouble collecting an account. However, there are ways of reducing losses, such as not allowing customers to exceed their credit limit and freezing credit when accounts are delinquent. The business owner-manager must keep several factors in mind when collecting delinquent accounts:

1. The older an account, the less likely it is that the money will be collected. Early action is needed.

2. If there are many delinquent accounts, time must be taken away from regular business duties to collect them.

3. When a good customer becomes delinquent the store will lose all of that customer's future business, hence the need to be prudent in the granting of credit.

4. Customer credit problems can create a dilemma for the business: its funds can become tied up, which impairs its ability to take advantage of cash discounts and meet its own credit payments.

How can the business deal with collection problems before they become serious? The first way is to keep good records. Who owes how much? Who is in arrears?

Exhibit 16-2 Sample Accounts Receivable Analysis

ACCOUNTS RECEIVABLE ANALYSIS, MONTH ENDING JUNE 30, 19—						
Name & Address	Under 30 Days	30–60 Days	60–90 Days	Over 90 Days	Total	Action Taken
William Adams 94 Elm Street	$ 80	$ 135			$ 215	
John Bickley 1324 Wadsworth Drive			$ 225	$ 75	$ 300	Will pay $1/3$ each of next 3 months.
Melinda Hudson 265 Fifth Street	$ 55				$ 55	
Harold Llewyln 2605 Fairfax Avenue				$210	$ 210	With collection agency.
Lucy Granada 381 Dorrell Drive		$ 50	$ 125	$ 25	$ 200	Will pay $1/2$ this month and $1/2$ next month.
⋮						⋮
TOTALS	$11,500	$3,500	$1,105	$500	$16,605	

What is being done about it? These questions can be answered with accounts receivable analysis. Exhibit 16-2 provides an example of an accounts receivable aging schedule. Note that some accounts have been outstanding more than 90 days. These are the critical ones and should be given primary consideration. The *Action Taken* column shows how the firm is following up on these accounts.[4]

A second useful rule of thumb is to compare monthly credit sales with monthly credit collections. If sales outrun collections, it means the firm has had a net increase in its outstanding credit. This, in and of itself, may not be bad. For example, during the winter holiday shopping season this may be a common occurrence. However, when the previous year's records are analyzed, there will be offsetting periods when credit collections outrun credit sales. If these patterns do not repeat themselves in the current year, it is a sign that credit is too easy to acquire, that collections are slipping badly, or that both of these things are happening.

TAKING APPROPRIATE ACTION   Exhibit 16-2 shows some actions that can be taken. The action that is appropriate for the situation is determined by the circumstances of the situation. In some cases, a discussion with the customer will indicate that he or she has overlooked the bill or wants to dispute some of the charges. These problems can be handled in a friendly, face-to-face conversation. Other times customers may have lost their jobs or overextended themselves and they owe money all around town. In this case, the owner should ask them to make some small payment on the bill each month. Also, if some of the merchandise can be returned it can be credited to their account.

---

[4]Robert A. Weissman and Reid L. Steinfeld, "Collecting Bad Debts," *Small Business Reports,* April 1990, pp. 43–47.

■ **SMALL BUSINESS OWNER'S NOTEBOOK** ■

Credit Insurance

Credit insurance provides commercial firms with protection from "catastrophic" bad debt losses. Of the several types of credit insurance available, the two issued most often are blanket and specific. Blanket coverage should be used by companies with several small accounts. Specific coverage is best used by companies that have a handful of major accounts.

Companies that tend to use credit insurance are those that have a few major accounts, those that are greatly affected by the economy, and those that make significant sales to high-risk customers. The benefits, of credit insurance include increased sales potential due to a willingness to extend more credit, improved receivables management due to a constant review and evaluation of customer payments, greater access to financing due to banker receptiveness to small firms protecting their cash flows, and improved business planning overall. The premium charged for credit insurance varies depending on several factors including the industry involved, the financial position of the company, and the credit ratings of insured accounts. Companies may use a strategy of self-insurance for smaller accounts and credit insurance for larger accounts.

Source: Thomas Owens, "Limit Bad Debt Losses with Credit Insurance," *Small Business Reports,* May 1990, pp. 38–42.

When many creditors are delinquent, personal contacts may prove difficult. In these cases, a form letter accompanying each bill should call the account's delinquency to the customer's attention. Some of the common appeals used in these letters include the is-there-anything-wrong or would-you-like-to-tell-us-your-story approach. Others urge the individual to be fair: "We sold to you because you told us you were honest. Are you now going to endanger that reputation by not paying?"

If these attempts at collection fail, there are still a couple of alternatives. One is to forget the matter, and on small accounts, this is exactly what the owner should do. It is costly to pursue collection past the letter-writing stage. Larger accounts, on the other hand, can be turned over to a collection agency. However, keep in mind that while this may result in success, the agency often takes a hefty fee, and the business will probably lose the customer. This action should be a last resort. (See Small Business Owner's Notebook: Credit Insurance.)

WHOLESALING CREDIT

Wholesalers sell to retailers, most of whom require credit. This is especially true in the case of small retailers. As a result, the wholesaler occupies a very important position. Refusal to give credit can result in a retail store's bankruptcy. On the other hand, an excessively liberal credit policy can also lead to problems for the retailer, and the wholesaler who extends the credit will have to bear part of the loss. How, then, should the wholesaler go about deciding who should get credit? A good place to begin is with credit analysis.

CREDIT ANALYSIS

If the retailer is large enough, it may be possible to learn its credit rating from an agency such as Dun & Bradstreet. Such agencies specialize in credit reporting and have financial data on thousands of businesses. Unfortunately, most retailers are small operations, so credit agencies do not have much information on them. In these cases, the wholesaler has to rely on past experience in judging the risk.

Astute wholesalers keep records on all their customers—what type of business they operate, what kinds of purchases they make, how much money they spend, and so on. These records provide information for gauging the amount of credit to allow and the terms of repayment to require. In particular, the wholesaler will have a good idea of the types of retail establishments that are a high risk and can then take the appropriate steps to ensure the safety of the credit line.

SERVICE BUSINESS CREDIT

Services are consumed as they are being rendered. A barbershop, a health spa, and a lawn-care business all sell nonreturnable products. As a result, service business credit is risky and it is less common than in other kinds of businesses. Nevertheless, many service enterprises are finding that they must offer credit in order to maintain their customers. Of course, this results in higher costs, which must be passed on to the customers.

MANAGING CREDIT

Service business credit is similar to retail credit in that the owner-manager follows the same steps in establishing a credit system. However, the control aspect is even more important, because there is no collateral or security upon which the business can fall back if the account becomes delinquent. All the owner can do is refuse further credit. Service establishments typically offer 30-day or 60-day charges limited to $100, so they do not stand to lose a great deal of money.

Additionally, it should be noted that credit is not as important to service enterprises as it is to other types of businesses. Quality is the major factor in drawing customers, and as a service business's reputation grows, so does its clientele. Credit plays a secondary role. (See: Small Business Success: Exotic Cuisine.)

MANUFACTURING ENTERPRISE CREDIT

Small manufacturing firms use credit as a sales tool in basically the same way as wholesaling establishments. However, the manufacturing enterprise has one distinct advantage: many of the wholesalers with which it does business have credit ratings. The same is true for retail or service establishments that buy directly from the manufacturer. Thus, a manufacturer's main concerns are obtaining credit information and establishing trade credit terms.

■ SMALL BUSINESS SUCCESS ■

Exotic Cuisine

 Long before any small business decides whether or not to make customer credit available, the company usually establishes a solid client base. Frieda's Finest/Produce Specialties is not a new venture by any means. Launched in 1962 by Frieda Caplan, it is a business that found a crack in the food industry, turned it into a niche, and then into a market. Today Frieda's Finest/Produce Specialties, Inc., is one of the best-known names in produce with over $19 million in sales in 1989.

Frieda's Finest/Produce Specialties began with mushrooms—fresh mushrooms. Few retailers at the time were able to market produce well, and Caplan's ability to do what other grocers could not gave her a start. With the advent of computers in the late 1970s, grocers realized that produce accounted for 30 percent of a store's profits, although it took up just 7 or 8 percent of the floor space. Frieda's Finest was ready to take advantage of this discovery and had been ready since 1962.

Frieda's Finest began as Produce Specialties, Inc., in a purple-trimmed stall in the Seventh Street Market in Los Angeles. After mushrooms came the Jerusalem artichoke, which is derived from the root of a sunflower. The company renamed the product the sunchoke and packaged it in order to keep customers from mistaking it for ginger root. Sales of the product shot up 600 percent in two months.

Since the sunchoke, Frieda's Finest has been making exotic produce user friendly with helpful hints, labels, and directions for cooking the more unusual items. The company was also responsible for promoting the Chinese gooseberry, now well known as the kiwi. Now the company is experimenting with marketing the green cactus pear, also known as the prickly pear. On the horizon is the winged bean from the Philippines. The company opens markets for unusual produce items, many of which previously may have been cultivated on no more than one acre of land.

Caplan attributes her success to outside factors. The most obvious is the societal trend toward healthier eating. She also claims that frequent-flyer plans have increased the customers' awareness of the exotic and raised the demand for unusual international cuisine.

Since only 100 plants have been cultivated out of 20,000 edible plants on this planet, it would seem that Frieda's Finest/Produce Specialties has quite a base from which to expand. The company provides scientists and growers with the market they need to explore and develop new fruits and vegetables, and these findings could eventually help to lessen the world hunger problem.

Source: Adapted from Dennis Rodkin, "Produce Pro," *Entrepreneur,* May 1990, pp. 138–44.

CREDIT INFORMATION

As noted earlier, one of the best places for a small manufacturing firm to get credit information is through Dun & Bradstreet. This agency publishes reference books that contain credit data on business firms. It also issues reports to members, supplies analytical information, and offers credit-checking services. These are available to members on a contract basis.

Additionally, credit information can be obtained through other groups such as local credit bureaus, sales representatives who are familiar with the firm, and personal interviews with the prospects during which key questions can be asked and a financial statement obtained. And then there are various special agencies that provide credit services to businesses. Many of these are affiliated with trade associations and have access to credit information on small firms. This often is released in the form of ratings books that indicate the prospect's general credit rating, current capital resources, paying habits, and other pertinent data. The latter include excessive returns of merchandise, unreasonable requests for service, troublesome practices, and chronic complaints without justification.

These types of sources can help the manufacturer construct a picture of how good a credit risk the prospect is. Based on this evaluation, a credit decision will be made.

The sale of exotic produce has made Frieda's Finest/Produce Specialties a success for thirty years.

CREDIT TERMS

Like other types of businesses, small manufacturers must be careful not to give credit to slow-moving accounts. When this occurs, vital working capital is tied up.

Most trade credit calls for payment within a given time period and, if the bill is paid early, a discount is given; that is, 2/10, net 30. In any event, the total bill must be paid within 30 days. For those firms that buy small quantities frequently, the billing may be under **middle-of-the-month (M.O.M.) terms;** that is, purchases bought before the middle of the month are billed as of the fifteenth. Buyers who pay by the twenty-fifth get a 2 percent discount, and the entire bill must be paid by the fifteenth of the next month.

Regardless of the billing cycle, the manufacturer must remain alert for delinquent accounts. In this regard, the controlling aspect of credit is similar to that employed by retailers. However, trade-credit terms vary. The larger the order size the more likely it is that the buyer will be given a greater discount or more lenient payment terms. In fact, many manufacturers give no discount unless a minimum order is placed. After all, the costs associated with filling a large order are not much greater than those for a small order. Thus, the discount serves to motivate the buyer to increase the order size while simultaneously ensuring greater profit for the manufacturer.

■ SUMMARY

Credit is an important sales tool for both consumers and businesses. One of the most popular forms of consumer credit is the charge account. The most typical forms are the 30-day charge and the revolving charge. Another is installment credit. Business firms, meanwhile, use trade credit in financing their operations.

Since consumer credit often results in the levying of finance charges, Congress passed the Truth-in-Lending Act. The Act has many provisions, but they are all geared to the same thing: providing information on exactly how much the credit will cost the user. This information is required for both charge accounts and installment loans.

Retailers often extend credit to their customers, and unless they are careful there is a good chance they will not be paid. As a result, the retailer needs to establish an effective credit system. The six most important steps in establishing a credit system are getting information about the customer with the credit application, evaluating the risk of extending credit to the applicant with the credit check, establishing a line of credit, setting the terms of payment, controlling the account, and taking appropriate action when an account becomes delinquent.

Wholesalers sell to retailers, and a refusal of credit can result in financial problems for a retailer. In making a credit decision, the wholesaler will try to obtain a formal credit report on the firm. If none is available, the wholesaler will look over the retailer's business and base the decision on a first-hand view of the operation.

Service establishments use credit similarly to retailers. However, credit is not the major factor in attracting customers to a service business. Quality of service is primary, and credit plays a secondary role.

Small manufacturing firms use credit in basically the same way as wholesaling establishments. However, since credit information on their customers is often available, their risk is reduced. Additionally, credit terms often vary with the size of the order, and the credit cycle may be set up to start in the middle of the month.

■ REVIEW AND DISCUSSION QUESTIONS

1. Explain how credit is a sales tool.

2. How does a 30-day charge account work?

3. When would a revolving charge be used? Explain how this type of credit works.

4. Who uses trade credit? How does it work? Be specific.

5. What are some things an individual must be told before opening a revolving charge account?

6. A number of things must be told to the consumer on periodic billing statements. List at least five of them.

7. Cite at least four things a customer must be told in an installment contract.

8. One of the most important things in giving credit is to establish an effective credit system. Describe the six steps of an effective system.

9. Describe at least two things a small business owner should do in controlling credit collections.

10. How do wholesalers go about extending credit to retailers? What does the owner-manager need to know about credit? Explain.

11. How important is credit to the small service enterprise? What does the owner of such a business need to know about credit? Explain.

12. How do small manufacturers get credit information on their customers?

13. Describe three kinds of credit terms small manufacturers give their customers.

Case Studies

Geraldine's Findings

■ When Geraldine Novak heard that her uncle had taken gravely ill, she hurried to the hospital. She learned that he needed surgery immediately, and would be confined to bed for at least ten weeks. Geraldine told her aunt, "If there's anything I can do, just let me know."

A few days later her aunt called her. "As you know," she told Geraldine, "Harold's store was just about a one-person operation. However, it looks like he won't be getting back there for quite a while. Since you're an independent sales broker and this is a slow time of year for you, we were wondering if you might be able to drop by the store a couple times a week to see if Sam needs any help with anything—actually just to help make sure the store will still be there when Harold gets back. I know Sam's a great salesman, but he knows nothing about the finances or things like that. We need some-one with some business experience to keep an eye on things for us." Geraldine told her aunt that she would drop by three times a week to see how things are going, pay the bills, and take care of general administrative matters.

While going through her uncle's accounts receivables this week, Geraldine found that a lot of people have 30-day charge accounts. When she aged the receivables, she found this:

DAYS OUTSTANDING	NUMBER OF ACCOUNTS
1–30	27
31–60	119
61–90	173
91 +	59

The total amount outstanding is $13,492, most of it in accounts more than 60 days outstanding.

When Geraldine told her aunt that a large number of customers have not been paying their accounts on time, her aunt did not appear surprised. "Oh, Harold has always had problems with that. Don't worry. I'm sure when he goes back he'll get everyone to pay their bills. It's just a matter of time."

Geraldine did not say anything more about the matter to her aunt. However, she wondered if she should try to collect the overdue accounts and take some action to prevent this from happening in the future.

1. Is the overdue account situation anything to worry about? Explain.

2. What might be the reason for this problem? Explain your reasoning.

3. If Geraldine were going to do something about it, what step(s) would you recommend? Be complete in your answer.

No Pangs of Conscience

■ When he opened his shoe store, Steve Alum knew that some customers would want to buy on credit, so he devised a credit application form. The form is quite simple. It asks for the person's name, address, telephone number, place of business, and two credit references. However, Steven never bothered to check the references. Since all credit was to be extended on a 30-day basis, he saw no problem in giving credit to those who asked for it. Of course, he did spend a few minutes talking to each applicant to see if the person appeared reliable, and a few times he did turn down a credit request. For the most part, though, credit was extended.

Now Steve is having a problem. Fifty of his approximately 200 charge customers are delinquent in their payments. Sending them bills every month is time-consuming and costly, but Steve is reluctant to give up on the accounts. Furthermore, many of the people still shop at the store, and while Steve refuses to give them further credit, this does not seem to worry them. They simply purchase for cash, and this makes Steve angry. Recently he told a friend, "They have money to buy the things they need, but they don't have money to pay me for the things they previously bought on credit. I can't believe it. Don't these people have any pangs of conscience?"

Steve is in a quandary. If he stops them from shopping at his store altogether, he will lose their new business. However, he needs to collect their old bills. If he pushes too hard he is afraid he will scare them off entirely.

Last week, Steve talked with his accountant, who told him that something has to be done. "Over $3,000 is owed to you by your customers. You can't afford to just write these bills off. Furthermore, they are sapping your working capital. You have to collect those bills—and soon. Otherwise, you're going to be in serious financial trouble."

1. What should Steve know about establishing a credit system?

2. How would you recommend that he go about resolving his dilemma?

3. For the future, what recommendations would you offer to Steve to prevent this problem from recurring? Explain.

You Be the Consultant

JEROME'S CREDIT PROBLEMS

The Curvall Auto Supply Company sells to large trucking firms, companies that own and operate their own trucking fleets, retail auto suppliers, independent service stations, and individuals who simply walk in off the street and ask for a particular item. The businesses with which Curvall deals all have credit arrangements with the company; the walk-in customers pay cash.

Recently, Curvall has been having some credit-related problems. First, it has been attempting to expand the number of trucking firms with which it does business. Credit terms to these firms have been 2/10, net 30. However, some of the companies they've been talking to are demanding 3/10, net 60. The owner, Jerome Curvall, is concerned that he will have to change the terms of credit for all the trucking firms if he alters his terms for the new customers. This will mean an increase in revenue but a larger amount of outstanding receivables and a greater risk to the firm. He is not sure if the change in credit terms is a wise strategy.

Second, Jerome has learned that a number of wholesalers to whom he has been selling are complaining that he is also selling to retailers, thereby infringing on their markets. Jerome has reaffirmed to them that his prices to wholesalers are more favorable than those to retailers because the wholesalers buy in much larger quantities. However, two retailers to whom he has been selling also buy in very large quantities, and Jerome has given the same discounts that he allows wholesalers who buy in those lot sizes. The problem Jerome sees here is that more and more retailers will try to bypass the wholesalers and buy from him in large quantities. If this pattern or buying behavior should persist, the wholesalers will no longer buy from him.

Of course, Jerome knows that five times more wholesalers than retailers buy from him. But the retailers have been increasing in number. If Jerome could deal directly with a large number of these retailers, each of whom was capable of acting as his or her own wholesaler, he would not have to worry about the complaints of the wholesalers. However, there is one very big problem that worries him. It is not difficult to get credit information on the wholesalers with whom he deals, but few of the retailers have a rating with Dun & Bradstreet or any other agency. Dealing with them is risky. In fact, an aging of his receivables reveals that none of the trucking firms have accounts outstanding more than 90 days and most of them are paying within 30 days. The wholesalers are a little slower, but Jerome's largest accounts are no older than 60 days. The retailers are the weak link. Sixty percent have been paying within 30 days, 20 percent within 60 days, 10 percent within 90 days, and the other 10 percent are over 90 days. Jerome found that 8 percent of his sales to retailers in the last year have proved to be uncollectible. In most of these cases, the retailer has gone out of business.

Finally, Jerome believes that if he can get on top of the credit aspect of his business he can use the information to help him in his advertising and promotion campaigns. However, he feels the first thing he must do is sort through all of the data, find out where his credit problems are, and take steps to resolve them.

■ **YOUR CONSULTATION** You have been hired as Jerome's consultant. First, provide him with some basic advice about how to establish a credit system. Second, give him your recommendations about how to deal with the wholesaler-retailer credit problem. Third, what would you suggest he do in collecting the late retail accounts, and how can he prevent late payments in the future? Finally, can an analysis of his credit business help him in developing an advertising promotion campaign? If so, explain how.

Part Five Case Study

BAR CODES, UNLIMITED: SELLING FILM MASTERS BY MAIL

BACKGROUND INFORMATION

You know them by those inch-long groupings of thick and thin black lines on a light background. They're bar codes, a system of written symbols used to quickly and accurately communicate product or item identification through electronic media. Bar codes are helping video owners solve a major headache—keeping track of hundreds of movie cassettes. They're helping book stores and book departments decrease cash inventory even while sales rise—by helping track thousands of titles quickly and easily. Professional offices such as that of lawyers, doctors, and accountants are using bar codes to bill time and to track client/patient documents that get passed around. Dosage control via bar coding is spreading rapidly in hospitals. The post office is installing a massive bar code sorting system aimed at cutting costs and improving the speed and accuracy of mail delivery. A major wood products manufacturer is planning to affix color-coded, pressure-sensitive Universal Product Code (UPC) labels on the end pieces of lumber. The airline industry is using bar codes to sort and track luggage more efficiently and accurately. And, penetration of bar coding in the food retailing industry, where it all began, is nearly complete.

BAR CODES, UNLIMITED

One supplier to the bar coding industry is Bar Codes, Unlimited, a small Dayton, Ohio operation started by Jay Dring in the spring of 1989. Prior to launching Bar Codes, Unlimited, Jay Dring had over twenty-seven years of retail experience, including ownership of his own retail store and eighteen years in sales with NCR corporation. In 1974, while with NCR, Jay helped introduce the Uniform Product Code symbol scanning system to the retail industry. In fact, he was a major player in the world's very first Bar Code Scanner installation in Marsh Supermarkets in Troy, Ohio, in 1974. Since then, he has been involved with thousands of other installations. All of Bar Codes, Unlimited's current business is developed through personal selling. Jay Dring now wants to test the viability of the direct response channel as the next step in his company's approach to marketing its products and services.

THE UNIVERSAL PRODUCT CODE

The key to the universal product code is its machine-readable bar code symbol for the 12-digit, all numeric code. This number is represented by a series of parallel light

This case was prepared by Herbert E. Brown, Wright State University, Paula M. Saunders, Wright State University, and Nabil Hassan, Wright State University, and is intended to be used as a basis for class discussion rather than to illustrate either effective or ineffective handling of the situation. Presented and accepted by the Midwest Society for Case Research. All rights reserved to the authors and by the MSCR. Copyrighted © 1990 by Herbert E. Brown, Paula M. Saunders, and Nabil Hassan.

spaces and dark bars which can be read by an optical scanner at the check-stand. The code number permits a computer to recognize the item. In most applications, there is no price or other information in the number. Instead, when read, the code number is sent to an instore, or remote, computer which contains constantly updated information, including price, on all items carried in the store, or items which are being monitored. The computer transmits back to the check-stand, or other input point, the item's price and description (which are instantly displayed on the customer's receipt tape) as well as relevant information on taxability, food stamp acceptance, etc. While doing this, the computer also captures and stores item movement information which can be aggregated, instantly compared or checked against other data, or analyzed and summarized in a wide variety of control reports.

FILM MASTERS

Film masters are the central ingredient in the bar coding process and are usually required whether the bar code will be printed directly onto a package label or onto pressure-sensitive labels which are later affixed to the package. Film masters are most easily understood as the bar code numbers translated into artwork. Technically, a film master is a negative or positive image of a Universal Product Code symbol that allows reproduction of the symbol. Because these are used to make printing plates, film masters are a critical element in any successful application of bar coding. The quality of the film master determines whether, and to what extent, the printed symbol will be scannable. Thus, if the translation from number to film master or artwork form is not done according to very strict rules, much can, and usually will, go wrong.

THE COST OF FILM MASTER/ADHESIVE LABEL FOUL-UP

Bar codes are usually printed on either adhesive labels or directly onto the product's packaging. Accordingly, poor bar coding quality results mainly from flaws either in adhesive labels or in the film masters used when printing adhesive labels or product packaging. A goof in either can be a major problem. For example, adhesive labels that customers can readily peel off will, in fact, often be peeled off by some customers. Some of these may even be placed on other merchandise as a way of getting the other merchandise for a lower price. Some very messy problems can result when adhesive labels do not adhere. For example, labels fell off a significant percentage of 50,000 packages of frozen smoked fish. Incorrect or unreadable codes can be a nightmare of cost and hassle. To see how a flawed film master adds up to a disaster for the brand's owner, one need only imagine a million units of a nationally branded item with a UPC code symbol printed from a plate produced from a flawed film master.

UNIFORM CODE COUNCIL

The chronology of events leading up to the present-day widespread use of the bar code technology and the Universal Product Code (UPC) dates back to about 1916. Rapid expansion of use began when the National Association of Food Chains initiated development of the UPC in 1969. Part of this included the establishment of an organization to act as a clearing house for manufacturers, retailers, and wholesalers participating in the system. This organization, the Uniform Code Council, Inc., headquartered in Dayton, Ohio (8163 Old Yankee Road, Suite J., 45458, 513-435-3870) is not a government agency. It is a private, voluntary organization formed specifically to control the issuing of manufacturers' code numbers, to provide detailed UPC information, and to provide world-wide coordination of bar coding for all member participants. The council's growing list of major sponsoring organizations include the Food Marketing Institute, the Grocery Manufacturers of America, the National American Wholesale Grocers' Association, the National Food Brokers' Association, and the National Grocers' Association.

Whenever a producer decides to sell a product through retail channels that use bar code scanners at their check-outs, a unique six-digit universal product code number which identifies the manufacturer must be obtained from the Uniform Code Council. (There is a one-time fee for this number that is based on retail sales volume and is a minimum of $300.) A five-digit number which identifies the specific item, and a twelfth check-digit, are added by the manufacturer or other number recipient. For example, the Crest toothpaste bar code number is 0 37000 00334 2. The UPC authorized unique manufacturer's (Procter & Gamble's) number is 0 37000. The item number, unique within Procter & Gamble's product line and added by Procter & Gamble, is 00334. The "2" is a check-digit. Scanners read the symbol, not the number. Thus, it is always the readability of the symbol and not the number that is at issue.

The above description is of the "A" version of the UPC Symbol. What is actually seen on Crest toothpaste is another version called the "E" symbol with the number: 0 373340 2 rather than 0 37000 00334 2. The zeros in the number have been suppressed. The "E" symbol is used on products when there is limited space for the symbol, such as on cigarettes, etc. The "E" version is constructed following the same rules as the "A" version and differs from it only in that some or all of the zeros in the "A" version code number are suppressed. This permits the symbol to be physically shorter without loss of information.

In either the "A" or the "E" case, the symbol must be printed to strict specifications, both as to size and location.

The "nominal" size is 1.020 inches high and 1.469 inches wide. This can be varied from 80 percent of nominal to 200 percent of nominal. No reduction, or expansion, beyond that shown in the UPC Symbol Specification Manual (a publication of the Uniform Code Council) is permitted. Violation of this rule can lead to poor scanning quality.

Placement of the code on the product package is also very critical because the more variation there is in symbol location, the more difficulty the check-out clerk will have in finding the symbol in order to pass it across the scanner. The Uniform Code Council supplies a "UPC Symbol Location Guidelines" manual which provides detailed, uniform rules for doing this.

The Uniform Code Council is not directly involved in the creation of film masters. It provides only manuals. Translating the code number into a machine-readable, bar code symbol that will appear on its product's package is totally the responsibility of the manufacturer. However, the council stands ready to provide additional informational assistance to insure that the number holder gets his or her bar code properly produced. This assistance includes offering new members lists of film master suppliers, lists of manufacturers of UPC label printing equipment, and lists of bar code consultants.

PRINTERS AND FILM MASTERS

Film masters have to be made in different specifications depending on whether flexography, gravure, or silkscreen printing will be used. For example, when using silkscreen, the printing process reproduces exactly what the film master dictates. However, if the printing is to be done using flexography, which uses a rubber plate, the pressure of the press will enlarge the bar code bars. To compensate for this, the plate bars must be smaller than the bar code specifications indicate. To make this happen, the film master must be correspondingly reduced so that plates made from them print correctly sized bar codes on packages or adhesive labels. These and other complexities motivate a majority of printers not to get involved in film master creation. As a result, users are often left with the responsibility for supplying their packaging or adhesive label printers with the film master. Users, in turn, nearly always find it cost-effective and expedient to turn to external suppliers for such services. By 1989, nearly 100 companies were known to be offering film master services. Among these was Jay Dring's firm, Bar Codes, Unlimited.

BAR CODES, UNLIMITED'S CURRENT PRODUCTS

Neither film masters nor adhesive labels are actually produced by Bar Codes, Unlimited. These are produced by suppliers. Bar Codes, Unlimited serves as a bar codes consultant and nationwide middleman or distributor for firms that actually make the film masters and adhesive labels. The company also serves both customers and suppliers as a kind of consultant-broker and quality control agency, making sure that the supplier produces correctly specified film masters and/or adhesives labels to exacting specifications for every customer. This, of course, demands a very close working relationship with suppliers. Dring had clearly established such a relationship by the early summer of 1990, and his fledgling company appears to be well on its way to success. Projected company sales, all of which are being made via direct personal contact by Dring, are approximately $150,000 for the 1990 fiscal year. At this time the firm has only two employees: Dring and a secretary.

BAR CODES, UNLIMITED'S CURRENT MARKETS

FOOD AND PHARMACEUTICAL Jay Dring's background and thorough familiarity with the checkout and scanning industry gave him instant credibility with several national chains in both the food and pharmaceutical industries. He chose to concentrate on these initially, selling them in person. Although film masters are a part of nearly every sale, adhesive labels are the most profitable part of his business.

THIRD PARTY SALES Dring also has had some success selling automotive accessory, food, and drug trade associations on "third-party" marketing of film masters and adhesive labels to their membership. Third-party marketing is a big business which involves selling the membership of a trade or other association under the auspices of the association. The buyer does business with the trade association, but the product or service is supplied by a third party. There are thousands of trade associations across the country. It appears, therefore, that these associations represented a very large and attractive market.

NEW MARKETS WITH DIRECT MARKETING POTENTIAL

As he continues to develop the food chains, trade associations, and pharmaceutical markets with in-person selling, Dring, like most good entrepreneurs, has begun to cast about for other markets and marketing approaches. Inspired by a continuing flow of new applicants for UPC numbers, Dring turned to direct mail as a method to get better leads from his current markets and possibly to make direct sales to others.

UNIFORM CODE COUNCIL NEW APPLICANT LIST   Each month approximately 800 applications for new UPC numbers are received by the Uniform Code Council in Dayton. When the applicant plans to print his symbol on a product's package, and usually when it has to be printed on adhesive labels (labels can be done on demand, without film masters, by many printing devices), a film master must be made for each of the products that the applicant plans to sell through a channel using bar code scanning. The names of the 800 applications accumulated during preceding months can be purchased from the Uniform Code Council for $.10 per name and used as a direct mail list.

There is, necessarily, a time lag between the time the applicant gets a number and the time the Uniform Code Council can make these names available. The Uniform Code Council has a cut-off date of two weeks before the names are made available. This delay works to allow a new UCC member to get his or her number and all UCC manuals before being solicited by film master suppliers. Thus, if a film master supplier buys the names every month, he would receive names of members who had joined the UCC between two and six weeks prior. By the time Bar Codes, Unlimited receives the names, many of the applicants have already transformed their UPC numbers into film masters and onto their packages. Nonetheless, for one reason or another, even after as much as six weeks, a sizeable percentage of this list is still in the market for film masters, adhesive labels, or consulting.

The Uniform Code Council list is not well-defined, and for its purposes, need not be. It is Dring's general belief that it contains a high percentage of "mom and pops" selling anything from cookies to ginseng roots. Small, but more sophisticated entrepreneurs, and large companies selling a new product through bar code scanning channels, are also thought to be prominent on the list. In sum, at the beginning of Dring's investigation, no one at Bar Codes, Unlimited knew for sure who was on a typical new list of applicants. (Note: The Uniform Code Council also markets entire category lists—pharmaceutical, industrial, apparel—and several subsets of food and grocery and food manufacturers.) Some of these lists number into the thousands. The purchase of a complete category list would enable Dring to approach all companies (or select companies within a category) known to have a Universal Product Code Number.

PRINTERS   On occasion, commercial printers and platemakers are competitors, but more often than not, both are also significant markets. New UPC recipients often turn first to their printers for help in translating their new UPC numbers into the proper symbols. Printers, in turn, not generally being specialists in the film master business but requiring a film master before they can proceed, often turn to someone else, such as Bar Codes, Unlimited for the service. Dring realized that these printers could be a major market for his services and that they would require unique promotions.

PACKAGED GOODS   Dring was also interested in an effort on the part of some major packaged-goods sellers to use bar codes to assess and increase the effectiveness of their promotional efforts. For example, a dog food seller promoted his dog food with specialized bar codes on the package. Contest entrants were asked to place these on an entry form sheet. When these were turned in for prizes, the seller could learn much about the who, what, when, and where of his dog food buyers. Initially, Dring was unclear as to exactly how this process worked, or even all of its purposes, but given the enormous amount of promotion going on in the packaged-goods industry, it sounded very promising to him.

OTHER MARKETS   It soon became apparent to Dring that bar coding was rapidly becoming used by many other industries and that although they may not be his most promising initial markets, they were certainly worth watching and contacting as soon as his resources permitted. Among those he noted were the hardware, home accessory, lumber, airline industries, and the post office.

COMPETITOR ACTIVITY

All of these markets were being pursued by a variety of direct mail competitors. At least thirteen of the firms pursuing the UPC applicants were known to be doing current mailings. This was known because a friend of Dring obtained a number for his product line and received thirteen different mailings offering him film master and related services. It was clear from the timing of the receipt of these mailings that all were buying the Uniform Code Council list and mailing it just as Dring planned to do.

Examination of the efforts of these mailers revealed a variety of approaches. Some asked for orders; other invited inquiries.

One of the simplest of these packages was a postcard. It had a bar code symbol on the top center of the front. Below this it had the firm's 800 number which was printed in large, bold print. On the back it had a sample bar code adhesive label. This led the eyes of the reader into a very simple message: the firm had been informed that the addressee had been assigned a manufacturer's number and that the firm was a qualified supplier of Bar Code Film Masters for UPC symbology. It went on to stipulate a vague "starting" per unit price and invited the addressee to call the 800 number for a quote. (Most prospects would not know it, but this competitor is a retired vice president of the Universal Code Council.) The other mailings range along a continuum of complexity all the way to one which came in an 8½" by 11" envelope containing an expensive brochure, a sales letter, several sample film masters, an order form, and even a small pamphlet analyzing when the use of bar codes was the right thing for a business to do.

All of the mailers offered quick turn-around on receipt of an order. Their prices ranged, or appeared to range, from ten to thirty-five dollars per film master. They "appeared" to range because exactly what could be received for whatever price was mentioned could not be known until the recipient accepted the mailer's invitation to call and discuss the firm's services and prices.

CHANGES IN THE COMPETITIVE ENVIRONMENT

In 1986 the typical firm offering film master services was run by a highly technical person who knew the bar code system and business thoroughly. At that time, bar code services were priced much higher, with film masters, for example, being sold for as much as one hundred dollars or more. Few mistakes were made by these suppliers because they knew what they were doing. Now, however, the field has attracted a large number of firms that some have termed "fly-by-nighters" who have only a very superficial knowledge of the technical details of the business, and in some actual cases, no real idea of what they are doing. This has driven both the prices and the quality of bar code services down and made the industry very competitive. This is particularly true when buyers can be convinced that one film master company is the same as any other, making price the only issue. This is untrue, but buyers often believe it.

ECONOMICS OF THE INDUSTRY

Most of the firms on the new applicant list are believed to be small; otherwise they would already have a bar code number and a well established bar coding system. Many of them are also believed to have only a few items, and most probably have only one or two items to be bar coded. Thus, the typical prospect on the list would need only one or two film masters. This distilled down to a very simple fact: there isn't much profit to be had selling film masters one at a time to this list, even at Bar Codes, Unlimited's current $19.95 price for one film master.

Bar Codes, Unlimited's average film master production costs are in the three to six dollar range, with the average direct variable production and warehousing cost per unit being about $5.00. The gross profit or marketing margin is, therefore, assumed to be approximately $15.00 dollars per unit. Economies of scale are present but very marginal in the production of film masters.

Low profit on film masters is offset by potential profits from adhesive labels and consulting. The situation most of the new bar code number applicants find themselves in, i.e., with existing inventories without bar codes on printed labels, etc., requires initial use of adhesive labels rather than printing directly onto the product package. That will come later. However, adhesive label orders could range upward to some very high and profitable numbers. For example, one book printer had 500,000 books with incorrect bar codes and had to "retrofit" them with adhesive labels placed over the original incorrect ones. Adhesive label orders from the new applicant list are estimated to fall for the most part in the five to fifty thousand label range.

Adhesive label costs to Bar Codes, Unlimited are in the following ranges:

1-5,000	$17-22.00/thousand,	Average	$18.50/thousand
5-10,000	11-17.00/thousand,	Average	14.00/thousand
10-25,000	3-6.00/thousand,	Average	4.50/thousand
25-50,000	1.50-3.00/thousand,	Average	2.25/thousand

Prices correspond to costs and normally reflect a 100% markup on costs. For example, an order for 12,000 might be priced at $9.00 per thousand which includes a markup which is 100% of costs, or 50% of selling price.

CURRENT DIRECT MARKETING PROGRAM STATUS

Dring's initial direct mail effort consisted of the letter shown in Exhibit V-1. The initial response to this letter, when mailed to the Uniform Code Council list, was virtually nil. However, after several weeks had elapsed, some calls did come in from

Exhibit V-1 Dring's Initial Sales Letter to the Uniform Code Council's New Applicants

---

BAR CODES, UNLIMITED, INC.
7651 East Von Dette Circle
Dayton, Ohio 45459
513-434-CODE

Dear U.P.C. Participant:

Your product is on the way to commercial success with the addition of the U.P.C. (Universal Product Code). Our firm is available to assist you in the implementation of your U.P.C. program. Bar Codes, Unlimited concentrates on product quality codes for a reasonable price and prompt service. Inferior codes can cause your product to be rejected by your customer.

PROFESSIONAL SERVICES

—Film Masters   —Symbol Verification
—U.P.C Consulting   —Prompt Service
—Implementation Planning   —Reasonable Price
—Pressure Sensitive Labels   —Customer Satisfaction

In 1974, I introduced the first U.P.C. symbol scanning system to the retail industry as well as federal and state agencies. My last 27 years of retail experience have afforded me the opportunity to demonstrate and install hundreds of scanning systems.

Bar Codes, Unlimited invites you to become a customer and grant us the opportunity to fulfill all your U.P.C. implementation needs.

John J. Dring
President

---

recipients and one of these turned into a significant sale. Dring thinks the results of his mailings should be much better and is thinking of consulting direct marketing professionals. Though he is not sure what they could know that could really help, he feels that there must be some way to use direct marketing to profitably access the Uniform Code Council list market.

Dring also has a near-term plan to generate leads among pharmaceutical companies. This could be a very profitable enterprise because pharmaceutical companies (which are already well established users of bar code scanning) sometimes buy hundreds of film masters each month. Unfortunately, it is not easy to determine who in pharmaceutical companies buys film masters. Thus, at this point, Dring is confused as

Exhibit V-2 Data Requested on Bar Codes, Unlimited's Order Form

On the "Date Needed" line, please be specific. Do not leave blank or use the terms "ASAP" or "Rush." Our manufacturing system makes use of the needed date as its priority for manufacturing sequence.

UPC VERSION   A—standard 10 digit version (excluding 1st and 12th digits)

                         E—zero suppression, 6 digit version (excluding 1st and 12th digits)

EAN VERSION   Standard 13 digit version (13th digit is for country) EAN stands for European Article Number.

NUMBER SYSTEM CHARACTER

0, 6, 7—General Merchandise items. 6 & 7 are also used in industrial applications

       2—variable weight items

       3—national drug code

       4—for retailer use without format restrictions

       5—coupons

       1, 8, and 9—not in use at this time

FLAG NUMBER   Please supply us flag numbers for EAN film masters

CHECK CHARACTER NUMBER   Please calculate and supply us with the check character number. It will be verified by the manufacturing computer. Should it be incorrectly calculated or an error made in the writing of the order, the symbol will be made according to the first eleven numbers on the order. However, the notation "Check character NBR: X (changed from Y)" will appear in the check character number portion of the film master carrier.

TWO AND 5 DIGIT SUPPLEMENTS   For use within the paperback and periodical industry. Leave this space blank if you do not want a supplemental master.

to how to go about generating leads in this industry. He feels, however, that the basic method has to be direct response of some sort.

The pharmaceutical company market, like most other markets, has many firms which already have UPC numbers. Thus, high potential prospects in the pharmaceutical market and in the other markets may or may not appear on the Uniform Code Council monthly lists. Those that don't may represent even higher potential customers than those who do, but for different reasons. Dring feels that his program for developing these markets may, therefore, have to include a very specialized approach.

INFORMATION NEEDED ON A FILM MASTER MAIL ORDER FORM

First-time film master buyers do not need to see an order form, nor do they need detailed instructions. However, they do have to supply detailed application information. This would have to be collected over the phone whenever a first time mail order buyer is being serviced. (Repeat customers are supplied with copies of an order form for use when faxing repeat orders to Bar Codes, Unlimited.) Some of the directions for completing Bar Codes, Unlimited's necessarily complex order form are shown in Exhibit V-2.

Exhibit V-2 *(cont'd)*

MAGNIFICATION   The decimal equivalent of the percentage of reduction or magnification. Example: .85 is a 15% reduction, 1.00 is nominal size, 1.23 is a 23% magnification. The magnification will be specified by your printer.

BAR WIDTH   Bars may be reduced or grown. You must fill in this column to achieve reduction or growth. Example: .002 would be a two-thousandth reduction, .000 would be no bar width reduction.

Note: Printing method for bar width reduction.

1—Offset = Minimum 1/2 thousandth to minus 3 thousandths.

2—Flexography—need to know straight rubber-Photopolymer rubber = minus 3 thousands to minus 6 thousandths. Photopolymer = minus 1 thousandth to minus 3 thousandths.

3—Gravure = no bar width reduction.

4—Silkscreen = plus 2 thousandths.

NEGATIVE (NEG.) OR POSITIVE (POS.)   Your printer will want either of the above depending upon his process and internal methods of production. Not all printers using the same process will specify or request a symbol with the same specification.

RIGHT READING EMULSION, UP OR DOWN   Your printer will specify either of the above depending upon his process and internal method of production. Not all printers using the same printing process will specify or request a symbol with the same emulsion.

FOR FLEXO BARRIER   Check this column only if you want a flexographic barrier around the symbol. The barrier will replace the corner marks on the master.

CURRENT ORDERING PROCEDURES

At the present time, Bar Codes, Unlimited has only one incoming telephone line. Calls on this line are handled by an electronic system which facilitates the receipt of fax orders but permits normal handling of other calls. Thus, when a fax call is received, the system automatically directs it to the fax machine. But when a customer calls over the regular line, the system allows either Bar Codes, Unlimited or the caller to switch the call to the fax line, eliminating the need for placing another call. Thus, after-hours customers can:

a. Fax an order to Bar Codes, Unlimited.

b. Call and leave a recorded message.

c. Call and leave a recorded message, and by depressing 11 on their telephones, fax an order or other information to Bar Codes, Unlimited. (The system informs the caller of this option.)

Fax orders received by 7:30 P.M. one day can be turned around by 10:30 A.M. the next day if the customer's need is urgent.

DRING'S DILEMMA

As he surveys his situation and options, John Dring is unsure of what to do. He's sure direct response marketing will work, but he's tried it once and it didn't. He's decided to turn to experts for assistance. You're the "experts." Show him why and how direct marketing will work for him or prove to him why another direct response effort will be futile.

DISCUSSION QUESTIONS

1. Are the products and services offered by Bar Codes, Unlimited amenable to direct marketing techniques? Suggest the most likely role or roles direct marketing might play in a successful Bar Codes, Unlimited marketing program.

2. Offer an overall framework for guiding development of a direct marketing program for Bar Codes, Unlimited.

3. What appears to be the best basic direct marketing strategy for Bar Codes, Unlimited? ■

Part Five Entrepreneurial Simulation Program

SPREADING THE WORD

How do your customers find out about your store? How do they discover who you are, where you are, what types of shoes you have to sell, and what specials are being offered in your store each month? You could sit back, hoping they will walk past your store and notice how well you have stocked and decorated it. Or else you could reach out and pull them in. This is the purpose of advertising. Advertising gets the word out and attracts the attention of potential customers before they decide where to shop. The more you advertise, the greater the likelihood that consumers will choose your store to buy their shoes.

The appearance and the placement of the advertisement is as important as its cost. In the computer simulation, however, cost is the only aspect that need be considered when making decisions regarding advertising. The assumption is that there is a direct correlation between cost and the other more subjective aspects of advertising. The effectiveness of advertising in the shoe store simulation is measured by how many dollars you allocate to it.

As a store owner, you have to decide how much to spend on advertising each month and where to place your advertising dollars. You are not required to design media or to select the placement of your messages, but you must develop a plan of action regarding the type and the extent of your advertising. How well you do this will help determine how many customers you will attract to your store.

Market research data tells you how much you are spending each month on advertising, by shoe type and by store image, as compared to your competitors. You have the option to purchase or not to purchase such information. You also have the option to place your advertising dollars toward the promotion of a particular type of shoe or into image advertising for your store. Specific advertising relates to special shoe offerings during a particular month, while image advertising serves the broader function of telling your potential customers what kind of store you have. The impact of specific advertising lasts only during the month for which the ad is placed. Image advertising, like improvements to decor, has a 50 percent carry-over from month to month.

Advertising plays a significant roll in the customer's decision as to which store to shop in. Any store owner who chooses not to advertise is risking a loss of potential sales. The impact of a store's advertising for a particular type of shoe depends on how much is allocated to that shoe relative to the amount spent by other stores. If a store spends $100 to advertise boys quality shoes in a given month and another store decides to spend $1,000 to advertise the same shoe, the attraction of the second store attributed to specific advertising will be ten times as strong, assuming the two stores are equivalent in all other aspects such as price, location, and decor.

You have been operating your store for several months now. Think back over the decisions you have made regarding advertising during this time period. Review in your mind the process you went through to determine how much to spend each month on advertising and how you allocated those dollars. Were your decisions proactive, based on the goals and objectives you previously identified for the store? Or were your decisions instead reactive, based on what the other stores were doing with their advertising budgets and placement? Always keep in mind that you are the owner and proprietor of your store. The decisions you make should be based on your logic and analysis, not the decisions of your competitors.

As you plan your decisions for the next month, review your marketing goals and objectives. How well have your advertising decisions matched these goals and objectives over the past few months? Remember the impact that advertising has in attracting customers to your store, and try to be more effective in using your limited monetary resources to advertise both your types of shoes and your image as a retail shoe store.

DISCUSSION QUESTIONS

1. Compare the amount that you have spent each month to advertise each type of shoe with the number of pairs you have sold. Use a measure like advertising dollars spent per pair of shoes sold for this purpose. Document what this tells you regarding the effectiveness of your advertising. What could you do differently as a result?

2. Compare the measure identified in question 1 to the gross profit margin (selling price minus wholesale cost) for each type of shoe that you carry and advertise. Use a ratio of the two values (advertising dollars over profit margin) in this analysis. How much does this ratio differ for the different types of shoes in your inventory? What does this tell you about the relationship between advertising and price for each specific type of shoe that you carry?

3. Assume that you spend $500 each month throughout the year to promote a quality image for your store. Compute the value attributed to quality image advertising from these expenditures for each of the twelve months. What is the value remaining at the end of December that is transferred to good will?

4. In addition to the $500 each month spent to promote a quality image, assume that you spend another $500 a month to advertise your quality men's shoe. Use the factor weightings for store selection given on page 13 of the *ESP Student Manual* and multiply your specific advertising and image advertising values each month by their relative weights. What insight does this give you regarding the value associated with the $500 per month spent for each type of advertising? Would you modify your monthly decision strategy as a result? Why? How?

Part Six

Finances and Inventory Control

■ *Cash is the lifeblood of a small business. In order to successfully manage cash and profits, the small business owner-manager needs to understand finances and inventory-control measures. The overriding objective of Part Six is to present some of the tools and techniques that are useful to the small business owner-manager.*

In Chapter 17, we explain the typical financial statements that are kept by small businesses. We also focus attention on how small businesses maintain their records.

In Chapter 18, we examine financial analysis and budgeting. Emphasis is placed on balance sheet analysis and income statement analysis. We demonstrate the use of financial analysis and budgeting to improve management effectiveness.

Chapter 19 focuses on purchasing and inventory control. In addition to knowing about financial statement analysis, the small business owner-manager needs to understand how to achieve ideal inventory levels. This calls for purchasing policies and inventory-control techniques.

When you have studied the material in Part Six, you will be aware of the importance of finances to the success of small business operations. You will also understand how financial analysis is carried out and know about techniques for controlling inventory.

Financial Statements and Record Keeping

Objectives

In order to control his or her operations, the owner-manager needs to understand financial statements and the basic fundamentals of record keeping. These two areas are interdependent in that financial statements are put together from the firm's financial records. To build an understanding of these areas, it is best to start by examining basic financial statements and then move on to record keeping.

The first objective of Chapter 17 is to study the balance sheet. We will analyze the accounts found on this financial statement and answer the question, "Why does the balance sheet always balance?" Then we will examine the various sections of a typical income statement. Our final objective is to look at the way in which small businesses keep their books. Particular attention will be given to the Sales and Cash Receipts Journal and the Cash Disbursement, Purchases, and Expense Journal. After you have studied the material in this chapter, you will be able to:

1. Define the term balance sheet.

2. Describe what a balance sheet looks like, giving particular attention to its three main parts.

3. Explain why a balance sheet always balances.

4. Define the term income statement.

5. Describe the major components of the income statement.

6. Explain what the Sales and Cash Receipts Journal and the Cash Disbursement, Purchases, and Expense Journal are and how they can be used for overall control.

7. Discuss the options available to the small business owner-manager in maintaining the company's books.

8. Explain how a small business owner-manager should go about deciding whether to use a computer for handling record keeping and financial control.

FINANCIAL STATEMENTS

The basic financial statements with which a small business owner-manager needs to be familiar are the balance sheet and the income statement. The following sections examine each of these in depth, providing a foundation for understanding the books of record needed by all small businesses. (The importance of Financial Statements is emphasized in the Small Business Owner's Notebook: Early Warning Signs of Financial Trouble.)

THE BALANCE SHEET

A **balance sheet** is a financial statement that reports a business's financial position at a specific time. Many accountants like to think of it as a picture that is taken at the close of business on a particular day, such as December 31. The closing date is usually the one that marks the end of the business year for the organization.

The balance sheet is divided into two parts: the financial resources owned by the firm, and the claims against these resources. Traditionally, these claims against the resources come from two groups: creditors who have a claim to the firm's assets and can sue the company if these obligations are not paid, and owners who have rights to anything left over after the claims of the creditors have been paid.

The financial resources owned by the firm are called *assets*. The claims creditors have against the company are called *liabilities*. The residual interest of the owners of the firm is known as *owners' equity*. When all three are placed on the balance sheet, the assets are placed on the left, and the liabilities and owners' equity are placed on the right. It looks like this:

ASSETS	LIABILITIES AND OWNERS' EQUITY

An **asset** is something of value that is owned by the business. In order to determine an asset, it is necessary to:

1. Identify the resource.

2. Provide a monetary measurement of the value of that resource.

3. Establish the degree of ownership in the resource.

Most **assets** can be easily identified. They are tangible things such as cash, land, and equipment. However, **intangible assets** also exist. These are assets that cannot be seen; examples include copyrights and patents.

Liabilities are the debts of the business. These may be incurred either through normal operations or through the process of obtaining funds to finance operations.

■   **SMALL BUSINESS OWNER'S NOTEBOOK**   ■

Early Warning Signs of Financial Trouble

The importance of financial statements for small businesses cannot be overemphasized. In order to keep careful track of a small firm's health, the manager *must* understand the balance sheet, income statement, and cash flow statement, as well as sales journals and purchasing journals. If these statements are understood, then managers can recognize the signs of financial problems *before* those problems ruin the business. The following list illustrates many of the early warning signs of financial trouble that small business managers need to be aware of:

- ☐ Declining profits despite increased sales
- ☐ Decreasing gross margins
- ☐ Dwindling cash flow
- ☐ Shrinking market share
- ☐ Receding sales volume
- ☐ Increasing interest expenses in relation to sales
- ☐ Swelling overhead expenses
- ☐ Irregular, inaccurate, or untimely internally-prepared financial reports
- ☐ Repeated failure to meet overly optimistic sales forecasts
- ☐ Continual stretching of accounts receivable
- ☐ Growing write-offs of uncollectible receivables
- ☐ Increasing payables in relation to revenues
- ☐ Credit limits nearing exhaustion
- ☐ Increased pressure from creditors to pay
- ☐ A continual need to float checks due to bank overdraft
- ☐ Declining debt-to-worth ratio
- ☐ Lack of controls over purchasing and personnel
- ☐ Slow-turning or out-of-balance inventories

Source: Adapted from Thomas Owens, "Keys to Turnaround Management," *Small Business Reports,* March 1990, pp. 38–42.

A common liability is a short-term account payable in which the business orders some merchandise, receives it, and has not yet paid for it. This often occurs when a company receives merchandise during the third week of the month and does not pay for it until it pays all of its bills on the first day of the next month. If the balance sheet was constructed as of the end of the month, the account would still be payable at that time.

Liabilities are divided into two categories: short-term and long-term. **Short-term liabilities** are those that must be paid during the coming 12 months. **Long-term liabilities** are those that are not due and payable within the next 12 months, such as, for example, a mortgage on the building or a five-year bank loan.

Owners' equity is what remains after the firm's liabilities are subtracted from its assets. It is the claim that the owners have against the assets of the firm. If the business loses money, its owners' equity will decline. This will become clearer when we explain why a balance sheet always balances.

UNDERSTANDING THE BALANCE SHEET

In order to fully understand the balance sheet, it is necessary to examine a typical one and determine what each entry means. Table 17-1 provides an illustration. Note that there are three sections: assets, liabilities, and owners' equity. Within each of these classifications there are various types of accounts. The following sections examine each type of account presented in the table.

CURRENT ASSETS   Current assets consist of cash and other assets that are reasonably expected to be turned into cash, sold, or used up during a normal operating cycle. The most common types of current assets are those shown in Table 17-1.

Cash refers to coins, currency, and checks that are on hand. It also includes money the business has in its checking account and savings account.

Accounts receivable are claims of the business against its customers for unpaid balances from the sale of merchandise or the performance of services. For example, many firms sell on credit and expect their customers to pay by the end of the month. Or, in many of these cases, they send the customers a bill at the end of the month and ask for payment within ten days.

The **allowance for uncollectible accounts** refers to those accounts receivable that are judged to be uncollectible. How does a business know when receivables are not collectible? This question can be difficult to answer; it is not known. However, let us assume that the business asks all of its customers to pay within the first ten days of the month following the purchase. Furthermore, an aging of the accounts receivable shows that the following amounts are due the firm:

NUMBER OF DAYS OUTSTANDING	AMOUNT OF RECEIVABLES
1–10	$325,000
11–20	25,000
21–30	20,000
31–60	5,000
61–90	7,500
91 +	17,500

In this case, the firm might believe that anything over sixty days old will not be paid and write it off as uncollectible. Note in Table 17-1 that there is an allowance for uncollectible accounts of $25,000, the amount that has been outstanding more than 60 days.

Table 17-1 Gallagher Corporation Balance Sheet
for the Year Ended December 31, 1991

ASSETS			
Current Assets			
Cash		$200,000	
Accounts receivable	$375,000		
Less: Allowance for uncollectible accounts	25,000	350,000	
Inventory		150,000	
Prepaid expenses		35,000	
Total Current Assets			$735,000
Fixed Assets			
Land		$330,000	
Building	$315,000		
Less: Accumulated depreciation on building	80,000	235,000	
Equipment	410,000		
Less: Accumulated depreciation on equipment	60,000	350,000	
Total Fixed Assets			915,000
Total Assets			$1,650,000
LIABILITIES			
Current Liabilities			
Accounts payable		$150,000	
Notes payable		25,000	
Taxes payable		75,000	
Loan payable		50,000	
Total Current Liabilities			$300,000
Long-term Liabilities			
Bank loan			200,000
Total Liabilities			$500,000
OWNERS' EQUITY			
Contributed Capital			
Common stock, $10 par, 40,000 shares		$400,000	
Preferred stock, $100 par, 500 shares authorized, none sold		—	
Retained Earnings			
Total Owners' Equity		750,000	1,150,000
Total Liabilities and Owners' Equity			$1,650,000

Inventory is merchandise held by the company for resale to customers. Current inventory in our example is $150,000, but this is not all of the inventory the firm had on hand all year. Naturally, the company started the year with some inventory and purchased more as sales were made. This balance sheet figure is what was left at the end of the fiscal year.

Prepaid expenses are those expenses the firm has already paid but that have not yet been used. For example, paying insurance on the company car every six months is a prepaid expense entry because it will be six months before all of the premium has been used. As a result, the accountant would reduce this prepaid amount by one-sixth each month. Sometimes supplies, services, and rent are also prepaid, in which case the same approach is followed.

FIXED ASSETS **Fixed assets** consist of land, building, equipment, and other assets that are expected to remain with the firm for an extended period of time. They are not totally used up in the production of the firm's goods and services. Some of the most common types are shown in Table 17-1.

Land is property used in the operation of the firm. This is not land that has been purchased for expansion or speculation; that would be listed as an investment rather than a fixed asset. Land is listed on the balance sheet at cost, and its value is usually changed only periodically. For example, every five years the value of the land might be written up so that its value on the balance sheet and its resale value are in line with each other.

Building consists of the structures in which the business is housed. If there is more than one building, the total cost of all the structures is listed.

Accumulated depreciation on building refers to the amount of the building that has been written off the books due to wear and tear. For example, referring to Table 17-1, the original cost of the building was $315,000, but accumulated depreciation is $80,000, leaving a net value of $235,000. The amount of depreciation charged each year is determined by the company accountant after checking with the rules of the Internal Revenue Service. However, a standard depreciation is 5 percent per year for new buildings, although an accelerated method is sometimes used. In any event, the amount written off is a tax-deductible expense. Depreciation therefore reduces the amount of taxable income to the firm and helps lower the tax liability. In this way, the business gets the opportunity to recover part of its investment.

Equipment is the machinery the business uses to produce goods. This is placed on the books at cost and then depreciated. The total amount is the **accumulated depreciation of equipment.** In our example it is $60,000. The logic behind depreciation and its effect on the firm's income taxes is the same as that for accumulated depreciation on the building.

CURRENT LIABILITIES Current liabilities are those obligations that will become due and payable during the next year or within the operating cycle. The most common current liabilities are listed in Table 17-1.

Accounts payable are liabilities incurred when goods or supplies are purchased on credit. For example, if the business buys on a basis of net, 30 days, during that thirty days the bill for the goods will constitute an account payable.

A **note payable** is a promissory note given as tangible recognition of a supplier's claim or a note given in connection with an acquisition of funds, as in the case of a bank loan. Some suppliers require that a note be given when a company buys merchandise and is unable to pay for it immediately.

Taxes payable are liabilities owed to the government—federal, state, and/or local. Most businesses pay their federal and state income taxes on a quarterly basis. Typically, the first payment is made on April 15 of the current year, and the others are made on June 15, September 15, and January 15 of the following year. Then the business closes its books, determines whether it still owes any taxes, and makes the required payments by April 15. Other taxes payable are sales taxes. For example, most states and some cities levy a sales tax. Each merchant must collect the taxes and remit them to the appropriate agency.

A **loan payable** is the current installment on a long-term debt that must be paid this year. As a result, it becomes a part of the current liabilities. The remainder is carried as a long-term debt. Note in Table 17-1 that $50,000 of this debt was paid in 1991 by the Gallagher Corporation.

LONG-TERM LIABILITIES   As we have said, long-term liabilities consist of those obligations that will not become due or payable for at least one year or within the current operating cycle. One of the most common is bank loans.

A **bank loan** is a long-term liability brought about by a loan from a lending institution. Although it is unclear from the balance sheet (Table 17-1) how large the bank loan originally was, it is being paid down at the rate of $50,000 annually. Thus, it will take four more years to pay off the loan.

CONTRIBUTED CAPITAL   The Gallagher Corporation is owned by individuals who have purchased stock in the business. Various kinds of stock can be sold by a corporation, the most typical being common stock and preferred stock. Only common stock has been sold by this company.

Common stock is the most basic form of corporate ownership. This ownership gives the individual the right to vote for the board of directors. Usually, for every share of common stock held, the individual is entitled to one vote. As seen in Table 17-1, the corporation has issued 40,000 shares of $10 par common stock, with which it raised $400,000. Although the term *par value* may have little meaning to most stockholders, it has legal implications; it determines the legal capital of the corporation. This legal capital constitutes an amount below which total stockholders' equity cannot be reduced except under certain circumstances (the most common being a series of net losses). For legal reasons, the total par value of the stock is maintained in the accounting records. However, it has no effect on the market value of the stock.

Preferred stock differs from common stock in that its holders have preference to the assets of the firm in case of dissolution. This means that after the creditors are paid, the preferred stockholders have the next claim on whatever assets are left. The common stockholders come last. As seen in Table 17-1, 500 shares of preferred stock were issued, each worth a par value of $100, but none have been sold.

RETAINED EARNINGS   **Retained earnings** are the accumulated net income over the life of the corporation to date. In Table 17-1, the retained earnings are shown to be $750,000. Every year this amount increases by the profit the firm makes and keeps within the company. If dividends are declared on the stock, they, of course, are paid from the total net earnings. Retained earnings are what remains after that.

WHY THE BALANCE SHEET ALWAYS BALANCES

By definition, the balance sheet *always* balances. If something happens on one side of the balance sheet, it is offset by something on the same side of this financial statement or on the other side. In either event, the balance sheet is again in balance. Before examining some illustrations, let us restate the **balance sheet equation:**

$$\text{Assets} = \text{Liabilities} + \text{Owners' equity}$$

With this in mind, let us look at some typical examples of business transactions and their effect on the balance sheet.

A CREDIT TRANSACTION   The Gallagher Corporation calls one of its suppliers and asks for delivery of $10,000 worth of materials. The materials arrive the next day, and the company takes possession of them. The bill is to be paid within 30 days. How is the balance sheet affected? Inventory goes up by $10,000, and accounts payable rise by $10,000. The increase in current assets is offset by an increase in current liabilities.

   Continuing this illustration, what happens when the bill is paid? The company issues a check for $10,000 and cash declines by this amount. At the same time, accounts payable decreases by $10,000. Again, there are offsetting transactions, and the balance sheet remains in balance.

A BANK LOAN   As seen in Table 17-1, the Gallagher Corporation had an outstanding bank loan of $200,000 in 1991. Let us assume that the company increases this loan by $100,000 in 1992. How is the balance sheet affected? Cash goes up by $100,000, and long-term liability increases by the same amount; we again have balance. However, what if the firm uses this $100,000 to buy new machinery? In this case, cash decreases by $100,000 and equipment increases by a like amount. Again, there is balance. Finally, what if Gallagher decides to pay off its bank loan? In this case, the first situation above is reversed; cash and long-term liability decrease in equal amounts.

COMPANY SELLS STOCK   Let us look at one final example. Suppose the company issues and sells another 40,000 shares of $10 par common stock. How does this action affect the balance sheet? (This answer is rather simple.) Common stock increases by $400,000, and so does cash. Once more, there is balance.

   With these examples in mind it should be obvious that the balance sheet *always* balances. Every entry has an equal and off-setting entry so that:

$$\text{Assets} = \text{Liabilities} + \text{Owners' equity}$$

In fact, taking this idea a bit further, keep in mind that in accounting language the terms *debit* and *credit* denote increases and decreases in assets, liabilities, and owners' equity. This table relates debits and credits to increases and decreases.

CATEGORY	A TRANSACTION INCREASING THE AMOUNT	A TRANSACTION DECREASING THE AMOUNT
Asset	debit	credit
Liability	credit	debit
Owners' equity	credit	debit

Applying this idea to the preceding examples results in the following:

	DEBIT	CREDIT
Credit Transaction		
Materials	$ 10,000	
Current liabilities		$ 10,000
Bank Loan		
Cash	$100,000	
Long-term loan		$100,000
Stock Sale		
Cash	$400,000	
Common stock		$400,000
	$510,000	$510,000

THE INCOME STATEMENT

The **income statement** is a financial statement that shows the change that has occurred in a firm's position as a result of its operations over a period of time. This is in contrast to the balance sheet, which reflects the company's position at a particular point in time.

The income statement reports the success (or failure) of the business during the period. In essence, it shows if revenues were greater than or less than expenses. These revenues are the monies the small business has received from the sale of its goods and services. The expenses are the costs of the resources used to obtain the revenues. These costs range from the cost of materials used in the products the firm makes to the salaries it pays its employees.

Most income statements cover a one-year interval, but it is not uncommon to find monthly, quarterly, or semiannual income statements. All of the revenues and expenses that were accumulated during this time are determined and the net income for the period is identified. Many firms prepare quarterly income statements but construct a balance sheet only once a year. This is because they are far more interested in their profits and losses than in examining their asset, liability, and owners' equity positions. However, it should be noted that the income statement drawn up at the end of the year will coincide with the firm's fiscal year, just as the balance sheet does. As a result, at the end of the business year the organization will have both a balance sheet and an income statement. In this way, they can be considered together and the interrelationship between them can be studied. We will consider this in greater depth in Chapter 18 when we look at some of the financial ratios that simultaneously analyze balance sheet data and income statement data.

A number of different types of income and expenses are reported on the income statement. However, for purposes of simplicity, the income statement can be reduced to three primary categories:

1. revenues

2. expenses

3. net income

Revenues are the gross sales made by the business during the particular time period under review. Revenue often consists of the money actually received from sales, but it need not be the case. For example, sales made on account are still recognized as revenue, as in the case of a furniture store that sells $500 worth of furniture to the Adams family today, delivers it tomorrow, and will receive payment two weeks from now. From the moment the goods are delivered, the company can claim an increase in revenue.

Expenses are the costs associated with producing goods or services. For the furniture store in the preceding paragraph, the expenses associated with the sale would include the costs of acquiring, selling, and delivering the merchandise. Sometimes these are expenses that will be paid later. For example, the people who deliver the furniture may be paid every two weeks and so the actual outflow of expense money in the form of salaries will not occur at the same time as the work is performed. Nevertheless, it is treated as an expense.

Net income is the excess of revenue over expenses during the particular period under discussion. If revenues exceed expenses, the result is a net profit. If the reverse is true, the firm suffers a net loss. At the end of the accounting period, all of the revenues and expenses associated with all of the sales of goods and services are added together, and then the expenses are subtracted from the revenues. In this way, the firm knows whether it made an overall profit or suffered an overall loss.

UNDERSTANDING THE INCOME STATEMENT

In order to fully understand the income statement, it is necessary to examine one and determine what each account is. Table 17-2 illustrates a typical income statement. It has five major sections:

1. sales revenue
2. cost of goods sold
3. operating expenses
4. financial expense
5. income tax expense

REVENUE   Every time the business sells a product or performs a service, it obtains revenue. This is often referred to as gross revenue or **sales revenue.** However, it is usually an overstated figure because the company finds that some of its goods are returned or some customers take advantage of prompt-payment discounts.

In Table 17-2, sales revenue is $1,750,000. However, there are also returns and allowances of $50,000. These returns are common for companies that operate on a "satisfaction or your money back" policy. In any event, a small business should keep tabs on these returns and allowances to see if the total is high in relation to the total sales revenue. If so, the firm will know that something is wrong with what it is selling and it can take action to correct the situation.

Deducting the sales returns and allowances from the sales revenue, the company finds its **net sales.** This amount must be great enough to offset the accompanying expenses in order to ensure a profit.

Table 17-2 Gallagher Corporation Income Statement
for Year Ended December 31, 1991

SALES REVENUE	$1,750,000	
Less: Sales returns and allowances	50,000	
Net Sales		$1,700,000
COST OF GOODS SOLD		
Inventory, January 1, 1989	$ 150,000	
Purchases	1,050,000	
Goods available for sale	$1,200,000	
Less: Inventory, December 31, 1988	200,000	
Cost of goods sold		1,000,000
Gross Margin		$ 700,000
OPERATING EXPENSES		
Selling Expenses	$ 150,000	
Administrative expenses	100,000	
Total Operating Expenses		250,000
Operating Income		$ 450,000
Financial Expense		20,000
Income before Income Taxes		$ 430,000
Estimated Income Taxes		172,000
Net Profit		$ 258,000

COST OF GOODS SOLD   As the term implies, the **cost of goods sold** section reports the cost of the merchandise sold during the accounting period. Simply put, the cost of goods for a given time period equals the beginning inventory plus any purchases the firm makes minus the inventory on hand at the end of the period. Note in Table 17-2 that the beginning inventory was $150,000 and the purchases totaled $1,050,000. This gave Gallagher goods available for sale of $1,200,000. The ending inventory for the period was $200,000, so the cost of goods sold was $1,000,000. This is what it cost the company to buy the inventory that it sold. When this cost of goods sold is subtracted from net sales, the result is the **gross margin.** The gross margin is the amount available to meet expenses and to provide some net income for the firm's owners.

OPERATING EXPENSES   The major expenses, exclusive of costs of goods sold, are classified as **operating expenses.** These represent the resources that have been expended, except for inventory purchases, in generating the revenue for the period. Expenses are often divided into two broad subclassifications: selling expenses and administrative expenses.

Selling expenses result from such things as displaying, selling, delivering, and installing a product or performing a service. Expenses for displaying a product include rent for storage space, depreciation on fixtures and furniture, property insurance, and utility and tax expenses. Sales, salaries, commissions, and advertising also fall into this category. Costs associated with getting the product from the store to the customer are also considered selling expenses. Finally, if the firm installs the product for the customer, all costs including the parts used in the job are considered in this total. Taken as a whole, these are the selling expenses.

Administrative expenses is a catchall term for operating expenses not directly related to selling or borrowing. In broad terms, these expenses include the costs associated with running the firm. They include the salaries of the managers, expenses associated with operating the office, general expenses that cannot be directly related to buying or selling activities, and expenses that arise from delinquent or uncollectible accounts.

When these selling and administrative expenses are added together, the result is **total operating expenses.** Subtracting them from gross margin gives the firm its operating income. Note in Table 17-2 that selling expenses are $150,000, administrative expenses are $100,000, and total operating expenses are $250,000. When subtracted from the gross margin of $700,000, operating income is $450,000.

FINANCIAL EXPENSE   The **financial expense** is the interest expense on long-term loans. As seen in Table 17-2, this expense is $20,000. Additionally, many companies include their interest expense on short-term obligations as part of their financial expense.

ESTIMATED INCOME TAXES   As noted earlier, corporations pay estimated income taxes and then at some predetermined time (for example, December 31), the books are closed, actual taxes are determined, and any additional payments are made (or refunds claimed). When these taxes are subtracted from the revenue before income taxes, the result is the **net profit.** In our example, the Gallagher Corporation made $258,000.

KEEPING THE BOOKS

The balance sheet and income statement are important financial statements. However, the small business also needs to keep adequate accounting records for control purposes.[1] The two most basic books of record are the Sales and Cash Receipts Journal and the Cash Disbursement, Purchases, and Expense Journal. (See Small Business Success: Managing by Opening the Books.)

SALES AND CASH RECEIPTS JOURNAL

The Sales and Cash Receipts Journal records daily income to the business. Table 17-3 on page 445 provides an example. Note that total sales on March 15 amounted to $520, and this was credited to the account. Of this amount, $210 was charged, resulting in $310 in cash taken in. Additionally, $150 in accounts receivable was collected. However, $10 was lost due to change errors by the employee running the cash register. The business deposited $450 in the bank.

Note that Table 17-3 distinguishes debits (DR) and credits (CR). In *income accounts,* credit is an increase to the account and a debit is a decrease. In *expense accounts,* a debit is an increase and a credit is a decrease. The total of debits (DR) and credits (CR) should be equal. When they are not, an error exists in the entries and the firm should look into the matter. Meanwhile, the total of the total sales column tells the firm how much has been sold during the period; this is the total used in the income statement.

[1]See David B. Byrd and Sandra D. Byrd, "Using the Statement of Change in Financial Position," *Journal of Small Business Management,* April 1986, pp. 31–38.

■ **SMALL BUSINESS SUCCESS** ■

Managing by Opening the Books

The days of keeping financial information away from employees are gone. Today, CEOs of the fastest growing small businesses are giving employees access to the company's financial statements. The list of companies includes Springfield Remanufacturing Center Corp. in Springfield, Missouri; Reflexite Corp. in New Britain, Connecticut; Reuther Mold & Manufacturing in Cuyahoga Falls, Ohio; Visual Technologies in Plano, Texas; Member Data Services in Carmel, Indiana; and Solar Press in Chicago, Illinois.

All of these companies are practicing "open book management." The idea is to let information permeate the organization. Because of computerization, greater demands on a manager's time, and the redefinition of work, many small businesses are passing responsibility down the managerial line. Employees are given complete access to balance sheets, income statements, cash flow statements, and so on in order to better understand their new responsibilities.

As employees become more knowledgeable about their companies, a greater sense of contribution arises. Companies, such as the ones mentioned above, are reporting increased productivity, reduced waste, employee-initiated cost savings, and higher profit levels, due to the open book policy. In order to establish this type of system, a couple of key steps should be considered:

1. *Demystify the strategy.* Clearly explain the company's goals to the employees.

2. *Report job profitability.* Keep employees informed about their jobs including the costs, productivity levels, and outcomes.

3. *Explain company performance.* Distribute all of the financial statements to every employee with clear explanations of the key figures.

4. *Post department revenues.* Chart the actual gross sales, budgets, and profits for each department. Allow every employee the opportunity to "track" the performance of their department.

Source: Adapted from John Case, "The Open-Book Managers," *Inc.,* September 1990, pp. 104–113.

CASH DISBURSEMENT, PURCHASES, AND EXPENSE JOURNAL

The Cash Disbursement, Purchases, and Expenses Journal is a record of expenditures of funds by the small business. Table 17-4 illustrates a page from this journal. Note that the debits and credits balance. If they do not, an error exists and the bookkeeper needs to check the figures to find it. Using this journal and the Sales and Cash Receipts Journal, revenues, expenses, and changes in balance sheet accounts can be determined and financial statements can be drawn up.

Table 17-3 Sales and Cash Receipt Journal

Date	Description and/or Account	Total Sales (CR)	Credit Sales (DR)	Collected on Accounts (CR)	Misc. Income and Expenses		Bank Deposit (DR)
					Income (CR)	Expense (DR)	
3/15	Daily summary	$520.00	$210.00	$150.00			$450.00
	Cash short					$10.00	
3/16	Daily summary	$635.00	$300.00	$210.00			$550.00
	Cash over				$5.00		
3/17	Daily summary	$410.00	$225.00	$175.00			$345.00
	Cash short					$15.00	

MANAGING THE BOOKS

A number of options are available to the small business owner-manager in maintaining the books. One is to turn the job over to an accountant who will come in once a month and take care of everything. However, since this is often expensive, it is the least popular. Another option is to have a full- or part-time employee keep the books. For example, many businesses hire a retired person or have one of their people learn how to keep the books. Still others use a freelance bookkeeper who also keeps books for a number of other firms. Working on a contract basis, the person spends a few hours each week maintaining each company's books. This arrangement is often no more expensive than a part-time employee bookkeeper.

Table 17-4 Cash Disbursements, Purchases, and Expense Journal

Date	Payee and/or Account	Check Number	Amount of Check (CR)	Merchandise Purchased (DR)	Gross Salaries (DR)	Payroll Deductions		Misc. Income and Expenses	
						Income Tax (CR)	Social Security (CR)	Income (CR)	Expenses (DR)
3/15	Acme Office Supplies	511	$ 75.00	$ 75.00					
3/15	Jackson Properties (rent)	512	$ 425.00						$425.00
3/16	Judson Materials, Inc.	513	$ 175.00	$175.00					
3/16	Anderson Materials Company	514	$ 100.00	$100.00					
3/17	Complete Furniture Rental	515	$ 90.00						$ 90.00
3/17	Payroll	516	$1,100.00		$814.00	$220.00	$66.00		

Finally, the owner-manager can personally maintain the books. The advantage of this is that the individual is constantly aware of his or her firm's financial situation. On the negative side, this takes time away from other management duties. As a result, most small businesses use part-time or free-lance bookkeepers.

SMALL BUSINESS COMPUTERS

In recent years, small computers and a variety of computer programs have been developed to handle such small business needs as bookkeeping, billing, and financial control.[2] Some of these machines currently sell for around $3,000 and can be of value to the business. Before buying one, however, two things should be done. First, a careful examination of the computer's potential uses should be made. Exactly what will it do? How much is it presently costing the business for these services? Is there anything the machine can do that is currently not available to the business? Overall, is the purchase of the machine a cost-saving decision? Second, rather than buy this computer is there a firm that provides these same services for a monthly fee? Would it be less costly to have this company do the job? The final decision must be cost effective.

Many small businesses find that they cannot afford the luxury of a microcomputer. A bookkeeper is all they need. Their accountant periodically reviews the books and brings them up-to-date. At the end of the year the accountant closes the books, prepares the income tax forms, and gets everything in order for the owner to send to the IRS. However, more and more entrepreneurs are finding that computerized services do pay off.

■ SUMMARY

The small business owner-manager needs to be familiar with two basic financial statements: the balance sheet and the income statement. The balance sheet reports a business's financial position at a specific time. This statement is divided into two parts: the firm's financial resources and the claims against these resources. The first, which consists of assets, is equal to the second which is made up of creditor claims (liabilities) and owners' equity. This results in the accounting equation: assets equal liabilities plus owners' equity.

A complete description of the balance sheet was presented, and accounts commonly found in each of the three sections of this financial statement were described. A balance sheet always balances because any change in assets is offset by an equal change in either liabilities or owners' equity or by an equal and opposite change in assets.

The income statement is a financial statement that shows the changes that have occurred in a firm's position as a result of its operations over a period of time. The five sections of the income statement are sales revenue, cost of goods sold, operating expenses, financial expense, and tax expense.

---

[2]Paul M. Mangiameli, Scott N. Cairns, and Joseph P. Matoney, "A Computerized Approach to Choosing Depreciation Options," *Journal of Small Business Management,* April 1985, pp. 34–40.

The two most basic books of record for a small business are the Sales and Cash Receipts Journal and the Cash Disbursement, Purchases, and Expense Journal. The first records daily income to the business. The second records the disbursement of funds by the firm.

In managing the books, a number of options are available to the small business owner-manager. The most common approach is to use an in-house or free-lance bookkeeper in conjunction with an accountant, who periodically balances the books, sees that the books are properly closed at the end of the fiscal year, prepares tax forms, and verifies that everything is in order for the new year. For keeping their books, billing, and maintaining financial control, some businesses purchase micro-computers. Before doing so, however, the owner-manager should compare the costs with the savings to ensure that the expenditure is economically justified.

■ REVIEW AND DISCUSSION QUESTIONS

1. What is a balance sheet?

2. Define these terms: *assets, liabilities, owners' equity.*

3. Describe the major sections of the balance sheet. What are the major accounts in each? Be specific.

4. Why does the balance sheet always balance?

5. What is an income statement?

6. Describe in detail the five major sections of the income statement.

7. How does the Sales and Cash Receipts Journal work? What types of information does it contain?

8. What is the Cash Disbursement, Purchases, and Expense Journal? What kind of information does it contain?

9. Explain why the two journals mentioned in questions 7 and 8 are the most basic books of records for a small business.

10. List the small business owner-manager's options in managing the company's books. Which option do you favor? Why?

11. Should a small business purchase a microcomputer for handling its bookkeeping, billing, and financial control needs? Explain.

Case Studies

Tell It to Barbara

■ Ted Carrington, primary owner and manager of the Carrington Company, has just received his year-end balance sheet from his accountants. His niece Barbara has been working with the corporation for three months, and Ted hopes she will like the work and want to stay with the firm indefinitely.

He has been introducing her to the various phases of the business by having her spend some time in each department. When this training period is over, he intends to ask her which area of the business appeals to her the most and offer her a position in it.

In familiarizing Barbara with operations, Ted believes it would be very helpful for him to run through the balance sheet with her and show her the firm's assets, liabilities, and owners' equity. (See the balance sheet accompanying this case study.) However, he knows Barbara has had no exposure to bookkeeping or accounting. Her high school program was strictly academic, geared toward getting her into college; in college she majored in English, thinking that she might like to be a writer. However, after working for a year in a publishing house as a copy editor while writing short stories on the side, Barbara decided she really did not want to be a writer. She then decided to try business. This is how she ended up in her uncle's firm.

Ted knows he will have to explain the balance sheet to Barbara in very simple terms. He has, therefore, broken it down into its three major parts and is currently making some notes regarding what he wants to say to her.

1. Help Ted out by defining an asset, a liability, and owners' equity in terms Barbara would understand.

2. How would you explain the following accounts to Barbara: inventory, accumulated depreciation on the building, and notes payable?

3. How would you explain retained earnings to Barbara?

Carrington Corporation Balance Sheet
for Year Ended December 31, 1991

ASSETS

Current Assets			
Cash		$ 40,000	
Accounts receivable	$140,000		
Less: Allowance for uncollectible			
accounts	7,000	133,000	
Inventory		40,000	
Prepaid expenses		2,000	
Total Current Assets			$215,000
Fixed Assets			
Land		$ 40,000	
Building	$100,000		
Less: Accumulated depreciation on			
building	30,000	70,000	
Equipment	70,000		
Less: Accumulated depreciation on			
equipment	40,000	30,000	
Total Fixed Assets			140,000
Total Assets			$355,000

LIABILITIES		
Current Liabilities		
Accounts payable	$ 16,000	
Notes payable	—	
Taxes payable	5,500	
Installment on long-term debt	10,000	
Total Current Liabilities		$ 31,500
Long-term Liabilities		
Bank loan		90,000
Total Liabilities		$121,500
STOCKHOLDERS' EQUITY		
Contributed Capital		
Common stock, $2 par, 25,000 shares authorized	$ 50,000	
Preferred stock, $100 par, 1,000 shares authorized; none sold	—	
Retained Earnings	183,500	
Total Owners' Equity		$233,500
Total Liabilities and Owners' Equity		$355,000

From Fashion Sense to Financial Savvy

■ Carla Ponti owns a boutique in a very fashionable shopping district. She opened the store eight months ago and has done very well every month. A primary reason for her success is that she knows fashion. Everything she buys is snapped up by her customers immediately. Two other fashion boutiques are on her street, and neither of them does as well as Carla's.

Two weeks ago Carla visited with her accountant, Susan. Carla does not know much about the financial side of her enterprise. As she put it, "I sell things for more than they cost me, so I know I make a profit. Outside of that, I'm in the dark." Carla's accountant prepared the following income statement for her.

Carla looked at the statement and asked Susan what it meant. Susan explained that it shows she is doing quite well. "I see," Carla said, "but I think you should tell me more. What *are* all these things, and what do I need to know about this information? Remember, I'm a fashion expert, not a financial expert."

1. What do the sales revenue and cost of goods sold sections indicate about Carla's business?

2. What does the operating expenses section indicate about the operation? Explain.

3. Overall, how well is Carla doing? Defend your answer.

Carla's Fashions Income Statement for Year Ended December 31, 1991		
SALES REVENUE	$450,000	
Less: Sales returns and allowances	25,000	
Net Sales		$425,000
COST OF GOODS SOLD		
Inventory, January 1, 1989	$ 25,000	
Purchases	200,000	
Goods available for sale	225,000	
Less: Inventory, December 31, 1988	30,000	
Cost of goods sold		195,000
Gross Margin		230,000
OPERATING EXPENSES		
Selling expenses	$ 20,000	
Administrative expenses	60,000	
Total Operating Expenses		80,000
Operating Income		$150,000
Financial Expense *Interest on Loans*		5,000
Income before Income Taxes		$145,000
Estimated Income Taxes		45,000
Net Profit		$100,000

You Be the Consultant

HAROLD'S PLAN

Harold Stratton has been in business six months, and things have been going very well for him. His sales last month were $21,500, which is quite good for his type of business. In fact, things are so good that Harold is thinking about expanding his business and increasing the number of items he offers.

Harold put in a call to his banker, Sheree Wyatt, who was delighted to hear from him. "I've really gotten off to a fast start," he told her. "However, I think that in order to keep the momentum going, I'm going to have to expand. I've been giving it some serious thought and have checked around and talked to some contractors. I think I can increase my floor space by almost 33 percent if I can get a loan."

Sheree congratulated Harold on his success and asked him when he could come in to discuss the matter. Harold suggested that they meet the following Monday, a time that proved ideal for Sheree. "When you come," she told him, "be sure to bring along your income statement for the last six months. I'd like to see exactly how well you've been doing." Harold promised that he would do so.

However, as soon as he had hung up he realized he did not have an income statement worked up. In fact, ever since he started the business he has simply watched his cash flow, paid his bills by check, and tried to have enough money in the cash register at all times. His bank account is sizable, but he does not know exactly how much profit he has made.

Harold realizes he should know these things, but he counts on his accountant to take care of all such matters. In fact, aside from having the sales slips and invoices on everything he has bought, Harold does not know for sure where he stands. His feelings about needing to expand are based on his estimate of actual business versus predicted business. Harold never guessed he would be selling as much merchandise as he has been.

In order to straighten out the situation and be prepared to talk to Sheree on Monday, Harold is going to call his accountant immediately. If his accountant can come over later in the week, perhaps he can prepare an income statement for Harold to take Monday. In any event, Harold is very interested in learning exactly how profitable his business has been. In addition, he will ask the accountant some questions about the income statement, including how to read it and what it all means.

■ **YOUR CONSULTATION**   Assume you are Harold's accountant. How would you explain the income statement to him? Also, explain to Harold how he can use it to help him control his business operations.

Financial Analysis and Budgeting

Objectives

One of the most effective control techniques for small businesses is financial analysis. Using the balance sheet and income statement, for example, ratio analysis can be carried out and financial problems identified before they become serious. Additionally, budgets can be used for helping set objectives as well as for monitoring performance. In Chapter 18 we will study both ratio analysis and financial budgeting.

The first objective of Chapter 18 is to study some of the balance sheet ratios used to examine a business's current and long-run positions. The second objective is to examine income statement and combination ratios used for obtaining further insights to a firm's financial strength. The third objective is to review some of the limitations of financial statement analysis. The final objective is to analyze financial budgeting, giving primary attention to sales and cash budgets. After you have studied the material in Chapter 18, you will be able to:

1. *Identify and describe the most useful balance sheet and income statement ratios.*

2. *Describe combination ratios that draw on data from both financial statements and provide the owner-manager with such vital information as inventory turnover and rate of return on equity.*

3. *Point out the limitations of financial statement analysis.*

4. *Explain how the sales budget and cash budget work and the value of each for control purposes.*

BALANCE SHEET ANALYSIS

In Chapter 17 we examined the component parts of the balance sheet. In this chapter we will undertake an analysis of this financial statement. In order to do so, it is necessary to compare a company's balance sheets for at least two periods of time. We will use the Gallagher Company's balance sheets for 1990 (from Table 17-1) and 1991. Their data are placed side by side in Table 18-1.

Many comparative methods are used in analyzing balance sheets. However, since small business owner-managers seldom need to use sophisticated techniques, we

Table 18-1 Gallagher Corporation Balance Sheet
for Years Ended December 31, 1990, and December 31, 1991

ASSETS		1990			1991	
Current Assets						
Cash		$125,000			$200,000	
Accounts receivable	$400,000			$375,000		
Less: Allowance for						
uncollectible accounts	40,000	360,000		25,000	350,000	
Inventory		135,000			150,000	
Prepaid expenses		50,000			35,000	
Total Current Assets			$ 670,000			$ 735,000
Fixed Assets						
Land		$315,000			$330,000	
Building	$315,000			$315,000		
Less: Accumulated						
depreciation, building	65,000	250,000		80,000	235,000	
Equipment	$420,000			$420,000		
Less: Accumulated						
depreciation, equipment	30,000	390,000		70,000	350,000	
Total Fixed Assets			955,000			915,000
Total Assets			$1,625,000			$1,650,000
LIABILITIES						
Current Liabilities						
Accounts payable		$245,000			$150,000	
Notes payable		50,000			25,000	
Taxes payable		100,000			75,000	
Installment, long-term debt		50,000			50,000	
Total Current Liabilities			$ 445,000			$ 300,000
Long-term Liabilities						
Bank loan			250,000			200,000
Total Liabilities			$ 695,000			$ 500,000
OWNERS' EQUITY						
Contributed Capital						
Common stock, $10 par,						
40,000 shares authorized		$400,000			$400,000	
Preferred stock, $100 par,						
500 shares authorized;						
none sold		—			—	
Retained Earnings		530,000			750,000	
Total Owners' Equity			930,000			1,150,000
Total Liabilities and Owners' Equity			$1,625,000			$1,650,000

will limit our discussion to ratio analysis. A **ratio** expresses a mathematical relationship between one item and another. In financial statement analysis, ratios are computed between various financial items. *These ratios are only indicators; any judgment regarding whether they are good or bad must be based on an understanding of what other firms in the industry are doing and how they are performing.*

Overall, two types of ratios are useful in analyzing the balance sheet: those that reflect the firm's current position, and those that reflect the company's long-run position. We now will examine both types of ratios.

CURRENT POSITION RATIOS

The company's current position is most commonly measured by three liquidity ratios:

1. working capital
2. current ratio
3. acid-test ratio

A **liquidity ratio** indicates the ease with which an asset can be turned into cash (or is already in the form of cash). A business with a high liquidity ratio is referred to as "highly liquid" and vice versa. Before examining liquidity ratios, however, keep in mind that high or low liquidity is not by itself good or bad. Before judging how good a ratio is, we must look at the industry and see what is considered good for the particular type of business.

WORKING CAPITAL   A company's working capital is not actually a ratio, but it is a very important measure of current financial position. The calculation for **working capital** is

$$\text{Current assets} - \text{Current liabilities}$$

For the Gallagher Corporation (Table 18-1) the calculation is as follows:

	1990	1991
Total current assets	$670,000	$735,000
Total current liabilities	− 445,000	− 300,000
Working capital	$225,000	$435,000

The company had $225,000 in working capital last year and $435,000 this year. This ratio shows that the firm has more than adequate capital to pay its short-term obligations. As a result, the business should have no trouble paying its bills as they come due.

Computing working capital is especially useful in determining a firm's short-term financial strength. Obviously, the company must have sufficient working capital to do business on a day-to-day basis. Inadequate working capital is often the first sign of financial difficulty for a firm.[1]

---

[1]See "Cash Management Audit," *Small Business Report,* August 1987, p. 28.

CURRENT RATIO   The **current ratio** is simply the relationship between current assets and current liabilities. It is one of the best-known and most commonly employed financial ratios.

For the Gallagher Corporation, the ratio is computed this way:

	1990	1991
Total current assets	$670,000	$735,000
Total current liabilities	$445,000	$300,000
Current ratio	1.51	2.45

The computation shows a substantial increase in the current ratio from 1.51:1 to 2.45:1. Is this good or bad? There are no hard and fast rules. However, a rule of thumb in recent years is that anything above 1.0:1 is satisfactory. On the other hand, 2.0:1 or more is generally considered satisfactory for a manufacturing firm. In the case of the Gallagher Corporation, the ratio has risen above the 2.0:1 level; the ratio is much better than before. Keep in mind, however, that a current ratio can be too high. For example, if industry comparisons show that most firms in the Gallagher Corporation's industry have current ratios in the neighborhood of 2.2:1, then a 5:1 ratio would be excessive.

ACID-TEST RATIO   The **acid-test ratio,** often referred to as the "quick ratio," is a measure of the firm's ability to quickly convert its current assets to cash for the purpose of meeting its current liabilities. In order to calculate the acid-test ratio, it is first necessary to determine which assets are most quickly convertible to cash. Aside from cash itself, accounts receivable (after allowing for uncollectible accounts) are included, because they can usually be sold quickly to banks and finance companies. Noticeably absent, however, are inventory and prepaid expenses; neither of these is convertible to cash in the short run.

The quick ratio for Gallagher (Table 18-1) is calculated as follows:

	1990	1991
Current assets (less inventory and prepaid expenses)	$485,000	$550,000
Current liabilities	$445,000	$300,000
Acid-test ratio	1.09	1.83

The trend from 1990 to 1991 is favorable. In fact, an acid-test ratio of 1.0 is considered satisfactory because it indicates that a company can easily pay all current liabilities within a short period of time.

LONG-RUN POSITION RATIOS

Although owner-managers are always interested in their firms' short-run position, it is important to consider long-run stability. Three balance-sheet ratios reflect a company's long-run position:

1. debt/asset ratio

2. equity/asset ratio

3. debt/equity ratio

DEBT/ASSET RATIO   The **debt/asset ratio** expresses the relationship between a company's total debt (liabilities) and total assets. This ratio tells the owner-manager how much of the firm's assets have been financed by debt and provides creditors with an indication of how much protection they have. If the ratio is very high, there is not much equity in the firm; most of the company's assets are being provided by debt. In such a case, creditors might be wise to refuse the company any more credit. Remember, when a firm goes out of business it usually cannot sell its assets for the dollar amount shown on the balance sheet. As a result, the total amount received by the creditors and owners is less than the amount of their claims on the balance sheet. However, the creditors have first claim to the assets, and sometimes nothing is left for the stockholders. The creditors' question is "Is there enough to prevent our having to settle for less than what is truly owed us?" The lower the debt/equity ratio, the more likely it is that the creditors will get their money back.

In the case of the Gallagher Corporation, the debt/equity ratio is as follows:

	1990	1991
Total liabilities	$695,000	$500,000
Total assets	$1,625,000	$1,650,000
Debt/asset ratio	42.8%	30.3%

As can be seen, the ratio has been reduced from 42.8 to 30.3 percent between 1990 and 1991. The creditors of the corporation have a greater degree of protection than before.

EQUITY/ASSET RATIO   The **equity/asset ratio** is computed by dividing the owners' equity by the total assets. It is the complement of the debt/asset ratio; that is, if the debt/asset ratio were 45 percent, the equity/asset ratio would be 55 percent.

The equity/asset ratio is of particular interest to investors because it indicates the percentage of total assets to which the owners have a claim. A very low equity/asset ratio is an indication that in the event of financial difficulties, the owners may receive little, if any, of their original investment. For example, if an equity/asset ratio is 10 percent, it means that 10 percent of the assets is owners' equity and 90 percent is due to debt. In case of dissolution, the creditors would be entitled to so much of the firm's assets that nothing would be left for the owners after the debtors were paid. Theoretically, then, the higher the equity/asset ratio, the more advantageous it is for the owners (and for the creditors).

The equity/asset ratio for the Gallagher Corporation is as follows:

	1990	1991
Total owners' equity	$930,000	$1,150,000
Total assets	$1,625,000	$1,650,000
Equity/asset ratio	57.2%	69.7%

Before continuing, one point merits our attention. It is *not* always advantageous to the firm to have the highest equity/asset ratio. Many times it is good business for the firm to borrow some money. This is particularly true when the rate of interest is less than the return the owners can generate with the funds. For example, if it costs 15 percent to borrow money from the bank but the business can make 28 percent on this money, then borrowing is indeed wise. The important thing is not to borrow *too much*. If the business does make 28 percent, it can put some of the profits back into the firm. The natural inclination is to make money on someone else's and not tie up one's own funds. However, sooner or later the business may grow large and accumulate so much debt that a slow down in the economy could drastically affect its ability to meet debt obligations. For this reason, the use of debt must be undertaken prudently. To have too little debt may deny the firm a source of funds with which to increase its profits. To have too much debt can be overburdening. By consulting industry statistics, the company can get an idea of a desirable "ballpark" equity asset/ratio.

DEBT/EQUITY RATIO   This ratio expresses the relationship between liabilities and owner's equity. A very high debt/equity ratio would indicate to the creditors that they are financing most of the business's operations. It would also indicate to the owners that their claim in the business is small.

In the case of the Gallagher Corporation, the debt/equity ratio is calculated as follows:

	1990	1991
Total liabilities	$695,000	$500,000
Total owners' equity	$930,000	$1,150,000
Debt/equity ratio	74.7%	43.5%

This comparison indicates that debt as a percentage of equity is declining. More and more of the firm's operations are being financed through owners' equity. This, of course, is a direct result of plowing back net profits into retained earnings, which in 1991 was $258,000 as noted in Table 17-2. As seen in the preceding calculation, owners' equity increased by this amount while total liabilities decreased. This trend should be viewed positively by both the owners of Gallagher and its creditors.

INCOME STATEMENT ANALYSIS

As with the balance sheet, there are financial ratios that can be used to analyze the income statement. Some of these use data from the income statement exclusively. Others, known as **combination ratios,** draw on data from the balance sheet and the income statement. Both types of ratio analyses are useful in evaluating a small business's income and profitability performance. In doing so, we will use the Gallagher Corporation's income statements for 1990 and 1991. See Table 18-2.

INCOME STATEMENT RATIOS

The balance sheet ratios provide indicators of short-run and long-run financial stability. The income statement ratios provide information on current operating performance and efficiency. Two of the most important are the operating expense ratio and the number of times interest earned.

Table 18-2 Gallagher Corporation Income Statement
for Years Ended December 31, 1990, and December 31, 1991

	1990		1991	
SALES REVENUE	$1,565,000		$1,750,000	
Less: Sales returns and allowances	$ 65,000		$ 50,000	
Net Sales		$1,500,000		$1,700,000
COST OF GOODS SOLD				
Inventory, January 1	$ 135,000		$ 150,000	
Purchases	$1,000,000		$1,050,000	
Goods available for sale	$1,135,000		$1,200,000	
Less: Inventory, December 31	$ 150,000		$ 200,000	
Cost of goods sold		$ 985,000		$1,000,000
Gross Margin		$ 515,000		$ 700,000
OPERATING EXPENSES				
Selling expenses	$ 125,000		$ 150,000	
Administrative expenses	$ 95,000		$ 100,000	
Total Operating Expenses		$ 220,000		$ 250,000
Operating Income		$ 295,000		$ 450,000
Financial Expense		$ 20,000		$ 20,000
Income before Income Taxes		$ 275,000		$ 430,000
Estimated Income Taxes		$ 125,000		$ 172,000
Net Profit		$ 150,000		$ 258,000

OPERATING EXPENSE RATIO **Operating expenses** are the expenses incurred in the normal day-to-day running of the business. They include selling and administrative expenses but not interest expense or income tax expense. The operating expense ratio is calculated by dividing the total operating expenses by net sales.

For the Gallagher Corporation for 1990 and 1991 the ratio is calculated as follows:

	1990	1991
Total operating expenses	$220,000	$250,000
Net sales	$1,500,000	$1,700,000
Operating expense ratio	14.7%	14.7%

The ratio has remained the same. Selling and administrative expenses are up almost 14 percent, but so are net sales. This is a good sign; it shows that operating expenses are being kept under control. (See Small Business Owner's Notebook: Cut Costs—Increase Profits.)

NUMBER OF TIMES INTEREST EARNED   A second indicator of financial stability is the number of times interest is earned on the long-term debt. This appears on the income statement as the financial expense. If a firm is just barely able to meet this expense, it may be in financial difficulty. Conversely, a business that is able to meet this financial expense easily is probably in sound financial condition. The number of times interest earned ratio is computed by dividing **operating income** (income before financial expense and income taxes) by annual financial expense.

■ SMALL BUSINESS OWNER'S NOTEBOOK ■

Cut Costs—Increase Profit

What do companies do when they are faced with a downward trend in profits? Do they cut costs across the board? Do they disband the research and development department? These, as a rule, are the worst ways to solve such a crisis. So what do they cut? Businesses normally reflect the 80/20 rule: 20 percent of products or customers tend to generate 80 percent of profits. Overhead and unprofitable product lines, then, are the best areas to cut for both short- and long-term health.

To determine which items are least profitable, the business should conduct a profit audit. Costs are first divided into three basic categories—direct variable product costs, strategic product costs, and shared overhead or indirect costs—and then the manager evaluates each one to determine how profits can be increased.

Direct variable product costs are the easiest category to calculate. Simply put, the direct material, labor, and energy costs involved in producing and delivering the product or service are identified.

Strategic product costs are the next category to be calculated. These costs are somewhat variable but are separated from direct variable costs because they tend to have a more long-term impact on sales. Strategic product costs include advertising, public relations, and other such expenditures.

Indirect overhead costs are the last category to be examined. Costs can and should be allocated to products, even if they are relatively "fixed" in the short term.

Once the costs are categorized, a profit audit can be conducted. The small business owner is then able to compare the products in the audit to determine what adjustments are needed in order to increase profits.

Source: Adapted from Harry S. Dent, Jr., "Do You Know Where Your Profits Are?" *Small Business Reports,* March 1990, pp. 14–18.

For the Gallagher Corporation that calculation is as follows:

	1990	1991
Operating income	$295,000	$450,000
Annual financial expense	$20,000	$20,000
Number of times interest earned	14.75 ×	22.5 ×

The ratio is very high for both 1990 and 1991. The firm should have no trouble paying its interest on the bank loan.

If the Gallagher Corporation wanted to be more conservative, as some owner-managers do, it could deduct income tax from operating income before dividing by annual financial expense. In this case the calculations would be as follows:

	1990	1991
Operating income	$170,000	$278,000
Annual financial expense	$20,000	$20,000
Number of times interest earned	8.5 ×	13.9 ×

The number of times interest is earned is now lower, but it is still more than adequate.

What really counts, however, is the trend from year to year. In the preceding calculations the trend is upward. As long as the ratio does not drop drastically, Gallagher should be able to more than meet its interest payments.

COMBINATION RATIOS

As mentioned earlier, some ratios show the relationship between items on the income statement and the balance sheet. Four of the most common are

1. inventory turnover
2. accounts receivable turnover
3. rate of return on total assets
4. rate of return on equity

INVENTORY TURNOVER   **Inventory turnover,** simply put, is the number of times, on average, that inventory is replaced during the year. A low inventory turnover indicates that goods are not selling very well; they are remaining on the shelf in the warehouse for extended periods of time. If already paid for, the inventory represents money that is tied up and not providing any return to the business. If the inventory was obtained on consignment, then the firm can send back whatever it does not sell, but it must pay the storage bill as long as the goods are on hand. Of course, a very high turnover may not be good, for it can indicate that the firm is continually running out of items and having to turn customers away. As a result, most companies want a turnover that is neither too low nor too high.

In computing turnover, cost of goods sold is divided by the average inventory. Ideally, average inventory is computed by adding the beginning inventory of each month from January of one year through January of the next and dividing by 13. This assures that there is no bias due to the traditionally lower inventory figures at the end of the calendar year. However, it is much easier to simply take the beginning inventory for the year, add it to the ending inventory, and divide by two. This gives an average that is satisfactory for most purposes. In addition, once the turnover is determined it is possible to calculate the average number of days to turn over, thereby providing the manager with a detailed view of the inventory picture.

For the Gallagher Corporation the place to start is with a computation of the average inventory for both 1990 and 1991. (See Table 18-2.) The calculations look like this:

$$\text{Average inventory} = \frac{\text{Beginning inventory} + \text{Ending inventory}}{2}$$

$$\text{For 1990:} \quad \frac{\$135,000 + \$150,000}{2} = \$142,500$$

$$\text{For 1991:} \quad \frac{\$150,000 + \$200,000}{2} = \$175,000$$

Then the number of times the inventory turned over is calculated using these values. And, finally, the average number of days to turnover is obtained by dividing the number of days in a year by the inventory turnover. These calculations look like this:

	1990	1991
Cost of goods sold	$985,000	$1,000,000
Average inventory	$142,000	$175,000
Inventory turnover	6.91	5.71
Days in a year	365 days	365 days
Inventory turnover	6.91	5.71
Average number of days to turnover	53 days	64 days

These calculations indicate an unfavorable trend. In 1990, Gallagher's inventory turnover was 6.91, while in 1991, it dropped off to 5.71. Additionally, in 1990 it took 53 days to turn over the inventory, while in 1991 it took 64 days. More and more time is needed to turn over the inventory.

What accounts for this increase? The calculations do not, in and of themselves, provide the answer. Perhaps, in order to increase its sales, the firm has been forced to carry more slow-moving items. That would increase inventory and result in a lower turnover. In that instance the decrease in turnover would not be a very negative factor. However, if the firm has simply been buying more goods in anticipation of higher sales, it should now reduce purchases and maintain lower inventories.

ACCOUNTS RECEIVABLE TURNOVER   The analysis of accounts receivable is similar to that of inventory turnover. It is a measure of how rapidly accounts receivable are being collected. In general terms, the higher this turnover, the better. A low turnover is usually regarded as unfavorable for two reasons: the interest expense in maintaining the receivables is increasing; and an abnormally high number of these receivables may well end up being uncollectible.

The accounts receivable turnover is computed by dividing net sales by average accounts receivable. Since we have no data for the Gallagher Corporation for 1989, we will use the accounts receivable for 1990 (from Table 18-1) and assume that the beginning and ending receivables were the same. This gives us an average of $360,000. Meanwhile, for 1991 (also from Table 18-1) the average receivables are

$$\frac{\$360,000 + 350,000}{2} = \$355,000$$

The calculations from here are as follows:

	1990	1991
Net sales	$1,500,000	$1,700,000
Average accounts receivable	$360,000	$355,000
Accounts receivable turnover	4.2	4.8
Days in a year	365 days	365 days
Accounts receivable turnover	4.2	4.8
Average age of accounts receivable	86.9 days	76.0 days

Overall, the trend for the Gallagher Corporation is favorable. Turnover has risen from 4.2 to 4.8 times, and the average number of days from sale to collection has declined from 86.9 to 76 days.

Many times, as a company's sales increase its accounts receivable also increase but the turnover of the receivables declines. This is often occasioned by a lenient credit policy that allows poor-risk customers to buy on credit. Such customers tend to purchase up to their credit limit and then fall behind in their payments. As a result, while sales are up, so are receivables, and the chance of collecting all of these accounts is very small. More and more must be written off as uncollectible. In the case of the Gallagher Corporation, this has not happened.

RATE OF RETURN ON TOTAL ASSETS   In addition to knowing the net income of the company, the owner-manager needs to know the rate of return the business is earning on its assets. The greater the amount of assets, the more income the firm should earn. In short, by comparing operating income and average assets, we can find out how well the firm has performed with its available resources. This ratio is known as the **rate of return on total assets** and is computed by dividing operating income by average assets.

Drawing on Table 18-1, Gallagher's average assets for 1991 were $1,637,500 [($1,625,000 + $1,650,000)/2]. We do not know its average assets for 1990 because we do not have 1989 figures. However, let us assume that the assets between 1989 and 1990 have remained the same, giving us an average of $1,625,000. The rate of return on total assets can be computed as follows:

	1990	1991
Operating income	$295,000	$450,000
Average assets	$1,625,000	$1,650,000
Rate of return on total assets	18.2%	27.3%

This return is very good. The 18.2 percent is far higher than what could have been obtained if the money had been invested in a bank note or simply left in a savings account. It is also a higher return than the 10 percent the firm currently is paying on its bank loan. In short, the company is making a fine return. In 1991 this return was 50 percent higher than in 1990; which indicates even better performance.

RATE OF RETURN ON EQUITY   While the rate of return on investment discloses how well management is performing with the resources available, the small business owner is also interested in how this translates in terms of his or her own investment. This can be determined by a simple calculation of the **rate of return on the common stockholders' equity.**

This computation for the Gallagher Corporation is as follows:

	1990	1991
Net income	$150,000	$172,000
Common stockholders' equity	$400,000	$400,000
Return on equity	37.5%	43.0%

Gallagher's rate of return on equity is extremely high. The owners have earned a return of 37.5 percent and 55 percent, respectively. Of course, it is important to analyze why Gallagher has performed so remarkably. If everyone else in the industry did as well, the conclusion would have to be tempered accordingly. If everyone else did poorly, we would want to investigate what makes Gallagher so successful. In either event, an industry comparison would be very helpful.

LIMITATIONS OF FINANCIAL STATEMENT ANALYSIS

Until now, we have been concerned with the various ways of analyzing financial statements. However, we need to moderate our remarks with some comments on the limitations of financial statement analysis.[2] Metcalf and Titard, two noted accounting experts, have stated such limitations this way:

1 Companies may have differing year ends which could cause a different composition of assets, particularly current assets. For example, one company may choose to operate on a fiscal year which comes at a low point in production. This causes its inventory to be at an exceptionally low level while its cash, marketable securities, and accounts receivable are unusually high. Another company, selecting a point for its fiscal year when accounts receivable is low, finds its inventory and cash positions at a high point. Of course, these problems, while confounding comparisons between companies, are of no importance when comparing the ratios for either company against itself over a period of time, because it will always be at either a low inventory level or a low receivable level at that time of year.

2 Companies may have acquired their property, plant, and equipment in differing years. Because the accountant follows a stable dollar approach in financial reporting, periods of inflation between times that two companies acquire assets may result in vast dollar differences between the amounts shown for two assets which serve the same purpose. Again, comparisons of one company's results over time is only mildly affected by this condition.

3 Companies may account for the same items using alternative accounting methods.

4 Finally, industry patterns cause significant differences between the amount and the relationship of a particular item to the total. For example, a company which takes more than a year to manufacture a particular machine, such as a printing press, tends to have a large inventory balance when compared to a company which is merely selling purchased items, such as a grocery store selling produce.[3]

These limitations illustrate that whereas the owner-manager can compare his or her own firm's financial statements from one year to the next in determining improvements or problems, care must be exercised in making comparisons with

---

[2]For example see Richard I. Levin and Virginia R. Travis, "Small Company Finance: What the Books Don't Say," *Harvard Business Review,* November/December 1987, pp. 30–32.

[3]Richard W. Metcalf and Pierre L. Titard, *Principles of Accounting* (Philadelphia: W. B. Saunders Company, 1976), pp. 203–204.

other firms. It is necessary to be sure that the firms chosen for comparison are indeed similar; that is, that they sell the same types of goods and services, are about the same financial size, and operate under similar economic conditions.[4]

FINANCIAL BUDGETING

Budgets are plans as well as control tools. As plans, they pinpoint objectives the small business wants to attain in areas such as sales, product-line growth, number of personnel, expenses, and the like. In each case, the owner-manager sets a target—such as sales of $230,000, 11 percent growth of product-line A, and increasing the number of personnel by two employees. Each of these is an objective. At the same time the company can incorporate these objectives into the financial budgeting process by asking itself what it must do to attain the objectives. One answer might be that it must increase sales by 25 percent. If the business can do that, the other objectives will be attained in the process.

However, without going into a long list of the objectives a small business might have, let us look at the two most valuable types of financial budgeting: sales budgets and cash budgets. Then we will examine some other budgetary considerations.

SALES BUDGET

The sales budget is the primary budget for the small business; once it is worked out, all of the other budgets flow from it. For example, if the owner-manager believes that sales next year will be $400,000, the business will want to stock inventory, hire personnel, and put together a marketing strategy based on this objective. Of course, the owner-manager needs more information than just the total sales figure. It is necessary to break down the dollar amount by month or quarter so that all of the other budgets can be tied to it. For example, if half the sales are expected during the first three months of the year, half of the production should be finished and ready for shipping during (or soon after) that period. Likewise, there will be greater cash and personnel demands on the business during that quarter of the year than during any other.

By linking the other budgets to sales, the owner-manager can adjust expenditures up or down depending on how things are going. If sales are greater than expected, production can be raised and the number of personnel can be increased. Conversely, if sales are slower, production can be temporarily halted and some employees can be let go.

How closely should everything be tied to sales? This depends on the size of the business. If the organization has sufficient capital to ride out a sluggish six months, the owner-manager need not be as concerned as if the firm were living hand-to-mouth and could not afford any financial setback. Depending on how closely things must be monitored, the firm can control operations on a weekly or biweekly basis, or let them go as long as three to six months. (For an example of controlled growth, see Small Business Success: Mother's Work.)

---

[4]For an interesting discussion see Charles W. Kyd, "How Are You Doing: If You Really Want to Measure Your Company's Performance, You Should Try Calculating Its Z Score," *Inc.*, February 1987, pp. 121–23.

■ SMALL BUSINESS SUCCESS ■

Mother's Work

Ten years ago, Rebecca Matthias was working as a civil engineer for a construction company when she helped her husband start a software firm. The experience sold her on the idea of entrepreneurship. When Matthias later became pregnant and continued to work, she had difficulty finding maternity clothing that looked professional. "It's hard for men to understand how much need there is for this kind of product," she said.

In 1982 Matthias used $10,000 of her own money to start Mother's Work, a company that would manufacture clothing for working women who were in their first trimester. Mother's Work began as a mail order company, but Matthias had difficulty finding a mailing list that just included working professionals in their third month of pregnancy. The lists she did find were old and the women were no longer pregnant. So instead of relying on mailing lists, Matthias placed ads in the *Wall Street Journal* and *The New Yorker*. She got plenty of requests for catalogs, but no orders. She telephoned a random selection of those requesting a catalog and asked what kinds of ads they preferred. She learned that she needed to introduce her fashions earlier for each season and that people liked color ads instead of black and white. She revamped the catalog, released it earlier the next season, and business picked up—slowly.

After two years of slow growth, Matthias came to the conclusion that her market was small, and that the mail order portion of it was even smaller. She decided to open retail outlets and then franchises. By 1985 there were three company-owned Mother's Work stores and eleven franchises. In that same year, the company was backed by a $250,000 investment, followed by another $500,000 in 1987.

The franchises were not as profitable as Matthias had hoped they would be, because she made only a wholesaler's profit rather than the high margins she had been accustomed to. In 1986, spurred by the influx of venture capital, she began systematically buying the franchises back. "It's a powerful combination when you sell what you make," she said.

Today, Mother's Work is made up of 15 franchises and 24 company-owned stores. Last year the company rang up $10 million on it's registers and is expecting sales to rise to $14 million this year.

Source: Adapted from Bob Weinstein, "From Here to Maternity," *Entrepreneurial Woman*, May/June 1990, pp. 55–58.

CASH BUDGET

Cash budgeting is vital to small business survival.[5] At the heart of the cash budgeting process is **cash planning.** Cash planning requirements for a small business are of two types: the daily and weekly cash needs for the normal operation of the business, and the maintenance expenses of the organization during this time period. The first relates to cash on hand for day-to-day operations. Usually the business estimates its needs for a 30–60 day period and then determines how much money it is likely to collect during this time. If a cash shortage is anticipated after comparing the inflows and outflows, then a line of credit or a short-term loan can be arranged.

The maintenance part of this budget takes into account such things as insurance, rent, payroll, purchases, services, and taxes. This more long-run view of operations provides the firm the opportunity to balance its annual cash needs. Exhibit 18-1 provides a sample cash budget form that can be used in accomplishing both the operational and maintenance objectives.

The first four lines in Exhibit 18-1 help determine the amount of cash that will be collected over the next three months. The *collection on accounts receivable* (line 2) is especially important and warrants discussion. Remember that many small businesses sell on credit. And while these obligations may be due within 30 days, some people wait 60–90 days—and others never pay. How much will be collected each month? In answering this question the owner-manager needs to examine past collections. For the sake of discussion, however, let us assume the business's records show that half of all sales are made for cash and the other half are paid over 90 days. Of this latter amount, 70 percent are collected the first month, 20 percent the second, 8 percent the third, and the remaining 2 percent are written off as uncollectable. Additionally, assume that sales were $8,000 in October, $10,000 in November, and $16,000 in December. Using these data, the owner-manager can determine both cash and accounts receivable collections. Table 18-3 shows these calculations.

Lines 5–12 in Exhibit 18-1 take into account those items for which the firm pays cash. Some of these outflows, such as administrative expense and repayment of the loan, will remain basically the same; others will rise or fall depending on the level of activity. For example, as production goes up, payroll and raw materials expenses will go up and vice versa.

Table 18-3 Cash and Accounts Receivable Collection Calculations

MONTH	CASH SALES	70% OF RECEIVABLES 30 DAYS OLD +	20% OF RECEIVABLES 60 DAYS OLD +	8% OF RECEIVABLES 90 DAYS OLD =	TOTAL COLLECTED ON ACCOUNTS RECEIVABLE
January	$4,000	5,600	$1,000	320	$6,920
February	$5,000	2,800	1,600	400	$4,800
March	$6,000	3,500	800	640	$4,940

Note: The accounts receivable collections constitute a flow of cash into the firm. By tracking this flow on a monthly basis, the owner can determine the amount of cash the business will have for operations.

---

[5]See Ray Thompson, "Understanding Cash Flow: A System Dynamics Analysis," *Journal of Small Business Management,* April 1986, pp. 23–30.

Exhibit 18-1 Cash Budget Form

CASH BUDGET
(for 3 months ending March 31, 19 ___)

	January Budget	January Actual	February Budget	February Actual	March Budget	March Actual
EXPECTED CASH RECEIPTS:						
1. Cash sales.....................						
2. Collection on accounts receivable						
3. Other income						
4. Total cash receipts..............						
EXPECTED CASH PAYMENTS:						
5. Raw materials..................						
6. Payroll.........................						
7. Other factory expenses (including maintenance)						
8. Advertising						
9. Selling expense						
10. Administration expense (including salary of owner-management).....						
11. New plant and equipment						
12. Other payments (taxes, including estimated income tax; repayment of loans; interest; etc.)............						
13. Total cash payments						
14. Expected Cash Balance at beginning of the month..........						
15. Cash increase or decrease (item 4 minus item 13)						
16. Expected cash balance at end of month (item 14 plus item 15)......						
17. Desired working cash balance						
18. Short-term loans needed (item 17 minus item 16, if item 17 is larger than item 16)..................						
19. Cash available for dividends, capital cash expenditures, and/or short-term investments (item 16 minus item 17, if item 16 is larger than item 17)....................						
CAPITAL CASH:						
20. Cash available (item 19 after deducting dividends, etc.)						
21. Desired capital cash (item 11, new plant and equipment)						
22. Long-term loans needed (item 21 less item 20, if item 21 is larger than item 20)..................						

Source: J. H. Feller, Jr., *Is Your Cash Supply Adequate?* (Washington, D.C.: Small Business Administration, 1973), Management Aids, No. 174.

Lines 14–19 of Exhibit 18-1 involve balancing the cash account, along with a determination of any short-term loans that will be needed and the amount of cash, if any, that will be available for dividends and short-term investments. Lines 21 and 22 help the firm to compare desired and actual cash available in order to see how much is available for capital investment.

OTHER BUDGETARY CONSIDERATIONS

Sales and cash budgets are not the only ones a small business needs for controlling its operations. There are others that are actually spin-offs of items on the cash budget form (Exhibit 18-1), including payroll, advertising, selling expense, and new plant and equipment budgets.[6] Depending on the size of the firm, these budgetary categories will be handled through the cash budget or broken out and given special consideration. For example in a manufacturing operation there will be a manufacturing and purchasing budget, while in a sales business there will be a selling expense budget. However, since the small business will not want to overburden itself with budgets there should be as few as possible.

As a result, the astute owner-manager uses the **exception principle of control** in handling budgetary problems. This principle holds that the owner-manager should be concerned with results that are extremely good or extremely bad, and not with things that go as expected. If sales for January are forecasted at $8,000 and end up being $8,200, there is little need for concern. However, if they are $15,000, the owner-manager should be concerned about filling the orders (if it is a manufacturing firm) or purchasing more materials or products (if it is a retail or wholesale operation). Likewise, sales of only $4,000 would be a sufficient deviation to warrant making some changes in the next month's budget by curtailing purchases, laying off some people, or taking other actions.

The most important thing to remember is that budgetary controls must be kept in their proper perspective. They are tools that help the business set goals and evaluate performance. If there are problems, budgets should help the owner-manager to pinpoint where and why they arose. For this reason, every budget should possess two characteristics: economy and timeliness. If the budget is too cumbersome or detailed, it may take $1 of effort to pinpoint a 50¢ problem. The budget must be worth its cost. Also, the budget should be timely; it should allow the owner-manager to collect, analyze, and interpret the information in time to take the required action. If the company runs on a fixed three-month budget but is subject to widely varying sales fluctuations, it may be out of cash before the budget period is over. In this case, the firm needs to budget for shorter periods of time—that is, a month at a time. Finally, remember that in most cases the owner-manager can rely on one or two budgets, such as the sales and cash budgets, and assume that if these are in line then everything else is okay. And, in most cases, the owner-manager will be right.

◼ SUMMARY

One of the most effective control techniques for small businesses is financial analysis. The balance sheet provides the owner-manager the opportunity to examine the

---

[6]See for example Stanley Block, "Important New Aspects of Financial Planning Following Tax Reform," *Journal of Small Business Management*, October 1987, pp. 40–46.

current state of the firm's assets and liabilities and the owners' equity. Some of the most useful ratios in this examination are the working capital ratio, current ratio, acid-test ratio, debt/asset ratio, equity/asset ratio, and debt/equity ratio.

The income statement can also be analyzed using ratio analysis. Two of the most common are the operating expense ratio and the number-of-times-interest-earned ratio.

Some useful combination ratios draw on data from both the balance sheet and the income statement. Four of the most common are the inventory turnover, accounts receivable turnover, rate of return on total assets, and rate of return on equity ratios.

The budget is another useful financial analysis tool. Small businesses must be careful not to have too many budgets, for the paperwork is time-consuming. By relying on a few—such as the sales budget and cash budget—the small business can maintain effective budgetary control. In handling budgetary problems, the astute owner-manager uses the exception principle of control. In this way he or she concentrates on major developments and not on minor problems.

■ REVIEW AND DISCUSSION QUESTIONS

1. How does a business compute its working capital? Give an example.

2. What does the current ratio tell the owner-manager? Also, what is a *good* current ratio?

3. Explain how the acid-test ratio differs from the current ratio.

4. Why would the owner-manager be interested in the debt/asset ratio? Equity/asset ratio? Be sure to explain in your answer what each ratio tells the owner-manager.

5. Which ratio is of greater interest to the owner-manager, the operating expense ratio or the number-of-times-interest-earned ratio? Support your answer.

6. How is inventory turnover computed? What does it tell the owner-manager?

7. How is accounts receivable turnover computed? What does this calculation tell the owner-manager?

8. Which is of greater interest to the owner-manager, the rate of return on total assets or the rate of return on equity? Support your answer.

9. List and explain three of the limitations of financial analysis.

10. How does a sales budget work?

11. How does the cash budget help the owner-manager control operations? Include a description of this budget in your answer.

12. Explain the value of the exception principle of control to the owner-manager.

Case Studies

A Case of Liquidity

■ The Compton Company's accountant put together the comparative balance sheet for 1990 and 1991, and gave it to Mr. Ed Compton, the company president. (See the balance sheet that accompanies this case study.)

Compton Company Balance Sheet
for Years Ended December 31, 1990, and December 31, 1991

ASSETS	1990			1991		
Current Assets						
Cash		$ 30,000			$ 40,000	
Accounts receivable	$100,000			$140,000		
Less: Allowance for						
uncollectible accounts	5,000	95,000		7,000	133,000	
Inventory		50,000			40,000	
Prepaid expenses		2,000			2,000	
Total Current Assets			$177,000			$215,000
Fixed Assets						
Land		$ 40,000			$ 40,000	
Building	$100,000			$100,000		
Less: Accumulated						
depreciation, building	25,000	75,000		30,000	70,000	
Equipment	$ 70,000			$ 70,000		
Less: Accumulated						
depreciation, equipment	30,000	40,000		40,000	30,000	
Total Fixed Assets			$155,000			$140,000
Total Assets			$332,000			$355,000
LIABILITIES						
Current Liabilities						
Accounts payable	$ 33,000			$ 16,000		
Notes payable	10,000			—		
Taxes payable	4,000			5,500		
Installment, long-term debt	10,000			10,000		
Total Current Liabilities		$ 57,000			$ 31,500	
Long-term Liabilities						
Bank loan		100,000			90,000	
Total Liabilities			$157,000			$121,500
OWNERS' EQUITY						
Contributed Capital						
Common stock, $2 par,						
25,000 shares authorized		$ 50,000			$ 50,000	
Preferred stock, $100 par,						
1,000 shares authorized;						
none sold		—			—	
Retained Earnings		125,000			183,500	
Total Owners' Equity			$175,000			$233,500
Total Liabilities and Owners' Equity			$332,000			$355,000

After looking at the statement for a few minutes, Ed told the CPA that he was very pleased with the company's performance in the last two years. The accountant agreed with his analysis, and they began talking about various balance sheet items. As they were engaged in their conversation, Mrs. Compton, Barbara, entered Ed's office. She has been working for the company for almost six months, and Ed is familiarizing her with the business.

Ed introduced Barbara to the accountant and told the accountant that he had been explaining the balance sheet format to Barbara just a few weeks earlier. "However, now that we have a comparative balance sheet we can calculate a few financial ratios and really see if our performance has improved this year."

Ed could see that Barbara did not understand this particular remark. He then turned to the accountant and said, "Why don't you and Barbara have a cup of coffee, and maybe you can explain something about financial ratios to her. I really think she should learn something about financial analysis, and who could teach her better than an accountant?"

The accountant agreed, adding that he had to be back to his office in an hour. "That's okay," said Ed. "Just give her a brief introduction to liquidity, and show her a couple of liquidity ratios." The accountant promised to do so.

1. What is meant by the term *liquidity?* Explain.

2. What types of ratios should the accountant compute in analyzing the corporation's liquidity? List them.

3. Calculate these ratios. What do they tell you about the firm? Be specific in your evaluation.

Still More Calculations

■ The owners of the Carrington Corporation want to get a detailed breakdown of their financial statements. (See the income statement and balance sheet that accompany this case study.) One way to accomplish this is through ratio analysis. They have examined the liquidity and profitability ratios and they have looked at their turnover ratios. However, two calculations have not been carried out yet: the operating expense ratio and the number-of-times-interest-earned ratio. The owners want to have someone help them compute both of these for the last two years and then draw some conclusions about what they mean.

In addition, the owners are concerned that they are not properly interpreting the financial statement analysis. "Should we interpret these data only in relation to our past performance, or do we need to compare them with figures from our competitors?" one of the owners asked. "Also, what's the effect of inflation on the data? I'd like to know how much faith we can put in these ratios."

1. What is the firm's operating expense ratio for the last two years? Show your calculations. What conclusions can you draw from these findings?

2. What is the firm's number-of-times-interest-earned ratio for the last two years? Show your work. What conclusions can you draw from these findings?

3. Are there any limitations to the use of financial statement analysis? Explain.

Carrington Corporation Income Statement
for Years Ended December 31, 1990, and December 31, 1991

	1990		1991	
SALES REVENUE	$500,000		$575,000	
Less: Sales returns and allowances	15,000		20,000	
Net Sales		$485,000		$555,000
COST OF GOODS SOLD				
Inventory, January 1	$ 60,000		$ 50,000	
Purchases	240,000		300,000	
Goods available for sale	$300,000		$350,000	
Less: Inventory, December 31	50,000		40,000	
Cost of goods sold		250,000		310,000
Gross Margin		$235,000		$245,000
OPERATING EXPENSES				
Selling expenses	$110,000		$110,000	
Administrative expenses	45,000		35,000	
Total Operating Expenses		$155,000		$145,000
Operating Income		$ 80,000		$100,000
Financial Expense		1,100		1,000
Income before Income Taxes		$ 78,900		$ 99,000
Estimated Income Taxes		31,372		40,500
Net Profit		$ 47,528		$ 58,000

Carrington Corporation Balance Sheet
for Years Ended December 31, 1990, and December 31, 1991

ASSETS	1990			1991		
Current Assets						
Cash		$ 30,000			$ 40,000	
Accounts receivable	$100,000			$140,000		
Less: Allowance for						
uncollectible accounts	5,000	95,000		7,000	133,000	
Inventory		50,000			40,000	
Prepaid expenses		2,000			2,000	
Total Current Assets			$177,000			$215,000
Fixed Assets						
Land		$ 40,000			$ 40,000	
Building	$100,000			$100,000		
Less: Accumulated						
depreciation, building	25,000	75,000		30,000	70,000	
Equipment	$ 70,000			$ 70,000		
Less: Accumulated						
depreciation, equipment	30,000	40,000		40,000	30,000	
Total Fixed Assets			$155,000			$140,000
Total Assets			$332,000			$355,000

(continued)

LIABILITIES

Current Liabilities

Accounts payable	$ 33,000		$ 16,000	
Notes payable	10,000		—	
Taxes payable	4,000		5,500	
Installment, long-term debt	10,000		10,000	
Total Current Liabilities		$ 57,000		$ 31,500

Long-term Liabilities

Bank loan		100,000		90,000
Total Liabilities			$157,000	$121,500

OWNERS' EQUITY

Contributed Capital

Common stock, $2 par, 25,000 shares authorized	$ 50,000		$ 50,000	
Preferred stock, $100 par, 1,000 shares authorized; none sold	—		—	
Retained Earnings	125,000		183,500	
Total Owners' Equity		$175,000		$233,500
Total Liabilities and Owners' Equity		$332,000		$355,000

You Be the Consultant

A REAL GOLD MINE

Things were not always easy for Mindy and Peter Whiting. When they opened their steak house they had an average of only five customers per evening for the first two weeks. Business really picked up after that, however, and one of the reasons was word-of-mouth advertising. Mindy and Peter gave their customers large, quality steaks at lower prices than anyone else in the area. Soon things were so good that the Whitings had to ask their customers to make reservations, especially for Friday, Saturday, and Sunday evenings.

One night Peter had to go out for an hour. When he returned he saw people lined up outside waiting to get into the restaurant. This is when he decided it was time to expand the operation by doubling the seating capacity. After some serious discussions with their banker and contractor, he and Mindy increased the size of the restaurant, hired more help, and began doing business on a much larger scale.

All this happened five years ago. Since then, business has remained brisk, and the Whitings are thinking about increasing the size of their restaurant again. This time they believe an increase in seating capacity of about 50 percent will be sufficient.

Peter and Mindy mentioned this to their accountant, and she expressed delight. "You're certainly not big enough to handle all of the people who want to eat in your restaurant. I think you could double your seating capacity without any trouble at all. You have a gold mine there."

When Mindy asked her if the business was sufficiently sound to afford the costs of the construction, the accountant explained that they would have no trouble getting the funding. "You have very good financial statements. There isn't a banker in town who wouldn't be happy to deal with you."

Peter was intrigued by this remark. "What do you mean by a very good financial statement? For example, all I know about the income is what the bottom line shows. I realize we make a very good profit every year, but bankers *must* look at a lot more than that. How does a banker know exactly how much money to lend us?"

The accountant tried to explain in general terms. "Well, Peter, there are a number of financial ratios that bankers compute using income-statement data. Also, a banker would put your balance sheet next to the income statement and make calculations that draw numbers from both of the statements. Based on the results, the banker would determine how much money the bank could safely lend you."

Peter was fascinated. "I wonder," he said, "what kind of analyses the banker would conduct."

■ **YOUR CONSULTATION** As Peter and Mindy's consultant, tell them the types of financial analyses a banker would carry out using the income statement. Then tell them the kinds of ratios the banker would calculate based on the income statement and the balance sheet. Finally, explain to them the role and importance of financial budgeting in maintaining a healthy financial position.

CHAPTER 19

Purchasing and Inventory Control

Objectives

Two of the most important control areas for small businesses are purchasing and inventory. The first objective of Chapter 19 is to define the term purchasing *and explain how this function is carried out. The second objective is to review some of the policies that guide small businesses in deciding how to purchase merchandise and materials. The third objective is to study how small business firms establish an inventory control system. Particular attention will be given to perpetual inventory systems, inventory valuation, the economic order quantity formula, and materials reserves. When you have finished studying the material in this chapter you will be able to:*

1. *Define the term* purchasing.
2. *Describe the five steps in the purchasing process.*
3. *Discuss the major purchasing policies employed by small businesses.*
4. *Compare and contrast a physical count with a perpetual inventory system.*
5. *Tell how an inventory valuation method can help a firm control its inventory.*
6. *Explain how the economic order quantity formula works.*
7. *Explain how reorder points are determined.*
8. *Describe the way small manufacturing firms attempt to balance the demand for components with those currently on hand.*

PURCHASING

Purchasing is the procurement of merchandise and materials. Retailers, wholesalers, and in certain cases, service establishments, buy merchandise to sell to their customers. Manufacturers purchase the materials they use in their production processes. In all cases, purchasing is vital to the success of the business; without an adequate supply of merchandise and/or materials, the firm would be unable to operate at maximum efficiency.

Regardless of the type of business, certain steps are taken in purchasing merchandise and materials. Businesses also are guided by certain policies as they carry out the purchasing function. The following sections examine these issues.

HOW PURCHASING IS DONE

Although the purchasing function is basically the responsibility of the owner-manager, it is often—especially as a firm gets larger—turned over to a purchasing agent. Working closely with the various departments, the purchasing agent learns what merchandise and materials are needed, what quality and quantity are required, and what sources need to be contracted in order to obtain them. This is accomplished through the following five steps.

STEP 1: ISSUE THE PURCHASE ORDER   Purchasing usually begins with the issuance of a purchase order. A **purchase order** specifies the item(s) or merchandise wanted, the number desired, a brief description of the item, and the price. This document often is sent to the supplier in triplicate. The supplier signs one copy and returns it to the firm, indicating acceptance of the order and the establishment of a contract. A second copy remains with the supplier so that he or she knows exactly what has been ordered. The last copy accompanies the merchandise so that the receiving department can check the purchase order against the accompanying invoice.

In some cases, the seller calls on the small business and personally takes the order. This is typical in the retail business, where suppliers go out and actively solicit business. When this is the case, the buyer places an order and receives a copy of the order document before the seller's agent leaves the store.

STEP 2: KEEP THE PURCHASE RECORD   The receipt for the purchase should be filed so that the firm has a record of the price and the credit terms for the purchased goods. Another important reason for such record keeping is that it lets the business know what orders it has outstanding. Then, if there is a problem meeting these financial obligations, steps can be taken to acquire the necessary financing.

STEP 3: FOLLOW UP ON PURCHASE ORDERS   Sometimes orders are not delivered on schedule. By keeping good records and knowing when merchandise or materials are due, the business learns which suppliers are reliable.

STEP 4: INSPECT THE GOODS   When the goods are received, they must be inspected. Were the right items sent? Is the quantity correct? Is the quality adequate? In answering the latter question, **sampling** is often employed. For example, a small manufacturer that has ordered bolts of a specific dimension and a particular tolerance will sample the shipment to determine whether it meets their specified level of **acceptability.** This may require that 98 percent of all bolts be within the specified dimensions. Out of 1,000 bolts, 100 may be randomly sampled; if 98 pass inspection, all are accepted. Otherwise, the shipment is judged unacceptable and returned to the supplier.

STEP 5: PAY FOR THE SHIPMENT   If everything is in order, the purchasing manager will notify the bookkeeper or finance department to make payment. Conversely, if the shipment is unacceptable, the purchasing manager will send a letter to the supplier explaining why the goods are being returned.

PURCHASING POLICIES

A **policy** is a guideline to thinking and action. It provides the owner-manager with direction for decision making by establishing some basic do's and don'ts. Within these parameters the owner or purchasing manager is free to operate. We will now examine some of the policies that direct purchasing decisions.

ETHICAL PURCHASING BEHAVIOR The individual charged with the purchasing function should solicit bids from suppliers so as to ensure that the firm is getting the best possible deal. However, it is unethical to show the bids or price quotations of one firm to sales representatives from other firms. Likewise, the acceptance of gifts from suppliers should not be allowed. Otherwise, the purchasing manager tends to favor suppliers that offer gifts, and the business is likely to end up paying more for its goods than if open competition among suppliers was encouraged.

MAKING VERSUS BUYING   Among small manufacturers there is the issue of making or buying component parts. Some arguments support making the parts themselves:

1. When there is idle capacity, it can be used for producing components.
2. By manufacturing components internally, the firm reduces its dependence on outside suppliers.
3. If the components being manufactured are under the protection of a patent, internal production helps to ensure the secrecy of the process.
4. Quite often it is cheaper to make components than to pay others to do so.
5. Internal production allows closer coordination and control of overall manufacturing operations.
6. When design changes are needed, they can be more effectively implemented with internal production.

On the other hand, sometimes it is more beneficial to buy component parts. Arguments in favor of buying the parts include the following:

1. It may be less expensive to subcontract the work than to do it in-house.
2. A shortage of equipment may make it impossible to manufacture the components in-house.
3. If demand for an item is seasonal, it may be wiser to subcontract than to underwrite the risk of manufacturing.
4. By occasionally purchasing from outside sources, a business can compare its own efficiency with that of subcontractors.
5. In industries where technological change can make equipment obsolete, subcontracting helps the business sidestep this risk.

Research shows that most small manufacturers produce many of their own components and subcontract the rest. However, the final make-or-buy decision should be based on cost considerations and the overall effect on short- and long-run profit.

PURCHASE DISCOUNTS   Many small businesses try very hard to take all available purchase discounts because of the savings involved. For example, on terms of 2/10, net 30, the business can save 2 percent on all early payments. If a particular material is purchased monthly, this can amount to a substantial saving over a year's time. In fact, in many cases it is worthwhile to borrow money to take advantage of these discounts.

DETERMINING SUPPLY SOURCES   In every industry, the specific sources of supply are well known. Wholesalers and retailers are aware of merchandise sources; manufacturers know which firms supply materials and components. The big question, therefore, is whether the business should rely exclusively on a few sources, or spread its purchasing among many.

Buying from only one or two suppliers can result in quantity discounts. It also allows the supplier to learn the business's varied needs, and the supplier will often make an extra effort to provide the best possible service. And if the company is having financial problems, the supplier may help the firm by providing lenient credit terms because the supplier wants to keep the customer.

On the other hand, if the supplier runs into problems and the business has failed to develop a secondary source, the firm may run out of merchandise or materials. Then there is the matter of price. Unless the small business shops around, it cannot be certain that it is paying the lowest possible price.

Most firms try to handle this problem by seeking competitive bids and finding the suppliers who offer the best terms. Then they check the reputations of these companies and strike a deal with the two or three who are considered the best, thereby ensuring themselves several sources of supply.

INVENTORY CONTROL

No small business should keep too much inventory on hand. When that occurs, money is tied up in goods that are simply sitting on the shelf or in the warehouse. Additionally, a **carrying cost** is associated with inventory; it costs money to keep inventory on hand. This carrying cost includes the expense of insurance (fire, theft), the physical space taken up in the warehouse (that is, $2 per square foot per year), and the finance charges associated with paying for the inventory. If we assume that carrying costs are 20 percent of the value of the inventory and the inventory turnover is low, these carrying costs are going to be high. Conversely, if the turnover is high, these costs will be low.

This table provides an example of a company that sells $100,000 worth of inventory annually:

ANNUAL INVENTORY CARRYING COSTS		
Turnover	Investment	Carrying Costs
1	$100,000	$20,000
2	50,000	10,000
3	33,333	6,667
4	25,000	5,000
5	20,000	4,000

From these numbers, it might seem that only a small amount of inventory should be carried. However, if inventory is very small—for example $20,000—the business is likely to encounter a large number of **stockouts.** This will result in the firm either placing a rush order for the goods or telling customers it cannot fill their orders. With a rush order the profit margin is greatly reduced (and sometimes totally eliminated) by the extra costs. With each unfilled order, the business foregoes a sale and risks losing the future patronage of a dissatisfied customer.

Thus, there are two sides to the inventory control dilemma, and the small business owner-manager must walk the tightrope between them.[1] In the remainder of this section, we will study how retailers, wholesalers, and manufacturers go about doing this. Service enterprises will not be considered specifically, since they do not have an inventory problem per se. (See Small Business Owner's Notebook: Strong Inventory Controls—Gearing Up for Growth or Resisting Recession.)

RETAIL INVENTORY CONTROL

A number of advantages are associated with retail inventory control. Three of the major ones are

1. Inventory stock can be balanced in relation to sales.

2. Primary attention can be given to the fastest moving, most profitable lines.

3. The ideal rate of stock turnover for each item can be determined.

Additionally, an effective merchandise control system can help the retailer develop a profitable marketing strategy for all goods in the store.[2]

TRACKING INVENTORY   How does the business know *exactly* how much inventory is on hand? The most common ways are to make a physical count and to keep a perpetual inventory.

Most small retail stores simply count the merchandise on hand periodically. This **physical count** may be tedious, but it does indicate what is in the store. A **perpetual inventory** approach is more sophisticated: a record is kept of everything that has been sold and everything that has been stocked. As a result, the number in the inventory book *should be* the actual amount on hand. When it is not, the owner-manager knows that pilferage (by employees or customers) has taken place or that mistakes have been made in the record keeping.

Many businesses use a combination of these two inventory approaches. A perpetual inventory record is kept, and an annual or semiannual physical count is made to ensure the accuracy of the records. This is how pilferage, theft, and mistakes are discovered.

INVENTORY VALUATION   Another commonly used method, approved by the Internal Revenue Service for income tax purposes, is the **retail inventory valuation** method.

---

[1]See "Inventory Management: Controlling Costs to Maximize Profit," *Small Business Report,* August 1987, pp. 50–53.

[2]See David F. Groebner and C. Mike Merz, "Solving the Inventory Problem for the Sale of Seasonal Merchandise," *Journal of Small Business Management,* July 1990, pp. 19–26.

■   **SMALL BUSINESS OWNER'S NOTEBOOK**   ■

Strong Inventory Controls— Gearing Up for Growth or Resisting Recession

Growing small firms typically invest too much money into inventories. If a larger inventory could be avoided, then the money could be used for growth or for cash reserves in times of recession.

One Chicago-based manufacturing firm, Skolnik Industries, Inc., has developed an early warning system against potential inventory problems that involves tracking five different kinds of financial relationships within the company. This system may be useful for other small manufacturers. The following five key functions are reviewed when using this system:

1. *Gross Margin Return on Investment*   This amount is calculated by subtracting the cost of a product's raw materials, direct labor, and factory overhead from its selling price and dividing that figure by the selling price. A 15 percent to 25 percent return should be expected on products.

2. *Inventory Turnover*   To calculate the turnover by product, divide the total number of units sold by the average number of units on hand (beginning total plus ending total divided by 2). The turnover rate should be 4 to 6 times per year.

3. *Percentage of Orders Shipped on Time*   This percentage should be monitored for each product. The aim is to achieve a 98 percent success rate, based on the delivery terms promised to customers. If the percentage drops below 90 percent, then inventory levels are too low.

4. *Length of Time to Fill Back Orders*   The number of days it takes to fill back orders should be watched and measured. If backlogs are increasing, then the inventory may need to be larger.

5. *Ratio of Customer Complaints to Shipped Orders*   The complaint ratio equals complaints divided by all orders shipped. If the ratio is larger than 2 percent, then the owner should be aware of problems in inventory or warehouse systems. Of course, each complaint needs to be analyzed for any additional underlying problems.

Source: Adapted from Jill Andresky Fraser, "Hidden Cash," *Inc.,* February 1991, pp. 81–82.

This method can be used by any store or department that sells goods without processing or altering them.

In addition to providing the owner with a closing inventory at cost or market value, whichever is lower, the method provides a means of maintaining a perpetual merchandise inventory and of keeping records on discounts to employees, markdowns, and shortages. Table 19-1 illustrates how this inventory method works. Note in the table that beginning inventory and purchases are recorded at both cost and

Table 19-1 The Retail Inventory Valuation Method

		COST	RETAIL
Beginning inventory		$100,000	$150,000
Purchases		40,000	60,000
Add: Freight and express charges		1,000	1,500
Goods available for sale		$141,000	$211,500
Markup (retail minus cost)	$70,500		
Dividing markup of $70,500 by retail cost of $211,500 results in a markup of 33%.			
Net sales	80,000		
Add: Discounts to employees, markdowns, and shortages	5,000		
Goods sold or disposed of at retail			85,000
Ending inventory			$126,500
Cost percentage (100% minus 33%)			67%
Ending inventory at cost		$ 84,755	
Cost of goods sold		$ 56,245	
Net sales	$80,000		
Less: Cost of goods sold	56,245		
Gross margin	$23,755		

retail value. Freight and express charges are added to the cost of inventory because these are expenses associated with obtaining the goods. The result is the value of the goods available for sale at both cost and retail.

Markups to the retail price are then computed, because this is money that will be received in revenue when the goods are sold. In this case, the markup is determined to be 33 percent.

Net sales are then entered. In this case, they are $80,000. To this has been added all discounts to employees, markdowns, and shortages for the particular period. The sum is the retail price of all the goods sold or disposed of during this time. By subtracting this amount ($85,000) from the retail price of the goods available for sale, the retail price of the goods still on hand is determined. However, all the owner really needs to know is the *cost* of the goods on hand. Since the markup is 33 percent, the cost is 67 percent, or $84,755. Subtracting this from the cost of the goods initially available for sale, namely $141,000, results in a cost of goods sold figure of $56,245. Finally, this cost of goods is subtracted from the net sales of $80,000, to arrive at a gross margin of $23,755.

Note that the markup of 33 percent was calculated without including discounts, markdowns, or shortages. However, these were added to sales to get the total value of the goods at retail. Thus, the calculated cost value of the closing inventory is less than actual cost. This is all right, however, because some of the goods were marked down. If the price trend had been upward and additional markups had been taken, they would be reflected in the calculation of the markup percentage, and the calculated cost would more closely approximate the actual cost.

This retail valuation method is widely recommended by small business experts. In particular, they like the fact that a perpetual inventory is maintained at retail prices and records are kept of all changes in these prices. This provides management with a record of all discounts, markdowns, and other changes. However, it should be noted that since markups vary somewhat by the type of merchandise, this inventory valuation method should be used within departments or with homogeneous merchandise classifications, not uniformly employed on a storewide basis.[3]

WHOLESALE INVENTORY CONTROL

Many small wholesalers keep track of inventory through the **observation method.** They look at how much inventory they have on hand and decide whether to reorder now or let things go a little longer. However, this is dangerous because it is notoriously inaccurate. Quite often, the business ends up with a stockout and cannot fill incoming orders, which costs the business money.

Having excess inventory also costs money, because the wholesaler's profit margin is greatly affected by the number of times inventory is turned over. Remember, most wholesalers work on low gross margin coupled with high turnover. They cannot afford to carry slow-moving merchandise. One way to avoid that is with an effective perpetual inventory record system.

PERPETUAL INVENTORY RECORD SYSTEM   In essence, this system requires the business to keep track of the various lines, noting beginning inventory, reorder points, and how much to repurchase each time. The logic is rather simple: by keeping a record of sales in each line, the owner-manager can balance supply and demand.

Here is the way it is done. First, the amount that should be reordered each time is computed. (This method will be discussed in the next section.) Second, the time it takes to receive the goods is determined. Third, the amount of merchandise most likely to be sold between the placement of the reorder and the receipt of the goods is calculated. Along with this information, the wholesaler knows both the minimum and maximum stocks for each line. The minimum is the amount on hand just before receipt of the new goods; the maximum is this minimum amount plus the newly purchased merchandise.

By keeping perpetual inventory records, the wholesaler is able to determine how many units constitute a **reorder point.** When the stock reaches this level, a new order is placed. Problems can result if it takes much longer to get the stock than it should and stockouts occur, and if sales variations during the reorder period are greater than anticipated and the firm ends up with much more (or less) inventory than expected. However, by carefully examining past reorder times and sales fluctuations, these problems can be minimized. (See Small Business Success: Keeping Inventory Down.)

INVENTORY CONTROL IN SMALL MANUFACTURING FIRMS

Small manufacturing firms face two inventory control problems. One is that of keeping a sufficient number of finished units on hand. In dealing with this problem, a perpetual inventory system similar to the one used in wholesaling is most appropriate. The other problem is that of keeping the needed raw materials and component parts on hand. These situations are often handled by reserving materials,

---

[3]See also William M. Bassin, "A Technique for Applying EOQ Models to Retail Cycle Stock Inventories," *Journal of Small Business Management,* January 1990, pp. 48–55.

■ **SMALL BUSINESS SUCCESS** ■

Keeping Inventory Down

Stanley Cohen is the founder of Vanity Fair and Playtime Products. Cohen's first venture, Vanity Fair, successfully manufactured and sold toy radios and other "adult" stereo products. However, in the early 1960s he entered the high-end stereo components industry and carried a large amount of inventory, expecting the demand for these higher quality stereo components to increase. Instead, the increase occurred in the television market. Cohen found that he was overstocked with stereo equipment and could not go after the market niche of color television. This blunder cost three million dollars. He was able to continue for another seven years before selling the business to Filter Flow, Inc. Filter Flow allowed him to stay on staff to set up manufacturing locations and sales markets in Hong Kong and Japan.

However, the experience taught Cohen to avoid over producing and carrying a high amount of inventory. In 1980, at age 51, Cohen founded Playtime Products to manufacture all kinds of toys ranging from race sets to dolls and play tools. Playtime produced toys only after obtaining a letter of credit from the customer. This approach kept the inventory down and gross margins up.

In 1983, Cohen decided to expand his product line to include the popular Cabbage Patch Kids. Cohen had a hunch that these stuffed dolls would end up being a success, and they turned out to be just the kind of gamble he was looking for. Company sales increased from $7 million in 1983 to $40 million in 1984. Today, Playtime Products manufactures and distributes a line of 80 children's toys and generates sales of $42 million.

Source: Adapted from Bob Weinstein, "Play It Again, Stan," *Entrepreneur,* December 1990, pp. 96–102.

thereby ensuring their availability when needed. Thus, two inventory issues need to be addressed: the economic ordering of materials and the reserving of materials for specific jobs.[4]

ECONOMIC ORDERING OF MATERIALS The manufacturer needs to determine the most economical amount to purchase at one time. In so doing, the firm can turn to a mathematical formula known as the **economic order quantity formula (EOQ).** Before examining this formula, let us examine the two most important order quantity components: order cost and carrying cost.[5]

Every time a firm places an order, some expenses are incurred. Contracting the supplier, tying up the order, and mailing it all cost money. Let us assume that for the

---

[4]See John H. Blackstone and James F. Cox, "Inventory Management Techniques," *Journal of Small Business Management,* April 1985, pp. 27–33.

[5]See Richard M. Hodgetts and Donald F. Kuratko, *Management,* 3rd ed. (San Diego, CA: Harcourt Brace Jovanovich, 1991), pp. 143–44.

Table 19-2 EOQ Computation: Trial and Error*

UNITS PER ORDER	ORDER COST	CARRYING COST (inventory/2 × $1)	TOTAL COST
100	$2,812.50	$ 50	$2,862.50
200	1,406.25	100	1,506.25
300	937.50	150	1,807.50
400	703.13	200	903.13
500	562.50	250	812.50
600	468.75	300	768.75
700	401.79	350	751.79
800	351.56	400	751.56
900	312.50	450	762.50
1,000	281.25	500	781.25
1,100	255.68	550	805.68
1,200	234.38	600	834.38

*Based on an order cost of $18.75 and an annual requirement of 15,000 units.

firm being analyzed this expense is $18.75 per order. Furthermore, the firm annually requires 15,000 units of a particular component. Given these data, if the company orders 100 units, **order costs** for the year will total $2,812.50 ($18.75 × 150 orders). Should the firm order 200 units each time, these order costs will drop to $1,406.25 ($18.75 × 75 orders). Additional order costs associated with varying order sizes are presented in Table 19-2. Note that at 1,200 units per order the annual costs decline to $234.38. Carrying this logic to the extreme, the firm could order 15,000 units at one time, thereby reducing annual order costs to $18.75. However, this would increase the carrying costs dramatically.

Carrying costs are the expenses associated with having inventory on hand. These include insurance, taxes, depreciation, obsolescence, and the interest on the inventory investment. Let us assume that these add up to 10 percent of the value of the component (which is $10), or $1. Additionally, it should be noted that a constant rate of depletion is assumed with the EOQ. This means that if 3,000 units are sold every 30 business days, 100 will be sold daily. Following this logic, the average inventory on hand will *always* be one-half of the number ordered. Thus, the actual cost of carrying the inventory is

$$\frac{\text{Number of components order}}{2} \times \$1$$

With an order of 100 units, the carrying cost will by $50; for 200 units it will be $100, and so forth. These data are presented in Table 19-2 for order sizes up to 1,200.

Note in Table 19-2 that the most economical order size is 800. However, there are two problems with this solution. First, it will take the business quite a bit of time to determine the ideal reorder size if every product line is to be analyzed this way. Numerous lot sizes will have to be determined for the purposes of zeroing in on the best one. Second, the owner does not know that 800 units is really the most economical order size, only that, of those in Table 19-2, 800 is the best. In short, learning what order size is ideal is a trial-and-error process.

To overcome these problems, the business can turn to the EOQ formula. It can be written this way:

$$\text{Economic order quantity} = \sqrt{\frac{(2 \times \text{Annual demand} \times \text{Order cost})}{\text{Carrying cost per unit}}}$$

For the firm being analyzed,

$$\text{EOQ} = \sqrt{\frac{(2 \times 15{,}000 \times \$18.75)}{\$1.00}}$$

$$= \sqrt{\frac{(30{,}000 \times \$18.75)}{\$1.00}} = \sqrt{\frac{\$562{,}500}{\$1.00}}$$

$$= \sqrt{562{,}500} = 750 \text{ units}$$

The firm should reorder in lot sizes of 750. This can be verified by referring it to the various lot sizes in Table 19-2. Order costs are $18.75 × 20 (if the firm orders 750 units each time, it will have to order 20 times to meet its annual requirement of 15,000 units), or $375. Carrying costs, meanwhile, will be 750/2 × $1, or another $375. Thus, the total cost will be $750. (See Figure 19-1.) By substituting data into the formula, a fast, accurate answer can be determined.

Figure 19-1

Graphic Representation of the Economic Order Quantity (EOQ) Formula

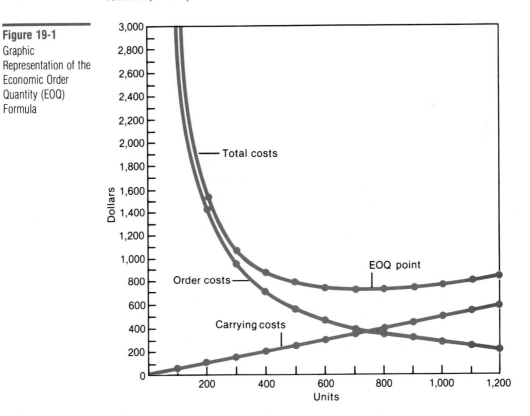

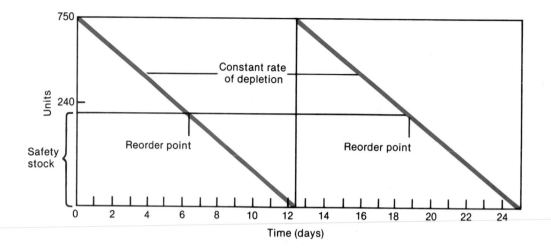

Figure 19-2
Graphic
Representation of
Reorder Points

DETERMINING REORDER POINTS When should the components be reordered? It depends on how long delivery takes and the rate of sales expected during this period. While this was noted before, let us reexamine it and tie the discussion to the EOQ answer. Let us assume that the business starts the year off with 750 units in inventory and that an average of 60 are sold each business day, of which there are 250 in a year. This gives an annual demand of 15,000 (60 × 250) units. Let us also assume that it takes two business days to fill an order.

Given this information, a reorder should be placed when 120 units are on hand. However, this may be cutting it a little close. The reorder may, on occasion, take three or four days to fill. Furthermore, every now and then there will be a larger-than-average daily demand, so 120 units may not be enough **safety stock.** A more conservative level would be 240. In this case, the reordering process would be graphed as shown in Figure 19-2.

Note the assumed constant rate of depletion. Every 12.5 days 750 units will be sold. On the ninth day an order is placed, and it is received just as the safety stock is exhausted, resulting in another 750 units for sale. If, over time, the firm finds delivery time or annual demand changing, appropriate adjustments can be made in both the quantity that is ordered and the amount of safety stock that is maintained.

MATERIALS RESERVES The inventory received is eventually scheduled for use in manufacture. The necessary components must be available when they are needed. This is done by balancing the amounts ordered and on hand with the amounts that are needed, using a well-designed ledger sheet. See Figure 19-3.

Note in Figure 19-3 that there are four major areas of consideration: the materials ordered, the balance on hand, the reserved materials, and the balance available. Here is the way our records are kept. When a material or component is depleted to the reorder point, a new order is placed. This amount, let us say 750 units, is entered in the *Ordered* section under both *Ordered* and *Balance*. If the firm wants to reserve part of this order for a special job, the number of items to be reserved is entered in the *Reserved* section under both *Reserved* and *Balance*. Let us say that this is not necessary in this particular case.

Date	Order Number	1. Ordered			2. Balance on Hand	3. Reserved			4. Balance available
		Ordered	Received	Balance		Reserved	Issued	Balance	

Figure 19-3
A Balance-of-Stores Ledger

Given this fact, the total of 750 is also entered in column 4, thereby increasing the *Balance Available*. The reason for this is that, at least theoretically, these materials will be received before the present quantity in the storeroom is exhausted.

After each transaction is entered on the ledger sheet, the **balance on order** (the amount ordered minus the amount received) and the balance on hand should be equal to the **balance on reserve** (the amount reserved minus the amount issued) plus the balance available. In this way, the ledger provides a continuous check on the accuracy of the entries. It is very much like a double-entry bookkeeping system.

In order to provide you with more experience with this system, we present the five rules that govern the posting of entries to the ledger. As you read these, refer to Figure 19-3 and follow the movement and logic of the numbers.

1. When materials are ordered, the amounts are posted to columns 1 and 4. In column 1, they are added to any amounts already in *Ordered* and *Balance*. Assuming none of these materials is being reserved, the amounts are added to the *Balance Available* (column 4).

2. When materials are received, the amounts are subtracted from *Ordered in column 1 and added to the Balance on Hand* (column 2).

3. If any materials are reserved, the amount is added to *Reserved* in column 3 and subtracted from *Balance Available* (column 4).

4. When materials are issued, having already been reserved, the amounts are subtracted from *Balance on Hand* (column 2) and *Balance* in column 3.

5. When materials that have not been reserved are issued, the amount is subtracted from both the *Balance on Hand* (column 2) and from *Balance Available* (column 4).

■ **SUMMARY**

Purchasing is the procurement of merchandise and materials. Since every small business must eventually repurchase things, an effective purchasing strategy is crucial to business success.

The purchasing function is usually handled by the owner-manager or purchasing agent. This commonly involves five steps. First, a purchase order is issued. Second, the purchase record is kept on file. Third, orders are followed up for purposes of ensuring delivery as scheduled. Fourth, the goods are inspected upon arrival and a decision is made regarding their acceptability. Fifth, payment for the shipment is made.

Most small businesses rely on a number of policies to help them make purchasing decisions. Four of the most common relate to ethical purchasing behavior, making versus buying, purchase discounts, and the determining of supply sources.

Inventory control is needed in balancing the amount of material and components on hand with the amount being used. If too little is on hand, the firm will continually face stockouts. If too much is on hand, the company's carrying costs will be high.

Retail firms control inventory through a physical count and/or perpetual inventory system. Another commonly used method, approved by the Internal Revenue Service for income tax purposes, is the retail inventory method. This method can be used by any store or department that sells goods without processing or altering them. In essence, the method provides the firm with a means of determining its gross margin.

Wholesale firms tend to use perpetual inventory control. The biggest problem they face is determining reorder points.

Small manufacturing firms can use the economic order quantity formula (EOQ) to balance their order costs and carrying costs and to determine reasonable reorder points. Another inventory control issue, unique to manufacturing firms, is the reserving of materials for use in processing or assembling goods. Small manufacturers find it helpful to develop a balance-of-stores ledger for keeping track of materials and components that have been ordered, reserved, and on hand.

■ **REVIEW AND DISCUSSION QUESTIONS**

1. What is meant by the term *purchasing?*

2. What takes place during each of the five steps in the purchasing process?

3. What is meant by the term *policy?* How can a policy help an owner-manager with decision making?

4. When deciding between making and buying components, what advantages of making the units in-house are considered? What are some advantages of buying components from others?

5. In addition to make-or-buy decisions, what other purchasing policies do small business owners need to know about? Identify and describe three of them.

6. How does a perpetual inventory system work?

7. How does the retail inventory method of evaluation work? Describe it in your own words.

8. How does the economic order quantity formula work?

9. How should a company go about determining reorder points? Explain in detail.

10. One of the problems small manufacturing firms have is that of maintaining adequate materials reserves. How can a business deal with this problem? Include a discussion of the balance-of-stores ledger in your answer.

Case Studies

Regina's Reorders

■ Homemaker's House is a large retail outlet that sells a wide variety of home appliances. They sell such things as washers and dryers, freezers, toasters, garbage disposals, food processors, and ice cream makers.

The owner, Regina Whortler, believes that a primary way of maximizing profit is to keep inventory to a minimum. "I know this is no easy chore," she explains. "If I have too little inventory on hand, I'll lose sales. If I have too much, the carrying costs can be very high. Nevertheless, it's a challenge I have to face if I'm going to stay in business. To help me balance my inventory, I rely heavily on the economic order quantity formula. Today Toni [her assistant] and I will be reviewing the reordering of some kitchen appliances that have reached the inventory reorder point."

Regina was referring to four goods—blenders, toasters, mixers, and ice cream makers. A review of the data associated with each reveals that each year:

☐ 1,000 blenders are sold. The order cost per blender is $20, and the carrying cost per unit is $1.

☐ 500 toasters are sold. The order cost per toaster is $30, and the carrying cost per unit is $1.33.

☐ 1,000 mixers are sold. The order cost per mixer is $50, and the carrying cost per unit is $1.98.

☐ 200 ice cream makers are sold. The order cost per ice cream maker is $100, and the carrying cost per unit is $4.

1. How many blenders should Regina reorder? How many toasters? If necessary, round your answer to the nearest unit.

2. How many mixers should Regina reorder? How many ice cream makers? If necessary, round your answer to the nearest unit.

3. If the annual demand for ice cream makers doubled and the carrying cost increased to $8 per unit, how would this affect the number Regina should reorder each time? Explain.

Making versus Buying

■ Wayne Erickson is the owner of a small manufacturing firm that produces specialty machinery. All of this machinery is made to order, which means that an order is placed with Wayne's firm before the machine is built. Given the specialized nature of the machines they manufacture, it would be foolhardy to build them first and then seek buyers.

However, Wayne has been having a problem. Some of the components for these machines have been costing his firm more and more to produce. One reason for this is that the materials are costing more. A second reason is that the company needs only a small number of each component, so the setup and processing costs are quite high. The result is that their costs are rising faster than the sales prices of their machines, and the profit margin is suffering.

One solution to this dilemma is for Wayne to subcontract the production of the various components and become more of an assembler. He is reluctant to do this because the company will then be reliant on outside manufacturers. "What if they're late with a shipment or don't produce high-quality components? What do I do then? As long as we manufacture these things in-house, I have control over my operation. If I give up this control, profits might suffer because I'll be late on orders due to stockouts. I'm really reluctant to let anyone else produce my products."

1. What advantages are associated with self-production?

2. What advantages are associated with subcontracting production?

3. What would you recommend that Wayne do? Support your answer.

■ ■ ▬▬▬▬▬▬▬▬▬▬▬▬▬▬▬▬▬▬▬▬▬▬▬▬▬▬▬▬ ■ ■

You Be the Consultant:

A MULTITUDE OF PROBLEMS

The Iznack Manufacturing Company has some inventory control problems. Its major problem is caused by the difficulty of keeping a particular component on hand. The component is used in the manufacture of a medium-sized office machine. Iznack builds for one of the nation's largest office machine supply firms. The company has been placing orders with Iznack for thirty of these machines monthly. However, in the last two months the firm has been able to deliver only twenty because of the shortage of the components.

There are a number of reasons for the shortage. One is that Iznack is unsure of how often to reorder. In the past, it has reordered when it had a five-day supply on hand. The supplier could fill the order in four days, so there was no problem. Recently, the reorder time has risen to twelve days, and more and more orders are running late. Consequently, Iznack has been increasing the size of each order. However, the question of when to reorder has gone unanswered.

Knowing how many units to order is another problem. Realizing that this is tied directly to the issue of not ordering soon enough, Ralph Iznack, the company president, has suggested trying to find an ideal number of units to reorder each time. However, all the purchasing manager has done is adjust the reordering period. If a large number of units were ordered, the manager would still let the number on hand be drawn down to a five-day supply and then reorder. Ralph is certain that there is a more systematic way of determining reorder times and inventory size.

The last problem with which the firm is having trouble is the scheduling of components for assembly. Sometimes components have been reserved for machines currently in assembly while other machines were complete except for that component—and the purchasing manager has refused to release the reserved components. The result is that the nearly complete machines have not been completed until new shipments of components were received.

In an effort to resolve these problems, Ralph has made a full investigation of the situation. He has made several discoveries:

1. The firm uses 3,000 of these components monthly.

2. The cost of ordering the units is $60 per order.

3. Each component costs $2.10, and the carrying cost associated with each is 20 percent of this value.

Although Ralph is unsure about how this information can help him resolve these problems, he is determined to analyze the situation and try to come up with the best possible answers.

■ **YOUR CONSULTATION** As Ralph's consultant, help him deal with these problems. First, tell him how many units he should order at a time. Second, advise him on how he can determine the reorder point. Third, make recommendations about how he should deal with the problem of scheduling components for assembly. Be sure to give your answers in clear and concise language.

Part Six Case Study

CLEVENGER LIGHTING

BACKGROUND INFORMATION

Phil Sladow started the Clevenger Lighting Company in the early 1980s when he and a group of investors bought the patent for a halogen gooseneck reading lamp from its inventor. Sladow and his original investors were forced to sell additional stock to finance their start-up costs, which included the purchase of molds, manufacturing facilities, and the initial marketing program. Along with the money came a board of interested investor/directors who were delighted with what Sladow, after a very slow and worrisome start, was able to do with the company.

COMPANY BACKGROUND

The product was initially sold through the traditional wholesale-retail channel, but when this approach proved to be only marginally successful, Sladow turned to the direct mail channel. Direct mail marketing was in its ascendancy in the early 1980s, and was used to market a rapidly expanding array of products and services, including innovative new products like the halogen lamp.

MARKETING INFORMATION

The unique halogen lamp was an ideal direct mail product. It was a product that needed to be explained. Product explanation, or selling, seldom happened in retail stores where retail service had already become, according to experts like Tom Peters, an oxymoron. In contrast, carefully crafted mailings could explain the product, bring it alive, and, unlike untrained retail clerks, point out unnoticed values to potential owners of the product. In addition, a direct mail package could be sent selectively, and therefore cost effectively, to carefully chosen lists of people.

The mail package included a thorough brochure and sales letter, along with a variety of involvement devices, such as, for example, paper coins that the reader is invited to insert in a slot on the order form, and puzzles that respondents can put together, and, in the process, get the sales message. The mail package had the effect of making Clevenger's halogen lamp offer really come alive. It also made the cash register ring. Sales, in fact, were being made as fast as the small manufacturing operation could manufacture, assemble and ship the lamps.

ADVERTISING INFORMATION

During this period, Clevenger's advertising had been in magazines such as *Atlantic Monthly,* the *New Yorker,* and *Harpers* for the most part. The advertising had centered on

Source: This case was prepared by Nabil Hassan and Herbert E. Brown, Wright State University, and is intended to be used as a basis for class discussion. Presented and accepted by the refereed Midwest Society For Case Research. All rights reserved to the authors and the Midwest Society for Case Research. Copyrighted © 1989 by Nabil Hassan and Herbert E. Brown.

the "higher order" benefits of the halogen lamp. Its bright, cool, focused light was presented as relaxing the harried young executive, while projecting an image of success to whoever might take note of the lamp in the executive's home or office.

Sladow soon found that it was less expensive and more profitable to produce a direct mail catalog and target it to the upscale yuppie market. He kept advertising in the same media, but now for leads to whom he could send catalogs. In a catalog, he could surround the unique lamp product with a variety of other closely related items purchased from other manufacturers, thereby spreading his marketing costs.

Clevenger prospered until 1985 when sales peaked at 40,000 lamps. This was one year after the hiring of Millie Christie as advertising manager. Since then, despite major soul searching and effort, and a move back into upscale specialty stores, sales have continued to decline. At present, in 1989, sales were at an annualized rate of 22,000 lamps.

CURRENT ISSUES

Encouraged by his inability to turn things around, and by his board, Sladow recently decided to look for some managerial help, possibly even a replacement for himself. He felt very fortunate when he found Jim Merchant, a Northwestern University MBA, who was ecstatic about the possibility of taking over the company as president. Merchant had been a consultant to the firm during its movement into the direct marketing channel and knew the business well. He also had experience in virtually all aspects of marketing and business while working for a national consulting firm. Thus, he appeared to be an ideal candidate. Sladow's board agreed, and Merchant was hired.

Merchant determined that his biggest problem was underutilized capacity. He felt the best way to attack this was by increasing sales. He also felt he had a margin problem, and determined that this could best be attacked through cost control. Here, he determined, variable costs were the primary issue. He also felt that advertising strategy was a potential source of the firm's difficulty, and asked Millie Christie, who has been in charge of Clevenger's advertising strategy since 1983, two years before the sales peak, to present her views on the firm's advertising program.

Millie felt somewhat defensive, and right, when she asserted that the fall-off in sales was not due to the advertising media or the advertising message. The direct response channel was not a problem either as she saw it. To Millie, the problem was quite simple: the lamp was priced too high. She pointed out that the targeted market was now saturated, and insisted that sales could not be increased unless the price was lowered, permitting her to address mass market segments that lie beyond "Yuppie Land."

THE PROPOSAL

Millie's proposal was to decrease the present $100.00 price to $90, proceed with advertising in mass media such as newspapers, in newsweeklies such as *Business Week*, on Top 40 Radio, and the like. Her goal was to reach far more potential customers than were being reached at present. She felt that this could be done while absolute marketing costs remained essentially unchanged.

President Merchant was skeptical but intrigued by Millie's ideas, and asked for a business and marketing analysis of the impact of her proposal. He asked her to first get together with Herm Agee, the controller, run "some numbers", and then find a pricing consultant to render some qualitative advice on the numbers and anything else that seemed pertinent to the case. The consultant, it turns out, is you.

FINANCIAL INFORMATION

Herm suggested that they calculate the additional sales necessary to reach break even under Millie's suggestions. He agreed to make an attempt to divide costs into their fixed and variable components as necessary for cost-volume-profit analysis. He also prepared the following list of fixed and variable costs and expenses. He used the least square method to classify costs into categories for 1988.

Fixed Costs and Expenses:	
Manufacturing Costs	$400,000
Marketing Costs	50,000
Administrative and General Costs	150,000
Total	$600,000
Variable Costs and Expenses:	
Manufacturing Costs	$ 40
Marketing Costs	20
Administrative and General Costs	10
Total	$ 70

Both Millie Christie and Herm Agee agree that they must first show President Merchant the amount of additional sales needed. Then their task will be to assess the probabilities of reaching and exceeding these sales levels. Agee's data contain three critical assumptions:

1. Material prices and labor wage rates have been stable in the recent past, and will stay that way for the foreseeable future.

2. Capacity is available for a sales increase.

3. An average of $30.00 worth of complementary, add-on merchandise is sold for every halogen lamp that is sold. The average variable costs associated with this merchandise is $10.00.

DISCUSSION QUESTIONS

1. What is Clevenger's break-even point in dollars (a) assuming the present sales price of $100 per unit and (b) the proposed sales price of $90. Assume that *Clevenger does not handle the additional merchandise, or that it is not being sold.*

2. What is Clevenger's break-even point in dollars (a) assuming the present sales price of $100 per unit and (b) the proposed sales price of $90. Assume that *Clevenger handles the additional merchandise, and that it is being sold.*

3. Determine the net additional halogen lamp sales necessary for Clevenger Company to break even under the new proposal without the additional merchandise. (Assume a sale price of $90.)

4. Determine the net additional halogen lamp and add-on product sales necessary for Clevenger to break even under the $90 halogen lamp price proposal.

5. Determine the net income or loss for 1988 if the Clevenger Company sells halogen lamps without add-on products, assuming:
   a) The sales price per unit is $100, and the sales volume remains the same, 22,000 units.
   b) The sales price per unit is $90, and the sales volume remains the same, 22,000 units.

6. Determine the maximum income for 1988 if the Clevenger Company sells halogen lamps without add-on products, assuming the proposed sales price of $90 per unit and the company is operating at its current level.

7. Take the position and argue that market value, not accounting costs, is what drives price.

8. Make a coherent argument as to what the market, cost, and competitive conditions would have to be for Millie's proposal to work.

9. Discuss other strategies that you feel Ms. Christie and Mr. Agee should propose to the president (alternate methods for increasing sales and profits and why these should work).

10. Note that in all of the above analyses allocated administrative and general costs were included as variable costs and deducted from price to determine the contribution margin, the contribution ratio, and ultimately, dollar and unit breakevens. Do you agree with this? Why or why not? ■

Part Six Entrepreneurial Simulation Program

HOW'S BUSINESS?

By now you should be an experienced shoe retailer. Over the months you have worked hard developing your market niche and trying to attract customers to your store. So if someone approaches you and asks, "How's business?," what would be your response? Will you really have an answer, or will you respond with a shrug of the shoulders and the words, "Still hanging in there"?

What is your indicator of success? Every month you receive an income statement and balance sheet along with feedback regarding sales by type of shoe. You also have an opportunity to purchase market research data comparing your decisions and performance with those of your competitors. How could you more effectively convert the data into information that would answer the question "How's business?" for yourself as well as for others?

One of the best ways is to develop and use a series of ratios based on the monthly data. Raw data can give you insights as to how well your store is doing, but comparisons with other elements of data from the same time period can provide even more revealing information. Such ratios can illustrate how well you are doing in one aspect of your business as compared with some other aspect of the business.

Many such ratios are available. They include ratios to analyze financial performance, ratios to evaluate operational decisions, and still others to measure the effectiveness of advertising disbursements. Those you ultimately select are the ones that directly relate to those aspects of your operation that you feel are important to evaluate on a monthly basis.

An example of a financial ratio is one that shows the relationship between sales and total monthly expenses. Since both numbers are always positive, the ratio could never be a negative number. Any value between zero and one would indicate a potential problem. It means that the store is spending more that month than it is taking in. The larger the ratio, the greater the probability of an increase in retained earnings. On the other hand, a high ratio obtained at the expense of advertising, decor, and/or insufficient inventory could result in a loss of future sales.

An example of an operational ratio would be to add the profit lost from missed sales to the carrying cost of inventory and then divide the sum obtained by dollar sales. The larger the ratio, the greater the excess in the number of dollars tied up in inventory, or the greater the loss of profit resulting from not having enough stock to sell. A small ratio value would indicate success in carrying an appropriate amount of inventory in the store.

An example of a ratio to evaluate advertising disbursements would be one that compares the percent of total dollars spent on specific advertising for a particular shoe against the percent of total sales for that type of shoe. This ratio would show the effect of advertising dollars spent on attracting customers to your store. Determining this ratio for each type of shoe carried in your store will indicate which type of shoe gets the greatest response each month for the limited dollars spent on specific advertising. Also, comparing the percent of total advertising dollars against the spread between income from and the cost of shoes sold, will demonstrate the effect of the advertising dollars spent by shoe based on the price charged per pair.

Ratios can provide insights regarding the success of operational decisions each month. In addition, they can provide comparisons across shoe type as well as comparisons of performance from month to month. Trend lines, when plotted, demonstrate the effectiveness of decisions made over a period of time.

So now when the question is asked, "How's business?," you should be able to respond based on the feedback obtained from each month's operation. You will become more proficient in the evaluation of your decision strategy and be able to fine-tune your monthly decisions to obtain more profit from your store's operation.

DISCUSSION QUESTIONS

1. Using data obtained during the months that you have been in business, compute the financial ratio described above for each month. Plot the ratio values obtained for each month on graph paper placing the month number on the x-axis and the ratio value on the y-axis. Describe what information can be derived about your decision strategy based on the plot of these financial ratios.

2. Using data obtained during the months that you have been in business, compute the operational ratio described above for each month. Plot the ratio values obtained for each month on graph paper placing the month number on the x-axis and the ratio value on the y-axis. Describe what information can be derived about your decision strategy based on the plot of these operational ratios.

3. Using data obtained during the months that you have been in business, compute the advertising disbursement ratio described above for each type of shoe carried in your store each month. Plot the ratio values obtained for each type of shoe on graph paper for a particular month, placing shoe type along the x-axis and the ratio values for the shoes carried on the y-axis. Prepare a plot for each of the last few months of operation. Describe what the plots tell you about your advertising decision strategy. Do the same for the other advertising disbursement ratio described above. Describe what those plots tell you about your advertising decision strategy relative to your pricing strategy.

4. Develop three other ratios that can be formulated from the monthly feedback obtained by your store. Compute the ratios for each month of operation and plot them, month by month, on graph paper. Identify the information that each ratio provides. Describe what each ratio tells you about the operation of your store.

Current Issues in Small Business

■ *The environment in which a small business operates is dynamic; it is constantly changing. Thus it is vitally important for the owner-manager to stay abreast of new ideas, trends, and techniques. Part Seven focuses on five important issues for small business.*

Chapter 20 focuses on the challenges of ethics, social responsibility, and crime in small business. The potential harm caused by unethical business practices, lack of social responsibility, or criminal activity is too great to be ignored. A basic framework for understanding these critical concepts is presented.

Chapter 21 examines the impact of computers on small business. The microcomputer is revolutionizing the way small businesses operate. Many tasks that were performed manually in the past, from financial analysis and record keeping to the typing of letters, are now computerized. Every small business owner-manager needs to become familiar with the basics of computers.

Chapter 22 deals with insurance. Various types of coverage—auto, fire, public liability, life, and health—are discussed. Guidelines for managing a business's overall insurance program are presented.

Chapter 23 examines the legal framework that confronts the entrepreneur of today. Contracts, warranties, agency, and bankruptcy are just a few of the topics discussed. An understanding of legal principles can help small business owner–managers to avoid potential legal problems.

Chapter 24 highlights some of the types of assistance available to small business through federal, state, and local government agencies. Financial and managerial assistance programs of the SBA are described. In addition, small business incubators are examined, and the chapter concludes with a discussion of recent legislation by Congress directed specifically at aiding small businesses.

Part Seven will acquaint you with some of the pressing issues that confront small businesses today. It would be impossible to present everything the businessperson needs to know in a book of any size, but combined with the material in Parts One through Six, Part Seven gives much insight into the dynamic issues facing every small business person every day.

CHAPTER 20

The Challenges of Ethics, Social Responsibility, and Crime for Small Business

Objectives

Honesty, integrity, and ethical behavior are key characteristics that growing businesses must strive to develop. The potential harm caused by unethical business practices, poor social responsibility, or criminal activity may never fully be understood. However, awareness of these elements is the first major step toward implementing them into a company's daily business activities. When you have finished studying this chapter, you will be able to:

1. *Describe the challenge of ethics in small business.*
2. *Explain the public's stereotype of business ethics.*
3. *Define codes of conduct for businesses.*
4. *Outline the levels of social responsibility for business.*
5. *Discuss the potential ethical leadership position of small business owners.*
6. *Describe the impact of crime on small business.*
7. *Examine the preventative methods for specific crimes such as credit card fraud, check deception, and shoplifting.*
8. *Describe internal crime including theft, embezzlement, and computer fraud.*

UNDERSTANDING ETHICS IN SMALL BUSINESS

Innovation, risk-taking, and venture creation form the backbone of the free enterprise system. The qualities of individualism and competition that have emerged from this system have helped to create new jobs (approximately 20 million in the last decade) and an enormous growth in new ventures (over 600,000 incorporations were started each year during the 1980s). However, these same qualities have also produced complex tradeoffs between economic profits and social welfare. On one hand is the success rate measured in profits, jobs, and efficiency. On the other hand is the quest for personal and social respect, honesty, and integrity. Ideally, society would provide one ethical norm to calculate the greatest good for the greatest number and, thus, help resolve such ethical dilemmas. However, to develop an ethical code that would suit all people in all situations is nearly impossible. To illustrate, a study by researchers Longenecker, McKinney, and Moore examined the ethical concern of small business owners regarding specific business issues.[1] The left side of Table 20-1 provides a list of the issues that owners believed needed a strong ethical stance. However, the right side of Table 20-1 lists the issues that the same small business owners viewed with greater tolerance in regards to demanding ethics. The contradictory nature of these findings prove that ethical decision making is a complex challenge due to the nature and personal perception of various issues.

In addition to the complexity of ethical decisions, society itself appears to have a negative opinion regarding ethics in business. In one study, 65 percent of those surveyed said that executives would do everything they could to make a profit, even if it meant ignoring society's needs.[2] Another study reported that a Darwinistic Ethic is now prevailing in business, which spreads a "profit-at-any-price" attitude among business owners and managers.[3]

Yet the public's perception is sometimes based more on a misunderstanding of the free enterprise system than a condemnation of it. One ethicist, Margaret Maxey, reminds us that in a complex world of changing technology and valuable innovations one cannot blame single individuals for the ethical problems in free enterprise. Rather, there must be an understanding of the total, systematic impact on the common good.[4]

Table 20-1 Ethical Views of Small Business Owners

	Issues that Small Business Owners View with Greater Tolerance in Regards to Ethical Position
1. Evaluating faulty investment advice.	1 Padded expense accounts.
2. Favoritism in promotion.	2. Tax evasion.
3. Reporting dangerous design flaws.	3. Collusion in bidding.
4. Misleading financial reporting.	4. Insider trading.
5. Misleading advertising.	5. Discrimination against women.
6. Cigarette smoking on the job.	6. Copying computer software.

Source: Justin G. Longenecker, Joseph A. McKinney, and Carlos W. Moore, "Ethics in Small Business," *Journal of Small Business Management*, January 1989, p. 30.

---

[1]Justin G. Longenecker, Joseph A. McKinney, and Carlos W. Moore, "Ethics in Small Business," *Journal of Small Business Management*, January 1989, pp. 27–31.

[2]Edward L. Hennessey, "Business Ethics—Is It a Priority for Corporate America?" *Financial Executive*, October 1986, pp. 14–15.

[3]Myron Magnet, "The Decline and Fall of Business Ethics," *Fortune*, December 8, 1986, pp. 65–72.

[4]Margaret N. Maxey, "Bioethical Reflections on the Case for Private/Free Enterprise," *The Future of Private Enterprise*, ed. Craig E. Aronoff, Randall B. Godwin, and John L. Ward (Atlanta, GA: Georgia State University Publications, 1986), pp. 145–64.

However, the general perception stereotypes business ethics as a contradiction in terms. It is a stereotype based upon three principle misconceptions that dominate society. First, profit and morality are necessarily incompatible. In other words, the pursuit of wealth is a barometer of success, yet, it is believed that wealth tends to corrupt individuals. Second, all ethical problems have simple solutions: there is always a right and wrong answer. This misconception is based upon an assumption that there is an absolute standard for judging moral conduct. Third, ethics is simply a matter of compliance with laws and regulations. While laws and regulations often emerge from ethical concerns, they are not *always* considered ethical.[5] (The legal argument versus the ethical argument over abortion is a good example.) In spite of these misconceptions, the fact remains that unethical behavior does take place. Why? A few explanations are possible:

1. greed
2. an inability to distinguish between activities at work and activities at home
3. a lack of foundation in the study of ethics
4. survivalist (bottom-line) thinking
5. a reliance on other social institutions to convey and reinforce ethics

Whatever the reasons, ethical decision making is a challenge that confronts every businessperson involved in large or small enterprises.[6]

ETHICAL PRACTICES AND CODES OF CONDUCT

In the broadest sense, ethics provides the basic rules or parameters for conducting any activity in an "acceptable" manner. More specifically, ethics represents a set of principles prescribing a behavioral code that explains what is good and right or bad and wrong; ethics may, in addition, outline moral duty and obligations.[7] The problem with most definitions of ethics is that they are static descriptions that imply that there are universal principles on which society agrees. With society operating in a dynamic and ever-changing environment, however, such a consensus does not exist. Continual conflict over the ethical nature of decisions is still quite prevalent. Therefore, a code of conduct within a business is a statement of ethical practices or guidelines to which an enterprise adheres. A variety of such codes exists; some relate to industry at large and others relate directly to corporate conduct. These codes cover a multitude of subjects, ranging from misuse of corporate assets, conflict of interest, and use of inside information, to equal employment practices, falsification of books and records, and antitrust violations.

---

[5]Robert A. Cooke, *Business Ethics: A Perspective* (Chicago, IL: Arthur Anderson & Co., Monograph, 1988).

[6]Charles R. Stoner, "The Foundation of Business Ethics: Exploring the Relationship between Organization Culture, Moral Values, and Actions," *SAM Advanced Management Journal,* Summer 1989, pp. 38–43; and see Cooke, *Business Ethics: A Perspective.*

[7]Verne E. Henderson, "The Ethical Side of Enterprises," *Sloan Management Review,* Spring 1982, pp. 38–46.

How prevalent are codes of conduct today? A study conducted in 1980 found that out of 673 chief executive officers, more than 75 percent reported having such a code.[8] In 1988 a survey of executives by *Personnel Journal* revealed that 72 percent of the organizations had published codes of ethics.[9]

Based on the results of such research, two important conclusions can be reached. First, codes of conduct are becoming more prevalent in industry. Management is not just giving lip service to ethics and moral behavior; it is putting its ideas into writing and distributing these guidelines for everyone in the organization to read and follow. Second, in contrast to earlier codes, the more recent ones are proving to be more meaningful in terms of external legal and social development, more comprehensive in terms of their coverage, and easier to implement in terms of the administrative procedures that are being used to enforce them.[10]

Of course, the most important question still remains to be answered: Will management really adhere to a high moral code? Many managers would answer "Yes." They have discovered that high moral conduct results in good business. One top executive put the idea this way:

> Singly or in combination, (unethical) practices have a corrosive effect on free markets and free trade, which are fundamental to the survival of the free enterprise system. They subvert the laws of supply and demand, and they short-circuit competition based on classical ideas of product quality, service, and price. Free markets are replaced by contrived markets. The need for constant improvement in products or services is removed.[11]

A second reason to improve the moral climate of the enterprise is to win back the confidence of the public. A change in the public's opinion of business would mark a true turnaround, since many people today question the moral and ethical integrity of companies and believe that businesspeople try to get away with everything they can. Only time will tell whether codes of conduct improve business practices. Current trends indicate, however, that the business community is working hard toward this objective.[12]

THE CHALLENGE OF SOCIAL RESPONSIBILITY

Over the last three decades, social responsibility has emerged as a major issue in the business world. Although it takes different forms for different industries and companies, the basic challenge exists for all.

---

[8]Bernard J. White and B. Ruth Montgomery, "Corporate Codes of Conduct," *California Management Review*, Winter 1980, pp. 81–85.

[9]*Personnel Journal*, September 1988, pp. 37–38.

[10]For more on this topic, see Donald R. Cressey and Charles A. Moore, "Managerial Values and Corporate Codes of Conduct," *California Management Review*, Summer 1983, pp. 121–27; and Steven Weller, "The Effectiveness of Corporate Codes of Ethics," *Journal of Business Ethics*, July 1988, pp. 389–95.

[11]Reported in Darrell J. Fashing, "A Case for Corporate and Management Ethics," *California Management Review*, Spring 1981, p. 84.

[12]Amitai Etzioni, "Do Good Ethics Ensure Good Profits?" *Business and Society Review*, Summer 1989, pp. 4–10; and also L. J. Brooks, "Corporate Ethical Performance: Trends, Forecasts, and Outlooks," *Journal of Business Ethics*, no. 8, 1989, pp. 31–38.

Table 20-2 What Is the Nature of Social Responsibility?

Environment	Pollution control Restoration or protection of environment Conservation of natural resources Recycling efforts
Energy	Conservation of energy in production and marketing operations Efforts to increase energy efficiency of products Other energy-saving programs (for example, company-sponsored car pools)
Fair business practices	Employment and advancement of women and minorities Employment and advancement of disadvantaged individuals (handicapped, Vietnam veterans, ex-offenders, former drug addicts, mentally retarded, and hardcore unemployed) Support for minority-owned businesses
Human resources	Promotion of employee health and safety Employee training and development Remedial education programs for disadvantaged employees Alcohol and drug counseling programs Career counseling Child day-care facilities for working parents Employee physical fitness and stress management programs
Community involvement	Donations of cash, products, services, or employee time Sponsorship of public health projects Support of education and the arts Support of community recreation programs Cooperation in community projects (recycling centers, disaster assistance, and urban renewal)
Products	Enhancement of product safety Sponsorship of product safety education programs Reduction of polluting potential of products Improvement in nutritional value of products Improvements in packaging and labeling

Source: Richard M. Hodgetts and Donald F. Kuratko, *Management,* 3rd ed. (San Diego: Harcourt Brace Jovanovich, 1991), p. 670.

Social responsibility consists of those obligations a business has to society. Table 20-2 presents some of the different areas affected by this societal obligation. The diversity of social responsibility opens the door for questions concerning the *extent* to which corporations should be involved.

In examining the stages or levels of socially responsible behavior that corporations exhibit, a distinct difference in the ways corporations respond becomes apparent. S. Prakash Sethi, a researcher in social responsibility, has established a framework that classifies the social actions of corporations into three distinct categories: social obligation, social responsibility, and social responsiveness (see Table 20-3). This framework illustrates the range of corporate intensity toward social concerns. Some firms simply react to social issues through obedience of the laws; others make a more active response, accepting responsibility for various programs; still others are highly proactive and are even willing to be evaluated by the public for various activities.

Another way to examine this concept is through the use of a social responsibility scale (see Figure 20-1). This scale extends from zero (minimum social responsibility response) to 10 (maximum social responsibility response). One represents the reactive form of obedience and 10 the proactive form of social support.

Only a few studies have examined different features of social responsibility in smaller firms. For example, an examination of 180 small business owners' perspectives on social responsibility found that 88 percent recognized social responsibility as part of their role in business.[13] Another study indicated that small businesses were more critical of their own performance than was the general public.[14] Even though the studies specific to ethics and small businesses are still emerging, a number of views are agreed upon. The research shows that differences in ethical environment,

Table 20-3 Classifying Corporate Social Behavior

DIMENSION OF BEHAVIOR	STAGE ONE: SOCIAL OBLIGATION	STAGE TWO: SOCIAL RESPONSIBILITY	STAGE THREE: SOCIAL RESPONSIVENESS
Response to social pressures	Maintains low public profile, but if attacked, uses PR methods to upgrade its public image; denies any deficiencies; blames public dissatisfaction on ignorance or failure to understand corporate functions; discloses information only where legally required	Accepts responsibility for solving current problems; will admit deficiencies in former practices and attempt to persuade public that its current practices meet social norms; attitude toward critics conciliatory; freer information disclosures than stage one	Willingly discusses activities with outside groups; makes information freely available to public; accepts formal and informal inputs from outside groups in decision making; is willing to be publicly evaluated for its various activities
Philanthropy	Contributes only when direct benefit to it clearly shown; otherwise, views contributions as responsibility of individual employees	Contributes to noncontroversial and established causes; matches employee contributions	Activities of stage two, *plus* support and contributions to new, controversial groups whose needs it sees as unfulfilled and increasingly important

Source: Excerpted from S. Prakash Sethi, "A Conceptual Framework for Environmental Analysis of Social Issues and Evaluation of Business Response Patterns," *Academy of Management Review* (January 1979):68. Reprinted by permission.

---

[13]Erika Wilson, "Social Responsibility of Business: What are the Small Business Perspectives?" *Journal of Small Business Management*, July 1980, pp. 17–24.

[14]James J. Chrisman and Fred L. Fry, "Public Versus Business Expectations: Two Views on Social Responsibility for Small Business," *Journal of Small Business Management*, January 1982, pp. 19–26.

Figure 20-1
A Social
Responsibility Scale

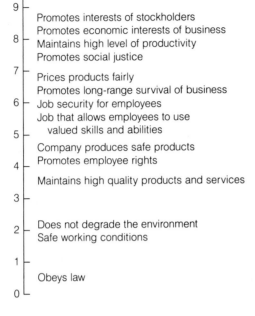

```
10 ─  Supports cultural/social activities

 9 ─
      Promotes interests of stockholders
      Promotes economic interests of business
 8 ─  Maintains high level of productivity
      Promotes social justice
 7 ─
      Prices products fairly
      Promotes long-range survival of business
 6 ─  Job security for employees
      Job that allows employees to use
 5 ─     valued skills and abilities
      Company produces safe products
 4 ─  Promotes employee rights

      Maintains high quality products and services
 3 ─

 2 ─  Does not degrade the environment
      Safe working conditions

 1 ─

      Obeys law
 0 ─
```

Source: Adapted from Kimberly B. Boal and Newman Peery, "The Cognitive Structure of Corporate Social Responsibility," *Journal of Management*, Fall/Winter 1985, pp. 71–82.

ethical precepts, and ethical perceptions, still exist between large firms and small firms. These differences stem from the structure of smaller firms, which require fewer professional specialists, less formality, and whose owner is more closely involved in the actual decision making. (See Small Business Success: From Domino's Pizza to a Honduras Mission.)

ETHICAL LEADERSHIP BY SMALL BUSINESS

Even though ethics and social responsibility present complex challenges for small business owners, the entrepreneur–owner's value system is the key to establishing an ethical organization. An owner has the unique opportunity to display honesty, integrity, and ethics in all key decisions. The owner's behavior serves as a model for all other employees to follow.

In small businesses the ethical influence of the owner is more powerful than in larger corporations because his or her leadership is not diffused through layers of management. Owners are easily identified and usually constantly observed by employees in a small business. Therefore, small business owners possess a strong potential to establish high ethical standards in all business decisions. (See Small Business Owner's Notebook: Twelve Questions for Examining the Ethics of a Business Decision for a guideline that small business owners can distribute to all managers).

■ **SMALL BUSINESS SUCCESS** ■

From Domino's Pizza to a Honduras Mission

Thomas S. Monaghan is famous as the founder of Domino's Pizza, a fast food franchise with 4,800 stores and $2.4 billion in revenues. However, Monaghan is rarely recognized for his efforts to help others that are less fortunate than himself.

For example, during the last few years Monaghan has worked with a Catholic mission in Honduras. He has donated $1 million to build a medical clinic, a dam that will provide electricity to 2,000 people, and an agricultural training center that will teach farmers about growing new crops and current farming techniques.

Tom Monaghan remembers what it was like to grow up deprived. His father died when he was four. His mother placed him and his brother in an orphanage so she could attend nursing school. When Monaghan graduated from high school in Ann Arbor, Michigan, he was on his own. He peddled newspapers, set up bowling pins, and then joined the Marine Corps. When he got out of the Marines he lost all of his savings to a con artist. Desperate for cash, he worked for his brother, who had bought a defunct pizza parlor in Ypsilanti, Michigan. Monaghan eventually traded a used Volkswagen for his brother's business.

Today, Monaghan drives a Cadillac, owns the Detroit Tigers baseball team, and continues to help the deprived people in Honduras. He reflects the growing trend: entrepreneurs giving back to society in order to improve the chances of success for others.

Source: Joan Delaney, "Making a Difference," *Venture*, December 1988, pp. 67–70.

Overall, small business owners must realize that their personal integrity and ethical example will be the key to ethical performance. Their values can permeate and characterize the organization. It is this unique advantage that creates a position of ethical leadership for small business owners.[15]

CRIME AND SMALL BUSINESS

The cost of crime has become a major cause of small business failure. The U.S. Chamber of Commerce reported in 1990 that 30 percent of all business failures result from the costs of employee dishonesty—that is, **internal crime.** Research shows that businesses with less than $5 million in annual sales are 35 times more likely than larger firms to suffer from business crime. Consider the following statistics from the

---

[15]G. Lynn Shostack, "Stand Up For Ethics," *Journal of Business Strategy*, May/June 1990, pp. 48–50; and Justin G. Longenecker, Joseph A. McKinney, and Carlos W. Moore, "Do Smaller Firms Have Higher Ethics?" *Business and Society Review*, Fall 1989, pp. 19–21.

■ **SMALL BUSINESS OWNER'S NOTEBOOK** ■

Twelve Questions for Examining the Ethics of a Business Decision

1. Have you defined the problem accurately?

2. How would you define the problem if you stood on the other side of the fence?

3. How did this situation occur in the first place?

4. To whom and to what do you give your loyalty as a person and as a member of the corporation?

5. What is your intention in making this decision?

6. How does this intention compare with the probable results?

7. Whom could your decision or action injure?

8. Can you discuss the problem with the affected parties before you make your decision?

9. Are you confident that your position will be as valid over a long period of time as it seems now?

10. Could you disclose without qualm your decision or action to your boss, your CEO, the board of directors, your family, society as a whole?

11. What is the symbolic potential of your action if understood? If misunderstood?

12. Under what conditions would you allow exceptions to your stand?

Source: Reprinted by permission of the *Harvard Business Review.* An exhibit from "Ethics Without the Sermon" by Laura L. Nash (November/December 1981). Copyright © 1981 by the President and Fellows of Harvard College. All rights reserved.

Federal Bureau of Investigation (FBI). In each of the last few years, white-collar crime has accounted for over $40 billion in losses. The FBI breakdown includes some startling figures: $100 million was accounted for by computer fraud; $1.1 billion was lost in credit-card and check fraud; and $7 billion was lost through embezzlement and internal theft. No small business owner-manager can realistically ignore this effect.[16]

These statistics bring home dramatically a major problem for today's entrepreneurs. While many owners are formulating their business plans and financial investment policies, their profits are vanishing from their financial sheets. If

---

[16]"Stealing $200 Billion the Respectable Way," *U.S. News and World Report,* May 20, 1985; "Costs of Crimes against Business," U.S. Department of Commerce, Washington, D.C., 1985; and "Preventing Crime on the Job," *Nations Business,* July, 1990, pp. 36–37.

these losses are ignored, bankruptcy can result. Fortunately, the small business owner-manager *can* combat these "quiet" crimes.[17]

CREDIT-CARD FRAUD

The use of consumer credit has grown tremendously in the past twenty-five years (Chapter 16). With this growth has come an increase in the fraudulent use of credit cards. Most of this fraud is committed with amounts of less than $50—in order to avoid merchant verification—and within seven days of the cards' theft. As a result, the small business owner's "front-line" defense is the salespeople and cashiers. They must have the knowledge and means to effectively thwart this type of crime.

RECOMMENDED PROCEDURES

Employees can take certain precautions to reduce credit-card fraud:

☐ SCRUTINIZE SIGNATURES   Compare the signature on the sales slip to the signature on the card.

☐ GET CREDIT AUTHORIZATION   If signatures do not match, call the authorization center for approval. Only the person whose signature is on the card is legally authorized to use the card.

☐ ASK FOR ADDITIONAL IDENTIFICATION   When legitimacy of an authorized card is suspected, request additional identification (driver's license with a photograph).

☐ USE "CODE 10"   This is the terminology for designating suspicious cards and users when calling the authorization center.

☐ THE "HOT CARD PROGRAM"   This is a joint effort of the credit card industry, local mall managements and security, and various state merchants' associations. Small business owners post listings of names and account numbers of recently stolen cards. This list is updated regularly and provided to small business owners.

CHECK DECEPTION

The passing of bad checks costs businesses millions of dollars annually. Small business owner-managers need to establish firm check-cashing policies.

DEVELOP EFFECTIVE POLICIES

A small business owner-manager should establish procedures for a sound check-cashing policy. The following are suggestions for such a policy:

☐ CHECK VERIFYING SERVICES   The small business owner-manager may want to contract with a check verification service. Such a service provides updated lists of people who have recently passed bad checks.

---

[17]See "Crime Prevention for Small Business," *Small Business Reporter* (Bank of America), January 1985.

☐ SUPERVISOR APPROVAL   In some cases, it is a good idea to require a second approval, usually by a supervisor, before a check is cashed.

☐ CHECK-CASHING CARD   By asking a customer to fill out a check-cashing card, the owner-manager can determine in advance whether or not to accept checks from the person.

☐ PHOTOGRAPHS   In addition to requiring identification, the owner may want to photograph each customer who cashes a check or applies for a check-cashing card.

☐ CHECK CASHING LIMIT   Establish a limit on the amount of checks to be accepted—and stick to it.

☐ IDENTIFICATION   In addition to a driver's license, ask for another piece of identification—an automobile registration card, major credit card, or ID card with a photo and signature. Unreliable sources of identification include a Social Security card, business card, bank book, work permit, insurance card, learner's driving permit, personal or business letter, birth certificate, library card, initialed jewelry, unsigned credit card, and voter's registration card.[18]

SHOPLIFTING

Shoplifting costs small businesses not only in lost merchandise but also in expenses incurred trying to prevent the crime. Some studies by retail organizations estimate that $5 out of every $100 of operating expense goes to theft or theft prevention. National figures indicate that one out of three small retail bankruptcies is caused by losses from shoplifting. With these figures in mind small business owners need to approach this problem in two ways: they must make employees aware of the problem, and opportunities for shoplifting must be eliminated or at least reduced.

EMPLOYEE AWARENESS

National statistics show that the largest percentage of shoplifters are between the ages of thirteen and nineteen, female, and able to afford the item taken. Nonetheless, every customer is a potential shoplifter.

Employees should be taught to look for certain actions more than for certain types of individuals. For example, a customer who returns to the same area often, rearranges merchandise, and sends salespeople away bears watching. Employees should also keep a close eye on customers carrying bulky items or wearing loose-fitting clothing. Bulky coats on a warm day or a big umbrella on a cloudless afternoon should make an employee take notice.

Most shoplifters are keenly aware that store clerks look for anything out of the ordinary. Although the decision to steal may have been made, employee alertness can still deter it.

---

[18]Leonard Kolodny, "Outwitting Bad Check Passers," U.S. Small Business Administration Management Aids No. 3.008 (U.S. Government Printing Office, 1984).

OPPORTUNITY REDUCTION

Opportunities for shoplifters can be reduced in a number of ways.[19] The primary ways involve alert employees, merchandise arrangement, and store layout.

Employees should greet customers as they enter the store and ask how they can be of assistance. Sales clerks should be able to see their areas at all times and never turn their backs on customers. Telephones at sales stations should be located accordingly.

Many stores require customers to check their parcels at the door when they enter. This practice is declining with the growing use of electronic tags and sensors. Upon completion of a sale, the clerk should give the customer a receipt for the purchase, place the merchandise in a bag, and seal the bag with the receipt attached so it is clearly visible.

Display counters should be low—no more than waist high. Mirrors mounted in corners can eliminate blind spots. Every station should be attended during business hours. Employees should arrange to have their stations covered when they need to be away even for a few moments.

Small, high-priced merchandise should be kept in locked display cases. If it is impractical to do this, keep them in the center of the store, away from the exits. Such items can be attached to the display case, requiring the salesperson to release a lock before giving them to a customer to look at. Displays can be arranged so that missing items are easily noticed.

Employees should be instructed to show only one piece of expensive merchandise at a time. It is much easier to keep track of one item than a half dozen or more. When a customer tries on clothes, the employee should note the number of articles taken into and returned from the fitting room.

Counters and display tables should be arranged so that there is no direct route to the exit. Some stores put turnstiles at entrances so that the only way to get out is through the checkout counter.

Clerks should be aware of the price of all articles. Ticket switching can be deterred by the use of price tags that are difficult to remove.

APPREHENSION, ARREST, AND PROSECUTION

While good deterrent systems will greatly reduce shoplifting, some people are not deterred. These individuals force the owner to turn to apprehension, arrest, and prosecution. In dealing with these people, the owner must remember that in order to make the charges stick, someone must

1. see the person take or conceal the merchandise,

2. identify the merchandise as belonging to the store,

3. testify that it was taken with the intent to steal, *and*

4. prove that the merchandise was not paid for.

If all four criteria are not met, the store can be open to countercharges of false arrest. **False arrest** need not imply police arrest, it simply means preventing a person

---

[19]"Reducing Shoplifting Losses," Small Business Administration Aids No. 3.006 (U.S. Government Printing Office, 1983); and Anthony J. Faria, "Minimizing Shoplifting Losses: Some Practical Guidelines," *Journal of Small Business Management*, October 1977, pp. 37–43.

from conducting normal activities. Furthermore, any physical contact (even a light touch on the arm) may be considered unnecessary and used against the firm in court.

In general, store personnel should never accuse customers of stealing, nor should they try to apprehend suspected shoplifters. If they observe suspicious behavior or an apparent theft in progress, they should alert the store manager or detective or the police.

It is wisest to apprehend shoplifters outside the store. The owner has a better case if he or she can show that the shoplifter *left the premises* with stolen merchandise. Outside apprehension also eliminates unpleasant scenes that can disrupt normal store operations. Of course, if the merchandise is of considerable value or if it is felt that the thief will elude capture outside the store, apprehension inside the store is warranted.

In either case, verbal accusation of the suspect should be avoided. The Small Business Administration (SBA) recommends that employees or owners identify themselves and then say, "I believe you have some merchandise you have forgotten to pay for. Would you mind coming with me to straighten things out?"

INTERNAL CRIME: THEFT, EMBEZZLEMENT, AND COMPUTER FRAUD

No matter how small the business is or how loyal the employees seem to be, internal theft is always a potential problem. Some experts in crime prevention report that 30 percent of employees steal from their employers.[20] Regardless of the reports and numbers, internal theft has been increasing steadily for the last twenty years. This increase can be attributed to a number of factors:

- □ HIRING PRACTICES   Hiring personnel without a careful check of background or employment references.

- □ PERSONNEL POLICIES   Failure to enforce strict, uniform rules for even minor infractions.

- □ EMPLOYER-EMPLOYEE RELATIONSHIP   Failure to establish a climate of trust, confidence, and respect for employees as well as incentives for outstanding and honest performance.

- □ THEFT OPPORTUNITIES   Failure to apply techniques that will thwart opportunities for employee theft.

- □ ECONOMIC CONDITIONS   Applications of "belt-tightening" and cost-cutting measures that lead to employee theft. During a recession, employees react to such things differently than they do during healthy economic times.

REDUCING THEFT OPPORTUNITIES

Another important way to cut internal theft is by reducing the opportunity for it.[21] This can be done in several ways, one of which is by controlling keys. A record should be kept of *all* keys issued and to whom.

---

[20]"Price Waterhouse Report on Inventory Shrinkage," *Executive Edition Retail Newsletters*, April 1986.

[21]Harry Bacas, "To Stop a Thief," *Nation's Business*, June 1987, pp. 16–23.

Employees should be required to use a designated entrance and exit, where they must leave their personal belongings. Employees should sign in (or "punch in") when they arrive for work and sign out when they leave.

The accounting system can be used to enforce accountability through a system of checks and balances. Employees should have separate functions; for example, the bookkeeper should never handle cash, and the person who makes purchases should not be the person who pays the bills. An independent auditor should be hired to audit the company's books every year.

Control of price marketing can be maintained by the use of a machine or rubber stamp (not handwriting). Only authorized personnel should mark merchandise prices. Unannounced "walk-throughs" or spot checks are a good way to check prices and inventory.

Protection against "back door thefts" is afforded by not allowing employees to park next to the back door or loading dock. The receiving door should be locked except when deliveries are being made.

EMBEZZLEMENT

Embezzlement is defined as a fraudulent appropriation of property by a person to whom it has been entrusted. Quite often an embezzler is an employee who occupies a position of trust and confidence. Embezzlers operate from the belief that they are smarter than the owner and that they can beat the system. However, this is not the case if the owner is familiar with the methods of embezzlement.[22]

TYPICAL SCHEMES

There are many ways to embezzle money from a business. These six are the most common:

☐ POCKETING CASH TRANSACTIONS An employee simply keeps the cash and does not record the transaction.

☐ LAPPING An employee temporarily holds receipts such as payments on accounts receivable. This is an ongoing scheme that usually requires employee access to the books.

☐ CHECK KITING An employee with check-writing authority takes advantage of "float" time (the number of days between the deposit of a check and collection of funds) by writing checks on and making deposits in two or more bank accounts.

☐ PAYROLL FRAUD An employee adds the names of friends, relatives, or fictitious persons to the payroll.

☐ TAKING KICKBACKS The firm's purchasing agent accepts kickbacks offered by suppliers to ensure continued buying from that supplier.

☐ PADDING This occurs in a number of ways. Two of the most common are for employees to inflate expense-account reports and to report excess overtime.

---

[22]Carol B. Gilmore, "To Catch a Corporate Thief," *Advanced Management Journal*, vol. 47, no. 1 (Winter 1982), pp. 35–59, and M. Green and John F. Berry, "Corporate Crime," Parts I and II, *The Nation*, June 8 and June 15, 1985.

INTERNAL SAFEGUARDS

Internal controls are the most effective measures for combatting embezzlement. A tight control system that is audited frequently and administered carefully will deny embezzlers the opportunities they rely on. The following suggestions are provided by the SBA.[23]

As emphasized previously, backgrounds of prospective employees should be checked carefully. Sometimes a few telephone calls or a few letters will be sufficient. In other cases, particularly for positions involving accounts and receipts, a credit bureau or similar agency should be used to run a background check. (Keep in mind that the rights of individuals must be preserved in furnishing, receiving, and using background information.)

A small business owner-manager should know employees to the extent that he or she may be able to detect signs of financial or other personal problems. If enough rapport is built up, employees may feel free to discuss such problems with the owner in confidence.

Only the owner-manager or someone else authorized to do so should place a person on the payroll. Usually a personnel manager, if the company has one, must approve additions to the payroll.

Company mail should be addressed to a post office box rather than the place of business. In smaller cities, the owner-manager may want to go to the post office personally to collect the mail. In any event, the owner-manager or a designated person should personally open the mail and make a **record of cash and checks received.** Checks or money orders payable to a company *can* be converted into cash by an enterprising embezzler.

The owner-manager personally should either prepare and make the daily bank deposits or compare the deposits made by an authorized employee with the record of cash and checks received. The person making the deposit must make sure to get a duplicate copy of the **deposit slip** or other documentation from the bank. If these jobs are delegated, the owner-manager needs to make an occasional spot check to see that nothing is amiss.

Bank statements and other correspondence from banks should be sent to the same post office box used for other business correspondence. If possible, the owner-manager should personally reconcile all bank statements with the company's books and records. This includes personally examining all canceled checks, including payroll checks, and endorsements for anything unusual.

Any employee in a position to mishandle funds should be adequately **bonded.** The owner-manager should let employees know that **fidelity coverage** is a matter of company policy. If would-be embezzlers know that a bonding company also has an interest in what they do, they may think twice before helping themselves to company funds.

Periodic spot checks of accounting records and assets can satisfy the owner-manager that all is well and that the plan of internal control is being carried out. The owner-manager should also personally approve all unusual discounts and bad debt

---

[23]"Preventing Embezzlement," Small Business Administration Management Aids No. 3.009 (U.S. Government Printing Office, 1983).

write-offs and approve or spot-check credit memos and other documentation for sales returns and allowances.

The signing of checks and approval of cash disbursements should not be delegated unless absolutely necessary. Payments should never be approved without sufficient documentation or prior knowledge of the transaction. All invoices and supporting data should be examined before checks are signed to make payment. A record should exist, showing that all merchandise was actually received and that the price seems reasonable; in many **false purchase schemes,** the embezzler does not record the receipt of the merchandise. All invoices should be marked "paid" at the time the checks for payment are signed to prevent double payment.

The owner-manager or other authorized person should never sign blank checks. When the authorized check signer goes on a vacation or business trip, someone else should be authorized to sign checks in his or her absence. All prenumbered checkbooks and other prenumbered forms should be examined from time to time to ensure that checks or forms from the backs of the books have not been removed for possible use in a fraudulent scheme. Preparation of the payroll and the actual paying of employees should be handled by different persons, especially if cash is involved.

COMPUTER EMBEZZLEMENT

The computer era has ushered in new embezzlement schemes. Many of those already mentioned are now being carried out. One study by the U.S. General Accounting Office of computer-related crimes in federal programs revealed that most computer crimes were committed by people with a limited knowledge of computer technology. The use of false input data represented the most common attempts at computer embezzlement.[24]

In light of this, controls on input are essential. The following suggestions can be helpful in developing a policy to control computer embezzlement:

- ☐ Make sure that the computer is programmed to reveal unauthorized use and program alterations.
- ☐ Develop an adequate audit system of transactions with updates.
- ☐ Separate the computer programmer and operator functions.
- ☐ Limit after-hours use of the computer.
- ☐ Make sure that programs contain a statement of ownership.
- ☐ Monitor and log all inputs and outputs.
- ☐ Use special devices and procedures to control access to the terminals and to financial and financially related files.

■ SUMMARY

This chapter described the challenges of ethics, social responsibility, and crime in small business today. The complexity of ethical decisions was discussed along with the misconceptions that society has in regards to business and ethics.

---

[24]Eugene T. Leininger, "Detecting and Preventing Accounts Receivable Fraud through Computer Systems," *Credit and Financial Management,* January 1981, pp. 18–20; David A. Bradbard, Dwight R. Norris, and Paramjit H. Kahai, "Computer Security in Small Business: An Empirical Study," *Journal of Small Business Management,* January 1990, pp. 9–19.

Codes of conduct are statements of ethical practices or guidelines to which a business adheres. These codes are becoming more prevalent in businesses and owners are emphasizing their importance to the business more than ever.

Social responsibility consists of obligations that a business has to society. These obligations may relate to the environment, energy, human resources, community involvement, or other such factors. It is apparent that small businesses are taking an active role in establishing socially responsive behavior.

Business owners can provide ethical leadership due to their personal involvement with the business. The owner's value system can permeate the business and become a standard of ethical performance.

Crime in small business is a major concern for business owners to confront. Credit card fraud has grown along with the increase in credit card use. Most fraudulently obtained items cost less than $50. When a card is stolen, it is usually presented to pay for a purchase by the thief within seven days of its theft. Cashiers and salespeople must be educated with regard to this problem.

The passing of bad checks costs businesses millions of dollars a year. Key items for salespeople to look for and guidelines for effective policies were highlighted in the chapter.

Shoplifting is responsible for a third of small retail bankruptcies. Employee awareness as well as reducing the thief's opportunities are vital in protecting small business from this crime.

Finally, internal theft is increasing because of weak hiring practices, lack of personnel policies, poor employer-employee relations, lack of theft prevention measures, and economic conditions. All of these areas must be considered in adopting business policies to help prevent this crime. Embezzlement and computer fraud are two of the more "glamorous" types of internal crime. They are difficult to detect and procedures must be carefully established in order to effectively control them.

There often is a fine line between success and failure in small business. Allowing unethical business practices, poor social responsibility, or criminal activity to diminish the chance for success is every bit as tragic for an owner-manager as a failure to understand a market segment or financial statements. Following the suggestions and guidelines in this chapter will not guarantee managerial and business success, but failure to recognize them will increase the likelihood of business failure.

■ REVIEW AND DISCUSSION QUESTIONS

1. Describe the complex nature of ethics in small business.

2. Explain the misconception that society has regarding business and ethics.

3. What is a code of conduct and how can it assist ethical practices?

4. What are the three levels of social responsibility that a business could exhibit?

5. How can small business owners assume an ethical business leadership position?

6. Briefly describe the size and scope of business crime in the United States today.

7. How can business owners prevent credit-card fraud? Offer some practical guidelines.

8. How does a check-cashing policy work, and why is it effective in preventing crime?

9. How can a manager deny opportunities to shoplifters? Cite at least two examples.

10. How does internal theft work, and why does it occur?

11. What is embezzlement, and what safeguards can be used to prevent it?

12. What is computer fraud, and what can owner-managers do to prevent it?

■■■
Case Studies

A Code of Conduct?

■ Things have not been going well at Robert Garcia's department store. According to the annual statements provided by his accountant, Robert has lost $9,000 due to internal theft. Given that his net profit margin is only 4 percent, he felt the impact severely. (His sales last year were $825,000.)

In reaction to this discovery, Robert has put extra pressure on his salespeople to "push" customers into buying expensive items. He is also considering raising prices even to the point of "gouging" the consumer on certain high demand items. Finally, he plans to computerize the store in order to keep better track of the inventory.

However, a close business associate of Robert's has suggested that the entire ethical foundation of Robert's business is the cause of his problems. The employees are responding to Robert's questionable attitudes with unethical and illegal activity of their own. The business associate has recommended that Robert consider a code of conduct for his entire organization.

Robert is frustrated and upset with the situation he is facing. He is seriously considering the suggestion of a code of conduct from his business associate. Robert is unsure of exactly what should be in the code of conduct and he ponders the value of such a document.

1. What exactly should be included in a code of conduct for Robert's business?

2. How could a code of conduct help the ethical foundation of Robert's business?

3. Is there anything else you would suggest that Robert do in this situation?

A Question of Guilt

■ Kathy Thomas began her job at a department store two weeks ago. Today as she was pricing some merchandise she looked down the aisle and noticed a customer loitering around the jewelry counter. She tried to watch closely as the customer tried on two or three necklaces at a time. The customer appeared to be tucking a necklace under her sweater when another customer came up and asked Kathy where the shoe department was located. When Kathy again looked at the jewelry counter, the customer had disappeared. The counter appeared to be missing a few necklaces, and Kathy was sure the woman had stolen them. She immediately reported the incident to her superior, Tom Jones. Together they searched up and down the aisles for the customer. Tom asked Kathy if she was sure the woman had lifted the merchandise. Kathy said that she was positive. Moments later they noticed the customer leaving the store, not carrying a store shopping bag. Tom ran out of the store after the customer and stopped her in the mall. Kathy began to doubt her judgment and hoped that Tom would not make a big scene.

1. Should Tom confront the customer outside the store?

2. What should Tom know about detaining or confronting a customer he suspects is guilty of shoplifting?

3. What type of training should the store give its employees for handling such situations?

You Be the Consultant

CRIMINAL LOSSES

Lucy and John Field opened an antique store in Aspen, Colorado, in 1980. Five years later they opened another one in Estes Park and they have plans to open a third in Denver. After watching a TV special on crime in business recently, Lucy began to question their protection from theft. Many of their antiques are worth several hundred dollars. While there is an electronic alarm system in their store, they have noticed some discrepancies in their inventories. They have always written these off as shoplifting. The TV program, however, made them begin to wonder whether shoplifting or employees is the real cause. Lucy and John know that several of their employees are seasonal residents. The reason they had never considered employee theft was because they give a 25 percent employee discount. Because their business has done well and has grown steadily, they've never questioned the honesty of the help.

Lucy suggested to John that they check over their accountant's books and the inventory procedures at both stores. John agreed, feeling that a complete audit of their business would be costly, especially with their new store in Denver about to open. They have been planning to purchase a computer to tie them closer to their other stores' operations. Lucy pointed out to John that the computer system could be another potential area for employee theft. All of a sudden crime has become a great concern for Lucy and John.

■ **YOUR CONSULTATION** Assume that Lucy and John have asked for your advice in developing a sound approach toward crime prevention. What measures would you recommend for internal control of the inventory? Would an audit be effective in determining the reason for their losses? What measures would you recommend for personnel selection since they hire largely from a transient population? Finally, will the computer system diminish or contribute to the potential for crime?

CHAPTER 21

Computers in Small Business

Objectives

Over the last ten years, the microcomputer has emerged on the business scene. This small, relatively inexpensive machine has revolutionized recordkeeping, financial analysis, and word processing—three of the most time-consuming activities of small businesses. The first objective of this chapter is to examine the nature of the computer. The second objective is to examine computer applications for small business. The third objective is to explain how a small business owner should go about making and implementing the decision to computerize his or her operations. When you have studied the material in this chapter, you will be able to:

1. *Describe the basic components of computers.*

2. *"Translate" some computer jargon.*

3. *Weigh the advantages and disadvantages of computers for a small business.*

4. *Discuss the major computer applications for small business.*

5. *Identify the steps in making and implementing a decision to computerize operations.*

NATURE OF THE COMPUTER

Computers have been around for a long time. The earliest ones, which arrived on the scene just after World War II, were really just giant calculators. Since then, computers have gone through a number of generations. Vacuum tubes have been replaced by silicon chips; calculation speed has been increased dramatically; size has been reduced to the point that some computers are actually portable, and prices have tumbled to the point where a small business owner can purchase a complete computer package for less than $10,000.

BASIC COMPONENTS

Despite the technological changes, however, the computer itself has remained the same. The machine still has three basic components: the input unit, the central processing unit, and the output unit.

The **input unit** allows information and instructions to be fed into the machine. For example, the small business owner may want a printout that lists the customers whose outstanding bills are more than ninety days old. In order to get this information, instructions must be entered into the machine that tell it what to do and how to do it. The most common input devices are the keyboard and magnetic disks.

The **central processing unit** has three parts. One is the **memory (storage) unit.** When the machine is given instructions it stores them in memory. As it makes calculations and computes results, these too, are temporarily kept in memory. The memory is a temporary storage facility. A second part of the central processing unit is the **arithmetic-logic unit.** This unit performs operations such as adding, subtracting, multiplying, and dividing. The third part of the central processing unit is the **control unit.** This unit interprets the instructions stored in memory and issues commands to the computer circuits for executing the instructions.

Technology has allowed for these three functions to be integrated onto a single "microchip." This is a small piece of silicon with electrical circuits etched into the surface of a chip that is about 1/4" square. In most small business computers, this chip is located in a small cabinet that is less than two feet square and 5" high.

The **output unit** provides the results of the computations or processing. This output is displayed on a **video screen** and may be run through a **printer,** which provides a hard copy in the form of a typewritten page (a **printout**). Typical examples of such output include current cash position, amount of inventory on hand, and accounts receivable position reports.

COMPUTER JARGON

In order to understand the role and function of computers, owner-managers need to educate themselves about what a computer can do for them, how much one costs, and what the benefits and drawbacks are for their specific business.[1] Thus they must first learn some computer jargon. It is not necessary to become a computer expert, but it certainly helps if the owner-manager and the computer salesperson can speak the same language.

The basic distinction in computer jargon involves the difference between hardware and software. **Hardware** is the term used to refer to the computer, the printer, and other physical equipment needed to run the machines. In the case of small business computers this also includes the typewriter keyboard that plugs into the computer. Additionally, since the computer itself often comes in two parts, a **video screen** and a **disk drive,** it is technically correct to avoid saying *computer* and refer to these parts by name.

Software is the term used to refer to the programs that operate the machine. In the case of most small computers, these programs are stored on a diskette. A **diskette** resembles a small, flexible phonograph record except that it has a special protective cover on it to prevent damage in handling. It is commonly called a **floppy disk.**

Another useful term is **microcomputer.** There are many types of computers. The smallest ones, which sit on desk tops (or lap tops) and contain tiny but powerful

---

[1]See Philip L. Cooley, Daniel T. Walz, and Diane B. Walz, "A Research Agenda for Computers and Small Business," *American Journal of Small Business,* Winter 1987, pp. 31–42.

micro chips, are called microcomputers. For all practical purposes, this is the computer of most interest to small businesses.

User-friendly describes computers and programs that are designed to be easily understood and used. For example, a special software program designed to print out the balance sheet and income statement of a company will require the user to learn certain instructions so that he or she can "talk" to the machine. The easier it is for the average person to learn how to use this software package, the more it is user-friendly.

Many other terms make up the vocabulary of "computerese," but these are some of the most important. As the small business person gets acquainted with computers and what they can do for the business, his or her vocabulary will grow. The most important thing to remember is that, so long as computer jargon is unclear to the individual, he or she needs to ask more questions before deciding to go ahead and buy a computer. What the individual does *not* know can make a big difference in terms of buying the right machine and programs and getting the necessary service.

COMPUTER ADVANTAGES AND DISADVANTAGES

Computers offer small businesses some very important advantages. On the other hand, there are drawbacks to their use. An owner-manager who is thinking about purchasing a computer must weigh these benefits and shortcomings.[2]

ADVANTAGES The most commonly cited advantage of the computer is its speed. Microcomputers can make calculations thousands of times faster than the average person can using paper and pencil. Additionally, when the micro is hooked up to a high-speed printer, an owner-manager can obtain printouts in a matter of minutes. It is not uncommon to find small printers that can generate a complete typewritten page of material in less than thirty seconds.

Another advantage is their accuracy. Using a simple program, an owner-manager can ask the computer to add up the accounts receivable, age them by thirty-day intervals, and know that the results are correct. So long as the information about the current state of the receivables has been fed in correctly, the output will be accurate.

A third advantage of computers is their storage capacity. Microcomputers now have sufficiently large memories that all of the company's records can be stored in the machine. It is not necessary to enter the information on floppy disks and feed it in every time a calculation is to be made. As a result, manipulating and updating data are simpler than ever before. (See Small Business Success: Researching Neural Networks.)

DISADVANTAGES On the other hand, there are some important drawbacks to computers. One is that despite their declining costs, some computers are not worth the money. Very small businesses really do not need a machine for keeping track of their accounts receivable, doing their billing, or updating their financial records. It is a lot cheaper to have an accountant handle all this on a monthly basis.

A second disadvantage—surprisingly—is that the computer requires the owner-manager and employees to assume *more* responsibility for running the business

---

[2]See Tom K. Massey, Jr., "Computers in Small Business: A Case of Underutilization," *American Journal of Small Business,* Fall 1986, pp. 51–60.

efficiently. For example, since it is now possible to get updated daily information on accounts receivable, there is no reason for allowing slow-paying customers to charge more purchases. Up-to-the-minute payment information is available, and before a credit purchase is permitted, the salesperson should check the customer's credit record. Fewer mistakes should be made. On paper this sounds fine, but in practice many people feel threatened by the responsibility. They like the old way of doing things: when a mistake was made, it was accepted as part of the price of doing business. In short, change scares some people, and the computer represents dramatic change.

COMPUTER APPLICATIONS FOR SMALL BUSINESS

A microcomputer can do many things for a small business. (See Table 21-1.) Most applications are tied directly to increased efficiency, usually by helping the firm to get better control of operations or cut costs. One study of small business owners found that the primary applications for computers were accounting, budgeting, inventory

Table 21-1 Some Common Computer System Applications

AREA	APPLICATION
Accounting	Accounts payable/receivables Budgeting Cash flow projections General ledger Payroll Tax accounting
Inventory	Warehouse control Materials resource planning Purchasing Economic order quantity
Production	Product mix determination Scheduling of production Setting due dates
Marketing	Sales analysis Price lists Competitor analysis Vendor information
Human Resources	Personnel files Employee benefits OSHA reporting Labor relations
Business Support	Word processing Report generation Graphics Data communication File management

Source: Adapted from Jatinder N. D. Gupta, Thomas M. Harris, and Donald F. Kuratko, "Effective Computer Selection for a Small Business," *Mid-American Journal of Business,* March 1987, p. 37.

■ SMALL BUSINESS SUCCESS ■

Researching Neural Networks

 Defining a target market can be one of a manager's most important business decisions, but for Neurogen, making this decision has become a problem. Neurogen Laboratories, Inc., founded in January of 1988 by Michael Kuperstein, is a laboratory dedicated to the research of neural networks, which are computer solutions based on the human brain. Kuperstein, who has a PhD in brain science from the Massachusetts Institute of Technology, originally founded Neurogen as a creative outlet after he was unable to find an acceptable academic job in Boston. Although the lab was originally funded by government grants, Kuperstein quickly realized that to extend the life of the lab he was going to have to find a way to make Neurogen profitable. He thought that the opportunity to commercialize what he was doing was tremendous. After all, Kuperstein was the owner of a proprietary technology with limitless applications.

Of the four major areas that apply to neural nets, Neurogen targeted two possibilities: robotic control and pattern recognition. The choice was made to pursue the pattern recognition field because of the speed in which a product could be brought to the market. Neurogen eventually focused on an application which had yet to be successfully implemented: the computer recognition of human handwriting. By the following April, Neurogen had a production prototype of a numerical recognition device called "Inscript."

The major problem for Neurogen was defining its target market. The product, Inscript, was a board and accompanying software tht fit any IBM PC/AT, and

(continued)

---

control, and word processing.[3] Generally, the applications fall into three categories: financial, word processing, and "what if" analysis applications. Many programs have been written for each area. We will examine these categories in more detail.

FINANCIAL APPLICATIONS

Financial applications include preparation of payroll, general ledger, accounts receivable and payable, and inventory control information and reports.

PAYROLL One of the most popular microcomputer applications is for preparing the payroll. Many software packages have been written to meet this small business need, and owners find that very little modification of the programs is required. Basically they can use a "canned" program. The best part of the payroll programs is that

---

[3]G. S. Nickell and P. C. Seado, "The Impact of Attitudes and Experiences on Small Business Computer Use," *American Journal of Small Business,* Fall 1986, pp. 37–48.

cost $60,000. A device such as this could be applied to many different fields, but Neurogen finally settled on seven large market possibilities:

- □ Banking
- □ Insurance
- □ Sales Ordering
- □ Credit Card Companies
- □ Mutual Funds
- □ U.S. Postal Service
- □ Internal Revenue Service

Neurogen decided to target banking, because it offered the easiest penetration into the market. However, a technical problem arose. The Inscript device could not read numbers that were touching each other, and the hand-written numbers on checks were often unreadable by the scanner. An idea derived from a trade show suggested a possible solution to the problem. Neurogen decided to pursue the form processing market. When forms, such as sales forms, are used, each number is placed in a separate box. This eliminated the readability problem. At this point, Neurogen had also hired a CEO, a move that allowed Kuperstein to resume his position as head of research. Its concentration on the form-processing market allowed Neurogen to open several other doors for itself including optical character recognition, which now accounts for about a quarter of its business. The company has estimated its sales to increase from $800,000 in 1990 to $75,000,000 by 1994.

Source: Adapted from Edward O. Welles, "Decisions, Decisions," *Inc.,* August 1990, pp. 80–90.

they take much of the manual effort out of preparing paychecks. However, they do not stop there. Many of the programs can also provide labor expense distribution and report by department and job. This allows a comprehensive cost control system to be established. They can also generate reports to meet government requirements, such as withholding and quarterly unemployment reports.

GENERAL LEDGER Another popular computer application is the general ledger. There are software packages that can prepare income statements and balance sheets, make debit and credit entries, print general ledger journal reports, run trial balances, consolidate accounts, and maintain month-to-date and year-to-date account balances through automatic journal posting. These programs eliminate the need for cumbersome ledger books and allow the business owner to know the company's financial state at any time. General ledger applications have proved particularly popular among small businesses that cannot justify hiring full-time bookkeepers.

ACCOUNTS RECEIVABLE Computerized accounts receivable programs provide a wide array of vital financial information to the small business. Some of the most common of these popular programs are invoice production, sales analysis, sales journal data, and customer balances. These programs also make it possible to print invoices, trial balance reports, customer lists and labels, sales analysis reports, and sales commission reports.

ACCOUNTS PAYABLE   Similar to the accounts receivable software packages, accounts payable programs allow the user to enter purchases and miscellaneous debits, process materials requisitions, generate vendor analysis reports, maintain vendor files, and update inventory control programs. Depending on the specific needs of the business, it is also possible to generate cash requirement reports and other types of information that will allow the business to manage its accounts payable efficiently.

INVENTORY CONTROL   Inventory control programs allow small businesses to turn over to the computer many of the activities we discussed in Chapter 19. For example, if inventory information is continuously reported, the computer can compare current stock levels with reorder prints and generate requisitions for additional inventory as required. Using these programs, it is also possible to keep accurate records on every item in a store—to know how well it is selling and how much inventory remains on hand. The only time the business needs to conduct a physical inventory is for comparing the actual number of items on hand with the number reported by the computer. Any discrepancy between the two numbers is resolved in favor of the physical inventory count, and the computer total is adjusted appropriately. The primary reason for comparing the numbers is to determine whether there has been any theft by customers or employees. This comparison can be made only if a physical inventory is carried out. Everything else discussed about inventory in Chapter 19—from determining the EOQ to plotting the rate of depletion—can be done by the computer. The amount of time saved by computerizing inventory management often pays a large percentage of the cost of computer installation.

WORD-PROCESSING APPLICATIONS

Perhaps the most popular nonfinancial use of computers in small business is for word processing. Word-processing software allows the user to enter, edit, save, retrieve, and print material. Until computerized word processing came along, the most effective way of typing letters and other documents was with electronic typewriters that could correct mistakes. Once a document was typed, copies could then be made on a photocopying machine. Document-oriented word processing equipment has changed all of that. Now, user-friendly word-processing programs allow the typist to call up a letter or other document on the video screen, correct mistakes by simply backing up and typing over the error, save the document, check the spelling, print a copy for review, retrieve the document and make any necessary changes, and then print it in final form. File copies do not have to be printed, since the document is already on the floppy disk (or whatever input device is being used by that particular computer), thereby saving the company filing expenses.

Another feature of word-processing programs is **wrap around,** meaning that the typist does not have to hit the return key at the end of a line; the program automatically "wraps" to the next line, allowing the typist to continue at full speed. Other

typical features include the ability to personalize correspondence to hundreds of recipients, maintain mailing lists by various categories, and produce professional-quality documents, reports, and correspondence in a variety of formats. The result is that typists are able to generate more work with fewer errors.

DESKTOP PUBLISHING

Another computer application that is becoming quite popular in small businesses is "desktop publishing." Essentially desktop publishing is an extension of word-processing combined with graphics. In the past, small businesses often had to send brochures, flyers, advertisements, and other documents to graphic artists and then to printers for preparation. Now with DTP software and laser printers, it is possible for a person with little training to produce professional looking documents in short periods of time. This can be a large cost-saving activity.

"WHAT IF" ANALYSIS APPLICATIONS

In recent years software programs for handling "what if" questions have begun to appear. These programs allow the businessperson to make certain assumptions and see the possible outcomes that are generated by them. For example, a small business owner-manager might feed in sales data for the last three years and then ask the question, "If sales continue to increase the way they have in the past three years, what will my income statement look like next year?" The individual may then make some modifications in the request by saying, "Okay. Now tell me what the income statement will look like if sales increase at only 90 percent of the rate they have over the last three years." The individual may then ask for an optimistic result by telling the computer, "Show me my income statement for next year if sales go up 10 percent faster than they have over the last three years." These projections are based on "what if" assumptions; that is, what if my sales increase (or decrease) by x percent? The projection shows what will happen to the business in financial terms.[4]

After looking at a number of annually forecasted revenues and expenses, the owner-manager can decide which is most likely to occur and make plans accordingly. The owner can also analyze capital expenditures, cash flows, and sales area potentials using the same basic approach. The programs that carry out these analyses provide for the data to be typed in long spread sheets to permit comparison of the figures in each column against the others. The ultimate aim, of course, is to help the owner-manager make realistic plans. All the individual has to do is ask realistic "what if" questions; the computer does the rest.[5]

FUTURE APPLICATIONS

The power of computer software is now allowing the emergence of "expert systems" in the small business environment. The function of an expert system (ES) is to mimic the skill of an expert or a small group of experts as it is used to solve a specific problem, usually involving diagnosis or prescription. While they have been used in medicine, engineering, and manufacturing for a decade, only recently has software been developed that would allow expert systems to be constructed quickly and at low cost in small business.

Although expert systems can make predictions and reasoned inferences, their general function is to give either direct or implied advice to managers who have a problem to solve or a decision to make.[6] Figure 21-1 illustrates the theoretical applications of expert systems in small firms.

It should be kept in mind that as the costs associated with computer technology decrease, and as friendlier systems are developed that allow small business firms access to computer capability without a high degree of computer sophistication, the applications of computer systems will become more widespread.[7]

Over 800 small businesses were surveyed recently to examine their information system usage.[8] It was found that the application of management information systems

---

[4]See Douglas J. Lincoln and William B. Warberg, "The Role of Microcomputers in Small Business Marketing," *Journal of Small Business Management,* April 1987, pp. 8–17.

[5]See James Williams, "Job Order Cost Accounting Information System," *Journal of Small Business Management,* April 1985, pp. 17–26.

[6]Jeremiah J. Sullivan and Gretchen O. Shively, "Expert System Software in Small Business Decision Making," *Journal of Small Business Management,* January 1989, pp. 17–26.

[7]Philip L. Cooley, Daniel T. Walz, and Diane B. Walz, "A Research Agenda for Computers and Small Business," *American Journal of Small Business,* Winter 1987, pp. 31–42.

[8]Albert Kagan, Kinnam Lau, and Keith R. Nusgart, "Information System Usage Within Small Business Firms," *Entrepreneurship Theory and Practice,* Spring 1990, pp. 25–36.

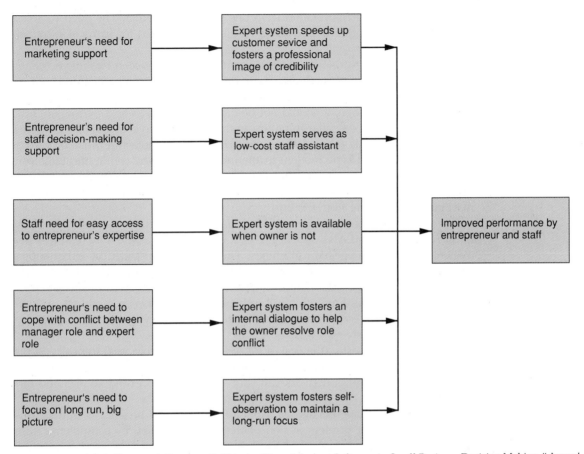

Source: Jeremiah J. Sullivan and Gretchen O. Shively, "Expert System Software in Small Business Decision Making," *Journal of Small Business Management*, January 1989, p. 21.

Figure 21-1
Theoretical Model:
The Uses of Expert
Systems

is unique to each small business sector. In other words, each particular segment of small business—retail, wholesale, manufacturing, service—has its own particular computer usage. However, wholesaling and retailing were found to be the most sophisticated software users. In addition, as small businesses develop in size, their information and computer systems needs increase in levels of sophistication.[9] Thus, the use and applications of computers in small business are continually increasing with the improvements and advancements in computer technology.

NETWORKING

As with many other business tools, smaller firms often find that having more than one computer can add to the productivity and efficiency of the business activities. Most small businesses that have purchased multiple computers soon find that

---

[9]Kagan, Lau, and Nusgart, 25–36.

they need to transfer information from one system to another. The need to access one computer to another is becoming very important, even for firms of extremely small size.

One of the easiest ways of facilitating communication between two microcomputers is through the use of **modems.** These devices enable a computer to use normal telephone lines to "talk" from one machine to another. Since this communication does tie up a phone line, it should not be considered or used as a permanent link. Both modems must be similar in nature so that there are no compatibility problems. The **"Hayes Standard"** (named for a popular modem manufacturer) has evolved as the de facto standard type modem in the industry. Also, the communications software package in use must enable the computers to pass information between machines. Modems are most frequently used to connect a firm's computer to a machine that is off site from the business.

Another form of networking that is becoming more popular in small firms is the **Local Area Network (LAN).** To use LANs, it is necessary to have a more or less permanent physical link between machines. This is usually provided by either copper wires or a coaxial cable (much like phone lines or cable TV). The computers are equipped with special input/output devices (normally in the form of special circuit boards that are installed internally) that enable this link between machines. As with the use of modems, communication software must be provided to allow control of the network.

While somewhat costly (the cost of a LAN may range from $100 to nearly $4,000 per computer on the network, depending on the complexity of the hardware and network software), a network can soon pay for itself in time savings and task efficiencies.

There are three major benefits of using a LAN. The first benefit is that expensive devices, such as laser printers or pen plotters, can be shared by computers on the network, thus eliminating the need to buy multiple devices. The second benefit is that a LAN allows improved communication, such as electronic mail, within the business. The third benefit is that LAN provides the ability to share software quickly. While these benefits may prove cost effective in the long run, not all firms need, nor can afford, a LAN. Like all computing applications, the situation must be carefully analyzed and studied before making a decision to install a permanent network.[10]

MAKING AND IMPLEMENTING THE COMPUTER DECISION

Research shows that many businesses buy a lot more computer power than they need.[11] The salesperson will show a number of different types of computers and what each can do. On the showroom floor, each machine is set up to be as physically appealing as possible. For example, the businessperson will see a graphic display of information or a multicolored pie chart showing sales breakdown and be impressed. The salesperson will then push a few buttons on the machine and show how other calculations can be made. It all looks so simple, and the speed at which the machine

---

[10]Nick Sullivan, *Computer Power for Your Small Business: A Guide from Home Office Magazine* (New York: Amacom Publishing, 1991).

[11]John M. Garris and E. Earl Baruch, "Small Business and the Computer Panic," *Journal of Small Business Management,* July 1983, pp. 19–24.

works seems to ensure instant information for decision making. Before leaving the showroom, the businessperson may place an order for the machine. Once the computer is delivered, however, a crisis seems to develop. Who will have access to the computer? How will people be trained to use it? How much will this cost? Exactly what functions or jobs will the machine perform? Who will make this decision? As the questions pile up, it becomes painfully obvious that insufficient planning accompanied the purchase of the machine. All of this could have been avoided if the company had done its homework before buying. This section explains how postdecision problems such as these can be avoided. (See Small Business Owner's Notebook: Watching Out for Pitfalls in Computer Implementation.)

■ SMALL BUSINESS OWNER'S NOTEBOOK ■

Watching Out for Pitfalls in Computer Implementation

 Although today's microcomputers offer tremendous potential for business operations, estimates show that one-third of the computers owned by small firms are underutilized, while another one-third are not being used at all. How can the small business owner counteract such problems in computer implementation? One study identified five critical pitfalls that must be avoided in order for small businesses to most effectively implement their computer systems:

1. *The hardware purchase strategy needs to be carefully reviewed.* The most common method of acquiring hardware is through a computer vendor. Therefore, choose a reputable firm that can provide on-going support for the small businessperson.

2. *The software should be purchased in correspondence with the hardware.* Understand the types of software that work best with the purchased hardware, and be sure that the software package fits the business's current and future needs.

3. *Plan for a smooth changeover to the computer system.* Prepare a written, step-by-step plan for implementing the data transition. Take care to avoid any "down" time that would affect the business's critical functions.

4. *Establish the good external support that is provided by a carefully drafted contract.* Either the computer vendor or the systems consultant may provide one, but in either case a thorough contract is needed to avoid misunderstandings or lack of support later.

5. *Prevent a lack of computer knowledge by training employees before and after the system is implemented.* Trade group conferences, readings on computers, or even continuing education courses are possible sources of knowledge for small business owners to pursue.

Source: John F. Schleich, William J. Corney, and Warren J. Boe, "Pitfalls in Computer System Implementation," *Small Business Reports*, January 1991, pp. 74–78.

LEARN ABOUT COMPUTERS

Many makes of microcomputers are on the market today. Three of the most popular are those from Apple, Compaq, and IBM. These are desktop models. For business owners who travel a lot, a portable microcomputer may be more desirable; two of the most popular are those from Toshiba and Zenith.

Every month, it seems, another new microcomputer arrives on the scene. At present there is a great deal of interest in smaller, more compact portables that can fit into briefcases. There is also a marked trend toward providing more memory and more user-friendly software in new product offerings. All of this means that the average small business owner-manager will be somewhat confused about which machine to buy. The best way to resolve this dilemma is to visit at least a half-dozen of the largest computer retail stores. In many cases, the salespeople will have very little hands-on knowledge of how to operate all of the machines they are selling. They will be able only to describe them and provide a brief operational display. Nonetheless, visits to a number of these retailers will acquaint the businessperson with what is out there.

If the entrepreneur is still somewhat confused or in doubt about various computers and what they can do, he or she can easily hire a computer consultant for a day for assistance. Many individuals know what is going on in the field, and their services are not expensive. These people will even work with the business later if it needs to have a software program specially adapted to meet its needs or if it needs to have a program written from scratch to handle a problem unique to the business.

ANALYZE THE BUSINESS'S SPECIFIC NEEDS

Once the small business owner-manager knows what is available, he or she can start looking for ways a computer could help the business. This investigation involves two important steps. First, the owner must examine how things are being done presently. If a person is preparing 200 payroll checks a month, this job could be computerized. If an employee is responsible for keeping track of inventory levels and reordering at the appropriate times, the computer could help this person work faster and more accurately. If an employee spends two days a week taking care of the accounts receivable and accounts payable, it may be possible to cut this person's work down to a half-day and give him or her additional responsibilities. As the owner-manager analyzes the business's specific needs, he or she can begin working out how a computer could help.

Second, as the list of things a computer could do for the firm is developed, the owner-manager should begin to determine exactly what he or she expects from a machine. This provides a shopping list that can be used in deciding which machine will give the best overall performance. The list also reduces the likelihood that the owner will buy a computer that does not meet the needs of the firm.

MAKE A COST–BENEFIT ANALYSIS

Some things are best done manually because computerizing them is too expensive. Additionally, some problems or jobs require special software packages that are extremely costly. For example, a special inventory control system package that would cut personnel time by fifteen hours a month might cost $15,000 to develop. And, if the business is paying its personnel an average of $9 an hour, it would take almost six years for the package to pay for itself. It is not worth the cost. The businessperson must compare the costs of doing things the way they are being done with computerizing them. In some cases the right decision is *not* to buy a computer, at least at the present time. In other cases the correct decision is to buy *now* because more and more new work can be put on the computer in the coming months, and the future cost savings will justify the purchase decision.[12]

FOCUS ON THE SOFTWARE, AND THEN ON THE HARDWARE

The first consideration in selecting a microcomputer is: What software is available. Businesses that need standard packages for handling the types of applications mentioned in the previous section need have no fear. There are many packages that can do these things. Those who need specially designed software, on the other hand, will have to contact consultants who specialize in designing software packages. Fortunately, most small businesses need very little "fine tuning" of standard packages.

Software packages dictate hardware decisions for a number of reasons. One is the amount of memory needed to run the programs. For example, simple word-processing packages usually require small amounts of memory; on the other hand, user-friendly packages typically need a lot more capacity, so a larger memory is required. Some programs, especially those that produce spread sheets with accounting and financial data, require wide-carriage printers. So, as the owner-manager finalizes software decisions, hardware choices become more obvious.

The first hardware choice should be the computer—that is, the video screen, the disk drive and the keyboard. Business associates and friends who have microcomputers and magazine articles that review those machines are good sources for judging the reliability of the various microcomputers on the market. Many businesses have opted for the IBM/PC because they are confident that the company will still be around in ten years. They are not so certain about other companies. Another reason for IBM's popularity is service; the company stands behind its product. However, many very good "clone" computers are also available. These machines often cost about one-third to one-half the price of a name machine and prove to be as serviceable as the better-known machines. The major consideration for purchase should be the machine's return policy (30 to 60 days is standard), its long term warranty (1 to 2 years), and the availability of an on-site service contract (most reputable firms do provide such contracts).

The second hardware choice should be the printer. Printers come in different sizes and configurations. Besides the carriage size, the other major consideration is type quality. There are two types of printers: dot-matrix and letter-quality. Dot-matrix printers are fairly inexpensive and extremely fast. They print characters by using a series of dots. The finished product, although not always eye appealing, is usually sufficient for most business needs. Many companies that provide their customers with itemized receipts use dot-matrix printers. For their purposes the quality of the printing is not very important, and the machine's speed allows them to print

---

[12]For a good discussion see Jatinder N. D. Gupta, Thomas M. Harris, and Donald F. Kuratko, "Effective Computer Selection for a Small Business," *Mid-American Journal of Business,* March 1987, pp. 36–40.

hundreds of receipts in an hour. Letter-quality printers are of two types: daisy-wheel and laser. A daisy-wheel printer is like a typewriter in that each character is typed individually. These printers type a double-spaced page in about a minute. A laser printer uses a photocopying-type process to produce letter-quality output rapidly. Laser printers can turn out six to ten pages per minute depending on the machine. In deciding between a dot-matrix and a letter-quality printer, the small business owner–manager should determine how important letter-quality output is to the business. If it is not needed, a dot-matrix printer is sufficient. A dot-matrix printer is the least expensive and will cost in the range of $100 to $400. A laser printer is the most expensive; it will cost in the range of $1,000 to $4,000.

The final hardware choice should be the peripherals, or extras. In most cases this decision does not have to be made immediately. Peripherals can be added later. One popular extra is a spindle, which allows information to be entered into the computer at the same time as other information is being printed. Another is a modem, which, as explained earlier, allows computers to "talk to each other." In most cases, these extras can wait until personnel becomes more familiar with the computer and can identify additional computer needs.

NEGOTIATE THE DEAL

When the business owner-manager has decided that buying a microcomputer is wise, his or her next step is to buy the machine. Table 21-2 presents some typical costs of computer systems. Bear in mind, however, that it is wise to negotiate the amount with the seller; most retailers are willing to make price concessions. For example, at many stores an individual can secure a 5–10 percent discount off list price. Many other retailers, in recognition of the competitiveness of the industry, will offer similar terms. On the other hand, except in the case of academics and certain other groups, IBM will not discount its computers.

The second part of the deal is for the necessary software. Some standard programs cost as much as $495. Typically the best way to handle this situation is to see how much the retailer wants for all the needed programs. For example, assume that a small business requires word-processing, inventory-control, and "what if" programs costing a total of $1,200, including operating manuals. This is a great deal of money, and most retailers would sell the package for $900. If the owner has nowhere else to turn, this is a good price. However, many consultants have these programs and will provide them at a very reasonable price as part of their assistance package.

Many software programs are protected by copyright and cannot be copied unless specific permission is obtained by the copyright holder. However, numerous software programs are available that users may copy. For example, many computer clubs hold weekly meetings where members discuss the availability of **share-ware programs**—programs that users are allowed to copy for little or no fee. Currently, approximately a thousand programs are listed under a "shareware" title. In addition, numerous programs can be obtained through mail-order catalogs for the price of the diskette (usually $5.00 or less) and a small fee.[13]

---

[13]A catalog that lists 700 such programs is *The PC-SIG Library: (Public Domain and User-Supported Software of the IBM-PC,* Fourth Edition (Sunnyvale, CA: PC-SIG, Inc., 1987).

Table 21-2 Typical Computer System Costs

ITEM	COST
Hardware	
Central processor	$600–4,500
Monitor	100–800
Disk drives	100–350
Hard disk	200–2,000
Printer(s)	200–3,500
Modem	350–3,500
Miscellaneous	up to 15% of system cost
Total for hardware	$2,000–20,000
Software	
Operating systems	$50–500
Accounting package	75–1,500
Spreadsheets, etc.	50–800
Data management	50–2,000
Word processing	75–750
Business graphics	100–600
Data communication	50–400
Custom-developed software	1,000–5,000
Annual Repair and Maintenance	up to 20% of system cost
Annual Computer Supplies	$1,500–4,000
Annual Staff/Personnel	$18,000–35,000
Education and Training/Conversion	varies with applications

Source: Jatinder N. D. Gupta, Thomas M. Harris, and Donald F. Kuratko, "Effective Computer Selection for a Small Business," *Mid-American Journal of Business*, March 1987, p. 39.

These cases demonstrate that significant cost savings are available with software that are perfectly legal. Again, remember that most copyrighted software is protected and should not be copied. Today only specialized programs need to be bought at full price. Everything else can be obtained at significant discounts.

Finally, there is the matter of service. What will the business do if something happens to the machine? While the likelihood of a breakdown is not very great, service costs are quite high. A service contract on machinery brought back to the retail store runs approximately 10 percent of the price of the hardware. (Software does not require servicing. If something happens to the program, a new copy is simply created from the original, which is always kept in reserve for making copies.) An annual service contract on a $5,500 computer and printer system will run about $550 the first year. If something major does go wrong, the expense can easily exceed $550. For this reason, small businesses are well-advised to buy service contracts. Because the quality and reliability of microcomputers improve each year, this may not be true in the future. For the time being, however, most service contracts are cost effective. Additionally, many retailers are moderately flexible on these contracts and will write a full-service agreement for 8–9 percent of the hardware price if the small business owner negotiates skillfully. Also remember that the competition within the industry is so great that it is not difficult to pit one retailer against another in order to get the lowest possible price.

IMPLEMENT THE DECISION

The last step in installing the computer is **implementation**—making the new system work. A number of problems can develop at this point.[14] One is that some employees may feel the machine is a threat to their jobs. This can be dealt with by explaining the functions the computer will be performing and assuring the employees that if anyone's work assignments are computerized, additional tasks will be found for them elsewhere in the firm.

Another common problem is employee resistance to using computerized information. Since the machine provides up-to-date data, personnel will be expected to understand the data and act on it. The way to facilitate this is to determine what kinds of computerized data are most useful to employees and then provide it in the most understandable, easy-to-use fashion. Employees need to be involved in the implementation process.

A third common problem is that, at least in the beginning, more attention must be given to straightening out problems uncovered by the computer. For example, if the computer printout shows that inventory stockouts are occurring because of slow vendor delivery, something has to be done about this. Either faster deliveries must be obtained from that vendor, or a new vendor must be found. The computer will help highlight problems; the owner-manager must be willing to deal with them.

Finally, there are usually some "bugs" in new computer systems. They can be expected, and time for working them out should be allowed.

A final problem currently on the rise is that of computer security. The small business owner needs to consider the safeguards appropriate for preventing physical damage to the computer due to such things as power surges, fire, and water. Recovery methods and procedures must be established to ensure against the loss of information; these include backup files, backup equipment, and so on. Also needed are management controls for protection against theft.[15]

■ SUMMARY

Computer size and price have now reached the point where small businesses can afford and benefit from these machines. Despite these technological changes, the basic components of the computer, have remained the same; they are the input unit, the central processing unit, and the output unit.

Computers offer some important advantages, including speed, accuracy, and storage capacity. On the other hand, there are some significant drawbacks. These include the facts that some computers are not worth the money and that their implementation often requires personnel to assume a great deal more responsibility for efficient operations.

---

[14]See John F. Schleich, William J. Corney, and Warren J. Boe, "Pitfalls in Computer System Implementation," *Small Business Reports,* January 1991, pp. 74–78.

[15]See Norman Pendegraft, Linda Morris, and Kathryn Savage, "Small Business Computer Security," *Journal of Small Business Management,* October 1987, pp. 54–60; also see David A. Bradbard, Dwight R. Norris, and Paramjit H. Kahai, "Computer Security in Small Business: An Empirical Study," *Journal of Small Business Management,* January 1990, pp. 9–19.

Computers have helped small business in many ways. Some of the most common applications have been for payroll, general ledger, accounts receivable, accounts payable, inventory control, word processing, and "what if" analysis. In making and implementing the computer decision, several important steps need to be followed: learn about computers; analyze the business's specific needs; make a cost-benefit analysis; consider the available software and then the hardware; negotiate the deal; and implement the system.

■ REVIEW AND DISCUSSION QUESTIONS

1. Identify and describe the three basic computer components.

2. Define the following terms: *hardware, software, microcomputer, user-friendly.*

3. What advantages are associated with using computers? What disadvantages? Identify three of each.

4. How can a microcomputer help a small company manage its payroll? General ledger? Accounts receivable? Accounts payable? Inventory control?

5. Perhaps the most popular nonfinancial use of computers in small business is for word processing. Explain this statement.

6. How does a "what if" analysis work? How is it valuable to small businesses?

7. Many experts believe that the first step in choosing a computer is to go out and learn about these machines. Explain the logic behind this.

8. Explain why a business should focus first on the software and then on the hardware? Why not do it in reverse order?

9. What should a small business owner-manager know about negotiating a deal to buy a computer? Offer at least three recommendations.

10. What kinds of problems often occur during the implementation of a computer system? Identify and describe two of them.

Case Studies

Liz's Decision

■ When Eileen Tisori arrived at her flower shop one morning she saw men carrying equipment into the children's clothing shop next door. The panel truck from which they were taking the equipment belonged to a firm called Computer World. Eileen unlocked her store, went in, and got ready for business. Later that morning when business was slow, she closed the store and went next door to visit with her friend Liz Ganarzski. The following conversation transpired.

Hi. What was all that equipment I saw men bringing in here this morning?

Let me show you! It's a new Apple computer that's going to help me keep track of my inventory and financial records. I spent about three weeks looking at computers and figuring out how they could help me run the store.

How are you going to use it?

Well, first I have to enter all of my records on these floppy disks. It'll take a couple of weeks, but the salesperson showed me how to do it. Then all I have to do is enter all sales and financial transactions and ask for status reports on everything.

Sounds great. But, gee, haven't you been keeping records all along?

Oh sure, but by hand. With the computer it's going to be a lot easier.

Eileen looked around the small children's store. It seemed to her that there was not enough inventory to justify a computer. However, she certainly did not intend to hurt her friend's feelings. "It looks like you've really modernized your operation. Well, I've got to get back to the shop. See you later."

Back in her store Eileen pondered whether Liz's computer decision was a wise one.

1. What are the advantages and disadvantages of a computer?

2. How does Liz plan to use her computer? Based upon your understanding of the case, what benefits will it provide her?

3. Was Liz's purchase a good one? On what do you base your answer?

Getting the Cart before the Horse

■ Bill Jackson owns a small manufacturing firm that produces and sells machine parts. Some of Bill's output is produced "to order"; that is, customers place orders for specific parts by phone, and the items are manufactured and then shipped to them. Over 70 percent of his sales, however, are to people who buy machine parts over the counter. The markup on these walk-in items is lower than on the "to order" items, because the customers run the risk that the parts will be out of stock. Most customers are willing to accept this risk rather than pay premium prices for made-to-order parts.

Bill has always used a perpetual inventory system, but he has come to realize that a computerized network would help him keep track of inventory better and improve his control of his operations. As a result, he has been looking at computer equipment for three months.

Bill started out by visiting a number of computer retailers and telling them what he needs. He believes he needs three personal computers, two dot-matrix printers, and a laser printer. He thinks this hardware should be sufficient to handle all his needs. Right now he's in the process of pricing this equipment and making final decisions regarding the computers' capability. He thinks he needs a hard disk drive in one of the three computers and color monitors for all of them.

Once he has purchased the hardware, he will look at the various types of software that are available and select particular programs that will help him balance and control inventory as well as handle word processing. "I hear there are some programs that can do all of this. On the other hand, some people tell me that most programs do only one thing well, and rather than purchasing a multipurpose program it's better to buy two or three different ones and link them all together. However, I can wait to decide on that until I've made my hardware decisions."

1. What mistake is Bill making in computerizing his operations? Explain.

2. Explain the difference between a dot-matrix printer and a laser printer? When would each be useful?

3. If you were advising Bill, what would you suggest? Explain.

■ ▬▬▬▬▬▬▬▬▬▬▬▬▬▬▬▬▬▬▬▬▬▬▬▬▬ ■

You Be the Consultant

TRYING TO GET CONTROL OF THINGS

Joanne Durker has always loved art and music. She majored in art in college and went on to get a master's degree in it. Fresh out of graduate school, she married and began to raise a family. She was active in community affairs and joined the Theatre Guild and Fine Arts Society.

Several months ago her youngest child started first grade, which gave her more freedom to pursue her interests during the day. She particularly enjoyed the Wednesday meetings of the Fine Arts Society. She also liked driving over to a large shopping center each Tuesday and Friday to have lunch with her friend Julia Bernstein, who had a porcelain store there. Julia's shop was centrally located and was one of the most popular in the mall. Some browsers voiced objections to the prices, but this never upset her.

"I buy only the best porcelain," she told Joanne. "Every year I go to the factories in Spain, England, and Denmark to select the pieces. Everything in my store is quality."

Two months ago Julia's husband took a job as senior vice-president of a large banking firm headquartered in Boston, and the Bernsteins began planning their move. Julia will open a porcelain shop in the Boston area but feels it is important to first learn about the competition and find a good location. Knowing how much Joanne loved art, she offered to sell her the store.

"You can pay me for the merchandise as you sell it. I'm not going to be able to open an new store in less than a year, and by then you should have sold all of the current inventory. And I'll help you get bank financing so you can replenish the merchandise."

The idea sounded fine to Joanna, and her husband was supportive. "You can open the store at 10:00, close it at 3:00 and be home before the kids get here. And it's a business you really know something about."

So Joanne took over the shop a month ago. She spent the first couple of weeks taking an inventory, reviewing orders, and waiting on customers. The biggest problem she had was keeping track of inventory—well over 1,000 items.

Julia had been able to remember everything because she had bought and placed all the pieces in the various showcases and shelves in the store. She had then filed the sales receipts by manufacturer. That is, all of the Boehm porcelain receipts went in one folder; all of the Spanky receipts in another, and so on. The sales price was placed on each item in the form of a letter code. For example, a

Boehm bird that cost $100 would have a retail price of $200, represented by the letters GZZ. G stood for 2, Z stood for 0. This way, Julia did not have to look up the sales price every time a customer asked about it.

Whenever an item was sold, Julia took the respective purchase invoice out of the file and put it into a sales folder. She later matched up sales revenues and expenses and kept her books in order. All she had to do was gather her monthly bills (for rent, electricity, and other expenses), add them to the cost of the goods she sold, and subtract the total from the monthly gross revenues. Every three months her accountant would spend an hour going over her records, making the necessary ledger entries, and preparing the state and federal forms that must be submitted.

Joanne explained Julia's recordkeeping procedures to her husband. He admitted that the system seemed pretty complex.

"You know," he said, "some microcomputers sell for less than $2,500, including a printer. If you could computerize all of your inventory and financial records, you'd have a better handle on where you are at all times."

Joanne thinks this might be a good idea. However, she knows nothing about computers or how they could help her manage her new procelain shop.

■ **YOUR CONSULTATION** Help Joanne out by explaining the advantages and disadvantages of computers to her. Then explain the specific applications a computer would have for her. Finally, tell her whether she should buy a micro. Be sure to defend your answer in terms of costs and benefits.

CHAPTER 22

Insurance Needs of Small Business

Objectives

Practically all small businesses carry insurance, if only minimum coverage against such calamities as fire, burglary, robbery, and public liability. The first objective of Chapter 22 is to present an overview of insurance. The second objective is to study the types of insurance that are commonly purchased by small business firms—auto insurance, fire insurance, workers' compensation insurance, public liability insurance, crime insurance, special coverage, life insurance, and health insurance. The last objective is to explain how to manage a small business insurance program. When you have studied the material in this chapter you will be able to:

1. *Define the term* insurance.

2. *Explain what auto insurance is and tell what types of coverage are available.*

3. *Discuss fire insurance and explain the importance of the coinsurance clause in determining how much an insurer will pay in case of a fire loss.*

4. *Discuss workers' compensation insurance, public liability insurance, and crime insurance.*

5. *Differentiate between term life insurance and whole life insurance, noting the benefits and drawbacks of each.*

6. *Review group life insurance, pension plan insurance, credit life insurance, and health insurance.*

7. *Outline the major steps a small business owner-manager should follow in managing an insurance program.*

WHAT IS INSURANCE?

Insurance is a cooperative method of pooling funds by which many people pay a small amount of money, a **premium,** to protect themselves against a potentially large loss. For example, what is the likelihood that Mr. Smith, a small business owner, will die this year? He is a 50-year-old white man. Recent mortality tables indicate that the chance of his dying this year is 6.42 percent. Furthermore, the tables show that Mr.

Smith has a life expectancy of 25.7 more years. Based on these statistics, an insurance company determines its policy rates.

Where do these statistics come from? The insurance industry compiles them on the basis of births and deaths in this country. Assuming that they are close to correct, it is likely that Mr. Smith has a long life ahead of him. So to protect his business against his unexpected death, he can buy a $10,000 life insurance policy today, assuming that he is in good health, at a very low price. How can the insurance company sell the policy at such a low rate? Because it will insure many people Mr. Smith's age and it knows that only a small percentage of them will die soon. So it will charge premiums equal to all of the death benefits it must pay plus something for administrative costs and profit for the firm. This is often referred to as **pooling the risks.** Everyone pays a little bit to insure against a given calamity, and whoever encounters the calamity receives the insurance proceeds.

In this chapter we will examine the types of insurance coverage available to small businesses. Before doing so, however, we need to define some important insurance terms:

- □ INSURANCE POLICY   Written evidence of the terms of an insurance contract.

- □ INSURER   The insurance company that is providing the coverage.

- □ INSURED   The person or business firm being insured.

- □ PREMIUM   The price being paid by the insured for the coverage specified in the insurance policy.

- □ BENEFICIARY   The person(s) or company(s) named by the insured to receive any money paid by the insurance policy.

- □ DEDUCTIBLE   A clause that exempts specified initial amounts of loss from the insurance policy. For example, the first $50, $100, or $200 loss may not be covered by the policy. The purpose of such clauses is to reduce the premiums.

- □ RIDER   Extra protection not provided by the standard insurance policy.

- □ ENDORSEMENT   The addition of new provisions to an insurance policy already in effect, to avoid having to rewrite the entire policy.

- □ INSURANCE AGENT   Person who acts for the insurer in arranging contracts with people or companies seeking insurance protection.

INSURANCE COVERAGE

Many types of insurance coverage are available to small businesses. Some of the most important are

1. auto insurance
2. fire insurance
3. workers' compensation insurance
4. public liability insurance
5. crime insurance

6. special coverage

7. life insurance

8. health insurance

Before examining them, however, it is important to realize that *not every* potential loss should be insured. It does not pay the company to insure against a trivial loss. Rather, it should be absorbed as a common cost of doing business. Likewise, if the cost of insuring is extremely high and the chance of occurrence is not very great, it may be better to **self-insure.** This means that the company will put aside money in a special fund to meet any losses incurred by certain events. For example, a company that is located next door to a fire station might feel there is very little chance of its suffering a major loss from fire. Thus, it might put its fire insurance premiums into a special fund and "bet" that it will be cheaper to self-insure than to buy coverage from an insurance firm.[1] Such a company has two choices: *assume* the risk or *shift* the risk via insurance. The following sections examine the major types of business insurance.

AUTO INSURANCE

Since auto accidents and auto thefts are so common today, businesses need to insure their cars. A number of types of auto insurance coverage are available. **Liability insurance** coverage protects the driver or owner against claims arising from auto accidents. There are two types of liability insurance: **property damage liability insurance,** which provides protection against claims or damage to other people's property resulting from an accident; and **bodily injury liability insurance,** which provides coverage of anyone inside or outside the vehicle who suffers personal injury because of the driver.

Additionally, most businesses carry some form of **medical payments insurance,** which is designed to meet the medical needs of the people in the auto. This coverage extends to all the occupants in the vehicle, regardless of which driver was responsible for the accident. Usually the coverage extends from $250 to $5,000 per person, depending on how much protection is desired. However, insurance firms commonly refuse to sell medical payment insurance unless the other types of liability insurance are also purchased.

In addition, there is insurance for protecting the owner's investment in the auto; this is called **collision insurance** and it covers the vehicle regardless of who was at fault in the accident. The coverage usually comes in two forms: full coverage and deductible. Under full coverage, 100 percent of any loss or damage caused by a collision is paid. Of course, for such coverage the premium is usually quite high. As a result, companies typically carry a deductible. Formerly it was common for a business to carry a $50 to $100 deductible. Today deductibles are higher, because it does not take much of an accident to surpass this deductible. The insurance companies have raised their rates on $50 and $100 deductible, and businesses realize that to keep their premiums low they now must opt for a $200 or $250 deduction. In the case

---

[1]See "Cutting Costs through Self-Insurance," *Small Business Report,* July 1986, p. 98.

of the firm that has a $250 deductible, for example, an accident in which the collision bill is $2,750 will result in the company paying the first $250 and the insurance firm picking up the remaining $2,500.

FIRE INSURANCE

In this country, forty buildings catch fire every hour. Thus fire insurance is very important to businesses. Fire insurance policies pay *either* the monetary loss at the time of the fire or the face amount of the policy, *whichever is lower.* For example, if a business carries a $300,000 policy on a building worth $250,000 the insurance company will pay $250,000 if a fire totally destroys the structure. On the other hand, if the firm carries only $200,000, the insurance company will pay a maximum of $200,000, depending on the terms of the policy.

Of course, few buildings are *totally* destroyed by fire. In some cases, the fire department can save part of the structure and some of its contents. As a result, many businesses used to **underinsure;** that is, for example, carry $150,000 of fire insurance on a structure worth $250,000. In order to prevent gross underinsuring, the **coinsurance clause** has been developed. This clause requires businesses to carry insurance equal to a certain percentage of the building's actual value. The percentage is usually 80 percent.

Let us take a look at how fire losses are settled on an 80 percent coinsurance clause. Consider a firm that has a building worth $250,000 and ensures it for 80 percent or $200,000. The insurance company would compute the payment in case of a total loss like this:

$$\frac{\text{Amount of insurance carried}}{\text{Amount of insurance required}} = \frac{\$200,000}{\$200,000} \times \$200,000 \text{ face value of policy}$$

$$= \$200,000 \text{ payment}$$

If the business is insured for only 30 percent of the value of the structure and there is a $100,000 loss, the insurance firm would pay less. Here is how the insurance company would compute the payments:

$$\frac{\text{Amount of insurance carried}}{\text{Amount of insurance required}} = \frac{\$75,000}{\$200,000} = \frac{3}{8} \times \$100,000$$

$$= \$37,000 \text{ payment}$$

Because the building was underinsured, the insurance company will pay the business firm only a portion of the total loss. Remember that the insurance company will pay no more than the amount of the insurance policy. If the face value of the policy is greater than the loss, the company will simply pay for the loss. Thus it does a business no good to overinsure.

If a business needs further insurance, it is obtained through **extended coverage** in the form of a **rider**—an addition to the policy. Extended coverage is purchased to cover risks such as storms, tornados, cyclones, hail, and smoke damage. Some companies also purchase **business interruption insurance,** which replaces earnings lost because of fire damage.

WORKERS' COMPENSATION INSURANCE

Every state has workers' compensation laws. Under these laws, employees who are injured on the job are entitled to compensation unless the injury was deliberately inflicted or caused by intoxication, although in many cases intoxicated individuals are covered.

In some states businesses must purchase workers' compensation insurance from the state; other states allow private insurance firms to compete with them for the business. Still other states let private insurance companies handle the entire matter themselves.

The cost of the insurance is borne by the business, with rates depending on the size of the payroll and the hazards of the industry. If an employee is injured, medical and hospitalization expenses are paid and the person receives a weekly wage. This wage is usually 50–70 percent of the person's regular pay. However, in order to avoid paying for minor accidents, most plans call for a waiting period of from two days to two weeks before any payments are made. Since most businesses are required to have this insurance, the owner-manager should shop for the lowest rates.

PUBLIC LIABILITY INSURANCE

Public liability insurance is designed to protect businesses from lawsuits by individuals who injure themselves on the company's property. For example, someone visiting the company plant slips in a puddle of water and hurts himself. Can he sue the firm? The answer is yes, and he just might win. In fact, many companies do not wait for a person to get a lawyer and sue; they report the accident to their insurance company immediately, and the insurer sends a representative to talk to the injured party. Without liability insurance the company could find itself in big legal trouble. After all, the property should be safe at all times. A liability policy reduces the risk associated with occurrences such as this. However, the cost of premiums has become a great concern for small business owners.[2]

CRIME INSURANCE

For many small business people, crime insurance is the least familiar kind of insurance. This coverage protects the firm against burglary, robbery, and so forth. This insurance usually covers loss of inventoried merchandise and safes, as well as any damage done by the burglar. These policies typically limit coverage to around $500 per loss.

And then there is the problem the business owner faces when employees steal from the firm. For example, the treasurer of the company might make off with $50,000 and bankrupt the firm in the process. One way of protecting the firm is through the use of **fidelity bonds.** These bonds are usually written to cover people who hold jobs in which they handle funds. Sometimes the bond covers a specific person or group; other times it covers a particular position, such as the chief financial officer. If a financial loss is caused by the dishonesty of any bonded employee, the insurance company will pay the amount specified in the policy.

---

[2]See "Coping with the Insurance Crisis," *Small Business Report,* November 1986, p. 42; and Fikry S. Gahin, "Spreading the Blame for the Liability Insurance Crisis," *Risk Management,* March 1987, pp. 48–52.

Similar coverage can be obtained for protecting the business against theft by employees. For example, in retail stores it is common for some of the workers to walk off with merchandise. While insurance will help, the cheapest way to protect against this type of loss is to prevent it from occurring in the first place with well-formulated procedures. (Refer to Chapter 20.)

SPECIAL COVERAGE

In recent years there has been an increase in the use of special coverage insurance. This insurance is not needed by every business but for those who do require such coverage, it can be extremely important. Two forms of special coverage insurance are political risk insurance and directors' and officers' liability insurance.

POLITICAL RISK INSURANCE   This type of insurance is important for small firms that do business overseas. Three basic types of coverage are available. One is **kidnap/ransom insurance,** which covers losses such as monies paid to those making ransom or extortion demands, reward monies paid for information leading to the arrest and conviction of those responsible for these acts, and post-kidnap expenses for those engaged in negotiating the individual's release, as well as medical, legal, travel, and other associated expenses. With the increase in kidnapping of businesspeople in foreign countries, this insurance is being purchased by many firms doing business overseas.

Expropriation insurance provides protection against the confiscation, nationalization, or expropriation of property held in a foreign country. Business firms can buy coverage for such tangible assets as plant, equipment, land, and inventories. Compensation is usually based on the difference between the value of the investment and the compensation received from the government that expropriates the assets. Firms doing business in Third World countries find this type of insurance to be very helpful in light of those countries' ever-changing political policies.

Another concern of firms doing business overseas is that they might be unable to convert the local currency back into domestic currency. Interest, fees, and dividends will be tied up in the host country if they cannot convert profits. **Inconvertibility insurance** protects against these losses. The insurance company will convert the monies into domestic currency at the exchange rates prevailing on the day the period of inconvertibility begins. Such insurance virtually eliminates the risk of businesses having their money tied up in a foreign country for an indefinite period of time.

DIRECTORS' AND OFFICERS' LIABILITY INSURANCE   When a business firm runs into problems, the directors and officers of the company may be sued by the stockholders. Directors' and officers' liability insurance provides protection against financial losses arising from such suits. While it may appear unlikely that stockholders of a small firm would sue the directors or officers, it is not uncommon. Whenever a company buys another firm or sells part of its current holdings and the decision proves to be a poor one, there is likely to be trouble from those stockholders who feel that they have been cheated. When this happens, directors' and officers' liability insurance can be extremely important.

LIFE INSURANCE (KEY PERSON INSURANCE)

Life insurance is very helpful to small businesses that wish to protect their operation in the event a key person dies. For example, if one of the partners were to die, the others might have a great deal of difficulty buying this person's interest from the heirs. However, if the company owned a life insurance policy on the individual and the beneficiaries were the other partners, they could use the proceeds of the policy to buy the individual's interest and thereby continue operations.

Or consider the case of the key executive who accounts for over $200,000 worth of business to the firm annually. If this person died the company might suffer a tremendous drop in sales, resulting in a loss of earnings of perhaps $50,000. However, a policy on the individual's life could tide the company over until another key person could be hired to replace the deceased one.

What type of insurance is best? The answer will vary, but in most cases businesses choose term life insurance rather than whole life insurance. Additionally, there are other types of insurance with which the business person should be familiar. These are discussed next.

TERM LIFE INSURANCE   Term life insurance provides coverage for a limited number of years. For example, a businessperson could buy a term life insurance policy of $10,000 for one year. Assuming that the individual is in good health and under fifty years of age, the cost of the policy would be quite low when contrasted with any other type of life insurance policy. This is because the cost of the insurance is based on the death benefits that will have to be paid to the number of people in this person's age category who die this year plus a small markup for administrative expenses and profit. Table 22-1 provides a mortality table. A close look at the table shows that the survival rate for people under fifty years of age is quite low.

However, there is one big danger in using term life insurance. The cost goes up as the person gets older. Notice that for black males the death rate at fifty is more than twice than at forty, and the rate at sixty is more than twice the rate at fifty. So term

Table 22-1 Life and Death Expectancies

AGE IN 1983 (YEARS)	LIFE EXPECTANCY (YEARS)					EXPECTED DEATHS PER 1,000 ALIVE AT SPECIFIED AGE				
		White		Black			White		Black	
	Total	Male	Female	Male	Female	Total	Male	Female	Male	Female
At birth	74.6	71.7	78.7	65.4	73.6	11.15	10.79	8.60	21.05	17.23
1	74.5	71.5	78.4	65.9	73.9	.75	.80	.59	1.22	.92
2	73.5	70.5	77.4	64.9	72.9	.59	.60	.47	1.00	.76
3	72.6	69.6	76.4	64.0	72.0	.47	.47	.37	.81	.62
4	71.6	68.6	75.5	63.0	71.0	.39	.39	.31	.66	.51
5	70.6	67.6	74.5	62.1	70.1	.33	.35	.26	.54	.42
10	65.7	62.7	69.6	57.2	65.2	.18	.19	.14	.30	.22
20	56.0	53.1	59.8	47.6	55.4	1.02	1.47	.50	1.81	.69
30	46.6	43.9	50.1	38.7	45.9	1.21	1.52	.59	3.49	1.33
40	37.2	34.6	40.4	30.2	36.7	2.05	2.35	1.27	5.89	2.81
50	28.3	25.7	31.2	22.5	28.1	5.42	6.42	3.56	12.97	6.98
60	20.3	17.9	22.6	16.0	20.5	13.33	16.76	8.89	28.35	16.01
70	13.5	11.5	15.1	10.9	14.1	29.70	39.52	20.78	51.45	30.79
80	8.1	6.9	8.8	7.1	9.0	66.98	90.04	53.49	93.33	62.99
85 & over	6.1	5.2	6.5	6.0	7.4	1,000.00	1,000.00	1,000.00	1,000.00	1,000.00

Source: U.S. National Center for Health Statistics, *Vital Statistics of the United States,* annual, 1985.

insurance provides inexpensive protection when one is young but becomes very expensive later in life. (Even when an insurance company is willing to issue the policy, it usually must be foregone.)

WHOLE LIFE INSURANCE   Whole life insurance, often called **straight life,** offers the policyholder a combination of protection and savings. The annual premium remains constant throughout the life of the policy. Except for term life insurance, whole life provides the greatest coverage at the lowest premium. Additionally, the policy builds what is called a **cash surrender value,** which is payable upon cancellation of the policy. The owner can borrow against the cash surrender value, often at a low rate of interest (6–8 percent).

If the business partners or associates are young and want to buy insurance to protect their business, whole life may indeed be cheaper over the long run. On the negative side, however, there is the problem of having to pay more for the policy than for term life insurance, at least for five to ten years. Additionally, some people object to having to pay an interest charge to borrow the cash surrender value that, in effect, belongs to them.

OTHER TYPES OF LIFE INSURANCE   In addition to term and whole life, business firms use a number of other types of life insurance plans. One of these is **group life insurance.** This is often a fringe benefit for the employees but can be used for the owner-manager as well. Usually, it is a one-year, renewable term policy with the employer paying at least a portion of the premium. The plan commonly requires no physical exam so everyone in the business can be covered regardless of health.

A second type is **retirement** or **pension plan insurance.** Many firms want to provide their employees with retirement income beyond that paid by Social Security. One of the most popular ways of doing this is to have an insurance agent set up a retirement and pension plan program. Most of these plans require the employer, and sometimes the employee, to put money into the plan each year. Money is then drawn from this fund to pay retirement benefits.

Finally, there is **credit life insurance,** which has grown rapidly in recent years because of the increased amount of credit purchases and short-term borrowing by consumers. This type of insurance guarantees repayment of installment contracts and personal loans in the case of the debtor's death. Banks, finance companies, and retailers use this type of insurance. Usually a policy is written on a one-year basis and covers all of the firm's credit customers. In turn, the cost of the insurance is passed on to customers as part of the price of merchandise. A great advantage of this insurance is that it reduces the risk of consumer borrowing for both lender and borrower.

HEALTH INSURANCE

Another major form of insurance is health insurance. Almost 80 percent of all Americans have health insurance in one form or another. Many of these policies cover both accident and sickness, and they may also cover surgical expenses, hospitalization, and loss of income during a period of disability.

Policies commonly carry some type of deductible such as $100 a year on medicines and another $100 per year on major medical. In these cases the insured must pay the first $100 personally, and after that everything is covered according to some formula. A common division is 80–20: the insurance pays 80 percent of the bill, and the insured pays the remaining 20 percent. Also it is common for the policy cover to specify that it will pay a maximum amount toward the hospital room. For example, the individual may be guaranteed payment to cover a double-occupancy room or $120, whichever is less. If the person wants an individual room, he or she must pay the difference.

This insurance is important to small businesses for two reasons. First, it is a common fringe benefit. Since most companies provide it in one way or another, it is required by firms that want to remain competitive. Second, getting into a group health policy at work is usually much cheaper than buying one on an individual basis. Thus, small business owners can obtain health coverage for themselves while providing an employee fringe benefit at the same time. (See Small Business Success: Health Insurance Software.)

TYPES OF COVERAGE   There are a number of types of health care coverage. One is **hospital expense insurance,** which covers room, board, routine nursing care, and minor medical supplies when a person is hospitalized. This insurance usually has a limit on the number of days it covers, tending to range from 21 to 365 days. It is also common to find a limit on daily hospital costs, such as a maximum of $400 per day for no more than 200 days.

Another type of coverage is **surgical expense insurance.** This covers the surgeon's fee and is usually limited by, among other things, where the surgery takes place. For an operation in New York City the policy may allow $1,800, whereas the same operation in Dallas may be covered only to the extent of $1,400.

A third type of coverage is **physician's expense insurance.** This is commonly combined with hospital and surgical expense insurance to provide what is called **basic insurance.** This insurance package typically covers in-house hospital costs, visits by the doctor, and other nonsurgical care including office visits and house calls.

Major medical insurance is a fourth type of coverage. It picks up where basic coverage leaves off, paying for most medical care whether or not the person is hospitalized. These policies have deductibles and often contain a limit such as $300,000 over the life of the policy.

A fifth type of coverage is **comprehensive medical insurance,** which pulls together the other four forms of coverage. Comprehensive policies are very popular and are the most common form of health insurance offered through group insurance plans.

A person's chance of becoming disabled is three times that of dying during his or her working years. As a result, in recent years, **disability insurance** coverage has become a part of most health insurance programs. While these policies specify a waiting period of one or more weeks before payments begin, they are very useful in replacing income when the insured is unable to work because of illness, injury, or disease.

SPECIAL COVERAGE INSURANCE   In addition to the types of health insurance already described, some special coverages are becoming more popular. Four of them are accident insurance, cancer insurance, supplemental hospital insurance, and

■ SMALL BUSINESS SUCCESS ■

Health Insurance Software

 Located on 10 acres of pasture land 30 miles north of Tampa, Florida, Tingley Systems, Inc., has an unusual ambience. Cattle graze around the building. Groves of citrus trees, birds, and wildlife loom in the distance.

However, CEO Margie Tingley and her employees are far from uncivilized. Inside the building they design state-of-the-art computer systems used by major health insurance companies—such as Kaiser Permanente, Aetna, Blue Cross, and Blue Shield—in 22 states and Puerto Rico. Their software products handle billing, membership management, and accounting for companies serving up to one million people.

Born in Helen, Georgia, a town of about 3,000, Tingley left high school to get married and had three children by age 21. During the birth of her last child, she ruptured two disks in her neck and was in so much pain she couldn't even lift her babies. To pay for child care and "to keep my sanity," Tingley took a job at her husband's Air Force base exchange. "Being a young mother of three, wearing a neck brace, and not having a high school diploma was tougher than making my first million," she says. But she persevered and continued working, first as a bookkeeper and secretary, then as an office organizer. She would take a job, learn how the company worked, and then spend three to six months straightening out the business's internal reporting and procedural operations. "I'd have the place totally organized and be bored to death," she remembers, "and then I'd move on."

Another setback occurred in 1975 when Tingley ruptured two spinal disks in an automobile accident. She was out of work for two long years, hospitalized frequently for back surgeries and therapy, and in so much pain she couldn't even walk down a flight of stairs. But Tingley's steely resolve won out.

Her big break came in the 1970s when she and her husband, William, designed the first health maintenance software system to organize paperwork and billing for health care companies. This was the first of nine software packages that make up the company today. The software package put together by the husband-wife duo would cost millions of dollars and require a team of 20 programmers if it were prepared for larger corporations today.

Tingley's attitude toward failure is apparent. "We have so many excuses to fail if we want to use them. It takes a lot of courage not to use those thousands of reasons for failure."

Source: Adapted from Kristin Von Kreisler-Bomben, "Programmers Prescription," *Entrepreneur,* November 1990, pp. 87–89.

dental insurance. Few small business owners pay the entire premiums on these. Quite often the owner shares the cost with the employees and in some cases makes it available to employees but pays none of the premium.

Accident insurance can now be purchased along with health insurance. This was not possible years ago when they were sold separately. Accident insurance covers people in the event of a particular accident or injury, providing a fixed payment such as $150 a day for 30 days in case of hospitalization of $15,000 for the loss of a limb.

Cancer insurance—and other dread disease coverage for that matter—provides a specific payment to the insured should he or she contract the disease. A typical example of coverage is $100 a day for each day in the hospital or $5,000 in the event of death. Since a large percentage of the population will, at one time or another, be subjected to some form of dread disease, these policies have become more popular in recent years.

Supplemental hospital insurance is designed to increase the employee's current hospital coverage. The policy pays a specified benefit, such as $100 a day for each day in the hospital to offset the costs of a hospital stay. For example, a person in the hospital for ten days might end up with a bill of $5,000. Assuming the typical 80 percent coverage, the individual owes $1,000 and the rest is covered by the person's comprehensive medical insurance policy. The $1,000 owed by the individual would be covered by the supplemental policy. In most cases, supplemental coverage does not take care of *all* extra expenses but goes a long way toward reducing the employee's direct, out-of-pocket expenses.

Dental insurance also has become popular. There are many things that it does not cover, in particular cosmetic dentistry (capping teeth to improve a person's looks). However, it does cover annual checkups, cleaning, normal fillings, dentures, and other routine work. Most of these policies, at best, are only partially paid for by the employer. They are often made available to employees as options.

HEALTH CARE INSURERS   Small business owners need to know where health coverage can be obtained. Basically, three types of organizations provide health insurance coverage.

The best known is Blue Cross and Blue Shield. **Blue Cross** pays for hospital services; **Blue Shield** pays for physicians' services. Both are actually intermediaries between the groups that need the services and the physicians and hospitals that contractually agree to provide the services. At the present time about 40 percent of the U.S. population is covered by some form of Blue Cross/Blue Shield protection. The employer provides this insurance by contracting the local Blue Cross/Blue Shield office and, working with their people, setting up an insurance package tailored to the needs of the personnel. This group policy is then available to everyone in the firm and extends to their immediate families as well.

Another health insurer is the **health maintenance organization (HMO).** HMOs have been around since the 1920s but, with the escalating costs of health care in recent years, their popularity has been increasing. In essence, an HMO is a prepaid insurance plan. The organization itself consists of a group of hospitals, physicians, and other health-care providers who have joined together to provide health services to members. An HMO is a "medical supermarket" that provides a broad range of services designed to get people well and keep them well. Those who join an HMO are given a list of participating physicians. They select one as their main physician, and if something happens to them that this doctor cannot treat, the doctor refers them to a specialist in the program who can. The cost of this insurance is usually shared by the employer and the employee. It is higher than Blue Cross/Blue Shield coverage initially because of its prepaid feature; that is, someone who visits the doctor usually pays a nominal amount such as $3 per visit. Many employees with young children or a chronically ill family member will opt for HMO coverage because it is cheaper than any other coverage in the long run.

A third kind of health insurer is **private insurance companies.** These firms are much smaller than Blue Cross/Blue Shield and the HMOs. Although they can provide the same types of coverage as their larger competitors, they are unable to meet the lower rates of those organizations. For this reason, private insurance firms tend to focus their efforts on specialized types of coverage that make direct cash payments, such as $500 in the case of an appendectomy or $1,000 for the removal of cataracts. These companies sometimes offer policies that are unavailable elsewhere and, as a result, can be excellent supplemental insurers.

A final alternative for small businesses is to reduce their health insurance expenses through cooperative efforts with other companies. These cooperatives are also known as "self-funded insurance co-ops" and "multiple employer welfare associates." The idea behind these groups is that a number of small businesses can share the risk of insurance by joining together as a purchasing group. The Federal Product Liability Risk Retention Act of 1981, later amended in 1986, allowed groups to provide liability coverage of any type if they share a common risk. While this option may not be viable for every small business, it is an alternative that may offer some relief from escalating health insurance costs. (See Small Business Owner's Notebook: Scams in Health Insurance.)

MANAGING THE INSURANCE PROGRAM

The material we have discussed to this point can be very helpful to the small business owner-manager in identifying the business's insurance needs and getting suitable coverage.[3] However, insurance is *not* a one-time thing; it is necessary to evaluate insurance needs continually. As a company grows new coverages may become necessary. Also, certain policies may have to be terminated and others picked up. For example, as a business grows in size the proprietor might use some of the company's funds to buy a small whole life insurance policy. If the business is terminated, the owner could continue to maintain the policy personally. However, it is unwise to buy a large, or a series of small, whole life insurance policies because the cost of maintaining them eventually becomes prohibitive. Instead, the businessperson should turn to term life insurance and get more coverage for the dollar. Of course, the cost of the insurance will rise each year, but it will take a long time before the cost of the term policy exceeds that of the whole life policy and, at least in the short run, term life insurance is a better buy. Later, when the business is more financially sound, it

---

[3]See Nancy A. Sutton, "A Comparison of Insurance and Pension Plans in Large and Small Firms," *American Journal of Small Business,* Fall 1986, pp. 15–22.

■ SMALL BUSINESS OWNER'S NOTEBOOK ■

Scams in Health Insurance

To combat the escalating cost of health insurance, many small businesses are searching for affordable, multiple-employer plans that allow a number of small companies to take part in a self-funded insurance cooperation. The plans are known as MEWAs, or Multiple Employer Welfare Associations. They are also sometimes called METs, or Multiple Employer Trusts. These plans attract small companies with cut-rate health-insurance premiums. But they often collapse or vanish when it's time to pay out big claims.

The self-funded plans most likely to run into trouble are those that lack reserves and rely entirely on premiums to pay claims. When the claims exceed premiums, they have no further resources.

In reality, many of these plans are nothing more than sophisticated pyramid schemes in which the ability to pay the claims of existing participants depends on the ability to attract more participants and thereby obtain more premium dollars.

A proliferation of health-insurance scams have gone virtually unchecked by either the states or the federal government until fairly recently. No one knows how many of the MEWAs use unethical practices, however, or even how many MEWAs exist nationwide.

Legislation has been proposed that would require MEWA promoters to file registration documents with the Department of Labor, making it easier for states to locate promoters and enforce state insurance laws.

Meanwhile, law-enforcement officials recommend that small companies be on guard against self-funded, multiple-employer health-insurance scams. Before buying a multiple-employer plan, research the MEWA thoroughly, ask for the plan's financial statement, press your insurance agent for details on what you are buying, and keep an eye on the plan once you have bought into it.

Source: Roger Thompson, "Beware of Scams," *Nations Business,* July 1990, p. 22.

will be able to afford higher premiums, so term life insurance may still be the best bet for the long run. In any event, the owner-manager must continue to review the various insurance policies to ensure that the business has the coverage it needs. The following guidelines can help the owner-manager to accomplish these objectives.

Formulate and write down a clear statement of your insurance philosophy. This will help the owner-manager clarify his or her thinking and will aid anyone helping the owner-manager manage the business's insurance. An illustration of such a policy is this: Insure all risks except those considered small in relation to the cash position of the firm; these will be borne by the business.

If you put another person in charge of your firm's insurance management, be sure the person understands his or her responsibility. Give the person all the necessary facts to do the job effectively. For example, be sure the person knows about any new operations being planned.

If you have more than one branch of operation, it is usually a good idea to centralize insurance responsibility. Handle all insurance coverage from the main office.

Have one agent handle your insurance. If there are several agents, they may not be able to view company problems from a sufficiently broad perspective.

Do everything possible to keep your losses down. Supervise and coordinate a loss-prevention program, including safety campaigns and safety rules.

Decide which kinds of risk protection are most important and most economical. With the insurance agent, investigate the various coverages and match them to the firm's needs.

Cover largest loss exposures first and the rest as the company budget permits. Use premium dollars where the need for protection is greatest. For example, some companies insure their cars against collision loss but neglect to purchase adequate liability coverage. This is a mistake. Collision losses seldom bankrupt a firm, but liability judgments often have.

Make proper use of deductibles. In many lines of insurance, full coverage is uneconomical because of the high cost of covering the first dollar of loss. A deductible can reduce the cost while still giving the business adequate coverage.

Review coverages periodically. Reviewing the policies greatly reduces the likelihood that the business will fail to increase limits of liability where needed or that the owner will be deprived of a rate reduction.

Check occasionally to see that the firm is getting its insurance for a reasonable price. Do not switch insurers every time a lower price is quoted, but do keep aware of average costs for the amount and types of coverage needed.

Analyze the insurance terms and provisions. When a firm attempts to save money by purchasing a cheaper policy, it sometimes discovers that the specific hazard it wanted to insure against is not covered because of a technicality. Or it learns that the insurer is able to offer the rate only by reducing services or following a very restrictive claims policy.

Insure the proper risk. Make sure that insurance is being purchased to handle the right risk. One small firm bonded its employees who handled cash but did not bond those who handled materials. One of the latter stole large amounts of merchandise, and the firm suffered an extensive and unrecoverable loss.

Find out if the firm can assume certain administrative duties required by the policies. If the company takes over some administrative chores, the insurance company may reduce the premium by more than the expense that will be incurred in performing the service.

Buy insurance in as large a unit as possible. In this way the firm can take advantage of the savings most insurers allow for large-unit policies. This is particularly true of many types of property insurance and life insurance. For example, the more property included in a single policy, the less expensive it is for the insurer to handle per unit.

■ SUMMARY

Insurance is a cooperative or group method of pooling funds in which many people pay a small sum, known as a premium, to protect themselves against a potentially large loss. There are many types of coverage that the small business person should know about. One is auto insurance. How much liability and medical payment insurance should the business carry on its cars? Should it also have collision insurance? These are questions that the owner and the insurance agent, working together, should be able to answer. It is important that the businessperson know about the types of auto insurance coverage and the benefits of each.

Most businesses need fire insurance. A coinsurance clause may require the firm to cover a certain percentage of the structure's actual value. If this is not done, the insurance company will pay the business only a portion of any loss it incurs. Other types of insurance discussed in the chapter are workers' compensation, public liability, crime insurance, and special liability coverage.

Two general types of life insurance are available, term life and whole life, each with its own advantages. Since term life is cheaper, most small businesses purchase it. Additionally, other types of life insurance plans, including group life insurance, pension plan insurance, and credit life insurance, may benefit the small business owner. Health insurance is a fringe benefit offered by many small businesses. Types of coverage and health care insurers were described in the chapter.

Some guidelines for managing a business's insurance program were listed. They point to the need for continually evaluating the firm's insurance requirements.

■ REVIEW AND DISCUSSION QUESTIONS

1. What is meant by the term *insurance?*

2. What does a small business owner-manager need to know about auto insurance? Explain.

3. An owner-manager has purchased a fire insurance policy in the amount of $100,000. The coinsurance clause requires 80 percent coverage, and the appraised value of the building is $100,000. How much will the insurance company pay if a fire loss of $50,000 is incurred? A fire loss of $80,000? A fire loss of $100,000? Show your calculations.

4. What does workers' compensation insurance cover? Public liability insurance? Explain.

5. How can an owner-manager insure against crimes such as burglary and theft?

6. What kinds of special liability coverage can a small business buy? Identify and describe two kinds.

7. In what way can an understanding of term life insurance and whole life insurance be of value to an owner-manager? Also, why would the owner-manager be interested in purchasing such insurance?

8. What is group life insurance; pension plan insurance; credit life insurance?

9. Explain what a small business owner needs to know about health insurance.

10. A new owner-manager has asked you for some guidelines to use in managing her business's insurance program. What would you tell her? Present at least six guidelines.

Case Studies

Covering the Risk

■ Jean, Jessica, and Joan Hardin are equal partners in their own business. They are also 30-year-old triplets. The women would like to purchase life insurance so that if something happens to any of them, the proceeds can be used to keep the company alive.

Their plan is for each to purchase $100,000 of term insurance and to name the other two as the beneficiaries. Thus if one were to die, the surviving sisters would each receive $50,000. "In this way, we would have money to hire the necessary people to replace the one who died and to buy out her share," explained Jean. "Each of us is critical to the overall success of our company. A loss of one would have a dramatic effect. Also, we estimate that the business is currently worth about $150,000 and that it should increase in value at the rate of about 10 percent a year. So if one of us were to die, the surviving partners would have to pay the deceased's estate $50,000. The insurance proceeds would allow us to do this and still keep the partnership intact."

The sisters have been considering both term and whole life policies. They will ask their insurance agent to recommend one. "We want as much protection as possible for our dollar," said Joan, "but we just don't know what type of policy will provide this to us. Nor do we know which insurance company would be best. However, I'm sure that our independent insurance agent can help us answer these questions and make the right decision. We have a meeting with her the day after tomorrow and we should have this entire matter taken care of within the next couple of weeks."

1. Which type of policy should the insurance agent recommend, term or whole life? Why?

2. Based on the data in Table 22-1, what can you tell the sisters about their life expectancy and the cost of insurance to them? Be complete in your answer.

3. If the sisters opt for term insurance, will their rates increase next year? Why or why not?

Fire Insurance Coverage

■ The Brinkler Corporation owns a two-story building three blocks from a large fire station. Brinkler is a small chemical firm and flammable products are always in the building. However, because of its rigid safety program, the company has never had a fire on the premises.

Last month the company's insurance agent made his annual appraisal. He valued the building at $500,000 and recommended that the firm insure the building for this amount. However, the company's financial officer did not believe that this was necessary for two reasons. First, the firm had never had a fire; its safety program was superb. Second, the fire station is so close. As a result, he felt that no more than $250,000 worth of damage could possibly be done regardless of the accident. For this reason the financial officer suggested that the firm carry only $250,000 worth of fire insurance and put the rest aside into a self-insurance fund. After thinking over the matter, the president of Brinkler decided to insure the structure for $400,000. He really wanted to insure for $300,000, but the insurance agent explained that because of the 80 percent coinsurance clause the structure had to be insured for at least $400,000 if the firm wanted 100 percent coverage. Otherwise, only a percentage of the loss would be covered.

Last night a major fire occurred in the building. Flames raged through the structure. Within fifteen seconds the fire alarm in the building went off, and a firetruck was on the scene within three minutes. Despite all of their efforts, however, the building was completely gutted, and nothing was saved.

The president tried to look on the positive side of things. "It could have been worse," he said. "We could have canceled our fire insurance altogether. Then where would be we?"

1. How much will the insurance company pay the Brinkler Corporation?

2. How much would it have paid if the company had insured the structure for $500,000?

3. What if the company had insured for $250,000? How much would it have received then?

You Be the Consultant

THE 50 PERCENT SOLUTION

The Redford Shopping Center is located in the southwest corner of a medium-sized city. The owner of the shopping center, Charles Redford, has had a fire insurance policy on the property since the mall was built three years ago. According to the terms of the policy, in case of a fire the insurance company will pay for damages caused by the fire and by fire-related events. The latter refers to damages that might be suffered by a store if it were inundated with water from firefighters' hoses.

The value of the shopping center has been placed at $4.5 million by an independent appraiser. Mr. Redford bought the land and personally directed the building of the shopping center. Because of his close relations and good credit rating with the city's largest bank, he was able to obtain a loan for 95 percent of the construction cost, which was $3.1 million. Since then, the city's suburbs have expanded in the direction of the shopping center, and its overall value has skyrocketed.

Last year the value was estimated at $3.9 million, and Mr. Redford insured the structure for 80 percent of this. This 80 percent figure is a minimum value that the insurance company will accept, based on its coinsurance clause, if the owner wants to be paid 100 percent of the fire damage or the face value of the policy, whichever is lower. This year, however, Mr. Redford felt that the estimate of $4.5 million was too high and that the premium for 80 percent coverage was too great. He therefore decided to insure the shopping center for 50 percent of its appraised value. Mr. Redford's insurance agent counseled against this action, pointing out that under the terms of the fire insurance policy, the company will not pay the full amount of any loss. However, if Mr. Redford continues to insure for 80 percent of the appraised value, the company will pay 100 percent of any loss up to the face value of the policy.

After giving the matter serious thought, Mr. Redford decided that the chance of a fire occurring in the shopping center was really quite small. Additionally, there is a fire station only eight blocks away. As he put it, "How much damage could really be done by a fire, no matter how bad it was?" So last month he purchased a fire insurance policy that covers the shopping center for 50 percent of its appraised value.

Last week a fire broke out in one of the stores in the middle of the shopping center. The fire spread in all directions. The alarm was not turned in to the fire department until at least thirty minutes after the fire had begun. Because the sixty-five stores are arranged in an S-shaped pattern, the flames were able to lick up the wall and travel along the ceiling from one store to the next. By the time firefighters arrived, the fire had been raging for almost an hour.

Forty stores in the central part of the center were totally destroyed and another twenty were badly damaged by either smoke or water. The shopping center will be closed for almost two months while repairs are being made. The overall damage estimate is $2.2 million.

■ **YOUR CONSULTATION** Assume that you are Mr. Redford's independent insurance agent. First, estimate how much the insurance company will pay toward the overall fire damage of $2.2 million. Second, offer Mr. Redford some advice regarding what he should do about providing adequate fire insurance coverage in the future. Give him some sound insurance advice.

Legal Concerns of Small Business

Virtually every day businesses enter into situations that involve potential legal problems. Normal transactions with suppliers, customers, employees, and competitors can develop into problems if there is a failure to understand certain basic principles essential to our legal framework. The objective of this chapter is to introduce certain fundamental legal concepts of which every small business person should be aware. When you have studied this chapter you will be able to:

1. *Define the term* contract.
2. *Explain what constitutes an agreement, what is meant by consideration, and what is meant by contractual capacity.*
3. *Explain the importance of legality of purpose and reality of consent.*
4. *Describe breach of contract.*
5. *Explain the duties and responsibilities of an agency relationship.*
6. *Define and describe the types of warranties.*
7. *Distinguish between voluntary and involuntary bankruptcy.*
8. *Define patents, copyrights, and trademarks.*

CONTRACT LAW

A **contract** is a legal agreement that can be enforced by the courts if either party fails to abide by its provisions. The small business owner-manager must understand the basics of contract law, keeping in mind that there is no substitute for a competent attorney. When a businessperson draws up a contract, it is always wise to have one's own lawyer look over the agreement and make sure that everything has been covered properly. At that time the lawyer should be able to give advice about possible contract problems and how they can be resolved.

This discussion of contract law will provide the fundamentals necessary for understanding these legal agreements. As a beginning, let us set a case before you and let you be the judge. Here are the facts:

Mrs. Jones has decided to sell her 500-acre farm. On March 3 she talks to Mr. Haseman, a real estate agent, who agrees to take the listing and find a buyer. On March 5 Mrs. Jones receives a standard written listing agreement from Mr. Haseman, which she is to sign and return. The agreement is dated March 4. The contract provides a 6 percent commission to the agent if he finds a buyer for the property at a specified price within 30 days. Mrs. Jones specifies that she will not take less than $250,000 for her farm.

Mr. Haseman receives the signed agreement on March 10. Noting that the letter was mailed on March 9, he changes the date of the agreement to read March 9 so as to ensure himself 30 days in which to sell the property.

On April 5 Mr. Haseman receives a deposit of $100,000 from Mr. Young, who had looked at the Jones farm two weeks earlier. Mr. Young tells Mr. Haseman that he will pay $250,000 for the property.

Mr. Haseman immediately calls Mrs. Jones and conveys the news. However, Mrs. Jones explains that her contract with him expired on April 3—30 days after March 4—and that she has gone ahead and sold the property to Mr. Mandel for $255,000.

Mr. Haseman then brings suit for his fee. He tells the court that he had sold the property within 30 days of the date the agreement was returned to him. Mrs. Jones's attorney argues that the original agreement was dated March 4, and that in order to change the effective date of their agreement, Mr. Haseman would have had to directly call this to her attention and get her okay, something he failed to do.

With which party would you side if you were the judge? Why?

The court held for Mrs. Jones, because it ruled that the contract had expired on April 3. If the real estate agent had wanted more time, he should have contacted Mrs. Jones and requested it.

How well did you do in resolving the case? If not too well, keep in mind that the average small business person does not know very much about contract law. Thus, our purpose here is to acquaint you with some of the major facets of contract law and make you aware of some of the things a small business owner-manager should do, or refrain from doing. (See Small Business Success: Knowing Your Legal Expenses.)

ESSENTIALS OF A CONTRACT[1]

The first thing the small business owner-manager needs to know about contracts is what they require in order to be legal and binding. The five essentials of a contract are

1. agreement
2. consideration

---

[1] For a thorough discussion of contract law, see Kenneth W. Clarkson, Roger LeRoy Miller, Gaylord A. Jentz, and Frank B. Cross, *West's Business Law,* 4th Edition (St. Paul, Minnesota: West Publishing Co., 1989), pp. 131–297.

■ **SMALL BUSINESS SUCCESS** ■

Knowing Your Legal Expenses

 Kamran Elahian had worked closely with his attorney, Arthur Schneiderman, to nurture two companies: CAE Systems, Inc., a design automation software company, and Citrus Logic, Inc., a semiconductor manufacturer. However, in October of 1989 Elahian received a statement from his attorney that contained only a total figure for legal expenses: $4,108.80. There was no explanation of what services were performed, nor was there a detailed description of the particular situation for which that fee related. Elahian phoned Schneiderman and demanded a detailed explanation. He received a complete itemized statement.

Today Elahian and Schneiderman still work together and the statements that Schneiderman submits are itemized so that they can be better understood. For example, partner's fees, associates fees, hours spent, duties performed, and specific situations (that is, raising financing, preparing statement, filing documents, and so forth) are delineated. Everything is clearly detailed on the legal statement.

For Kamran Elahian, understanding the legal bill is important. His latest venture, Momenta Corp., a portable computing service, has raised approximately $12 million in venture capital and legal fees amounted to $40,000. During 1990, Momenta's entire legal bill totaled $119,000. Thus, it has been extremely important to both Elahian and Schneiderman to satisfy each other's understanding of the legal expenses.

Elahian believes that keeping abreast of his legal expenses helps him to maintain a strong working relationship with his attorney. Irritations in business relationships are prevalent enough without adding this type of misunderstanding. Every small business owner should be able to interpret his or her legal expenses. After all, if a half-hour telephone conversation with an attorney costs $200 then maybe the small business owner should review the importance of such a call.

Source: Nancy Rutter, "Controlling Legal Costs," *Inc.*, February, 1991, pp. 90–91.

3. contractual capacity

4. legality

5. reality of consent

These essentials are explained in the sections that follow. Emphasis is given to the key elements a small business owner-manager should understand about each one.

AGREEMENT

The first, and most important, element of a contract is agreement. In order for **agreement** to exist there must be a reasonably definite understanding between two or more parties. What the small business person needs to realize is that there must be an **offer** by one party followed by an **acceptance** from the other, in order for agreement to be present.

REQUIREMENTS OF AN OFFER   There must be an **intent to contract.** Sometimes when people talk business they do so only in *exploratory* terms and there is no agreement; hence there is no contract. For example, George says to Andy, "How much do you want for that new machine you have advertised in your brochure?" Andy consults his price catalogue and says, "It costs $2,000," George replies, "Heck, that's too much money. The most I could afford to pay would be $1,600." The two men chuckle and hang up. The next day the machine is delivered to George's business along with an invoice for $1,600. Does George have to pay for the machine? No, he does not. He did not contract with Andy. He merely told him what his top offer would be. He was still in the preliminary negotiation stage. If Andy were interested in selling at $1,600 he should have followed up and said, "If you are serious, I will sell it to you for $1,600." Then, if George agreed, there would have been a contract.

The same is true of advertising. Advertisements are invitations to make an offer. For example, Mary writes an ad, delivers it to the newspaper, and sits back waiting for the customers to come to her sale. To her surprise she gets more than three times the number of expected customers. All of them have seen that she has priced handknit sweaters at $26 while everyone else in town is selling them for $65. Actually, Mary made an error when writing the ad; she meant to write $62 but she reversed the digits. Does Mary have to sell the sweaters for $26? No. An advertisement is considered by the courts to be a preliminary negotiation rather than a firm offer to sell. When the customers show up and demand the sweater for $26 she can refuse, pointing out that the actual price is $62 and ask them to make an offer at that price or leave the store.

In order for an agreement to exist, the offer must be **reasonably definite.** This means that the terms must be specific enough that a court can determine when the parties to the contract have lived up to their promises. For example, Harry promises to sell Martha his car for $3,700 with "credit terms to be arranged." Martha agrees but then decides to back out. Can she do so? Yes, she can, because the statement, "with credit terms to be arranged" is vague; Harry's offer lacks reasonable definiteness.

An offer must be **communicated** for a contract to exist. For example, Kuratko advertises a reward for the return of his lost textbook. Hodgetts, not knowing of the reward, finds the textbook and returns it to Kuratko. Legally, Hodgetts is not entitled to the reward since the offer had not been communicated to him.

TERMINATION OF THE OFFER   It is also important for the small business person to realize that under certain conditions an offer can be terminated. One instance is when the person who made the offer simply revokes it by communicating with the other party and calling off the deal. This will not work if the offer contains a promise that it will stay open for a given period of time or if the other party has an option contract. An **option contract** exists when a seller says, "I will give you the exclusive right to buy this land for $100,000 at any time during the next thirty days in return for $500." In this case the seller cannot revoke the offer during this thirty-day period.

Another way an offer can be terminated is if the offeree notifies the offeror that he or she does not intend to accept. A third way is if a sufficient amount of time has elapsed. For example, if a person offered to sell someone an acre of land for $5,000 three years ago, the offeree could not hold the person to the offer today because a significant amount of time has elapsed. In this case the offeree's failure to act promptly terminated the offer.

REQUIREMENTS OF ACCEPTANCE In order for acceptance to be present, it must be **unequivocal;** that is, the offeree must agree to the offer as stated. If the offeree says, "I will not give you $1,000 for that lumber, but I will give you $900," this is *not* an acceptance. It is a *rejection* of the offer followed by a *counteroffer.* Now it is up to the seller to accept or refuse.

It is also important to know that in most cases silence does constitute acceptance; acceptance must be communicated. For example, a manufacturer sends a business owner a letter that reads, "If I do not hear from you within ten days I will assume that you want these 5,000 shirts and will mail them to you." The owner is not required to buy these shirts because he or she did not ask for them. Remember, however, that the business owner cannot keep the shirts without paying for them. This, too, is illegal. They should be returned—at the manufacturer's expense.

If the person being offered the goods or services decides to accept, when does the acceptance take place? The courts have held that *an acceptance is effective when it is communicated to the person who made the offer* (or the person's agent), but *revocation is effective only when it is received.* For example, Dolores receives a letter from a manufacturer offering her some products at a reduced rate. She calls the manufacturer and accepts. At this point an acceptance takes place, and the manufacturer can ship the goods. However, there are some fine points of law when it comes to acceptance, and the owner-manager should have a general knowledge of them. The most important point is known as the implied agency rule.

If the parties negotiate a contract through the mail or by telegram, there is a lapse of time between when the offeree initiates the message of acceptance and the time the offeror receives the message. In some cases it becomes important to determine the *precise moment* acceptance became effective—particularly if the acceptance is delayed in reaching the offeror (or never reaches the person at all) or if the person who has made the offer attempts to revoke it before receiving an acceptance. In these cases the courts rely on the **implied agency rule.** This rule holds that when an offeror sends an offer through one means of communication, he or she is implicitly designating that means of communication as the one to be used by the offeree in accepting. If the offer is made by mail, the acceptance should be sent back by mail. If it is, the acceptance becomes effective the moment it is deposited in the mailbox in a properly addressed and stamped envelope. Even if the letter is delayed or lost, the offeror cannot assert that a contract has not been created.

CONSIDERATION

A second major requirement for a contract is consideration. Simply put, **consideration** is something of value that is given to the offeror by the offeree. What constitutes consideration? A primary means the courts have used to answer this question is the detrimental test.

THE DETRIMENTAL TEST   Whenever a person seeks to hold another party to his or her promise and the latter claims there was no contract because there was no consideration, the courts usually inquire as to whether the former party incurred a **detriment**—a loss of some kind—under the contract.

PERFORMANCE OF PREEXISTING OBLIGATIONS   A second era of importance in studying consideration is that of **preexisting obligations.** If someone does something in carrying out a contract, it may constitute consideration; however, if what the person does is required by preexisting obligations, it does not constitute consideration. For example, if a police officer captures a burglar for whom a reward has been offered by a local merchant, the officer cannot demand the reward. She is required by her job to capture criminals and is merely carrying out a preexisting obligation.

MUTUALITY OF OBLIGATION   Another thing the small business owner-manager must know about consideration is that there must be **mutuality of obligation;** that is, both parties are tied to the agreement.

CONTRACTUAL CAPACITY

The individuals who are parties to the agreement must be *able* to contract. In some cases they are not. A group that can constitute a contractual capacity problem for the small business person is minors.

THE MINOR   In most states a **minor** is someone who is under 18 years of age (in some states it is someone under 21 years of age). The risk in dealing with minors is that, virtually without exception, contracts with minors are *voidable at their option.* This means that a minor can escape contractual obligation at his or her option by merely letting the other party know the decision prior to the time the minor reaches the age of majority or within a reasonable time thereafter.

WHEN THE MINOR IS LIABLE   Once a minor reaches the age of majority, he or she has the ability to ratify earlier contracts. Usually this takes the form of complying with the conditions of the contract. For example, Ellen has purchased a typewriter for $20 down and $20 a month. If she continued to pay for the typewriter for any length of time after reaching the age of majority, this constitutes **ratification** of the contract and she must continue to abide by the agreement. Analogously, if George bought a car one year ago and it is now nine months since he reached the age of majority, the courts will not let him void the contract. He has waited too long.

Additionally, a minor cannot disaffirm *every* contract. Agreements calling for the purchase of goods that are **necessaries** create at least a partial responsibility for the minor. This liability is usually established as the reasonable value of the goods actually used. For example, Diane goes into a clothing store and buys a warm jacket for winter wear. When the winter is over she returns the coat, tells the store manager she is a minor, and asks for her money back. Can she disaffirm the agreement? Not completely, because the coat was *necessary* for the cold winter. The court would rule that she must pay its reasonable value at the time of purchase. However, it is important to remember that the minor's liability is dependent on the existence of a necessary; if the good is *not* ruled to be such, the individual can void the entire contract. In one such case a young couple were living with the husband's parents but wanted a place of their own. They bought a mobile home and lived in it for two years. Just before they reached their majority the couple disaffirmed the contract, announced that they would no longer make payments on the promissory note, and asked for a return of their money. Judgment was held in their behalf because the mobile home did not constitute a necessary. Because they *could* have lived with the parents, they did not require their own home. As a result, they were entitled to disaffirm the contract.

INSANITY AND INTOXICATION   An individual who is adjudged insane cannot be held responsible for any contracts he or she signed while in this condition. The courts will set them aside. Likewise, if someone was intoxicated when a contract was entered into, many courts will set aside the agreement. However, it should be noted that the person who is asking the court to set aside the agreement must be able to prove that he or she was so intoxicated at that time that the terms of the contract were unclear.[2]

LEGALITY

The fourth requirement of a contract is **legality of purpose**—a contract that is in violation of the law cannot be enforced. For example, if someone makes a bet with another person and then refuses to pay, the law will hold (except in Nevada and New Jersey) that the contract for the bet was illegal and will thus refuse to enforce it. Likewise, in most states there are statutes requiring persons who engage in certain professions, trades, or businesses be licensed. Lawyers, physicians, real estate brokers, and contractors are typical examples. A contract with someone who is not duly licensed is nonbinding. For example, if someone provides a businessperson with legal advice but the individual is not licensed as a lawyer, the businessperson is not required to pay the bill.

Usury (charging excessively high interest rates for a loan), restraint of trade agreements (such as price fixing or monopolizing), and **exculpatory clauses** (unreasonably one-sided or unfair liability statements) are all examples of potentially illegal contracts.

THE EFFECT OF ILLEGAL CONTRACTS   As a general rule, illegal contracts are unenforceable. As a result, neither party to such a contract is given any assistance by the courts. However, there are times when the courts will intervene because to do otherwise would create an unfair hardship.

One time when the courts will rule on an illegal contract is when, for example, a business has purchased fire insurance from an insurance firm. Unknown to the business, however, the company is not licensed to sell insurance in the state and when a fire destroys the company's office building, the insurance firm refuses to pay on the grounds that the contract is illegal. The courts will step in and require payment.

The courts will also step in if they feel that the parties are not equally at fault. For example, Harry forges a warehouse receipt, which makes it appear that he is the owner of certain goods stored at a warehouse. He takes the receipt to a trucking company and asks the company to deliver the goods to his place of business. The

---

[2]John R. Allison and Robert A. Prentice, *The Legal Environment of Business,* 3rd ed. (Hinsdale, IL: The Dryden Press, 1990), p. 194.

trucking company does so, unaware that Harry is not the owner of the goods. In this case, although the contract is illegal, the company is entitled to receive its transportation charges from Harry.

Finally, if a contract calls for several things to be done, one legal and the others illegal, the courts may require the first to be carried out but not the others. For example, Mary promises to pay Cindy $300 for a painting and $300 more for a vase. However, the painting does not belong to Cindy and she had no business promising to sell it. Nevertheless, the second part of the contract is binding and the courts will allow Mary to buy the vase for $300 even if Cindy protests, claiming that the entire contract is null and void because one part of it called for the performance of an illegal act.

REALITY OF CONSENT

The fifth requirement for a contract is **reality of consent.** This is missing when the agreement is tainted with fraud, innocent misrepresentation, or mistakes.

FRAUD OR MISREPRESENTATION   Deception with the intent of misleading another person constitutes **fraud,** which can take numerous forms. For example, there is misrepresentation of fact in the case of a horse owner who sells someone a horse, telling the buyer that the horse's mother was a champion. Based on this statement, the buyer agrees to pay a price far in excess of the horse's real value. However, keep in mind that statements of such things as opinion ("I think this painting is a very good investment"), prediction ("This land is bound to double in value within a year"), or value ("This building is worth at least $100,000") are not regarded as fraud by the courts because the average person would recognize that they are not meant to be factual statements in the true sense of the word. However, if the person who makes the statements is regarded as an expert, the courts *may* hold that the individual is guilty of fraud. This is particularly so when the buyer relies heavily on the seller's experience.

Likewise, if a lay person makes a statement of law such as "This land has been zoned for apartment buildings, so you will have no trouble getting an okay to build a high rise here," then a person who acts upon the statement as if it is true can seldom maintain an action for damages. The courts feel that since the individual is a lay person, the buyer should know better than to rely on the person's statement. The buyer should check out the accuracy of the fact before purchasing. However, in recent years the courts have begun changing their stance and holding that sellers who *should* know the law by virtue of their occupational or professional status, can be found guilty of fraud if they make an erroneous statement upon which the buyer relies. For example, if the individual who was selling the land was a real estate broker, he or she should know how the land was zoned, and an action could be brought if the realtor misrepresented (even innocently) such a key fact.

Additionally, *silence can constitute fraud.* For example, if a businessperson is buying a second-hand automobile and the dealer knows that it has a cracked motor block, the dealer is required to call this fact to the buyer's attention. Likewise, if one of the parties to a contract occupies a position of trust or has a personal stake in the contract, he or she must speak up. For example, Henry tells Susan about a competitive business that is for sale and urges her to look into it and make an offer. If Henry is a silent partner in the firm and has an ownership interest, he must tell this to Susan.

Otherwise, if the deal proved injurious to Susan she could claim that Henry misled her and that if she had known he was part-owner she would have looked the deal over more closely. Or consider the case of Al who tells Chuck that this is a good time to buy stock in the XYZ Corporation. Chuck does so, unaware that Al is a major stockholder, has inside information that the firm is going to go bankrupt, and is slowly getting rid of his shares. Finally, it should be noted that in some cases an individual will give false information by remaining silent. For example, Jack takes out an insurance policy for $500,000 but does not tell the company that three years before he had a minor heart attack. The next month Jack has a second heart attack and dies. If Jack had been open about the matter, the company would have turned him down for insurance. Therefore, once the firm learns about his prior condition, it will refund all premiums and refuse to pay the face value of the policy to his estate. Jack committed fraud in not revealing his prior heart attack.

In determining whether to award damages in the case of fraud, the courts generally require the party bringing the suit to show that he or she has suffered financial loss as a result of the misrepresentation. However, sometimes the injured party simply wants his or her property or money returned. In this case the party asks the court to merely rescind (cancel) the contract, and a showing of financial injury by the innocent party is usually not required.

MISTAKES   Contracts are sometimes set aside by the courts because a mistake was made by one of the parties. The only time a plea of mistake is accepted by the courts, however, is when the mistake was one of fact; and the only time courts allow this is when both parties to the contract were mistaken about some important fact or when one of them was mistaken and can show that the other party knew, or should have known, of the mistake at the time the contract was made. When both parties are mistaken, a **mutual** or **bilateral mistake** exists. When only one person is mistaken, it is a **unilateral mistake.** As we said earlier, rescission is ordinarily not allowed unless the mistake was (or should have been) apparent to the offending party.

WHAT FORM SHOULD THE CONTRACT TAKE?

Many people believe that contracts are never enforceable unless they are in writing. Oral contracts, however, are just as enforceable as written ones if their terms can be established in a court of law. The problem here, of course, is that with an oral contract it may be difficult to establish what was agreed upon, since each party is relying on its memory and bias. For this reason, it is typical today to put most contracts in writing, especially those that involve money. Additionally, certain contracts *must* be in writing under what is known as the **Statute of Frauds:**

1. any contract calling for the sale of land or an interest in land
2. any contract that will not be performed within one year
3. a promise by one person to pay the debt of another
4. any contract that involves the purchase of real property valued at $500 or more[3]

---

[3]Kenneth W. Clarkson, Roger LeRoy Miller, Gaylord A. Jentz, and Frank B. Cross, *West's Business Law,* 4th ed. (St. Paul, MN:, West Publishing Company, 1989), pp. 246–47.

It is safest to use a written contract for *all* but minor matters. In this way, if there is a problem with the contract, the businessperson can spend his or her time trying to get performance or an award for damages rather than arguing over the terms of the contract that were initially agreed upon. (See Table 23-1 for a list of the important elements in sales contracts.)

BREACH OF CONTRACT

If both parties to a contract fulfill their obligations, each should have benefited from the arrangement. Unfortunately, sometimes a **breach of contract** occurs—one party fails to perform according to the terms of the agreement. If this party declares bankruptcy or can prove that some special problem prevented the fulfillment, such as a heart attack making it impossible for him to paint the office on the agreed-on date, the courts may excuse performance. On the other hand, if one party simply refuses to comply with the agreement—for example, because the painter realizes that the agreed-on price was too low and he will lose money on the job—then the other party can bring a lawsuit for breach of contract.

The party instituting the suit is called the **plaintiff,** and the party against whom the suit is brought is called the **defendant.** After hearing both sides of the case, the court will reach a conclusion and issue a judgement. In the case of small businesses, it is common for suits to be filed over failure to pay. For example, John paints Paul's business offices and Paul says the job is of poor quality and will not pay for it. In such cases the conflict usually never gets to court; the attorneys usually work out a settlement. Of course, if this proves impossible, the parties can go to court, and a judge will decide the matter.

Table 23-1 Important Elements of Sales Contracts

OFFER AND ACCEPTANCE	1. The acceptance of unilateral offers can be made by a promise to ship or by shipment itself. 2. Not all terms have to be included for a contract to result. 3. Particulars of performance can be left open. 4. Firm written offers made by a *merchant,* the duration of which is three months or less, cannot be revoked. 5. Acceptance by performance requires notice within a reasonable time; otherwise, the offer can be treated as lapsed. 6. The price does not have to be included to have a contract. 7. Variations in terms between the offer and the acceptance may not be a rejection but may be an acceptance. 8. Acceptance may be made by any reasonable means of communication; it is effective when dispatched.
CONSIDERATION	A modification of a contract for the sale of goods does not require consideration.

Table 23-1 *(continued)*

REQUIREMENTS UNDER THE STATUTE OF FRAUDS	1. All contracts for the sale of goods priced at $500 or more must be in writing. A writing is sufficient so long as it indicates a contract between the parties and it is signed by the party against whom enforcement is sought. A contract is not enforceable beyond the quantity shown in the writing. 2. Exceptions to the requirement of a writing exist in the following situations: a. When written confirmation of an oral contract *between merchants* is not objected to in writing by the receiver within ten days. b. When the oral contract is for specially manufactured goods not suitable for resale to others, and the seller has substantially started to manufacture the goods. c. When the defendant admits in pleadings, testimony, or other court proceedings that an oral contract for the sale of goods was made. In this case the contract will be enforceable to the quantity of goods admitted. d. When payment has been made and accepted under the terms of an oral contract. The oral agreement will be enforceable to the extent that such payment has been received and accepted or to the extent that goods have been received and accepted.
PAROL EVIDENCE	1. The terms of a clearly and completely worded written contract cannot be contradicted by evidence of prior agreements or contemporaneous oral agreements. 2. Evidence is admissible to clarify the terms of a writing: a. If the contract terms are ambiguous. b. If evidence of course of dealing, usage of trade, or course of performance is necessary to learn or to clarify the intentions of the parties to the contract.
UNCONSCIONABILITY	An unconscionable contract is one that is so unfair and one-sided that it would be unreasonable to enforce it. If the court deems a contract to be unconscionable at the time it was made, the court can (1) refuse to enforce the contract; (2) refuse to enforce the unconscionable clause of the contract; or (3) limit the application of any unconscionable clauses to avoid an unconscionable result.

Source: Kenneth W. Clarkson, Roger LeRoy Miller, Gaylord A. Jentz, Frank B. Cross, *West's Business Law*, 4th ed. (St. Paul, MN: West Publishing Company, 1989), pp. 324–25.

EFFECT OF STATUTE OF LIMITATIONS

Every state has a **statute of limitations,** which provides that after a specified number of years have elapsed, breach of contract claims are not allowed. For example, in many states the statute allows a person who has done work on a house and not been paid six months to file a lien against the owner. If the lien is not filed during this time, the plumber, electrician, or whoever else did the work is not allowed to pursue the claim. The statute does not discharge the debt; it merely provides a defense against a breach of contract claim. If legal action is brought, the defendant can plead the statute and defeat the claim. However, if the party agrees either verbally or in writing, after the statute has run out, to make good on the contract, the entire obligation is revived and the period of limitations begins anew. The party again places itself in jeopardy. Any small business owner who finds, thanks to the statute, that a claim against the firm was filed too late is wise to let the matter drop.

WARRANTIES

A **warranty** is a seller's promise or statement of fact about a product. There are several types of warranties as well as disclaimers that may be included with the sale of a product. Table 23-2 provides an overview of the specific types of warranties, how they are created, and their possible legal defenses.

Table 23-2 Understanding Warranties

TYPE OF WARRANTY	HOW CREATED	POSSIBLE DEFENSES
Warranty of title	Upon transfer of title, the seller warrants— 1. That he or she has the right to pass good and rightful title. 2. That the goods are free from unstated liens or encumbrances. 3. When the seller is a merchant, that the goods are free from infringement claims.	Specific language or circumstances excluded or modified warranty.
Express warranty	As part of a sale or bargain, a seller may create an express warranty by— 1. An affirmation of fact or promise. 2. A sale by description. 3. A sample shown as conforming to bulk.	1. Statement that is purported to create warranty was an option. 2. Specific language or conduct negated or limited warranty.

Table 23-2 *(continued)*

Implied warranty of merchantability	This warranty arises when— The seller is a merchant who deals in goods of the kind sold.	1. Warranty was specifically disclaimed (disclaimer can be oral or in writing, but must mention *merchantability* and, if in writing, must be conspicuous). 2. Sale was stated to be "as is" or "with all faults." 3. The buyer examined the goods and is therefore bound by all defects that were found or should have been found. If the buyer refused or failed to examine, the buyer is bound' by obvious defects. 4. Course of dealing, performance, or usage of trade.
Implied warranty of fitness for a particular purpose	This warranty arises when— 1. The buyer's purpose or use is expressly or impliedly known by the seller, and 2. The buyer purchases in reliance on the seller's selection.	1. Specific disclaimer excluded or modified warranty (disclaimer must be in writing and be conspicuous. "There are no warranties which extend beyond the description on the face hereof."). 2. Same as items 2–4 under merchantability, above.
Implied warranty arising from course of dealing or trade usage	This warranty is created by prior dealings and/or custom of trade.	Warranty was excluded by specific language.

Source: Kenneth W. Clarkson, Roger LeRoy Miller, Gaylord A. Jentz, Frank B. Cross, *West's Business Law,* 4th ed. (St. Paul, MN: West Publishing Company, 1989), pp. 394–95.

EXPRESS WARRANTY

Express warranties are a seller's words or actions that indicate clearly a particular condition, performance, or quality in the goods or services that the buyer relies on in deciding to purchase. Samples, demonstration models, printed documents, and statements of salespeople all constitute express warranties if the buyer clearly relies on that information.

IMPLIED WARRANTY

Implied warranties are automatically transferred in a sale *unless* they are "disclaimed" in a clear and noticeable fashion. Implied warranties include

- WARRANTY OF TITLE   implies that the title to the goods is valid.
- WARRANTY OF MERCHANTABILITY   implies average quality in the merchandise. ("Fit for the ordinary purposes for which such goods are sold"—UCC Sec. 2-314, 1-C).
- WARRANTY OF FITNESS   implies that goods or services selected for specific purposes will, in fact, serve those purposes.

These examples of warranties indicate to the small business person that concern for consumers and their purchases is essential in today's sales agreements. In 1975, the Magnuson-Moss Warranty Act was passed by Congress to require complete disclosure in warranties and to clearly define the requirements of full and limited warranties. According to the Act, *all* warranties must include the following:

- a prominent declaration of the nature of the warranty—full or limited
- a clear explanation of the items covered under the warranty (no fine print)
- a statement of the remedy available to correct a defective product
- a definition of how long the warranty lasts
- a name, address, and telephone number for customer warranty service
- a legal notice informing the customer that certain legal rights exist and that they may vary from state to state

FULL WARRANTY

A **full warranty** must meet these specifications:

- Defective products will be repaired or replaced free.
- Products will be repaired within a reasonable time of the complaint.
- The consumer will not be required to do anything unreasonable to get warranty service.
- Anyone who owns the product during the warranty period has a valid warranty.
- If the product cannot be repaired after a reasonable number of attempts, a replacement or refund will be made.
- Registration of the product is not required; it is only voluntary for the seller's records.
- Implied warranties cannot be disclaimed.[4]

LIMITED WARRANTY

A **limited warranty** offers less protection and imposes various limitations or conditions. Examples of such limitations include the following:

---

[4]Information adapted from the Federal Trade Commission Manual for Business, *Warranties: Making Sense out of Warranty Law.* U.S. Government Printing Office, 1988.

☐ covers parts replacement only (does not cover labor)

☐ covers repairs only

☐ is nontransferable

☐ allows only pro rata refunds

☐ may impose handling charges

☐ is valid *only* if a registration card is returned

☐ Implied warranties cannot be disclaimed but may be limited in duration.

PRODUCT LIABILITY

Most states allow any person in the chain of distribution to be sued for breach of warranty. Any consumer who suffers personal or property damage from a faulty product may seek remedies against the manufacturer. Design, inspection, labeling, instructions, and identification of any potential dangers in products are the responsibility of the manufacturer. Due care must be exercised in product safety in order for manufacturers to avoid liability for negligence in lawsuits.[5] (See Small Business Owner's Notebook: Understanding Depositions.)

AGENCY LAW

An **agency relationship** is created between two parties when one party, the **agent,** agrees to represent the other party, the **principal,** subject to the principal's control. Acting as a representative for purposes of business affairs, an agent is bound to perform certain duties. In the same manner, a principal is bound by certain duties.

FIDUCIARY RELATIONSHIP

In general, agency law is based on the Latin phrase *qui facit per alium, facit per se* ("one acting through another is acting for himself"). Thus, a relationship of extreme trust and confidence is formed. This special relationship is known as a **fiduciary relationship.** The duties of an agent are

1. to perform
2. to notify and account
3. to be loyal

The duties of principal are

1. to compensate and reimburse
2. to cooperate
3. to provide safe working conditions

Agency law permits simultaneous business transactions to be carried on. A small business, owner-manager does not have to handle all situations personally, but he or she should be aware of the legal duties and responsibilities involved in the use of an agent when delegating authority and responsibility.

---

[5]Marisa Manley, "Product Liability: You're More Exposed than You Think," *Harvard Business Review,* September/October 1987, pp. 28–36.

■ **SMALL BUSINESS OWNER'S NOTEBOOK** ■

Understanding Depositions

A deposition is the collection of oral testimony, under oath, that is documented prior to a trial. Attorneys gauge the strength of their cases based, in part, upon the vital information collected in depositions. Since many product liability cases, or other lawsuits, may involve this process, the small business owner needs to keep the following recommendations in mind when asked to provide a deposition:

☐ *Don't over-rehearse.* While preparation for a deposition is important, don't rehearse "pat" answers with your attorney.

☐ *Relax.* Come to the deposition well rested, relaxed, and dressed as if you are attending a business meeting or going to court.

☐ *Take your time.* Be sure you understand the question.

☐ *Never guess what the question means.* Ask for clarification so that you do not make a mistake.

☐ *Tell the truth.* Remember, testimony is given under oath and any attempt to hide something will usually come out during trial.

☐ *Avoid exaggeration.* Unreasonable estimates of time and distance, for instance, will be used against you later.

☐ *Don't volunteer information.* If you can, answer with "yes" or "no." After answering, stop.

☐ *Speak clearly.* A court reporter is attempting to capture every word.

☐ *Don't let them wear you out.* Don't be afraid to ask for rest breaks.

☐ *Don't get angry.* A pleasant demeanor is important. If you lose your temper, you may get defensive and try to justify your position instead of sticking to the question.

Source: James Rollin Miller, "The Legal Deposition," *Small Business Report,* February 1990, pp. 68–70.

BANKRUPTCY

As noted in Chapter 2, few businesses declare bankruptcy; typically, businesses are voluntarily dissolved for various other reasons. The SBA reports that only 10 percent of the firms that cease to exist do so because they are bankrupt.[6]

Bankruptcy occurs when a debtor's financial obligations are greater than his or her assets.[7] The objective of bankruptcy law is to allow debtors to straighten out their

---

[6]*The State of Small Business: A Report to the President* (Washington, D. C.: U.S. Government Printing Office, 1990), p. 148.

[7]See Reuben Abrams, "Warning Signs of Bankruptcy," *Nation's Business,* February 1987, pp. 20–22.

financial affairs and/or provide for an orderly and equitable distribution of the company's assets among the creditors.

FEDERAL BANKRUPTCY REFORM ACT OF 1978

The most recent change in the federal bankruptcy law was enacted in 1978. This revision has been particularly helpful to small businesses that have to declare bankruptcy. In the case of sole proprietorships, in which business and personal assets are the same, the law limits what creditors can take. Protected assets include house equity of $7,500; motor vehicle equity of $1,200; $200 on each personal item (clothing, books, furniture, and the like); $500 of personal jewelry; another $400 of property; and tools of one's trade and/or prescribed health items up to a maximum of $750 in value. In the case of a husband and wife filing joint bankruptcy, these amounts are doubled. Additionally, certain states provide even higher allowances. California, for example, allows the head of a household to exempt $30,000 in home equity.

On the other hand, the 1978 law has tightened the use of business bankruptcies to prevent people from using them for the sole purpose of escaping legitimate business debts while protecting their personal assets. It is now much more difficult for businesses to hide assets from creditors, and it is easier for creditors to force involuntary bankruptcy. However, it is important to stress that whenever possible a business should attempt to work things out with the creditors; bankruptcy should be a last resort.

WORKING THINGS OUT

Perhaps the most common way of working things out and thereby avoiding bankruptcy is through an **extension agreement.** Under this agreement, the creditors give the firm an extension of payment terms. For example, in the case of a small business owner who owes a bank $10,000, an extension agreement might give the individual a six-month **grace period,** during which no payment of principal or interest would need to be made, and six more months during which only interest on the debt would be paid. At the end of this time the owner would again start paying both interest and principal. An extension agreement gives the owner time to catch his economic breath. By the end of this period the individual should have turned things around and again be able to start paying off the loan.

Another popular approach to working things out is the **composition agreement.** Under this arrangement creditors agree to take a reduction in the amounts owed to them. This arrangement, quite obviously, is not as attractive to creditors as the extension agreement, but it does give all parties a chance to clear up the matter quickly and get on with other business.

If either an extension or the composition agreement is used, it is common for the creditors to demand some role in the management of the business. For example, in an extension agreement, creditors often have the right to approve any pay raises for employees or plans to expand operations. In this way, they keep their fingers on the business's pulse and protect their investment at the same time. If the owner is unwilling to go along with an extension agreement or the creditors are unwilling to accept a composition agreement, bankruptcy is often the only avenue available.

VOLUNTARY AND INVOLUNTARY TERMINATION OF OPERATIONS

Bankruptcy can be either voluntary or involuntary.[8] **Voluntary bankruptcy** takes place when the debtor files a petition of bankruptcy in federal court. In the Bankruptcy Act, this is known as **Chapter 11,** or **reorganization bankruptcy.** In the petition the debtor declares that the liabilities of the business exceed its assets and asks the court to divide the assets in an equitable way among the creditors. If the court agrees, the debtor is given a new start, having been legally freed from the remainder of the old financial obligations.

An **involuntary bankruptcy** occurs when creditors file a petition in federal court charging that the debtor has committed an *act of bankruptcy.* In the Bankruptcy Act, this is known as **Chapter 7,** or **liquidation bankruptcy.** Table 23-3 outlines the major types of business bankruptcies. Many acts constitute bankruptcy, some of the most common are

1. transferring property for the purpose of defrauding creditors
2. failing to pay interest when it becomes due
3. failing to pay principal when it comes due
4. concealing property
5. admitting in writing an inability to pay debts

When creditors bring a bankruptcy proceeding, the court notifies the debtor of the action. It is then the obligation of the debtor to deny or admit the alleged act of bankruptcy. If the individual denies the charge, the court will investigate the claim to determine its validity. If the creditors are wrong, the matter is settled. If the creditors are right, the court will appoint a referee who will notify the creditors to submit their claims to the court. The assets of the business are then turned over to a *trustee* who will administer them or operate the firm during the period of bankruptcy proceedings. The *order of claim on assets* is as follows:

1. all court costs, including the expense of the trustee, lawyers, and other people approved by the court
2. employee wages earned within three months prior to the start of the proceedings and limited to $600 per employee
3. all reasonable expenses of those creditors who opposed the liquidation plan finally agreed to by the court, as well as reasonable expenses incurred by the creditors in obtaining evidence resulting in the conviction of any person violating the Bankruptcy Act
4. all taxes
5. debts, in order of priority established by law

---

[8]For a thorough discussion, see Kenneth W. Clarkson, Roger LeRoy Miller, Gaylord A. Jentz, and Frank B. Cross, *West's Business Law,* 4th ed. (St. Paul, MN: West Publishing Company, 1989), pp. 567–85.

Table 23-3 Bankruptcy: An Overview of the Chapters

ISSUE	CHAPTER 7	CHAPTER 11	CHAPTER 13
Purpose	Liquidation.	Reorganization.	Adjustment.
Who can petition	Debtor (voluntary) or creditors (involuntary).	Debtor (voluntary) or creditors (involuntary).	Debtor (voluntary) only.
Who can be a debtor	Any "person" (including partnerships and corporations) except railroads, insurance companies, banks, savings and loan institutions, and credit unions. Farmers and charitable institutions cannot be involuntarily petitioned.	Any debtor eligible for Chapter 7 relief; railroads are also eligible.	Any individual (not partnerships or corporations) with regular income who owes fixed unsecured debt of less than $100,000 or secured debt of less than $350,000.
Procedure leading to discharge	Nonexempt property is sold with proceeds to be distributed (in order) to priority groups. Dischargeable debts are terminated.	Plan is submitted; and if it is approved and followed, debts are discharged.	Plan is submitted (must be approved if debtor turns over disposable income for three-year period); and if it is approved and followed, debts are discharged.
Advantages	Upon liquidation and distribution, most debts are discharged, and debtor has opportunity for fresh start.	Debtor continues in business. Creditors can accept plan, or it can be "crammed down" on them. Plan allows for reorganization and liquidation of debts over plan period.	Debtor continues in business or possession of assets. If plan is approved, most debts are discharged after a three-year period.

Source: Kenneth W. Clarkson, Roger LeRoy Miller, Gaylord A. Jentz, and Frank B. Cross, *West's Business Law,* 4th ed. (St. Paul, MN: West Publishing Company, 1989), p. 582.

PATENTS, COPYRIGHTS, AND TRADEMARKS

Intellectual property is protected by the federal government through the use of patents, copyrights, and trademarks. These affect the small business person in the form of start-up ventures, innovations, or simply proprietary information gained by employees and competitors. Each type is discussed in the following sections.

PATENTS

A **patent** is granted to an inventor for developing a "product" or a "process." Thus, an actual physical product or a particular manufacturing process can be protected. A patent is issued by the federal government and grants the owner the right to make, use, sell the particular product or process for seventeen years without infringement.

A patent contains two parts: (1) a disclosure statement describing the invention, and (2) a set of claims covering the exact particulars to be protected by the patent. These claims state the protection from infringement and allow the individual to license other people to use the patented article in return for a percentage of sales revenue, which is paid to the patent holder in the form of royalties.

Patent law is a very complicated and technical area. An attorney specializing in patent law should be consulted. Such attorneys are familiar with the patent office and its procedures as well as the technical aspects of the patent process.

One final note is important. Pursuing a patent can be expensive. The product or process should be distinctive enough to warrant protection, and this investment in protection should be expected to pay off later on.[9]

COPYRIGHTS

According to the copyright law (revised in 1978), a **copyright** protects the author of written material for the extent of his or her life plus fifty years. One can *claim* a copyright by simply using the notice of copyright on any written work. These elements are needed: (1) a copyright symbol © or the word *copyright,* (2) the year, and (3) the name of the author.

Registration of a copyright is filed with the U.S. Copyright Office by paying a small fee and submitting the appropriate registration document. The copyright grants the individual the exclusive right to reproduce and distribute the material to the public. It prohibits derivations, based on the work and any performance or display for profit. The **fair use doctrine,** however, allows limited reproduction of the material for purposes of criticism, comment, reporting, teaching, scholarship, or research without any infringement of the copyright.

TRADEMARKS

The Federal Trademark Act of 1946 provides for registration of names and symbols used for products involved in interstate commerce. The *use* of a trademark establishes the rights, rather than just the registration of that trademark. For example, if a small

---

[9]See Ronald D. Rothchild, "Making Patents Work for Small Companies," *Harvard Business Review,* July/August 1987, pp. 24–30.

business's area of operation will only be local without expansion to other regions, there is no need for registration, since *using* the name or mark in the local area establishes the trademark rights. Problems can arise if the business expands into other areas, however. In order to prevent competitors from using the name in other regions, registration is needed.

Professional trademark searches vary in cost. A local search may begin at $300, with larger national searches (including registration) reaching a cost of $2,000 to $2,500. The small business owner-manager needs to keep in mind the extent of the business and the possible need for a distinct and protected trademark.[10]

■ SUMMARY

A contract is a legal agreement that the courts will enforce if either party breaches the agreement. The five essentials of a contract are agreement, consideration, contractual capacity, legality, and reality of consent.

The first, and most important, element of a legal contract is agreement. For agreement to exist there must be a reasonably definite understanding between the parties. Some of the most important elements of an agreement are intent to contract, reasonable definiteness, and communication. Under certain conditions an offer can be terminated.

The second essential of a legal contract is consideration, something of value that the offeree gives to the offeror. What constitutes consideration? One way in which the courts answer this question is with the detrimental test. Finally, in order for consideration to be present there must be mutuality of obligation; both parties are tied to the agreement, and neither has an "out."

The third essential of a legal contract is contractual capacity. Minors, except when buying necessaries or having misrepresented their age, can void contracts if they choose. So can persons who made contracts when they were adjudged insane or so intoxicated that they could not understand the terms of the contract.

The fourth essential of a legal contract is legality of purpose. Contracts that violate the law are not enforceable. Usury, restraint of trade, and exculpatory clauses are usually sufficient grounds for setting aside an agreement.

Finally, there must be reality of consent. This is missing when the agreement is tainted with fraud, innocent misrepresentation, or mistakes. In these cases the contract will be set aside by the courts.

A breach of contract occurs when one party fails to perform according to the terms of the agreement. Usually these disagreements are worked out without going to court. If they are not, the aggrieved party must initiate action before the statute of limitations expires.

Warranties are logical extensions of contract law in that they are a promise the producer makes to the buyer. There are two major types of warranties, limited and full, each of which carries specific rules and limitations.

---

[10]See Thomas M. S. Hemnes, "How Can You Find a Safe Trademark?" *Harvard Business Review,* March/April 1985, pp. 40–48.

Agency law involves transactions in which one party (principal) is being represented by another party (agent). This relationship involves a fiduciary (extreme trust) responsibility and dictates certain duties for both parties.

Bankruptcy occurs when a person's (or firm's) financial obligations are greater than his or her assets. Bankruptcy laws allow debtors to straighten out their financial affairs and/or make an orderly and equitable distribution of the assets among the creditors. If an extensive agreement or a composition agreement cannot be worked out, bankruptcy is usually the only alternative for a troubled firm. Bankruptcy can be either voluntary or involuntary.

Finally, intellectual property is protected by the federal government in the form of patents, copyrights, and trademarks. Patents are designed to protect investors from infringement for a period of 17 years. Copyrights, according to the 1978 amendments to the law, protect an author and his (her) written works for his (her) life plus 50 years. The only legal exception is the fair use doctrine, which outlines specific uses of copyrighted material that do not violate the copyright law. The trademark law is designed to protect distinct names or symbols used in interstate commerce. While local use may not demand formal registration, a regional or national business should consider such formal registration in order to protect its trademark or trade name.

◼ REVIEW AND DISCUSSION QUESTIONS

1. What is a contract?

2. One of the most important things affecting whether or not there is agreement in a contract is reasonable definiteness. What does this term mean?

3. One of the best ways to determine if there is consideration is to apply the detrimental test. How does this test work?

4. Ted, a city detective, arrests a man who robbed a large bank of $1 million. All the money is recovered and the bank president is elated. To express his thanks, the president sends Ted a thank you letter. However, Ted would prefer the $20,000 reward the bank offered for the return of the money and tells the president so. Does the bank legally owe Ted this money? Explain.

5. The Wilshire Brothers signed a contract to buy a ski lodge from Charles Anderson. Unknown to the parties, the lodge burned to the ground the day before the signing. Is the contract enforceable?

6. Does a contract have to be in writing? Must any contracts be in writing? Explain.

7. When does a breach of contract occur? What impact does the statue of limitations have on a plaintiff's right to bring a lawsuit? Explain.

8. What are the two distinct types of warranties. Discuss the differences between them.

9. What is a fiduciary relationship? What is its importance to agency relationships?

10. Compare and contrast voluntary and involuntary bankruptcy.

11. How do patents, copyrights, and trademarks each involve legal protection for intellectual property?

Case Studies

Clara's Legal Problems

■ Clara Bowman is having a bad week. Everything seems to be going wrong for her. Clara owns a job placement service. She charges a fee to place people in jobs. Last month she helped Jennifer Hargrove find employment. After Jennifer's first week on the job she stopped in to see Clara again to thank her for helping her find work and happened to mention that she needed to buy a good used car. Clara told her that she was trying to sell her business car and would sell it to her at the wholesale price. Jennifer agreed to buy it. Two days later Jennifer brought Clara a check, and Clara gave Jennifer title to the car. Monday Jennifer called Clara to say that she was not happy with the car and that she is returning it to her. She went on to say that she knows she can get all of her money back because she is a minor.

To make matters worse, Clara received a call from Sydney Brown yesterday. Sydney told her that although he appreciates her finding a job for him when no one seemed interested in him because he has only a high school education, he is a minor and is disaffirming the contract and will not pay Clara her fee.

Then earlier today Justin Wingate called Clara. Clara had talked with Justin several times in the last three months and had met with him last week to seal a contract whereby he would take a job at Arkwright Industries. Clara's fee was to be 10 percent of his first year's salary, and it would be paid by Arkwright after Justin had worked there a week. Justin said he had thought some more about the job change and decided to stay with his present employer. "I know I signed a contract saying that I would accept the offer from Arkwright, but to be frank about it, I had had too much to drink and was not thinking clearly. I don't want to leave Monmouth, Inc. I'm staying where I am."

1. Can Clara take any legal action against Jennifer Hargrove? Why or why not?

2. Can Clara successfully sue Sydney for her placement fee? Explain.

3. Can Clara successfully sue Justin for the placement fee that she is about to lose? Why or why not?

The Anguished Author

■ Pat Chadwick is an editor for a large publishing house. On Monday, September 1, he received a review of a manuscript for a new novel in the mail from one of his most reliable reviewers. Whatever this person tells him about a novel, Pat abides by. A note with the manuscript said, "This is great. I'd sign the guy immediately."

Later that morning Pat dictated a letter to the author. He asked the author to read the enclosed contract, discuss it with his attorney, and if he agreed with the terms, mail it back. Meanwhile, if the author had any questions, he was to call Pat collect. Pat mailed the letter, along with a contract, the same day.

The author received the contract, but before he could sign it he got a telegram from his agent. The agent said that she had shown the manuscript to another publisher, who was willing to top any other publisher's offer. The author called his agent and told her Pat's terms. The agent called back later in the day and said that the editor she had talked with was willing to give a higher royalty rate and a larger advance on the book than Pat. The author told his agent to go ahead and make the deal. Meanwhile, he wrote Pat a short note thanking him by saying that he was going to sign with a different publishing house. The letter was postmarked Friday, September 5, at 9 A.M.

At 11:00 A.M. that day the agent called the author to tell him that the other deal had fallen through. The author still had the contract Pat had sent him, so he read it to his agent. She recommended that he accept the offer. However, his revocation letter was already in the mail.

Unsure of what to do, he called Pat and explained the situation. Pat said he was happy to have the author on the team and that all he needed to do was sign the contract and put it in the mail. The first letter of revocation would be ignored.

The author hurried down to the post office and mailed the signed contract to Pat. He then went into a nearby tavern for a beer, where he told the story to his friend Jeff. Jeff, although not a lawyer, said he wondered if there really was a contract. "Your letter of revocation is going to get to your publisher's desk before your letter of acceptance. This may negate the contract and call for a whole new deal."

Now the author is worried. He would really like to know if he has a contract or not.

1. If the author's revocation letter reaches Pat before the letter with the signed contract, is the deal off?

2. Did calling Pat directly have any influence on the contract?

3. Is everything all right, or is Jeff correct in his warning to the author? Explain.

You Be the Consultant

THE TV CONTRACT

Gloria wanted to surprise her parents at Christmas with a television set. She went to a major retail chain store, looked over the sets, picked one out, and paid for the set in cash.

However, just as the salesman was calling the delivery department to ask them to bring the set from the stockroom, he remembered that six TVs were about to go on sale. They had been floor models, and the store was selling them for 15 percent off. They, also, were down in the storage area, and he asked Gloria if she might be interested in buying one of these "slightly used" models. He explained to her that they had the same warranty as new TVs had and that it was

impossible to tell they had been floor models. Additionally, the store still had the boxes in which they had come, so they could easily be repackaged and wrapped as Christmas presents.

Gloria was intrigued and suggested that they go to the delivery area and look at the sets. One of the sets was virtually the same set Gloria had selected on the sales floor. This one cost only $650 with the discount. Gloria agreed to buy it, and the salesman had the delivery department box the TV and take it to her car.

Meanwhile, he and Gloria went back to the sales floor and he wrote up the ticket. As he did so, he told Gloria that he had failed to note one thing. Since it was a floor model, it was a final sale; it could not be returned, although of course, the store would provide service and honor its warranty. Gloria said that was fine with her, and the salesperson wrote on the sales slip "final sale." Gloria signed the sales slip indicating her acceptance of the terms, paid him, and left the store.

At Christmas, Gloria's parents were overjoyed with the present. However, there was a slight problem. The color of the wood frame on the television was too light for their living room. Gloria's mother asked if Gloria could return it for a model with a darker wood finish. Gloria agreed to do so.

She called the salesperson and asked him to exchange the TV for one with a darker wood finish. The salesperson said he could not do that because floor models were final sales. Gloria then told him that she was only seventeen years old, and that she was voiding the contract. The salesman told her he did not understand what she meant. Gloria, thereupon explained that she was a minor and could not be held liable for a contract. She wanted her money back and she wanted them to pick up the TV as soon as possible.

The salesman was aghast. He reiterated that all sales of floor models were final and reminded her that she had signed the sales slip, indicating that she understood and was willing to abide by this term.

Gloria said again that she was not liable for the contract and demanded that the salesperson talk to his manager immediately. "If I don't hear from you in an hour, I'll have my father's attorney talk to you," she said.

The salesman promised to call back as soon as possible.

■ **YOUR CONSULTATION** Help the salesman out. Is Gloria right? Can she demand that the seller pick up the TV and give her her money back, or is she bluffing? What is the store's responsibility in this case? What rights does Gloria have? Explain.

CHAPTER 24

Government Assistance to Small Business

Objectives

Governments are well aware of the importance of small business to the economy and the general well-being of society and, thus, seek ways to encourage entrepreneurship. Every person in small business needs to know about the many kinds of assistance available to them through the federal, state, and local governments. The objective of this chapter is to give you this information. Chapter 24 will explain the many kinds of programs of the U.S. Small Business Administration, the small business incubator concept, three very important laws passed by Congress in the 1980s, and the White House Conferences on Small Business. When you have studied this chapter, you will be able to:

1. Explain the objectives of the SBA.

2. Discuss the various types of loan assistance available from the SBA.

3. Explain the other types of SBA assistance—including courses, conferences, workshops, clinics, and counseling.

4. Tell what small business incubators are, and describe the types of them and the services they provide.

5. Explain three legislative acts that address public policy with regard to small business.

6. Discuss the importance of the White House Conferences on Small Business, and list the major recommendations of the 1986 Conference.

WHAT IS THE SMALL BUSINESS ADMINISTRATION?

Most small business owner-managers prefer to "go it alone" without using outside consultants or advisors. What advice they do get is usually from their banker or lawyer. Many of them fail to realize that many types of government assistance are available to them and that in most cases, this help is free. One of the agencies is the Small Business Administration (SBA); the SBA does many things to assist new enterprises. However, government assistance does not end there. The U.S. Department of

Commerce and state departments of commerce are also very active in promoting small business.

The Small Business Administration was discussed briefly in Chapter 8 when we studied how to raise money for start-up operations. However, there is much more to the SBA's activities than simply participating with banks in securing the necessary funds. Since its creation in 1953, this agency has provided many kinds of assistance—financial and nonfinancial—to small businesses. Congress has directed the agency to take the lead in identifying and analyzing small business problems, to be the voice and advocate of small companies, to foster and coordinate research of small business problems, and to initiate ideas and innovations that will increase the opportunities for small businesses to get started and compete with other companies on an equitable basis.

> The Agency strives to carry out this mandate by ensuring that small business concerns receive a fair proportion of government purchases, contracts, and subcontracts, as well as of the sales of government property; making loans to small business concerns, state and local development companies, and victims of floods and other catastrophes; licensing, regulating and lending to small business investment companies; improving the management skills of small business owners, potential owners, and managers; and conducting studies of the economic environment.[1]

FINANCIAL ASSISTANCE

A primary kind of SBA help is that of financial assistance. The agency guarantees bank loans and loans money to state development companies for supplying long-term loans and equity capital to small business concerns. These state development companies are corporations organized by a special act of the state legislatures. They operate statewide and try to assist the growth and development of business concerns in the area. The SBA can loan a state development company as much as its total outstanding borrowing from all other sources, and the loans can be for as long as twenty years at variable interest rates.

The SBA also works with local development companies made up of citizens whose primary purpose is to improve the particular local economy. To be eligible for this kind of loan, the citizens must invest their own personal money. With at least 75 percent of the members living or doing business in the community, these local corporations assume responsibility for the projects they sponsor. The development company loans are commonly used to buy land, build new factories, acquire machinery and equipment, expand or convert existing facilities, or provide other forms of assistance to small business. When making such loans the SBA often participates with banks, insurance companies, pension fund groups, and/or state agencies.

The SBA also helps small businesses get disaster loans. If a calamity such as a tornado strikes a small company and causes damage, the agency can help arrange a loan to get the firm back on its feet. It can also participate in loans to small firms that have suffered substantial economic injury because they were unable to process or

---

[1]"SBA: What It Is . . . What It Does," (Small Business Administration, U.S. Government Printing Office, 1974), p. 1.

market a product for human consumption because of disease or toxicity resulting from either natural or undetermined causes. The SBA can also help the following types of companies:

1. a small firm that is suffering substantial economic injury as a result of being displaced or being near federally aided urban renewal and other construction projects, any of which necessitate the need to relocate or reestablish the place of business

2. a small firm that is operating a coal mine and has to make changes in its equipment, facilities, or operations in order to meet the standards of the Federal Coal Mine Health and Safety Act of 1969

3. a small business that has to make changes in its equipment, facilities, or operations in order to comply with the requirements of a U.S. Department of Agriculture order or the Occupational Safety and Health Act of 1970

4. a small business that has suffered, or will suffer, substantial economic injury as a result of the closing of a military installation by the federal government

All of this assistance is loan-related. However, the SBA also helps small businesses obtain a share of government contracts. In fact, it holds meetings where small business people can learn contracting and subcontracting opportunities. Finally, the SBA tries to help businesses by providing them with management assistance.

PROCUREMENT ASSISTANCE

Each year federal, state, and local governments contract with private companies for billions of dollars' worth of goods and services. At the federal level the SBA has sponsored the Procurement Automated Source System (PASS). The objective of PASS is to help small businesses obtain a fair share of government contracts. Once a week all government requests for bids are sorted by computer, and information is sent to companies that have the necessary expertise to bid on these jobs.

At the state and local levels small businesses learn about upcoming contracts through Information Bid (INFO BID). INFO BID provides small business owners with initial marketing assistance to identify governmental bodies and private industries that are seeking bids for particular goods and services. The small business person is encouraged to request that his or her firm be placed on the appropriate bidders' list so that future bidding opportunities can be received directly.

CONTRACTS FOR SOCIALLY AND ECONOMICALLY DISADVANTAGED

Section 8(a) of the Small Business Act authorizes the SBA to enter into contracts with other federal agencies to supply goods and services that those agencies need. The SBA then subcontracts the actual performance of the work to small businesses that are owned and controlled by socially and economically disadvantaged persons. The objective of the Section 8(a) program is to help eligible firms become independently competitive.

To be eligible for the Section 8(a) program, a small business must be least 51 percent owned, controlled, and daily operated by one or more socially disadvantaged persons. These individuals are those who have been subjected to racial or ethnic prejudice or cultural bias because of their identification as members of certain groups. African Americans, Native Americans, Hispanic Americans, Asian-Pacific Americans, and Asian-Indian Americans have all been officially designated as socially disadvantaged. Members of other groups can also be given contracts under the Section 8(a) program, but they must show proof of social disadvantage.

Since the Section 8(a) program is basically a business development effort, it provides for business development funds. These funds, in some instances, allow firms to purchase needed capital equipment to improve efficiency and for growth. The program also provides for advance payments to assist the companies in meeting their financial obligations prior to completion of the contract.

VETERANS AND WOMEN

In every SBA office, a person is designated as the Veterans' Affairs Officer (VAO). This individual is the contact and resource person for information on SBA programs designed to assist Vietnam veterans. In addition to financial help (see chapter 8), the SBA offers veterans management assistance and help in procuring contracts.

Executive Order 12183 of May 18, 1979, requires federal agencies to take affirmative action in support of businesses owned by women. To carry out this order, agencies are required to make special efforts to advise women of business opportunities and preferential contracting programs for which they may be eligible. In support of this order, the SBA encourages women entrepreneurs to seek assistance and counseling from its various offices and branches. One of the most helpful in this regard is the Small Business Development Center.

SMALL BUSINESS DEVELOPMENT CENTERS

Small Business Development Centers (SBDCs) are funded by the SBA and provide a full range of small business assistance services by drawing together local, state, and federal resources. This assistance takes a number of different forms, including courses, conferences, clinics, and counseling.[2]

SBDCs cosponsor business management *courses* with public and private educational institutions and business associations. The courses are usually of two types: some deal with starting a new business, and others concentrate on specific aspects of small business such as advertising, budgeting, loan applications, and so on.

SBDC *conferences* typically run a day in length and cover such topics as working capital, business forecasting, and diversification of markets. SBDC *workshops* often deal with capital requirements, sources of financing, types of businesses, organization, and the choice of location for the enterprise. *Clinics* zero in on specific problems of small business people in a particular industry. The SBDC plans these classes and provides speakers, outlines, visual aids, sound movies, and case studies for the instructors, as well as publications to be used by those attending. A small fee is sometimes charged for participation, but most of these programs are free.

The SBDC furnishes individual assistance to small business people who have management problems. It also counsels prospective entrepreneurs who want management assistance or information on specific types of business enterprises.

---

[2]James J. Chrisman, R. Ryan Nelson, Frank Hoy, and Richard B. Robinson, Jr., "The Impact of SBDC Consulting Activities," *Journal of Small Business Management,* July 1985, pp. 1–11.

In addition to the SBDC's regular staff of professionals, small business people can benefit from the services of organizations such as SCORE (Service Corps of Retired Executives) and ACE (Active Corps of Executives). The SBDC draws counselors from this pool of talent as required by the needs of the particular business. The assigned counselor then visits the owner at his or her place of business, observes the operations, analyzes the problems that are being faced, and offers a plan of action for resolving the situation. Except for out-of-pocket expenses, this service is free. Today there are approximately 400 SCORE and ACE chapters, consisting of 2,000 volunteers, spread throughout all fifty states, Puerto Rico, Guam, and the Virgin Islands.[3]

SMALL BUSINESS INSTITUTES (SBIs)

The purpose of the SBI is to bring together business school faculty, seniors, and graduate students to provide individualized counseling to small business owners. The SBI provides professors with the names, addresses, and descriptions of problems confronting small businesses in their area. The professors then assign teams of students to visit with, counsel, and make formal written reports to the small business owner. The costs associated with this counseling are paid by the SBA. Today, more than 500 universities have SBIs.

SBA LITERATURE

One of the best places to turn in finding small business assistance is the literature provided by the SBA. Some of these materials are available for the asking; others cost money. (See Small Business Owner's Notebook: SBA Publications: Management Aids.)

Free material can often be obtained from a local SBA office, although these offices tend to be reluctant to give out more than five or six pieces at a time. Coming in and asking for fifty free management aids is likely to elicit a frown from the SBA representative. The office may have only a single copy of some of these aids on hand, so they prefer to have an individual look some of these over and leave them at the office. If there are any in large quantity, an individual may take them. The way to be sure you get all the publications you want is to write directly to the SBA in Washington, or leave your name and address at the local office and ask them to get the literature. If the owner-manager is willing to wait for delivery, he or she can obtain copies of everything.

These aids are continually changing. Some are being added to the list and others are going out of print. For this reason their stock numbers are not in numerical sequence. A list of management assistance publications can be obtained by writing the U.S. Small Business Administration, Washington, D.C. 20416, and requesting Form SBA 115A. The publications available are listed in the Small Business Owner's Notebook: SBA Publications.

In addition, there are for-sale booklets. A list of these booklets can also be obtained by requesting Form SBA 115B from the SBA.

---

[3]Donald G. Anderson, Dennis J. Elbert, and James R. Floyd, "Training of SCORE/ACE Counselors: Attitudes and Needs," *Journal of Small Business Management*, July 1985, pp. 31–36.

These management aids, small marketers' aids, small business bibliographies, and for-sale booklets are all very useful. However, the businessperson who has run into a problem that cannot be solved by simply reading the literature on the subject can attend seminars to get some on-site consulting through the SBA.

DEPARTMENTS OF COMMERCE

Departments of commerce at both the federal and the state levels are also important sources of assistance for small businesses. An excellent example is the case of international trade opportunities. Although many small businesses are unaware of it, all commerce departments are very interested in encouraging and promoting small business ventures in overseas markets.

The U.S. Department of Commerce, for example, provides a wealth of published information on international economic indicators, global market surveys, and foreign economic trends and their implications for the United States. They also make available brochures and booklets that describe how to conduct business overseas. For example, their pamphlet *A Basic Guide to Exporting*[4] offers information related to assessing export potential; researching foreign markets; selecting sales and distribution channels; communicating overseas via letter, cable, and/or telephone; locating foreign representatives; drawing up agreements; financing exports; shipping products; and promoting product sales overseas. All of these topics, and many more, are spelled out in detail in the pamphlet.

The SBA also supports this federal effort by offering publications and management assistance. For example, district office staff will work to provide would-be exporters with one-on-one counseling by volunteers with international experience; counseling through the SBDC; assistance from professional international trade counseling firms; referral to public- and private-sector groups offering in-depth knowledge in the area; and export training. There is also an SBA export revolving line of credit loan program for which companies may qualify.

At the local level, state departments of commerce are very active in promoting export. These firms and agencies offer services ranging from international consulting assistance to export management companies to commercial banks with international departments. Such assistance is extremely helpful to small businesses entering overseas markets.

SMALL BUSINESS INCUBATORS

A growing number of communities are experimenting with small business "incubators" in an attempt to develop and retain business.[5] A **small business incubator** is a building designed to house businesses just starting up at very low rents; support services are provided to help the businesses during their formative stages.

---

[4]*A Basic Guide to Exporting* (Washington, D.C.: U.S. Department of Commerce, 1988).

[5]David N. Allen and Syedur Rahman, "Small Business Incubators: A Positive Environment for Entrepreneurship," *Journal of Small Business Management,* July 1985, pp. 12–22.

■ **SMALL BUSINESS OWNER'S NOTEBOOK** ■

SBA Publications

Management Aids

MAs recommend methods and techniques for handling management problems and business operations.

Financial Management and Analysis

MA 1.001 The ABC's of Borrowing

MA 1.002 What is the Best Selling Price?

MA 1.003 Keep Pointed toward Profit

MA 1.004 Basic Budgets for Profit Planning

MA 1.005 Pricing for Small Manufacturers

MA 1.006 Cash Flow in a Small Plant

MA 1.007 Credit and Collections

MA 1.008 Attacking Business Decision Problems with Break-even Analysis

MA 1.009 A Venture Capital Primer for Small Business

MA 1.010 Accounting Services for Small Service Firms

MA 1.011 Analyze Your Records to Reduce Costs

MA 1.012 Profit by Your Wholesalers' Service

MA 1.013 Steps in Meeting Your Tax Obligations

MA 1.014 Getting the Facts for Income Tax Reporting

MA 1.015 Budgeting in a Small Business Firm

MA 1.016 Sound Cash Management and Borrowing

MA 1.017 Keeping Records in Small Business

MA 1.018 Checklist for Profit Watching

MA 1.019 Simple Break-even Analysis for Small Stores

MA 1.020 Profit Pricing and Costing for Services

Planning

MA 2.002 Locating or Relocating Your Business

MA 2.004 Problems in Managing a Family-Owned Business

MA 2.005 The Equipment Replacement Decision

MA 2.006 Finding a New Product for Your Company

MA 2.007 Business Plan for Small Manufacturers

MA 2.008 Business Plan for Small Construction Firms

MA 2.009 Business Life Insurance

MA 2.010 Planning and Goal Setting for Small Business

MA 2.011 Fixing Production Mistakes

MA 2.012 Setting Up a Quality Control System

MA 2.013 Can You Make Money with Your Idea or Invention?

MA 2.014 Should You Lease or Buy Equipment?

MA 2.015 Can You Use a Minicomputer?

MA 2.016 Checklist for Going into Business

MA 2.017 Factors in Considering a Shopping Center Location

MA 2.018 Insurance Checklist for Small Business

MA 2.019 Computers for Small Business—Service Bureau or Time Sharing

MA 2.020 Business Plan for Retailers

MA 2.021 Using a Traffic Study to Select a Retail Site

MA 2.022 Business Plan for Small Service Firms

MA 2.024 Store Location "Little Things" Mean a Lot

MA 2.025 Thinking about Going into Business?

General Management and Administration

MA 3.001 Delegating Work and Responsibility

(continued)

MA 3.002 Management Checklist for a Family Business
MA 3.004 Preventing Retail Theft
MA 3.005 Stock Control for Small Stores
MA 3.006 Reducing Shoplifting Losses
MA 3.007 Preventing Burglary and Robbery Loss
MA 3.009 Preventing Embezzlement

Marketing
MA 4.003 Measuring Sales Force Performance
MA 4.005 Is the Independent Sales Agent for You?
MA 4.007 Selling Products on Consignment
MA 4.008 Tips on Getting More for Your Marketing Dollar
MA 4.010 Developing New Accounts
MA 4.012 Marketing Checklist for Small Retailers
MA 4.013 A Pricing Checklist for Small Retailers
MA 4.014 Improving Personal Selling in Small Retail Stores
MA 4.015 Advertising Guidelines for Small Retail Firms

MA 4.016 Signs in Your Business
MA 4.018 Plan Your Advertising Budget
MA 4.019 Learning about Your Market
MA 4.020 Do You Know the Results of Your Advertising?

Organization and Personnel
MA 5.001 Checklist for Developing a Training Program
MA 5.004 Pointers on Using Temporary-Help Services
MA 5.005 Preventing Employee Pilferage
MA 5.006 Setting Up a Pay System
MA 5.007 Staffing Your Store
MA 5.008 Managing Employee Benefits

Legal and Governmental Affairs
MA 6.003 Incorporating a Small Business
MA 6.004 Selecting the Legal Structure for Your Business
MA 6.005 Introduction to Patents

Miscellaneous
MA 7.002 Association Services with Small Business
MA 7.003 Market Overseas with U.S. Government Help

Small Business Bibliographies

SBBs list sources of information on business management topics.

0101 Building Service Contracting
0104 Radio-Television Repair Shop
0105 Retail Florists
0106 Franchised Businesses
0107 Hardware Stores and Home Centers
0111 Sporting Goods Store
0112 Drycleaning
0114 Cosmetology
0115 Pest Control
0116 Marine Retailers
0117 Retail Grocery Stores
0122 Apparel Stores
0123 Pharmacies
0125 Office Products

0129 Interior Design Services
0130 Fish Farming
0133 Bicycles
0134 Roofing Contractors
0135 Printing
0137 Bookstore
0138 Home Furnishings
0142 Ice Cream Shop
0145 Sewing Centers
0148 Personnel Referral Service
0149 Selling by Mail Order
0150 Solar Energy
0201 Break-even Point for Independent Truckers

(continued)

Starting Out Series

SOSs are one-page fact sheets that describe financial and operating requirements for selected manufacturing, retail, and service businesses.

1. Handcrafts	31. Retail Credit and Collection
2. Home Businesses	37. Buying for Retail Stores
3. Selling by Mail Order	72. Personnel Management
9. Marketing Research Procedures	75. Inventory Management
10. Retailing	85. Purchasing for Owners of Small Plants
12. Statistics and Maps for National Market Analysis	86. Training for Small Business
	87. Financial Management
13. National Directories for Use in Marketing	88. Manufacturing Management
15. Recordkeeping Systems—Small Store and Service Trade	89. Marketing for Small Business
	90. New Product Development
18. Basic Business Reference Sources	91. Ideas into Dollars (Inventors' Guide)
20. Advertising—Retail Store	92. Effective Business Communication

---

Source: Small Business Administration (U.S. Government Printing Office, 1988).

The particular support services provided vary, but the following services are usually available insofar as possible or needed:

□ FINANCIAL SERVICES   Venture planning, legal and tax consulting, accounting and financial consulting, loan advice and programs, compensation and benefits planning, and banking relations.

□ MANAGEMENT SERVICES   Business planning, legal advice, strategic growth consulting, inventory management, organizational structure advice, and location and layout planning.

□ OPERATIONS SERVICES   Clerical, word processing, telephone answering, copying machines, and painting capabilities.

Based upon initiative and dimensions, four types of incubators are prevalent today:

1. Publicly sponsored: These are organized and managed through city economic development departments, urban renewal authorities, or regional planning and development commissions. Job creation is the main objective.

2. Nonprofit-organization sponsored: These are organized and managed through industrial development associations of private industry, chambers of commerce, or community-based organizations with broad community support and/or a successful record in real estate development. Area development is the major objective of these incubators.

3. University-related: Many of these are spin-offs of academic research projects. Most are considered science and technology incubators. Their major goal is to transfer the findings of basic research and development into new products or technologies.

4. Privately sponsored: These are organized and managed by private corporations. Their goal is to make a profit—and in some cases, to make a contribution to the community.[6]

While the differences allow for flexibility in developing an incubator, they may also confuse and actually inhibit the initiative. Jeffrey King and David Allen point out that due to the various sponsoring organizations, the purposes of incubators differ and, thus, so will their expectations and outcomes. "Different organizational purposes translate into different organizational arrangements."[7] For example, the publicly sponsored or nonprofit organization-sponsored incubators are aimed at the creation of job opportunities, economic development, or building rehabilitation. The university-based initiatives seek to transfer academic research into viable technologies as well as to create additional research opportunities for students. Finally, the privately sponsored incubators are aimed primarily at profit and investment opportunities and, thus, seek high-growth firms as tenants. Table 24-1 lists differences that may exist between private-sector and public-sector incubators.

Overall a small business incubator removes some of the obstacles that must be overcome by a small business as it starts up and expands. An incubator does this by

1. offering below-market-rate leasing with flexible terms

2. eliminating building-maintenance duties and responsibilities

3. allowing tenants to share equipment and services that would otherwise be unavailable or unaffordable

4. increasing entrepreneurial awareness of, and access to, various sources of assistance and information

5. increasing the tenants' visibility in the community

6. providing an environment where small businesses are not alone, thereby reducing anxiety during start-up

7. allowing tenants to provide their services or products to other incubator tenants

Small business incubators are becoming increasingly attractive to economic development areas because of the benefits that can be derived from them. The benefits include the following:

1. Underutilized property can be transformed into productive property.

2. Public-private partnerships can be created and strengthened.

3. The community's economic base can be diversified.

4. The community's image can be enhanced as the incubator becomes a center for innovation and entrepreneurship.

---

[6]Donald F. Kuratko and William R. LaFollette, "Examining the Small Business Incubator Explosion," *Mid-American Journal of Business,* Spring 1986, pp. 29–34.

[7]Jeffrey M. King and David N. Allen, "Public and Private Approaches for Developing Small Business Incubators," *Small Business in the Entrepreneurial Era: Proceedings of the Thirtieth World Conference of the International Council for Small Business,* June 1985, pp. 392–410.

Table 24-1 Comparison of Privately Supported and Publicly Supported
Small Business Incubators

CHARACTERISTIC	DIFFERENCE
Size and Tenant Capacity	Privately sponsored are twice the size of publicly sponsored facilities and have a median tenant capacity of 45, compared to 14 for public initiatives.
Governance	Publicly sponsored incubators have executive or advisory boards; privately sponsored do not.
Tenant Selection	Publicly sponsored criterion is job creation potential with stricter entry standards; privately sponsored incubators seek profit potential in their tenants and thus do not have strict entry barriers.
Exit Policy	Public facilities have a time limit on tenant residency; private incubators tend to allow residents to stay or grow out of the facility.
Rent	Private incubators charge higher rents (usually 2 or 3 times more than public facilities) per square foot.
Services	While both sectors have centralized services, the concentration is different. Privately sponsored tend to provide physical and human services (e.g., space, secretarial, maintenance, conference rooms, etc.); publicly sponsored concentrate more on financial and business services.
Financial Sources	Privately sponsored incubators have a majority of the financing sources in the private sector (77% according to King and Allen, 1985); publicly sponsored initiatives are widely distributed among private, governmental, and industrial development financial sources.
Operating Revenue	Both types of incubators (public and private) utilize the money from rent and services for their operating income. The difference is in the additional nonrent revenue needed to operate the incubator. Publicly sponsored incubators receive most of this revenue from government sources. Privately sponsored incubators rely to a great extent upon private sources, which allows them the opportunity to receive, on the average, more money.
Staff	Private incubators have larger staff than public facilities (medium size of 5 as opposed to 1.7). Consulting staff size tends to be about the same; however, the incubator managers of privately sponsored facilities possess more business experience than their public counterparts.
Growth Pattern	Publicly sponsored incubators, which place greater emphasis on job creation, have registered a higher level of growth in employment (157%) than privately sponsored incubators (31%). However, in sales growth, the privately sponsored facilities, which placed emphasis on net profit of the tenants, demonstrated a larger increase (75%) than the public facilities (35.2%).

Source: Donald F. Kuratko and William R. LaFollette, "Examining the Small Business Incubator Explosion," *Mid-American Journal of Business,* Spring 1986, p. 31. Information adapted from Allen's (1985) studies and Mihailo and Campbell (1984).

5. The neighborhood may be revitalized.

6. Employment opportunities are created.

Currently interest in the incubator concept is intense, as evidenced by the number of new developments being proposed. In 1988, the SBA reported that over 200 incubator projects had been established and that many more were in the proposal stage.

As can be seen in the lists of benefits, the incubator concept has value for business and community alike. Service, processing, and manufacturing firms can prosper in this environment. A new direction has been given to economic development efforts and to the establishment of small businesses. (See Small Business Success: Hatching Young Companies.)

■ SMALL BUSINESS SUCCESS ■

Hatching Young Companies

Small business incubators are successfully nurturing new companies across the United States. In one study, conducted by the firm of Pryde, Roberts, and Associates, of 556 small firms housed in 13 incubators, only 13 businesses failed after moving out of the incubator. Another study conducted by Control Data Corporation of its licensed incubators showed that 91 percent of the businesses started in incubators succeed. One of the newest and largest incubator projects is located in San Pedro, California.

The San Pedro Venture Center is an example of the expanded developments that incubators can foster. This new center has eleven buildings on 10 acres and can house 125 new businesses. It currently provides office space that ranges from 490 to 785 square feet or warehouse space that ranges from 580 to 1,400 square feet. Each space functions independently with its own air conditioning, lights, heat, restrooms, and a transformer to control power.

The incubator services in the San Pedro Venture Center include access to a FAX machine, photocopying, secretarial services, a conference room, a mail room, and professional services, such as tax, legal, and accounting consultation. The fees are based upon which services the small business uses.

The goal of this new venture center is to establish 1,350 new jobs over the next five years. In its first five months of operation, 30 new jobs have been created.

There are currently 330 incubators in the United States and that number is expected to increase to 1,000 by the year 2000. Small business incubators like the San Pedro Venture Center may be the key to hatching young companies in the years to come.

Source: "Business Incubators Hatch Young Companies," *Small Business Success,* vol. 2, 1989, pp. 24–26.

NEW LEGISLATION

The 1980s witnessed the legislation of several "milestone" laws that offer small businesses some objective considerations. The three major ones are discussed here.

REGULATORY FLEXIBILITY ACT

"Reg-Flex" was passed in 1982 and recognizes that a business's size has a bearing on its ability to comply with federal regulation. It puts the burden of review on government to ensure that legislation does not impact unfairly on small businesses. According to the SBA, the major goals of the act are

1. to increase agency awareness and understanding of the impact of their regulations on small business;

2. to require that agencies communicate and explain their findings to the public; and

3. to encourage agencies to provide regulatory relief to small entities.

The SBA Chief Council for Advocacy monitors the agencies for compliance.

EQUAL ACCESS TO JUSTICE ACT

Also passed in 1982, this act provides for a greater balance between small business and regulatory bodies. The act specifies that if a small business challenges a regulatory agency and wins, the regulatory agency must pay the legal costs of the small business. The act has five main points:

1. Either the government or the business may initiate litigation.
2. Bad faith by the agency does *not* have to be proven.
3. Substantially justified actions must be demonstrated by the agency.
4. To receive an award, the business does not have to prevail on all issues.
5. There is no dollar limit to the awards.

PROMPT PAYMENTS ACT

This act was developed to help small businesses collect money they are owed by federal departments with which they have contracted to do business. It requires bills to be paid in 30 days but allows a 15-day grace period. If this is not respected, the interest penalty charges are to be assessed from the 30-day point.

In addition, the act states that any disputes over a portion of the contract do not allow the federal agency to withhold the entire payment. The disputed section may be withheld, but the remainder of the contract must be paid.

The penalties imposed (interest charges) are to be paid from that agency's present funds; additional appropriations to cover late-payments charges are not to be allowed.

WHITE HOUSE CONFERENCES

Passage of these three acts was a direct result of the 1980 White House Conference on Small Business. Small business owners from across the nation met at this conference to discuss specific concerns that impact on them. As a result, major legislation was enacted to address those concerns.

Because the conference proved to be successful, a second conference was held in 1986. In preparation for that conference, individual state conferences were held to determine agenda items and elect delegates. Thus 1,823 delegates converged on Washington with 371 agenda items, which were eventually reduced to sixty recommendations. Table 24-2 lists the top twenty items that emerged from those recommendations. The list is significant; it represents the deliberations of thousands of owners of small service, manufacturing, and retailing businesses. (More than three-fourths of the delegates employed fewer than fifty people.)

The conference was attended by 985 "official" observers, 400 members of the press, and 163 visitors from forty foreign countries.[8] The conference's impact will continue to be felt through the 1990s. Its recommendations will assist the framers of public policy in the same manner as those of the 1980 conference.

---

[8]*A Tribute to Small Business* (Washington, D.C.: U.S. Small Business Administration, Office of Private-Sector Initiatives, 1987), pp. 11–32.

Table 24-2 1986 White House Conference Recommendations
(number of votes received)

1. **Liability Insurance:** Reform tort laws; create standards for product, professional, and commercial liability; ensure that insurance is available and reasonably priced. (1419)

2. **Mandated Benefits:** Prohibit government-mandated employee benefits. (1360)

3. **Unfair Competition:** Protect small business from government and nonprofit competition. (1267)

4. **Deficit Reduction:** Adopt a constitutional amendment to balance the Federal budget. (1175)

5. **Department of International Trade:** Create a cabinet-level department of international trade. (1173)

6. **Entrepreneurial Education:** Promote entrepreneurial education and free enterprise in schools, and require the teaching of foreign languages and global economics. (1161)

7. **Davis-Bacon Act:** Repeal the Davis-Bacon Act, which requires contractors to pay "prevailing" (often "union") wages on Federal contracts. (1156)

8. **Social Security:** Freeze employer contributions and cover all workers in the system. (1152)

9. **Liability Insurance:** Enact product liability legislation that will set uniform liability standards and limit punitive damages. (1146)

10. **Equal Access to Justice:** Include the IRS in the Equal Access to Justice Act and the Regulatory Flexibility Act; amend the Regulatory Flexibility Act concerning judicial review; make disputes with the Internal Revenue Service subject to binding arbitration; make the IRS pay for the cost of its errors. (1137)

11. **Finance:** Create new capital formation and retention vehicles for small business. (1109)

12. **Taxation:** Enact capital gains tax provisions to defer taxes on proceeds received by a qualified business, and establish lower rates for assets held two to five years. (1075)

13. **Small Business Administration:** Maintain SBA as independent agency. (1051)

14. **SBIR:** Re-authorize the Small Business Innovation Research (SBIR) Program. (1043)

15. **Protect Technology:** Protect intellectual property nationally and internationally. (1034)

16. **Investment Tax Credit:** Retain the Investment Tax Credit (ITC). (972)

17. **War on Drugs:** A "War on Drugs" to solve the drug problem. (964)

18. **Procurement:** Increase federal government awards to small business by simplifying the procurement process and strengthening the small business set-aside program. (948)

19. **Finance:** Ensure equal access to commercial credit for all small business, and prevent discrimination on lending to women and minorities. (931)

20. **Retirement:** Promote the private retirement system in the small business community by increasing parity between large and small plans and between private and public plans and by simplifying the regulations governing pensions. (861)

The sixty recommendations approved by the delegates were presented to the President, Executive Branch, and the Congress for consideration. Of the sixty recommendations approved by the delegates to the 1980 White House Conference on Small Business, thirty-eight became law.

Source: "A Tribute to Small Business: America's Growth Industry," (Office of Private-Sector Initiatives, Small Business Administration, 1987), pp. 15–30.

■ **SUMMARY**

The SBA provides assistance of all types, financial and nonfinancial, to small businesses. This assistance takes many forms. Much of the financial assistance involves making direct loans, participating in loans, and guaranteeing of loans to small companies. The agency offers numerous management-assistance publications free of charge. Other types of assistance provided by the SBA include the co-sponsoring of management courses, conferences, workshops, clinics, counseling, Small Business Institutes, and Small Business Development Centers.

The chapter also examined small business incubators. The types of incubators and their dimensions and services were discussed in order to provide a better understanding of this emerging development concept.

The last part of the chapter discussed recent legislation by Congress that aids small businesses, specifically the Regulatory Flexibility Act, the Prompt Payments Act, and the Equal Access to Justice Act. In addition, the 1981 and 1986 White House Conferences on Small Business were discussed and the top twenty recommendations of the 1986 Conference were presented.

■ **REVIEW AND DISCUSSION QUESTIONS**

1. What are the overall objectives of the SBA?

2. In what ways can the SBA assist a small business financially?

3. How does the SBA go about counseling small business people? Include a discussion of SCORE, ACE, and the Small Business Development Centers.

4. Explain the value of the Small Business Institute to fledgling entrepreneurs?

5. What are small business incubators? Explain the four major types, and identify some of their benefits to small firms.

6. Identify the three legislative acts concerning small business passed in the 1980s.

7. Explain the significance of the two White House Conferences on Small Business.

8. List ten key recommendations from the 1986 White House Conference.

Case Studies

Attacking the Cause

■ It was not easy for Mack McKenzie to get a loan. He visited four banks and was turned down four times. However, Mack was desperate, knowing that if he could not raise $22,500 he would have to close his doors. Then he learned about the Small Business Administration (SBA) and applied for a loan with them. Working closely with an SBA representative, he finally was able to get a bank to give him the necessary loan, which the SBA guaranteed. All of this happened four months ago.

Since that time Mack's cash on hand has declined drastically, and he is going to need another loan. However, he is reluctant to go back to the SBA because he believes they will turn him down. After all, they just got him a loan that was supposed to carry him until the end of the year when his sales would start increasing, his cash flow would go up, and he would be able to repay the money.

Mack decided that the best thing to do would be to look over his operations and see why he was having cash flow problems. After doing so he arrived at what he feels is the answer, and it surprises even him. Apparently Mack does not really know that much about how to manage his business, nor does he understand a great deal about how to market his product. The weak finances of his operations, he has concluded, are just a symptom of poor management. The bank could lend him *another* $25,000, and he would soon need *more*.

Therefore, Mack has decided to seek management advice. In particular, he would like some consultant to help him organize his business properly and increase his overall sales through better advertising and selling practices. Since the SBA helped him out of his last problem, he is going to ask them for consulting assistance.

1. Will the SBA be able to help Mack with management and marketing problems? Explain.

2. What specifically will the SBA be able to do to assist Mack? Bring SCORE, ACE, and the SBI into your answer.

3. In addition to helping out with loans and management assistance, what other benefits does the SBA provide to small businesses? Be specific.

Does Gerald's Small Business Need Incubation?

■ Gerald Matthews has developed a business plan for a new computer sales, service, and consulting operation. His proposed venture would develop clients throughout the region. One of his close friends and advisors, Charles V. Sursa, a bank vice president, examined his plan and mentioned the possibility of starting this business in the new incubator facility now being completed in their community.

Gerald had never heard of a small business incubator and asked Charles a lot of questions about it. All Charles knew is that the incubator is housed in a remodeled warehouse building near downtown and that it will lease inexpensive space to new start-ups. It is intended to save new businesses substantial start-up and administrative costs.

The opportunity sounded good to Gerald, but he wonders if his business can qualify. And, even if he could get a space in this new incubator building, would it be appropriate for his business? Gerald is determined to learn more about the incubator.

1. What is an incubator, and what services are typically provided for small start-up firms?

2. What specific things should Gerald examine to help him decide if the incubator is right for him?

3. How do incubators differ? Which type of incubator would be ideal for Gerald?

You Be the Consultant

A LITTLE OF EVERYTHING

The Adams Corporation did very well during its first year. Maybe this initial success lulled it into a false sense of complacency. In any event, everything has been going wrong lately. The company has had to obtain an additional $5,000 line of credit at the bank because it ran into cash flow problems. At the same time, three of the top salespeople have quit, claiming that the company's compensation program is not sufficient. They now have positions with Adams' main competitor. Finally, some problems seem to be developing among the remainder of the work force. The owner, Andy Adams, believes it is simply a matter of poor morale. "We're not as much of a team as we used to be," he said recently. "That old esprit de corps is missing."

Last week Andy was talking to his banker, relating some of the problems he has been having in the company. After listening to him for a while she said, "You really need to get a consultant in there to look things over."

Andy explained that he was unwilling to pay a consultant's fee. "Who has $300 to $500 a day to spend on consultants?" he asked. "What I need to do is get a couple of books on business management, read them carefully, and see if I can't pick up some tips on how to straighten out the situation."

This is when his banker raised the issue of the Small Business Administration. "Don't you have a loan with us that's guaranteed by the SBA?" she asked, reaching for his file. "Sure, I got that when Charlie Williams was handling my account. Just before he left and you took it over."

As his banker verified this last statement she said, "You know, the SBA provides lots of assistance to small businesses, especially those that have loans with them. If you really feel that you need some help, why not go by their office and see what they can do for you?"

Andy liked the idea. When he left the bank he went to the SBA office immediately and asked to speak to someone about getting assistance. He was sent in to talk to Ed Wheatley. After explaining his problem in general terms, Andy asked Mr. Wheatley if the SBA could help.

"Oh, I think we can give you some assistance," he said. "It's really a matter of determining how we can best help you. We have loans, literature, courses, counseling, and a whole lot more. What exactly do you think you need?"

Andy pondered the question for a moment and then said, "I don't know. Maybe I'd better have a little of everything."

■ **YOUR CONSULTATION**   Act as an informal consultant to Andy and answer the following questions: What is the Small Business Administration? What specific types of assistance does it provide to small business? What would *you* recommend for Andy's firm? Be specific.

Part Seven Case Study

ETHICAL QUESTIONS IN PROFESSIONAL AND ORGANIZATIONAL RELATIONSHIPS

INTRODUCTION

Ross Larson, a successful professional in management consulting and executive search work, was involved in a discussion with his friend, Les Curtis, a management professor at a large business school. The conversation centered on several of the ethical issues which have visibly characterized American business in the past few years.

After wide-ranging give and take, the focus sharpened, concentrating on specific situations in which Larson had been involved in his consulting and search assignments. With two degrees in engineering, Larson had spent several years in technical assignments and project management with one of the nation's best known consulting firms. He went on his own principally in the search business, in 1976.

The four situations which follow all confronted Larson with ethical questions. In analyzing these incidents, he sought to draw upon his knowledge of management custom and practice, his experience with specific industries, his own personal sense of ethics, and the code of ethics published by the Association of Executive Search Consultants, Inc., a professional/trade group in his field. The code is included here following the description of the fourth incident.

THE CONGLOMERATE

For many years, Ross Larson has conducted executive recruiting assignments for several divisions of a major conglomerate. In determining the appropriate relationship with a large and complex organization, Larson has placed considerable reliance upon the code of ethics of the AESC (appendix), which is designed to enhance and encourage professionalism in the practice of executive search. One of the specific canons of this code stipulates that members ". . .will not recruit or cause to be recruited any person from the defined client organization for a period of two years after the completion of such assignment unless the member firm and client agree in writing to an exception."

Executive recruiters frequently have access to and develop contacts with senior and middle managers in a client's organization during the course of a search. The "hands-

Source: This case was prepared by Cyril C. Ling, Illinois Wesleyan University, and is intended as a basis for class discussion rather than to illustrate either effective or ineffective handling of the situation. Names of firms and individuals have been disguised.

Presented and accepted by the refereed Midwest Society for Case Research. All rights reserved to the author and the MSCR Copyright © 1990 by Cyril C. Ling.

off" provision in the Code of Ethics is designed to ensure that a recruiter does not use this access to the detriment of a client. Larson not only subscribes to this Code but includes the above "hands-off" statement in all of his proposal letters.

Shortly after completing an assignment for this major conglomerate, Larson was retained to find a Chief Financial Officer for United Financial, a financing company. His research led to a candidate who was currently employed by the financing subsidiary of the conglomerate. This subsidiary was a separate corporation established by the conglomerate, and the conglomerate held all of the finance subsidiary's stock. Larson never worked for this subsidiary. In fact, he had never met anyone employed by this company and he had no knowledge of its organization or management.

Larson was convinced that approaching the candidate in the conglomerate's subsidiary would not violate the *spirit* of the "hands-off" provision in the Code of Ethics and in his proposal letters. However, he recognized that the conglomerate's CEO could take a very broad construction of "defined client organization," restricting him from considering the candidate in the financing subsidiary. On the other hand, he was obligated to render a thorough and diligent effort to find the best candidate for the chief financial officer position.

PIERCE, ADAMS, AND JEFFERSON

When Ross Larson established his own search business upon leaving Pierce, Adams, and Jefferson, his relationships with his former firm and colleagues remained cordial. He did several recruiting assignments for P.A. & J during the first two years of his new venture. He also worked for several other clients, including ILM, Inc., a consulting firm, but not a competitor of P.A. & J.

The president of ILM called Larson to tell him that ILM was seeking a new Vice President to handle a significant portion of its consulting business. ILM was already looking at several candidates and, while Larson was not retained to find additional candidates, ILM's president did ask him for the names of possible additional candidates. ILM offered to pay Larson his standard fee if one of his candidates was hired. Larson immediately thought of Steve Roberts, one of his former colleagues at P.A. & J. Roberts aspired to be a P.A. & J Vice President but had been passed over several times.

Larson called a Senior VP at P.A. & J whom he knew he could take into his confidence. The Senior VP told him that Roberts would never be promoted to VP at P.A. & J because the P.A. & J President did not believe Roberts had the full range of skills believed to be necessary to be a VP at P.A. & J. Larson then called Roberts. He did not tell Roberts of his conversation with the Senior VP. Roberts admitted he was unhappy and frustrated over his inability to gain a promotion. He expressed interest in the ILM position. Larson told Roberts that before he could introduce him to ILM he (Larson) would have to talk to P.A. & J President, Mack Michaels. Roberts gave Larson permission to call Michaels.

Larson called Michaels, a close personal friend, and explained the ILM position and his interest in presenting Roberts as a candidate. He did not tell Michaels of his conversation with either Roberts or the Senior VP, nor did he ask for permission to present Roberts to ILM. When asked about Roberts promotability at P.A. & J, Michaels said, "I don't see why Steve couldn't be promoted, but no one has made a convincing case to me yet that he should be promoted." Michaels concluded by saying, "I'll be very upset if you pull Steve out of here." Larson thanked Michaels for his time and comments and ended the conversation.

Larson reflected on these conversations for several days. Roberts was a friend who was unhappy and who was not going to be promoted at P.A. & J. Larson knew Michaels well enough to know that his comment about no one making a convincing case for Roberts' promotion really meant that Michaels believed a convincing case could not be made now or in the future. Larson presented Roberts to ILM. Roberts was hired.

Michaels was furious. He claimed Larson used intimate knowledge about P.A. & J against the firm. Michaels decreed that Larson be banned from future assignments with P.A. & J. One year after being hired by ILM, Roberts was fired because ILM found his management style too abrasive.

THE PERSONNEL MANAGER

IAB Inc. was conducting its own search for a Personnel Manager. Although the organization was not using the services of an executive recruiter, Ross Larson was asked to make recommendations of candidates. He had done many searches for IAB and knew the organization well. He was not retained to conduct a search; his recommendations would be based on contacts previously established during the conduct of his business. IAB was particularly interested in hiring an individual with a strong recruiting background.

Two finalists emerged. Mr. Grant was nominated by Larson; Mr. Lee responded to an IAB ad. Larson knew Grant from prior interviews. Grant was an experienced professional well qualified to manage IAB's personnel function. He had done some recruiting but it was not a significant strength. IAB also asked Larson to interview Lee.

Larson interviewed Lee for two hours and concluded that Lee had good recruiting experience and capability but was generally of average capability in the other areas associated with the personnel function. However, Larson felt uncomfortable with Lee personally. He felt there was something about Lee's demeanor and personality that would eventually make him ineffective in the IAB environment. He did not share any of his misgivings with IAB because he had no "hard" evidence or data to support them. Furthermore, he thought IAB executives might think he was being self-serving trying to promote Grant's candidacy. It would obviously be to Larson's advantage to have "his man" as IAB's Personnel Manager. Therefore, Larson told IAB that he believed Lee "could do the job IAB needed to have done."

Lee was a disaster. He had serious psychological problems. He was a manic depressive. After several months of bizarre behavior, IAB arranged for Lee to be admitted to a psychiatric care facility. Treatment was not successful. Lee was fired. Grant was hired and had a long, very successful career at IAB.

HELPFUL INFORMATION?

Ross Larson was retained to find a Director of Human Resources for a $200 million plastics business listed on the American Stock Exchange. Larson's client contact was the business' Chief Financial Officer. Larson had placed several key managers in one of the company's two operating divisions, including the division's General Manager.

As a result of continuing contacts with this division, which accounted for about 40% of the company's sales, Larson knew this division was enjoying record sales and profits.

Larson identified three candidates for the human resource position. After reviewing the candidates' backgrounds the client asked Larson to arrange for him to interview each candidate. Even though Larson had already interviewed each candidate at length, the client asked him to sit in on the interviews. The interviews were held on a Tuesday in December, three weeks before the close of the fiscal year, at an airport hotel.

During each interview, the Chief Financial Officer talked extensively about the company's history, prospects, financial health, management style and, in general terms, business strategy. No financial data not previously available in annual or quarterly reports was presented.

Although Larson already knew most of the information the CFO presented, he did learn about some aspects of management style and strategy he had not known before. During his flight home he reviewed in his mind the CFO's comments along with what he had previously known about the company. The next day he bought 250 shares of the company's stock at $11-1/2 per share. The stock is thinly traded and 100-share days are not unusual. Early in January the company announced record earnings, and the stock advanced to over $20 per share.

AESC, Association of Executive Search Consultants, Inc.

CODE OF ETHICS

I. Professionalism

Executive search consulting is a professional endeavor. A profession is characterized by the objectivity, integrity, and thoroughness of its practitioners. Members will maintain the highest standards of professional work and behavior so that their actions reflect favorably on the Association, its members, their clients and candidates. In this endeavor, members will serve their clients in a professional manner, including the performance of at least the following services before proposing any candidates:

A. Meetings with the client to develop understanding of the client's organization and needs and the position to be filled;

B. Written documentation outlining the position description, scope, and character of the services to be provided;

C. Thorough independent research on the nature and the needs of the client organization;

D. Comprehensive search for qualified candidates;

E. Thorough evaluation of potential candidates, including in-depth personal interviews, verification of credentials, and careful assessment of the individual's strengths and weaknesses, in order to provide an adequate basis for independent and expert recommendations to the client; and

F. Either before or after presentation of a candidate, but prior to final selection by the client, performance of comprehensive reference checking.

Any practices that do not embody the above process cannot be objective, are adverse to the client's best interest, undermine independent judgment, tend to bring disrepute to the profession, and are in violation of this code.

(continued)

II. Qualifications
Members will accept only those assignments that they are qualified to undertake on the basis of full knowledge of the client situation and the professional competence and capacity of the consultants involved. Assignments accepted will be based on a comprehensive written document outlining the scope and character of the services to be provided.

III. Client Relationship
Members will, in each assignment undertaken, define, preferably in writing, what constitutes "the client organization." The member will not recruit or cause to be recruited any person from the defined client organization for a period of two years after the completion of such assignment unless the member firm and client agree in writing to an exception. The member will disclose to the client limitations arising through service to other clients that may affect the scope of the search assignment in the event that a client retains a member to conduct a search and any other firm has already been retained by the client, the member shall assure that its retention is fully disclosed to such other previously retained firms.

IV. Confidentiality
Members shall regard as totally confidential all information concerning the business affairs of their clients and of candidates.

V. Promotion Activities
Members will conduct all firm promotion, public relations, and new business activities in a manner that involves no representations, express or implied, that are false, deceptive, unsubstantiated, or that otherwise have a capacity to mislead.

VI. Promotion of Competition
It is the policy of AESC and its members to promote free and fair competition in the provision of executive search consulting services. Neither AESC nor any member will engage in any unlawful restraint of trade, unfair method of competition, or other violation of the antitrust laws.

DISCUSSION QUESTIONS
1. Why is "defined clients organization" such an issue in this situation?

2. Is there an identifiable factor which explains why this situation developed so negatively?

3. Did Larson put himself in the role of "inside trader"?

4. Is this a legal or ethical issue? ■

Part Seven Entrepreneurial Simulation Program

VACATION TIME
It is time for a well deserved vacation. You have dedicated many hours to the store, developing a plan of action, purchasing inventory, setting prices for your shoes, allocating scarce advertising dollars, and much more. The experience you obtained running the store enhanced your ability to make the necessary decisions each month. You found that the other stores were always looking for ways to attract your customers, and

you learned to be ever alert to changes in the retail shoe market in order to meet your goals.

Now you need to get away from it all, perhaps to some remote location where you cannot be called every time a decision needs to be made back at the store. This raises a problem. How can you leave the store and still be certain that the person placed in charge in your absence will make the same monthly decisions that you would make if you were still there running the store? You want to take a vacation, but at the same time you believe your expertise in making the decisions each month is indispensable for the success of the store. This conflict places you in a dilemma.

Think back on the insecurity you felt making the monthly decisions when you first opened the store. There were so many variables to consider and so much data to absorb and analyze at the end of each month. During those first few months you were operating in a heuristic decision-making mode. You knew your current status and had an idea as to what you wanted your store to attain by the end of the month, but you had not established a well-defined process or sequence of steps available to tell you how to reach your objective. Month by month you made your decisions and ascertained from the feedback the success of those decisions for your store. Each month you adjusted your course of action and, through this process, formulated a more appropriate set of decisions.

Except for franchises, this is the way it is with new retail businesses. You develop, month by month, a better understanding of the best course of action for your store. Even with a franchise there is no guarantee that your decisions will produce the monetary success you hope for. The entrepreneur, establishing a new retail business, must understand and be willing to accept the fact that successful patterns of decision making are developed based on a great deal of experience and perhaps several unforeseen catastrophes along the way. This is how the successful retailer learns how to make good decisions. The process the retailer develops is referred to as an algorithm.

An algorithm is a well-defined sequence of steps that, if followed correctly, will lead to a desired result. When you made decisions each month for your store, and modified them the following month based on the feedback you obtained, you were developing a decision-making algorithm. This algorithm was personal and unique. It was formed around your decision-making style and was designed to attain the goals of your enterprise. If your algorithm were applied to someone else's store, it would probably not be as appropriate to making the necessary monthly decisions.

Computer programs and other quantitative techniques can be very helpful in developing and applying an algorithmic process for your store. The ability to set up a spreadsheet or to write a computer program in a language such as BASIC are very useful skills for developing and applying an algorithm. These technological tools are themselves based on an algorithmic process. If the algorithm you develop conforms with how you make the necessary decisions, it could be used to represent your desires even when you are away.

The algorithm could also be used to do "What if. . ." analysis prior to making the decisions. You could modify one of the variables, such as price, to get some idea of the effect of the change on the desired outcome. Using this approach eliminates the need to gain all of your insight by trying out new ideas in the monthly operation of your store only to find out after it is too late the idea was not so good after all.

It is vacation time and you are eager to spend some time away from it all. Do you have a decision-making algorithm ready to pass on to the person who will take over for you, or is your presence indispensable for the operation of the store?

DISCUSSION QUESTIONS

1. Based on the experience you have gained running your shoe store, describe how shoes should be ordered each month. Document your instructions in such a way that another person could follow them and make the same decisions that you would make regarding shoe purchases, assuming you were still actively managing the store.

2. Describe how prices should be established each month. Document your instructions in such a way that another person could follow them and make the same decisions that you would make regarding pricing, assuming you were still actively managing the store.

3. Describe how the advertising budget should be determined and allocated each month. Document your instructions in such a way that another person could follow them and make the same decisions that you would make regarding advertising, assuming you were still actively managing the store.

4. Plan a party or some other joyous event to celebrate the conclusion of your recent endeavor in the retail shoe business. If you made money, rejoice in the fact that you've done it once and could do it again, next time for real. If you lost money, rejoice in the fact that your life savings are still in your bank account and that you had this chance to work out the problems before committing your money to a retail business venture. Either way, you have a lot to be thankful for.